RUSSIA
A HISTORY

RUSSIA

A HISTORY

SIXTH EDITION

By Sidney Harcave

State University of New York at Binghamton

J. B. LIPPINCOTT COMPANY

Philadelphia & New York

TO NORAH

This book is designed as a concise presentation of Russian history for those to whom the subject is relatively unfamiliar. For that reason, an organization neither strictly chronological nor strictly topical has been used. If the intricately plotted story of Russia is told in an undeviating date-after-date manner, the separate threads of the plot may become snarled for the reader. To prevent that, certain threads have been separated for particular consideration at points where it is possible to do so without disrupting the sequence. If those separate threads were continuously parallel, it would be possible, of course, to simplify the study of them by following each from its beginning to its end. But the story is not plotted that way; its threads are woven together in an irregular manner. In one place, a single character may sustain it; in another, a group; in another, an idea; in another, the impelling current of world history. And those sustaining elements appear and reappear singly and in varying combinations. Consequently it seems advisable, in an introduction to Russian history, to keep the whole story moving chronologically while the threads are picked out topically, here and there, and considered in their relation to the moving whole.

Arbitrary decisions have been made not only about method of presentation but also about proportion. In a work of this length it would be impossible to cover all periods of Russian history, giving equal weight to each, without sacrificing detail and interpretation to such an extent that the result would be little more than an outline. Therefore some parts have been emphasized at the expense of others. The greater emphasis has been given to the periods following the establishment of the empire, those during which there is a marked interrelation of Russian and world history. At the same time, an effort has been made not to slight those aspects of the earlier periods which affect directly the developments in the later.

In dealing with dates, the transliteration of Russian words, and the translation of Russian terms, the practices followed are intended to facilitate reading and understanding. Russia used the Julian calendar until 1918; but, since most readers will have learned their modern history according to the Gregorian calendar, dates since 1582 are given according to that system of time-reckoning in order that they may be readily associated with dates learned in other historical study. In the transliteration of Russian terms, surnames, and place names, popular usage rather than any standard system of transliteration is followed. As far as possible, Russian terms are translated into English. Often, in the case of terms for which no English equivalents exist, the English terms most nearly equivalent are used with explanation. Common English equivalents are used for all Russian given names.

To supplement the material included in the body of the book, a selected bibliography is provided. All titles listed are in English; but, for the convenience of those with facility in other languages, bibliographies with fuller listings are cited. The index, also, contains a supplementary feature: it gives, in addition to conventional itemization, the birth and death dates of most of the Russians mentioned in the text.

In assembling the materials for this book, I had the advantage of being able to draw upon the works of many who have done detailed research work in various aspects of Russian history; I humbly acknowledge my debt to them and trust that my efforts may serve to lead some readers to the richer fields which they have opened. Others contributed much to the actual preparation of the book. Friends and colleagues offered encouragement and suggestions; the Champlain College librarians patiently provided needed materials from far and wide; and my students, by their questions and responses, often set me to reorganizing and rewriting in an effort to clarify and vivify ideas or information presented to them. While the work was in progress, the Russian Research Center of Harvard University made it possible for me, through participation in its refugee interview project among Soviet displaced persons in Germany, to acquire a broader understanding of Soviet Russia.

Three individuals gave me personal assistance for which this mere mention is wholly inadequate payment. To Edward A. Schmitz, who prepared the end papers and all the maps, I am grateful not only for his craftsmanship but also for his patience and co-operation in fitting the maps to the text. To my wife, Norah Harcave, who edited the manuscript, assisted me at every stage in its preparation, and compiled the index, I offer thanks which cannot possibly be commensurate with the help she gave. To Professor Frederick S. Rodkey, of the University of Illinois, who read the entire work in manuscript, I am particularly indebted; his scholarly criticism and friendly advice served me profitably on countless points. Whatever imperfections persist in the book may be charged to my own limitations.

Preface to Sixth Edition

In revisions made since the publication of the first edition, that part of the text dealing with the period before Peter the Great has been expanded, later chapters have been reorganized or rewritten, a final chapter has been added to deal with the post-Stalin era, and supplementary materials have been extensively changed to bring them up to date and improve their usefulness.

S.H.

Binghamton, New York
January, 1968

CONTENTS

PREFACE

MAPS

ILLUSTRATIONS

PART 1

Growth of People and Polity

CHRONOLOGICAL OVERVIEW

862 Legendary founding of
Russian State

964–972 Reign of Svyatoslav

978–1015 Reign of Vladimir

c. 990 Conversion of Russians to
Christianity

1019–1054 Reign Yaroslav the Wise

1113–1125 Reign of Vladimir Monomakh

c. 1147 Founding of Moscow

1223 First Mongol invasion

1240 Capture of Kiev by Mongols

1325–1341 Reign of Ivan I

1359–1389 Reign of Dmitri Donskoi

1380 Victory over Mongols by
Dmitri Donskoi

1462–1505 Reign of Ivan III

1478 Annexation of Novgorod
by Muscovy

1480 Overthrow of the Mongol
rule

1505–1533 Reign of Basil III

1533–1584 Reign of Ivan IV

1547 Coronation of Ivan IV as
"Tsar"

1552 Conquest of Kazan

1556 Conquest of Astrakhan

1584–1598 Reign of Feodor I, last of
Rurik dynasty

1589 Establishment of Russian
Patriarchate

1598–1605 Reign of Boris Godunov

1604–1613 Time of Troubles

1613–1645 Reign of Michael, first of
the Romanov dynasty

1645–1676 Reign of Alexis

1667 Treaty of Andrusovo
Schism in the Church

1676–1682 Reign of Feodor III

ONE / THE BEGINNINGS OF THE RUSSIAN PEOPLE

The history of Russia is the history of a people who shared a common culture for many centuries before being united in a common political organization. These people were the descendants of certain Slavic tribes that migrated to what is now Russia and were there transformed from a group of tribes into a nation. Unfortunately their lives before the ninth century A.D. cannot be traced in exact detail; but, from various sources, enough may be pieced together to make a fairly reliable outline.

Slavonic ancestors

EARLY HISTORY.   Although our specific knowledge of the Slavs before the Christian era is based upon scanty and inconclusive evidence, we may presume that, during their early concentration as a group, they were still a primitive people, somewhat beyond the nomadic stage, speaking primitive Slavonic, a language of the Indo-European group. At that time the Slavs had not learned to write, and none of their contemporaries, so far as we know, recorded the activities of these early ancestors of the Russians. The available archaeological data concerning them is meager and not particularly useful. So we are forced to base our conception of them chiefly upon philological evidence. The fact that a place bears a name of early Slavonic origin may lead to the inference that it was inhabited by the early Slavs, and the fact that the early Slavonic language included many words relating to agriculture and few relating to handicraft may suggest the priority of agriculture in their way of life. However, our conclusions based upon such reasoning are limited, for our knowledge of the early Slavonic language itself is inferred from the languages that developed out of it, and the gaps in that knowledge are so great that many of the conflicting hypotheses based upon it cannot be satisfactorily supported.

It is generally agreed that the Slavs existed as an ethnic group as early as the seventh century B.C., but there is less agreement about the region in which they began their development. Whereas some have placed it in the Carpathian Mountains and others have located it along the Danube, the most widely accepted hypothesis is that it was the region including what is now eastern Poland, the western Ukraine, and western White Russia. The first known written reference to the Slavs was made in 77 A.D. by Pliny the Elder. Later ones—among them, items in the writings of Tacitus, Ptolemy, and Procopius —added to the record; but, until the sixth century, it was a slim record and an ambiguous one. It is believed that during the first five centuries of the Christian era, a period characterized by mass movements of peoples throughout Asia and Europe, the Slavs took to the road. Their migration was a slow but continuous process, which cannot be dated with accuracy. However, it is known that by the sixth century they had separated into three groups, which had moved in different directions and grown apart culturally and politically under the varying influences of the regions through which they had passed or those in which they had settled.

DIVISIONS.   On the basis of the directions in which they migrated, the early Slavic tribes may be divided into three groups: the western, the southern, and the eastern. The western Slavs (ancestors of the Poles, Czechs, and Slovaks) migrated toward the Elbe, the Oder, and the lower Vistula rivers. They came under the influence of Western European culture and eventually adopted the Roman Catholic faith and Latin alphabet. The southern Slavs (ancestors of the Serbs and the Bulgarians) pushed across the Carpathian Mountains into the Balkans, there to come under the influence of Byzantine culture and to adopt the Greek Orthodox faith and the Cyrillic alphabet. The eastern Slavs (ancestors of the Russians) made their way eastward toward Lake Peipus, Lake Ilmen, the Dnieper, the Oka, and the upper Volga. They also were affected by the Byzantine culture and consequently developed many cultural traits similar to those of the southern Slavs but differing markedly from those of the western Slavs.

The land of settlement

THE RUSSIAN PLAIN.   The migration of the eastern Slavs brought them to the region now known as the Russian plain, the nature of which was to

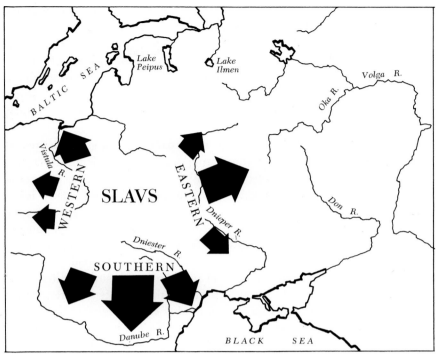

DRAWN BY EDW. A. SCHMITZ

MAP 1. Dispersion of the Slavs

have a definite and extended influence upon their further development.

The Russian plain, part of the great Eurasian plain, extends from eastern Europe to central Siberia and from the Arctic Ocean southward to the Carpathian Mountains, the Black Sea, the Caucasus, the Caspian Sea, and the mountains of Central Asia. It is uniform neither in vegetation nor in topography, but it is relatively level. Except for the Ural Range, which forms a north-south bisector of the plain, its elevations do not rise above 1,200 feet. Even that range, the highest peak of which is only 6,183 feet above sea level, is on the whole gentle in contour and cut by valleys that permit easy transit from the European to the Asiatic parts of the plain.

On the basis of soil and vegetation the plain may be divided into east-west belts, each with characteristics differing from those of the others. That part extending from the Arctic Ocean to a line following roughly the Arctic Circle is known as the tundra region. Below it is the forest region, the southern boundary of which may be traced through Kishinev, Kazan, and Omsk. The remainder of the plain is almost all steppe (grassland) except in Central

Asiatic Russia; there, below the fiftieth parallel, lie a region of semi-desert and, still farther south, one of desert.

To the migrating Slavs, the tundra, semi-desert, and desert were not inviting: the cold tundra region was barren except for mosses and lichen, and the other two were unfit for agriculture and grazing except near the few oases and rivers. The forest and steppe, however, were comparatively attractive, and the history of the migrants and their descendants came to be largely the history of those regions.

The forest and the steppe, though not separated by a sharp boundary, were marked by definite and contrasting features that determined their desirability—though not always their availability—to the would-be settlers. The first, a region of fine woodlands, occasional hills, and many lakes, promised an abundance of fuel and game as well as some opportunity for agriculture. But the attraction of the forest was not equal to that of the steppe, the area of broad plains and limitless horizons, where an agricultural people could expect nature's co-operation in the pursuit of a livelihood. Practically all of it could be cultivated, and some of it was of surpassing fertility—that part later known as the black soil belt, one of the most fertile areas in the world, beginning in the Ukraine and continuing eastward through the south central portions of European Russia and into Siberia. There were occasional forests and many ravines in the steppe, but the expanses of flat, open grassland were common enough to be typical.

CLIMATE.   Inevitably the incoming Slavs found their lives directed somewhat by the climate of the Russian plain. Whatever their attitude toward it, there can be little doubt that only a hardy people would have chosen to endure it.

Since the plain is too far from large bodies of water to benefit from their moderating influence, its climate is one of seasonal extremes: hot summer, cold winter, short spring and fall. The length of the seasons varies, depending on location, but the climatic pattern is surprisingly uniform;[1] it is likely to be as hot in Archangel in July as it is in Astrakhan, some fifteen hundred miles to the south, and both cities may have the same degree of frost in January.

The Russian winters are severe because the country is exposed to north and northeast winds that sweep down from the Arctic, their intense coldness undiminished by any opposing warming influences. A considerable snow cover accumulates during the winter, and almost all rivers freeze over. Kiev

---

[1] It is only in the regions adjoining the plain, those acquired comparatively late in Russia's history, that the pattern changes. Among these are the permanently frozen areas in the far north; the Transcaucasian mountains and subtropical lowlands, where many climates are represented; and the Central Asian desert and semi-desert expanses.

DRAWN BY EDW. A. SCHMITZ

MAP 2. Vegetation Belts

will experience perhaps two and a half months of hard frost; Moscow, nearly four and a half; and Archangel will live with it for half of the year. Leningrad generally has a longer winter than does Moscow, but it has frequent thaws as a result of its proximity to the Gulf of Finland.

Throughout the Russian plain, spring comes late and quickly, often bringing heavy rains and floods from rapidly melting snow and ice. The Volga has been known to rise as much as forty feet in some spring months, and the low areas near Kiev are inundated yearly as the ice breaks up at the end of April.

WATERWAYS. Another natural aspect of the Russian plain that must have weighed heavily as a factor in any of the early peoples' decision to choose it for settlement was its system of excellent waterways. Apparently the same aspect has continued to influence the Russians, whose reliance on waterways, to the general neglect of their roads, has become traditional. The waterways of the plain—about 75,000 miles in combined length—have always been helpful in overcoming the drawbacks of its great expanse. The rivers are numerous, long, navigable, and accessible to one another. Together with the lakes, they make water transportation possible in almost any direction. For that reason they have served not only as connections between the several parts of the country but also as natural avenues of expansion.

Three rivers in particular—the Dnieper, the Volga, and the Neva—have

been prominently associated with the growth of Russia. The Dnieper, empty-
ing into the Black Sea, was the focus of activity when Russia was developing
under the influence of Byzantium. It marked the main line of an important
trade route, passing through Kiev and on to Constantinople, capital of the
Byzantine Empire. And, as the Russian state developed, the significance of
the Dnieper increased.

The Volga River, although it figures in the first centuries of Russian
history, was of secondary importance until about the eleventh century, when
it began to serve as a major axis of development. From then until the fifteenth century, political and economic centers were to grow strong in the area
drained by the upper Volga and one of its tributaries, the Oka River; notable
among them were Ryazan, Moscow, Vladimir, Rostov, Suzdal, and Tver.
Moscow, ultimately to dominate the area, was linked to the Volga by the
Moscow River, itself a tributary of the Oka, and smaller accessible rivers.
Yet it was not until the end of the sixteenth century that the entire river and
the great Volga basin, an area equal in size to Germany, England, and France
combined, came under Russian domination. Control of the mighty Volga,
longest of all European rivers, provided Russia with access to the trade routes
of Asia via the Caspian Sea, into which it flows, as well as a base for expansion into Siberia and Central Asia.

Being only forty-five miles in length, the Neva River is obviously not
among the great rivers of Russia; yet it is doubly noteworthy. In early centuries it served as a link in important and extensive trade routes. And, from
the beginning of the eighteenth century, when it came under complete
Russian control, it has represented Russia's tie with Western Europe, providing direct maritime access by way of the Gulf of Finland, at its mouth. The
French historian Alfred Rambaud undoubtedly simplified history but nevertheless made a striking point when he wrote, "The Dnieper made Russia
Byzantine, the Volga made her Asiatic: it was for the Neva to make her
European."

In contrast to the excellent internal waterways, the water connections
between the Russian plain and the outside world have always been poor. In
fact, for many centuries Russia was landlocked, having no access to any sea.
As she developed, many of her wars were fought for the purpose of gaining
maritime outlets. Even now, for an area of its great size, European Russia has
access to an exceedingly short coastline (about 5,500 miles in length), consisting of stretches along the Arctic Ocean and the Black, the Baltic, and the
Caspian seas. The Arctic coast, which accounts for half of the coastal boundary, affords only the most out-of-the-way communication with other coun-

tries and that only during the few months when the ice is broken sufficiently for navigation. Northern ports on the Baltic are more often than not icebound and closed to navigation during the middle of the winter, and the northern part of the Caspian is often frozen. It is easy to understand why the problem of outlets to navigable waters has engaged attention in all periods of Russian history.

Development before 862

FIRST FOOTHOLDS.   When the eastern Slavs began to establish themselves on the Russian plain, they found other ethnic groups in possession of parts of it. In fact, it had been inhabited for many centuries before their arrival; excavations have turned up traces of human existence in the area during the Stone Age and have shown that habitation continued down through the succeeding ages. No people who came before the Slavs had succeeded in creating a culture and polity of sufficient strength to support an enduring claim over the plain. But, at the time of their arrival, the Slavs probably met opposition that, although it did not drive them from the plain, was strong enough to divert them from what must have been their first choice, the steppe lands; and they finally had to accept a foothold where they could manage to maintain it at the time, in the forest region. There, for centuries, they and their descendants had to content themselves with second-best lands.

CLAN LIFE.   In the sixth century the eastern Slavs were far behind their neighbors of the steppe region, particularly those under Byzantine influence, in all phases of their development. Their basic social and economic unit was the clan, representing a rough kind of equality. Clan members lived in closely grouped rude homes, often no more than dugouts. For livelihood they hunted, fished, trapped, collected honey, and tilled the soil. Their clearing of land for cultivation with their primitive wooden plows (actually little more than sharpened branches of trees) involved the tedious work of killing trees by stripping them of bark and attempting to rid the soil of their roots by grubbing them out and setting fire to them; to have prepared an acre after a month of work by horses, oxen, and men was considered normal progress. Of necessity under such conditions, their chief concern was merely to maintain existence. In some years their primitive economy would offer nothing but the threat of starvation, and whole tribes would be compelled to move in search of new lands. Even when nature was kind, their security was tenuous, for at all times they had to face the likelihood of expulsion at the hands of stronger tribes.

The level of their cultural achievement was reflected in their religious conceptions. For them the world was an inscrutable region, full of malignant and good spirits that might be found anywhere: in rocks, streams, trees, animals, and even in human beings. Over these spirits reigned gods who controlled the forces of nature—gods such as Perun, the master of thunder and lightning; Stribog, the controller of winds; and Svarog, the god of the firmament. To obtain their blessings men needed to make sacrifices and offer prayers before silver- and gold-covered idols. No priests were required to perform religious services; but sorcerers, witches, and magicians were often called upon to placate the evil spirits, to interpret omens, and to foretell changes in the future.

Another reflection of their cultural level was their political organization. It was a simple one, but adequate for their simple needs. As a body of equals under the leadership of an elder, the clan was the custodian of customary law and the source of justice. And above it was the loose organization of the tribe, the usefulness of which was to unify the clans when strength of numbers was needed for defense or aggression.

The cultural and political development of the eastern Slavs involved a gradual change during the period from the time of their appearance on the Russian plain (probably in the sixth century) to the time when they began the creation of their state (in the ninth century). It was a change made requisite by the physical and human environment in which they found themselves, one offering both risks and rewards. Powerful foes threatened them with extinction while rich trade routes, fertile lands, and well-stocked forests and rivers gave promise of a good future to those who could survive to enjoy it. And, since survival in this region was more appealing to them than a renewal of the nomadic practices of their forebears, they began to make the changes necessary to insure it: to construct more permanent homes, to strengthen their means of protection, to plan for a more reliable economy, and to combine their small political units into larger ones.

NEIGHBORS AND OPPONENTS ON THE PLAIN.   By 862 A.D., the date traditionally used to mark the beginning of the Russian state, the eastern Slavs had come into contact with many non-Slavic peoples in the European part of the Russian plain. Some of them had moved on; some had remained. Of the latter, the most numerous were the Finno-Ugrians, the Bulgars, and the Khazars.

The Finno-Ugrians (so called because of their languages, which are of the family to which modern Finnish and Hungarian belong) consisted of several small tribes, lacking in military skill. Living in the northern forest land between the upper Volga and present-day Finland, they had no organized state and presented no military threat to other peoples.

The Bulgars and Khazars, settled chiefly in the steppe, had come to whatever eminence they had in that region by invasion and conquest. The steppe lands, geographically accessible and economically desirable to invaders, had been and would continue to be the home of warring peoples who succeeded one another to dominant power. Most of the invaders were Asiatic by origin, nomadic by habit, and warlike by necessity. This, briefly, was the order of their succession: the Scythians had driven out the Cimmerians, only to be displaced by the Sarmatians; the Sarmatians had been ousted by the Goths, who in turn had fallen before the Huns; the Huns had been succeeded by the Avars, who were followed by the Bulgars and Khazars.

The Bulgars,[1] a Turcic people, were originally nomads, but they began to till the soil and make permanent settlements when they reached the Russian plain. By the beginning of the eighth century, they had organized themselves as a state. From their capital, known as the "Great City," near the confluence of the Kama and Volga rivers, they ruled much of the middle Volga and the Kama basins until the arrival of the Mongols, in the thirteenth century. Their mercantile activities brought them into touch with the lands of the Finno-Ugrians and with Byzantine, Central Asia, and Transcaucasia. From the Arab regions, they learned of the Moslem faith, which they adopted in the tenth century.

South of the Bulgar lands were those of the Khazars, chief threats to Bulgar security. The Khazars, of whose antecedents little is known, established themselves at the mouth of the Volga in the seventh century, with Itil (near modern Astrakhan) as their capital. At its greatest extent, their state dominated an area extending west to the Dnieper, east to the Urals, south to the Caucasian Mountains, and north to the Bulgar lands. With trade as their chief interest, the Khazars maintained contacts with an area even more extensive than that touched by the Bulgars. In the middle of the ninth century, their ruling class was converted to Judaism, but they continued to preserve a tradition of tolerance to other faiths. By the end of the tenth century, the Khazar state was going the way of most of its predecessors in the steppe: it had been conquered, and the culture of its people was disappearing.

---

[1] Some of the Bulgar tribes migrated westward to an area along the Danube, which owes to them its name (Bulgaria) but not its Slavic culture.

It would be useful to assess the extent to which their non-Slavic neighbors and opponents influenced the eastern Slavs as they sought to make a home for themselves on the Russian plain. However, the records are not adequate for that: although we know something of the Finno-Ugrians, the Bulgars, and the Khazars, we must assume that there were also other peoples who should be considered but of whom we have no record. And we must further assume that there was some cultural continuity from one period to the next despite the rise and fall of various peoples, and that the eastern Slavs were, to some extent, heirs of all who had gone before. We know, for example, that Kiev had been settled long before it became the home of the Slavs, but we cannot identify the earlier inhabitants nor evaluate their contributions to their Slavic successors.

There is some support for the belief that the eastern Slavs were culturally more advanced than the Finno-Ugrians but not as advanced as the Bulgars and Khazars. It would follow that they would be likely to be givers in their contacts with the Finno-Ugrians and takers in their contacts with the Bulgars and Khazars. Available evidence indicates that intermarriage between Slavs and Finno-Ugrians was common and justifies the belief that some Finno-Ugrian tribes assimilated Slavic culture. About the relations between the Slavs and the Bulgars little is known. But, since some of the Slavic tribes were either in alliance with the Khazars or were subjected to them, there is more information about the Slav-Khazar relations. Even this information, comparatively extensive though it has become, is difficult to evaluate since it lends itself to varying interpretations. However, it makes clear the fact that, in their relations with the Khazars, the eastern Slavs found themselves face to face with a culture more complex than their own and that they adopted much of it. Many documents survive to indicate that eastern Slavs acquired from the Khazars their mercantile interests and skills, among others, and that they participated in the intricate and extensive trading life of which Itil was the center.

BEGINNINGS OF EXPANSION.   As they were increasing in experience, the eastern Slavs were also gaining a measure of strength in numbers and possessions near the Baltic area inhabited by tribes of Lithuanians, Letts, and Livs; and farther inland, to the east, they managed to claim territory already settled by tribes of the Finno-Ugrian group. But, because they expanded the area of their occupation slowly, by the end of the ninth century they occupied only a small portion of what is now European Russia, their chief settlements reaching north to Lake Ladoga, south to the middle Dnieper, and east to the Oka River.

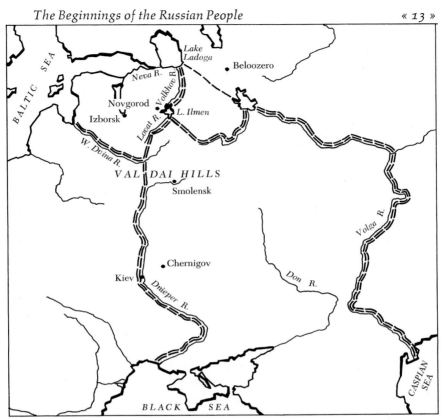

DRAWN BY EDW. A. SCHMITZ

MAP 3. Trade routes and towns in the ninth century

At the same time, as it became evident that the expanding group interests could be best served through a larger organization, the clan lost its importance and towns began to develop among the Slavic settlers. The growth of their towns was aided by the economic revival of the northern and western parts of Europe and the resultant extension of trade between Europe and Asia, part of which was conducted along routes running through areas of Slavic settlement. The most important of these routes, known as the River Road, stretched from the Baltic to the Black Sea; and the next in importance led to the Caspian Sea by way of the Western Dvina River or Lake Ladoga and the Volga. Along the River Road were developed the leading Slavic towns: Kiev, Chernigov, and Novgorod. These and other towns profited from the growing trade by providing furs, honey, wax, and slaves for transport by Slavic and non-Slavic merchants to Constantinople and to the Arab Empire.

There the cargoes were exchanged for silks, perfumes, spices, spears, swords, and precious metals—items to be sold on the return trip to the Baltic.

It was in their towns along the River Road that the eastern Slavs became acquainted with the powerful warrior-merchant Varangians, who, when away from their native Scandinavia, led a life of dual nature, pillaging where they could and trading where they could not pillage. Because of their superior prowess as warriors the Varangians were able to determine the extent of their relations with the Slavs, sometimes carrying them to the point of profit for both sides, sometimes pressing beyond that point—to profit for themselves only.

The growth of towns and the attendant widening of areas of contact brought important political, social, and economic change in the lives of the eastern Slavs. In each town there was developed a simple organ of authority, the common council, consisting of the adult male residents; and from time to time this council would appoint a prince who, with his warriors, assumed the duty of protecting the town. With increasing security, the more enterprising among the townsmen were able to advance materially, and class distinctions based upon accumulated wealth began to appear. Often those with wealth and social position would begin to seek power also, sometimes arranging with the appointed prince to get it.

Many leaders strengthened the position of their towns by subjugating weaker ones or by uniting theirs with stronger ones for common protection. As a result, such towns as Kiev, Novgorod, Chernigov, Smolensk, Beloozero, and Izborsk became the centers of widely expanded political units. But with all their expansion, it was not until the eighteenth century, when the descendants of the pioneer Slavs annexed the northern coast of the Black Sea, that the steppe could properly be called Russian. Until that time, an uncertain and disputed frontier existed between the Russians and their enemies to the south and east.

Many pitfalls are to be encountered in studying the beginnings of a nation that still exists. It is tempting, for instance, to consider a nation's existence as proof that its continuation has been inevitable; yet the study of history does not warrant such a belief. That the eastern Slavs succeeded in creating an enduring polity in a land where other peoples, apparently stronger and more advanced, had failed, was not preordained. The eastern Slavs themselves might have disappeared as an ethnic group had not certain unpredictable events taken place.

A more dangerous pitfall is the tendency, sometimes called *presentism*, to think of past institutions and behavior as identical with institutions and behavior of the present when they are discussed in modern terms. Lack of more precise terms is some justification for this somewhat loose use of modern ones in discussing the past. And the historian may argue that, since he is dealing with antecedents, he is justified in using modern terms for early institutions from which later ones have evolved. The study of the development of the early Russian polity lends itself easily to *presentism*, especially when such terms as *nation* and *state* are used. Therefore it is necessary to keep alert to the fact that those terms are being applied to an entity lacking many of the attributes that we commonly associate with them.

Kievan Russia

DEVELOPMENT OF THE KIEVAN STATE.   The chief source of the early history of the Russian nation[1] is the *Russian Primary Chronicle*, a record

---

[1] The term *nation* as used here refers to a historically developed community of people having a common language and culture.

The Slavs receiving the Varangians

begun probably by the Kievan monks in the second half of the eleventh century.

According to the *Chronicle*, the Varangians, confident of their superior strength, began to exact tribute from the Slavs in the middle years of the ninth century. That led to dissatisfaction, which caused the Slavs to rise against them and drive them out, back to Scandinavia. But soon such disorder arose from the Slavs' efforts to govern themselves that, in 862, they implored the Varangians to return and rule them. Three Varangian brothers, Rurik, Sineus, and Truvor, answered the call and came with their armed followers. Rurik established himself as prince in Novgorod; Sineus, in Beloozero; and Truvor, in Izborsk. Within two years Sineus and Truvor died, leaving Rurik in control of their areas. While he gave his attention to his enlarged principality, his followers—Slavic and Varangian—ranged farther afield, establishing themselves in Kiev and building up extensive trade connections. After Rurik's death, in 879, his son Igor was recognized as the heir to his territory and power; but since Igor was then only a child, his kinsman Oleg ruled in his stead until he came of age, then served prominently under him. Oleg proved to be more ambitious than Rurik had been in expanding and strengthening his principality. He took over the city of Kiev and established there the central control of the many other cities and towns he brought under his rule —including the important trading centers Smolensk and Novgorod. Thereafter his Slavic and Varangian followers (all now being called *Russians*— from the Varangian designation *Rus*) profited by better-organized protection for their established settlements and greater safety in the promotion of commerce with Byzantium. Thus was laid the foundation for Kievan Russia, a state that was to be ruled by successive princes of the Rurik dynasty.

Since the *Chronicle* is the chief source for the history of Kievan Russia, it is unfortunate that not all of the portion dealing with the ninth and tenth centuries can be taken as verified historical fact. In writing of the early period, the monks had to rely for the most part on accounts handed down orally. Such accounts, always more suspect than written ones because they can be more easily distorted without detection, should be validated by other sources before being accepted as fact. But much of the *Chronicle* material dealing with the early period, because of the lack of other sources, can be neither confirmed nor denied with any degree of certainty. As a result, scholars have disagreed sharply on some crucial matters covered by the *Chronicle*. The identification of Rurik, for example, is the subject of much dispute. One eminent scholar doubts him as a historical person; another is convinced that the exact place and time of his birth is established—Denmark, in the year 800; and a third accepts him as a historical person but identifies him as a Slav, not a Varangian.[1]

Despite their disagreement over many minor and some major matters, most historians agree on the broad outline of early Russian history. It is not likely that the Russian state was created by a single act such as the alleged calling of the Varangians in 862. It is almost certain that the state evolved slowly and that, even before 862, there existed, in such places as Kiev and Novgorod, eastern Slavic political entities resembling city-states. It is generally accepted that, during the second half of the ninth century, the Varangians established military and political mastery over the eastern Slavic settlements; that they succeeded in forming the kernel of a state with Kiev as center; that they assumed the ruling power in the Kievan state; and that,

[1] Various approaches to the early history of Kievan Russia will be found in these works: George Vernadsky's *Ancient Russia* and *Kievan Russia*, Michael Florinsky's *Russia: A History and an Interpretation*, N. K. Chadwick's *The Beginnings of Russian History*, P. Kovalevsky's *Manuel d'Histoire Russe*, H. Paszkiewicz's *Origin of Russia*, M. Hrushevsky's *A History of Ukraine*, and A. L. Mongait's *Archaeology in the U.S.S.R.*

during the tenth century, the term *Russian* was applied both to the nascent state and to its people. It is probable but not certain that there was a Rurik (whether or not he existed, the dynasty of princes that ruled Russia until its last reigning member—Feodor—died, in 1598, claimed descent from him). Many other points in the narrative are subjects of dispute; of particular note is that pertaining to the Varangian origin of the name *Rus*, which many believe to be of eastern Slavic origin.

The term *state*, when applied to the early Russian polity, refers to a weak union of city-states. It can reasonably be assumed that the Varangians did not intend to found a state but sought only to establish political authority sufficient to make themselves secure in their pursuit of trade, pillage, and tribute. Whether or not Kiev, Novgorod, and the other cities submitted willingly to the new rulers is not known. It is probable, however, that the natives and the rulers found much mutual benefit in the new relationship: the Varangians had a base from which to operate, and the natives were provided protection by the Varangian military strength. The state was at first a conglomerate of Varangian and eastern Slavic institutions. The new rulers concerned themselves with those functions of a state that relate to the making of war, the collection of tribute, and the conduct of foreign relations. They left the remaining functions, such as the maintenance of internal order and the settlement of disputes, to the jurisdiction of the existing native institutions. The result was a division of authority and power. That there were occasional conflicts, resolved sometimes in favor of the Slavs, is attested by the fact that the common councils of the cities were often successful in establishing their right to select or reject princes sent to rule them.

Gradually a coalescence and a reshaping of Varangian and native institutions were achieved, and the cleavage between rulers and ruled was narrowed to the point of disappearance by the process of cultural assimilation that led eventually to the Slavification of the Varangian princes as well as their military retinues. At the same time, a fusion of the foreign and native upper classes was being brought about through the inclusion of upper class natives in the military forces and through intermarriage. Those who claimed descent from Rurik retained their identity as a ruling family but, within a few generations, they could no longer be identified as foreigners.

STRENGTHENING OF THE KIEVAN STATE. By the beginning of the tenth century, the new rulers were strongly enough established in Kiev to use it as a bastion from which to protect their trade on the lower Dnieper, hitherto a hazardous stretch for all who followed that route to Constantinople. Now, at the beginning of each winter, they went into the country to exact tribute—slaves, furs, honey, wax, perhaps money—and, when the ice broke on the river in the spring, they were ready to lead the trading expedition south. Slavic merchants, their wares bought on the market, were permitted to join the princes and their armed followers, whose trading capital was derived wholly from tribute. After sacrifices were made to the pagan gods, the long journey to Constantinople would begin from a point just south of Kiev. Although the broad, dirty yellow waters of the Dnieper were safely navigable at the beginning, the trip could not be expected to be an easy one. Farther south, the boats would encounter narrow and turbulent rapids through which passage was impossible with the use of either oars or sail, and it would be necessary to portage the small craft along the shore for a few miles. Below the rapids, the chief danger came not from natural obstacles but from hostile and predatory nomads. But the Varangians' handling of such irregular and unpredictable features was successful often enough that a very profitable Byzantine trade was established, the risks being more than offset by the gains.

As the tenth century advanced, the princes strengthened Kiev still further by expanding its power over the tribes and towns along the River Road and bringing new areas into the state it dominated. But their progress was neither fast nor easy. They usually entrusted the administration of the outlying territories (principalities) to relatives, who as often as not were more concerned with dethroning their kinsman in Kiev than with embellishing his authority; and the state remained hardly more than a loosely articulated polity. Moreover, it was constantly beset by outside enemies, particularly by the Khazars and the Pechenegs, who competed with it for the southern trade routes. Yet for many years the Kievan princes succeeded in keeping their enemies at a safe distance and in holding in check the ambitions of the lesser princes. At the same time, they kept up trade relations with the Byzantine Empire and gradually made them secure by repeated demonstrations of Kievan military strength, sometimes carried as far as Constantinople and often followed by favorable treaties.

Svyatoslav, who became Prince of Kiev in 964, was a strong ruler whose ambition was to extend the state far beyond its previous boundaries. He turned first to the east, conquered the Khazars and annexed their lands on the lower Volga and the Don. Then, at the request of the Byzantine emperor, he turned his forces west—against the Bulgars on the Danube—and there gained more territory for the Kievan state. But his ambition overreached itself. His campaigning extended Kiev's military power to its very limits, and both the Pechenegs and the Byzantine emperor were ready to take advantage of that fact. The Pechenegs made such aggressive gains against him that they threatened Kiev itself, and the Byzantine emperor forced him to give up the Danubian territory. Svyatoslav tried to rally his defenses; but before he could make good any of his loss, he was killed (in 972) in an encounter with the Pechenegs.

After Svyatoslav's death, his sons dissipated their heritage by fratricidal conflict, from which Vladimir (978–1015) emerged as victor. He was faced with the immediate task of re-establishing order in a diminished and weakened realm, and he managed to accomplish it, building again on the strong economic foundations laid in previous years.

CONVERSION OF RUSSIA.   The most outstanding occurrence during Vladimir's reign was the conversion of the Russians to the religion that had long been the central element of Byzantine culture: the Christian religion as supported by the Holy Orthodox Apostolic Eastern Church—known more conveniently as the Eastern Orthodox or Greek Orthodox Church. It had come into being as a result of the many schisms that had destroyed the original unity of the Christian Church. Because of the schisms, two major religious centers had developed, Rome and Constantinople; and although the final break between those centers did not come until 1054, two distinct and separate religious organizations had been formed by the ninth century: the Roman Catholic Church, with its center in Rome, and the Eastern Orthodox Church, with its center in Constantinople.

The Eastern Orthodox Church, developing under the influence of the Byzantine Empire, acquired certain distinctive characteristics: (1) it was marked by Greek—rather than Roman—influence; (2) it was dominated by the Byzantine emperors; (3) it had four ecclesiastical heads of equal authority —the bishops of Alexandria, Antioch, Jerusalem, and Constantinople, each of whom was designated as a patriarch and given supreme ecclesiastical authority within his area (although the Patriarch of Constantinople, by virtue of his proximity to the emperor, appeared the most exalted).

During the tenth century many members of the Russian upper classes were affected by the more advanced Byzantine culture and religion, and it was only natural that the ruling princes inclined toward the faith of Byzantium. About 988, Vladimir was received into the Eastern Orthodox Church. Two years later he proclaimed Christianity the faith of his realm and ordered all his subjects baptized (acts for which he was later canonized). Following that, a branch of the Church was organized in Russia as a metropolitanate, with Kiev as its center. Its head, known as the metropolitan, was appointed by the Patriarch of Constantinople. Until 1237 the appointed metropolitans were, with few exceptions, Greeks; and, in the beginning, the bishops and priests were generally Greeks or Bulgarians.

Diffusion of Christianity in Russia was a gradual process, beginning with the upper classes and spreading slowly to the lower urban classes and even more slowly to those of the rural regions. Secret worship of the old heathen gods continued for many centuries, and pagan elements even found their way into the rituals of the new faith. But gradually, as houses of worship were built, monasteries established, and native clergy trained, Russians began to look to the Church as their spiritual center. In time, piety became so pervasive that the country was known as "Holy Russia."

The language of the Church in Russia was Church Slavonic, not Greek. The Eastern Orthodox Church generally followed the practice of using in its services the vernacular of the regions into which it penetrated; but since Church Slavonic, which had been developed in Bulgaria, was so closely related to the language spoken in Russia, it was used there as the religious language. The alphabet of Church Slavonic, based mainly on the Greek alphabet, had been developed in the latter part of the ninth century by the missionary Cyril in order to make possible the translation of religious literature into the vernacular of the southern and western Slavs and thus facilitate their conversion. Cyril's brother, Methodius, had translated the Bible into Church Slavonic, and translations of other religious texts had followed. Those translations were the first written literature made available to the Russians and became the models for their own religious literature. Their secular literature also employed Church Slavonic until about the eighteenth century.

OPPOSING POLITICAL FORCES.   At the beginning of the eleventh century certain elements in Kievan Russia were favorable to the creation of a nation from its various parts: a common language, a common religion, common social and economic institutions, and a common ruling dynasty. Moreover, out of the fusion of Slavic and Varangian peoples there was developing a vigorous and creative society, prime requisite for a dynamic nation.

On the other hand were forces making for disunity. Kievan Russia lacked a strong tradition of political cohesion. It lacked also any satisfactory rule of monarchical succession, although the House of Rurik held uncontested political power. The ruler, by that time known as the Grand Prince, was head of the realm, and the princes (his uncles, brothers, and sons) shared in the administration of it; yet there was no established manner of inheritance. Often, when a grand prince died, Kiev, as the seat of his power, simply lost its authority and prestige until the disputes among the rival claimants for the grand princely throne were settled—usually by armed might.

At times, before the country could recover from the debilitating effects of a struggle over the succession, it would be further weakened by additional rivalries between prince and prince or between prince and incumbent grand prince. Moreover, the princes usually thought of themselves as autonomous rulers rather than as faithful lieutenants of their superior in Kiev. That attitude often led the common councils of strong cities such as Novgorod and Chernigov to abet the princes who opposed Kiev, their reason being the justified expectation that a weak grand prince was likely to mean strong local government.

The period following the death of Vladimir, in 1015, illustrates well the common political difficulties of Kievan Russia. For many years the country was torn by the struggle for ascendancy among five of Vladimir's sons. The oldest, Svyatopolk, began a quick ascent through the murder of two of his brothers but met his match in the person of another brother, Yaroslav, Prince of Novgorod. Yaroslav defeated Svyatopolk in 1019, brought Kiev under his control, and undertook to establish himself as Grand Prince. His position was contested, in turn, by the remaining brother, Mstislav, with whom he was forced to divide the realm; and, until his death, in 1036, Mstislav ruled that part lying east of the Dnieper, while Yaroslav ruled the remainder.

During the years that Yaroslav (known as the Wise) ruled alone, the disruptive forces were temporarily halted. Those years, 1036–1054, were notable because they marked the last period during which the Grand Prince of Kiev actually governed all of the country, the time of the greatest territorial expansion of Kievan Russia (see map on p. 24), and a noteworthy period of progressive development. Kievan economic relations with both European and Asiatic countries were so expanded during this time that Kiev became an accepted meeting place of Byzantine, Arabic, Dutch, Polish, Hungarian, and Scandinavian merchants. With Byzantine help the impressive cathedral of St. Sophia was built in Kiev; schools and libraries were established; scholars and artists were encouraged; and the people were urged toward useful pursuits. Such progress led one traveller, Adam of Bremen, to call Kiev "Constantinople's rival and the most brilliant of ornaments." Although Kievan Russia was tied most closely to the Byzantine Empire economically and culturally, it was beginning to make dynastic ties—so important in those days—with other parts of the world also. Yaroslav himself was related by marriage to the kings of England, France, Norway, and Poland.

THE DARKENING YEARS, 1054–1223. The factors that made Yaroslav's reign a brilliant one did not persist after his death but gave way to the sub-

Yaroslav the Wise   Andrei Bogolyubsky

The features of these busts by archaeologist Michael M. Gerasimov were determined on the basis of data derived from skeletal remains.

versive factors that had been in restive abeyance during his reign. The next two centuries of Russian history were characterized by two concurrent processes: (1) the decentralization of political authority and (2) the decline of Kiev as the center of Russia.

Unwittingly Yaroslav contributed to the dispersion of power that followed his death. In the hope of preventing internecine strife and preserving the unity of the realm, he left to each of his six heirs the administration over one specified area and enjoined the five younger ones to obey the oldest, who would rule as Grand Prince of Kiev. He hoped thus to establish a regular rule of succession, but many of the princes refused to be bound by any rule except that of force. Ironically, his own testament was used to promote disunity: in 1097, his descendants, meeting at Lyubech and parcelling out the various principalities, justified their actions by contending that each was entitled to the lands that Yaroslav had assigned to his father. Yaroslav had intended to divide administration, not possession; but the princes, supported by the common councils of the cities, looked upon their principalities as possessions over which they were sovereign. It followed then that the Grand Prince of

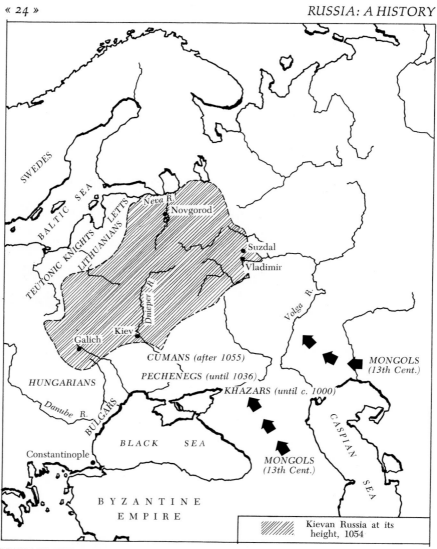

MAP 4. Chief threats to Kievan Russia

Kiev was just another prince, distinguished only by the grandeur of his title and his control over Kiev.

Historians are not in agreement about the nature of the princely succession in the years after 1054. Klyuchevsky, the most distinguished of Russian historians, claims that a system of rotation operated during the period of decline: upon the death of a grand prince, the eldest son would vacate the principality he held and assume the title and rule over Kiev while the younger princes would move up in the hierarchy of principalities. But the very evidence used by Klyuchevsky has been used by other historians to discount the idea of a system of rotation. All agree, however, that the authority of the grand prince gradually declined while the autonomy of the principalities increased.

Although the central administration was losing prestige, the idea of a Russian realm, at least as the patrimony of the House of Rurik, continued in force. And some change was being effected in the attitudes of the princes; they were now expected at least to respect one another's lands. In the conference at Lyubech it was agreed that if one prince attacked another, the rest "with the aid of the Holy Cross" would move against the aggressor. The agreement was often violated, but the idea behind it had some influence. Of greater influence—and perhaps of greater import to the country—was their agreement to unite against outside forces.

In 1113, the succession brought to Kiev a grand prince strong enough to stay the disruptive forces again for a short time—Vladimir Monomakh, grandson of Yaroslav. He made an effort to draw the rival princes into a peaceful agreement and, although he failed to establish a workable organization among them, succeeded in keeping relative peace among them for a period of twelve years. During that time, the nomads on the Russian borders were held off and Kiev was given a chance to regain some of its former prosperity. But he was not able to convert the forces of disintegration to forces of construction, and after his time they ate into the structure of the state even more rapidly than before.

To the effects of the interprincely wars that sapped the strength of Kiev must be added the effects of the incursions of nomads, which, except for the period of Vladimir Monomakh's reign, became increasingly destructive. Between 1061 and 1210, the Cumans (known to contemporaries also as Polovtsy or Polovcians) made fifty major attacks on Russian territory, usually in the Kievan region. The nature of these attacks is illustrated by this statement, from the *Chronicle* account of one that ended in the suburbs of Kiev in 1096:

> . . . Bonyak, that godless, mangy thief and bandit, came suddenly to Kiev for the second time. The Polovcians almost entered the city, burned the suburbs about the town, and then attacked the monastery. The godless sons of Ishmael slew the brethren in the monastery. . . . Then they set fire to the shrine of the Holy Virgin. . . .[1]

[1] Samuel H. Cross and O. P. Sherbowitz-Wetzor (trs. and eds.), *The Russian Primary Chronicle* (Cambridge: The Mediaeval Academy of America, 1953), p. 183.

The Cumans endangered not only the security of the city but also its trade with Constantinople, which they made more and more hazardous at a time when it was already becoming less profitable because Byzantium, itself suffering from barbarian attacks and internal decline, was losing its economic strength. By the middle of the twelfth century, signs of the decadence of Kiev and its environs were evident in the movement of many people from this dangerous and impoverished region to safer and more flourishing Russian principalities to the west and north.

These principalities—among them Rostov-Suzdal, Novgorod, Polotsk, Smolensk, Galicia, and Volhynia—were now practically independent, recognizing no higher authority than their own princes and often at war with one another. But they still felt themselves bound by family and ethnic ties and were sometimes moved to common effort by an enemy. Although Kiev had no authority over them, the member of the family holding the title of Grand Prince was in that city, as was also the Metropolitan of the Orthodox Church in Russia; so the various princes could not but give it some thought, whether of respect or jealousy; and it became, naturally enough, one of the sought-after goals in the princely warring.

In 1169, Andrei Bogolyubsky, Prince of Rostov-Suzdal, took Kiev and subjected it to ruthless plunder and looting. However, though he assumed the title of Grand Prince, Andrei refused to make Kiev his residence. Instead he installed his brother Gleb as its prince while he himself returned to live in Vladimir, which now became capital of Rostov-Suzdal as well as seat of the grand prince.

After Bogolyubsky's humbling of the once proud capital, the Russian nation was no longer, properly speaking, Kievan Russia. And further changes were to come, for it was entering a new period of development, during which it was to meet and be affected by enemy forces more powerful than any encountered in the earlier periods. From the Baltic region were to come the Lithuanians, Germans, and Swedes. From the southwest were to come the Poles and the Hungarians, pressing toward eastern conquest, particularly in the Galician principality. And from the east were to come those whose threat was greatest of all—the Mongols (called Tatars by the Russians), fierce and well trained warriors who swept into Russia from the Transcaucasian region. MONGOL CONQUEST.   Although the Mongols were successful in their first efforts against the Russian princes, defeating them at Kalka, near the Sea of Azov, in 1223, they did not push their conquest at that time. Returning to Asia, they allowed thirteen years to elapse before their next onslaught; and during that time, the Russians apparently gave no particular thought to

A twelfth century painting showing (top) citizens of Novgorod with their icons; (center) negotiations between Novgorod and Suzdal being disrupted as Suzdal archers, in right background, shoot at icon; and (bottom) Novgorod, directed by angel, in combat with Suzdal.

them. But the Mongols were not idle; they were consolidating their power over most of Asia and preparing for an extensive campaign into Europe. In 1235, their leaders met at Karakorum, the Mongol capital, to work out final plans; and in the following year, the campaign began with a successful attack on the Volga Bulgars and the Cumans. The Russian princes appeared not to sense the approaching danger until the Mongols had crossed the Volga, and then their attempts to organize a unified resistance failed because of the old intra-family rivalries and animosities. As a result, Ryazan, the first of the principalities to be attacked, met the Mongols unaided. Its lands were devastated and its chief city, Ryazan (from which the principality took its name), was captured on December 12, 1237, after a siege of six days. The Mongols, as was their custom with those who resisted, slaughtered the survivors and then moved on, overcoming the hastily prepared Russian defenses with fire and sword. They took Vladimir in February, 1238. Then they turned their attention to the army of that principality, which had taken a position outside the city; and on March 4, they routed the army and killed the Grand Prince, Yuri Vsevolodovich. Their next objective was to be Novgorod; but, when they had advanced to within about sixty miles of the city, they found that the spring thaws had made the roads nearly impassable. So the leaders, deciding the campaign unfeasible under the conditions, gave the order to return south in order that men and horses might have a period of rest.

The next Mongol invasion began in 1239 and resulted in the fall of Kiev in 1240. From that area the invaders continued west into Hungary and Poland until, in 1241, they were compelled to suspend operations because of political changes in the Mongol Empire. During the next year, they set up headquarters at Sarai (on the Volga, near present day Volgograd) and established their rule. The Russian principalities that had been conquered and those that had agreed to submit now acknowledged Mongol suzerainty; and Novgorod, although still unconquered, later acknowledged it also, out of weakness.

RUSSIA DIVIDED.   The disintegration of Kievan Russia had been accomplished before the coming of the Mongols; and the country now had the added burden of foreign control. Yet the situation was not as bleak as it was to become, for others who coveted the Russian lands were still unsated and aggressive.

As the Mongols completed their conquest of southern Russia, the Swedes and Germans attacked from the north and west—but with less success. In 1240, Prince Alexander of Novgorod defeated the Swedish forces in an

DRAWN BY EDW. A. SCHMITZ

MAP 5. Russia in the fourteenth century

engagement on the banks of the Neva.[1] Two years later, in a dramatic battle fought on the ice of Lake Peipus, he defeated a German force consisting of members of the military monastic order known as the German Knights. These victories relieved the principality of Novgorod from immediate physi-

[1] For his victory on the Neva, the Russians remember him as Alexander Nevsky. For his defense of Orthodox Russia against the enemies of the Church, he was later canonized.

cal threats but did not make it strong enough to refuse tribute and homage to the Mongols.

In the western and southern principalities, Lithuania was becoming a threat that not even the Mongols could meet successfully. About the middle of the thirteenth century, the pagan, illiterate, and powerful Lithuanian tribes formed a state that, within a century, absorbed lands stretching from the Black Sea to the Baltic and including the Russian principalities of Polotsk, Smolensk, Chernigov, Volhynia, and Kiev.

The political breakup continued as the westernmost of the Russian principalities, Galicia, was lost by the Mongols to Poland in the 1340's. In that region, Mongol control had been only nominal and, in the century between the Mongol invasion and the Polish annexation, Galicia had been less affected by Mongol demands than by Polish-Hungarian rivalry over its territory. In the end, Poland took the winner's share; Moldavia (now a part of Rumania) annexed a small tip of Galicia; and Hungary gained only some new subjects, immigrants from Galicia who had crossed the Carpathian Mountains into Hungarian lands.

From the second quarter of the thirteenth century until the second half of the fifteenth, no part of what had been Kievan Russia was free of foreign domination. As a result, the subsequent political and cultural history of the Russians was determined by two sets of influences: those exerted by foreign rulers and those that survived from the centuries before their advent.

Post-Kievan Trends

CRISIS.   With the disappearance of the Kievan state, some different turn of events might easily have sent the Russians to join the Scythians, the Cimmerians, the Khazars, and others in the historical discard. Some of them were assimilated by their conquerors, others were not. And it was the survival of the unassimilated ones as a distinct ethnic group that made possible, but by no means guaranteed, the further growth of the Russian nation. In the middle of the thirteenth century, their vital need was a state. All that was left of their former state was the title of Grand Prince, held now by the princes of Vladimir.

Within what had been Kievan Russia, there were three areas any of which might have served as the center of future Russian political growth and one of which was finally to do so: the principality of Novgorod, the principalities under the rule of Lithuania, and the principalities of the Volga-Oka region under Mongol rule. These areas were unequal both in specific advantages and in general characteristics; the final choice among them was to be determined by those qualities most favorable to lasting political leadership.

NOVGOROD.   Politically, Novgorod followed a path strikingly different from that of other Russian principalities. While in others the urban councils were weakened or crushed by the princes, in Novgorod there was taking place what may be called, with some reservations, the extension of the democratic tradition. The princes of Novgorod retained the status of chief magistrates, but that meant so little in view of the limitations placed on their powers by the common council that it was customary to speak of the principality as a republic.

The chief reason that the principality of Novgorod had been able to dominate its princes was the fact that the thriving commerce of the city Novgorod had produced a citizenry of considerable economic and political strength. The city's position, near the head of the ancient River Road, made possible the command of trade routes leading to the Dnieper and Volga basins, to the fur producing areas of the north, and to the rich trade of the Baltic Sea. It served also to put the city outside the center of princely conflicts. In short, Novgorod had developed in striking contrast to most Russian cities of the time; and the extent of her wealth and the nature of her political life accentuated that contrast.

The impression of direct democracy that had been created in Novgorod was due to the fact that all citizens were included in the common council and that its apparent powers were quite broad, including even the right to elect bishops. Its meetings were frequent and lively (often ending in bloody street fights between contending factions). However, Novgorod's "democracy," like that of many contemporary mercantile republics in Italy and Germany, was more apparent than real. The Council of Notables, a much smaller body than the common council, was the actual source of policy and was in fact nearly independent of the common council, to which it was in theory responsible. Yet, democratic or not, Novgorod was a conspicuous exception to contemporary trends in Russia; and, had it not lacked the military power to impose its will upon the other principalities, it might have served as a model for political life quite different from the one eventually followed by the rejuvenated state. As it was, Novgorod's national influence was limited to playing one neighbor against another in order to maintain its own security.

LITHUANIA.   Many historians speak of Lithuania in the thirteenth and fourteenth centuries as a "Russian-Lithuanian" state. It is believed that, during that period, Russians outnumbered Lithuanians in the state two to one and that they were culturally in advance of them. It was therefore natural that Russians should be prominent in civil administration and military life. Theirs was the official language of administration, a fact explained not only by Russian influence but also by the Lithuanians' lack of a written language. Another fact favoring the Russians was that, although most Lithuanians clung to paganism for some time, those who wavered turned not to Catholicism but to Eastern Orthodoxy.

The Russian principalities under Lithuanian rule remained so, with little change, until the end of the fourteenth century. It is conceivable that the chief city of Lithuania, Vilna, might have become the center of a new phase of Russian political development had not another foreign influence been officially imposed upon it. In 1386, Jagiello, ruler of Lithuania, became King of Poland by marrying its Queen Jadwiga; and for nearly two centuries the dynasty created by this marriage ruled Poland and Lithuania, gradually displacing Russian influence in the latter. During most of this period, Poland and Lithuania were in theory separate states, united only through their monarch; but, as time passed, their relationship grew closer and was characterized by increasing Polish influence. Among the upper classes of Lithuania (particularly among those of Lithuanian origin, but also among those of Russian descent), the Polish language and the Roman Catholic faith displaced the Russian language and Eastern Orthodoxy. Some of the influence of Russian culture and the Orthodox religion persisted, especially among the lower classes in the former Russian principalities; and Vilna continued to be a center of Russian culture, but it was no longer a potential center of Russian political power.

THE NORTHEASTERN PRINCIPALITIES.   In the end, Russian political leadership came not from Novgorod, not from Lithuania, but from the northeastern principalities. So called because they included the north-eastern part of the realm once ruled by Kiev, these were the principalities that, along with Novgorod, formed the Russian holdings of the Mongols. It was in this area, comprising the basins of the Oka and the upper Volga, that the Great Russian branch of the Russian people began to evolve and in which the political future of Russia was to be decided.

That leadership fell to the northeastern principalities may seem a matter for wonder. In their location they were less favored by nature than were other parts of what had been Kievan Russia, and they were under the apparent handicap of Mongol domination. Yet they had several advantages that ultimately outweighed the negative factors.

Even though the Volga-Oka region did not provide the rich opportunities that were natural to the immediate vicinities of Kiev and Novgorod, it offered the means of insuring a satisfactory livelihood. Its complex river system permitted trade in many directions, although the accessible markets were less desirable than those with which Kiev had dealt. Its arable lands, wrested from the forest, were not as fertile as those to the south; but the soil was productive enough to sustain a growing population. Thus, though its geographical setting was not the most desirable, it had the advantages necessary to encourage a vigorous people to grow stronger, given favorable political circumstances.

Mongol rule, paradoxical as it may seem, was a favoring political circumstance. The new rulers, despite the fact that they considered the conquered Russian principalities as integral parts of the Mongol Empire, generally found it more convenient to preserve the existing system of princely rule and to use the princes as agents than to replace the system with a purely Mongol administration. And, although the Mongol rulers themselves became Moslems, they tolerated the Orthodox Church. As a result, the ruling class of the northeastern principalities remained Russian and Orthodox while its counterpart in Lithuania, after 1386, was shifting to Catholicism and learning to speak Polish. Moreover, while the former Russian principalities under Lithuania were being merged with the Lithuanian state and, later, the Polish-Lithuanian state, the northeastern principalities retained their separate identity under a Russian ruling class supported by the Orthodox Church, which regarded the northeastern princes as allies against the threat of the Catholic West. Thus these princes, almost as if by default, found themselves in the position of leadership.

New political centers in Mongol Russia

NATURE AND EFFECTS OF MONGOL RULE.　The gradual restoration of a Russian political entity was a process in which many factors were in operation and many influences at work. At first, the Mongols demanded the most immediate consideration.

By the middle of the thirteenth century, the Mongols had established an empire reaching from China to Eastern Europe. It was governed from the imperial capital at Karakorum, in Mongolia, by the Great Khan (chosen from among the descendants of Genghis Khan, founder of the empire). To make administration practicable, the vast realm was divided into several parts, each under a khan selected from the family of the Great Khan. One such part was the Golden Horde, which governed the defeated Russian principalities as well as the middle and lower reaches of the Volga basin and the western parts of Siberia and Central Asia. The khan of the Golden Horde, the capital of which was Sarai, on the lower Volga, was legally the deputy of the Great Khan; but, as time went on, the khans of Sarai became increasingly free of effective control by the Great Khan, and the Golden Horde was soon to become (in fact, if not in theory) an independent empire.

While the khans administered the northeastern principalities through their princes and tolerated the activities of the Orthodox Church, they expected evidence of proper subordination to Sarai. Princes could not assume their titles and their possessions nor could officers of the Church take office except with the consent of the khan. He usually accepted existing practices of princely succession, thus preserving the rights of the descendants of the House of Rurik, but he could and did remove rebellious princes and, when princes were in dispute over succession, exercised the right to settle the matter as he saw fit.

Indirect as it was for the most part, Mongol rule over the Russian principalities was both visible and tangible. The princes were constantly reminded that they were vassals of the khan by the presence of Mongol civil agents and troops, by frequent orders to make the long trip to Sarai with their families and retainers, by oft-repeated Mongol interference in local affairs, and by punitive expeditions (some fifty in number during the period of Mongol suzerainty) to put down unrest or to settle princely squabbles.

Above all, the Russians—princes as well as commoners—felt the "Tatar Yoke," as they called Mongol rule, in the constant and heavy demand from Sarai for revenue to support the government and recruits to replenish the armies of the Golden Horde. Even though the Russian princes were soon permitted to replace Mongol agents as tax collectors for the khan, the double burden of taxation and military levies for both the Golden Horde and the local principalities remained heavy for those who bore it.

There has been much debate over the lasting effect of the "Tatar Yoke." Some have blamed the Mongols for all that they deplore in later Russia: absolutism, Muscovite centralization, cultural backwardness, and isolation from the West. Others have treated Mongol rule as a bloody but relatively minor episode in the history of Russia. Certainly it is difficult to assess Mongol influence because many—probably the most important—aspects of that influence were indirect and therefore elusive. Yet the results of Mongol rule should not be dismissed lightly. Napoleon at least indicated a proper emphasis when he remarked that to scratch a Russian was to find a Mongol.

The Russian upper classes not only adopted a number of Mongol social customs but also took into their ranks Mongol nobles who, for one reason or another, chose to live and marry among them. They also borrowed many fiscal and administrative practices from the conquerors: their coinage, transportation system, and military organizations show direct Mongol influence. And it is possible that they acquired from the same source the idea of state monopoly of liquor production.

Although the effect of Mongol rule on the political structure of Russia is difficult to evaluate, it can be indicated. Princely power, in the latter part of the fifteenth century, at the end of Mongol rule, was more nearly autocratic than it had been in the days of Kievan Russia, when the powerful urban councils had been instruments for preserving a democratic tradition. The Russian princes, it is true, had already begun to undermine this tradition before the invasion; but the Mongols accelerated the subversion of the common councils, for it was more in their interest to support a prince subservient to the khan than to recognize a common council that, more often than not, was in opposition to Russian prince as well as Mongol khan. The result was that, by the end of the fifteenth century, the common council had all but disappeared (the Novgorod council was one of the few exceptions) as an effective counter-balance to princely power, and the movement toward absolutism was thus facilitated. Absolutistic tendencies were probably also reinforced by the example and influence of the Mongol state system, which required complete submission of the subject to the all-powerful state.

The great changes in the Russian economy between the thirteenth and fifteenth centuries cannot be ascribed solely to the Mongols; yet the immediate effects of their ruthless destruction of the Russian cities, probably as extensive as the long-range consequences of the "Tatar Yoke," must not be overlooked. Nevertheless, had the Mongols never entered the country, Russia would still have been adversely affected by the rapid decay of the Byzantine Empire, which began in the thirteenth century and made possible the Turkish conquest of Constantinople in the fifteenth. The urban population of Russia (by estimation, since figures are lacking) was much less in the Mongol period than it had been in the Kievan, and it did not reach its former level again until the nineteenth century. During that time the urban contribution to the general economy was necessarily lowered. Many urban artisans had died at the hands of the first Mongol invaders and others, willing or not, had entered Mongol service. Consequently there was a definite decline in the production and in the quality of artisan goods; some handicrafts—e.g., the making of cloisonné enamel—ceased entirely, not to be resumed for several centuries. The economy of the cities (with the exception of Novgorod) suffered also from the loss of many of the old trade routes to Byzantium and Central Asia and the accompanying decline in available profits. Thus trade in general became less extensive and less profitable than it had been when Kiev was at its height.

Still further change resulted from the Mongol-imposed isolation from the West. Before the coming of the Mongols, Russia had established many ties with the West and had achieved a level of civilization which compared favorably with that of contemporary England and Germany. But, restrained from Western contacts, the country fell behind in comparative progress; while the West was entering the age of complex urban life, of universities, of Humanistic literature and Renaissance art, Russian civilization remained static or retrogressed. Patriotic Russian writers have argued that, because of the situation during this period, the West is indebted to Russia for holding off the "Asiatic hordes" while the West was advancing its civilization. Such an argument distorts certain facts of history: Russia was not responsible for limiting the Mongol advance in Europe; and many of the Russian princes, far from being unselfish defenders of "European civilization," were shamelessly servile toward the Mongols. It is true, of course, that Russia was for several centuries on the embattled border of European civilization and paid heavily for a position not of her own making. But it must be remembered that an area on which the Mongols had imposed their rule was the one finally to dominate, restore, and shape the rest of Russia.

GENERAL POLITICAL DEVELOPMENTS.   The northeastern principalities continued, during the period of Mongol domination, to act insofar as possible as independent polities, each with its own capital, army, and system of government. Their numbers varied with the ups and downs of fortune, but there were usually a dozen or more of them (including Rostov, Suzdal, Tver, Ryazan, Vladimir, Pereyaslavl, Starodub, and Seversk) vying with one another for power. The ruling families were of the House of Rurik, but they tended to break up into separate subdynasties, each regarding its principality as family property to part of which each son had a claim. It was customary that the senior member of a family would rule as prince of the entire principality but administer only the principal city and its environs while the other adult male members of the family—also having the title of prince—would administer other parts of the principality; upon the death of the senior member, all would be rearranged. In a sense, this was little more than the system of rule that had prevailed in Kievan

Russia, but it was now applied to a dozen or more distinct polities rather than to one.

Of all the ruling families in the northeastern principalities, the one finally to achieve control and hold it to the end of the Rurik dynasty (in 1598) was that descended from Yuri Dolgoruky, Prince of Rostov until 1157. This family held its supremacy, at various times, from the princely seats of Rostov, Suzdal, Vladimir, and Moscow.

Among the principalities, Rostov and Suzdal were at first the chief contenders for political pre-eminence. Rostov, located on Lake Nero, gained importance as early as the ninth century and became a city of considerable wealth and renown. Suzdal, established later at a favorable site on the Kamenka River, soon reached a status equal to that of Rostov. The two, in time, came under the rule of the same prince; and, by the twelfth century, it was common to speak of them as Rostov-Suzdal.

A newcomer among cities, Vladimir, having been established on the Klyazma River about 1108, outstripped the older rivals after becoming the choice of Andrei Bogolyubsky, son of Yuri Dolgoruky, for his residence rather than Rostov or Suzdal (which had served his forebears) or Kiev (which he had just taken). Vladimir was never to become a great city, but for about two centuries, it served, insofar as any city of the time may be said to have served, as the capital of Russia. And, since Prince Andrei had won the title of Grand Prince, his successors could claim some shadow of seniority over the other Russian princes. In fact, his successors used the title "Grand Prince of Vladimir and All Rus," which was recognized by the Mongols as conferring on its holder the right to speak for the other princes. Vladimir gained yet another distinction when the seat of the Metropolitan of the Orthodox Church was transferred to it, in 1300. While the senior member of the family ruled from Vladimir, junior members were assigned to various parts of the principality or to Novgorod, which was generally willing to accept princes from the Grand Principality of Vladimir (Alexander Nevsky was one of them).

Among the less important centers administered by members of the ruling family was Moscow. The earliest reference to Moscow in the Russian historical chronicles is dated 1147; hence, although its origin may pre-date that year, 1147 is officially accepted as the founding date of Moscow. Little is known of it before the latter part of the thirteenth century, when Daniel, son of Alexander Nevsky, served as prince. During his reign and that of his son Yuri, Moscow was a crude, small town, dominated—as were other Russian towns and cities—by a fortified center known as a *kremlin*.

CHANGING NATURE OF PRINCELY RULE.   Within the various principalities, there was a tendency toward fragmentation as the number and
ambitions of the princes increased. That tendency was sometimes curbed
in instances involving the lands of princes strong enough to check the
ambitions of members of their own families; and at times it was reversed
by those whose forces were powerful enough not only to handle the problems of their own principalities but also, perhaps, to annex the lands of
others. Such princes earned the favor and support of the Church, which felt
that its interests would be served best by political unification of the principalities. Now and then, the fragmentation of princely holdings was forestalled also by direct personal action—as happened when Gleb Vladimiro-
vich, Prince of Ryazan in the first half of the thirteenth century, had the
other six princes of his realm assassinated.

Another important factor in the political life of the principalities was
the necessity that each prince maintain a group of professional men-at-
arms. The upper ranks of these developed into a separate class, known
as boyars, who served under conditions that varied from place to place.
Generally, however, being assigned land in return for the furnishing of
military contingents and for the performance of military and administrative duties, the boyars developed into a landholding aristocracy. Since land
was plentiful and fighting men were scarce, they were often able to
consolidate and expand their rights. In many of the principalities, they
were able, for example, to compel the recognition of their land rights even
when they failed to serve the prince who had engaged them or, worse yet,
when they were serving another. Where possible, the princes enforced a
system of land-tenure under which the boyar's right to the land was recognized only as long as he served the prince who had granted the land. Even
under this system, boyars were free to enter the service of another prince,
relinquishing their holdings and taking their fighting men, without in-
curring the taint of treason. Because they were powerful, boyars were able
to continue the institution of the Boyars' Duma (or council), which had its
beginning in the Kievan period. In the several principalities, the Boyars'
Duma served as a consultative council; but the prince, while recognizing
the right of its members to a hearing, usually stood fast on princely prerogative in matters of state. Limited though it was at certain times and places,
the power of the boyars was great enough to give them a sense of general
independence and to make the princes conscious of them as potential opponents.

RISE OF MUSCOVY.   Among the cities contending for pre-eminence, none was more favorably situated than Moscow. Its geographical location, near the center of the Russian lands, combined with the accidents of history and the strength of its rulers, gave it extraordinary advantages for growth. Its early princes, noted in the table on page 40, laid the foundation.

Because of its position on the Moscow River at a point where that river was crossed by the trade route connecting the Oka and the upper Volga, its princes were able to develop it as a strong commercial center from which to control an expanding principality, then known as Muscovy. In time, the princes of Muscovy brought their realm to political pre-eminence by establishing strong political power within it, appropriating for it certain national symbols, and expending their political and military power over neighboring areas.

Prince Ivan I (known as Kalita, or Moneybag) advanced the fortunes of his patrimony by two important steps. First, he persuaded the Metropolitan to move the seat of the Church from Vladimir to Moscow, thereby gaining for his city dignity and influence as the spiritual center of Russia. Then, by a combination of bribes to the Mongols and the use of force against his neighbors, he gained the confirmation of himself as Grand Prince of Vladimir and All Rus. His two immediate successors, Simeon and Ivan II (the Red), held his gains. And Grand Prince Dmitri, who followed them, enhanced the position of Muscovy still further when he defeated the Mongols on the upper Don, in 1380. Although the Mongols recovered from their loss to Dmitri—thereafter known as Dmitri Donskoi (of the Don)—his effort and initial success served to rally a degree of national feeling around the Muscovite rulers as challengers of the foreign oppressor. The next two in the princely line, Basil I and Basil II, were hard pressed to maintain their heritage against the incursions of Lithuanians and Mongols and the efforts of rivals for the throne. Yet Basil I managed to add a little to the Muscovite territory, and Basil II strengthened the independence of the metropolitanate at Moscow by opposing the arrangement made at the Council of Florence to unite the Eastern and Western Churches.

By the middle of the fifteenth century, the princes of Muscovy had gone far toward establishing their pre-eminence among the Russians, and their strength was gaining a widening respect.

Genealogy of Early Moscow Princes[1]

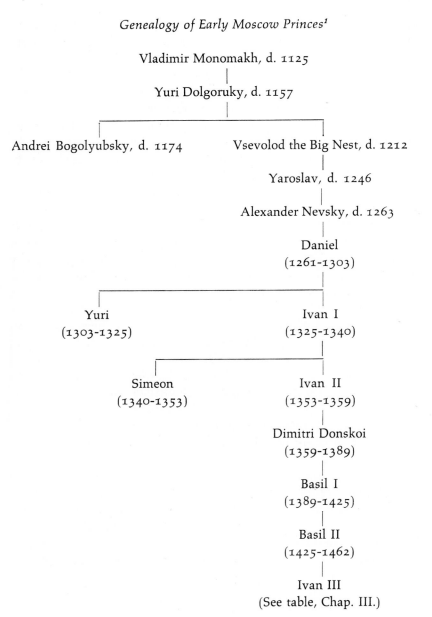

Vladimir Monomakh, d. 1125

Yuri Dolgoruky, d. 1157

Andrei Bogolyubsky, d. 1174   Vsevolod the Big Nest, d. 1212

Yaroslav, d. 1246

Alexander Nevsky, d. 1263

Daniel
(1261-1303)

Yuri   Ivan I
(1303-1325)   (1325-1340)

Simeon   Ivan II
(1340-1353)   (1353-1359)

Dimitri Donskoi
(1359-1389)

Basil I
(1389-1425)

Basil II
(1425-1462)

Ivan III
(See table, Chap. III.)

[1] This table of genealogical relations and those that follow are not complete but contain only information considered pertinent in relation to the text. Dates in parentheses above indicate periods of rule over Moscow.

During the fifteenth and sixteenth centuries, the Muscovite principality advanced to the status of empire through developments involving rapid geographical expansion, establishment of an autocratic form of government, and enserfment of the agricultural population. Those developments, closely interrelated, came about during the reigns of Ivan III (the Great), Basil III, and Ivan IV (the Terrible). The period of their accomplishments was followed by one of decline; and after the Rurik dynasty ended (in 1598) there came a period of crisis during which it seemed that Russia might not survive as a state. But when a new dynasty was finally established, that of the Romanovs, the country resumed the course that had been set during the century and a quarter under the three strong Muscovites of the Rurik line.

Genealogical Relations of Rulers, 1462-1598

Ivan III. . . . . Sophia
(1462-1505)   (niece of Byzantine Emperor)
                        Basil III
                        (1505-33)

                        Ivan IV
                        (1533-84)

                        Feodor I
                        (1584-98)

Evolution of imperial characteristics

EXPANSION OF MUSCOVITE
CONTROL.   When Ivan III, son of
Basil II, became Grand Prince of
Muscovy, his realm consisted of
about 15,000 square miles. Small as
that area may seem in comparison
with the territory of Russia some
four centuries later (about one-sixth
of the world's land surface), it was
a sizeable holding for a prince of
that day. And during his and succeeding reigns it was progressively
expanded. Circumstances favoring
that expansion were (1) a succession
of three able and energetic rulers,
(2) the disintegration of the Golden
Horde, and (3) the vigorous Russian
colonization of newly annexed areas.

SOVFOTO

Ivan III

It fell to Ivan III not only to accelerate the growth of Muscovy but also
to invest it with new and important goals. His predecessors had conceived
of themselves as princes more or less equal to other Russian princes, all
engaged in the struggle for survival and power. But Ivan III believed that
the title of "Grand Duke of Vladimir and All Rus," won by his forebear
Ivan I, was more than a symbol. To him it was the legal basis for his claim
that he was head of the Russian state and that he should, by right, rule over
all the lands previously held by Kiev—including those parts now in alien
hands. Thus he justified the initiation of an undertaking (continued by
his successors and later known as "the gathering in of the Russian land")
to bring those lands again under a central administration. However, claims
were one thing, reality another: the patrimony left by Basil II in 1462 was
not as large as the one claimed by Ivan III, nor was it a secure one. At
that time, as Klyuchevsky points out, a relatively short journey would take
one from the city of Moscow to hostile neighboring lands—the still strong
and contentious principality of Tver, fifty miles away, or the frontier of
Lithuania, sixty miles away. Moreover, although the Golden Horde was
disintegrating, there were dangerous Mongol armies no more than sixty

miles to the south and less than 300 miles to the east. Such difficulties notwithstanding, the grand princes pursued their campaigns for re-uniting the Russian lands. That they made progress in their efforts must not be credited to national irredentism as it is now understood, but rather to Muscovite desire for power and profit.

To strengthen the position of Muscovy, Ivan III and his successors engaged in extended conflicts with other Russian princes and with the Mongols; but it was against Lithuania and its more powerful partner, Poland, that the chief enmity was directed. Ivan III set the tone when he declared that between his realm and Poland there could be no peace, only "truce in order to draw breath," as long as any parts of his patrimony were under Polish control. The same relentless attitude was adopted toward Lithuania with the result that Muscovy was at war with that country during forty of the years between 1492 and 1582.

One of the first goals in Ivan III's crusade was the acquisition of Novgorod, at that time economically superior to Moscow but militarily inferior. When he found an excuse for an attack on Novgorod (the fact that its upper classes were friendly with the arch-enemy Poland-Lithuania) Ivan was soon able to reduce it to a tribute-paying status. That was in 1471; and seven years later, he brought it to the point of actual capitulation, annexed its territories, and deported its suspect upper classes to the interior of his realm. His success was a great gain for Muscovy, but it might have been greater had he not required assurance that his new acquisition be free of foreign influence: in his zeal, he expelled most of the foreign merchants from Novgorod, thus crippling the foreign commerce of the city and lessening its income.

Under the same pretext for attack, friendship with Poland-Lithuania, Ivan overcame Prince Michael of Tver and annexed his principality in 1485. Then, with those two important principalities under his control (in addition to a number of minor ones that he had been able to acquire with the little effort), he began a war to regain the Russian lands under the control of Poland-Lithuania. He continued it intermittently from 1492 to 1502, when he was granted control over some of the border territories of Western and Little Russia.[1]

While he was establishing dominion over others, Ivan III was still a

---

[1] In those days the term "Little Russia" referred to the principalities of Galicia and Volhynia. The term "Western Russia" was employed in two senses: to designate all of the former Russian principalities under Lithuanian and Polish rule, and to designate only those areas that now form White Russia.

tribute-paying vassal of the Golden Horde. He was paying tribute more or less regularly but, at the same time, gradually becoming all but independent of the dictates of Sarai, for internal dissensions were rapidly sapping the strength of the Golden Horde and making difficult its exercise of suzerainty. Nevertheless, Khan Akhmad, then struggling to maintain his Mongol rule, did not intend to give up his authority over Moscow and, encouraged by the promise of Lithuanian aid, decided on a punitive expedition to compel Ivan to submit. In 1480, Akhmad led his troops across the southern part of Muscovy to the Ugra River, a tributary of the Oka. There, at the Lithuanian-Muscovite border, he waited for Lithuanian military support while Ivan hurriedly mobilized Russian forces to meet him. For seven months, the Russian and Mongol armies faced each other, waiting for a battle that was never fought. The Lithuanian forces did not appear; and Akhmad, having lost hope of the fulfillment of Lithuanian promises and uncertain of the loyalty of his own forces, finally gave the order to retreat, thus forfeiting any further claims of the Golden Horde on Muscovy.

To the Russians, the bloodless battle at the Ugra River in the year 1480 means "the overthrow of the Tatar Yoke." However, although that date marks the end of the general Mongol rule over Russia, two things must be kept in mind: that the effective power of the Golden Horde had been weakened before 1480, and that vestiges of Mongol control continued for several generations thereafter. The Golden Horde disappeared as a state in 1502, but from its pieces were formed a number of Mongol khanates, among them the khanates of Crimea, Astrakhan, Kazan, and Western Siberia. And some of these continued to threaten Muscovite security and to receive tribute of some kind from Moscow until the middle of the sixteenth century. None the less, Muscovy was in fact a sovereign state after 1480, and its exercise of independence overbalanced the persisting tokens of Mongol rule. To Ivan III, the year 1480 meant the end of vassal status for his realm, and he began to use the title "sovereign" and to insist that foreign rulers treat him with appropriate respect.

Basil III, overshadowed in fame by his father and in notoriety by his son, is often overlooked, but he merits consideration as a successful executor of the Muscovite policy of expansion. When Pskov, already subject to Moscow dictates, became restive, he ordered the arrest of its leading citizens and, in 1510, ended its independence and annexed its lands. Four years later, after two years of war with Lithuania, he took Smolensk. Possession of this excellently fortified and strategically located city gave the Russian ruler control of the western approaches to his capital and greatly enhanced his security. He next seized the principality of Ryazan (in 1517), using the secret negotiations of its prince with the Crimean Khan as justification for annexation. And with Ryazan in his hands, Basil could claim domination of all the northeastern principalities for Muscovy.

The next in line of rulers, Ivan IV, was the first to make territorial gains against the Mongols and to carry Muscovite power beyond the Russian lands. For years, the Mongols had kept up a continuous border warfare, raiding, looting, and kidnapping (the khanate of Kazan alone holding over 60,000 Russian prisoners in 1551); and neither Russian diplomacy nor military force had been able to check them. Ivan IV, however, threw such strength against them that he succeeded in capturing Kazan in 1552 and Astrakhan in 1556, bringing the entire Volga basin under Muscovite control and opening it to Russian colonization. The fall of Kazan also opened the way to Russian expansion into Siberia, where the only bar to further movement was the Khanate of Western Siberia. In 1555 its khan also was forced, in order to save any of his power and wealth, to accept the suzerainty of Moscow. Then the subjugation of Astrakhan, in the following year, placed Russian power on the Caspian Sea and opened the way to commercial and diplomatic relations with Persia and the states of Central Asia.

Unfortunately Muscovy's incorporation of the lower Volga region led to new frontier trouble. To the east of it was still another remnant of the Golden Horde, the unfriendly Nogai Horde, whose restless warriors were a constant threat; and to the west were the everwarring Don Cossacks, who took their name from the Don River, which flowed through their land. The latter, an independent, democratic organization of Russian frontiersmen with a fighting force of about 10,000 men, soon agreed to end their resistance and, in return for a subsidy of arms and flour, to become an ally of Moscow against the Mongols of the Crimean region. Their help was needed in that quarter because the Crimean Khan (since 1475 a vassal of the Ottoman Empire), who now controlled not only the Crimea but also the entire coast of the Sea of Azov, kept up a perpetual harassment of neighboring lands. However, Ivan IV was diverted from his planned offensive against the Crimean Mongols by what he considered the greater need for an advance toward the Baltic.

A foothold on the Baltic would provide an outlet to Western European markets where Muscovy could buy needed arms and wares. At that time the routes by way of the Baltic were virtually blockaded by hostile powers—Poland-Lithuania and Livonia, and the Russians could reach their

SOVFOTO

Ivan IV: a painting (1897)
by V. M. Vasnetsov

former Western European markets only by the circuitous sea route from Archangel. That route, established by the English in 1553, was excessive in length and navigable only during the summer months. Tantalizingly near at hand, however, were ports on the Baltic coast and the Gulf of Finland. Most important of them was Riga, at the mouth of the Western Dvina River, "whose banks," Ivan IV is credited with saying, were "worth their weight in silver, whose waters, in gold." Riga was no more than 125 miles from the nearest point of the Muscovite border; but between them stood the Livonian Order of the German Knights, a military monastic order, which held Courland, Livonia, and Estonia. In 1558 Ivan IV began an attack on the Livonian Order, opening a conflict that continued intermittently for twenty-four years and went into historical records as the Livonian War. To gain protection, the order dissolved itself; and its head, under the title Duke of Courland, became a vassal of Poland. Livonia then united itself with Poland-Lithuania, and Estonia placed itself under the protection of Sweden. Poland-Lithuania took up the defense against Ivan and was later joined by Sweden. The war continued with varying success until 1571, when the Crimean Mongols took advantage of Ivan's preoccupation to make a raid on Moscow. Ivan turned to the defense of the city and drove the Mongols back to what he considered a temporarily safe distance; then he gave his full attention again to the Livonian War and kept it going for another ten years. Finally both sides, weary of fighting and incapable of achieving decisive victory, agreed in 1582 to a cessation of hostilities on terms that left the Baltic coast in the hands of Poland-Lithuania and Sweden.

Although Muscovy's strength proved insufficient to support all of Ivan IV's dreams and although he fell short of his territorial goals, his gains were sufficient to round out an empire.

ESTABLISHMENT OF AUTOCRATIC, MONARCHICAL GOVERNMENT. As the territory of Muscovy was being expanded, the status of its ruler was being transformed from that of a grand prince with limited power to that of a sovereign, autocratic monarch. The changed status as well as the growth of Muscovite holdings is indicated in the following words, used by Ivan IV in reference to himself:

> We, the great sovereign, Tsar and Grand Prince Ivan of All Russia, of Vladimir, Moscow, Novgorod, Tsar of Kazan, Tsar of Astrakhan, Sovereign of Pskov and Grand Prince of Smolensk, Tver, Yugra, Perm, Vyatka, Bulgar, and others, Sovereign and Grand Prince of Nizhnii-Novgorod, Chernigov, Ryazan, Polotsk, Rostov, Yaroslavl, Beloozero, hereditary Sovereign and Master of the Livonian land of the German Order, of Udora, of Obdoria, Kondia, and all the Siberian land and ruler of the Northern land. . . .

The power of the grand prince of Moscow grew at the expense of princes and boyars in annexed principalities, of the boyars in Muscovy, and of the relatives of the grand prince. As principalities were annexed, their princes and boyars were taken into the service of Moscow, their former positions being given to new administrators, usually loyal to Moscow rather than to the locality in which they served.[1] To the extra power thus achieved, the grand prince added still more from a nearer source, his immediate family. It had been customary, in the early years, for the immediate family of the grand prince of Moscow to share in the rule and revenues of the new as well as the old holdings of Muscovy, but now custom was being ignored with respect to the new and slowly forgotten with respect to the old. These changes were effected by Ivan III, Basil III, and Ivan IV without direct declaration of intention; they pretended to respect the rights of their relatives, but their acts belied their pretensions. Ivan III set the example for change. When a brother died without heirs, the lands he had administered were not shared with the surviving brothers but were absorbed into Ivan's holdings. And when a brother was so unfortunate as to spend his last days in prison, his sons dying in exile, the property of his family reverted to the grand prince. Ivan III declared that each action

[1] The princes of annexed principalities and their descendants retained their princely titles (hence the large number of princes in latter-day Russia), but their status was in most respects no different from that of boyars.

he took was justified by particular circumstances; none the less, each contributed to the establishment of a new policy, that of concentrating power and holdings in the hands of the grand prince. By 1584, the ruler had direct control over most of the Muscovite lands, his position having been achieved through acts analogous to those of earlier English and French kings who, in their realms, had managed to annul the territorial claims of one lord after another. The formula "one and indivisible" was not completely applicable to the Russian realm by 1584, but the conditions for its application were rapidly being created.

While the power of Moscow was increasing and the number of principalities was decreasing, the rights and influence of boyars were being greatly affected. As the principalities that claimed their services came under the rule of Moscow, the right of the boyars to leave the service of one prince for that of another lost its meaning, of course. At first, some transferred to the service of Lithuania; but such transfer, though once sanctioned, came to be regarded as an act of treason, the penalty for which was confiscation of land and punishment of the family. Thus the boyars became tied to the service of Moscow. At the same time, their status as privileged men-at-arms was being weakened. Their property rights, which had been considered hereditary, were gravely threatened as Ivan III and his two successors extended the practice, begun on a small scale in earlier generations, of granting lands *conditionally* in return for military and administrative service. Some boyars received additional lands under the new terms, but the recipients were more likely to be men from the lower classes or foreigners who had migrated to Russia. The growth of the class of service nobles (as those who held the land conditionally were called) caused the grand prince to become less dependent upon the boyars for their services in official posts or for their provision of fighting contingents and less inclined, therefore, to respect their hereditary rights.

The situation of the boyars became actually precarious at their number under Muscovite rule increased, for the grand princes began to view them as threats to the throne. The boyars were not always blameless; many of them were turbulent and contentious, and some conspired with internal and foreign enemies against the rulers. In time, it was understood that differences between boyars and ruler would be settled by violence, a means accepted by both sides; and the grand princes, having more power and greater resources than the boyars, could, and often did, surpass them in its use.

Violence was not limited to the settlement of differences involving boyars; it might be invoked by the grand princes for all degrees of mal-feasance or suspected connection with such. In his resorts to violence, Ivan IV, nicknamed *Grozny* (usually translated as *The Terrible*, sometimes as *The Dread*), went far beyond the calculated brutality of his father and grandfather. Combining the "soul of a wild beast" (Klyuchevsky) with the avowed conscience of a man of God, he followed the practice of having masses said for the souls of those whom he had killed with his own hands (among them, his son Ivan) and those whose executions he had ordered. His victims (numbering 4,000 or more) came from many classes, though his chief suspicions were centered on the aristocratic families. His rule was to strike down any, high or low, who opposed him or whom he suspected of disloyalty. So great were his obsessive fears that, in 1564, he divided the realm into two parts, leaving one part to its traditional administration and placing the other under the rule of a body of officials whose actions and appearance (they were outfitted with black horses, black garments, and—to suspend from their saddles—dogs' heads and brooms) were in-tended to strike terror into the hearts of traitors and warn them of the penalty for treasonable acts. This bizarre administration, known as *oprichnina,* had no lasting historical significance, but it contributed to the further weakening of the boyars.

Although the grand princes, despite differences, continued to consult the Boyars' Duma, they managed to undermine its influence even while ostensibly recognizing it as a consultative body. Ivan IV's chief act of undermining was to create a second body, the Assembly of the Land *(Zemsky Sobor),* also with consultative status. To the new body he called representatives of the princes, boyars, government officials, church-men and merchants; but he gave them no collective authority. The Assem-bly of the Land met only at his pleasure and discussed only what he wanted it to discuss. It could give advice—if inoffensively worded—but it could not direct. Yet it served to lessen the importance of the Boyars' Duma and to supply the ruler with the myth of popular support.

Such calculated maneuvering, combined with the direct actions of the grand princes, had developed in Moscow, by the time of Ivan IV's death (in 1584), a powerful throne supported by a politically weak service nobili-ty—in striking contrast to neighboring Poland's weak throne dependent upon a powerful landed aristocracy.

While the aspiring Muscovite princes were extending their power, they were also assuming certain imperial characteristics hitherto attributed to the Byzantine emperors. Religious and political events in the Byzantine

Empire had brought about a situation which made that possible. When the Empire, under attack by the Turks, appealed to Western Europe for aid and, in order to strengthen that appeal, agreed in 1439 to the reunion of the Eastern Orthodox and the Roman Catholic churches, it exposed a weakness from which the Russian rulers were to profit. Although the reunion did not result in any substantial aid to Constantinople nor in the renewal of church unity, it convinced the hierarchy of the Orthodox Church in Russia that Constantinople had fallen from grace. And it took little rationalizing to establish the idea that Russia was the only remaining citadel of Orthodoxy and that the rulers of Moscow should succeed the Byzantine emperors as the defenders of the true faith. As a clergyman of the early sixteenth century expressed it: "Moscow is the successor of the great world capitals: ancient Rome and the second Rome—Constantinople; Moscow is the third Rome, and there will be no fourth."

The fall of Constantinople to the Turks, in 1453, marking the end of the Byzantine Empire, left another opening, of which Ivan III was to take advantage. When he married the niece of the last Byzantine emperor, in 1472, he declared his right to many of the imperial attributes and symbols. He at once gave himself the title of "Tsar-Autocrat chosen by God" (tsar being the Russian form of Caesar). He also appropriated as his own the double-headed eagle used on the seal of Byzantium.[1] Thereafter the grand princes of Moscow were generally accepted as tsars, although Ivan IV was the first to be formally crowned (1547) under that title.

The claims of the Muscovite rulers to imperial status were endorsed by two legends that were being circulated and accepted as fact near the end of Ivan III's reign. One of them declared that the descendants of Rurik had the right to rule in Eastern Europe by virtue of a grant of authority made to one of them by Augustus Caesar. The other related an incident in which an emperor of Byzantium acknowledged Vladimir Monomakh as his equal and sent him the cap worn by emperors as a symbol of the Russian prince's imperial status. The latter legend received particular emphasis, and "the cap of Vladimir Monomakh," a replica of the alleged original, was used in the coronation of Russian rulers as long as the monarchy lasted.

As an important support for the theoretical foundations of tsarism, Ivan IV sought to have the Orthodox Church in Russia established as a separate patriarchate with Moscow as its seat. That was not accomplished

---

[1] The double-headed eagle served as the imperial symbol of Russia until 1917.

during his reign; but when it was, in 1589 (by a decision of the Patriarch of Constantinople—later to be approved by all patriarchs), the tsars thereby received additional support for the assumptions upon which they had been acting for many years: that they were politically omnipotent in their realm, holding office by the grace of God and acting as guardians of the true faith.

The tsarist claim to authority was not unchallenged. It was fought by boyars, whose efforts took the form of a struggle for individual prerogatives and status rather than that of support for a rival political system. It was contested by some prelates who had the strength to defy secular rulers, even while the Church as a whole supported the theory of absolutism and accepted subordination to the state. And its palpable effects were resented by the oppressed peasants, who expressed themselves in scattered and unorganized revolts, though theirs was no political movement against the concepts of tsarism. Thus it cannot be said that tsarist authority was established beyond question by the end of the sixteenth century; yet the theoretical claims of tsarism had been formulated and were to remain unaltered for over three centuries.

RISE OF SERFDOM AND LANDLORDISM.   Simultaneously with the extension of the political power of grand princes and tsars, changes were occurring in the relations between those who tilled the land and those who owned it. Resulting from those changes were the elimination of free peasant proprietorship, the transformation of free peasants into serfs, the growth of extensive landholding, and the subjugation of the landlords by the state— all complex and interdependent developments.[1]

In the early Kievan period, there was no landlord class; the aristocracy (a military one) was supported by the proceeds of trade and war; and cultivated land was in the hands of peasants living in village communes. At that time, modern concepts of private property in land (such as the right to sell or mortgage it) did not exist, but the peasants had some notion of property, believing that they owned the land on which they lived and from which they drew their sustenance.

By the twelfth century, the system of large-scale landholding had begun to appear. Ruling princes, the military aristocracy, churches and monasteries, and members of the upper stratum of the peasantry were becoming landlords, acquiring their holdings from the distribution of conquered lands, by the clearing of untilled land, by purchase, or by seizure of the

[1] Cf. Jerome Blum, "The Beginnings of Large-scale Private Proprietorship in Russia," *Speculum*, October, 1953, 776-790.

"black land" (the designation heretofore popularly used for land that was considered peasant property). Large-scale land-holding was accompanied by the refinement of property rights and by the divorce of land ownership from land tillage. Some of the labor on the new estates was provided by slaves, but most of it by tenant farmers.

Although the peasants had for generations looked upon "black land" as their own, their ownership was not recognized by the state, which often distributed such land unceremoniously to the nobility or winked at landlord seizure of it. There is evidence that, by the beginning of the sixteenth century, the idea of peasant proprietorship over "black land" had disappeared in the central regions of Muscovy but that it was still preserved in such outlying regions as those on the border of the White Sea. The typical peasant was now the tenant farmer, still retaining his position in the village communal organization but having the right to till the soil and live off its products only through payment of dues-in-kind, labor, or money, and often finding it necessary to add to his burden of obligation by borrowing seed and tools from the landlord. The tenant-landlord relationship was a contractual one, implying reciprocal obligations that could be ended only under stipulated conditions: the landlord could not expel the tenant until the end of the agricultural year—that is, until the harvest was over; and the tenant was obligated to work until the end of the year, when he was free to leave if he had paid his debts.

The tenant-landlord relationship left the peasants a degree of freedom; and it was not uncommon for them to move from one place to another, perhaps leaving old worn-out land for new, responding to tempting inducements from other landlords, seeking the lands still free from landlords, or simply escaping their insupportable debts. The landlords sought at first to restrict and ultimately to end the right of their tenants to leave thus; and, by the end of the fifteenh century, the limited contractual obligations were being gradually changed into immutable ones, thereby initiating a process that ended a century later with the actual transformation of tenants into serfs. The growth of the service nobility was undoubtedly a major factor in this transformation: the state, in order to insure itself of the service of this class, had to provide its members with a secure source of income; and since land alone was not sufficient when labor was scarce and mobile, the state had to guarantee labor to work the land. Moreover, the state recognized a double profit from tying the peasants to the land; members of the service nobility would be more content with the rewards of their work, and governmental revenues would be more easily collected from the restricted peasant taxpayers.

The gradual enserfment of most of the tenant farmers was achieved during the sixteenth century. It began when the rights of the landlords over indebted tenants were increased and made more binding: tenants who could not pay their debts lost their freedom, and those who escaped before discharging their debts were subject to forced return. The mobility of debt-free tenants was lessened by further restriction of the period during which they could leave their landlords. Whereas they had once been allowed to leave after the harvest, they were now subjected to the stipulations of the law codes of 1497 and 1550, which allowed them to leave only during the week preceding St. George's Day (November 26) or the week following it. Finally, the prohibition of departure under any circumstances was imposed—tentatively in 1581, according to generally accepted indirect evidence, and permanently in subsequent years.

While the peasants were being tied to the land, the landlords were being tied to the state. Although the service nobles, by the very nature of their contracts, were more dependent upon the state than the boyars were, the distinction between the rights of the two groups was lessened in the sixteenth century as the state ignored more and more of the older nobility's privileges. Meanwhile, the obligations of service nobles were being made more specific and onerous. A decree issued by Ivan IV in the middle of the century, including and codifying previous legislation, specified that the male noble's service to the state began when he was fifteen years of age and ended when death or disability prevented further discharge of duties. The decree specified also the size of the military contingents that nobles were obliged to provide, each being determined by the extent of the estate and the amount of the stipend that the noble received from the government.

Thus a nearly complete ring of obligations had been forged: the peasant was obliged to help maintain the landlord and the state—by payment of dues to the first and taxes to the latter; the landlord was obliged to support the state as a soldier or as an administrator; and the state was obliged to guarantee the landlord economic security. But the ring remained incomplete, for there is no evidence that the state acknowledged any serious obligation to the peasant.

The crisis of tsarism

END OF A DYNASTY. The rulers immediately following Ivan IV were unable to hold their inheritance intact, for they were not strong enough to establish security in an empire welded together by force. At Ivan's death, the throne passed to his son Feodor I, an incompetent makeshift of a man, who willingly permitted his brother-in-law, the boyar Boris Godunov, to direct the business of the state in his stead. Godunov was an able man, but he could not quell the unrest that was increasing throughout the country as a result of the establishment of tsarist rule, the terrorization of the boyars, the enserfment of the peasantry, and the imposition of economic burdens to support the protracted wars of the growing empire. Before long, he himself became the object of intrigues led by disgruntled boyars. And when Dmitri, the only surviving brother of Tsar Feodor, died, in 1591, the rumor was started by some—and later accepted by many— that Godunov had ordered his death in anticipation of his own succession to the throne. Still the reign limped on without any serious trouble until the death of Feodor, in January, 1598. Then matters grew toward a crisis.

Since Feodor left no male issue, the dynasty of Rurik was ended, and the question of succession was open. Boris Godunov was still ruler in fact, if not in name; but he did not make the impolitic move of crowning himself. Instead, he revived the Assembly of the Land (which had been neglected since the time of Ivan IV), taking care to select assemblymen who would support him, and let it be known that he would accept the crown only if it were offered to him by that body. And, in February, he was duly requested by the Assembly of the Land to become the tsar of Russia.

Despite the nature of his selection and the fact that the boyars were still covertly plotting against him, Tsar Boris began his reign with three relatively untroubled years. However, in 1601, with the beginning of a three-year famine, the general restiveness began to assert itself.

THE TIME OF TROUBLES. By 1604, after three years of famine and increased hardships, the restive boyars and desperate peasants were in a dangerous mood. The boyars of Moscow opened the way for action against Tsar Boris by supporting a pretender to the throne, an obscure noble who claimed that Ivan's son Dmitri had not died in 1591 and that he himself was Dmitri, the rightful heir. The King of Poland, anxious to fish in Russia's troubled waters, immediately gave his recognition to the false Dmitri and helped in the preparation of an army of Poles and disaffected Russians (including many Cossacks) to assist him in taking the throne. When that army marched into Russia, it touched off a series of civil wars that lasted for nine years—a period aptly called the Time of Troubles.

The forces of the Tsar, much stronger than those of the pretender, repulsed the first attacks. But Boris' death, in 1605, turned the advantage

COURTESY NEW YORK PUBLIC LIBRARY

Feodor I, last tsar of the Rurik dynasty (St. George, patron saint of Russia, depicted at upper right)

to the opposition. His son, who had succeeded him (as Feodor II), was deposed, and the false Dmitri was proclaimed tsar. The new ruler did not have the support of all disaffected groups, however; one faction of the boyars, disapproving of his pro-Polish leanings, conspired against him. And in 1606, they killed him and placed one of their own number, Basil Shuisky, on the throne. During his four-year reign, the boyars made a desperate effort to regain the political and economic position they had lost in the preceding century and a half, but they soon found themselves facing the fact that other groups wanted adjustments also. Minor nobles who were jealous of boyar advantages, Cossacks, national minorities still not reconciled to Russian rule and, above all, Russian serfs saw in the instability of political authority an opportunity to assert themselves. Within a short period after the installation of Basil Shuisky, nearly half of Russia rejected Muscovite control, the greatest disaffection appearing in the southern and eastern regions. In many of the troubled areas, the news of the death of the false Dmitri was not believed, and disbelief provided a justification for not acknowledging the new tsar. Rebellion flared up in such places as Nizhnii-Novgorod, Astrakhan, and Chernigov. Several of the outbreaks coalesced into one during the summer of 1606, when a former slave, Ivan Bolotnikov, presented himself as a leader. His appeal was primarily to the peasants, who wanted both freedom and improved living conditions, but he was supported for a time also by many of the minor nobility; and from these sources he was able to assemble a large though poorly organized military force, with which he began a march on Moscow. When the rebels finally reached and besieged the capital, the chance of their success seemed good, but it was frustrated when the nobles among them began deserting out of fear that an uncontrolled peasant revolt might ensue. Bolotnikov's followers were compelled to withdraw, retreating before the forces of Tsar Basil but con-

Boris Godunov, depicted with symbols of the imperial power: (in left hand) *the scepter,* (in right hand) *the orb,* (on head) *the cap of Vladimir Monomakh*

tinuing to fight until October, 1607. Then, having been promised mercy, Bolotnikov surrendered with his troops. But mercy was not granted; he was blinded and drowned. With that, the main revolt was over, but for a few months rebellious activities, inspired by the efforts of the Bolotnikov forces, continued along the Volga with no far-reaching results. Thus, the first major uprising in Russia passed into history, having failed but having served nevertheless as a warning of the potential power of the peasantry.

Now Tsar Basil faced trouble from another direction. A second false Dmitri—this one, a member of the lower classes—arose to claim the throne. False Dmitri II, as he was called, advanced into Russia at the head of troops supplied by Poland and supplemented by contingents of Cossacks. To oppose him the Tsar turned to Sweden for military support and received it in return for the cession of Karelia and the renunciation of Russian claims to Livonia. The ensuing struggle, marked by double-dealing and treachery on both sides, was chaotic and ludicrously confused. Russian boyars and generals changed sides so often that many of them became known as "birds of passage"; the Swedish forces deserted Basil; and the Poles dropped False Dimtri II and began an independent campaign. Finally, in 1610, Basil was overthrown by his erstwhile supporters, and the Poles advanced to Moscow.

There followed an outburst of national feeling that could not have been predicted. It came at the urging of Patriarch Hermogen, who, despite imprisonment by the Poles, was able to send out proclamations calling on the people to drive out the foreigners. A popular army was formed but failed in its first attempts to free Moscow. Then two strong leaders appeared to give the army inspired and effective direction: Kuzma Minin, a merchant, whose encouraging speeches and administrative ability complemented the military skill of the other, the nobleman Dmitri Pozharsky. Under those two, the popular army moved on to Moscow and, in October, 1612, broke the resistance of the Polish troops and regained the city for Russia.

Russia under the First Romanovs, 1613–1682

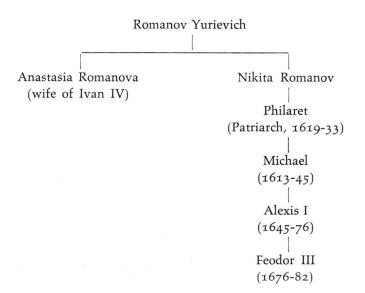

Romanov Yurievich

Anastasia Romanova
(wife of Ivan IV)

Nikita Romanov

Philaret
(Patriarch, 1619-33)

Michael
(1613-45)

Alexis I
(1645-76)

Feodor III
(1676-82)

In 1613 an Assembly of the Land, made up of representatives of the clergy, the boyars, the service nobility and some peasant and urban delegates, elected Michael Romanov as Tsar. He was of Russian boyar stock and distantly related to the first wife of Ivan IV. With him, a new line came to power, the Romanov dynasty, which was to rule Russia from 1613 to 1917.

RESTORATION OF STABILITY AND AUTHORITY.   During the reigns of the first three Romanovs, Russia regained a measure of internal political and economic stability. Order was gradually restored in the government, the outlying areas were again brought under the control of Moscow, and there was a satisfactory revival of internal and foreign trade. But the hope of many, that the Romanovs would not assume the absolutist authority of earlier tsars, was not fulfilled.

Tsar Michael was compelled to share his power for a time with the Assembly of the Land, which had elected him. He was not strong enough at first to rule without its support nor could he exact, without the assent of at least part of the governed, the heavy taxes required for the restoration of the government and the continuation of the effort to oust the Swedes and the Poles, who had not retired after the Time of Troubles. From 1613 to 1622 he kept the Assembly of the Land in continuous session, and during that time he eased his burdens by signing a treaty of peace (1617) with

Meeting of the Assembly of the Land, 1649

Sweden. Thereafter he called the Assembly only infrequently, for he was then able to keep up a strong military force and support his sovereignty with little aid. In 1634 he concluded a treaty with Poland, giving up the mighty fortress city of Smolensk but gaining Polish recognition and temporary relief from outside opposition. By the time of his death, in 1645, the tsarist power was so fully re-established that his son Alexis was able to ascend the throne as a matter of course, without the sanction of the Assembly of the Land. The Romanovs did not intend that the Russian monarchy become an elective one. Tsar Alexis followed his father's example in giving little attention to the Assembly of the Land. Its one contribution of note during his reign was the confirmation of a revised code of laws in 1649, and its last full meeting during his reign was held in 1653. The Boyars' Duma did not suffer the same fate as the Assembly of the Land; it continued to meet, but it had no power independent of the tsar. In short, after a brief period of accommodation, the Romanovs restored the full autocratic power of the throne.

REVOLT OF VOLGA PEASANTS. Just as the first Romanovs disappointed many who expected a mitigation of autocracy, so they disappointed the peasants who hoped for an improvement in their lot. Although the tsars did not share their political power with the nobility, they did cater to the nobility's economic interests at the expense of the peasantry and, in so doing, tightened the bonds of serfdom.

During the seventeenth century, peasant unrest was endemic in many regions, particularly along the Volga. That was a region, still frontier in character, to which many peasant malcontents had fled to escape onerous conditions on the estates in other parts of the country and to which many Cossacks had migrated because of dissatisfaction with growing class divisions in their former home areas. The Cossacks, having a tradition of independence which the peasants did not have, often supplied leadership in peasant revolts in that region. One such revolt, begun in 1667 under the leadership of the Cossack Stenka Razin, proved so successful that within three years the peasants and Cossacks had gained control of almost the entire lower Volga region. Tsar Alexis was finally able to suppress them and execute Razin, but the revolt was not quickly forgotten. It had indicated the fury and strength that could be expected from a united and well-led peasantry, and it confirmed the government in its policy of keeping a strong hand upon them. That defeat, however, so discouraged the peasants that no more large-scale risings were undertaken for almost forty years. During that time they were bound more firmly then ever before in their enserfment.

ANNEXATION OF THE EASTERN UKRAINE. Another revolt to engage the attention of Tsar Alexis was one with antecedents in the complicated past history of the Little Russians.

In 1569, when Lithuania and Poland were united in one state by the Union of Lublin (after nearly two centuries of personal union under a common dynasty), the Ukrainian (Little Russian) provinces passed from the administration of Lithuania to that of Poland. But the conflicting interests in the provinces remained the same: the majority of landholding nobles were Catholic Poles and the minority Orthodox Ukranians, the middle class was Jewish, and the peasantry was Orthodox Ukrainian. It was a combination destined for trouble since the native Ukrainians looked upon the Poles and Jews as "aliens"; the peasants hated the Polish landlords and the Jewish stewards, bailiffs, and estate agents who had taken service with them; and religious differences added to the general animosity among them.

In the sixteenth and seventeenth centuries, many of the native Ukrainians moved into the disputed frontier region of the lower Dnieper. Here, free from direct Polish rule, they were able to organize an autonomous community with

headquarters on an island in the Zaporozhe district, south of Kiev. The price
of freedom was frequent warfare, for in this region Poland and the Ottoman
Empire, aided by the Crimean Khan, were still carrying on their old contest
for supremacy. The Ukrainian position was maintained largely by frontier
fighters called Cossacks (as were the frontiersmen in Russia), properly known
as Zaporozhian but commonly called Ukrainian. The Cossacks governed their
community through democratic assemblies and an elected leader (*hetman*).
Poland, of course, did not favor the existence of this Orthodox, autonomous
Cossack community but, being unable to suppress it, made use of it by
recognizing its autonomy in return for promised help against the Turks. So
the Zaporozhian Cossacks fought the Turks for Poland, but they felt no
compunction about turning and fighting the Poles themselves when it seemed
expedient.

Meanwhile religion was becoming a more prominent matter of disagreement among the mismated peoples of the Ukraine. In the second half of the
sixteenth century, at the height of the Counter-Reformation, the Polish
Jesuits, leading a vigorous movement to stamp out Protestantism, attempted
to bring the Eastern Orthodox in Poland-Lithuania into the Catholic Church.
Several Orthodox bishops responded by negotiating an agreement with the
Pope whereby the primacy of the Pope and the Catholic position on matters
of dogma would be accepted by the Eastern Orthodox in return for the
privilege of retaining the Eastern Orthodox rites, the continuation of the use
of Church Slavonic in services, and the exemption of parish priests from the
rule of celibacy. This agreement was approved by some of the Orthodox
clergy at a meeting held in Brest in 1596; and the Union of Brest, as the
compromise came to be known, went into force. A minority of the Orthodox
clergy and laity accepted the Union of Brest, thus becoming Catholics (of the
Byzantine rite)—later to be known in Eastern Europe as Uniats. However,
most of the Ukrainians as well as the White Russians rejected the Union of
Brest and religious disagreement continued.

Finally the accumulated discontent broke out in a series of Ukrainian
peasant revolts, in which the Zaporozhian Cossacks, whose influence and
support extended into the interior of the Ukraine, took a leading part. The
most notable of the revolts was the one begun in 1648 under the leadership
of Bogdan Khmelnitsky, who was later elected hetman of the Cossacks. For
almost six years his rebel forces held out alone, massacring Poles and Jews
throughout the region. Then, finding themselves hard pressed by the better-
organized Polish forces, they turned to Tsar Alexis for aid. He responded
favorably by offering, in exchange for Cossack allegiance, to help them throw

off Polish rule and to recognize and respect an autonomous Cossack government in the liberated Ukraine. His offer was accepted by a Cossack assembly meeting at Pereyaslavl (now known as Pereyasavl-Khmelnitsky), near Kiev, in 1654; and the rebels received their aid from Moscow. Still Poland was able to maintain the defense for many years, even though she was at war with Sweden part of the time. Forced to ask for an armistice at last, in 1667, the Poles signed an agreement with the Russians at Andrusovo (near Smolensk) to cease fighting for thirteen and a half years. Their arrangements included also Poland's agreement to Russian retention of that part of the Ukraine lying east of the Dnieper and to Russian occupation of Kiev for two years (the city to be returned to the Poles at the expiration of the occupation).

The acquisition of the eastern Ukraine and Kiev (the city was not returned to the Poles) was to have far-reaching consequences for Russia. It was the first successful step toward the acquisition of the whole of the Ukraine. It placed Russia on the border of the Ottoman Empire, which directly controlled most of the northern littoral of the Black Sea. And it brought a difficult administrative problem because the Cossacks of the eastern Ukraine, who had fought Poland to gain freedom, were not willing to accept a new master in Moscow. To them the important part of the agreement of 1654 was the one that concerned autonomy; whereas, to Moscow the important part was the one that concerned allegiance to the tsar. It was almost inevitable that the relations between the autonomous eastern Ukraine and the autocratic government in Moscow should prove a source of trouble.

SCHISM.   At the time when Russia was taking a political interest in the Ukraine, another situation involving Ukrainians was developing in the Russian Orthodox Church. Some of the Ukrainian Orthodox clergy, having taken residence in Moscow during the first half of the seventeenth century, were beginning to acquire great influence in the ecclesiastical circles of that city and to point out errors in the religious texts and ritual of the Russian Church. That they were given a measure of respectful attention was due to the recognition of their thorough and strict education and their close adherence to the spirit and practice of the parent church in Constantinople, from which the Russian Orthodox Church had allowed itself to deviate somewhat since it was not under the jurisdiction of the Patriarch of Constantinople, as was the Orthodox Church in the Polish Ukraine. As their influence grew, they began to urge the need for correction in the Russian Church, and many came to support their position.

Nikon, who came to the patriarchal throne of Moscow in 1652, considered their criticisms justifiable and immediately turned the Russian Church to the

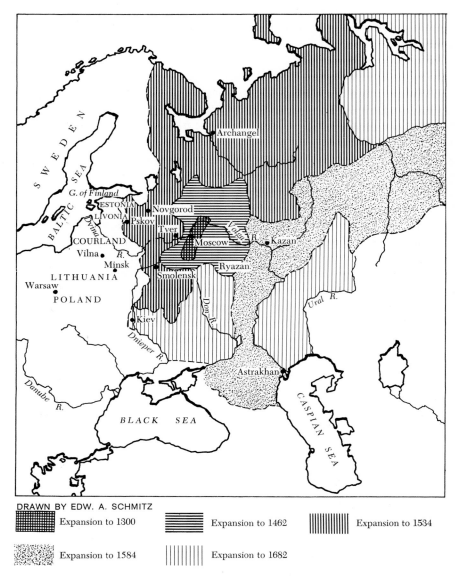

DRAWN BY EDW. A. SCHMITZ

Expansion to 1300   Expansion to 1462   Expansion to 1534

Expansion to 1584   Expansion to 1682

MAP 6. Growth of the Empire to 1682

task of eliminating from the ritual the innovations that had crept in during
the course of centuries. The Ukrainian clerics proffered their aid in making
the needed corrections, and Nikon accepted it. His impulse to do so may have

been political as well as religious; Moscow was then hoping to establish dominion over the Ukraine, and if the differences between the Ukrainian and the Russian Churches could be eliminated at the same time, the chances of subordinating the Ukrainian Church to Moscow would be greater.

The reform of the ritual was begun in 1653. At the distance of over three centuries, the changes made then appear of little moment. But to many of the Russian Orthodox the slightest alteration in religious practices that they had been taught to regard as sacred and inalterable appeared to be the work of the devil, and they were quick to interpret the reform as an inspiration of foreigners who were seeking to corrupt "Holy Russia." Nikon carried out the reforms with a heavy hand, arousing among both clergy and laity an opposition to the changes as well as to the manner in which they were being put into effect. At the same time he was alienating Tsar Alexis by his insistence on the power and prerogatives of the patriarchal office. At the instigation of the Tsar, a Church council was called in 1666 to deal with the Patriarch and with his reforms, which Alexis supported. The council removed Nikon from office and imprisoned him in a monastery, but it supported his position to the extent of anathematizing, in 1667, all who opposed the reforms he had begun. Still the opposition grew; and even after many of its leaders had been arrested and burned, their followers continued to reject the changes with vehemence. Thousands committed suicide rather than face the necessity of living under the reign of the Anti-Christ, whom they expected to appear soon, and thousands more left the reformed Church. Those who left— known as schismatics or as Old Believers—were vigorously persecuted by the government. But they survived to become a strong group in Russia.

After the reforms the Ukrainian Orthodox Church maintained close relations with the Russian Orthodox Church, but it did not agree to place itself under the jurisdiction of the Moscow Patriarchate until 1687.

THREATENED WEAKENING OF THE THRONE.   When Alexis died, in 1676, his fourteen-year-old son took the throne as Feodor III. He was a sickly and incompetent youth, unable to direct the affairs of his realm. Consequently, various factions at court began battling for the power that he could not exercise. His mother's family, the Miloslavskys, finally gained the advantage and, with the aid of other politically experienced nobles, managed to sustain the strength of the throne in Feodor's name.

The most striking domestic measure of his reign was one affecting the government and military services: the reversal of the old practice of assigning posts to nobles on the basis of their family status rather than on the basis of ability. Activity in foreign affairs was concentrated principally upon a conflict with the Ottoman Empire, which began in 1676 after the Turks had won part of the western Ukraine from Poland. This, the first of many direct conflicts with the Turks, led Moscow to attempt the creation of a European coalition against the Sultan. However, that effort failed; and, the fighting having ended indecisively with an armistice in 1681, it remained for Feodor's successor to resume the struggle.

FOUR / RUSSIA IN 1682

The year 1682, when the reign of Feodor III came to an end, is a convenient point at which to make a survey of the life and institutions of Russia. After that, the country entered a period of great change, revolutionary in some of its aspects. But the course of that change was determined in part by the Russia of 1682.

A contemporary writer, Yuri Krizhanich, based an interesting prophecy upon what he observed in Russia during the latter part of the seventeenth century:

> Wisdom, like courage, wanders from people to people. Certain peoples were in ancient times favored with all the sciences and are today ignorant—the Egyptians, Greeks and Jews. Others were uncultivated and wild in ancient times but are today renowned for their craftsmanship and for every kind of wisdom—the Germans and the French. . . . Let no one say that for us Slavs the road to learning must be forever closed by heavenly decree and that we can not and may not devote ourselves to learning. . . .
>
> We see among other peoples that if the state reaches a high point of power, the arts and sciences begin to bloom among them. Therefore we believe that the time has now come also for our people to devote themselves to the study of the sciences. . . .

The people

RUSSIANS.   In 1682, not all Russians were subjects of the tsar, nor were all subjects of the tsar Russians. In the territory claimed by Russia at that time neither the Russian language nor the Eastern Orthodox faith was common to all inhabitants. Russian culture, diffused chiefly by colonization, came slowly to newly acquired areas because the push of colonization was itself slow. Russian colonists were well established in annexed lands west of the Volga and along the river itself, but that area was still marked by frontier traces. East of the Volga, Russian settlement was noticeably thinner; and east of the Urals there were few Russians, mostly merchants, Cossacks, miners, and brigands. However, of the 9 million people living within the Russian Empire in 1682 (an estimated number based on tax records), most were settled west of the Volga and most were Russians, culturally homogeneous though racially heterogeneous. They spoke an essentially common language, had a common faith, participated in a common culture, and shared the memory of centuries of a common past. But racially they were a mixture of Varangian, Finnic, and Slavic stocks, each of which was itself a product of racial mixture. The Russians, it must be remembered, are an ethnic group, not a racial one.

How many people who might be classified as Russians lived outside of Russia cannot be definitely determined, but the number was considerable. The region now known as Carpatho-Ukraine was inhabited by people whose speech was akin to Russian and whose religion had been Eastern Orthodox; but, cut off from the main body of Russians by the Carpathian Mountains, they developed a distinct dialect and, under Hungarian Catholic influence, became Uniats. They had no contact with Russia until the end of World War II. In Bukovina, particularly in the northern part, were people of the Russian ethnic group, but their land was absorbed into the polity that later became Rumania.

The bulk of the Russians who were not subjects of the tsar, those occupying the former Russian principalities collectively designated as Western Russia, were subjects of the king of Poland-Lithuania. These Russians, as a result of several centuries of existence under a foreign rule, had developed characteristics and customs differing from those of the Russians in the northeastern principalities, under Muscovite rule. Moreover, within Western Russia itself, because distinguishing characteristics developed among the people, two groups came to be identified: the White Russians (in the north) and the Ukrainians (in the south). Therefore the Russian people are generally divided into three branches: the Great Russian, the White Russian, and the Ukrainian. The notion that these three constitute a single Russian nation has caused prolonged controversy, much of it inspired by nationalistic considerations. Some insist that Ukrainians are, and have been from the very beginning of the Kievan state, a nation separate and distinct from that of the Russians; and comparable but less sweeping claims are made for the White Russians. However, historical evidence does not justify the designation of the three groups as separate nations in the seventeenth century. At that time, they were simply divisions of the Russian people.

For some time before 1682, various terms had been in use to designate the areas inhabited by Russians. One was *Ukraina*, which means *border land*, and is the origin of the word *Ukraine*; but it was usually used with reference only to part of the area composing the modern Ukraine, the whole area being more commonly called *Little Russia*. The area that now forms the White Russian S.S.R. was then sometimes called *White Russia*, and Muscovy was often designated as *Great Russia*. Tsar Alexis used the title "Tsar of All Great and Little and White Russia" although he did not, in fact, rule all. That these various terms were in use indicates that regional differences had already been developing under differing political rule.

By the late seventeenth century, the Great Russians, the Ukrainians (the term *Ukrainian* is more convenient than *Little Russian*), and the White Russians had developed distinguishing differences in dress, customs, and speech—of which the last is most noteworthy. The speech of the Ukrainians and White Russians had been subjected not only to the usual regional influences that make for dialects but also to the influences of the Polish and Lithuanian languages. The following will illustrate the differences that, as a result, developed in their speech: the Ukrainian for *head* is *holova*; the White Russian is *halava*; and the Great Russian is *golova* (Great Russian has no *h*).

Although their dialects differed, the three groups had a common written language, Church Slavonic, used in the liturgy and literature of the Orthodox Church (most of the literate Russians were of the clergy). Had a vigorous secular literature in Ukrainian and White Russian developed, these dialects might have developed speedily into national written languages. But for two centuries they remained little more than dialects used mostly by the lower classes, while Great Russian, which was used in the development of a vigorous secular literature, finally became the literary language of all. Great Russian became also the dominant spoken language, used by the majority of educated Russians; and even the Ukrainians and White Russians used it, when under Russian rule, until the growth of their nationalism in the late nineteenth century drew them again to a preference for their own dialects.

The White Russians of 1682, the majority of them still subjects of Poland-Lithuania, did not show any marked sense of identity as a group. In fact, group identity among them was precluded at an early date by the Polish

Catholic assimilation of their upper class, a process that helped to atrophy their development generally. At the end of the seventeenth century, most White Russians were poor and, except for some of the clergy, illiterate peasants.

The Ukrainians were considerably stronger as a group than the White Russians. During the first half of the seventeenth century, an active cultural revival was begun in their central city, Kiev, which became the focus for the expansion of education and the importation of Western European ideas. Despite the fact that Kiev was under Polish control until the Khmelnitsky revolt, this revival was Ukrainian in the sense that those who provided leadership were natives, although their efforts were directed toward the Orthodox Church rather than toward specifically Ukrainian matters. They were the ones who might have served as the core of the Ukrainian educated class, just as the self-governing Ukrainian (or Zaporozhian) Cossacks might have provided the political leaders of the Ukrainian nation if they had achieved an enduring autonomy. But, by 1682, Moscow was already beginning to undermine, and would soon destroy, Ukrainian Cossack autonomy; and the idea of a Ukrainian state was again receding from reality.

In addition to the Ukrainian Cossacks, there were other Cossack groups —those of the Don River, the Yaik (later called the Ural) River, and the Terek River—and they too were autonomous. The Don, Yaik, and Terek Cossacks, though all of Great Russian origin, considered themselves separate peoples, and essentially they were. As bands of venturesome men, they drew away from the more thickly settled regions and sought the southern and eastern frontiers of Russia, there to become the feared and fearless warriors whose exploits mark many pages of Russian history. In their outposts, they tilled the soil, raised horses, trapped, hunted, and fought the enemies of the tsar or—if so moved—the regular forces of the tsar. At first, like the Ukrainian Cossacks, they formed a democratic society, sharing in power and profit and electing their own leader (called *ataman*); but by the end of the seventeenth century social cleavage was becoming evident among them in the development of a ruling class of landholding officers. Finally the several groups of Cossacks ceased to welcome into their ranks any more refugees from inner Russia and became closed hereditary bodies.

Of the three branches of the Russian nation, the Great Russian was most important. As the empire spread eastward, it took the lead in colonization; and, even in the south of Russia, where the Ukrainians were in the forefront of the colonizing movement, the Great Russians had an influence. The White Russians were then, as they are now, the least numerous and least influential of the three.

NATIONAL MINORITIES.   The number of non-Russian groups in the Russian state had been quite small until the sixteenth century, when Moscovy began to annex non-Russian areas. Thereafter, although the Russian people formed the core and constituted the great majority of the population, national minorities and their significance grew as Russian expansion grew; in fact, Russia was becoming a multinational state.

At the end of the seventeenth century, the most noteworthy national minorities were the Finno-Ugrians, the Turco-Tatars, and the Siberian tribes. The people of Finno-Ugrian stock were typified by the Karelians, living north of Lake Ladoga; and related to them by language were the Voguls, Mordva, Cheremis, and Votiaks of the upper and middle Volga region. The various ethnic groups collectively classified as Turco-Tatar—the Bashkirs, the Kazan Tatars,[1] and the Crimean Tatars—were scattered throughout the middle and lower Volga basin, the approaches of the Caucasus, Central Asia, and the approaches of the Urals; they were, for the most part, Moslem in faith and Mongol in descent. East of the Urals, as far as the coast of the Pacific, lived many peoples, most of whom were organized in clans or tribes and who differed sharply from one another in religion and language. Among them, various stages of cultural and economic development were represented; the Samoyedes, making their home in the northern part of European Russia and Siberia, were perhaps the most primitive, and the cattle- and horse-breeding Yakuts, on the Lena River, were among the strongest and most advanced.

Moscow had no fixed policy toward national minorities; in fact, it did not recognize nationality as a basis for differentiating among peoples. Russia, like other Christian (and Moslem) states, classified its subjects on the basis of religion; one was simply Orthodox, Moslem, Catholic, Jewish, or pagan. If he were not Orthodox, he was not of the true faith in the judgment of the state and the Church and should be persuaded or compelled to be baptized in the Eastern Orthodox faith.

Whether or not Moscow recognized national minorities, it had to deal with them. And, although it did not devise a definite or consistent policy, it followed certain precedents in dealing with non-European peoples absorbed into the Russian Empire by eastward expansion. The early treatment of the Khanate of Kazan, annexed by Ivan IV, provided such a precedent. It was characterized by the imposition of Russian administration, the introduction of Russian colonists, and the toleration of existing native institutions. The imposition of Russian administration was facilitated by the extermination or removal of most of the Kazan ruling class and the confiscation of their lands

---

[1] The term *Tatar*, rather than *Mongol*, is used in Russia, and there are still Tatars living in Russia.

(which were distributed to Russian service nobles or to the Church). Then Russian peasants, most of them serfs, were brought in to provide labor for the estates of the nobles and the Church. Soon Russians outnumbered the surviving native Bashkirs and Kazan Tatars, who were usually left to their own devices as long as they paid their taxes. Ivan IV justified his campaign against Kazan as a crusade to convert the infidels and the heathen; but, in the next two centuries, very little energy was devoted to proselytizing the natives. Although the remaining native groups lost some members through marriage with the Russian colonists or through voluntary conversion, on the whole they preserved their separate identities and distinct culture as they continued to live side by side with the Russians.

Once Moscow had established its rule over any national minority, it tended to permit the subject people to adhere to their own faith, customs, and language. And the Russian Orthodox Church, although it conducted missionary work, rarely used force in its activities. Perhaps in the heat of war, Russian soldiers might burn Catholic churches or drown Jews, as they did during the conflicts with Lithuania, but these were incidents rather than the execution of policy.

Generally speaking, the attitude of the Russian government toward the Jews was quite different from that displayed toward other groups. Until the early sixteenth century, the government permitted the small groups of Jews in various Russian cities to live in peace but viewed their religion with deep abhorrence. And when, at the end of the fifteenth century, a heretical group known as the "Judaizers" sprang up in Novgorod and Moscow, Ivan III was convinced that it was the work of the Jews. It was stamped out by force, and Moscow decreed that Jews could no longer live within the Russian Empire. Officially the ban on Jews continued in force until the latter part of the eighteenth century, but it was sometimes violated. In the Ukrainian territory acquired in 1667, where the number of Jews was considerable, enforcement of the ban was particularly difficult, and Jews in that area found it possible to remain, though prevented from moving into other parts of the empire.

The economy

AGRICULTURE.   The economy of seventeenth century Russia was a natural one, based on the cultivation of the land by serf labor. But it was so lacking in uniformity that it cannot be properly called a system.

The land was divided among various holders—the boyars, the princes, the service nobility, the Church, the tsar, the state, and a few free peasants. The boyars and princes who still possessed lands held them by hereditary right. The service nobility held land only as a reward for service, and their right to it was dependent upon the continuation of their service; they were attempting, however, to transform their temporary right into a hereditary one. The Church, a large landholder in Russia as in most other countries at the time, held its lands theoretically in perpetuity; but the state could—and did, from time to time—assert the right of confiscating lands belonging to the Church. As the first among the princes, the tsar held great tracts of land in hereditary right; they were known as the crown lands. In addition, he had disposition of certain tracts known as state lands, over which the legal proprietor was the state rather than the tsar himself. The few free peasants who held land were to be found mainly in the far north and the far south, removed from the centers of population. The absence of reliable data makes it impossible to give the exact distribution of land among the various classes of landholders; but it appears that about 60 per cent was held by service nobles, princes, and boyars; about 13 per cent by the Church; and the re-mainder by the state and the free peasants.

In the cultivation of the land the peasants utilized simple techniques which were about the same as those employed in other European countries of the period. Most of them employed the prevalent open-field system, laying out long, narrow, unfenced strips for cultivation according to either the "three-field" or the "continuous" plan. The three-field plan, under which one field in three lay fallow each year, was followed mainly in central Russia. Elsewhere the "continuous" plan was followed; under it, a field would be tilled continuously until is ceased to yield, then would be allowed to lie fallow for an extended period. The chief agricultural implement was the oxen- or horse-drawn wooden cultivator (*sokha*), a multitoothed instrument with a moldboard for turning over the soil. It was narrow and did not plow deeply, but it was practical enough for the difficult terrain of the forest region. Other implements in common use were crude hoes, wooden harrows, and sickles. Manure was used as a fertilizer in a few districts, but productivity was de-termined principally by the nature of the soil. Few animals were raised to provide food or raw materials; in most areas only horses and oxen, used as draft animals, were to be found.

Agriculture under such conditions could support only a subsistence economy. Of the produce that the peasant was permitted to keep, he con-sumed the greater part, occasionally having a small surplus to exchange for goods or services in his village. And the portion that went to the landlord, the Church, or the state was generally required for direct consumption, not for the market. Even if agricultural production had been higher, sale would have been limited because the Russian market for farm produce was small, foreign markets distant, and transportation costly. However, some of the wealthier landholders managed, in the later years of the century, to begin marketing some grain along with the hides and timber for which they had previously established a market.

HANDICRAFT.   In the towns and cities that had grown up as centers of governmental, ecclesiastical, or commercial life, there had developed concentrations of artisans supported by handicraft. In some of the centers, the artisans worked on a single specialty. Those in Yaroslavl, for example, specialized on mirrors; those in Vologda, on ironwork; those in Kaluga, on wood products. In other centers they grouped themselves according to their various specialties. In and around Moscow, which was representative of such centers, there were many separate neighborhoods of special craftsmen, among them smiths, weavers and armorers. The peasants also, particularly those in the poorer agricultural areas of the forest region, contributed to the production of handicraft. They eked out their livelihood by offering handmade articles for sale or using them as part-payment of dues to their landlords.

The handicraft of Russia compared unfavorably with that of Western Europe both in technique and in organization. By Western standards, the tools used were antiquated: carpenters, having no saws, hewed their boards with axes; metallurgists used small, manual bellows in their foundries; and weavers worked at the simplest of looms. And, whereas the Western artisans had their guilds, the Russian artisans had as yet no organization through which to improve their lot economically or politically.

INDUSTRY.   Russian industry had made a mere beginning by the end of the seventeenth century. The state was the principal customer for industrial products, and its chief needs were military supplies. One of the first industrial establishments in the country, an ironworks near Tula, was typical of the few set up during the century. It was erected, with governmental permission, by a Dutch merchant, Andrew Vinius. In return for the government's allowing him to use the labor of enserfed peasants during the winter months to supplement the work of the few free peasants he could hire, Vinius provided some of the iron needed by the state. That arrangement proved satisfactory to both parties, and the ironworks grew to be one of Russia's largest.

In addition to ironworks, supported mainly by the state, there were a few other industries, supplying home and foreign markets. The most important of them were salt and potash industries, the returns from which helped to make some families of the country outstandingly wealthy. One was the Stroganov family, whose members rose from peasant beginnings to great affluence, supported mainly by their salt works. Their combined interests used the services of some 15,000 free and serf laborers. Another, the boyar family of Morozov, drew a yearly profit of about $200,000 from industrial enterprises, chief of which were potash works. Such success, however, was not widespread, and the few who attained it were able to hold their positions because the demand was not then sufficient to encourage competition.

TRADE. Internal trade reflected the state of production; it was limited and specialized. Moscow's trading center (known as the Chinese City) was the model for lesser ones throughout the country. It was composed of rows of crowded little shops, hardly more than glorified sheds, arranged by specialty —one row for the sale of laces, another for woolens, another for fish, and so on to the limit of items for sale. Often from two to four shopkeepers would own and share a single shop twenty feet long and ten feet wide, but occasionally some entrepreneur would own as many as fifteen of them. Established trading centers were supplemented by periodic fairs to which peasants would bring their agricultural and handicraft products, urban artisans would bring their wares, and merchants and shopkeepers would come to buy and sell domestic as well as foreign produce.

Among the traders, the merchants were considerably above the economic level of the petty tradesmen. In this period they were introducing the practice of buying in bulk the products of the craftsmen's skills and storing them in warehouses until the market became favorable. Some were beginning to specialize in import or export. And of those who were amassing great wealth, some were aspiring to political influence.

After the sixteenth century Russia's foreign trade expanded in spite of the fact that the old Baltic routes to Western Europe were under the control of unfriendly nations. After English navigators opened the route by way of the White Sea to Archangel, English traders were granted the most favorable conditions for trade in Russia. They were followed by the Dutch, and soon foreign trade was thriving. International summer fairs were organized at Archangel and patronized by traders from many countries. There the Russian merchants could sell grain, hides, timber, potash, luxury items such as silk (originally purchased from eastern traders in Astrakhan), and furs, which they had bought or seized in Siberia; and they could buy woolens, spices, and such luxury items as the Russian market demanded.

Before 1667 foreign merchants were given the right to ship goods to and from Persia, India, and Central Asia through Russia. After that, however, as a result of pressure from Russian merchants, the government deprived foreigners of that right and gave the Moscow merchants a monopoly over transit trade.

Classes and masses

THE NOBILITY.   At the apex of the Russian social hierarchy stood the nobility—the boyars, princes, and service nobility. Theirs were the privileges and responsibilities of a ruling class, for they were the administrators, the military leaders, and the landholders. The boyars and princes, with their hereditary status and proud lineage (many tracing their families back to Rurik), considered themselves socially above the service nobility. The latter, however, had certain advantages. They were a numerically larger group, and they were of essential importance to the existing form of government. Moreover, although their noble status was not legally hereditary, many families among them were beginning to make it practically so by keeping the faith and favor of the tsar, thereby retaining their holdings and being able to pass both their wealth and their position to succeeding generations.

The Russian nobility differed from the nobility in such countries as Poland, France, and Spain in two important respects. In the first place, they did not attain the sense of corporate unity found among the noble classes in those countries. That was the consequence of their defeat by the tsars in the struggle for power. After the defeat they were unable to hold their ranks stable, for the tsars were continually advancing non-nobles to noble status. From time to time the nobility attempted to close its ranks to new additions, but it never succeeded. Consequently, although the noble class of Russia was relatively larger than that of other countries, it never achieved comparable status.

The Russian upper class differed from the upper classes of Western Europe also in the nature of its family life. In the period of Mongol control, the ruling families of Muscovy had adopted the institution of the *terem*, which required the virtual isolation of the women of the family from all males except the head of the household and the servants; and its practices were continued until the eighteenth century. Noblewomen lived in a separate part of the home and were not permitted to meet male guests of the house nor to leave the house except on the rarest of occasions. Ruled by such restrictions, social life among the nobles could not develop the influence it had in other countries.

THE CLERGY.   The clergy of the Russian Orthodox Church, like that of the

West, was divided into regular and secular branches and marked by sharp class differentiation. The regular clerics—that is, those who had taken monastic vows and who lived according to monastic rules, were known as the black clergy; and the secular, who lived among the laity and ministered to their spiritual needs, were known as the white clergy.

The prelates of the Church—the bishops, the metropolitans, the abbots, and the patriarch—were drawn exclusively from the black clergy. They controlled the great economic wealth of the Church and directed its political influence. Representatives of this branch were numerous and often powerful in the government. The most influential before the end of the seventeenth century had been the Patriarch Philaret, the power behind the throne during the reign of his son Michael Romanov.

The white clergy, the lower class of the Church, were the parish priests. In accordance with the rules of the Eastern Orthodox Church, they were permitted to be married. Therefore they became a hereditary group. Sons of parish priests might leave the service of the Church, and sons of laymen might become parish priests; but generally the calling passed from father to son. The white clergymen were on the whole a poorly educated and poverty-ridden lot; many were barely literate, some wholly illiterate, and most of them lived on but a slightly higher material plane than did the peasants among whom they served. Their position was further degraded by the fact that they were subject to corporal punishment by their superiors.

THE MIDDLE CLASS.   One of the peculiarities of Russian development has always been the absence of a strong middle class. No single reason can be given for the continuation of that peculiarity; it has been maintained by various parallel and interacting political and economic circumstances down through the history of the country.

The reason that a strong middle class did not develop before and during the Kievan period is obvious: the ruling class, the minority, held and directed the urban centers as if they were hereditary family estates, and few were able to rise from the majority class into positions of security and independence there. After the decline of Kievan Russia, the country did not develop an economically vigorous and politically independent urban class, such as that which became the middle class of Western Europe, because the general economic decline at that time and the subsequent rapid rise of a centralized and powerful state were added to the original drawbacks to such development. In Western Europe the growth of urban political and economic strength preceded the development of royal absolutism, and the urban middle class was able, therefore, to maintain some independence and much power even after the rise of absolutism. In Russia the process was reversed: the urban middle class began to develop after the power of the throne had been firmly established and was not able to assert itself in the face of tsarist power. That circumstance forestalled the development of a corporate feeling among the members of the middle class and lessened their chances of gaining political influence.

THE PEASANTRY.   The peasants were the most numerous and the least influential class in Russian society. As has already been noted, they were becoming enserfed at a time when serfdom was declining in Western Europe. And their status, low as it was in the seventeenth century, was to become even lower before it was to improve.

Peasant social life at that time was built upon family and village organization. The family usually spanned three generations and consisted of an elder couple, the couple's unmarried sons and daughters, the married sons and their wives and children—all living together and operating as a single social and economic unit under the domination of the oldest man.

Families lived together in small villages rather than on scattered farms. The ordinary village was physically a collection of perhaps a hundred wooden or earthen huts; socially it was a unit directed by the family heads. Out of the village social organization there had grown up, by the seventeenth century, an important organization known as the village commune (*mir* in Russian), the original purpose of which was to regulate economic and legal relationships within the village.

The communes had developed along diverse lines in different parts of the country until the time that the government began restricting and taxing the peasants; thereafter they began to show more common characteristics. Almost every commune had these features: (1) it was based upon the family, not the individual; (2) its membership was hereditary, but newcomers could be admitted; (3) its internal affairs were regulated by the heads of the families under the leadership of peasant elders elected from among them; (4) its state taxes were apportioned among the families by the elected elders; (5) its family heads worked out a periodical redistribution of the land assigned to the commune; and (6) it—not the individual family—was the economic unit with which the landholder dealt.

The Russian Orthodox Church

ORGANIZATION, DOGMA, AND RITUAL.   The basic unit of the Eastern Orthodox Church was the parish, through which contact between the clergy and the laity was made; the parishes were organized into bishoprics, each under a bishop chosen from among the black clergy; several bishoprics formed a metropolitanate; and all the metropolitanates in Russia were united as the Patriarchate of Moscow and All Russia. At the head of the patriarchate, ranking fifth and last in order of precedence among the patriarchates of the Eastern Orthodox Church in 1682, stood the patriarch, chosen by the prelates of the Church from among themselves, almost invariably with favored consideration to the wishes of the tsar.

The organization of the Church was developed around its central function, the saving of souls; it was recognized as the only instrument of salvation, and the priests serving it were considered indispensable intermediaries between God and man. The priests were ordained by the bishops, whose importance in the Church is illustrated by the following declaration made by a synod of Eastern Orthodox prelates held in Jerusalem in 1672:

> The dignity of the Bishop is so necessary in the Church, that without him, neither Church nor Christian could either be or be spoken of. For he, as a successor of the Apostles, having received the continued succession by the imposition of hands and the invocation of the All-holy spirit [and by] the grace that is given him of the Lord of binding and loosing, is a living image of God upon the earth.[1]

The Eastern Orthodox Church based its dogma and ritual on the Old and New Testaments, the writings of the Church Fathers, and the decisions of the first seven ecumenical councils (the first held in the year 325, and the seventh in 787). From these sources derived the creed of the Church, which has not been altered since. In most respects it did not differ from the Roman Catholic Church; and, until the eleventh century, the two were parts of one religious community, in which the Bishop of Rome was recognized as the first in order of precedence among the patriarchs.

Seven sacraments were recognized by the Eastern Orthodox Church: Baptism, Confirmation, Holy Orders, the Eucharist, Marriage, Penance, and Unction. And while the Orthodox explanation of some of the sacraments and their administration differed somewhat from the Roman Catholic explanation and administration, the two churches had no quarrel over the number and the significance of the sacraments. Rome and Constantinople accepted the same sources of authority for dogma and ritual but disagreed in the inter-

---

[1] Quoted in R. M. French, *The Eastern Orthodox Church* (London: Hutchinson's University Library, 1951), 90-91.

pretation of what was stated or meant by some of the sources. Rome argued that, according to the Trinitarian Creed, the Holy Spirit proceeds from the Father and the Son; Constantinople, that the Holy Spirit proceeds from the Father and *through* the Son. Rome came to believe that all priests should be celibate; Constantinople, that the rule of celibacy should not apply to parish priests. The Eastern Orthodox Church differed from the Roman Catholic also in permitting the laity to partake of both the bread and the wine in the sacrament of the Eucharist, in having the congregation stand throughout the services, and in forbidding the use of graven images to represent holy figures (allowing only two-dimensional representations). In addition, it refused to acknowledge the Roman theory of the primacy of the pope, holding to a belief in the equality of the patriarchs, thus later permitting the organization of the Eastern Orthodox Church as a loose union of self-governing churches.

Conflicts of interpretation as well as political rivalries between Rome and Constantinople finally led to a schism in 1054, when Pope Leo IX anathematized those who accepted the interpretations of the Patriarch of Constantinople. The schism was regretted by many, and efforts were frequently made to reunite the two churches. In 1439, at the Council of Florence, most of the representatives of the Eastern Orthodox Church agreed to reunion, but their action was disavowed in many parts of the Eastern Orthodox world, notably in Russia. The Union of Brest (see p. 60) was an act of actual reunion, but it affected a relatively small group among the Eastern Orthodox. So the schism continued; and, as far as the Russian Orthodox Church was concerned, even Protestants were more tolerable than Roman Catholics.

CHURCH, STATE, AND NATION.   The Church and the state had been intimately connected in Russia since the time that Vladimir made Eastern Orthodox Christianity the state religion. The creation of the Russian patriarchate strengthened the ties by removing the Church in Russia from the jurisdiction of Constantinople. And the new status of the Church enhanced its nationalistic character, for it had become not only the state Church but also—at least in name—a self-governing national institution. It is proper, therefore, to designate it after 1589 as the Russian Orthodox Church rather than the Eastern Orthodox Church in Russia.

Independence from Constantinople did not mean complete independence for the Church since the concept of Caesaro-papism (which implied subordination of church to state) was still a threat to its independence. Although the concept was sometimes challenged by Russian metropolitans and patriarchs, as it had been by those of Byzantium; and although the position of the head of the Church was strong, from the time of Nikon's removal from the office

Cathedral of the Assumption, where tsars were crowned. It was constructed in the Kremlin during the years 1475-1479.

of patriarch (1666) until the separation of the Church and the state in 1918, the state was the dominant power in the relationship. The tsar, it is true, did not assume the position of head of the Church, as did the rulers in the Protestant countries, but he exercised commanding power over its personnel and property.

The relation of the Church to the state, which was eventually to weaken the vitality of the Church, gave it many immediate advantages. It was the official custodian of the true faith. It could call on the state to punish apostasy or heresy, for a person born a member of the Church was not permitted to leave it or to hold to beliefs or practices rejected by the religious authorities. It could expect state support in its proselytizing activities and feel free of competition from the missionary work of other religions since the state forbade it. It was assured of additional membership if any of those Russian subjects born outside the Church were to be compelled by the state to accept Christianity—though the chances were that such people would be allowed to continue in what was considered a life of error. And, with its broad powers of censorship, the Church could determine to a great extent the nature of the reading matter available to any Russian, whether Orthodox or non-Orthodox.

In return for such advantages, the Church supported the state by buttressing the theories of autocracy with theological arguments, among them the argument that submission to the will of the tsar was the religious duty of all subjects. Equally important was the national leadership that the Church supplied, notably in the Mongol period and in the Time of Troubles. The Church also strengthened the national feeling in general by convincing its followers that not only was the Orthodox faith the true one but also that Russia, more than any other country, was the bastion of orthodoxy (especially now that Byzantium was in Turkish hands).

INFLUENCE.   The influence of the Church was so extensive that to indicate all the areas it pervaded would require a cataloging of nearly every aspect of Russian life. Art, literature, music, education—all were, in essence, within the religious domain, and secular activities in those fields were still weak. Tsar Alexis illustrated the temper of religious Russia in his devotion to pious activities, which employed most of his time, and in his insistence upon the approval of his confessor before almost every undertaking, even the observation of a staged play. Contact with those outside the faith was supposed to make one unclean, and Russians, therefore, were not ordinarily permitted to go abroad. In Moscow, foreigners were segregated, for even to eat with a non-Christian—or, for that matter, with a Catholic or Protestant—was to become unclean.

For the majority of Russians, the rhythm of life was set by the Church. The events of birth, marriage, and death were colored by its activities. Its lengthy services provided a test of the faith and endurance of the believer, who, when not prostrating himself, remained standing for several hours, almost incessantly crossing himself. Saints' days were as frequent as in the Catholic world; and periods of fasting, more lengthy and rigorous. Of all the holidays, Easter was the most significant: probably at no other time was the feeling of religious exaltation higher than when, after all had marched around the church, the priest announced that "Christ is risen!"

Icons, paintings of religious subjects, were given places of honor and prominence in all Orthodox homes, even carried to the harvest and to war. The Russians revered particularly those icons accepted by the Church as having miraculous powers. Of these, the best known is the *Wonder-working Virgin of Kazan,* associated with Ivan IV's taking of Kazan.

Monasticism, a prominent feature of Russian religious life, was marked by a heritage from the earlier days of Eastern Orthodoxy when solitude and asceticism were the ideals. The Monastery of the Caves, in Kiev, the most important and most revered monastic establishment in Russia, was in the ascetic tradition. Here monks might immure themselves in underground cells, some for as many as forty years, to pray and meditate, sometimes to fast for days or weeks. The dominant type of monastic life, however, was that of the organized establishment, following rules laid down by St. Basil in the fourth century and elaborated by St. Theodore of Studius in the ninth. In such monasteries monks or nuns ate and prayed together and engaged in work, perhaps cultivating the land or transcribing manuscripts. Sometimes, by establishing themselves beyond the limits of Russian settlement, monks served as pioneers of the colonizing movement. Solovetsky Monastery, established in the fifteenth century on an island in the White Sea, was one that served such a purpose. It was one of the fortified monasteries of Russia, which could give protection to the areas in which they were located as well as to the monks within them. Around Moscow itself were several such monasteries, providing an outer defense ring for the city.

The Trinity Monastery of St. Sergei, north of Moscow, which ranked next to the Monastery of the Caves in importance, illustrated the many-sidedness and far-reaching influence of monastery life. It was founded in the fourteenth century by St. Sergei of Radonezh and soon became the goal of many pilgrims. Tens of thousands—in later centuries, as many as 100,000—came each year to view the remains of St. Sergei, said to be miraculously preserved, to kiss his coffin, and to worship. In time, the monastery acquired many villages, including more than 100,000 serfs. Its resources enabled it to provide a small army in case of war and to defend itself from attack, as when it successfully held off a Polish army of 30,000 for sixteen months in 1608 and 1609. It was also a focus of national feeling: its founder, St. Sergius, supported Dmitri Donskoi in his decision to fight the Mongols, and monks from the monastery were important agents in stimulating the popular movement that swept Russia clear of invaders in the Time of Troubles.

For the Orthodox, the monastic life was the only completely Christian life. If a believer could not take monastic vows, he could at least make pilgrimages to monasteries and holy places, and the custom of doing so was widely practiced, many walking barefoot for months to reach their destinations. The coveted goals were the Holy Places and Orthodox monasteries in Palestine and Mt. Athos, in Greece, the most important monastic center of the entire Eastern Orthodox Church.

In the first seven centuries of its existence in Russia, the Orthodox Church had become deeply rooted and, being the bearer of superior moral and cultural influences from outside, had raised the moral and cultural level of the people. But it was only one influence among many in a country that was still backward and still tolerant of many practices and many kinds of behavior that produced results inconsistent with the aims of the Church. Moreover, Russia could not evade the universal truth that piety is susceptible to adulteration and, in some persons, it may come to be little more than ritualistic observance of the letter of Church requirements.

Arts and learning

GENERAL STATUS.   Russian arts and letters at the end of the seventeenth century were still largely religious in nature, and literacy was limited principally to the clergy and the upper class. There was no cultivated leisure class patronizing literature, music, and painting and no educated class concerning itself with the advancement of thought and learning. What there was of cultural enthusiasm was being attracted to Moscow, but that city could not yet be called a cultural center. The recency and nature of its development were reflected in the generally rude and provincial character of its society. And those who pursued the arts and learning were a minority who received little attention.

FOREIGN ELEMENTS.   The Byzantine culture that was introduced to Russia along with the Eastern Orthodox Church in the tenth century had a noticeable effect upon the Russian way of life. But it did not make the deep impression it might have because its introduction was followed by an extended period of continuous warfare that retarded cultural development in Russia and because contacts with Byzantium were considerably lessened after the twelfth century. The next foreign contact of any note, that with the Mongols, produced no general cultural change of significance, and toward the end of the period of Mongol hegemony, the Russian princes began to turn to the West. Ivan III and his successors hired gunsmiths, military engineers, officers, metallurgists, naval architects, and manufacturers from England, Holland, Sweden, France, and Germany; but, since the tsars were interested in improving only the technical and military skills, they did not invite those who might have assisted in other phases of the country's development.

Foreign cultural influences were not entirely lacking, however. At the end of the reign of Tsar Feodor III, there were some 18,000 foreigners in Russia. A large portion of them lived in a suburb of Moscow, where they were allotted a special district known as the German Settlement (since the Russians employed the same word, *nemets*, for Germans specifically and for foreigners collectively). They introduced not only Western technical skills but also certain manners and material amenities that were taken up by some members of the upper classes. Somewhat deeper cultural influences came from the Ukraine, where the Kiev Academy, established in 1631, became a center of learning and from which many well educated clergymen went to Moscow and there introduced to others the works of the medieval scholastics of the West. That contribution was supplemented by the introduction from Poland, Serbia, and Bulgaria of other translated European writings, including some classics and some popular novels and tales.

The intellectual effects of these first Western contacts were quite limited. Generally speaking, there was not as yet enough intellectual ferment in Russian life to offset the large measure of fear and suspicion of the West that existed, particularly among the clergy and the masses. The opposition to outside influence, which had been so definitely expressed in the religious schism, was frequently revived in acts of mob violence against foreigners in the cities. The hope of eventual profit from that influence lay with the few who were daring enough to accept whatever good there was in it, regardless of popular disapproval.

EDUCATION.   The level of education was a fair index of Russian culture at this time. There were a few Church schools, in which the most meager instruction was given; some clerics took children, by arrangement with parents, into their homes for instruction; and the upper aristocracy sometimes engaged tutors, usually from the Ukraine, Poland, or Western Europe. Still there did not exist, except in the Ukraine, even a rudimentary elementary school system; and higher education, either clerical or lay, had hardly made a beginning. One notable effort toward improving the situation was made in 1649, when a number of able monks educated at the Kiev Academy were brought to the Monastery of St. Andrei, near Moscow, to teach Greek, Latin,

Slavonic languages, rhetoric, and philosophy. But even that effort, which aimed at the establishment of a university, was not carried to fruition.

The lack of educational faciltites kept the Russians in a retarded state of knowledge; they were generally ignorant of the contributions of Greece, Rome, and Western Europe[1] in such fields as theology, philosophy, science, and mathematics—fields in which they had yet to make any contributions of their own.

How limited the country was in secular learning is illustrated by the general state of its mathematical and scientific knowledge. Of mathematics, some arithmetic and less geometry were known. Arabic numerals had just been introduced, and until their use had been thoroughly mastered, multiplication and division presented difficulties. Euclidean geometry was unknown, and what was taught under the heading of "geometry" bore little resemblance to it. Astrology was still respected as a science, and the works of Copernicus, Kepler, Harvey, Gilbert, Vesalius, Descartes, and Galileo were not known.

Though Russia was a pious country, even in religious learning it was unsophisticated. Few of the clergy had the necessary knowledge of Greek or Latin to be able to read the important books in religious philosophy and theology, and even if they had acquired the skills, they would still have lacked the intellectual preparation necessary to a full appreciation of such works.

PRINTING.   With learning in such a backward state, it is not surprising that the art of printing came to Russia late. In the 1550's, a century after Gutenberg, the first books were printed in Moscow. Even then the innovation was not welcomed; a mob, spurred on by the copyists' fear of the new technology, wrecked the first printing establishment. The number of titles printed in the beginning was small, less than twenty in the first fifty years in Moscow; but production was speeded up considerably after 1613. The products of the printing presses were primarily religious in character. And they were limited to those works that presented few technical problems to the printers; a complete copy of the Bible was first printed in Moscow in 1663.

LITERATURE.   The first written literature widely distributed in Russia, Greek religious works translated into Church Slavonic, comprised tracts on ritual, dogma, and church law, lives of the saints, and collections of sermons. Six centuries later, available literature was still of the same gen-

---

[1] There is no intention to suggest that India, China, and the Moslem world had nothing to offer Russia. The fact is that Russia was part of the Western World, and we are here concerned with its place in that world.

eral nature; translations of secular Byzantine, early Greek, and Latin works were very rare.

A native literature developed slowly, few original works being written before the eighteenth century except for practical purposes. Fortunately, historical curiosity prompted original efforts by some of the clerics, who became the first historians of Russia. The most prominent of their early works, the *Primary Chronicle,* has been mentioned earlier. The chronicles that followed it were similar in nature and displayed the faults of any contemporary historical work: little discrimination between the important and the unimportant, and the treatment of fact and hearsay as of equal reliability. Together the historical chronicles constitute an important body of source material, and may be considered as of some literary merit.

Most of the early writings were motivated by immediate needs or problems. An eminent example is the *Domostroi* (House-Orderer), the work of the sixteenth century priest Sylvester, in which he gives counsel on the management of home and family. There were also a number of polemical writings dealing with moot questions of religion and politics. Among the most interesting of the religious polemics are those of the sixteenth century clerics Nil Sorsky and Joseph, Abbot of Volokolamsk, who express opposing views on the relationship between Church and state. Another contribution of merit was made by the priest Avvakum, who died at the stake in 1681 for his persistent opposition to the reforms of Nikon. His autobiography, justifying his beliefs and actions, is a work distinguished by a powerful style and the daring use of vernacular Russian rather than Church Slavonic. Of the writings on the political questions of the day, the polemics exchanged by Ivan IV and Prince Andrei Kurbsky have become most famous. Kurbsky, who left the service of Russia for that of Lithuania, wrote bitter invectives against the terrorism of the tsar; and Ivan responded with skillful sarcasm, demonstrating an unusual literary ability.

Although the Church discouraged popular literature, censuring it as the work of frivolity, laymen composed songs, ballads, and tales. Usually those imaginative compositions were transmitted orally by wandering reciters, but a few of them were written. There is one oustanding example of a long written composition dating probably from the late twelfth century: a prose poem, *The Campaign of Igor,* describing a military campaign of Prince Igor in 1185. But few works even approximating belles-lettres were produced in Russia before the eighteenth century.

FINE ARTS.   Russia's early achievements in the fine arts were greater than those in the field of literature. The chief patron of architecture, paint-ing, and music was the Church. And, as was to be expected, the first mas-ters and the first models in the construction of churches, the painting of frescoes and icons, and the composition of music for religious services were Byzantine. However, the native Russian artists, after a period of imitating their Greek teachers, began to introduce vigorous and independent variations in their work despite the conservatism of the Church, which regarded innovations as potentially impious. By the seventeenth century, Russian architects, painters, iconographers, and painters had created much that was both original and highly artistic. Yet the Church was powerful enough to restrain the impulse toward original creation and, by frowning upon the living folk art, to block an important source of inspiration.

Consequently, the development of a sophisticated secular art was de-layed until the late eighteenth century. And when it did begin to flourish, it was imitative of Western art, having insufficient Russian tradition upon which to build.

PROMISE FOR THE FUTURE.   By the end of the seventeenth century three influences were distinguishable in Russian arts and letters: the cleri-cal, the upper class secular, and the folk. The Church, which had displayed such vigor in the first centuries after the conversion of the country, was beginning to lose its position as literary and artistic leader. That position was gradually passing to an upper class which was soon to become secular in its outlook and which, even now, was showing a slight inclination to turn to Western European secular art and literature for inspiration. Folk art, condemned by the Church and ignored by the upper class, was con-tinuing in its limited way. In short, the formal arts and letters were in the cocoon stage, growing but far from maturity.

The state

GOVERNMENT.   The first three Romanovs, it has been seen, reaffirmed the principles of tsarism which had been established in the fifteenth and sixteenth centuries, returning to the crown the absolutism against which no institutional nor legal checks existed. Tradition and prudence still re-quired circumspection on the part of the tsar in dealing with the service nobility and boyars, but those groups had not been able to develop a corpo-rate status recognized in law and embodying privileges that the tsar could not violate.

Since the Assembly of the Land had declined, there remained only the older Boyars' Duma to represent the governed in any active way. But it had failed in the efforts to transform itself into a legally constituted body with a clearly established set of rights and duties, and it was now an ineffectual body of tsar-approved men, giving advice when consulted, performing administrative tasks when permitted.

The administrative machinery of Russia, like that of many countries at the time, was in a disorderly state. There was no clear line between the tsar as a landholder and the tsar as a sovereign, and distinctions between the several organs of government were just as indeterminate. Administrative offices *(prikazy)* were set up as new problems arose. Some, like the Little Russia Office, were organized on a territorial basis; others, like the Office of Ambassadors, were set up on a functional basis. Often several offices dealt with the same function; military affairs were the province of at least four distinct offices of equal status, and a number shared the right to collect taxes. Many exercised judicial as well as administrative powers in their spheres. In all, there were more than forty heterogeneous offices in the muddled scheme of government. An effort was made to provide some coordination through the formation in 1658 of an Office of Secret Affairs, the duties of which were to supervise the work of other offices, especially those concerned with diplomatic and military affairs, to keep an eye on foreign diplomats in Moscow, and to handle the tsar's private affairs. But, although it performed many of the functions associated with a royal chancellery, it did not bring order into the imperial administrative system.

In local government, as well as in the imperial government, there was a tendency toward centralization. Because of the chaos resulting from the Time of Troubles, the first Romanovs had found it necessary to develop some new forms of local government. On the Polish frontier, where fighting was frequent, and in Siberia, where imperial power was being pushed eastward, local administration was left in the hands of powerful military governors. Elsewhere the office of cantonal governor *(voyevoda)* was established for the administration of cantons, made up of regional groups of towns, cities, and rural areas. The cantonal governor was appointed by the central authorities and responsible to them. He was assisted by a locally chosen reeve with authority over the judicial matters of the canton. Individual cities, towns, and rural areas within the canton were under various forms of government, some representative, some appointive, and all subject to the orders of the cantonal governor.

In the absence of a clear delineation of functions, many governmental offices took it upon themselves to issue legislation, thereby adding to the general confusion. To remedy the situation, the government undertook in 1648 to bring together and organize all existing legislation. The result was the legal code of 1649, which remained operative until 1833. It had the merit of systematic organization, but it showed a great lack of intelligent jurisprudence. That it lasted for nearly two centuries, according to Klyuchevsky, was not proof of its quality but rather of "Russia's long sustained ability to dispense with a satisfactory code."

Although the government claimed omnipotence, except perhaps in Church affairs, the range of its activities was, by modern standards, narrow; its major concern was war or the preparation for war. Yet it did not have a well-trained, regular military force. The core of the army was provided by the service nobility in times of war, but the number was insufficient for the needs of the state. To supplement it, several permanent regiments, composed of troops known as the Streltsy (the Archers) were created in the sixteenth century. The Streltsy, who were stationed in Moscow and other leading cities, could not properly be called professional soldiers because in times of peace they carried on the regular work of other callings while remaining under military control. Needing still more men than those supplied by the service nobility and the Streltsy, the first Romanovs began to hire foreign mercenaries and, when they proved unreliable, to form regiments of Russians, recruited into service and drilled and commanded by foreign soldiers. Such regiments were usually organized in times of emergency and disbanded at the end of the immediate need for them. Altogether, the Russian army was a poorly organized, poorly equipped, and very expensive organization. It is estimated that in 1680 nearly half the income of the state was spent on military requirements.

This emphasis on the military had two important consequences: to support the army, the government began to seek new means of increasing state income; and to eliminate inadequacies and improve the army, it began to make arrangements for acquiring the military techniques of Western Europe.

FOREIGN POLICY.   The destruction of Kievan Russia and the development of a new center of political power in Muscovy had a lasting effect on Russian foreign policy. Whereas Kievan Russia had maintained political and economic ties with many European and Near Eastern countries, Muscovite Russia began in relative isolation from them. Until the days of Ivan III, Muscovy's role in European politics was roughly analogous to that of

Afghanistan in modern times. After the fifteenth century contacts were gradually increased, but as late as the second half of the seventeenth century only England, Holland, Denmark, and Sweden maintained continuous diplomatic ties with Moscow.

Foreign policy was affected also by the fact that Muscovy grew up in the heart of a great plain, stretching from Western Europe deep into Asia and offering few natural obstacles to Russian expansion or to foreign aggression. To use a military figure, Muscovy had the advantages and disadvantages of interior positions. When in an expansive mood, it could move in any of the directions of the compass, the choice of direction depending upon the value of the prize sought or its political and military accessibility. On the other hand, the country was subject to attack from any direction. That situation has helped to determine Russian foreign policy through the centuries, often making it expedient for the government to shift diplomatic or military emphasis from one point to another—at times as much as six thousand miles removed from each other.

The history of Russian foreign relations has given support to a famous statement of Lord Palmerston: that nations do not have permanent friends or permanent enemies, only permanent interests. In the early centuries of its growth, the Russian nation acquired many interests which, if not permanent, have at least proved enduring. They might have been cut short in the beginning but for the fact that while Russia was gaining inner strength, her neighbors, one by one, weakened. One can imagine the result if the Golden Horde, Sweden, the Livonian Order, and Poland had maintained themselves at the peak of their power. Muscovy would have been still-born or, at best, would have survived as a satrapy of one or another of those powers (a condition with which it was closely threatened during the Time of Troubles). As it was, each of those powers, with some pressure from Russia, either declined or perished, and the Russian empire could further its interests at their expense.

One of the most enduring of Russia's interests has already been mentioned, the gathering-in of the Russian land, an interest that led to persistent conflict with Poland. At first, the pursuit of that interest seemed rather futile, for Poland was superior in power and internal stability. However, as the Russian throne was being strengthened by the tsar's mastery of the landed aristocracy, the Polish throne was being weakened by the rising power of the Polish landed gentry, and Russia's military position with respect to the major enemy began improving.

At the same time another interest was pressing for attention: the

gaining of a foothold on the Baltic seaboard. That eventually drew the concentration of attention to Sweden, then controlling not only Estonia and
the territory around the Gulf of Finland but also Livonia, with the coveted
seaport of Riga, which had been wrested from Poland early in the seventeenth century.

A third interest was the stabilization of the southern frontier, where
the continued aggressions of the Crimean Khanate made it difficult to
develop the agricultural regions that Russia was acquiring in the steppe
region. By the second half of the seventeenth century Russia had built up a
complex line of southern defenses reaching from Kharkov, in the Ukraine,
to Simbirsk, on the Volga. It included garrisons in fortified cities, blockades
in isolated areas, and frontier patrols—all manned by soldier-farmers. As
that line was slowly advanced to the south, a decisive struggle became
inevitable between Russia and the Crimean and other Mongols, who, with
the support of the Ottoman Empire, ruled the Black Sea coast.

In the Caucasus also, since the acquisition of Astrakhan, a Russian
interest was growing despite the counter-interests of the Ottoman Empire
and Persia in that region. When the native inhabitants appealed to Moscow
in the seventeenth century for aid against the aggressors, Russia was
occupied with other wars and could give only moral support; but the day
was to come when attention and strength could be turned to that region.

In the Far East, Russian interest was concentrated on a drive across
Siberia to the Pacific. After the fall of Kazan, in 1552, Russia had only
to overcome the khanate of Western Siberia in order to push expansion
into Sibera. In 1598 the last of the Siberian khans was defeated by Russian
troops, and the road eastward was then clear except for the opposition of
a few weak native tribes. The remainder of the drive did not require troop
operations, and in about two years adventurers and merchants had carried
the Russian flag across Siberia to the Pacific. In 1644 some of them turned
south to the Amur River, but there their advance was halted by Chinese
troops. That was the first contact between Russia and China.

The extension of power over Siberia made Russia a Eurasian state, but
the Asiatic portion of it remained for some time unimportant except as a
source of revenue. At the end of the seventeenth century Russia was
essentially a European state. To be sure, it was still only a "little cloud no
larger than a man's hand" on the horizon of European diplomacy, but it
was becoming a factor in the affairs of Poland, Sweden, and the Ottoman
Empire, which were of some diplomatic moment in Europe.

PRELUDE TO CHANGE.   By the middle of the seventeenth century Russian society had attained, in most respects, a condition of equipoise. It is true that certain things weighed heavily upon the people: the requirements of a state continually at war, the brutality of autocracy, and the hardships of serfdom. Yet generally they accepted those burdens and made the best of a society organized about the focuses of tsardom and Orthodoxy.

A thin wedge of doubt was entering the minds of a few, principally members of the upper classes, with whom the ways and thoughts of the more progressive West had found limited favor. But among the masses and within the Church, foreign customs and knowledge stirred not only disapproval but also active opposition. The majority were convinced that Russia, "the third Rome," stood superior and alone in a sinful and heretical world.

The only outside influence of any significance was that admitted by the government itself, the influence of Western technology; and it was limited. In admitting it, the government was in no sense acknowledging any need for change in the fundamental institutions of Russia or in the aims of governmental policy; it was simply acknowledging the need to improve the fiscal and military position of the state in order that it might continue those institutions and that policy.

Western technology later proved to be the introductory factor in a general program of "westernization," but at the end of the seventeenth century that consequence could not be foreseen.

PART 2

Consolidation and Expansion

CHRONOLOGICAL OVERVIEW

Rulers

1682-1696	Ivan V, co-tsar	1741-1762	Elizabeth
1682-1725	Peter I	1762	Peter III
1725-1727	Catherine I	1762-1796	Catherine II
1727-1730	Peter II	1796-1801	Paul
1730-1740	Anna	1801-1825	Alexander I
1740-1741	Ivan VI		

Chief Events

1700-1721	Northern War
1703	Founding of St. Petersburg
1709	Battle of Poltava
1721	Abolition of the Patriarchate
	Treaty of Nystadt
	Acceptance of title of 'Emperor" by Peter I
1722	Establishment of Table of Ranks
1725	Establishment of Academy of Sciences
1726	Creation of Supreme Privy Council
1733-1735	War of the Polish Succession
1753	Abolition of internal tariffs
1755	Establishment of the University of Moscow
1756-1763	Seven Years' War
1757	Establishment of the Academy of Arts
1762, Mar.	Manifesto on Freedom of Nobility
July	"Palace Revolution"
1764	Secularization of Church lands
1767-1768	Meetings of Legislative Commission
1772	First partition of Poland
1773-1775	Pugachev Revolt
1774	Treaty of Kutchuk-Kainardji
1785	Issuance of Charter of the Cities
	Issuance of Charter of the Nobility
1786	Publication of program for educational system
1792	Treaty of Jassy
1793	Second partition of Poland
1795	Third partition of Poland
1805	Formation of Third Coalition
1807, July	Treaty of Tilsit
1809, Sep.	Treaty of Friedrichsham
1812, May	Treaty of Bucharest
June-Dec.	Napoleonic campaign in Russia
Sep.	Battle of Borodino
1815, June	Final Act of Congress of Vienna

In the period between 1676 and 1725, three princes and two regents succeeded to power in Russia, but only one of them attained fame as a ruler. Peter I, who came to the throne in 1682, rose to the stature of Peter the Great through a forty-three-year reign which has become one of the most famous and controversial in Russian history.

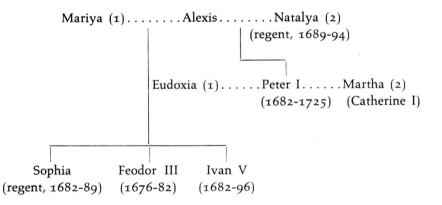

In an effort to evaluate Peter's reign, unending debate has been carried on by two schools of thought whose labels have changed with the times but whose essential arguments have remained the same. The adherents of one school, known since the nineteenth century as the Westerners have held that Russia before the time of Peter was a European country which had, for valid reasons, lagged behind its more mature cousins of the West and that the most important task in Peter's time was to close the gap between Russia and them—in short, that Russia needed the treatment of Westernization and that, when Peter administered it, he was doing the right and proper thing. Adherents of the other school, commonly known as the Slavophiles, have argued that Russia needed nothing from the outside world, that as the bastion of Eastern Orthodoxy it had developed a unique European civilization which should have been allowed to follow its preordained path of development, a path far better than that of Western Europe; in their opinion, Peter did Russia a disservice by his introduction of Westernization.

Each school has interpreted history to suit itself and winnowed the facts to select those that support its argument. Perhaps the proper evaluation of Peter lies somewhere between their extreme judgments. Certainly the fact that he was present and active at the time of Russia's precipitation into the general European scene does not justify the allocation of all blame or of all credit to him. Peter was no *deus ex machina* who did with Russia as his fancy pleased. He was definitely influenced by the policies of his predecessors, even though his interpretation and execution of those policies were determined by his own vigorous nature.

Irregular preparation for power

EARLY YEARS. Peter's childhood was spent under conditions that had a lasting influence upon his development. He was trained for an uncertain future in the midst of a struggle for imperial power, the outcome of which might determine whether he would succeed to the highest position in Russia or meet his death at the hands of a mob.

Peter (*b.* 1672) was the fourteenth child and the third son of Tsar Alexis I. Upon the death of his father, two elder half-brothers stood between him and the throne, the physically weak Feodor and the mentally deficient Ivan; and family division made the prospect of his succession even more remote. Alexis' first thirteen children were born of his first marriage, to Mariya Miloslavsky; and Peter was born of his second, to Natalya Naryshkin. When Feodor succeeded to the throne, in 1676, the numerous children and relatives of his mother moved into positions of power and influence, while the Tsarina Natalya and her son Peter were sent off to an imperial estate near Moscow to live in relative obscurity.

There for six years Peter received the customary training for one of his birth: a great deal of unguided physical exercise (in his case, chiefly playing with military toys) and instruction in reading, writing, religion, and Russian history. After that, his formal education was supplemented by the informal and brutal lessons of politics; for the Patriarch and a large number of the court aristocracy, having withdrawn their support from those in power, returned him and his mother to the Kremlin to await the appropriate time for action on their behalf. When Feodor died (1682) they proclaimed the ten-year-old Peter tsar. That act was met at once by strong resistance from the family of the half-brother Ivan, then sixteen years of age, and under their encouragement the Streltsy attacked the Kremlin. Peter was a witness of the attack and saw many of his mother's supporters beaten or decapitated by the drunken Streltsy. The conflict was settled by the proclamation of Ivan as co-tsar of Peter and the designation of Peter's ambitious half-sister Sophia as regent during the minority of the co-tsars. Peter and his mother were then returned to the country estate.

Thereafter his education and training were of his own making. He found military games and arts to his taste and spent his time at them. From the nobles in his retinue, servants, professional soldiers from the German quarter and men supplied by the government, he selected the best to make up two personal regiments. He furnished them with arms and quarters and drilled them himself, unopposed by the regent Sophia. At the time he was certainly no threat to those in power; he was just a precocious boy who found his pleasure in the activity of the drill field, the camaraderie of the barracks room, and the work of the smithy and carpenter shop rather than in the gentlemanly pursuits of horsemanship, the hunt, and falconry. He became a large (nearly seven feet tall) youth, raw-boned and nervous, who enjoyed above all to work with his hands at tasks auxiliary to military pursuits. His manners grew coarse and his intellect, other than in military and mathematical matters, was left uncultivated. But he was becoming settled in his likes and dislikes. As he developed his friendships with rough soldiers and technicians, he came to despise his half-sister Sophia, the court aristocracy, the ecclesiastical hierarchy, and the center of their activities, Moscow.

When he was seventeen, the duty of marriage was pushed upon him, and he married a girl for whom he showed no later affection, Eudoxia Lopukhin.

CONTEST FOR POSITION. Meanwhile, able and power-loving Sophia ruled the country, sometimes enlisting the aid of her lovers, ambitious men who were willing to overlook the fact that she was personally unattractive—according to a contemporary, "immensely fat, with a head as large as a bushel and hairs on her face." Peter showed little interest in

her handling of political affairs until she began using the title of Autocrat
and taking on the airs of the titular ruler. Then he asserted bitter resentment of her pretensions, and around him and his mother there gathered
many "outs" who hoped to become "ins" by the removal of the regent.
When the information came to Peter in August, 1689, that Sophia was
assembling the Streltsy in the Kremlin and intended an attack upon him,
he began to make plans for a military counterblow. Thereupon, Sophia,
believing in the strength of Peter's troops and doubtful of the reliability
of her own, relinquished her position. She was sent to a convent; her
supporters were removed from office, some exiled and a few executed; and
Peter and his followers came to power. The co-tsar Ivan continued his
inconsequential way until his death, in 1696, but he was of no moment
in the government. The Tsarina Natalya was allowed to assume the regency,
and Peter again returned to his earlier pursuits.

GRADUAL ASSUMPTION OF POWER. Peter's transformation from an
unreined youth into a ruler was a gradual one. As long as his mother was
regent, he felt free to pursue his personal interests. He employed himself
mainly at military games with his two regiments. Once, having found
fascination in shipbuilding, he went to Archangel to study the foreign ships
in the harbor. Even at the time of his mother's death, in 1694, he did not
take over the direction of the government but left it in the hands of court
officials. He performed his first activity for the state in 1695, when he
decided to take part in Russia's renewed fighting with the Crimean Khan
and his overlord, the Turkish Sultan. He participated, as a bombardier
sergeant, in the attack on Azov, a port near the mouth of the Don. There
he not only fulfilled his military duties in the attack but he also meddled
in the direction of it; and when it failed, some blamed his meddling. That
was his initiation into the affairs of the state—appropriately, the military
ones. He followed it, in the next year, after the death of Ivan, by moving
to Moscow and beginning to take an interest in political affairs also.

One of his first acts as an independent tsar was to renew the attack
on Azov, this time with a navy to assist the land forces. Although the
ships he provided were hastily constructed and manned, they gave such
advantage to the Russians that they were able to take the port. That victory
convinced the Tsar of the importance of a navy for Russia and, in characteristic fashion, he turned all energy to the problem of providing one.
His immediate aim was the construction of a Black Sea fleet with Azov
as a base; and, as the first step toward its realization, he immediately sent
off fifty noblemen to Western Europe to study navigation, seamanship

and shipbuilding. Then, in 1697, he himself set out to undertake the same study in England, Holland, and Venice, traveling incognito as a humble member of a Russian diplomatic mission which was visiting those places for the purpose of creating a military alliance against the Ottoman Empire. In so doing, he set a precedent; no tsar before him had ever left the country.

The venture proved worthwhile. The Tsar's party observed the shipyards of Holland and England and learned much which was later put to advantage in their own country. Peter himself learned first hand many of the skills of a shipwright, and, to insure such skills for the program he was planning, he hired nine hundred Dutch naval men for service in Russia.

In 1698, while in Vienna en route to Venice, Peter received news of a revolt of the Streltsy; and he abandoned his tour and returned home. The rising of the Streltsy had been subdued before he arrived, but it had a cruel and bloody aftermath. Suspecting that Sophia and possibly some of the nobility were responsible for the disorder, he conducted an intensive investigation but failed to uncover any solid evidence to support his suspicions. Nevertheless he compelled Sophia, who was already in a convent, to take the vows of a nun and subjected her to heavy guard. Under his personal supervision, he had more than a thousand of the Streltsy publicly hanged, decapitated or broken on the wheel. Then he ordered the disbanding of the group and forcibly scattered the survivors throughout the country. By those acts, he removed two thorns from his flesh: Sophia and the Streltsy.

There was still a third thorn, his wife, the unloved Eudoxia. To rid himself of her, he resorted to the current method of terminating a marriage, compelling her to become a nun. He refused her even the company of their young son Alexis, for he was the heir to the throne and was to be reared under the Tsar's direction.

ACCEPTANCE OF DUTIES. After his return from Western Europe, Peter no longer shirked or shared his responsibilities; he gave himself wholeheartedly to both the foreign and the domestic affairs of Russia and allowed himself no further intermission from them.

He was then twenty-six years of age, a physically and mentally powerful man, strikingly different from his moderate and pious father, Alexis. He was earthy in his tastes and manners, impatient of weakness or failure, derisive of precedent and tradition, warm-hearted, yet cruel when the need or mood arose. He was to make a strong impression on his contemporaries, but not a pleasant one.

In 1698 Peter was full of plans for the future: he wanted to build a navy, improve the army, strengthen the fiscal structure of the state and advance Russian power. But, despite any program of reform he may have had in mind, the circumstances of his reign—and perhaps his own temperament as well—were to dictate to him extemporized policies and decisions the total effect of which was to be disorder rather than synthesis.

Expansion of the empire

DIPLOMATIC PREPARATION. Since Peter's diplomatic mission of 1697-98 had not succeeded in promoting an alliance against the Ottoman Empire, it seemed expedient that Russia end the state of war with that power. Peace in the Black Sea area would free Russia to pursue what seemed to be the immediate possibility of gaining some of the old goals on the Baltic. Sweden had lost her powerful king, Charles XI, in 1697, and in his place there now sat the sixteen-year-old Charles XII. The situation tempted Peter, and he was encouraged by conversations he held in 1698 with Augustus II, King of Poland and Elector of Saxony, who agreed that their chances of gain at Sweden's expense were brighter than ever before. In the following year Russia, Poland and Denmark formed a secret alliance, Poland and Denmark agreeing to begin an early attack on Sweden and Russia promising to join them as soon as peace was concluded with the Turks.

Peace negotiations between the Ottoman Empire and those powers with which the Turkish forces had been warring—Austria, Poland, Venice, and Russia—had begun in 1698 at a congress held in Karlowitz. The other powers had been able to agree on their settlements in the following year, but at that time Russia and the Ottoman Empire could agree only on a two-year truce. In 1700, however, they reached a more binding agreement, by which a truce for thirty years was declared and Russian possession of the Azov area was acknowledged. As soon as the news of this agreement reached Peter, he ordered his troops, which had been ready for some time, to march on the Swedish fortress of Narva, in Estonia.

THE NORTHERN WAR.   The war begun so lightly dragged on for twenty-one years; and the young Charles proved to be a brilliant, even if erratic, opponent. Before Russian troops reached Narva, Charles had forced Denmark to withdraw from the war. The Russians, 35,000 strong, failed to

Peter the Great

take Narva; and with a relieving force of 8,000 Charles defeated them handily. Then, in the justified belief that Russian military strength was not an immediate threat, he left a small holding force in Narva and began a major effort against Augustus, whose Polish and Saxon troops had invaded Livonia. He drove the invaders from their Livonian gains, pushed them back upon their own soil, and continued the fighting there.

Charles' choice of objectives was a godsend to Peter, for it gave him time in which to renew his forces. He raised new levies of troops from the peasantry, hastily trained a new corps of officers, strengthened his artillery, and improved his supply services. By such measures he built upon the remnants of the defeated army a new one, trained and organized under new methods which were to endure far beyond the war.

While he waited for an opportune time to renew full-scale fighting, Peter sent troops, arms and money to Augustus, who was meeting the full force of Charles' attack, and took advantage of the main Swedish army's preoccupation elsewhere by directing attacks on Estonia, Ingria, and Livonia. From Pskov, which he had fortified after the defeat at Narva, he began a series of sorties in 1701 and, within the next three years, had taken most of those three provinces from the small Swedish forces left by Charles. Those gains gave Russia control of the Neva River and the southern shores of the Gulf of Finland. Peter at once took steps to protect his gains. In 1703, at the mouth of the Neva, he established a new town, which he named St. Petersburg in honor of his patron saint. In addition, he established the Sts. Peter and Paul Fortress on the island facing the town and built a shipyard on the shore of Lake Ladoga.

Charles, driving on into Poland, defeated Augustus and sponsored the election of a new Polish king, Stanislaw Leszczynski, in 1704. The following year, Peter, having decided to help Augustus (who had retired to his Saxon possessions) to regain his throne, resumed large-scale warfare by dispatching an army into Poland. But within a few months the Russians were forced to retreat, and the indefatigable Charles again turned on Augustus. The former king was compelled to sign a peace in 1706, renounce the alliance with Russia and forfeit all claims to the Polish throne. Then Peter also, lacking allies, decided to seek peace with Charles, but the latter was not interested in peace proposals; he had a grandiose scheme by which he hoped to end all danger from Russia.

In November, 1707, Charles set his scheme into operation. He sent a combined military and naval force to attack St. Petersburg and Ingria while he, with the main Swedish forces, moved eastward. By the summer of 1708 it appeared that he was ready to march on Smolensk. Instead he turned south to join forces with the head of the autonomous political organization of the eastern Ukraine, the Hetman Mazeppa, who had been negotiating with Sweden for some time. In the hope of ending Russian control in his lands, Mazeppa had planned to call for a revolt and take the rebels over to the side of Sweden; but Moscow anticipated him. When, in the fall of 1708, he began the planned revolt, loyal Russian troops razed his headquarters and seized key positions in his region. He managed to reach Charles with a few troops, but the great Ukrainian rebel army which the Swedish king had included in his calculations never materialized. Consequently when winter came, Charles found himself in the heart of the Ukraine, his troops exhausted by the campaign, greatly depleted by the harsh Ukrainian weather, and lacking support among the population. Fighting was suspended until the spring of 1709, and by that time the Swedish forces were a sorry lot. When they finally met Peter's forces, which had come to relieve the besieged Russian garrison of Poltava on July 8, 1709, the well-fed, well-trained Russians virtually annihilated them. Charles and Mazeppa left their men and escaped to Turkish territory. Peter was greatly encouraged. The Battle of Poltava gave him his first victory over the Swedish army in an organized encounter. Moreover, its weakening effect upon Sweden enabled Augustus II to regain the Polish throne.

The war was far from won, however. Charles persuaded his Turkish host to join the fight, and in November, 1710, the Ottoman Empire declared war on Russia. Peter opened a quick offensive, but he soon regretted his haste. His troops were no match for the Turkish forces; and he counted himself fortunate when, in July, 1711, he managed to make peace with the Sultan—even at the price of Russian cession of Azov.

Again the war moved to the Baltic. There the new Russian navy made a successful debut, aiding the army in establishing control of the Gulf of

Finland; Saxony and Denmark once more entered the fighting against Sweden, and Prussia and Hanover soon followed. Charles, whose maneuverings had finally led to his somewhat inglorious expulsion from the Ottoman Empire, returned to Sweden in 1714 to head his forces. At the time, advantages were on the side of the anti-Swedish coalition, but it failed to make the most of them; although it had potential preponderance of forces, its members did not work together effectively enough to overpower the Swedish armies. As it was, when Charles died, in 1718, the warring nations were ready to end the war, providing only that each retain some gains from it. Intermittent negotiations began and, one by one, the nations made peace.

TREATY OF NYSTADT. Russia and Sweden finally signed a treaty of peace at Nystadt in 1721. By its terms Russia received Livonia (including the prized city of Riga), Estonia, Ingria, and a part of Karelia. In return, she promised to recognize the previous rights of the inhabitants of the ceded regions and not to restrict their religion.

Russian acquisition of the Baltic provinces and Ingria had far-reaching effects on both the foreign and the domestic affairs of the country. Sweden was weakened by her losses to Russia, the cession of holdings in Germany to Prussia and Hanover, and the deterioration of her internal political life. As a result, she became a second-rate power while Russia emerged as a major power in the Baltic. And that change in status led to a shift in Russia's relations with Prussia, England, and France. Prussia, having acquired the major Swedish holdings on the German shore of the Baltic, could not ignore Russian interests on that sea and in Poland. England, whose ties with Russia had been primarily commercial, now saw her in a different light—as a possible disturber of the balance of power in Europe. France, too, began to think of Russia in relation to the maintenance of a balance of power and to look upon Sweden, Poland, and the Ottoman Empire as buffers against her. In short, Peter, in "opening a window to Europe," had also opened Pandora's box.

The Treaty of Nystadt brought about significant changes also in Russia's commercial situation. Having numerous ports on the Baltic and the Gulf of Finland now, Russia no longer needed to use only the White Sea route from Archangel to Western Europe. In consequence, the proportion of Russian foreign trade handled by English and Dutch vessels decreased as Russia became more independent commercially, and the domestic center of commerce shifted from the region around Archangel to the Baltic and the Gulf of Finland.

In conformity with treaty obligations, Russia did not tamper with the existing institutions of the newly acquired provinces. Even so, the inhabitants of Ingria and the Karelian territory became integrated with the Russians. On the other hand, the economic and political life of Livonia and Estonia continued under the domination of the German landed nobility, merchants and clergy, who constituted a small minority of the population in those provinces. The majority of Livonia's inhabitants were Letts, ethnically close to the Lithuanians. At the time of Russia's acquisition, they were serfs attached to the land of the German nobility, and they remained a submerged people of whom little was heard until the nineteenth century. The serf labor in Estonia was supplied by the Esths, related by culture to the Finns. However, life in both Livonia and Estonia was German in appearance: the language of politics, commerce, and religion was German, and the predominant faith Lutheran. Peter and his successors until the end of the nineteenth century accepted the status quo in those provinces and showed enough satisfaction with the dominant class there—called Baltic Germans—to admit many of its members to prominent positions in the Russian government and army.

EASTERN AFFAIRS.   Although the war with Sweden was foremost in Peter's mind during most of his active reign, he did not neglect Russia's commercial and political interests in the Far East and in Central Asia.

After Chinese troops had turned the Russians back from the Amur River in 1685, it became evident that some understanding would have to be reached about the boundary between Siberia and China. Such an understanding was reached in 1689 and embodied in the Treaty of Nerchinsk, setting the boundary at the Yablonovoi Range, north of the Amur. After that, Peter sought to extend commercial relations with China. In 1719 he sent a mission to Peking to work out trade arrangements, but it was not successful. Nor was any definite progress made toward that end until two years after Peter's death; in 1727, by the Treaty of Kyakhta, Russo-Chinese commercial relations were established and Russia was permitted to maintain a religious-diplomatic mission in the Chinese capital.

For the extension of Russian interests in Central Asia, Peter made plans which were overly ambitious and illusory, but prophetic. He dreamed of controlling the land and water routes to India and of diverting the eastern silk trade through Russia. He dreamed also of changing the course of the Amu-Darya River—then flowing into the Sea of Aral—back to its old channel to the Caspian (a project undertaken nearly two and a half centuries after his time—during World War II).

At that time, Persia controlled portions of the eastern trade route which Peter coveted for Russia; and when his diplomatic agent in Persia informed him that internal political difficulties in that country would make Russian military intervention possible, he was anxious to make the move. Having the victory over Sweden behind him, he declared war on Persia early in 1722 and set out with a military expedition, which moved from Astrakhan down the western shores of the Caspian. The ensuing war was brief. In 1723 Persia was forced to sign a treaty of peace which would give Russia the city of Baku and much of the western coast of the Caspian. However, the Shah of Persia refused ratification, and the plan of expansion through that region had to be abandoned for the time.

RECOGNITION OF THE EMPIRE-BUILDER. Even though Peter could not carry out all his imperial plans, he achieved enough to gain the country's acknowledgment of his stature as an empire-builder. During the festivities which followed the Treaty of Nystadt, the Governing Senate (*see* p. 109) offered him the titles of "Emperor" and "the Great," which he accepted after a first diplomatic refusal. The titles signified an appreciation of the position and recognition to which Russia had advanced as a result of its miliary achievements under the direction of Peter. Thereafter, the official title of Russian rulers was Emperor instead of Tsar, although the latter persisted in common usage.

Domestic affairs

DEVELOPMENT OF THE ARMED FORCES. In the early years of his reign, Peter saw the need for a large regular army and navy recruited on a systematic basis and trained by better methods; and, after the defeat at Narva, an improved military organization was hammered out according to his specifications.

The ranks of the regular army were filled by calling up men on the basis of a ratio of recruits to taxpaying population, the ratio varying with the needs of the service. Both the voluntary and the involuntary recruits, taken mainly from the peasants, were placed in service for twenty-five years, during which only death, incapacity, or decrease in the needs of the army could bring legal release. New levies of recruits occurred whenever need arose to enlarge the army or to fill gaps caused by death, injury, or desertion. All recruits received standardized basic training in Western techniques before being assigned to military units, and some also received specialized instruction in newly created artillery and engineering schools.

Officers were drawn from the boyars and service nobility. They received training either in the line regiments or in the Preobrazhensky and Semenovsky Guards Regiments, which had been created out of Peter's two play regiments.

At Peter's death, Russia had one of the largest armies in Europe: nearly 200,000 regular army men and about 100,000 irregulars (mostly Cossacks and Mongols). In accordance with the growing European practice, the infantry was treated as the "queen of the arms," supported by cavalry, artillery, and engineers.

The navy, conceived by Peter and built under his direction, had grown, by 1725, to thirty-five ships of the line, ten frigates and hundreds of lesser vessels—together requiring the services of 28,000 men. A nautical school, a naval academy, and a mathematical school had been established to provide technical training for naval service men.

The support of the army and navy accounted for two-thirds of the state's budget in 1725. The magnitude of the military preparations and the burden which they imposed may be seen by a comparison: Russia, with a relatively undeveloped economy, an inefficient fiscal system, and a population of some 13 million, was supporting armed forces almost equal in size to those of France, then the wealthiest state in Europe, with a population of 19 million.

FISCAL REFORMS.   One of the most pressing problems of the Petrine regime was that of finance. Peter found the Russian treasury in its customary state of deficit, tax payments in arrears, and the coinage debased. He wanted to reorganize the fiscal system, increase the national wealth, and bring a larger portion of it into the treasury. But conditions made it impossible for him to undertake a long-range program to accomplish those ends; most of his measures were designed to meet the need of the moment— at all times greater than the state income.

For an immdiate increase in income, he created new state monopolies and introduced a new form of direct tax. The monopolies were a good source of revenue, for through them the government was able to set ruthless price increases on items in popular demand—oaken coffins, for example, the price of which was advanced to four times that previously charged by private merchants. However, the most profitable and lasting fiscal innovation of the period was the poll tax—or soul tax as it was often called. Previously the basic direct tax was a tax on each household, except those of the landholders and the clergy. But it was decided in 1718 that a direct tax on each adult male (soul), exclusive of the landholders and clergy, would be more efficient and more profitable. In preparation for its introduction, an enumeration of taxable males was made and a tax register compiled. The enumeration (the first of its kind in Russia and probably not wholly accurate) showed about 5.5 million taxable males, of whom about 78 per cent were privately owned serfs, 19 per cent state-owned or free peasants, and 3 per cent urban dwellers. The poll tax, as applied to them, provided nearly half the government revenue, and it continued to be one of the main sources of state income until its abolition, in 1886.

ECONOMIC POLICIES.   Peter's economic policies were essentially mercantilistic—in line not only with earlier Russian policies but also with those of contemporary Europe. He sought to preserve a favorable balance of trade, to increase the Russian store of bullion, and to prevent the importation of articles which could be produced within the country.

Above all, he sought to supply Russian military needs from domestic sources rather than from the foreign sources upon which his predecessors had relied. Great emphasis was placed upon the development of metallurgy, arms manufactories, shipyards, and military clothing factories. The state encouraged private enterprise in those fields by providing subsidies, guarantees, and special privileges to entrepreneurs willing to organize new establishments. And since there was a lack of free labor, the state provided a labor force by detailing state peasants to the mines, factories, forests, and shipyards; by permitting nobles who entered industry to use their own serfs; or sometimes by granting manufacturers the right to purchase villages of serfs. If such incentives failed to interest a sufficient number of private industrialists in any field, the government itself would go into production.

In 1725 there were about two hundred industrial establishments in the country, most of them developed as a result of the Petrine policy. It was a striking development, but it did not represent a spontaneous growth of industry, rather a growth forced by the government. The state had become the chief promoter and the chief customer of industry, and it was to retain that position for many years to come.

Peter's plans for the improvement of the domestic economy involved also the encouragement of economic relations abroad. In the hope of increasing the wealth of Russia, he encouraged Russian merchants to enter foreign trade and sent many of them abroad to study Western methods. And to accelerate the transportation of goods to and from the ports he planned to increase the usefulness of the inland waterways by a system of canals. Of those constructed, the most important was that connecting the Volga and the Baltic Sea.

Although agriculture was the chief source of Russian wealth at that time, little was done to raise the level of agricultural production. The government sponsored the cultivation of some new crops, such as tobacco (hitherto under religious ban) and grapes; but on the whole, the old crops and old methods prevailed.

SOCIAL CHANGES.   The growing need of the state for soldiers, administrators, taxpayers, and laborers resulted in the extension of a principle already implicit in the political organization of Russia—that every subject owed service or a combination of service and taxes to the state.

The service nobility had long been the chief source of military officers and officials, but their number was insufficient for Peter's requirements. To make up for the lack, he added thousands to the roster of the service nobility and tried to insure against any shirking of service. Many of that class had been evading their military and governmental duties, but Peter limited the practice by the type of punishment he meted out for it: forced labor or loss of land. One group of noble youths (including the brother of the Grand Admiral of the Fleet) who attempted evasion were put to work at pile-driving in a canal.

To prepare sons of the service nobility for responsibility, Peter ordered, in 1714, the creation of a system of compulsory schools for noble youths between the ages of ten and fifteen, at which they would learn the three R's. At fifteen they were to enroll as enlisted men in the guards regiments if their families were of the upper nobility; or in the line regiments, if they were of lower rank. The schools, representing the first experiment in lay compulsory education in Russia, were a failure, and most of them did not last beyond the period of Peter's reign.

Further regulation was imposed upon the service nobility through the introduction, in 1722, of the Table of Ranks. Every responsible position, military or civil, was classified in one of fourteen ranks, and advancement from one to another was strictly regulated. Young noblemen were required to enter service in the lowest rank, from which they could rise by merit to the top. Persons of common origin also might enter the lowest rank and, if able to advance to the upper ones, might thereby acquire noble status. The Table of Ranks and the premises upon which it was based would have produced a complete fusion of the bureaucracy and the nobility if Peter's successors had followed his example in applying it; but as soon as he died, opposition to the principle of obligatory service began to weaken its application. However, the Table of Ranks remained in effect as a system of bureaucratic classification until 1917.

In an effort to strengthen the economic base of the service nobility, Peter introduced two changes in land tenure in 1714. He legalized the generally observed practice of treating their holdings as hereditary, thus eliminating one of the chief distinctions between boyars and service nobility. And he halted the gradual diminution of estates (resulting from the practice of dividing them among all heirs) by denouncing the practice of division and requiring that each estate be devised intact to only one heir.

Change in peasant status under Peter came about chiefly through the application of the poll tax. Previous distinctions in the degree of attachment of peasants to the landholder were now disregarded in the determination of taxes; and all, except the few free peasants, were classified either as privately owned serfs or as state peasants. The result was a further hardening of the system of serfdom.

Not even the urban dwellers were exempt from change. Peter wanted to encourage the development of the mercantile and artisan classes and, to that end, introduced among them some of the practices that he had observed abroad. The one of most lasting effect was the formation of guilds under franchises issued to the wealthier merchants and artisans.

ADMINISTRATIVE INNOVATIONS. Because the central and local administrative machinery of Russia proved unequal to the tasks imposed upon it by his policies, Peter made changes in it as needs arose. When he was through, Russia had a very different set of administrative bodies.

The nearly defunct Assembly of the Land met in limited session for the last time in 1698; it was not abolished but simply allowed to lapse. The Boyars' Duma had lost many of its functions; and Peter completed its dissolution, creating in 1711 a new body, the Governing Senate, which assumed the former functions of the Boyars' Duma and many new ones. He originally intended that the Senate serve as an executive body in his absence from the governmental center, but he soon transformed it into a permanent body to supervise the work of central and local administration. Since its members were appointed and held office at the pleasure of the sovereign, it could not be expected to offer any potential challenge to the throne.

The old central offices were the next to feel the effects of the reformer's zeal. Peter sent emissaries to study the central administrative organs of the major European countries; and they returned with the conviction that the Swedish collegiate system, under which the central departments of government were directed by colleges (or boards), was best. In 1718 Peter put that system into operation in Russia. The old offices were swept away and their functions coordinated in nine colleges—such as the College of Foreign

Affairs, the War College, and the College of Mines and Manufacture—each operating under the direction of a collegiate board consisting of a centrally appointed chairman, vice-chairman, and several other members.

Local government, which had failed to meet the requirements of the central government in fiscal and administrative activities, was even more thoroughly revamped. In 1708 the entire realm was divided into eight provinces,[1] each directed by an appointed governor with a large staff of assistants.

The energy shown by Peter in the reorganization of administration was not matched by the success resulting from his efforts. Many of the innovations he introduced endured until the end of the Russian Empire, but their functioning was usually so imperfect that administrative reform continued to be one of Russia's major problems.

SUBORDINATION OF THE CHURCH.   The Church, already weakened by the schism, was further debilitated by Peter. Although he was devout, he had little patience with the Church when it offered the slightest political opposition to him. He believed that the Church should be subordinate to the state and should serve its interests.

Since the Russian Orthodox Church was national in its organization, it could not present the same opposition to the ambitions of an absolute monarch as that presented by the international Catholic Church in the West; yet there was ample room for conflict between patriarch and tsar. During the reigns of Michael and Alexis, the strong patriarchs Philaret and Nikon had shown that the power of the Church could be raised to a level which might make it able to challenge the power of the state. Adrian, the patriarch at the time of Peter, was not a strong figure, but even he publicly denounced many Petrine reforms as irreligious.

When Adrian died, in 1700, Peter, not finding a suitable candidate for the patriarchal throne, did not permit the election of a successor; and, as the years passed, he showed a decreasing desire to permit the vacant post to be filled. In 1721 he abolished it completely and introduced into the ecclesiastical organization the collegiate principle of the secular departments of government. The Patriarchate was replaced by a spiritual college known as the Holy Synod, composed of eleven members of the higher clergy appointed by the Tsar. Shortly thereafter, Peter added another functionary, the Over-Procurator, to the membership of the Holy Synod. The duty of the Over-Procurator, a layman, was to supervise the work of the Holy Synod on behalf of the state. Thus, in effect, the Russian Orthodox Church became a department of

[1] The Russian name of this unit, *guberniya*, is often translated as *government*, but *province* is used here and in following chapters to avoid confusion.

the government, and its clergy became servants of the state. The subordination of the Church to the state was almost complete.

RESTRICTION IN AUTONOMOUS AREAS.   The efforts to subordinate all classes and institutions to the demands of the state resulted finally in the extension of central control to two areas that had hitherto been autonomous: the land of the Don Cossacks and the Ukraine.

The Don Cossacks had placed themselves under allegiance to the tsar, but they did not intend to give up their liberties and privileges. Peter's attitude toward them was divided: he valued their military assistance, but he disapproved of their political independence. In 1707 a revolt that broke out in a Don Cossack village under the leadership of Kondrati Bulavin opened the way for government interference. The revolt spread widely among the Don Cossacks and the neighboring serfs before internal dissension broke its force and drove its leader to suicide in 1708. Then, after regular troops had rounded up the remaining rebels and restored order, central control was extended in the region, and the government deprived the Don Cossacks of much of their land. Finally, in 1723, they were deprived of the right to elect their commander (*ataman*), and he was thereafter appointed by the tsars.

The story of the Ukrainian Cossacks followed almost exactly that of the Don Cossacks. After the abortive revolt of Mazeppa, Moscow interfered more and more in the hitherto autonomous Cossack government of the eastern Ukraine. The power of their elected hetman was circumscribed; and in 1722 he was subordinated to the newly created College of Little Russia, an arm of the central government. Thereafter the Ukrainian Cossacks, like the Don Cossacks, had the shadow of autonomy but not the substance.

CHANGES IN MANNERS AND MORES.   When Peter returned, in 1698, from his tour abroad, he outraged Russian sentiment by ordering that all his male subjects shave their beards and adopt Western European dress. Actually, conformity to the new style was enforced only among those closely associated with the Tsar (exclusive of the clergy) yet probably no other action of Peter's has been given so much symbolic importance. It seemed to indicate a drive for Westernization both because it compelled Russians to pattern their outward appearance after that of the Western European and because it broke with Russian tradition, which attached deep religious significance to the untrimmed beard and set the style for customary Russian dress. The drama of the action made it appear more symbolic than it really was. Peter's motives were primarily utilitarian: he felt that Western appearance would help to promote Western habits of work. That his order offended Russian feeling was a matter of indifference to him.

The Tsar's energy left little about him untouched, but everything he ordered was for one purpose—to fit his subjects for their proper roles in the Russian Empire. Wanting everything connected with the government to be properly appointed, he insisted upon the improvement of social manners among government officials and military officers. He ordered them to study at home and abroad in order to learn the habits of gentlemen, and he required that they practice what they learned. That some corrections were needed is indicated by the nature of some of the admonitions which were included in the book of etiquette which he ordered published for the nobility—for example, that the gentleman should refrain from fingering his nose in public, spitting in the middle of a group, and picking his teeth with a knife. Among the Western social practices encouraged by Peter were ballroom dancing and salon gatherings for both men and women. Their introduction, of course, necessitated the abandonment of the *terem*, which had required the isolation of upper-class women.

The calendar and the alphabet received the Tsar's attention also. According to the old Russian calendar, the year began on September 1, and the years were numbered from the creation of the world. In 1699 Peter had the Russian calendar brought into line with the Julian calendar, generally used in Protestant Europe until the middle of the eighteenth century.[1] In addition, since the 42-letter alphabet of Church Slavonic had become cumbersome and antiquated in some respects, he ordered the preparation of a revised one of thirty-six letters (known as the civil alphabet) which excluded obsolete letters and simplified others. The civil alphabet was employed for lay purposes while the older one was retained in use by the Church, thus increasing the divergence between the written religious and lay languages.

A NEW CAPITAL.   The spirit of the Petrine reforms was given concrete expression in the transfer of the Russian capital from Moscow to the newly established St. Petersburg. The latter had been built by forced labor in what seemed to most Russians a foreign, desolate swamp. Yet Peter loved the place from its beginning; he called it his "paradise" and, during the worst days of the Northern War, he was prepared to return to Sweden all of his conquests except this one. When begun, St. Petersburg was intended to serve as a naval base and fortress for the protection of Russia's northern acquisitions. As such it was generally considered a proper undertaking in spite of the fact that to build it on the marshy land chosen for it entailed great ex-

---

[1] Russia did not adopt the Gregorian calendar until 1918. Consequently the Russian calendar fell behind that of Western and Central Europe. It was eleven days behind in the eighteenth century, twelve in the nineteenth, and thirteen in the twentieth. All dates in this book are given according to the Gregorian calendar.

pense and years of hardship in defiance of climate, disease and danger from the Swedes. But when Peter declared his intention of making it the capital city, there was dissatisfaction. Officials were disgruntled at being forced to leave their comforts, build new homes in the rough city, and endure the isolation and raw climate of the region. To the people in general the abandonment of Moscow for St. Petersburg seemed an even greater act of defiance of Russia's past than had the shaving of beards. Still the Tsar, emotionally attached to the new city and hating Moscow, went ahead with his plans. The transfer of government offices was begun in 1714, and by 1718 it was virtually completed. In time, St. Petersburg became the commercial as well as the administrative capital of Russia. It became also the most Europeanized of all the cities, having come into being with no ties to the country's past; and it remained a lasting symbol of the Europeanization of Russia.

Russian reaction to Peter

THE CHIEF OPPOSITION.   The impulse to adopt Western techniques in the army, civil administration and economy—and thereby to disrupt the customary life of the country—came, as has been seen, from the Tsar, not from the people. Therefore it could hardly be expected that the public attitude toward Peter's reforms would be enthusiastic; it was not. However, the peasants, groaning under new burdens, were the only ones to express overt opposition on a large scale. Between 1704 and 1711, there were three extensive rebellions in which peasants took the major part. One, which broke out recurrently during the period 1704–11, involved the Bashkirs, other Tatars, and the Finno-Ugrians along the Volga; another broke out in Astrakhan and lasted from 1705 to 1706; and the third was the Don Cossack revolt from 1707 to 1708. As was usual with peasant revolts, these lacked program, unity, and organization; and after the last nests of rebels were cleaned out in 1711, peasant unrest became inarticulate for the remainder of the reign.

The clergy, naturally, looked dimly at the actions of the Tsar. But the Church had lost its capacity for independent political action and could offer no effective opposition.

THE CHIEF SUPPORTERS.   Peter drew his greatest support from the class to which he devoted the greatest amount of attention, the nobility. Of course, his heavy-handed insistence that each member of the nobility improve each shining hour did not meet with a gracious acquiescence. Many attempted to escape the duties imposed upon them; some feigned illness or tried to hide in some obscure official corner when called to military service, and the noble students impressed into the schools more often than not played truant. Yet, on the whole, the Tsar carried the nobility with him—for two good reasons. In the first place, the many whom he added to the ranks of the privileged gained more from the positions, preferment, land, and serfs which they received than they lost by accepting the duties which went with their privileges. In the second place, the nobility as a whole were given a more secure hold over serfs and land than they had ever enjoyed before. It may be said that Peter had applied to the nobility the technique of the proverbial peasant who coaxed his donkey along by dangling before him a carrot suspended from a stick. The nobility would have preferred the carrot without the stick, but they lacked the corporate strength and tradition to resist the coaxing sovereign.

Peter had the support also of an able body of lieutenants whom he had succeeded in gathering around himself, men who carried out his policies while he was alive and attempted to carry on his work after his death. "Peter's fledglings," as his lieutenants have been called, were chosen by merit and rewarded with the friendship of the Tsar as well as with lands and titles. Typical of the "fledglings" was Alexander Menshikov, who was with Peter from his boyhood days and who was regarded by him as "my brother." Enemies said that Menshikov had sold meat pies in his youth; if he had, that fact would not have altered Peter's friendship for him. He was at the Tsar's side on most occasions and undertook and executed the most responsible civilian and military assignments at his bidding. In return, he received the titles of "prince" and "field marshal" and was given vast estates. Even though Peter often raged against him and once declared, "Menshikov was conceived in iniquity, born in sin, and will end his life as a rascal and a cheat . . .," he always forgave him. Menshikov was one among many able men who were attached to their sovereign by affection, admiration, and favors.

The succession

THE LEGATEE. Although Peter followed in large part the policies marked out before his time, the scale and the intensity of his execution of those policies were determined by his own personality. It would take another Peter to hold the tempo which he had set. But the heir apparent, Alexis, was no Peter. The Tsar sought to provide his son with the training required for the duties he was to inherit, but Alexis developed according to another pattern. He had little love for his father and little admiration for his father's ways, being attracted to theology rather than to military science and to the company of the clergy rather than that of the court.

Peter had as little patience with what he considered his heir's short-comings as with those of any subject. He alternately bullied and entreated Alexis to become a man. But, whereas Peter's contemporary, Frederick William I of Prussia, succeeded in bludgeoning his son (the future Frederick the Great) into manhood, Peter failed. Alexis would often malinger to escape duties assigned him by his father; and, worse yet, he developed friendships with those who hoped to undo many of the Petrine reforms once their author was dead and Alexis was on the throne.

In 1716 a crisis was precipitated by the Tsar's ordering his son into the army. Instead of obeying, Alexis fled with his mistress to Vienna, where he received the protection of the Holy Roman Emperor. However, when a mission from his father promised him complete freedom from punishment if he would return to Russia, he foolishly relented. On his return, he and his friends were subjected to tortures in an effort to prove that he had been plotting against his father. Regardless of the outcome, Peter's mind—as in the cases of Sophia and Eudoxia—was implacably set: Alexis had to go. But this time the punishment was more severe, for Peter could not permit the survival of a son whose succession would bring into power the enemies of the existing regime; in June, 1718, Alexis was condemned to death for thinking of rebellion. The final execution, however, eluded Peter's hands, for soon after learning of his condemnation Alexis died of a combination of terror, the aftermath of savage torture, and constitutional frailty. He left behind him a three-year-old son named Peter; but, under the circumstances, the child could not be expected to be favored as heir. The succession would go to another.

After Peter had put his wife Eudoxia away in a convent, he had become fond of Martha Skavrenska, a young girl of Livonian peasant origin, the mistress of his friend Menshikov. She became the Tsar's mistress, bore him two children, Anna and Elizabeth, and in 1712, after adopting the Orthodox faith and taking the name of Catherine, she was publicly married to him. Despite occasional derelictions, Peter was deeply devoted to her, and some believed that he intended to make her his successor. That may have been true; if so, he did not carry out his intention. In 1722 he denounced the principle of primogeniture and asserted that he and those who should follow him were free to choose their successors. In the following year, he arranged

A statue (commonly known as "The Bronze Horseman") honoring Peter the Great, commissioned by Catherine the Great and created by E. M. Falconet

that Catherine be recognized as Empress, but he did not name her as his heir. When he died, in January, 1725, the succession was open to contest.

THE LEGACY.   What had Peter to pass on to his successor? The dynamic and pervasive character of his reforms can easily lead to an exaggeration of his accomplishments, and the apparently symbolic meaning of some of his measures can lead to a misinterpretation of his intents.

Was he an abject admirer of Western European culture who sought to remake Russia on a European model? Not at all. He once remarked to one of his aides, "For a few score years only shall we need Europe. Then shall we be able to turn our backs on her." He was a Russian tsar—albeit unlike any who had come before him—who sought to strengthen his patrimony. To do so he had to borrow some Western techniques and technicians, but he did not borrow for imitation's sake. He had little interest in Western art, letters, or philosophy, his chief interest being in Western sciences and in Western skills in shipbuilding, military organization, and statecraft.

Like his fellow monarchs of Europe, Peter sought the enhancement of the international position of his country and the strengthening of his throne within his country. He succeeded in the first aim. The Northern War made Russia a European power. The groundwork for that success had been laid by his predecessors who had built up the Russian state, but the final step was his; and the final step was most important. Commercially and diplomatically Russia was now closely linked with Western Europe. She was also now open to increasing Western European cultural influences. But that was, from Peter's point of view, merely a by-product of his work, not the goal of his efforts.

In strengthening his throne, Peter was less successful. It is true that he increased the imperial power by abolishing the Boyars' Duma and by completing the subordination of the Church to the state, of the serfs to the nobility, and of the nobility to the throne. But he failed, as all his successors were to fail, in establishing an efficient, honest administrative machine to implement the supreme autocratic power lodged in the throne. That failure resulted not so much from his own shortcomings as from the material that Russia provided. Other absolute monarchs of his period inherited fairly well-established executive and judicial institutions and traditions, and they found in the middle classes of their countries useful cadres for administration. Peter found none of those things. To provide the personnel for his government he had only a landed aristocracy on which to rely; and to secure their support he, like earlier rulers, had to intensify the subjugation of the peasantry to them. The result was to saddle Russia with the debilitating institution of serfdom without securing a reliable administrative class.

Another feature of the legacy he left was a widening gap between the rulers and the ruled. In the beginning of the seventeenth century, the upper and lower classes had at least the bond of a common culture and tradition. After Peter, that bond grew more and more tenuous. The ruling nobility became more Europeanized and so divorced in speech, manners, costume and outlook from the masses that two distinct cultures were evident in Russia. That separation was not Peter's intention, nor did it come about in his time; but many of his measures helped in making it possible.

The period of thirty-seven years following Peter's death bore many of the characteristics of the Time of Troubles. It will be recalled that the Time of Troubles had come when, after nearly a century and a half of strong tsars, the reign of weak Tsar Feodor made possible the breaking of tensions among

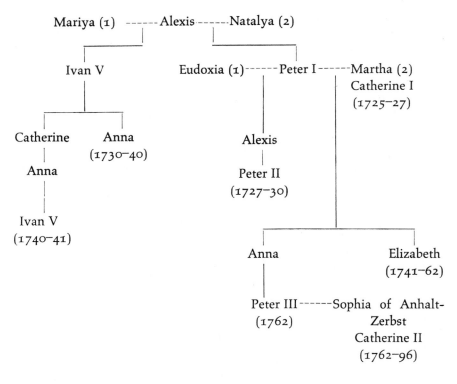

those who had suffered by the strengthening of the throne. The difficulties which arose after Peter's time were less serious than those of the previous century, but the succeeding rulers allowed them to run a comparable course.

By 1725 the throne had again reached a peak of strength. But the balance of forces which Peter had finally achieved was an unstable equilibrium that was kept from toppling only by the pressure of war and by his personal strength. Now the country was released from the requirements of war and was no longer restrained by the hand of a strong autocrat. The years between 1725 and 1762 included the reigns of six rulers, three female and three male. Of the women, the first was amiable but incapable, the second neither amiable nor capable, and the third reasonably acceptable. Of the males, the first was a child, the second an infant, and the third an adult with the personality of a child. The situation invited the results which were produced during the period: an upset of the balance, a redistribution of power, and a weakening of the throne.

Contest for power-behind-the-throne

MENSHIKOV'S CHOICE.   Within a few hours after the death of Peter the Great, two groups were proposing successors. The "fledglings," led by Menshikov, wanted to retain their powerful position at court and to continue the Petrine policies. To them Catherine seemed the most suitable choice for monarch. The boyars and other nobles of the upper ranks wanted to establish an oligarchic rule in which they would have a leading part. They favored young Peter and were making plans to insure his succession. However, when Menshikov appeared with the guards regiments to support the wishes of the "fledglings," they saw that they had no choice but to agree to the enthronement of Catherine.

Catherine had neither the desire for power nor the qualities of a ruler. Consequently Menshikov, the strongest and greediest of the "fledglings" and Catherine's former lover, became the dominant influence in the government. But his arrogance and his desire for money and position incited such strong opposition that his influence could bring him no permanent gains.

A COMPROMISE.   When it became apparent to Menshikov that he might be ousted by a coup on the part of the upper nobility, he hastened to compromise with them. In 1726 he agreed to the creation of the Supreme Privy Council, made up of six members including himself and representatives of both the "fledglings" and the upper nobility. Its establishment not only eased

the tension between the main contestants for power but also officially relegated the Governing Senate to a subordinate position in the government.

The Supreme Privy Council assumed the right to advise the Empress,
examine the principal affairs of state and issue decrees. Thus the government
became, in effect, an oligarchy; but because of Menshikov's continued con-
nivings it was an unstable one. When the Supreme Privy Council obtained
Catherine's agreement to name Peter the heir to the throne and to provide
that the Council act as regent during his minority, Menshikov at once began
to plan the marriage of his daughter to the future emperor. And when
Catherine died, in 1727, leaving the twelve-year-old Peter to succeed her, he
lost no time in beginning his domination of his intended son-in-law. But his
efforts to gain power were so overt that they forced the nobility once more
to unite against him in defense of their own interests. They finally managed
to displace him from the favor of the young Emperor and to secure the
imperial signature to his dismissal and exile.

BRIEF ASCENDANCY OF UPPER NOBILITY.   Even then, the matters at
court were not satisfactorily resolved, for the noble families would not co-
operate in the division of the power they had gained. Following the ousting
of Menshikov, the noble family of Dolgorukys began to assume the powers
of the deposed favorite; and an equally distinguished family, the Golitsyns,
came out in opposition to it. Neither was able to establish itself; for in 1730
Peter II died suddenly from smallpox, and a new succession problem was
presented.

The Supreme Privy Council, in which both the Dolgorukys and the
Golitsyns were represented, finally agreed that Ivan V's daughter Anna, now
the widow of the Duke of Courland, be named Empress. They planned with
her succession to secure their own positions by requiring that, in order to
have their support, she accept certain secret limitations upon the power of
the throne that would, in effect, place the chief power of the state in the
hands of the upper nobility. Anna agreed to the limitations with which the
Supreme Privy Council surrounded the offer of a crown because she was
anxious to escape from the provincial life of Courland. But when she arrived
in Russia, she found a situation that made it possible for her to have the
crown and autocratic power as well.

COUNTERMOVE.   A number of the lower nobility, having been excluded
from the right to share the gains made by the upper nobility, had formed an
opposition. With the support of the guards regiments, they called upon Anna
to assume complete control. That she did, denouncing all restrictions on her
imperial power. The country waited to see whether or not she would use that

power to restore all authority to the throne or to work out a plan which would accommodate the interests of both throne and nobility.

Period of concession and suppression

AMBIVALENT POLICY.   The new Empress was not complacent, as the first one had been. She was a mature woman (thirty-seven years of age) who liked the feel of power and the pleasures which the employment of power would bring. Moreover, she had sufficient political acumen to understand what measures were necessary to maintain her position. Realizing that her ultimate security depended upon the avoidance of trouble with the nobility, she was willing to meet some of their demands. On the other hand, she was not adverse to using brutal force to prevent any encroachment upon the autocratic power she chose to retain for herself.

CONCESSIONS TO THE NOBILITY.   When Anna came to the throne (1730) the nobles were still seeking mitigation of what they considered the excessive requirements of service to the state. One of their complaints, that against the Petrine requirement that nobles serve in the ranks of the army before receiving commissions, met with favorable response from the Empress. In 1731 she established in St. Petersburg the Corps of Noble Cadets, to provide officer training for sons of the nobility. Upon completion of training in the Corps, the young men were to enter the army as officers or to enter the administrative services at a grade in the Table of Ranks equivalent to that of military officer. Since its enrollment was limited, not all sons of the nobility profited from the new institution; yet it was appreciated as an indication of a break with the Petrine system.

Another general complaint was based upon the requirement of continual service from the nobility until old age, death or injury rendered them unfit for service. Many estates had languished because no male members of the landholding families had been permitted to remain at home to manage them. Anna made an adjustment there by means of an imperial manifesto, issued in 1736, permitting the head of each noble family to select one son to remain on the estate, free from all compulsory service. Other male members of the family were still required to render service, but the term of service was now limited to twenty-five years, beginning at the age of twenty. A further concession which pleased the nobles was one whereby they were granted the right to determine the punishment due a serf who attempted to escape. These concessions left the nobility far from the realization of their hope for com-

plete freedom from obligatory service, but Anna showed no intention of
going beyond them.

SAFEGUARDING THE AUTOCRACY.   Instead of seeking further means
of mollifying the nobility, Anna gave her attention to means of safeguarding
her autocratic power and protecting herself from the ambitions of the upper
nobility who had shown their hand in 1730. She ordered the chief members
of the Dolgoruky and Golitsyn families exiled, imprisoned or executed; and
all others who had plotted against her or who had been found guilty of con-
templating conspiracy were treated with unrelieved harshness. Twenty
thousand persons were sent into exile; and hundreds, regardless of age or sex,
were tortured or maimed. The Empress was demonstrating her mastery, but
she was at the same time prodding the mastered into acute resentment. Her
terroristic methods only bred more plots, and the terror had to be continued.

GERMAN INFLUENCE IN THE GOVERMENT.   Since she feared and mistrusted the native upper nobility, Anna allowed Russians in hardly any
government posts of importance. Instead she invited foreigners, most of
them Germans from Courland, to assist her in governing Russia. The chief
influence went to her lover, Ernst von Biron, who immediately set about to
enrich himself with power, money, lands, and titles. His chief avocation was
the breeding and handling of horses, and a special governmental office was
created to look after his horses. Count Andrei Ostermann, a German who
had begun his service under Peter the Great, was given charge of foreign
affairs. Count Burkhard Christoph Münnich, another German who had begun
his distinguished career under Peter, managed military affairs for the country. Baltic German gentry were imported wholesale to staff two newly created
guards regiments, the Ismailovsky Foot Guards and the Cavalry Guards.
Naturally the spectacle of a Russian government dominated by Germans
fanned resentment among the Russians, who began to speak suspiciously of
a "German Party." There was no such party in the sense of a group having a
community of interest or policy among Anna's aides, but their precedence in
the governmental hierarchy was sufficient to warrant the development of a
strong opposition to them.

To assure the continuation of her favorites in the government, Anna,
having no direct heir, chose her infant nephew Ivan to succeed her and
provided that, if she should die before his maturity, Biron should serve as
regent.

Her selection of an heir prevented an immediate struggle for the crown
after her death (October, 1740), but it did not prevent a struggle for power.
As planned, the six-weeks-old Ivan became Emperor Ivan VI, and Biron

assumed the duties of regent. But Biron, hated both by the Germans in office and by the Russians, could neither prevent the boiling over of the long pent-up popular resentment nor bottle up the ambitions of his rivals. Within less than a month after the accession of Ivan VI, the regent was on his way out. Münnich, supported by the Preobrazhensky Guards, arrested him and sped him on his way to Siberia. Then Münnich himself became the power behind the throne, a position which he held only a few months before he was forced to give way to Ostermann.

Meanwhile, the Russian nobles in the Preobrazhensky Guards, in addition to a great number of other Russians who were united in disgust with the squabble for power in St. Petersburg and in hatred for the foreigners in the government, were looking with favor upon another claimant of power (and of the throne as well)—Elizabeth, the thirty-two-year-old daughter of Peter the Great. In December, 1741, Elizabeth, followed by the Preobrazhensky Guards, marched into the imperial palace, arrested the infant Emperor and his entourage, and proclaimed herself Empress. Ostermann and Münnich soon joined Biron in his Siberian exile. The Russian government was again in the hands of Russians.

Progress toward equilibrium

AN ACCEPTABLE RULER.   Elizabeth, although she had lived inconspicuously apart from political life, assumed her new position with apparent confidence and ease. Like her father, she favored an active and vigorous life, but she was not as passionately devoted to the affairs of state as he had been. That was perhaps to the good, for it is doubtful that Russia could have borne the weight of two rulers of Peter's kind in such close succession. She was wise enough to continue the extension of privileges to the nobility, to discontinue the excesses of Anna, and to replace the Germans among the court counsellors by Russians. She surrounded herself with able advisers and turned over to them much of the responsible work of the government. The two decades of her reign were marked by relative peace, prosperity and fiscal stability. FURTHER CONCESSIONS TO THE NOBILITY.   As a first step toward relieving the strain in relations between the throne and the people, Elizabeth ended the policy of terror introduced by Anna and allowed the return of members of prominent noble families, including the surviving Dolgorukys and Golitsyns, who had been exiled. Then she gave her approval to a number of measures for the further satisfaction of demands for improvement in the status of the nobility in general.

The nobles were granted new rights which tightened their hold on the peasants: (1) the exclusive right, as individuals, to own serfs (a right hitherto shared by all individuals who could afford to own serfs); (2) the right to ascribe free peasants as serfs to noble estates (a right exercised principally in the regions where serfdom had hitherto been rare, the newer regions in which Elizabeth allotted estates to her favorites and supporters); (3) the right to exile serfs to Siberia; and (4) the right to decide whether or not serfs might marry.

Additional privileges increased both the independence and the power of the nobility. Arrangements were made whereby they could borrow money from a state bank for the improvement of their estates. The term of their compulsory service was appreciably shortened by the introduction of the practice of inscribing the infant children of noblemen in the registers of regiments and counting the years of service from the date of inscription. And their power in local administration was increased by granting to the nobles in each canton the right to select from among themselves the administrative chief of that canton. In short, Elizabeth's reign went far toward establishing the Russian nobility as a provincial landowning class concerned chiefly with the management of their land and endowed with complete power over their serfs and local administration.

DOMESTIC IMPROVEMENTS UNDERTAKEN.   Elizabeth's reforming energy was spent principally on the nobles and the social life of her court. Her one act which applied to the general domestic situation was a striking one: the abolition, in 1753, of most of Russia's internal tariffs and duties. That step set a policy for Russia considerably in advance of the policies then operative in other countries. Another act initiated but not carried out was the revision of the antiquated legal code of 1649. Elizabeth appointed a commission in 1754 to make that revision and then left it to work at its own discretion, producing no positive results.

INTRODUCTION OF A NEW PHASE IN EUROPEANIZATION.   Elizabeth's devotion to what she considered the good life reflected itself in the life of the capital city. Peter had given little attention to making St. Petersburg attractive as a center of court life, and his successors had likewise neglected it. Elizabeth, however, tried to reproduce there the glitter of Versailles. She ordered the construction of great palaces and encouraged social activities in which the dress, ceremony, and festivity of the French capital were carefully copied. It is true that many of the palaces were of wood, that the roofs leaked, and that the social elite displayed unrefined manners despite their newly acquired elegance; nonetheless, the process of Europeanization was progressing. During this time the French language, French manners and French fashions gained a popularity among the Russian aristocracy which was to be maintained for over a century.

Threatened relapse into domestic conflict

PROBLEM OF SUCCESSION. Elizabeth was foresighted enough to try to forestall a renewal of the succession problem. Her foresight was admirable but her choice was deplorable, for it fell on one whose early training predestined him to be a misfit in Russia. She chose Charles Peter Ulrich, the son of her sister Anna, who had married the Duke of Holstein. Being the great-nephew of Charles XII of Sweden, the boy had been trained in the expectation that he would inherit the Swedish throne; he had been taught the Swedish language and reared in the Lutheran faith. He had chosen as his idol and model, however, Frederick the Great of Prussia, and he had come to believe that a Prussian officer combined in himself all the admirable qualities of humanity.

In 1742, when he was fourteen years of age, Elizabeth brought him to Russia and began preparing him as her successor. His name was cut to the simple name of Peter and he was given a new religion, Russian Orthodoxy. Two years later he was married to the fifteen-year-old German princess Sophie of Anhalt-Zerbst, who also was required to adopt a new name, Catherine, as well as the Russian Orthodox faith. At fourteen Peter was an unprepossessing youth, lacking in balance, judgment, integrity, and charm; and as he grew older his defects multiplied. He loathed Russia and Russian Orthodoxy. In total disregard of them, he surrounded himself with riff-raff from Germany and spent his time in carousing. Catherine, although bred for obscurity and treated disdainfully by the reigning Empress, proved herself to be clever, quick and—as it soon became evident—scheming. She made many friends and, in contrast to her husband, adapted herself to Russia. To compensate for the unhappiness she found in her marriage with Peter, she began to accept lovers among the men about the court. In 1754 she gave birth to a son, Paul, whose parentage Peter disclaimed but whom Elizabeth accepted as legitimate and took under her care for training.

Around the court several groups, disgusted with Peter's childish behavior and open admiration for the king of Prussia, began planning to displace him when he succeeded to the throne and to make his wife the ruler. However, when Elizabeth died, in January, 1762, her nephew began his rule as Peter

III; and the opposing groups restrained themselves, waiting for a propitious time to turn their disaffection into action.

FINAL CONCESSION TO THE NOBILITY.   If Peter had permitted himself to be guided solely by the advisers whom he inherited from his aunt, he might have survived. In a few cases, he did accept the counsel of his advisers and, in so doing, won some approval for himself. Among those on whose counsel he sometimes relied were some who favored the complete abolition of the requirement of compulsory service by the nobility. As a result of their influence Peter issued, in March 1762, the Manifesto on the Freedom of the Nobility, ending the obligatory service of nobles to the state except in time of emergency. That manifesto climaxed the series of concessions begun at the death of Peter I; and upon its issuance, the Russian state became a monarchy dependent upon a privileged nobility.

MOUNTING RESENTMENT.   Peter soon forfeited the little popularity he had gained through his manifesto. He continued consistently to subordinate the Russian interests to those of his native Duchy of Holstein and to favor Frederick the Great with his slavish adulation. When he went so far as to attempt to Prussianize the Russian army he made a fatal mistake; that undertaking alienated the politically powerful guards regiments and caused them to turn their support to the growing opposition.

He also offended the clergy by his tolerance of Old Believers, his contempt for the Orthodox Church, and, finally, by an edict providing for the secularization of the Church lands.

All his personal faults might have been excused if he had not been in the eyes of the Russians, a foreigner who was using the Russian throne for alien ends. As it was, he lost the support of the nobility and the army and so aroused popular antipathy that, when his overthrow came—six months after his coronation—it had the character of a minor revolution.

"PALACE REVOLUTION."   The opposition was urged to action by Catherine's current lover, Gregory Orlov. He and his brothers, with the support of the guards regiments, had practically completed the preparations for a move against the Emperor when, on July 8, 1762, one of the conspirators was arrested. Two days later, seeing that immediate action was necessary, Catherine proclaimed herself the sole ruler of Russia and, dressed in the uniform of the guards, rode dramatically (perhaps in imitation of Elizabeth) at the head of the guards to arrest Peter.

A week after his arrest, Peter was murdered by friends of Catherine. She had not ordered his death, but she did not punish his murderers. The public was informed that his death had resulted from an old affliction which had finally broken his health.

SEVEN / THE THRONE SECURED: 1762-1796

The first problem which Catherine II faced was that of establishing her position as ruler, a position which, despite the ease of the coup of 1762, was not secure against pretenders and rivals. Closely related to it were the problems connected with the demarcation of the respective spheres of autocracy, nobility and peasantry. In addition she had two major, long-range problems: the improvement of the administrative machinery of the country and the maintenance and enhancement of Russia's position among the powers.

Time proved that her qualities were sufficient to sustain her in the handling of those problems. She was a diligent student of statecraft who had prepared herself well, during her twenty years in St. Petersburg, by spending much time in careful and judicious reading and in attendance to the words of experts. She developed into a master strategist with strength to be her own first minister and to play the most active and decisive role in the affairs of her realm.

Her policies in respect to the domestic and foreign problems of Russia were closely related; but to understand how she solved her first problem, that of making the throne secure, it is well to consider certain aspects of her domestic policies apart from the foreign (taken up in Chapter 8).

Pending problems

POSITION OF THE SENATE.   In the first years of her reign, Catherine proceeded slowly, dealing with the immediate problems which she had inherited from her predecessors. One of them concerned the Senate, which had

Catherine the Great

fallen into an anomalous position after the creation of the Supreme Privy
Council. By her efforts it was returned to its original position as set by Peter
I, that of a directing body. It was divided into six departments, each of which
was to supervise one or more of the administrative or judicial departments
of the government. As a body its duty was to co-ordinate the work of those
departments—with due consideration, of course, to the wishes of the ruler.
TEMPORARY ADJUSTMENT IN LOCAL GOVERNMENT.   At the same
time that she was strengthening the central government, Catherine was
working in the direction of decentralization with respect to local government.
In the second year of her reign she endowed the governors of the provinces

with supreme power over all institutions in their areas and extended their freedom in dealing with local problems. She did not do that because of any favor for decentralization as such but because of her realization that efficient local government required some autonomy.

POSITION OF THE NOBILITY.   One of the measures of Peter III which demanded her immediate attention was the liberation of the nobility from compulsory state service. She knew that if she failed to support that measure she might endanger her hold on the throne; the noble guards regiments which had made her empress could just as easily undo their efforts. In 1763 she appointed a commission to consider Peter's Manifesto on the Freedom of the Nobility. She did not act upon the commission's report—a favorable one —until 1785; but it was clear from her attitude that the nobility had little to fear, that she regarded them with cautious respect and that she would be more likely to strengthen than to weaken their position.

SECULARIZATION OF THE CHURCH LANDS.   Another measure she inherited from Peter III, the secularization of the Church lands, presented more complexities. The fate of the ecclesiastical estates had occupied Russian rulers since the fifteenth century. The estates were too valuable to be ignored; but, despite temptation, the state had refrained from contesting the Church's right to them because of reluctance to invite conflict. The complete sub-ordination of Church to state in 1721 had called special attention to the problem, but no definite action had been taken until Peter III had somewhat precipitately ordered the secularization of the Church lands.

Catherine hastened, in August, 1762, to renounce her husband's action in order to gain the support of the clergy; but hers was only a maneuver. The nobility favored secularization, hoping to participate in the fruits of it, and their attitude encouraged the Empress. In April, 1764, feeling sufficiently secure in her position, she ordered the confiscation of all lands of churches and monasteries and their transfer, together with all peasants, to the juris-diction of a governmental department known as the College of Economy. It was a major step, for the lands carried with them nearly a million adult peasants—more than 10 per cent of the population of Russia proper. Those peasants, known thereafter as "economic peasants," were required not only to pay to the state the regular poll tax but also to make an annual payment in cash in lieu of the dues and services which they had rendered to the Church. Thereafter the government allocated a yearly sum for the support of the Church and for the salaries of all the clergy except the parish priests, thus increasing the dependence of the Church upon the state.

After the confiscation, Catherine did not acquiesce to the wishes of the nobles that the newly acquired lands be distributed immediately among them; instead she added the lands to the state's reserve. That addition gave the government an increased source of income and at the same time gave the Empress a surplus from which to draw when she wanted to distribute land as largesse to deserving nobles.

REVISION OF THE LAW CODE.   From Elizabeth, Catherine inherited still another unfinished task, that of revising the Code of 1649. What she actually accomplished toward a revision was negligible, but the scope of her efforts was considerable.

Beginning in 1764, she spent two years, with some assistance, in the preparation of instructions for those who were to be assigned to the task of revising the code. Her instructions did not deal with the essential problem of revision, but rather with the general problem of the government of Russia. They consisted chiefly of observations reflecting the thoughts of eminent eighteenth century writers (particularly Montesquieu, in his *Spirit of Laws*) interpreted in such a way as to show that autocracy was best suited to Russia's needs.

The intended convocation of a legislative commission was announced in December, 1766. Certain groups were instructed to elect representatives to the commission and to prepare instructions to assist them in their work. The nobility, urban inhabitants, members of the central governmental institutions, the Cossacks, and a few of the non-serf peasant groups were to form the main body of electors. Serfs and the clergy were not invited to participate.

In August, 1767, the Legislative Commission opened its formal sessions with the participation of 564 delegates, who arrived with 1,500 sets of instructions from their constituents. Despite the omission of the largest component of the population, the serfs, it had the broadest representation of any assembly which had been called in Russia since the last full Assembly of the Land, in 1653. The full sessions of the Commission, which continued for nearly a year and a half, were occupied with the reading of the sets of instructions, discussion of existing laws and proposals for their revision. The reading of the instructions provided a good insight into the state of mind of the groups represented. Peasants asked for improvement in their position; merchants demanded an increase in their privileges; and others complained of the inadequacies of local government. The consideration of the laws revealed that the nobility were intransigently opposed to any change which would lead to the modification of their privileges or to the amelioration of the status of the serfs. Actually the full sessions accomplished nothing beyond an exposition of needs and a demonstration of disagreement on the nature of remedial steps. More substantial work was done by subcommittees, however; they formulated some conclusions which were later embodied in laws issued by Catherine. Yet not a single piece of positive work in the codification of the laws had been completed when, in December, 1768, Catherine ended the meetings on the ground that many of the delegates needed to report for military service in the war against the Ottoman Empire. After the end of that war, the Commission was not reconvened.

To assess the work of the Legislative Commission is to assess the enigmatic character of the Empress. Some see her as an enlightened despot, an empress-*philosophe* who gave her subjects an opportunity to reform Russia but gave up in disgust when she saw their incapacity for the task. Others see her as an adroit schemer who, attaching the plumage of a *philosophe* to the body of an autocrat, called the Legislative Commission merely to give the semblance of popular participation in the activities of her regime. Certainly it seems inaccordant with her policies that at any time she should have seriously considered allowing the status of the nobility to be weakened or that of the serfs to be improved. Perhaps she genuinely hoped that the Commission would revise the code in such a way as to leave the existing social structure of the country intact. In any case, the reason given for its adjournment was not the real one; she was tired of its work—or lack of work—and wanted to see the end of the body which she had gathered with such fanfare.

The failure of the Legislative Commission was to be repeated on many occasions in the nineteenth century when Russian emperors summoned other commissions to examine reforms, only to dismiss them before their work could be done. Usually the cause of failure was the incompatibility of any serious reform with the maintenance of the existing system of autocracy and noble privileges.

Suppression of threatening forces

THE LOWER VOLGA, DANGER ZONE.   In the 1770's a dangerous threat to the stability of the regime arose in the lower Volga basin, where suppressed groups were, as usual, ready for revolt. The complaints of the Russian peasants in that region had been augmented by the extension of serfdom, the enlargement of noble rights over serfs and the intensification of noble exploitation of them. All their uprisings in the past had resulted in failure, but they remained receptive to the call of revolt because no other form of expression was available to them. The Bashkirs of the region were also ready for rebellion. After the Russian conquest of their territory in the sixteenth century they had found increasing cause for discontent; the Russian assimilation of that area had involved the seizure of native lands and their transfer to Russian landlords, the imposition of heavy taxes and, after a period of toleration, the exertion of pressure on the natives to give up their Moslem faith in favor of Russian Orthodoxy.

Cossack military leadership and organizations were available to the rebellious groups, as they had been in the revolts led by Stenka Razin and Bulavin. Some of the Cossacks themselves had grievances that had been developing since the time of Peter the Great because of the increasing domination by the central government and the increasing class differentiation within their own groups. The upper-class Cossacks had sought special privileges and an increasing share of the land and, to protect their status, had made common cause with the central government at the expense of the lower-class Cossacks. In 1771 and 1772 small-scale revolts by the discontented Don and Yaik Cossacks broke out, and, when they were suppressed, the government deprived the Cossacks of their privilege of self-government. After that, they became more restive than ever, anxious to regain their old status by the only means they knew—fighting.

THE PUGACHEV REVOLT.   The dissident groups were roused to a major effort by Emelyan Pugachev. He was a Don Cossack who had deserted the Russian army after serving with it in two wars. In order to give himself a strong position as leader of the discontented, he assumed the guise of Peter III, who, he declared, had not died in 1762 but had escaped and hidden under the name of Pugachev. As Peter III, he promised his followers that he would restore the Cossack privileges, free the serfs from their landlords (who would be promptly hanged), release the Old Believers from religious perscution, and end the oppression of all. As for Catherine, he would send her to share the fate of Sophia and Eudoxia. The guise he chose was a fortunate one because the peasants believed that Peter III had tried to free them but had been prevented by the nobility. Their hope had never been to improve their condition through the extinction of autocracy, rather to see the ascendance of a benevolent autocrat. Most of them accepted Pugachev's claim as genuine and expected to see their hopes fulfilled. Even if they had not accepted his claim, his program of emancipation would have been sufficient incentive for them to follow him.

In September, 1773, Pugachev with a following of Yaik Cossacks began the rebellion, moving up the Yaik River. Other Cossacks, serfs, Bashkirs, Old Believers, and outlaws hastened to join them. By October they had reached

Orenburg, the chief administrative center of the Ural region; there they laid siege until March, 1774. They defeated the first regular forces sent to relieve Orenburg, and their success encouraged outbreaks all along the lower Volga. Serfs and Cossacks murdered landlords and government officials by the hundreds while the Bashkirs and other Mongols, less discriminating, took their revenge on Russians of all classes. During the winter of 1773–74 the rebellion was in full swing from Kazan to Tsaritsyn on the Volga, along the Yaik River, and in the Ural regions. Pugachev, meanwhile, established his headquarters near besieged Orenburg, where he set up an "imperial" court and began to create the skeleton of a governmental organization.

There was alarm in St. Petersburg when it became evident that what had at first appeared to be a minor Cossack revolt had assumed the character of a mass uprising. Late in 1773, the Empress assigned to General Alexander Bibikov the task of crushing it. He was finally able, in April of the following year, to compel Pugachev to raise the siege of Orenburg. Then the rebel forces scattered and the fighting died down. But pacification did not follow, for Bibikov had died in the midst of the fighting, and his successor was not able to take advantage of his gains. The revolt flamed up again and, by July, while Pugachev was taking Kazan, serfs were in successful revolt at Nizhnii-Novgorod.

However, the government was able by that time to send additional troops into the struggle. The rebels were overpowered near Kazan, and Pugachev fled south along the Volga, hoping to renew his forces among the Don and the Yaik Cossacks. The government troops followed and finally defeated his forces in September, 1774, near Tsaritsyn. Pugachev escaped with a few followers and sought refuge among the Yaik Cossacks, but he was soon seized by a group of upper-class Cossacks and turned over to the central authorities. On January 21, 1775, he was executed in Moscow before a large crowd of greatly relieved nobles.

All that remained was to punish the other rebel leaders and restore order. To insure against a repetition of the rising, central control over the Don and Yaik Cossacks was made more stringent than ever; and, as a final gesture, the town in which Pugachev had been born was destroyed and the Yaik River renamed the Ural River.

Establishment of internal stability

LOCAL ADMINISTRATIVE REFORMS. The Pugachev revolt provided an immediate impetus for domestic reforms. Close cross-examination of the

captured rebel leaders revealed the causes of discontent among the peasants
—most of them already known. But the existence of peasant discontent as
judged by Catherine required not the easing of peasant conditions but the
strengthening of the nobles in their rights and powers so that they would be
more able to suppress that discontent.

The early successes of the revolt had emphasized the inadequacies of
local administration still remaining after Catherine's early reforms, and immediate steps were taken to remove them. In 1775 the Empress decreed an
altered system of local government which was to last (with a few modifications after 1861) until 1917. The chief aims of the alterations were the reduction in size of the administrative units, the clear demarcation of official
functions, and the strengthening of the local administrative power of the
nobility. The number of provinces was increased to fifty, the areas of each
being thereby reduced so that it would include only about 300,000 to 400,000
inhabitants; and the provinces were subdivided into districts of about 20,000
to 30,000 inhabitants each. Each province was directed by a governor and a
staff appointed by the crown. The staff consisted of four boards—one each
for administration, criminal cases, civil cases, and financial affairs. A few
provinces were grouped in two's or three's under an all-powerful governor-
general. The offices of the provinces were appointive, and those of the districts were elective (usually filled by representatives of the district nobility).

A striking innovation in the decree of 1775 was the provision that in
each province there was to be a Committee of Public Assistance, headed by
the governor, which was to concern itself with problems of public health,
education and social work. To say that the creation of those committees
resulted in a new era of governmental attention to social welfare would be
an exaggeration; but their creation did signify that the government accepted
—in principle, at least—the responsibility for the provision of schools, hospitals and charitable institutions. The actual fulfillment of the responsibility
was slow in coming.

CHARTER OF THE CITIES.   Ten years later Catherine and her advisers,
using as a guide the corporate organization of cities in the Baltic provinces
of Russia, worked out a reformed type of government for all Russian cities.
By the Charter of the Cities, issued in 1785, each city was made into a
municipal corporation consisting of all the free, property-holding residents
and having elected officials. For purposes of representation the propertied
residents were divided into six classes, determined chiefly by occupation
and income; and the classes were given equal representation in a city council
(duma), which deliberated on civic affairs, selected municipal officers, and

imposed special municipal taxes. The scheme did not satisfactorily fulfill the hopes of the Empress. The development of genuine municipal self-government was hindered by the class division of the electorate, the denial of franchise to those without property, the absence of civic tradition, and the continued interference of the central government. Yet this system remained in operation for nearly a century.

ESTABLISHMENT OF ESTATES.   Behind the transformation of the local administration by the measures of 1775 and 1785 lay a general motive, that of settling the population of Russia (with the exception of privately owned serfs) into estates; that is, into legally recognized social groups such as the nobility, merchants, artisans, and state peasants—each with its own set of privileges and duties, each with its own courts. The aim was to model Russian society after that of the Baltic provinces of Livonia and Estonia, where the estates were rigidly defined. In actuality, the measures taken at this time succeeded in bringing only one estate, the nobility, into true corporate organization.

CHARTER OF THE NOBILITY.   The commission which had been appointed in 1763 to examine Peter III's Manifesto on the Freedom of the Nobility had affirmed, in principle, the basic tenets of that manifesto; and the nobility had proceeded to exercise the rights granted by it. However it was not until 1785 that their rights were legally and specifically defined. In that year Catherine issued the Charter of the Nobility, codifying the rights and privileges which the nobility had gradually acquired since 1725 and giving them a corporate organization. The Charter provided that (1) the nobles were to be exempt from all compulsory administrative and military service; (2) they were to be free from taxation; (3) they were to hold absolute rights over their lands and all their products—vegetable, animal, and mineral; (4) their noble status was hereditary and applicable to wives and children; (5) they might be tried only by their peers; and (6) they were exempt from any form of corporal punishment.

It provided further that all nobles should be organized into corporate bodies both at the level of the district and at the level of the province. In each district they were to form an association which would elect, every three years, a marshal of the nobility; and in each province a similar organization would elect from the district marshals, every three years, a marshal of the nobility for the province. In addition the noble association of the province was granted a number of special rights: (1) to choose certain of the local officials, (2) to maintain genealogical tables of the nobility, (3) to discuss the work of the governors or governors-general, (4) to address petitions directly to the crown or Senate, and (5) to maintain out of their own funds hospitals, schools and other special services for the nobility.

The Charter of the Nobility established the nobles in a very secure position. Their rights, privileges and property were no longer dependent upon service, and yet they retained first choice of important administrative and military stations. In local government they had a position of primacy, and in central government they retained a position of influence. The enhancement of their rights, however, did not diminish the autocratic power of the throne, which could still legally take away all the rights which it had bestowed. But since throne and nobility were united by common interests and since the throne still relied upon the nobility, the arrangement was to remain an agreeable one until 1917.

FURTHER RESTRICTION ON THE PEASANTRY.   Catherine and her advisers gave much consideration to the peasant question, but they always arrived at the same conclusion: the maintenance of the nobility (and hence, of the throne) required the continuation of the serf system. And the steps they took led to a deterioration in the legal conditions of the serfs rather than an advance.

During Catherine's reign the institution of serfdom was widely extended. She distributed from the state domains, including lands seized from the Church, vast estates together with their peasants, as favors and rewards. Gregory Potemkin received lands on which were 40,000 peasants who became his serfs, and the Orlov brothers received 50,000 peasants. In all, more than 800,000 peasants were transferred to the status of privately owned serfs by such grants. During the latter part of the reign the number of serfs was increased still further by the extension of the system of serfdom to those portions of the Ukraine where serfdom had not previously been established.

As the number of serfs increased, the rights of serfs were further diminished. In 1767 they were forbidden to bring to the authorities any kind of complaints against their masters, thus being denied the last redress against abuses. It is true that masters were forbidden to inflict capital punishment upon their serfs; but they could exile them to Siberia, sentence them to hard labor for insolent behavior, flog them, and punish them by sending them to the army for twenty-five years of service (and if a serf were killed by his master, the act usually went unpunished). Moreover, although serfs could not leave the land of their own will, masters could sell them off the land. Newspapers of the time often carried advertisements of offers to sell serfs alongside those offering cattle and dogs. Legally, the serfs of Russia were virtually in the category of chattel.

ECONOMIC ADJUSTMENTS AND DEVELOPMENTS. In Catherine's measures dealing with the economic life of Russia there appeared the same contradiction between theory and practice that appeared in her other measures. In theory she followed the physiocrats, who believed in the minimum of governmental interference with the operation of economic "laws." In practice she followed a course dictated by her own interpretation of what any particular situation demanded—sometimes physiocratic, sometimes mercantilistic. She removed many restraints on trade by abolishing some state monopolies, ending export duties, and liquidating much of the government's interest in industry; but she left in operation many mercantilistic policies of earlier rulers.

Prominent among her economic measures were those leading to the encouragement of colonization and the founding of new cities. Following the example of other European rulers—particularly those of Prussia—who invited industrious immigrants to build up backward regions, she encouraged the colonization of the sparsely settled lands on the Volga by offering inducements in the form of subsidies and tax exemptions to foreign colonists there. Thousands of Germans were attracted to the Volga, where they built up prosperous agricultural communities in the regions of Saratov, Samara, and Tsaritsyn. These Volga Germans, as they were later called, established themselves so well that they were able to resist assimilation and maintain their own culture in those regions until World War II.

Other undeveloped areas were incorporated into Russia by conquest during this period. They were at first given into the hands of the Empress' favorite Potemkin for improvement. Among those placed under his administration was the promising area on the Black Sea coast between the Don and the Dniester rivers, which was given the name of New Russia. Since it attracted few Russians at the time, the government encouraged immigrants from abroad; and many responded—Albanians, Serbs, Bulgarians, Moldavians, Wallachians, and Greeks. A number of new cities were established there, many of which failed but a few of which flourished. One of the most important was Odessa, founded in 1794 with a polyglot population of Greeks, Italians, and Russians, which became one of the great commercial centers of Russia.

When the Crimea was annexed, in 1783, Potemkin undertook to direct the improvement of that area also. He constructed Sevastopol as a naval base in 1784 and then turned his attention to the general development of the peninsula. He permitted the Crimean Tatars to remain; but since they had not developed the land, he induced foreign settlers to take residence there. He even proposed that the English send some of their convicts to the Crimea rather than to Australia, but nothing came of his proposal. Other immigrants came, however, and soon new settlements and new industries were developing throughout the area.

CHANGES IN THE UKRAINE AND THE BALTIC PROVINCES. The eastern Ukraine and the Baltic provinces presented unusual problems for Catherine. Both regions maintained political institutions different from those of Russia; and it was almost inevitable that a strong central government, despite old treaties and agreements, would attempt to assimilate them completely and impose upon them the institutions of Russia. They had been left relatively undisturbed since their acquisition, mainly because of the Russian rulers' preoccupation with other problems. But Catherine was able to give some of her bountiful energy to them. Her policy was to promote the extension of Russian political institutions and centralized control as far as was conveniently and safely possible.

In the administration of that policy in the eastern Ukraine, the special privileges and institutions of that region were, one by one, abolished between 1764 and 1785. The autonomous rights of the Ukrainian Cossacks and landowners were ended, and the Cossack organization of the Ukraine was dissolved, its members being distributed among regular cavalry regiments. Serfdom, as has been noted, was extended to the region, and the Ukrainian landowners were allowed to share with the Russian nobility in the rights granted by the Charter of the Nobility. In 1778 the local administrative organs of the Russian Empire replaced the traditional ones, and by 1785 the political assimilation of the eastern Ukraine was complete. The peasants still clung to their ancient speech habits and customs, but the landed nobles gradually came to consider themselves an integral part of the Russian nobility and to give up Ukrainian characteristics.

The process of integration was not so complete in the Baltic provinces of Livonia and Estonia as it was in the Ukraine. It will be recalled that, under the Treaty of Nystadt, the inhabitants of those areas had been permitted to maintain their traditional organs of government and system of law. Catherine was not prepared to ignore the terms of that treaty, but she did attempt to introduce parts of the Russian administrative system and fiscal policy into the provinces. In 1783 she imposed upon them the system of provinces and governors. She also required the payment of the poll tax by the Baltic peasants. Those measures did not make any real changes in the life of the provinces, but they indicated central control; beyond that the Empress did not dare to go.

Personal influence of Empress Catherine

DEVELOPMENT OF THE IMPERIAL COURT. Although Catherine's domestic reforms were of great concern to her subjects and although, to her credit, many of them endured, they did not reflect the brilliance for which her reign is known: that was to be seen chiefly in her administration of foreign affairs and in her development of the imperial court. Under Elizabeth the court had acquired some life but no polish; under Catherine both were added. Architects, gardeners, music teachers, cooks, and fencing masters were imported by the dozens from France and Italy to transform St. Petersburg physically and socially. Sumptuous palaces were built not only for the court but also for the Empress' favorities. For Potemkin, who had already been given the Anichkov Palace, erected by Elizabeth, the magnificent Tauride Palace was built in commemoration of his success in the Crimea. Others were rewarded likewise in proportion to their favor with the Empress.

The court was dominated, as in the time of Elizabeth, by French influences. And it gradually became a center of literature, painting, sculpture, and music—all favored and encouraged by the Empress. In her efforts to be a patroness of culture, Catherine constructed a palace—later known as the Hermitage—where she might place her fine foreign purchases: the libraries of Diderot and Voltaire and a great collection of paintings, among them some of the best examples of the work of French, Italian, and Dutch masters.

Not a little of the attraction of Catherine's court arose from its display of ostentation; she and her courtiers vied in the garish spending of money. She presented to her lovers jewels worth hundreds of thousands of rubles (at a time when a young serf could be bought for ten rubles). One noble spent thirty thousand rubles to present a court spectacle; another spent three thousand rubles on the soup course of a special dinner. One courtier owned two thousand dogs, which required the services of several hundred grooms. There was probably no court in Europe at the time in which extravagance was so conspicuously flaunted as in that of St. Petersburg.

The notoriety of the court was provided in great part by the numerous love affairs of the Empress herself. The most fantastic stories of her private life were circulated and accepted as true. Actually her morals, private or political, were no worse than those of her contemporaries. Her amours gained special attention because of the fact that she was a woman and the fact that she chose so many lovers—at least twenty-one. Although most of them were politically inconsequential and exercised no influence upon her policies, three became highly important in political and military activities: Gregory Potemkin, Gregory Orlov, and Platon Zubov. And all were expensive. A new lover usually received an initial gift of 100,000 rubles, and other gifts followed as long as he remained in favor. Even a discarded lover might continue to remain on the Empress' payroll; Orlov was granted, in addition to all the estates which he had received, an annual pension of 150,000 rubles after his retirement from favor. Undoubtedly the most important of the lovers was Potemkin. His term as favorite was only from 1774 to 1776, but he remained the friend and adviser of the Empress until his death, in 1791.

"GREATNESS."   Until the last seven years of her reign, Catherine did not permit her personal life to interfere with her rule. Although she usually chose her lovers for their appeal, she chose her advisers and officials for their ability. Among the most notable of them were Potemkin, administrator, soldier and colonizer; Peter Rumyantsev, general and administrator; Alexander Suvorov, one of the greatest of Russian generals; and Nikita Panin, statesman. They were all men whose ability she trusted and respected but not men by whom she would allow herself to be dominated. She made decisions; they executed them. The balance she maintained in that relationship helped to establish her in the esteem of her contemporaries. Voltaire, one of her admirers, called her the "Semiramis of the North" and a Russian "Minerva," and all were willing to concede the justification of her being called "the Great," being thereby recognized as worthy of rank with Ivan III and Peter I.

Period of relaxation

CHANGES IN THE EMPRESS.   Catherine's domestic policies declined in effectiveness during the concluding years of her reign as she herself declined in ability and energy, turned against ideas she had formerly patronized, and began to worry about the succession.

In 1789, at the age of sixty, she selected the last of her lovers, the young cavalry officer Platon Zubov, who had little to recommend him except his physical beauty. Catherine became so infatuated with him that, despite his conspicuous lack of ability, she allowed him to exercise a powerful political influence at court. That brought about a relaxation of central authority and invited insubordination at the lower levels of government. For the remainder of her reign domestic affairs suffered both from the lack of positive direction and from the lack of central support for established policies.

During these years the French Revolution ended Catherine's flirtation with the ideas of the French radical *philosophes* and led her to reverse her attitude toward them. She denounced the revolutionaries, encouraged Louis XVI to resistance, and offered asylum in Russia to aristocratic émigrés from France. When she received news of the French monarch's decapitation, she was prostrated. She became seriously concerned also about the spread of the "French plague"—as she termed the revolutionary ideas—being determined that Russians should never entertain the notion that "shoemakers" could run a government. The imperial policy became therefore one of rigid opposition to any expression of revolutionary ideas. The latitude of expression which had previously been permitted was now denied. Those who continued to support the ideas of the French radicals were punished, and those Russians who had participated in the revolutionary events in France were ordered home. At the same time Catherine bore down heavily upon any within her realm who dared to criticize the imperial regime, even prohibiting the publication of the satirical journals which she had previously encouraged and to which she had even contributed anonymously. Her alarm was excessive, for there was actually more sympathy in Russia for the victims of the French revolution than for the revolutionaries. French aristocratic émigrés found warm reception among the Russian Francophiles in St. Petersburg (the kind of reception which Russian aristocratic émigrés were to find in Paris after 1917). But the Empress had grown distrustful in her old age; and, although she was neglecting her imperial duties, she was determined to keep up evidence of authority.

FINAL PROBLEM.   Further worry was added to her last years by the prospect that the throne would be occupied by her son Paul. Since his early education had been under the supervision of the Empress Elizabeth, Catherine had not developed a maternal feeling toward him. Moreover, since 1762, he had been a potential rival for the throne; from the time of Peter III's overthrow there had been recurring evidence of conspiracies aimed at dethroning her and crowning Grand Duke Paul.[1] It was a trying situation: Catherine, on the one hand, disliking and working against her son;

---

[1] The male children of the rulers of Russia were given the title of Grand Duke and the female children that of Grand Duchess.

Paul, on the other, having little respect for his mother, seeing in her the ·murderer of his father. Catherine gave all her affection to Paul's two sons, Alexander and Constantine, whom she kept separated from their father. It was generally believed that she planned to designate her older grandson, Alexander, as heir to the throne; but she did not take any formal action to disown Paul. So the succession remained just another unsettled problem to distract the Empress from further concern with the programs which she had so energetically initiated in earlier years.

It is generally agreed that Russian presence at the Congress of Karlowitz in 1698-99 constituted the acceptance of Russia as a full member of that system of Christian European sovereign states which recognized one another by the maintenance of diplomatic relations and which, in common, accepted a body of international law embodied in the Peace of Westphalia (1648) and elaborated by subsequent treaties.

With that diplomatic coming of age, Russia was admitted into the small group of powerful states which, after the Peace of Utrecht (1713), dominated European affairs by maintaining the doctrine of the balance of power. That doctrine implied that the great powers were the agents for preserving a balance among themselves, but it did not limit the pursuit of their aggressions elsewhere.

At the time when Russia was accepted as one of the European sovereign states, neither her status as a power nor the degree of her involvement in balance-of-power politics could be predicted. The great powers in European politics were France, England and Austria; Prussia was still in the process of becoming a great power. Russia had no stake in their war of diplomacy west of the Elbe, including the race for empire in which France and England were engaged and the international competition for power in Spain and Italy. However, east of the Elbe—in the Baltic, in Poland, and in the Ottoman Empire— she had interests of outstanding importance. And since those areas also were important in the European balance-of-power politics, Russia was drawn more and more deeply into the complicated diplomatic and military struggle for power in which Europe was involved during the eighteenth century.

Focuses of Russian foreign policy in 1725

THE BALTIC QUESTION.   Since both Russia and Prussia had strengthened themselves on the Baltic at Sweden's expense during the Northern
War, Russia had no trouble in making common cause with Prussia for the
maintenance of the status quo in that region. France might have disturbed
their security there if she had maintained her traditional support of Sweden;
but, toward the end of the Northern War, French leaders came to feel that,
since Swedish power was in such a deplorable decline, it would be advantageous to establish amicable relations with Russia and Prussia in regard
to that country. Accordingly, in 1717, Russia and France signed a treaty
whereby the latter agreed not to make any new agreements with Sweden
hostile to either Russia or Prussia. Peaceful relations in that region were
further assured by a shift in the internal politics of Sweden: control of the
government was passing into the hands of men who were resigned to
Sweden's losses and to her decline in international importance. Since they
were willing to accept the status quo, Russian-Swedish relations were maintained without untoward event until that complacency in government was
overcome, in 1738.

THE POLISH QUESTION.   The Polish Question, on the other hand, continued to be a source of international friction. Since the middle of the
sixteenth century Poland had been in a state of continuous decline, and by
the early eighteenth century she had become economically stagnant, politically divided and militarily insignificant. The process of decay had been
hastened by two peculiar features which had been imposed upon the country's government: the elective form of the monarchy and the political
supremacy of the nobility. Candidates for the throne were compelled to
bargain with the nobility in order to secure election, promising retention
or extension of noble rights, offering bribes, or pledging rewards. If the
nobility had been united they could have used their bargaining power to
great advantage; but they were not united, and they often broke into factions supporting different candidates.

Under such circumstances, the foreign powers interested in Poland—
Russia, Sweden, France, Prussia, and Austria—could easily intervene in
her internal affairs; and they often did so. Moreover, because of Poland's
internal weakness and her lack of natural frontiers, it was inevitable that
the question of her continued existence as a state be raised sooner or later.
But she was too valuable a prize to be allowed to go to any one power;
and as long as several great powers with conflicting interests could exer-

cise their influence there, no single power would be in a position to take over the state.

Russia probably went as far toward dominating Poland as any one power could. After Augustus II regained the throne as a result of the Russian victory at Poltava, his friendliness toward Russia made it possible for the Russian ambassadors in Warsaw to manipulate Polish political affairs to their country's advantage. Yet Russia did not press her advantages to the point of territorial acquisition. Since the end of the seventeenth century, Russian policy had been concerned with increasing Polish friendship and dependence to the end that Polish aid might be assured in the struggle against Sweden. When the Northern War was over, Russia continued to use that friendship and dependence to turn the balance of power in eastern and northern Europe in her favor. Until 1772 her policy toward Poland was aimed at securing and maintaining a preponderance of influence for herself—or, if necessary, for herself and her allies—and at preventing any inimical power from gaining major influence in that country.

In order to understand developments in the Polish Question, it is necessary to consider briefly the policies of other powers in regard to it. France treated Poland as a pawn in her diplomatic game, trying to use that country in the French struggle against Austria and relying upon it as a buffer to Russia. Austria, contrariwise, sought to use Poland against France. Neither of those countries had any territorial ambitions in Poland itself. Prussia, however, had territorial ambitions: she wanted the Polish lands at the mouth of the Vistula River. On the whole the interests of the four powers were in conflict; but Russia, Prussia, and Austria had one common interest: the limitation of French influence in Poland. Therefore Austria was willing to accept the preponderance of Russian influence, knowing that Russia would act as a check to her enemy France; and Prussia was willing to accept it as long as it served to keep Poland weak and did not develop into complete control.

THE EASTERN QUESTION.   Another question which embroiled the European powers in the eighteenth century was the Eastern (or Turkish) Question. The Ottoman Empire, unlike Poland, was not yet a weak power. The zenith of the Turkish military power in Europe had been reached by the end of the seventeenth century; but the Ottoman Empire in 1725 was still a powerful state, controlling the northern coast of the Black Sea, a region coveted by Russia, and the Balkan Peninsula, into which Austria was trying to push. It was only a matter of time before Russia and Austria would recognize the Ottoman Empire as a common enemy and each other as allies. Opposed to them stood France and, in lesser degree, the other powers—all intent upon preventing any excessive increase in Russian or Austrian strength at the expense of the Turks.

POTENTIAL SUPPORT AND OPPOSITION. Having interests so involved with those of other European powers, Russia was forced to find supporting friends and, unavoidably, to face opposition. She could count on Prussia as a friend insofar as the Baltic and Polish questions were concerned; on Austria, with respect to the Eastern Question and, to some extent, the Polish Question. As opponents there were France, Sweden, Poland, and the Ottoman Empire, whose opposition might be combined in various ways as the Baltic, Polish and Eastern problems coalesced in international diplomacy. French diplomacy would seek to use Sweden, Poland, and the Ottoman Empire as counters to either Austria or Russia whenever possible; but, for the time being, it would not seek to break friendly relations with Russia. As for the other opponents, Sweden and Poland, Sweden and the Ottoman Empire, or Poland and the Ottoman Empire might be expected at some time to find common advantage in opposing Russia.

Great Britain had few direct political interests in Eastern Europe, but she had been disturbed by the sudden growth of Russian power during Peter's reign. If it had been feasible, she would have liked to prevent any further increase in that power; however, Russia was not a major preoccupation of the British in 1725.

International developments 1725-1763

MAINTENANCE OF POLICY. From 1725 to 1763 Russian foreign policy showed a clear continuity despite the fact that, after Peter's death, Russia's power in international affairs declined temporarily as a result of the succession of weak or short-lived rulers. His successors contributed to the decline by permitting a relaxation in the state's demands on its subjects which resulted in a lessening of Russian military strength. Moreover, the weakness of the throne made a firm foreign policy difficult of attainment and allowed foreign intrigue to develop at the court of St. Petersburg. A major source of intrigue was France, whose diplomatic representatives attempted to take advantage of the existence of hostile factions in Russia. Still a general continuity in foreign policy was maintained, principally because many of Peter's "fledglings" retained their influence in the delineation of that policy and because it was subjected to no great test in the relatively untroubled years immediately following Peter's reign.

WAR OF THE POLISH SUCCESSION: 1733-35.   In 1733 the calm was broken by events brought about through the death of the king of Poland, Augustus II. A year before that time King Louis XV of France had proposed that, on the death of Augustus, Russia support the candidacy of Stanislaw Leszczynski, the father-in-law of Louis XV. The proposal had been rejected by Russia on the advice of Count Andrei Ostermann, then in charge of Russian foreign affairs, who felt that its acceptance would strengthen French influence in Poland and would offend Austria, who opposed the candidacy. When Leszczynski was elected king by a large majority of the Diet, a militant minority denounced the election as invalid, and civil strife broke out immediately.

Within a week Russia had sent troops into Poland, and they had been joined by the Polish malcontents. The war which followed assumed a European character when Austria, nominally Russia's ally in the struggle, became engaged in hostilities with France, Spain, and Sardinia on various fronts. The fighting in Poland itself was confined principally to engagements between the Russian troops on the one hand and the poorly organized Polish troops of King Stanislaw, supported by small French contingents, on the other. Stanislaw was soon forced to flee the Polish capital, Warsaw, and take refuge in the fortified city of Danzig. Then the Russian land forces, aided by a Russian fleet which sailed across the Baltic to Danzig, besieged the city, defeated the French forces which came to its relief, and finally captured it in June, 1734. Stanislaw again managed to escape, but he now realized that without full French aid—which would not be given—he could not hope to win.

Meanwhile the Russians had assembled a rump Diet of the few Polish deputies who had opposed Stanislaw and, on October 6, 1733, secured the election of the son of Augustus II as king of Poland under the title of Augustus III. Sporadic fighting continued in Poland for another year, but Stanislaw's cause was a hopeless one; the Russians were in command.[1] In 1736 Stanislaw announced his abdication from the throne which he could not hold, and the regular Polish Diet accepted Augustus III, the Austro-Russian candidate. Under his rule, Poland became increasingly feeble—

---

[1] During the war one event of significance for Russia took place outside of Poland: some of her forces were sent, in 1735, to the aid of the Austrians fighting on the Rhine. To the major states, that was tangible evidence of her increasing growth toward the status of a European power with interests reaching into the West.

a sovereign state in theory but actually a sphere of influence of Russia, Austria, and (to some extent) Prussia.

RUSSO-TURKISH WAR OF 1736-39. The hostilities over the Polish Succession were no sooner ended than Russia, along with Austria, was at war with the Ottoman Empire. While Russian forces had been engaged in Poland, France had urged the Sultan to attack Russia, but he had been engaged in a war with Persia at that time and had not been able to oblige. In fact, it was finally Russia who took the initiative, influenced by the evidence of Turkish weakness in the struggle with Persia.

In the spring of 1736 Russian troops began an attack on the Sultan's vassal and Russia's perennial enemy, the Crimean Khan. For the next three years fighting continued intermittently, at great cost to the Russians as well as to the Turks and Crimean Tatars. Though the Russians concentrated their attack on the Crimea, they sent one force into the Turkish province of Moldavia to give relief to the Austrians, hard pressed by the Turks in that region. By 1739 the military advantage lay with the Russians, but the untimely decision of Austria to sign a separate peace with the Sultan forced the Russians to follow. The Treaty of Belgrade (September, 1739), which brought the Russo-Turkish war to an end, did not bring Russia the gains for which there had been hopes. By its terms the Ottoman Empire agreed to transfer Azov to Russian possession, on the condition that the city's fortifications be razed, and Russia agreed not to maintain a fleet on the Black Sea.

RUSSO-SWEDISH WAR: 1741-43. The demonstration of Russian military prowess against the Turks alarmed France, who had been hoping to see Austria's chief ally weakened by the war. Looking about for possibilities of further engaging Russian energies, she found one in Sweden in 1738. There a turn of political affairs had brought to power a war party anxious to restore Swedish power and to regain Swedish losses to Russia. Encouraged by French subsidies, the new Swedish leaders began to adopt a hostile policy toward Russia, even offering secret—though negligible—aid to the Turks. They went so far as to mass troops near the Russian frontier, waiting for a favorable opportunity to open hostilities.

Meanwhile in St. Petersburg French diplomats were engaged in still another offensive, the purpose of which was to weaken or break the Russo-Austrian friendship. It developed out of the question of the Austrian succession. The Austrian ruler Charles VI had secured the promises of the major powers that, upon his death, they would recognize Maria Theresa as heir to all of his domain. However, when he died, in 1740, Frederick II of Prussia, aided by France, attacked Austria in an effort to enforce his claim to the Austrian territory of Silesia, thus starting the War of the Austrian Succession. Although Russia sent no immediate aid, the majority of the leaders remained faithful to Austria and denounced the Prussian action. France hoped, nevertheless, that with proper manipulation the Swedish crisis and the Russian court discord on the Austrian question could be used to place Russia in a difficult position.

With French persuasion, Sweden declared war on Russia in August, 1741. At the same time, the French ambassador to St. Petersburg was encouraging Elizabeth to unseat Ivan VI and to dismiss Ostermann, chief proponent of the Austrian alliance. In December, 1741, she did, as has been noted, proclaim herself Empress and exile Ostermann.

However, the carefully laid plans of France were soon in process of disruption. Sweden no longer had the power of the days of Charles XII and, in short order, lost all of Finland to Russia. In August, 1743, the Peace of Abo was signed by Sweden, giving Russia a generous area in southeastern Finland and promising the succession to the Swedish throne to Adolf Frederic, a member of the Holstein-Gottorp family. Russia might perhaps have kept all of Finland, but Empress Elizabeth favored generosity in return for the assurance that the Holstein-Gottorp family would reach the Swedish throne; her nephew and heir presumptive, Peter of Holstein-Gottorp, might thus strengthen his future claims to the crown of Sweden.

ALIGNMENT AGAINST FRANCE.   French plans were disrupted in yet another respect. Ostermann was gone, but Russia did not end her support of Austria. Elizabeth chose, as Ostermann's successor, Alexis Bestuzhev, who had begun his career in the service of Peter the Great; and he, like the former counselor on foreign affairs, based his policy on support of Austria and enmity toward France. He went even further than that. Any enemy of France was, in his thinking, a friend of Russia; so he decided that Russia should cultivate the friendship of England, arch-enemy of France. On the other hand, he decided that any friend of France was an enemy of Russia; therefore he counted Prussia as an inimical power.

After the completion of the war with Sweden, Bestuzhev attempted to bring Russia into the Austrian war, but the court was so divided by opposing factions and beset by the intrigues of the ambassadors of Prussia and France that he could not get sufficient support for his plan. Elizabeth herself was at first unfavorable to entry because Austria had opposed her ascension to the throne. In time she was convinced, however, that neither France nor Prussia should be permitted to become too powerful; and in 1745 she agreed that Russia enter an alliance with Austria against Prussia.

Later, at the end of 1747, England consented to subsidize a Russian army to be sent against France. Such an army, numbering 30,000, was despatched to the Rhine, but it had no opportunity to engage in fighting before the end of the war.

DIPLOMATIC REVOLUTION.   In the next few years of peace, Bestuzhev attempted to bolster Russia's relationships with Austria and England. There was no problem insofar as Austria was concerned, but England was not anxious to tie herself down. In September, 1755, England finally agreed to a convention by which she would furnish a subsidy to Russia, and Russia, in turn, would provide 30,000 troops to be used against Prussia when the need should arise.

However, within a few months after the signing of the convention, all of Bestuzhev's plans collapsed as the diplomatic constellation of Europe changed. In 1756 Prussia abandoned her French alliance and formed one with England. France, for the time being, dropped her age-old enmity toward Austria and concluded a defensive alliance with that country against Prussia. Those shifts left Russia in a peculiar position: she was invited to join the new alliance of her old friend Austria and her old enemy France; at the same time she was under commitment to aid England against Prussia, and Prussia was now in alliance with England.

Readjustment of Russia's diplomatic position, now imperative, was influenced by two considerations: sympathy for Austria and opposition to the extension of Prussian power. Since the Anglo-Russian Convention of 1755 and the Anglo-Prussian Treaty of 1756 were, in Russian judgment, mutually exclusive, it was decided to consider Russian obligations toward England at an end and to accept the invitation to join Austria and France in their alliance.

THE SEVEN YEARS' WAR: 1756-63.   In 1756 Prussia again went to war against Austria, this time to protect the acquisitions she had made in the War of the Austrian Succession. Russia entered the war because of a desire to halt Prussian growth and, in the seven years of fighting which followed, served as an unwilling ally of France and an indirect opponent of Prussia's ally England. From the Russian point of view the alliance with France, though necessary, was distasteful; and no effort was made to develop it into close friendship. The position of opposition to England was considered purely accidental, and during the war Russia engaged in no hostilities against that country. For Russia, the war was against Prussia only.

As the fighting progressed, Russia's major forces took part and contributed materially to the checking and weakening of Prussia. Despite bad generalship, poor military organization, and inadequate support from Austria, Russian troops gave a good account of themselves through superiority in numbers and the show of extraordinary personal courage. Yet Frederick the Great of Prussia managed to hold his own, and neither Austria nor Russia was able to do more than win occasional battles. In August, 1759, the Russians and Austrians, with 70,000 men, defeated and nearly destroyed Frederick's army of 53,000 at Kunersdorf, near Frankfort-on-the-Oder. But the strategic results of the victory were lost because of friction between the Austrian and Russian generals; instead of pressing on, the Russians returned to their base of operations. The Russian army resumed the fighting in 1760 and, in October of that year, was able to occupy Berlin for a few days; then, after exacting tribute and damaging the city, it retreated.

That the war dragged on so long was due to the dogged insistence of the rulers of Russia and Prussia. Empress Elizabeth was determined to fight until Prussia had been crushed. And Frederick, even though at the end of his resources, declared dramatically—and perhaps not candidly—that he wanted to die on the field of battle.

Elizabeth's determination was shared neither at her court nor in the courts of her allies. In St. Petersburg the heir, Peter, openly expressed his admiration of Frederick and his wish to see the war end, while others felt that the war was too costly and perhaps without purpose. Austria and France, feeling the burden of the prolonged fighting, were anxious for peace. When Elizabeth died, in January, 1762, the decision to cease fighting was made immediately by the new emperor, Peter III. He offered his revered Frederick unconditional peace; and in May, 1762, the Treaty of St. Petersburg was signed, bringing the war officially to an end.

Perhaps it is true, as some have argued, that Peter's action was not entirely indefensible, that Russia could have gained nothing by continuing the struggle at so great cost to herself. In any case, his action was a complete reversal of the Elizabethan policy, and his offer of unconditional peace eliminated Russia's chance to secure concessions from Frederick. Nevertheless, once the fighting was ended, the Russians had no desire to renew it; and when Catherine succeeded Peter, in July, 1762, she made no effort to do so.

Extension of Russian power: 1763-1796

RUSSIA'S POSITION IN 1763. Between 1725 and 1763 Russia's foreign involvements, expensive in terms of men and money, had brought little territorial advantage. But during that period the gains made by Peter the Great had been maintained, the hold on Poland had been strengthened, and Russian superiority over Sweden and, in some measure, over the Ottoman Empire had been demontsrated. In addition Russia had gained increasing respect for her military power and diplomatic prowess. What was to be made of that established position among the powers depended now upon the direction of a new—and stronger—sovereign.

Catherine's conquest of the throne coincided with new developments in European diplomacy which were of immediate influence upon her direction of foreign policy. The combinations produced by the diplomatic revoultion preceding the Seven Years' War had not survived that war; focuses of interest were changing. France, temporarily a weakened power, relegated continental affairs to a secondary position and set as her chief goal the recapture of the colonial possessions which she had lost to England during the war. The French practice of employing whenever possible the Ottoman Empire, Sweden, and Poland against Russia was not abandoned, but French influence in Central and Eastern Europe from 1763 until the rise of Napoleon was minor and of little consequence to Russia. Austria now placed greater store on her continuing struggle with Prussia for hegemony in Central Europe than on her traditional drive against the Ottoman Empire. Prussia, although her position as a great power had been confirmed by the recent war, was not in a position to continue an aggressive foreign policy and now sought, rather, to secure the gains which had been made. Prussia's alliance with England was at an end, and Frederick was intent upon gaining other friends; above all, he wanted to make certain that, in the event of war, Russia would be a neutral or—better still—an ally.

Of the great continental powers, Russia was in the most fortunate position. Though the cost of war had been heavy, it had not fallen as heavily upon her as upon the other powers. No fighting had taken place on Russian soil, nor had Russian resources been severely strained by the war effort. Even more important was the fact that Russia was free of any real concern for her own security. The states which had formerly threatened her were now either weakened or decadent. Sweden could hardly be classed as even a second-rate power; Poland was only the ghost of a state; and the Ottoman Empire, even though still a military power, was on the defensive.

CATHERINE II'S POLICY.   The times were favorable for a Russian ruler with an aggressive foreign policy, and Catherine II proved to be such a ruler. The nature of her policy was no novelty in eighteenth century

Europe; the practice of the times was based on the assumption that strong powers must grow stronger at the expense of others. Catherine's policy, which provided for an active extension of Russian power abroad, was marked by two interrelated aspects: the achievement of pre-eminent influence in the European system of states and advancement, as opportunity presented itself or was manufactured, at the expense of the three weak neighbors. Broadly speaking, she sought to acquire for her country an influence in European affairs such as Louis XIV had acquired for France nearly a century before. The achievement of that aim would not only insure the country's prestige but would also make possible the influencing of European balance-of-power politics in Russia's favor.

Although there was no reason for Russia to fear attack by any single major power, there was reason to fear the formation of hostile coalitions which could frustrate the immediate aims of Russian foreign policy. Therefore, the necessity in 1763 was again to readjust relationships with the great powers. The chief counselor in Russian foreign affairs, now Count Nikita Panin, proposed a system known as the Northern Accord, by which Russia in combination with the northern powers—Prussia, Poland, Sweden, Denmark, and England—would offset the new combination of Austria and France. His plan did not gain the complete approval of the countries concerned; but, on paper, the Northern Accord remained the guiding principle of Russian foreign policy until 1780. In reality, it was only partially realized and often forgotten. Only one aspect of the projected system was of real moment; that was the combination with Prussia.

ALLIANCE WITH PRUSSIA. Catherine herself favored the prospect of an alliance with Prussia, and was in a position to set a high price: Prussian support in Poland. The need for that support arose in October, 1763, when King Augustus III died and rival candidates for the Polish throne were proposed. One faction of the Polish nobility favored a candidate with pro-French orientation, while another favored a native candidate acceptable to the Russians, Stanislaw Poniatowski. As before, the issue was decided by forces outside of Poland. Both France and Austria opposed the candidacy of Poniatowski, but France was unwilling and Austria unable to affect the decision. Prussia, in return for an alliance with Russia, agreed to support Poniatowski; and in September, 1764, the Diet, influenced by the distribution of bribes and the threat of Russian and Prussian military intervention, chose him king.

Thus begun, the Russo-Prussian alliance of 1764 remained operative until 1780 and was the most constant of Russia's ties during that period.

By it Russia was committed to give aid if Prussia were attacked by Austria. Prussia, in turn, agreed to give military aid if Russia were attacked by a third power other than the Ottoman Empire or the Crimean Khanate; in case the attack came from either of those two sources, the Prussian military aid would be replaced by a subsidy. The two states were further committed to follow a joint policy in Sweden and Poland to preserve the existing political institutions, which would insure continued weakness in those countries; in the latter, military force was to be employed, if necessary, to prevent any change in the existing government. In Poland protection was to be extended also to the rights of Protestants and Orthodox.

The alliance, though appreciated by both powers, was not born of love. Prussia had no wish to strengthen her partner in Poland, nor did Russia wish to share her influence in that country with Prussia. The arrangement was made viable only by Frederick's fear that Russia might support an Austrian attack on him and by Catherine's concern over the possibility of an Austro-Prussian combination against Russia.

FLARE-UP OF THE POLISH AND EASTERN QUESTIONS. By 1768 internal attempts to strengthen Poland's political structure had apparently been halted; the Diet had been compelled to extend the rights of the Orthodox and Protestants; and in February of that year the Polish government had been forced to agree to a treaty whereby Russia guaranteed the Polish constitution—in reality, gained the right to intervene in Polish internal affairs. Poland had become, in modern political terms, a protectorate of Russia. Catherine regarded her immediate aims as achieved, but a Ukrainian and a Polish revolt held her attention for a time.

The Polish Ukraine had been restive under the double burden of Polish persecution of Orthodox believers and economic subjugation of the peasantry, and a series of minor revolts had occurred there during the first part of the eighteenth century. In 1768 a major revolt broke out among the Polish Ukrainian peasantry and Cossacks, reminiscent of the Khmelnitsky uprising of 1648. The Polish Government, helpless against the rebels, asked for Russian troops, and they were supplied. Russia's position was a reversal of that of 1648, when aid had been given to the Ukrainian rebels; but Catherine justified it on the grounds that the agrarian revolt might spread to Russia if not quelled. The Russian troops soon subdued the rebels, known as *Haidamaks* (Brigands), and the task of final pacification of the peasants was left to the Polish landlords.

At the same time that Russian troops were overcoming the anti-Polish revolt, an anti-Russian revolt was in the making. After the treaty of February, 1768, was forced upon Poland, a group of Polish nobles de-

cided on resistance both to the Russian control and to the extension of
privileges to the Orthodox and Protestants. They were supported in their
decision by France, then able to offer little material support but willing to
provide military leadership for a rebellion. Having their headquarters in
the city of Bar, in southern Poland near the Turkish frontier, the rebels
called themselves the Confederation of Bar. Russian troops were sent against
them but, in spite of early successes, did not succeed in stopping the rebellion. It continued sporadically for four years.

Like most Polish troubles, this one did not remain confined within
the borders of Poland. The rebel leaders turned to the Ottoman Empire
for help. And the Sultan, encouraged by French and Austrian advice, was
moved to help them not only to settle old scores with Russia but also to
prevent complete Russian domination of Poland, which would facilitate
a Russian attack upon the Ottoman Empire. His first act was to demand
that Russia withdraw her troops from Poland. When Russia refused—as
expected—he declared war and immediately formed an alliance with the
Confederation of Bar. The Polish and Eastern Questions were now merged.

The Turkish declaration of war was made in the latter part of 1768,
but hostilities did not begin until the following year. The Russians took
the initiative in order to prevent the union of Turkish troops with those of
the Confederation and, in April, 1769, sent troops across the Dniester into
Turkish territory. By September they were in Bucharest. Then, pressing on
against Turkish armies superior in number, they gained control of the
Danubian principalities of Moldavia and Wallachia by the following summer. Meanwhile a Russian naval squadron had set out from the Baltic
around Europe to the Aegean Sea for the support of the Balkan Christians,
who were expected to rise against the Sultan. Its leader, Alexis Orlov, landed the ships on the coast of Greece in February, 1770, called upon the Greeks
to revolt, and, receiving an indifferent response from them, set sail once
more. In the latter part of June, supported by a newly arrived squadron,
his ships attacked and destroyed the Turkish fleet in Chesme Bay, facing
the island of Chios.

The Russian victories produced most unpleasant reactions in Vienna
and Berlin. Austria had in the past aided Russia against the Ottoman
Empire, but the Russian and Austrian territorial aims had not then been
in conflict. Now the situation was different; Russia was at Austria's back
door, in Turkish territory on which Austria had her eye.[1] Austria's response
to it was to mobilize troops on the Turkish frontier and to sign a secret

---

[1] This was the first instance of the serious Russo-Austrian conflict of interests in
the Balkans, which was to end in 1914 in the First World War.

alliance with the Ottoman Empire. War between Austria and Russia seemed likely.

FIRST PARTITION OF POLAND. The situation was disquieting to Frederick the Great. By terms of the Russo-Prussian alliance, Prussia was required to furnish Russia financial subsidies during the war with the Ottoman Empire; yet if Russia should defeat the Turks, she would gain extended territories, while Prussia would have nothing to show for her support except a depleted exchequer. Furthermore, if a war should break out between Russia and Austria, Prussia would be required, by terms of the agreement, to fight. Frederick had no desire for a new war of uncertain outcome. His strategy, therefore, was to play on the Russian fear of an Austrian attack and to persuade Russia to renounce the Danubian conquests, accepting in "compensation" a share of Polish territory (of which Prussia and Austria should also receive shares in "compensation" for Russia's acquisition).

By 1771 Catherine came around to Frederick's view, realizing that Russia was exhausted by warfare with the Turks and Poles and seeing no advantage in fighting still another power, Austria. The tripartite negotiations were completed in 1772. Maria Theresa, the ruler of Austria, remonstrated against the moral blackness of a partition of Poland, but, as Frederick remarked, the more she cried the more she took. Russia agreed to abandon any territorial claims on the Danubian principalities in return for the right to annex that portion of Poland which now forms Soviet White Russia. Prussia was to receive what was later known as Polish Prussia (exclusive of Danzig), and Austria was to receive Galicia, western Podolia, and part of the Cracow region. These concessions of Polish soil were confirmed by treaties, which powerless King Stanislaw was compelled to sign with the three powers.

TREATY OF KUTCHUK-KAINARDJI. The Russo-Turkish war had yet to be finished, and both sides were anxious to see the end of it. Serious peace negotiations began in the summer of 1772 but broke down on Russia's insistence that the Sultan recognize the independence of the Crimea. The renewal of Russian military operations, however, soon compelled the Turks to acquiesce; and, in July, 1774, Russian and Turkish representatives signed a treaty of peace at Kutchuk-Kainardji, a village just south of the Danube in the region which is now Bulgaria. By terms of the treaty, the Ottoman Empire agreed to several particularly weakening concessions: (1) the Crimea was declared independent; (2) the coast of the Black Sea from the Dnieper to the Bug was ceded to Russia; (3) navigation of the Black

Sea, hitherto regarded as a Turkish lake, was to be open to Russian ships; and (4) Russian merchants were to have the right of passage through the Straits. Russia, for her part, agreed to evacuate Bessarabia. Wallachia, and Moldavia in return for the Turkish promise to protect the Christian faith and to provide good government in those provinces; but she reserved the right to make representations to the Turkish government on behalf of the inhabitants of those provinces if the Turkish promise were not kept. The Ottoman Empire made a pledge also to respect the rights of Christians throughout the Empire and agreed that Russia might appeal to the Sultan at any time on behalf of the Turkish Christians.

The Treaty of Kutchuk-Kainardji proved to be one of the most important treaties in the history of Russia, for both economic and political reasons. Just as the Treaty of Nystadt had brought the realization of Russian aims on the Baltic, so this treaty assured the aims on the Black Sea. There was, however, one major difference between the two: unlike the Treaty of Nystadt, the Treaty of Kutchuk-Kainardji raised more problems than it solved—and many of them are still unsolved.

Economically Russia's acquisition of a permanent foothold on the Black Sea was a major gain, for it made possible the consolidation of her control over the rich, grain-producing lands north of that sea and gave her access to important ports from which to export surplus grain.

The political significance of the treaty was international in scope. Its provisions opened an aspect of the Eastern Question which was to plague European international relations for a century and a half. In substance it was now a question of which powers would fall heir to the territory of the "Sick Man of Europe." Russia appeared to be insuring for herself the role of chief heir, but that position was to be contested; and at least one major conflict, the Crimean War, was to be fought over it. More specifically, the treaty granted to Russia certain rights which would inevitably lead to subsequent disputes: (1) the right to protest on behalf of the Danubian principalities, a right which could be used as a pretext for interference in the affairs of the principalities; (2) the right of appeal on behalf of Turkish Christians, which could easily serve as a pretext for interference in Turkish affairs; and (3) the right to send commercial ships through the Straits, a right which, if Russia sought to extend it, would certainly bring involvements with the Ottoman Empire as well as other powers since the Straits were an inland waterway of the Empire and the sole means of navigation between the Black and Aegean seas.

SHIFT OF POSITIONS AMONG POWERS.   In 1774 Russian prestige

abroad was higher than it had ever been, but Catherine sought to lift it still higher. Her first opportunity came in 1778, when Austria's ambition to gain Bavaria led to armed conflict with Prussia. Catherine offered Russian mediation in the affair and was able to lead the warring powers to a peaceful settlement in 1779. That act of mediation indicated the strength of Russia's new influence and added somewhat to her diplomatic stature.

In 1780 Catherine took another opportunity to apply Russia's international leadership, this time in opposition to the British disregard of the rights of neutral shipping on the seas. To defend those rights Catherine organized the League of Armed Neutrality, consisting at first of Russia, Denmark, Sweden, and Prussia; later, of other powers as well. Although the achievements of the League were negligible, its organization emphasized Russian influence to the point that Great Britain began to re-examine her policies toward Russia.

The following years saw a general re-examination of policies which resulted in a rearrangement of the blocs of European powers. In 1780 Maria Theresa died and was succeeded by her son, Joseph II. He, seeing that France had allowed her efforts against England to take precedence over her diplomatic support of Austria, sought to renew the ties of his country with Russia. The time was propitious for a reunion between them. The Russo-Prussian alliance expired in 1780; and Catherine, whose interest in Poland—the chief reason for alliance with Prussia—was for the moment secondary to her interest in the Ottoman Empire, saw a possibility of renewing Russo-Austrian co-operation against the Turks. Accordingly, in 1781, Russia and Austria were united by a defensive alliance. With that alliance, the last vestiges of Panin's Northern Accord were gone. Prussia, isolated, was beginning to court England; and England, concerned about Russia's Turkish policies, was beginning to seek ways of bolstering the Ottoman Empire and preventing Russia from reaching the eastern Mediterranean.

ATTEMPTED PARTITION OF OTTOMAN EMPIRE.   For Russia, the net effect of the abandonment of Prussia in favor of Austria was encouragement to further expansion to the south. Since the conclusion of the Treaty of Kutchuk-Kainardji, Catherine, Potemkin, and others had been at work on a plan, known as the Greek Project, by which that expansion might be accomplished. It provided, in the first place, for Russian acquisition of the Crimea, the western Caucasus, and the coast of the Black Sea from the Bug to the Dniester. An even more ambitious feature of the project was the proposal to expel the Turks from Europe and to divide their territory into three main parts. One part, comprising the western provinces of the Balkan peninsula, was to be given to Austria. Another, including Moldavia, Wallachia, and Bessarabia, was to become a Russian-controlled buffer state under the ancient Roman name of Dacia, which was to be administered by Potemkin. Most of the remainder of the Balkan peninsula would form the territory of a recreated Byzantine Empire, with its capital at Constantinople. Catherine's second grandson, born in 1779, was named Constantine in the anticipation of his eventually ruling the new Byzantine Empire. The other great powers would receive small grants of territory or privileges as palliatives.

After the completion of the Russo-Austrian alliance, Joseph II agreed to the Greek Project, but not without misgivings that Catherine was attempting to divert him by this fanciful project when her real aim was to employ Austrian support to aid Russia in completing her conquest of the northern coast of the Black Sea from the Kuban to the Dniester. Although he held fast to the alliance, he tried to discourage Catherine from any actions against the Ottoman Empire which would require Austrian support.

In 1783 Russia annexed the Khanate of Crimea which had been, in effect, under Russian control since its "independence" was declared in 1774. That act might have provoked war with the Turks but for the fact that France and Prussia, anxious to prevent a war in which Austria would support Russia, were able to prevail upon the reluctant Sultan to recognize the Russian seizure. The Sultan, however, was not resigned to Russia's action in the Crimea, and his patience was severely tried by further Russian acts: interference in Moldavia and Wallachia and encouragement of rebellion against Turkish rule in the Caucasus. When he finally learned of the Greek Project, he knew that action could not be postponed; and, in August, 1787, he demanded that Russia give up the Crimea. Russia, of course, refused; and the refusal was followed immediately by a Turkish declaration of war. Joseph II, bound by his alliance with Russia, declared war on the Ottoman Empire in January, 1788. The first two years of the war went slowly. The Austrian military effort against the Turks was far from effective; the Turks showed greater resistance than they had shown twenty years earlier; and England was working behind the scenes to make it difficult for Russia to give adequate attention to the Turkish struggle.

England, now beginning to replace France as the supporter of the Ottoman Empire and Sweden against Russia, offered her diplomatic support to the Sultan and at the same time, to divert some of the Russian forces from the Turkish front, encouraged Sweden to declare war on Russia. The

Alexander Suvorov

diversion was temporarily successful. The Russian Baltic Fleet, under orders to sail to Greece and promote a rebellion there, was forced to remain in the Gulf of Finland to protect St. Petersburg from the Swedish fleet; and Russian troops were sent into Finland to meet the Swedish forces there. The Russians were victorious in both efforts, and Sweden asked for peace. In 1790 the Russo-Swedish war was brought to an end with no change in the frontiers of the two countries.

Meanwhile the Austrian assistance had been sagging. And after the death of Joseph II, in 1790, Austria signed a separate peace (1791) with the Turks.

The Swedish war and the Austrian defection helped to destroy the hope for realization of the Greek Project, but the war between Russia and the Ottoman Empire continued. In the summer of 1789, General Alexander Suvorov had begun a Russian offensive in the Danubian principalities and had been making brilliant gains (on one occasion, with 7,000 men, outmaneuvering a Turkish army of 100,000). In September, 1790, he captured the allegedly impregnable Turkish fortress of Ismail, near the mouth of the Danube. That victory spurred the Russians to greater effort to end the war quickly by pouring more troops into the fighting.

The Russian threat was now becoming more ominous to the English. William Pitt, the British Prime Minister, began to prepare a diplomatic coalition to force Russian agreement to a modification of her territorial demands; and, if threats failed, he intended to use force. British public opinion, however, was against Pitt; British commerce with Russia was great, and many influential Englishmen felt that their country had no vital interests in the Ottoman Empire. In the spring of 1791 Pitt, facing the opposition of Parliament, retreated from his plans.

Deserted by the English and hammered by the Russians, the Turks asked for peace. On August 11, 1791, they signed the preliminary articles; and on January 9, 1792, they signed a treaty of peace at the city of Jassy, in Moldavia. By the Treaty of Jassy, Turkey agreed once more to the

Russian annexation of the Crimea with adjacent lands extending east to the Kuban River and ceded the Black Sea coast between the Bug and the Dniester—in short, conceded the Russian possession of the northern shores of the Black Sea. At last Russia had completed the conquest of the steppe and established herself securely on the Black Sea. With the Dniester as her western boundary in that area, she set her next western goal in the Turkish province of Bessarabia. And her eastern boundary, set at the Kuban, was to serve as a bridgehead for further expansion into the Caucasus.

ATTEMPTED POLISH DEFIANCE.   For many years Russia's wars had been Poland's opportunities, and the Swedish involvement and the Russo-Turkish war ending in 1792 were no exceptions. Poland had taken another opportunity for independent action. Pitt's plans for a European alliance against Russia, led by England and supported by Prussia, had given hope to the large number of Polish nobles who wished to throw off Russian control; and a strong political movement to strengthen the Polish state and weaken or expel Russian influence had developed. In March, 1790, Poland and Prussia had concluded a defensive alliance aimed at Russia. That alliance had given the anti-Russian Poles the needed courage; and, on May 3, 1791, they had forced through the Polish Diet a new constitution, making the monarchy hereditary and strengthening the governmental structure. That had been an overt act of defiance to Russia, and under ordinary circumstances a Russian army would have been hurried into Poland to whip the Diet into retraction. But at that time Catherine and her advisers, though enraged by the contumacious act of the Diet, had decided to hold Russian fire until the end of the war with the Ottoman Empire.

The support which the Poles had expected began falling away just when Russia was freeing herself from the Turkish war. By April, 1792, Austria was at war with revolutionary France; Prussia, already becoming lukewarm in support of revivified Poland, was also soon at war with France; and neither Austria nor Prussia could or would stand by Poland under the circumstances. Catherine, meanwhile, was encouarging the formation of an anti-French coalition, which would help to divert attention from Poland. Knowing the probable outcome of Russia's interest, Austria and Prussia began talk of territorial compensation for themselves in Poland in the event of another partition.

SECOND AND THIRD PARTITIONS OF POLAND.   Events developed in Russia's favor. The upper Polish nobility, regretting the loss of their power under the new constitution, formed themselves into a party and called on Russia for support. Their call gave Catherine an excuse for intervention.

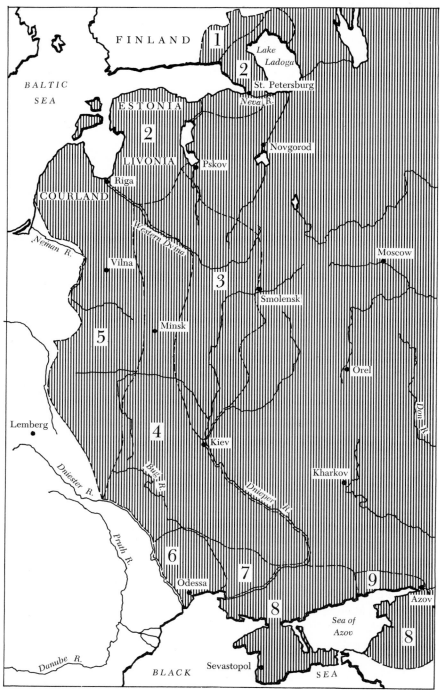

FINLAND

BALTIC
SEA

Lake
Ladoga

St. Petersburg

Neva R.

ESTONIA

Novgorod

LIVONIA

Pskov

Riga

COURLAND

Neman R.

Western Dvina

Vilna

Moscow

Smolensk

Minsk

Orel

Don R.

Lemberg

Kiev

Dniester R.

Bug R.

Dnieper R.

Kharkov

Pruth R.

Odessa

Azov

Sea of
Azov

Danube R.

Sevastopol

BLACK   SEA

DRAWN BY EDW. A. SCHMITZ

In May, 1792, she sent about 100,000 Russian troops into Poland with the declared aim of "restoring Polish liberties," and within a few weeks King Stanislaw was compelled to sign an armistice in which he agreed to annul the Constitution of May 3, 1791.

Prussia, in fear that Russia might seize all of Poland, demanded compensation. Russia met the demands by signing with Prussia, in January, 1793, the Treaty of St. Petersburg, by which Prussia received Danzig, Thorn, and the area known as Great Poland, and Russia received most of Lithuania and the western Ukraine. In the following year, Russia compelled a rump diet to accept the second partition and then demanded that the Polish army be reduced to an insignificant number. That demand touched off a final Polish revolt, led by Kosciuzsko. It was at first so successful that Prussia felt compelled to send troops into Poland to relieve the menaced Russians. But the tide soon turned, and a new Russian army, under Suvorov, succeeded in defeating the rebels and capturing Kosciuzsko.

Austria insisted that she be compensated for her exclusion from the second partition and that she be included in any new ones. To satisfy her, the third partition of Poland, which ended its existence as a state, was completed in October, 1795. By the treaty signed at that time, Austria gained the remainder of the Cracow region; Prussia received Mazovia, including Warsaw; and Russia was given the Duchy of Courland (nominally a vassal of Poland but actually under Russian control since 1737) and what remained of Lithuania and the Ukraine.

The Polish partitions made Austria, Prussia, and Russia territorial neighbors and bound them during the next century by their common interest in preventing the resurrection of an independent Poland. The Polish Question was destined to become the concern not only of these three powers but also of all Europe. Some tried to interpret it as a moral question; one French clergyman argued that as a result of the partitions Europe was living in a state of mortal sin. However, when it is remembered that Europe in those days found it possible to accept even worse crimes against morality, one may

MAP 7. Acquisitions in Europe during the eighteenth century *(see facing page)*.
  1) Treaty of Abo, 1743.
  2) Treaty of Nystadt, 1721.
  3) First Partition of Poland, 1772.
  4) Second Partition of Poland, 1793.
  5) Third Partition of Poland, 1795.
  6) Treaty of Jassy, 1792.
  7) Treaty of Kutchuk-Kainardji, 1774.
  8) Annexed 1783 (annexation recognized by Treaty of Jassy, 1792).
  9) Treaty of Belgrade, 1739.

judge that such arguments carried little weight. Actually it was Polish nationalism rather than European conscience which kept the Polish Question alive.

Collectively, the gains Russia received from the partitions were sizable and valuable: the Duchy of Courland with its ice-free ports; Lithuania; and almost all of the Ukraine except for Galicia (with its mixed Polish, Jewish, and Ukrainian population), which Austria had acquired. Now, with the exception of Galicia and Bukovina (largely Ukrainian in population), which Austria had received from the Ottoman Empire, the territories embracing the three branches of the Russian people—Great Russians. White Russians, and Ukrainians—were united in the Russian Empire. In addition, Russia had become the home of substantial minorities: Jews (who formed a portion of the urban population of the annexed areas), Poles, and Lithuanians.

SUMMARY.   During her reign, Catherine II had successfully asserted Russia's position as one of the five great powers of Europe. She had added to Russia a broad belt of rich territory, from the Baltic to the Black Sea, the western boundary of which lay in the heart of Central Europe. Together the newly acquired regions brought Russia much wealth, new centers of domestic and foreign commerce, and new taxpayers and soldiers. They brought also the disquieting promise of increased Russian involvement in European diplomatic complexities.

NINE / SOCIO-ECONOMIC AND CULTURAL

DEVELOPMENTS: 1725-1796

I n the years between the death of Peter the Great and that of Catherine the Great, the socio-economic and cultural development of the Russian Empire did not keep pace with its political development. By the end of the eighteenth century, the political might of the empire, having been secured at home, had been expanded to great-power proportions; yet economically and culturally the Russian people remained among the most backward in Europe. The struggle for power had absorbed the energies which might have been turned to domestic improvement, and the forces which had retarded development in the past were still in operation.

Population changes

GROWTH. In the eighteenth century, the Russian population, which in previous centuries had been slow and uneven in growth, began to increase phenomenally. The population of Europe as a whole increased rapidly in this century, but the Russian increase was—and has continued to be—exceptional. In 1725 the people of Russia numbered 13 million; by 1796, they had increased to 36 million. The latter figure includes the population of lands annexed by Catherine II; but even without those lands the population would have been 29 million (more than doubled, by natural increase, within the span of Catherine's life, 1729–96). At the end of the century Russia had the largest population of any state in Europe, although its density was still low in comparison with that of the population of the others. Of the many reasons offered in explanation of this great increase, one of the most plausible is that, with the increase of arable land in the Russian Empire and with the rise of agricultural productivity, larger families could be supported by the land. MOVEMENT. The growth in population was accompanied by a general movement from the rural to the urban centers and from the less productive to the more productive areas. Between 1725 and 1796 the number of urban inhabitants increased from about 300,000 to 1.3 million. The old center of Russia, with Moscow as its focus, became the most densely populated region of the country, and Moscow and St. Petersburg led the cities in increase.

More significant was the movement of population to the south and southeast of Moscow, along the Don and lower Volga basins, and into the Ukraine and New Russia. It was a movement, generally speaking, from the forest to the steppe—especially to the black soil regions of the steppe, where fertility and sparse settlement gave promise of the greatest opportunities. Russia, like the United States, was a country of frontiers; and it was only natural that, as the frontiers were opened, the population would flow into the better regions. During this century, as has been seen, the process of opening those regions was speeded up. Usually it had followed a regular sequence: conquest, erection of defenses, pacification of the native inhabitants, and, finally settlement. Toward the end of the century, the final step was in full progress; soldiers, often the first settlers, were being joined by Great Russian and Ukrainian civilians, and occasionally by foreign immigrants invited by the government to aid in the building up of the new regions.

Social changes

THE NOBILITY. The increase of privileges for the nobility reached its height in the second half of the century, a period which has been called the golden age of the nobility. At that time, free from obligations to the state, secure in their power over their serfs, certain of preferment in state service and well endowed with serf labor, they enjoyed such prosperity, security and freedom as they had not experienced before and were not to experience in succeeding periods.

For most of the nobility the material conditions of life were easy. Those with fewer than twenty-five serfs were considered poor and could often be found working alongside their serfs. The typical estate used the services of from 100 to 500 serfs and provided its owner an ample, though not luxurious, life by the standards of his class. Landowners with from 500 to 1,000 serfs were accounted men of wealth, and their number was relatively high. In the minority were the nobles—usually those who had been especially favored by the state—with giant estates worked by tens of thousands of serfs. One of Peter I's generals was able to leave his son 60,000 serfs, and by marriage the son added 80,000 more. Alexis Orlov bequeathed to his heirs 30,000. One of Catherine II's advisers, Bezborodko, owned 16,000 serfs in 1796. And out ahead of all was Count Sheremetev, with 300,000.

In return for the good life which they led, the nobility gave comparatively little in return. Of course, at court the higher nobility helped wield the power of the throne; and in the provinces the lesser nobility dominated the administrative organs of local government, selected serfs as recruits for military service and generally served as guardians of law and order. Many of them contributed also to the arts and sciences, and a few—very few—gave some thought to the economic improvement of the country. But, on the whole, they were content to siphon off the wealth of the country without adding to it by energetic and devoted service.

SERFS.   As the century was kind to the nobles, it was proportionately unkind to the privately owned serfs, whose number was large and whose condition was more onerous than ever before. Serfs now constituted a little more than 50 per cent of the entire peasant population. They predominated in the older areas of settlement—that is, in pre-Petrine Russia, and in the lands acquired by the partitions of Poland. In the more recent settlements, in the south and east of European Russia, they formed a much smaller proportion of the peasant population; in the extreme northern and southern regions they were few in number; and in Siberia they were rarely to be found.

The serfs were of two roughly defined classes: those who worked on the land and those who worked as domestics. Of the first class, some discharged their obligations to the landowner by the payment of cash and kind (*obrok*), while others were obligated for labor service (*barshchina*) in the landowner's fields. In some cases, both money payments and labor were required of them, but generally they served under one system or the other.

The cash-and-kind payment system predominated in the northerly non-black soil regions, where the returns from agriculture were comparatively low. The landlords in these regions usually parcelled out all the arable land of their estates to the serfs and retained for their own use the forests and pastures. Such an arrangement was highly satisfactory for the landlords, for it provided them a predictable source of income and left them free from the duties of management. Many of them lived apart from their holdings, in the towns or—if they could afford it—in St. Petersburg. Since they usually engaged in administrative or military services which rarely provided adequate salaries, they squeezed as much as possible out of their serfs in order to live up to the social requirements of their positions. Although that practice often weighed heavily on the serfs, it brought them one advantage: relative freedom from supervision as long as their obligations were met. And that freedom made it possible for them to engage in handicraft or find extra work in the villages in order to earn money for making their cash payments and supplementing the meager living they could make on the land.

The condition of those who owed labor service to their lords was generally worse than that of those who owed cash-and-kind. They were the ones in the black soil regions, where the returns from agriculture were good and where the landlords ordinarily reserved for their own use a large portion of their arable land and required their serfs to cultivate it. During each week of the agricultural season, the serfs in such cases usually worked three days, of eleven to sixteen hours each, on their own plots and three days on the lord's (a limit which some estate owners stretched—in a few cases, to as much as six days); and during the winter they performed other types of labor on the estates. In addition, they were required to pay some dues in kind—perhaps chickens, pigs, berries, or flax. Under this arrangement, the landlords often managed their own estates. Among those who did so, there developed a type comparable to the landed gentry of other countries—gentlemen farmers who administered their estates with care and industry. Others—and they were many—lived in the towns or cities, as did those who required cash-and-kind, and left the care of their estates to stewards, whose chief duty was to force the serfs as far as possible in the interests of the landlords.

The domestic serfs were assigned no plots of land, but were required to work in or about the homes of the landowners. Most of them were household servants, but some served as blacksmiths, carpenters, stableboys, or watchmen, and some were placed in charge of the landlords' children. In wealthy homes the service of a hundred or so domestic serfs was required—in some, as many as eight hundred. Great nobles who had a fancy for drama or music often recruited talent from their domestics, organizing theatrical or operatic companies composed entirely of serfs and, on occasion, selecting those of most promising talent to be sent abroad to study.

STATE PEASANTS.   After the secularization of the Church lands in 1764, almost all peasants who were not serfs belonged to the category of state peasants since their master was then the state. In most cases state peasants had a right, vested in tradition, to cultivate specific tracts of land, for which they owed dues to the state in cash, kind, or labor—generally lower than serf dues. Although most of them were tied to the land, as were the serfs, they had a legal standing in law, which was denied to the serfs. And they were further favored by being less subject to brutal and arbitrary treatment.

Among them, law and custom had created a variety of statuses, and they may be divided roughly into two categories based upon the freedom or lack of freedom which their status dictated. The lower category included peasants who could claim hardly any degree of freedom. It was made up of five well-defined subcategories: economic peasants, court peasants, possessional peasants, admiralty peasants, and crown peasants. The economic peasants—so called because they were under the jurisdiction of the Economic College of the government—made up the largest of the subcategories and constituted nearly 30 per cent of all state peasants. They cultivated the lands which had once belonged to the Church and paid dues—at first in kind and later in cash —to the state. In addition, they worked occasionally at the building and repair of roads and bridges. Of those in the other subcategories, the court peasants worked on the lands directly under the jurisdiction of the imperial court, generally paying dues in cash; possessional peasants worked in the factories, to which they were assigned by the state; admiralty peasants worked in the forests which supplied timber for the navy; and the crown peasants, fewest in number, served on the estates of members of the imperial family.

The other main category, that of the black-plowing peasants, stood much higher with respect to the amount of freedom allowed those included in it— about 20 per cent of the total number of state peasants. They were located chiefly in the extreme north, in Siberia and in the lower Volga basin. Like other state peasants, they were obliged to pay cash dues to the state and to provide services, but they had the advantages of personal liberty (tenuous, of course, since the state could change their status at any time) and limited property rights.

FREEHOLDERS.   The only group whose status was equivalent to that of the free, land-owning peasantry of the West was composed, in the main, of descendants of soldiers who had served on the southern and eastern frontiers of Russia and who had been assigned land in return for their services. Such peasants—known in some districts as freeholders and in others as old service serving people—made up about 6 per cent of the total peasant population.

URBAN CLASSES.   The comparatively slow growth of industry and commerce held back the development, both in numbers and influence, of the urban classes. The total urban population of Russia in the second half of the century was about the same as that of London in the same period. Of the slightly more than two hundred population centers classified as cities at that time, most were sleepy, muddy centers of provinces or districts which came alive only during fairs. Few of them provided any municipal services or attempted to do so; as late as 1762 only sixteen cities had a yearly budget of more than a thousand rubles. True urban life was limited to such cities as St. Petersburg, Moscow, Kiev, and a few of the seaports.

Catherine II, in her Charter of the Cities, organized the bulk of the urban inhabitants into six classes. The most important and influential was the merchant class, which was subdivided into the first, second and third guilds —so called, but actually not guilds in the Western sense of the word. Membership in the guilds was determined by the size of a merchant's capital, the wealthiest belonging to the first guild and the poorest to the third. Most of the merchants were men of comparative wealth, despised by the nobility, and themselves indifferent to the rest of society. They retained their conservative view, held to the old Muscovite customs (including the wearing of the old style of dress and the pre-Petrine beards) and rejected the Westernisms of the nobility.

Of the other five legal classes only the artisans had an organization of any significant proportions. In accordance with the Charter of the Cities, they were grouped in craft organizations resembling guilds. Each craft had its separate organization, elected its officers and laid down regulations concerning apprenticeship and the general nature of its work. Although the artisans were numerous, their share in the direction of community life was negligible in comparison with that of the wealthy merchant class.

Those who did not have membership in any of the classes were listed by the cities as being "persons of various ranks" (*raznochintsy*). Their number was made up of those who had left one legal class without finding their place in another—perhaps sons of priests or of merchants who had not followed the callings of their parents. From the ranks of this declassed group, usually young men of some education, were to come many of the country's intellectuals and radicals.

THE CLERGY.   The successive steps by which the Church declined until it became in fact the dependent, spiritual department of the government inevitably affected the position of the clergy. The members of the upper clergy, although continuing to be treated as members of the ruling class, lost greatly in influence and prestige. Some individual prelates managed to retain influence, but their number was small. The lower clergy were less affected by the altered position of the Church. They might now be called upon to perform for the government such duties as reading and explaining governmental decrees to parishioners or reporting on seditious activities among the laity, but generally they continued their traditional duties and retained their traditional position in society. The only significant change for them during this century came in 1796, when they were finally freed of the liability to corporal punishment at the hands of the upper clergy.

The economy

AGRICULTURE. The eighteenth century brought some changes in the agricultural scene: increased production, extension of the market for farm products, and greater geographical specialization in production. Techniques changed only slightly because the existence of a large, cheap labor force (now increasing with the new population growth) and the opening up of new land for cultivation made it possible to increase production without altering techniques; and the conservatism of the peasants and the landlords was such that changes were not likely to be made until necessity forced them. With increased production, there was a surplus for the market, but not a large one; most farm products, as before, were for direct consumption. But those which were available for sale were finding a widened market both within Russia and abroad.

The increasing role of money in the Russian economy during this period helped to bring about a regional shift in agricultural emphasis. Where agriculture was less rewarding, in the nonblack soil regions particularly, many peasants forsook farming as their main pursuit and began to concentrate on household industry or on work in the cities as their chief source of income, leaving the cultivation of their plots of land to the women and children of the family. About one-fourth of the adult male peasants in the nonblack soil regions thus changed their mode of livelihood by the end of the century. This shift was indicative of a growing geographical specialization, the black soil regions becoming more important as a source of farm products and the nonblack soil regions becoming more dependent upon non-agricultural sources of income.

INDUSTRY. There was a comparatively rapid growth in mining, metallurgy, manufacture, and handicraft because of the increase in governmental requirements of manufactured goods and metallurgical products for the army and navy, the enlargement of the urban population, and the rise in the standard of living of the nobility. That growth was limited, however, by the absence of capital, the lack of a voluntary labor force, and the low living standard of the great mass of the people.

As the number of mines and foundries multiplied, the number of ascribed peasants increased accordingly. In 1719, about 30,000 adult male peasants were ascribed to metallurgical establishments; and in 1796, over 300,000. A foundry or mine, whether operated by the state or an individual, might have ascribed to it the peasants of several villages, often brought from hundreds of miles away. As in earlier periods, the ascribed peasants continued to cultivate their land, being assigned to the mine or factory during certain months of the year, when they were paid—poorly paid—for their labor. During the century many of the state-owned establishments were transferred to individuals, generally favorites of the court, who were permitted to continue the use of ascribed peasants.

Conditions of labor were harsh and primitive. The servile laborers were often flogged for petty offenses and cheated of their earnings by brutal and venal owners, government officials, and overseers. One of their most frequent complaints was that they were required to work away from the land during the harvest season, a requirement forbidden by law but in common practice nonetheless. Although the use of ascribed labor under such conditions was uneconomical in the long run, the state encouraged it in order to obtain the needed metal products. At times, though, the evil rebounded; many of the peasant outbreaks during the century occurred among the ascribed peasants.

As demand encouraged them, many new factories were established in such cities as Moscow, Vladimir, and Kazan, and others on the estates of nobles who wished to have them near their source of labor. Yet, although their growth in numbers was rapid, the factories had but a modest place in the Russian economy. They were not large, as can be judged from the fact that in 1796 there were probably no more than 100,000 workers in all of them; and their output was limited by the fact that they were operated by techniques which were no more advanced than those of household industry. Most of them produced textiles, chiefly those in demand by the government for the armed forces but also some for the domestic market, now growing as the nobility and wealthy urban classes increased their demands for finer cloths in quantity. In addition to the textile factories there were some producing such luxury goods as crystal, porcelain and stained glass.

The nobles, because of their privileged positions, had a great part in the development of manufacturing. One of their chief advantages was easy access to the use of serf labor at a time when the free labor force of the country was small. Merchants, it is true, had been permitted to buy serfs for factory work; but the nobles succeeded in having that right denied to them in 1762, when the sale of serfs for factory work was prohibited by law. Yet the merchants, fortified by wealth and business acumen, were able to establish themselves in some parts of the textile industry, finding laborers wherever they could among the relatively small number of free men.

HOUSEHOLD PRODUCTION.   A large part of the fabricated goods in the eighteenth century came, as before, from peasant households rather than from factory production. In some sections of the central and northern provinces, merchants who were unable to get labor for the establishment of factories, provided raw material for home workers and collected and marketed the finished products. Because of the peasants' eagerness to earn money and the merchants' assumed right to fix the price in their own interest, the scheme was popular with both parties; and in many villages, every family would be employed in doing piece-work for some merchant. With such beginnings, extensive "home industries" grew up in bootmaking, ikon painting, and pottery and tool manufacture.

COMMERCE.   Several factors combined to increase the volume of domestic and foreign commerce during the century: the expansion of agricultural and industrial production; the growth of cities, the development—even though a slow one—of a money economy; and governmental actions, such as the abolition of the internal tariffs in 1753. However, commerce was still hampered by the slowness of improvement in the transportation facilities. There were no roads worthy of the name before the eighteenth century, and none was constructed during the century; most goods were transported by water in the warm seasons and on the frozen snows in winter. Therefore the cost of transportation was generally high—in some cases prohibitively high. At the end of the century, for example, when the price of rye in Moscow was nearly three times that in Kiev, the cost of transportation would have made profitless any movement of Kievan rye to the Moscow market.

Foreign commerce continued to develop after the time of Peter's acquisition of the Baltic ports, and England remained the chief customer. Between 1725 and 1796 the value of Russian exports increased about ten-fold; and, as at the beginning of her foreign trade, Russia still exported more than she imported. That was a situation resulting from her protectionist policy and the fact that there was small demand for foreign goods in Russia. The general pattern of the foreign trade was indicative of the country's relative industrial backwardness, showing the sale of raw materials and the purchase of finished goods. The principal products of export were flax, hemp, grain, iron, fur, timber, and naval stores; and imports included textiles and finished metal-ware (from the European countries) and silk, spices and cotton (from Persia, the Ottoman Empire and China). The commercial activities of St. Petersburg, Riga, Reval, and—after the Polish partitions—Libau increased steadily; and, in the last years of Catherine II's reign, the newly acquired southern ports of Odessa, Kherson, and Taganrog also began to figure in Russia's foreign trade, especially in the export of grain.

Religion

STATUS AND INFLUENCE OF THE CHURCH.   The Russian Orthodox Church, having begun to lose its power and influence by the end of the seventeenth century because the schism had driven away the Old Believers and increased its dependence upon the state as a police agent against the schismatics, was subsequently weakened still more by the increasing tendency toward secularization in political and cultural life. The spirit of secularism was apparent particularly among the nobility, who, despite their formal adherence to the Church, were rapidly rejecting its spiritual tutelage. It may be said that the Church by the end of the eighteenth century had come to have little function beyond that of guarding and administering orthodoxy. The cultural life of the country was developing outside its gates while it simply preserved but did not add to its heritage.

SCHISMATICS AND SECTISTS.   For a significant minority the Russian Orthodox Church did not serve even as the administrator of ritual. It is estimated that during the eighteenth century about 15 per cent of the population were Old Believers, who practiced their beliefs outside the Church under the conviction that they, rather than the established Church, were adherents of the true faith. After an initial period of intense persecution following the schism, the attitude of the government toward the Old Believers became milder, and they found it possible to live unmolested lives either by paying special taxes and openly practicing their faith or by posing as communicants of the Orthodox Church and practicing it in secret. Catherine II favored them by removing most of their legal disabilities and setting aside for them special areas near Saratov, on the Volga.

Since the Old Believers would not recognize the authority of the Orthodox Church, they found themselves, in time, without priests; for the power of ordination of priests was the bishop's, and they had no bishop. But a little manipulation of principles helped the majority of them to resolve their difficulty and to insure themselves a supply of priests: they simply agreed to accept from the established Church any ordained priests who were willing to disavow the reforms of Nikon and join them. A few radicals among them, however, broke completely with the idea of an organized church, declaring that the maintenance of the true faith did not require a formal religious organization and that believers could practice their religion without the aid of priests. This group, known as the Priestless, having little organizational unity, soon began to split into smaller bodies which were never able to gain much strength.

In contrast to the Old Believers, who considered themselves the true Orthodox, were the adherents of small Christian sects who had developed or accepted completely non-Orthodox concepts. Of these sects, three are noteworthy: the Khlysty (Flagellants), the Skoptsy (the Castrated), and the Dukhobors (Wrestlers of the Spirit). All three believed in the possibility of the reincarnation of the divine spirit in a human body and were inclined to accept the claims of persons who proclaimed themselves to be the divine spirit reincarnate. The Khlysty, who were first organized at the end of the seventeenth century, attempted to achieve a truly religious spirit through religious song and dance, which often assumed a licentious character. The Skoptsy, an eighteenth-century offshoot of the Khlysty, proclaimed the practice of asceticism as the only proper means for finding the spirit of religion. Shortly after its inauguration as a separate sect, the Dukhobors, who emphasized the search for the inner spirit of religion, were formed. Despite extreme persecution (which, in the latter part of the century, became so rigorous that the Dukhobors were first condemned to death and then to exile), the sects continued to grow and proliferate, appealing to the small minority who could find no religious sustenance in the Orthodox Church or among the Old Believers.

Learning, letters, and art

FOREIGN INFLUENCE.   As the cultural influence of the Church over the upper class declined, it was replaced by foreign secular influences. It has been seen that, from 1725 to 1740, Germany was the major source of foreign influence and that, after 1740, France became the accepted model of civilization. However, the influence of Germans and German culture was not completely displaced; much of the foundation work in the development of Russian scholarship and learning in the eighteenth century was performed by Germans.

EDUCATION.   In the first half of the century, the development of education made only halting steps. Peter I's plans for a system of practical, secular education for the upper class were not realized. Many of the schools which he had so laboriously created collapsed after his death; but a few of his technical, military, and naval schools survived, and some of the schools he had established for the education of noble youths were transformed into theological seminaries. His hope that the Academy of Sciences[1] would become a university was not achieved, although a university was created in connection with the Academy in 1748—a spectral institution attended by a mere handful of students.

Secondary education (but not of the type for which Peter had planned) made a beginning in the first half of the century. That was because the nobility, who still claimed education as their reserve, wanted secondary schools for the training of their children in the gentler arts. A fair example of the type they wanted was the school of the Corps of Noble Cadets. It provided for the younger pupils a program including fourteen hours a week in the study of French, six in dancing, six in Russian and less than one in religion; for the advanced pupils, one day a week for military practice, and the remainder of the time for such subjects as French, drama, and astronomy. In addition to it, several private and state-supported secondary schools were opened to satisfy the demands of the nobles and some of the wealthier merchants. One of the private schools was the famous Ellert's Academy, where the use of French was compulsory and a lapse into Russian was punished by a sharp crack on the knuckles.

In the second half of the century, general progress was more rapid but not always steady. High among the achievements was the government's opening of the first enduring Russian university, the University of Moscow, in 1755. It incorporated three schools: law, medicine, and philosophy, employing French and Latin as the languages of instruction. But few were ready to take advantage of it; in 1785 only eighty-two were in attendance in all schools, and in 1795 the law school enrolled only one. In connection with the new university, two secondary schools (gymnasiums) were opened, one reserved for the children of the nobility and the other for non-noble children. Then, for girls only, Catherine II sponsored the opening in St. Petersburg (1764) of the Society for the Training of Daughters of the Nobility, generally known as the Smolny Institute. Non-noble girls were admitted there also, but received instruction separately from their noble schoolmates. Although the

---

[1] Peter planned the Academy, but it was not opened until a few months after his death.

number of secondary schools was growing, it was quite limited until the last years of the century; education at that level was still carried on largely by private tuition and a small number of private boarding schools.

Even though little was accomplished toward the creation of an educational system during the days of Catherine II, she gave much attention to the matter of education. That she did not achieve better results was due partly to the fact that her ideas were vague and often contradictory. On the one hand, she wanted a large system of schools in which there would be no class distinctions; on the other hand, she had no wish to tamper with the social order. Moreover, at the time when she was trying to promote an ambitious and expensive scheme of education, she was pursuing a foreign policy the implementation of which was so expensive that the state treasury could not endure any additional drain for education. The inevitable consequence was a wide gap between conception and accomplishment. Plan after plan was considered and dropped. Finally in 1786 an educational commission which had been organized by Catherine in 1782 published what was considered a definitive program for a Russian educational system. This program, prepared by the Serb Yankovich de Mirievo and modelled on that followed by Joseph II in Austria, projected an integrated system providing elementary schools in each district seat, from which pupils might continue through progressively higher schools to any one of four state universities. At the time of its publication several elementary schools, with a total enrollment of 400, were opened; and by 1796 there were 316 elementary and secondary schools with 18,000 pupils —a small number from a population of 36 million. None of the projected new universities was opened, for there proved to be a lack of both money and personnel.

As it was conceived, that over-all program was statist and, in a sense, democratic. At the time of its initiation, private schools were ordered closed; education of the laity was intended to be thereafter a state monopoly, and the new schools were to be open to all classes. But in the face of protest from many nobles, the initial concept was modified, and the reopening of boarding schools for noble children was approved.

INTELLECTUAL LIFE.   Intellectual activity in Russia during the first half of the century was led by foreigners. The Academy of Sciences, to give one example, had in its first years one Russian, two French, two Swiss, and twenty German members. However, by the midpoint of the century, there had begun to appear a solid core of Russian intellectuals with an active interest in ideas and scholarship. Yet they sought their principal inspiration not from the older culture of Russia but from that of the West. Many went as students to the universities of France and Germany and, when they returned, introduced to Russia the French and German works of philosophy, political thought, and science.

In general the product of the native intellectual effort of the century was modest and imitative, but the foundation of truly original Russian literature and scholarship was being laid. A definite evidence of the growth of interest in learning and letters was the rise in publication of books; in 1726 less than a dozen titles were published, and by 1796 the number had grown to 233. Further evidence was to be seen in the formation of several learned societies for study in specialized fields, a typical one being the Free Economic Society (organized in 1765), devoted to the study of agriculture. But the commanding position was maintained by the Academy of Sciences,[1] which, from its inception, took all knowledge as its province—whether in the field of the natural and social sciences or that of the humanities.

Interest was rising also in the accumulation and organization of knowledge about Russia, particularly in the fields of history, ethnography, and geography. The Academy of Sciences sent two major scientific expeditions to study Russia's easternmost possession, Kamchatka, and began the publication of geographical studies. Gerhard Müller, a member of the Academy, systematized a collection of historical materials and, as archivist of the Russian foreign office, organized the documents on Russian foreign relations. Vasily Tatishchev, who had served as a civil official and army officer under Peter I, began the collection of historical sources in the 1730's and wrote a pioneer history of Russia which has earned him the name of father of modern Russian historiography.

Few Russians engaged in original and significant work in the natural sciences and mathematics. But among the foreign members of the Academy of Sciences were several distinguished in those fields, outstanding among them the mathematician Leonard Euler and the Bernoulli brothers.

The most eminent Russian scientist and scholar of the century was Michael Lomonosov, a man of genius and breadth of knowledge comparable to that of the German Leibnitz. His prominence was the more striking because of the fact that he was one of the few Russians of achievement in that period to come from the lower classes. He worked in a number of fields, writing a history of Russia, composing verse, and publishing a distinguished work on Russian grammar; but he reached his greatest heights in his linguistic work and in his theoretical investigations in thermodynamics and physical

---

[1] The Russian word for science, *nauka*, means knowledge of all kinds.

Michael Lomonosov

chemistry. He postulated a series of hypotheses concerning the composition of gases, the conservation of matter and energy, and the nature of heat which anticipated the discoveries of Lavoisier, Dalton, and Joule; but since most of this work was not published, it did not reach the attention of Western European scientists until the following century.

Important as it was, the nascent work in the natural and social sciences was probably less important for the future of Russia than were the eighteenth century beginnings made in the informal cultivation of political and social thought. A small group of Russian intellectuals were coming under the influence of the works of Hobbes, Locke, Pufendorf, Grotius, and the French *philosophes.* After 1750, their thinking was reflected in a number of periodicals featuring articles on philosophy, politics, social questions, and literature; and learned gatherings in the salons of the aristocratic intellectuals became forums for their exchange of ideas. Catherine II herself corresponded with the leading French *philosophes* and helped to spread their influence in Russia. Montesquieu and Voltaire in particular had a great vogue among the upper nobility, some of whom were sincerely interested in their views, others of whom were merely following the current fad.

The study and expression of political ideas opposed to the prevailing ones were not completely new to Russia. In the past there had been those who had phrased their opposition to the conditions about them in ideological terms, and throughout the country's history there had been movements of limited protest among both the upper and the lower classes. However, those movements had generally not questioned fundamentals such as tsarism or orthodoxy but had limited themselves to seeking improvements within the existing institutions; they had sought not the abolition of tsarism but better tsars, not the rejection of orthodoxy but orthodoxy cleansed of alien elements. Pugachev, it is true, had called for the abolition of serfdom, but he had accepted the essence of tsarism—if he could be tsar.

What was new in the intellectual life of Russia was the beginning, in the latter part of the century, of a systematic, critical examination of the existing institutions. As those concerned with that examination were realizing their common interests, a new social group was in the process of gestation, the intelligentsia. (That term did not come into use in the eighteenth century, but the group in formation was later to be designated by it.) At this time it was made up of educated individuals who appraised the contemporary scene with some degree of dissatisfaction. Among them were some members of the nobility, later known as the "repentant nobles," and some of the "persons of various ranks" from the urban population. University students, who were in later years to provide the mass base for the intelligentsia, were still few.

Critical as they usually were of the life about them, most of these intellectuals were far from revolutionary in their ideas. Some, like Prince Michael Shcherbatov, were in favor of a limited monarchy which would guarantee personal rights; but the majority had less specific programs in mind. Nicholas Novikov was one of the first whose thinking and activities were of a nature specific enough to bring him to the attention of the Empress. As one of the pioneers in the development of journalism and book publishing, he founded periodicals in which the excesses of government and landowners were satirized; published the works of Voltaire, Diderot, and Rousseau; and opened bookshops which became centers of discussion. In the 1770's he became one of the leaders of the Masonic movement in Russia. Inspired by English and German examples, the Russian Free Masons aspired toward a religious humanitarianism which had little in common with either Voltairean deism or Russian Orthodoxy. The Moscow Masonic lodge, to which Novikov belonged, exercised a wide social and intellectual influence, and, under its auspices, numerous educational and humanitarian activities were undertaken. It organized in 1787 a successful drive for relief of famine victims—probably the first large-scale humanitarian effort ever made in Russia.

Catherine II saw dangerous possibilities in the activities of the Masons and, after the French Revolution, took measures to restrict them. Novikov, as a leader, was condemned without trial to fifteen years of imprisonment. But her alarm was not to be quieted by that act; her attention was soon drawn to an even more alarming trend, represented by the work of Alexander Radishchev, one of the "repentant nobles." Radishchev had written for a number of the satiric journals, but the work which brought him to the attention of the Empress was his *Journey from St. Petersburg to Moscow*, which he printed privately in 1790. In it, all too graphically, he denounced the evils of serfdom and the iniquities of landlords and bureaucrats. He left no doubt of his wish to see serfdom abolished and, by his eulogy of Cromwell for the decapitation of Charles I, made clear his abhorrence of absolute monarchy. When a copy of the book reached Catherine, she denounced its author as a "greater villain than Pugachev." She had the work burned and its author given a death sentence (later commuted to exile in Siberia). Radishchev may be considered the first of the modern Russian revolutionaries.

ARTS AND LETTERS.   With the growth of an educated leisure class, there gradually developed a demand for literature, drama, and other art forms. But the upper class generally ignored native developments in the arts and sought their spiritual and aesthetic sustenance in France, Germany, England, and Italy, importing foreign musicians, composers, architects, painters, and sculptors to meet their needs. At first, most of the Russian artists sought to follow the trend and to learn Western techniques either by study with the foreign artists in Russia or by study abroad, and Russian writers studied and imitated foreign models in fiction, poetry, and drama. By midcentury a few native Russian artists and writers were being accepted, and by the end of the century they were beginning to crowd out the foreigners. But the native products of the period were, with few exceptions, imitative; the great age of Russian art and literature was still in the future.

Among the arts, the theater and architecture were distinguished for their vitality. A constant and appreciative audience for the theater developed among the upper and middle classes, first in the two capitals[1] and later in other cities. As its entertainment demanded more and more productions, many traveling companies were formed to provide them. In 1756 Elizabeth established the first permanent theater. Usually both the plays and the manner in which they were staged and acted were patterned after those of the French classical theater. Russian acting, however, began to develop its own vigorous style, and a few playwrights tried their hand at themes which were not imitations of the French. The most original and able of the Russian playwrights was Denis Fonvizin, whose comedies of social satire were the best of the century.

The development of architecture received its greatest stimulation from the court and the nobility. St. Petersburg, under Elizabeth and Catherine II, was transformed by non-Russian architects into a beautiful city. Elizabeth employed as her chief architect the French-trained Bartolomeo Rastrelli, who designed many of the capital buildings. When Catherine came to power, she appointed different architects, and the rococo style of Rastrelli was discontinued in favor of the classicism of the Italian Giacomo Quarenghi, leading court architect and the designer of the Academy of Sciences. In contrast to the architecture of St. Petersburg, that of Moscow showed more continuity with Old Russia. There the men commissioned to plan mansions and private churches for the wealthy achieved a blend of Old Russian and Western European styles. Throughout the remainder of the country, wealthy landlords, building in stone, generally copied St. Petersburg styles; and the lesser landlords and the merchants, employing the cheaper and more plentiful wood, followed the lead of Moscow.

While the great artistic monuments of the period were the work of foreigners, realization of the need for native artists was not wanting. In 1757 Elizabeth established the Academy of Arts, dedicated to the improvement of educational facilities in the fine arts. In its first years, the graduates of the Academy were given little attention, but their successors were to become leaders in native art.

Literature, to be the crown of Russian artistic achievement in the nineteenth century, was just getting its start in the eighteenth. One of the great drawbacks was the fact that an acceptable language of literature had not

---

[1] Even after St. Petersburg became the capital, Russians retained their regard for the eminence of Moscow and spoke of the country's "two capitals" when referring to its two largest cities.

been decided upon. Church Slavonic had for centuries served as the written language (although it was about as far removed from the spoken language as Latin from Italian), but since the seventeenth century there had been an increasing disparity between Church Slavonic and the written Russian used for secular purposes. Some still argued that the language of the Church was the only appropriate one for elevated writing; others argued that to continue the use of Church Slavonic would be to make writing unintelligible to most Russians and that the vernacular should therefore be adopted. The victory went to those favoring the vernacular. By the end of the eighteenth century, literary Russian was marked by the vocabulary and forms of the spoken language of the educated, although some elements of Church Slavonic were still retained.

The slow maturation of the literary language and the excessive dependence of Russian writers upon foreign models made difficult the creation of work of lasting merit during this period. The writings of Nicholas Karamzin did more than those of any other single person to help set the standards of the new literary Russian, but little of his work in belles-lettres has borne up well. Gavrila Derzhavin was the most able poet of the time, and Lomonosov wrote some lyrics which are still appreciatively read; but no great poetry was written in Russia before the end of the Napoleonic wars.

The small, urban middle class shared a little in the new cultural development, especially in that phase devoted to the theater, the passion for which was apparently not limited to any class. Literature also reached the literate among them—that is, literature in its less sophisticated forms. Although the translations of foreign belles-lettres and the original Russian efforts in the field were read only by the small, educated upper class, there was a growing demand by merchants, government clerks, servants, and urban artisans for the humbler and more palatable literary fare provided in sentimental and romantic novels, fairy tales, biographies of Russian saints and famous criminals, old folk ballads, and dream books. (Many of the educated upper class, too, while ostensibly disdaining such "trashy" products as fit only for the servants' hall, read them privately.) This middle-class literature slowly penetrated the countryside also as the few peasants who could read passed on to the illiterate the new tales of romance, crime, and adventure and read to them the printed forms of their own old folk tales and ballads.

While Russia's main energies were employed in the wars and diplomatic maneuverings connected with the Baltic, Polish, and Eastern Questions, little attention could be spared for the French Revolution. Even if attention had not been otherwise engaged, the immediate ideological effect of the Revolution upon the Russian people would have been slight, for there were no leaders nor class in Russia for whom the revolutionary ideas had any appeal. At the time of its beginning, some of the Russian Francophiles were pleased with the turn of events, but their pleasure waned as the significance of the revolutionary activity became apparent. At court antipathy was immediate.

However, when subsequent events restored France to the rank of a great state, the balance of power was upset again; and twenty-three years of intermittent warfare were required to restore it. As a power of the first order, Russia could not avoid becoming deeply involved in the conflict. It engaged the attention of three successive rulers.

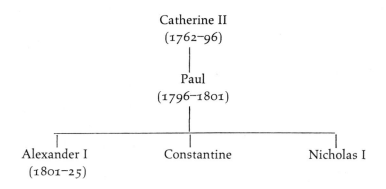

Catherine II
(1762–96)

Paul
(1796–1801)

Alexander I   Constantine   Nicholas I
(1801–25)

Russian position: 1789–1796

CATHERINE II'S INITIAL ATTITUDE.   From the first day of revolutionary disturbance in France, Catherine's abiding belief in the monarchical principle led her to give Louis XVI financial aid and to offer moral support— even to the extent of requiring that all Frenchmen residing in Russia take oaths renouncing the revolutionary government of their homeland.

She also spurred the formation of the First Coalition among anti-revolutionary governments; but when England, Austria, and Prussia had joined the lesser powers in that coalition, she felt thereby freed for what was of more immediate concern to her. She had no intention of participating in war against France until she had settled with Poland, and she felt more certain of being able to make her settlement when she was assured that Austria and Prussia would be embroiled with France. Although she piously declared that her activities in Poland were part of the common struggle against Jacobinism, she was careful to keep them under her personal direction.

GRADUAL CHANGE.   Once the third partition of Poland was completed, in 1795, Catherine was ready to turn her attention to France. By that time all of Europe was disturbed, not only by the French revolutionary ideology but also by the resurgence of French military might and aggressive ambitions. France was then, after three years of war against the First Coalition, master of The Netherlands; she had proved her strength and was still in a position to offer successful resistance to those combined against her. Catherine was concerned about this show of strength; but when Austria and England urged Russian intervention, she hesitated, for she did not feel that her country's vital interests were yet actually menaced.

In 1796 circumstances were altered. French victories had compelled one member after another of the First Coalition to make peace until only Austria and England remained. To force Austria out of the war, the French began a three-pronged attack. Two of the attacking armies fared badly; but the third, under the then little-known General Napoleon Bonaparte, defeated the Austrian armies in northern Italy and appeared to have a good chance of pushing on to Vienna. For Russia, this threat to Austria was far more important than French acquisition of The Netherlands had been. Moreover the French aim as it was revealed in 1796, to dominate the German scene, threatened Russian interests very definitely. Russia could not permit the growth of French power—whether it be the power of the monarchy or of the republic—in Central Europe. Catherine was at last ready to act. Suvorov, now a field marshal, was placed in command of 60,000 men and instructed to prepare for a march to northern Italy in support of Austria. But before

Catherine could complete her plans, she died; and the imperial power passed into the hands of her son, Paul.

Russian involvement under Paul

UNSTABLE LEADERSHIP.   The forty-two-year-old Emperor who came to the throne in 1796 had, from birth, been subject to influences which contributed to the formation of an unstable personality. One of his teachers had said of him: "Paul has an intelligent mind, in which there is a kind of machine held in check only by a thread; if the thread breaks, farewell to intelligence and reason." He was not mad in the clinical sense, but his behavior was most erratic. As for his attitude toward his mother, her friends, and her policies, it had always been one of detestation.

Paul had given much thought to foreign and domestic policies during his period of waiting for the throne. He had even sought to take part in affairs of state but had been warned off by his mother. When he finally came to the throne, he was determined to be a forceful ruler, and he had a set of policies which—to his mind, at least—were clear and coherent. That he assumed power when Russia faced a critical decision on foreign policy did not worry him; he had his plans. He was resolved not to follow in his mother's footsteps; and he declared at once that Russia would abandon her former aggressive policies abroad and seek to live in peace. But Paul was soon to find that even an autocrat might not be a free agent.

FORCED POLICY.   Catherine's plan to send Suvorov to Austria's aid was first on the order of business for the new Emperor; and, in consonance with his alleged aim to bring Russia a new era of peace, he decided not to carry it out. Yet he could not ignore the changes which were taking place in Europe. Austria, without help, was compelled in October, 1797, to agree to the Peace of Campo Formio, which made France master of Italy and strengthened her position along the Rhine. The First Coalition was at an end, and only England remained at war with France. This enhancement of French power along with the diminution of that of Austria and Prussia presaged a turn in European politics which would be highly unfavorable to Russia. Even Paul, anxious as he was for peace, realized that a powerful France, whose ambitions were apparently without limit, must be stopped. He hoped at first that this end could be accomplished by negotiation—that Russia as mediator, with the diplomatic support of Austria, Prussia, and England, could arrange for a general peace settlement whereby France would renounce some of her conquests in return for the assurance that she could keep her other conquests without anxiety about a new war. Russian diplomacy pursued this hope during 1797 and 1798, but to no avail. It became increasingly clear that France was in no mood for *quid pro quo* and that she was, moreover, planning to stir up trouble in Poland.

French activities in the eastern Mediterranean finally prodded Russia into activity. In the summer of 1798 Napoleon led a naval-military expedition eastward, aiming ultimately at the British possessions in India. En route, he captured Malta, the site of a military monastic order of which Paul considered himself protector. That act, to the quixotic mind of the Emperor, was the worst offense of the French, but their further operations in the Mediterranean area were of a kind which he could not ignore. When Napoleon, attacking Egypt in order to cut British trade routes to India, provoked war with the Sultan (the suzerain of Egypt), Russia was faced by the fact that France, whose policy had included the preservation of the balance of power in the Near East, was now on the point of disrupting that balance. The situation forced a reversal of alignments, a movement common to power politics: Russia promised the Ottoman Empire, her traditional enemy, naval support against the Sultan's traditional friend, France. And with that, the old pattern was discarded.

THE SECOND COALITION. In December, 1798, Russia and England began to form a new combination against France, the Second Coalition. Prussia, reluctant to resume fighting, did not join; but Austria was willing. Plans for offensive action were formulated and pushed forward as fast as possible. Russia's part was to provide several large forces to combine with the Austrians against the French in northern Italy and Switzerland. Field Marshal Suvorov, whom Paul had sent into retirement, was recalled at the request of Austria and England to act as commander-in-chief of the Austro-Russian armies.

In Italy, in the spring of 1799, the combined forces gained some victories. But from the beginning there was friction between Suvorov and his Austrian colleagues over military strategy. And as the campaign progressed, there was conflict over the fate of the Italian territories freed from French control. The critical disagreement came when Suvorov declared his intention of taking his armies from northern Italy and driving into France. The Austrian Emperor, Francis II, categorically forbade him to follow that plan and withdrew the Austrian contingent serving under him.

In the hope of restoring Austro-Russian amity, William Pitt suggested a new plan of attack. Suvorov was to abandon his own plan and begin a march to Switzerland, where he would relieve the main Austrian forces and the Russian troops engaging the French there. Simultaneously an Anglo-Russian expeditionary force would land in Holland and begin an offensive. Austria agreed to Pitt's plan (apparently in order to get the Russians out of Italy), and Emperor Paul also assented—over the protest of Suvorov.

The Swiss plan failed, chiefly because of Austria's actions. While Suvorov was marching north toward the mountain passes of Switzerland, the French began a diversionary offensive (in August, 1799) against the combined Austro-Russian forces already in Switzerland. Thereupon the Austrian troops were pulled out of the theater, leaving a numerically inferior Russian army to prevent the French from breaking through to reach the mountain passes. When Suvorov finally brought his troops over the passes, against the most difficult conditions of terrain, weather, and enemy opposition, he found that the Russian army in Switzerland had already been defeated. With only 15,000 men, a number dangerously inferior to that of the French, he was helpless. Under the circumstances, there was no alternative; Paul ordered him to extricate himself and march his troops back to Russia. At the same time, Paul informed Austria that Russia would give no further support to a country which, in his opinion, had acted so perfidiously.

Russia was still an ally of England, and the Anglo-Russian attack on the French in Holland had been in progress during the events in Switzerland. A Russian naval squadron had transported 12,000 soldiers to join the British; and the combined forces, under the command of the Duke of York, went into action in September, 1799. In the first engagements the Russians lost about one-fourth of their men and complained sharply that the British had not given them adequate support. By the middle of October it was necessary to end the fighting and admit that the campaign had been a failure. An armistice was signed, and the remaining English and Russian contingents were permitted to withdraw. The news of this failure helped Paul to a final decision: on October 22, he announced the Russian withdrawal from the Second Coalition.

DIPLOMATIC TURNABOUT.   During the following year Russian foreign policy veered from Francophobia to Anglophobia. The abrupt change is often attributed to the mental foibles of the Emperor, but he probably gave some consideration to certain circumstances which had changed during 1799. Napoleon had written off the Egyptian campaign as a failure and returned home, and the mood in France had become favorable to a termination of war. In November, 1799, he and his fellow conspirators had ousted the Directory and given France a new form of government, the Consulate, with Napoleon as First Consul. Meanwhile England had acquired the upper hand in the eastern Mediterranean in consequence of a victory over the French there, and she now appeared as a threat to Russian aspirations in that part of the world.

Paul's new foreign adviser, Count Feodor Rostopchin, proposed a plan for Russia's handling of the changed situation: that Russia should concentrate her attention on the partition of the Turkish Balkans, where France, he predicted, would support Russia in return for Russian support against England; and that, for general satisfaction, Austria and Prussia should receive territorial compensation—the former in the Balkans, the latter in the north of Germany. By that arrangement, England would be isolated, and a new peace settlement satisfactory to France, Austria, Prussia, and Russia would be reached. Napoleon, sensing the new direction of Russian policy, independently proposed a Franco-Russian alliance through the strength of which the two countries could take portions of the Ottoman Empire and move on to attack the British in India. He suggested also that the two powers might agree on the nature of a general European settlement. Paul gave evidence of his tentative approval of the plan and allowed negotiations to be begun. Then in January, 1801, without having reached definite agreement with Napoleon, he ordered the dispatch of about 20,000 Don Cossacks to attack British India; and in February their ill-conceived and ill-prepared march began. But when it reached Orenburg, from which it was to move to the southeast across Central Asia, it was stopped by governmental order. Paul had been assassinated.

Those who had plotted the Emperor's death were opponents of his anti-British policy, and they expected that his son and successor, Alexander, would change that policy. They were not disappointed; one of Alexander's first acts was to notify England that Russia was resuming friendly relations with her.

Alexander I and the Third Coalition

TENTATIVE PEACE. Paul's withdrawal from the Second Coalition helped to bring peace—or, at least, an interruption of war—for a short period. Austria, unable to overcome the French, agreed to a peace in

1801. Then Russia's reversal of policy suggested to Napoleon that it would be prudent to seek a cessation of hostilities with England in order to fight another day; and in 1802 France and England signed the Peace of Amiens. For a time thereafter Europe appeared to be at peace, but several potential threats to peace were in the making. The dynamism of France's foreign policy, strengthened by Napoleon's ascent to power, had not exhausted itself; and her plans still called for the domination of Central Europe and Italy and the reduction of the British naval power. Moreover Austria and Prussia could not reconcile themselves to their subordinate positions, nor could Russia for long accept the disruption of the balance of power.

FORMATION OF THE THIRD COALITION.   When France and England resumed warfare in 1803, Alexander did not bring Russia into the conflict but turned his attention to the formation of a combination to oppose Napoleon in Germany. England, of course, was eager to gain allies and in April, 1805, signed with Russia the Convention of St. Petersburg, an offensive alliance to which other powers were to be invited. This was the keystone of a new coalition against France, the third. The convention pledged each signatory to fight the war to the finish and to refuse a separate peace. Its effectiveness would depend upon the success of the original signatories in securing the adherence of Austria and Prussia and the minor powers, for their plans called for a combined allied military force of 500,000 exclusive of the British contingents. But the Third Coalition never reached the goals of its architects. Of the minor powers, only Sweden could see any profit in joining; and Prussia, weakened and exposed to French attack, was not disposed to excessive risk. Austria was likewise hesitant to encourage new hostilities, but could not afford to stand apart.

AUSTERLITZ.   When, in the latter part of 1805, the allies began their operations against France, the forces they had been able to raise were far smaller than they had planned. Napoleon, on the other hand, was able to put many more men into the field than had been expected, and prospects on the continent were in his favor. Yet the continental fighting brought one advantage to the British: the French army then being collected on the French coast in preparation for an invasion of England had to be recalled to meet an Austrian army in Bavaria in October, 1805; and in the same month, the English were able to defeat the French fleet at Trafalgar. But on the continent Napoleon gained and kept the upper hand. In December, meeting a combined Russo-Austrian army at Austerlitz, in Moravia, he won one of his most notable victories and turned the opposing forces back with heavy losses. Immediately thereafter Austria signed peace with

France. Alexander, although he refused to end hostilities, agreed to an armistice whereby the Russian army was permitted to withdraw peacefully from Bohemia.

JENA. The period after Austerlitz was another one of diplomatic and military maneuvering. Alexander wanted to resume the struggle with France, but finding sufficient military support on the continent was a difficult undertaking just then. Prussia wavered between opposition to Napoleonic policies in Germany and fear of a new Napoleonic attack, and Russian relations with England were becoming strained because of the continued highhanded British policy toward foreign shipping and British opposition to Russian aims in the Near East. So, rather than fight alone, Alexander authorized secret negotiations with France for a separate peace. Napoleon agreed to a treaty committing France to evacuate Germany, but he soon showed that he had no intention of living up to such a commitment. Alexander therefore announced that he would not sign the proposed treaty. Prussia also recognized the new threat to Germany, and she now entered the war, only to suffer a smashing defeat at Jena in October, 1806, and then to lose Berlin to the French. Napoleon did not follow up his victories over Prussia, however, for he saw a better target. The Prussian defeat at Jena had left the Russian armies, which were grouped east of Warsaw, in an exposed position; and he realized the possibility of directing a sweeping offensive against them, forcing them out of the war, gaining a free hand in Germany and then concentrating all his military energy on the effort against England.

FRIEDLAND. To implement his plans Napoleon persuaded the Sultan to make an attack on the Russian flank, an attack which opened a long war but aided him very little. He counted, too, on raising the Poles on his side and recruiting from among them additions to his main armies advancing across Poland against Russia; but he failed in that effort. Decisive fighting began early in 1807. The Russians, aided by small Prussian units, bled the French armies but could not halt them. The climax came at Friedland, in East Prussia. There, in June, the French won an expensive victory over the badly led and numerically inferior Russian forces, which then retreated across the Neman River and took a stand near Tilsit.

CHANGING ATTITUDES. Both Alexander and Napoleon had been rethinking their policies before the Battle of Friedland, and that engagement apparently brought them to the point of change. The Russian troops were exhausted and their generals wanted at least an armistice. Napoleon had won battles but had not gained his major aim, a decisive victory over

Russia. He was still not on Russian soil; and Russia still had her armies, which were closer to their base of men and supplies than the French to theirs. Since he could not defeat Russia, Napoleon felt that he might, by supporting Russian aims in the Balkans, interest Alexander (as he had interested Paul) in joint action against England. And Alexander was amenable, for he had come to believe that the defeat of Napoleon was improbable and that Russia should make what profit she could from the circumstances.

Period of strained alliance with France

TREATY OF TILSIT.   Within two weeks after the Battle of Friedland, Alexander and Napoleon began their negotiations. The Russian forces had remained on the eastern bank of the Neman, facing Tilsit on the western bank, the location of the French. For protocol's sake it was decided that Alexander and Napoleon should meet at the midpoint of the river, and on June 25, 1807, they began their talks aboard a raft constructed for the purpose. There they reached an agreement on fundamentals and began the framing of a treaty of peace and alliance. On July 7 they signed the Treaty of Tilsit, an action which gave Prussia heart to sign a treaty of peace with France two days later.

At Tilsit, Alexander accepted the territorial and political changes which Napoleon had imposed upon Europe and agreed that those portions of Poland taken by Prussia in the partitions should be formed into the independent Duchy of Warsaw, with the King of Saxony as its sovereign. At the same time, a secret treaty was signed whereby Russia agreed to aid France against England if the latter would not make peace, and France agreed to aid Russia in her Turkish troubles. For Russia the crux of the secret treaty was the part concerning the Ottoman Empire: Russia was to offer peace; and if the conditions offered were refused, France and Russia would agree on the means to be used in "liberating" from the Turks all of the Empire's European territory except Constantinople and Rumelia (the southern half of present-day Bulgaria). In less mellifluent words, the agreement meant that Napoleon would look favorably on Russian territorial expansion in the Balkans at the expense of his recent ally, the Sultan, but would not agree to Rusian acquisition of Constantinople and the adjacent territories—a prize too valuable to be given away lightly.

The peace of Tilsit was badly received in St. Petersburg. Napoleon was held in contempt by the court nobility, whose doors had been opened to the Bourbon émigrés, and they disapproved of Napoleonic France as heartily as they had disapproved of revolutionary France. The general opinion in Russia was that Europe could not return to normalcy until Napoleon were defeated and dethroned and the Bourbons were once more in Paris. On the other hand, England was popular there despite her many annoying policies, for she was Russia's best customer in foreign trade.

Alexander seemed to be repeating the mistakes of Paul. Yet from the point of view of the political morality which guided European foreign policy, as well as from other points of view, the new course could be defended. Russia needed peace. Her internal economic situation was grievous, her armies were weakened, and no other continental power was able or willing to join her in the struggle. Until 1807 she had fought France on foreign soil, but the French were now on the border of the Russian Empire. It seemed that peace with France might bring relief from a positive threat and provide hope for expansion in the Balkans. Yet strong as the argument for peace was, the alliance against England did not seem entirely defensible. The grievances against England were minor in comparison with the importance of that country's trade and her potential aid against France (to be expected surely to upset the status quo again).

Undoubtedly both Alexander and Napoleon, in true diplomatic tradition, entered the alliance with their fingers crossed. Certainly Napoleon was little disposed actually to give Russia a free hand in the Balkans, for the eastern Mediterranean figured prominently in his schemes of empire. If Russia were to be given any concessions in the Balkans, he would want in return substantial aid against Britain. But Alexander, while sincere in his antipathy toward England, was far more interested in the Near East than in a major military effort against England. There were also other loci of conflicting aims: Germany and the new Duchy of Warsaw, where Alexander would oppose the strengthening of the French position and Napoleon would assuredly promote it. There was, in fact, little community of interest other than in the cessation of mutual hostilities.

FIRST TEST OF TILSIT.   Despite the plans laid at Tilsit to end the Turkish conflict, it continued. Russia's Near Eastern ambitions were now pressed hard by Count Nicholas Rumyantsev, Alexander's Minister of Foreign Affairs and one of the few at court who approved of the Tilsit policy. Russia called for French support, but France was reluctant to help, knowing the Russian ambitions—which soon came to include Constantinople and the Straits. The war moved slowly because Russia could not afford at that time to put all her forces into it; some were engaged in a conflict with Sweden and others were required as a reserve against a possible act of unfriendliness by France. So it was not until 1811, when Alexander felt that another war with France was near, that the Russo-Turkish hostilities were brought to an end. As the price of peace, the Sultan agreed to the Treaty of Bucharest in May, 1812, ceding Bessarabia to Russia.

CONFLICT WITH BRITAIN. Meanwhile, England's quick reaction to Tilsit had been to take the offensive in the Baltic in order to prevent the formation of a bloc of Baltic powers under Russian auspices. As a means of compelling Denmark to abandon any idea of joining such a bloc, the British fleet was sent to attack Copenhagen in September, 1807; and some British warships were sent on into the Baltic as a demonstration against Russia. But Russia was not impressed in the expected manner; in November, St. Petersburg broke diplomatic relations with London. The two countries were soon involved in a war which was not to be concluded until 1812. As far as actual fighting was concerned, it was a rather tame war, generally confined to minor British naval attacks on Russian shipping. Commercially it was more significant; it impelled Russia to join Napoleon's Continental System, aimed at excluding British goods from the continent. And that act brought losses rather than gain to Russia, for it cut her off from the supply of many raw and manufactured products and ended the income hitherto gained from exports to England.

WAR WITH SWEDEN. England's attitude made Russia more conscious of the importance of Sweden, at the time allied to England; and diplomatic energies were turned toward forcing that country to break with the British. When diplomacy proved fruitless, Russia declared war on Sweden in February, 1808, and soon thereafter opened fighting in Finland. Coercing Sweden proved a longer and more difficult undertaking than had been anticipated, for the Swedish troops, aided by Finnish guerillas, fought well. Since Alexander regarded the war as a major effort and since Napoleon had not objected to it, increasing numbers of Russian troops were dispatched to Finland until Sweden was compelled to ask for peace. In September, 1809, the Treaty of Friedrichsham brought the war to an end, with the Swedish cession of Finland and the Aland Islands.

FRANCO-RUSSIAN ESTRANGEMENT. Although the French alliance had indirectly enabled Russia to obtain Finland, French policies elsewhere were straining the tenuous amity between the two countries. In the Near East, France was proving more of a hindrance than an aid. Her Continental System, to which Russia was committed, was not only costly but also trouble-making for the Russian government, now being beset by complaints of the landowners who were feeling the effect of the decline in foreign trade. Moreover, Napoleon, although engaged in a difficult war in Spain, was strengthening his control over Austria, Prussia, and the Duchy of Warsaw.

In 1809 a more immediate strain was put upon the Franco-Russian relations as a result of the renewal of hostilities between Austria and France. Napoleon asked Russian support against Austria, but since such support would have been contrary to Russia's basic interests, it was not given. Nevertheless, Austria was defeated and, in October, 1809, agreed to peace terms which included the cession of Galicia and its incorporation into the Duchy of Warsaw. Alexander saw in that arrangement, despite Napoleon's protestations to the contrary, a preliminary to the restoration of the kingdom of Poland under the French aegis. His anxiety was not illusory; France had been giving encouragement in one form or another to Polish nationalist hopes since 1795.

By the end of 1809 both Alexander and Napoleon were beginning to believe that resolution of the issues between their countries could be brought about only through war. Neither country could afford the luxury of a new war at that time; yet neither could afford to make concessions which might prove fatal if war should come. For the next two years, both followed policies which made war inevitable.

To strengthen his Continental System, Napoleon extended his control in northeastern Europe, breaking promises made at Tilsit; and in 1810 Alexander began in effect to abandon the ruinous Continental System, opening Russian ports first to hitherto prohibited neutral goods and, in the next year, to British goods. In the Duchy of Warsaw both competed for the support of the Polish nationalists; there France gained the advantage. By 1811 the imminence of war was so evident that military preparations were begun on both sides. Alexander secretly assembled troops on the border of the Duchy, while Napoleon began secretly to round up troops throughout the empire and from among his cowed German allies. The secrets were badly kept, and each soon became aware of the other's troop movements.

As things stood, Alexander would have been willing to take the offensive if he could have been certain of support from the Poles, but reports on Polish sentiment were unfavorable. Anyway, he was beginning to accept the view of many of his generals that, since Napoleon could count on superiority of numbers, Russia's initial strategy should be based upon planned retreat before the French in order to wear them out. The initiative, therefore, lay with Napoleon; and it appears that by August, 1811, he had definitely decided to attack. Unable to defeat England, unable to crush the revolution in Spain, and threatened by conflict with Russia, he chose to resolve his difficulties by concentrating his forces for a quick victory over Russia; once this was done, he could force Alexander into a new alliance with France or make Russian military might ineffective by erecting a new kingdom of Poland as a buffer state on her border; then he could turn on England.

By the spring of 1812 the French forces, numbering 600,000 of the Grand Army—including 30,000 sent from Austria, 20,000 from Prussia, and thousands more squeezed out of the former German states—were ready on the western side of the Neman. On paper the odds were in Napoleon's favor. However, many of his allies were far from dependable. Prussia would have been prepared to fight on the Russian side if the French forces had not been so threateningly close; and Austria had secretly avowed that her heart belonged to Russia. Also to his disadvantage, Napoleon had failed to recruit the Ottoman Empire and Sweden for his coalition. The Ottoman Empire was too weak to fight; and Sweden, already opposed to French policy, had the Russian offer of support in gaining Norway to balance against Napoleon's offer of Finland, a less valuable and more costly prize. Still another advantage came to Russia when she and England ended their drawn-out war at a time when all forces were needed against France.

Napoleon's invasion of Russia

THE OPPOSING FORCES.   In June, 1812, Napoleon led about 500,000 men of the Grand Army across the Neman River into Russian territory, having left about 100,000 on the border as reinforcements. Opposing them were the Russian forces of about 200,000, grouped in three armies—two facing the invaders and the third held in reserve. One of the front armies, under General Prince Michael Barclay de Tolly, was based at Vilna. The second, led by General Prince Peter Bagration, one of Suvorov's former aides, faced the French in southern Lithuania. Napoleon's strategy was to attack and destroy the armies separately. The Russians had no clear plan of action; although Alexander had shown favor for the policy of planned retreat, that policy had not been made the basis of any consistent strategy. The Russian military moves during the first months, retreat and avoidance of pitched battle, were tactical rather than strategic.

The French army was not as formidable as its size indicated. Napoleon's plan to move this vast aggregate at a speed necessary to cut off the Russian retreat required cohesion and high morale, but neither was possible. Little more than half of the men were French, and they were of a much lower caliber than those under Napoleon's earlier command. The motley character of the soldiers, inadequate services of supply, lack of medical care, and the strangeness and hostility of the countryside in which they were operating—all made for poor morale. The supply of so large an army was a particularly difficult problem. Its base of supplies, Danzig, was too distant; and it was unable to live off the country as French forces had so often done in the past. To its weaknesses must be added also the fact that Napoleon was losing the sure touch which had once so consistently given him victory.

THE RUSSIAN RETREAT.   The Russian leaders' hastily improvised manner of retreat drew the French army rapidly away from its base of supplies and brought it into immediate trouble. The loss of horses, due to a lack of provender, was soon hampering the cavalry and artillery, while the infantry was being cut down by demoralization and desertion. Badly supplied and poorly disciplined, many men were separated from their units and fell prey to disease or attack by civilians.

At first the populaton of Russian Lithuania and White Russia were not hostile to the invaders. In some sections serfs rebelled against their masters in the hope that the French would support them, but Napoleon apparently had no intention of promoting class warfare. Soon the looting and pillage by the French troops lost for them whatever sympathy there may have been among the peasants. Then, as they approached Smolensk, they found themselves in regions populated by Orthodox Great Russians, who were more responsive to the appeals of Alexander than had been the Lithuanians, White Russians, and Poles of the areas over which they had passed. There the patriotic feelings of the peasants finally led them to follow the call of the government to harass the invaders and to "scorch the earth" in order to prevent supplies from falling into their hands. There is still dispute over the intensity of their patriotic response, but there is no doubt that they did contribute to the defeat of the French. At least, their effort was effective enough to cause Napoleon to rant against what appeared to him unorthodox methods of warfare.

Along the route of the main military operations—from Vilna through Smolensk to Moscow—Barclay de Tolly retreated more rapidly than the French advanced. Bagration, despite French attempts at interception, managed to join his forces to those of Barclay de Tolly at Smolensk and there, in August, they made a determined but unsuccessful effort to stop the French. When Barclay de Tolly decided on further retreat, Bagration unwillingly agreed to it.

The continued retreat alarmed the court circles in St. Petersburg. There had been no major fighting inside Russia since Poltava, but now the road to Moscow was open and Napoleon the Mighty was on that road. The court distrusted the Fabian tactics of Barclay de Tolly and approved the ideas of Bagration, who felt that the Russians should stand and offer resistance. Alexander, acceding to court pressure, finally turned over the command to Field Marshal Michael Kutuzov, although he had a great personal distaste for the man. Kutuzov had a brilliant reputation, and it was generally felt that he alone could stop Napoleon.

BORODINO.   Kutuzov, like Barclay de Tolly, believed in Fabian tactics; but since the condition of his appointment was that he prevent Napoleon from reaching Moscow, he regrouped the Russian forces and prepared to resist at a point seventy miles west of Moscow, near the village of Borodino. The main encounter there, which took place on September 7, was a tactical victory for the French, who gained most of the contested objectives. But it was a costly victory; they lost about 30,000 men (49 of whom were generals) of the 130,000 thrown into the battle, while the Russians lost 35,000 (among them, Bagration) of their complement of 120,000. Although Borodino was lost, the Russian army was still strong enough to continue fighting.

After the defeat, Kutuzov's generals were divided between retreat and further resistance, but he decided in favor of retreat—which meant the abandonment of Moscow. "The loss of Moscow," he declared, "does not mean the loss of Russia." Following his plan, the Russian army marched through and beyond Moscow, took up new positions, and waited. The civilian population of Moscow, about 240,000 were ordered to evacuate the city, and all but a few thousand obeyed the order. A virtually empty city waited for Napoleon.

MOSCOW.   Early in the campaign Napoleon had declared that he would not go beyond Smolensk, that if he had not defeated the Russians before Smolensk, he would organize the conquered territory during the winter of 1812-13 and wait for a later opportunity to go on. However, his anxiety for a decisive victory pulled him beyond Smolensk—to Borodino and then to Moscow. When he entered Moscow, in September, 1812, his army was broken in force and depleted in number, the main part, with him, numbering only 103,000. Yet he tried to persuade himself that the loss of Moscow would compel Alexander to agree to peace. Even when his peace proposals were ignored, he held to his belief and waited in Moscow for five weeks.

On the first night of the French stay, Moscow began to burn. The origin of the fire has never been established beyond doubt, but the general conviction is that it was accidental in origin. Since the Moscow fire deparment had been evacuated and there was no means of checking the conflagration, it continued for over a week, destroying about three-fourths of the city's wooden buildings and adding to the demoralization of the French troops.

While Napoleon stayed in Moscow, the Russians undertook no major military actions but contented themselves with harassing that part of the French forces which remained between Moscow and the border. They were able to do that quite effectively with the regular Russian units released for action in 1812 at the end of the Turkish war, with Cossack detachments, and with small groups of hastily organized peasant militia. Still Napoleon waited, hoping that Alexander would come to terms and apparently little concerned over the prospect of winter. It was an unusually mild autumn, and he remarked that travelers were liars, that Russian weather was not bad at all; in fact, it was more pleasant than that of Fontainebleau. Finally, at the end of five weeks, he was convinced that Alexander would not give in and that he might as well retreat. His plan was to establish winter headquarters in a more secure place to the west—perhaps Smolensk or Vitebsk—and, if possible, to leave troops to hold the conquered regions.

THE FRENCH RETREAT.   In October the retreat from Moscow began. The line of march was to be first to the south—to Kaluga and perhaps to Tula, and then west. There were seemingly sound reasons for the choice of that route: (1) there were good stores at Kaluga and supplies at Tula: (2) winter quarters could be established at Kaluga if necessary; and (3) it was hoped that Kutuzov would follow and thus be drawn away from his position, which, in Napoleon's estimation, was too threateningly close to Smolensk.

It soon became apparent that the movement could not be carried out as planned. Kutuzov cut off the line of march to the south, and the French were compelled to retreat along the line of their previous advance: the devastated route from Moscow to Smolensk to Vilna. To add to their difficulties, Kutuzov's forces, marching at a safe distance parallel to their line, made repeated darting forays upon them whenever there was a chance to destroy a unit or seize supplies. Actually it was a rout rather than a retreat, but Napolean still believed in his star and hoped that he could establish his winter headquarters either in Smolensk or in Vitebsk. He expected to find fresh troops and supplies at Smolensk; but when he arrived there, late in October, he was disappointed. So, with the 42,000 men now remaining from those who had left Moscow with him, he continued the retreat, the situation growing more desperate with every mile. Cold weather set in, and his forces faced the inexorable maneuvers of General Winter in addition to the continuing flank attacks by the Russians. He continued to hope that he would find new troops or stores at each succeeding stop, but he found only repeated disappointment. Finally, he decided to give the army into the command of Joachim Murat and to hurry on to Paris in order to raise new levies and, at the same time, to deal with some pressing domestic problems which had arisen. Early in December, he set out, leaving Murat with orders to hold the remaining forces at Vilna until help could be sent. But Murat, finding Vilna untenable, was forced to lead the remnant of the army out of Russian territory to the western bank of the Neman, where he joined the reinforcements left there by Napoleon at the beginning of the invasion.

The War of Liberation

NEW PLAN.   Kutuzov established new headquarters at Vilna and waited. He and many others argued that, in view of the losses already sustained, Russia should not carry the fight beyond the Neman but should take steps to dissociate herself from Western European affairs. However, Alexander and his adherents wished to continue the war until the French were defeated; and, needless to say, Alexander made the decision—to fight on. In January, 1813, the Russian army crossed the Neman into the Duchy of Warsaw.

NEW COALITION.   By that act, Russia became the moving force of a new coalition. Austria and Prussia, though nominally still allies of France, now began to feel that support of Russia could lead to a victory over Napoleon. The first gesture in the direction of support was made by the Prussian General Count Johann Yorck von Wartenburg, commander of the Prussian troops that had been pledged to protect the flank of the French army. On his own decision, he suspended hostilities against the Russians, thus allowing them greater freedom of movement.

Under Russian attack, Murat's forces retreated rapidly across the Duchy, and the Russians followed to the borders of Prussia. On February 28, Frederick William III finally agreed to a treaty of alliance with Russia against Napoleon, and his forces were linked with the Russians in the continuing offensive. On March 4, after a successful thrust against the French holding Berlin, the allied troops entered that city. Encouraged by the turn of events, Austria began to change her position; and, in June, she became a member of the new coalition. England, likewise impressed by the prospects, promised subsidies and arms to the allies. Napoleon's control over Central Europe was breaking, and Alexander of Russia now seemed to be the inspired leader of a crusade against him.

DEFEAT OF NAPOLEON. Napoleon, having hastily assembled new forces, faced a formidable coalition in the latter part of 1813. Large-scale fighting in Saxony re-emphasized a fact which had been evident for some time: that the spark of Napoleon's military genius was dimming, that he could no longer turn the impossible into the actual. In October he was defeated by superior numbers at Leipzig and was compelled to order a disastrous retreat, which ended on March 31, 1814, with the triumphal entry of the allied troops into Paris.

Now, unquestionably, Alexander dominated the scene; for, although the defeat of Napoleon had been the work of many nations, it had been his decision which had started the final rout of the French emperor, and it had been he who had led in the formation of the victorious coalition.

Adjustment to peace: 1814-1815

ALEXANDER'S POLICY. No sooner had the battles of war ended than the conflicts of peace-making began. The formulation of peace settlements was dominated by the four major powers: Russia, Austria, Prussia, and England; and, among them, Russia's influence was at a higher point than it had ever been.

To determine the Russian policy in the period of adjustment to peace it is necessary to analyze the deeds of Alexander and to disregard many of his words. By 1815 he had succumbed to a mood of religious mysticism and had begun to speak of ordering affairs of Europe on the basis of justice and morality. He considered himself an inspired man who had received a call from on high. To one of his aides, he declared: "When God gave power and success to my arms, He wished me to secure the peace of the world." But most of his actions showed little sign of his pious sentiments, and an examination of his mysticism would provide few clues to Russian foreign policy in 1814-15.

It has been widely believed that the Russian policy of this period was Alexander's personal policy and that his opinions were at variance with those of his court on fundamental issues. Often he did ignore the majority opinion of his upper nobility; but he did not stray far from the line followed by his grandmother in trying to make Russia an arbiter in European affairs, nor did he forget the traditional Russian interests in Poland, the Near East, and the Baltic. With Finland and Bessarabia already in Russian hands, his immediate territorial interest was fixed on Poland. With respect to the larger question of restoring the balance of power in Europe, he felt it necessary to make certain that France be neither strong enough to endanger the peace nor weak enough to be dominated by other powers. He believed that, to assure such a situation, Napoleon should be removed from the throne and a stable French government should be established—necessarily a constitutional monarchy, since the French people would not endure the return of absolutism.

THE PEACE.   The four powers dealt first with the problem of France. On May 31, 1814, they signed with Louis XVIII, the new Bourbon king, the First Treaty of Paris, by which France was required neither to pay indemnities nor to give up any territory held by her before the war. The mildness of the treaty was in accord with Alexander's aims, as was also Louis' immediate granting of a constitutional charter to his people.

One of the most involved problems facing the peacemakers was that concerning the future of the Duchy of Warsaw. The King of Saxony, the sovereign of the Duchy, had been very loyal to Napoleon; and all agreed that he should be severely punished; certainly, that he should lose the Duchy. The problem was what to do with that territory. Alexander had promised Austria and Prussia that he would support the dissolution of the Duchy and the return to them of those portions which they had held before the Napoleonic wars—that is, the restoration of the boundaries of 1795. But he now faced a conflict of his own making; he had given support to Polish nationalist hopes on the eve of 1812 in order to counter Napoleon's appeals to those hopes, and to maintain that support would be to withdraw that which he had promised to Austria and Prussia. He resolved the conflict, in 1814, by disregarding his promises to those countries and proposing the project of transforming the Duchy into a new Kingdom of Poland with himself as king. To compensate for that, he proposed that Prussia take Saxony and that Austria choose her compensation elsewhere. Frederick

DRAWN BY EDW. A. SCHMITZ

MAP 8. *European Russia in 1815*

William III, who played second fiddle to Alexander, was amenable. But Metternich, Austria's foreign minister, was apoplectic at a proposal the fulfillment of which would bring powerful Russia even deeper into Europe. England was equally outraged. Her foreign secretary, Castlereagh, slyly suggested the complete restoration of Polish independence, an idea alien to Alexander's mind. The matter caused a threatening rift among the powers—Austria and England on one side, Russia and Prussia on the other; and tempers ran so high that on one occasion Alexander challenged Metternich to a duel. With troops in the Duchy and in Saxony, Alexander could afford to exercise his natural stubbornness.

When the Congress of Vienna met, in September, 1814, to settle the territorial and political questions left by the destruction of the Napoleonic Empire, the disposition of the Duchy was still undecided. And it continued to be a subject of concern until May, 1815. Then Alexander agreed to the terms of a minor compromise: that Danzig and the province of Posen be returned to Prussia, that Galicia be returned to Austria, and that the remainder of the Duchy become the Kingdom of Poland, ruled by Alexander and his heirs under a liberal constitution. These terms were embodied in the final act of the Congress of Vienna on June 8, 1815. It should be understood that the lands which Russia had previously acquired by the partitions of Poland were not to be part of the new kingdom but remained an integral part of the Russian Empire. The new Kingdom of Poland, with a population of 3 million, came to be known as "Congress Poland" because it was created at the Congress of Vienna.

The signature of that final act of the Congress was hastened by the news of the defeat of Napoleon at Waterloo, after his attempt to regain the throne of France. And the same incident served to frighten the powers into an attitude of harshness toward France. Prussia now favored the adoption of strong measures; but Russia and England, with an eye on the balance of power, were more temperate. In the end, they made a compromise by which Napoleon was exiled to distant St. Helena; and Louis XVIII was compelled to sign the Second Treaty of Paris, by which France suffered minor loss of territory and was required to pay an indemnity and to allow occupation of parts of her territory for five years. In addition, the four powers signed a treaty of friendship and alliance (November 20, 1815) which bound them to concerted action in the event of a renewal of French aggression or the return of a Bonaparte to the throne of France and which pledged them to meet periodically to consider problems affecting the peace. That treaty became the basis of the Quadruple Alliance, the members of which were pledged to

preserve all the territorial and political provisions agreed upon at Vienna.
THE HOLY ALLIANCE. In the course of his toying with mystic religious
concepts of his duties, Alexander met, in June, 1815, the Baroness Julie de
Krüdener, who was a devotee of a then fashionable variety of mystic pietism.
He found in her doctrines support of his own somewhat amorphous beliefs;
and, during later meetings with her and her friends and disciples, he formulated the ideas which were later embodied in the Holy Alliance.

He initiated that organization by persuading the Austrian and Prussian
rulers to join him in signing, in September, 1815, a declaration by which
they were bound in "holy alliance" to govern their realms and to deal with
one another in the spirit of the basic Christian principles of justice, peace,
and charity. The other monarchs of Europe were invited to join them and,
with few exceptions, they did. But the Holy Alliance never gained the respect
of the professional politicians of the period. On the whole, they regarded it
with distrust or contempt. Castlereagh called it "sublime mysticism and
nonsense." Metternich saw it as a smokescreen for Alexander's aggressive
schemes. Actually it committed its members to nothing but platitudes, and it
proved to be of little influence in the subsequent conduct of either the foreign
or the domestic affairs of any country.

PART 3

Bureaucratic Russia

CHRONOLOGICAL OVERVIEW

Rulers

1796-1801 Paul

1801-1825 Alexander I

1825-1855 Nicholas I

Chief Events

1797 Law on Primogeniture

1802 Creation of ministries

1809 Constitutional project of Speransky

1810 Establishment of the State Council

1816 Beginning of the military colonies
Organization of the Union of Welfare

1819 Opening of the University of St. Petersburg

1820 "Mutiny" of Semenovsky Guards Regiment
Troppau Protocol

1825 Decembrist Revolt

1826 Creation of the Third Section of the Imperial Chancellery

1829 Treaty of Adrianople

1830-1831 Polish Revolt

1833 Publication of revised Code of Laws
Münchengrätz and Berlin agreements

1837 Creation of Ministry of State Domains

1841 Straits Convention

1855-1856 Crimean War

1856 Treaty of Paris

During the period of the Napoleonic Wars and in the decade following them, Russia began to show signs of internal strain; the system of society and government bequeathed by Catherine II was beginning to lose its equipoise. Basic to the growing imbalance was the continuing peasant unrest, now becoming so extended that the institution of serfdom itself was being questioned. Another contributing factor was the evident inefficiency of administration, in the attempted correction of which the emperors unwittingly increased the imbalance. They tended to make changes in the organization of government which emphasized the role of professional bureaucrats at the expense of the nobility. That situation brought to the nobles a dim awareness that things were amiss, and a small minority of them began to realize the need for fundamental change in the country. Before long, wider attention was to be focused on the emerging question: could the existing system of society and government be maintained indefinitely without fundamental change?

Period of regression: 1796-1801

SAFEGUARDS FOR THE STATE.   Despite Paul's febrile desire to undo what his mother had done, to degrade those whom she had honored, and to honor those whom she had ignored, he did not stray as far from the traditions of the Russian throne as some of his more extreme acts might suggest. He set Novikov and Radishchev free, but that act did not indicate his approval of their ideas; he was simply undoing something that Catherine had done. At the same time, he continued her policy of keeping Russia safe from foreign revolutionary or liberal contacts. He prohibited the private publication of books, increased the stringency of censorship, decreed the prohibition of importations of foreign books and music, and recalled Russian students from foreign universities. Those and other measures indicated that he was just as zealous in maintaining the safeguards of the state as his predecessors had been.

SAFEGUARDS FOR AUTOCRACY. While attempting to forestall the dangers from outside, Paul did not neglect those he observed within the country. During the years of his exclusion from state affairs, he had reflected on the history of the Russian throne since the death of Peter I and had come to the conclusion that the many palace revolutions had been made possible by Peter's law on the succession, that the law had made the death of a monarch an invitation to intrigue. He had seen how the uncertainty of the succession had given the nobility repeated occasion for their maneuvering to gain increasing independence and how they had been able to use the guards regiments as instruments of their turbulence. Therefore, when he came to the throne, he was determined to make changes which would discourage intrigue and insure a more stable and powerful autocracy.

On the day of his coronation, April 16, 1797, he published a law establishing the principle that the crown should descend in the direct male line, thus ending for all time, he thought, the uncertainty over the succession. He followed that by rescinding many of the rights and privileges of the nobility, among them the right to corporative organization and freedom from corporal punishment, which had been granted them by the charter of 1785. And, as a final safeguard, he withdrew from the guards regiments the privileges and preferential treatment which had bolstered their power. Those changes were the first evidences of his plan, consistent but unrealizable, to insure the throne against threat or limitation by any class or group.

FEEBLE AGRARIAN REFORM. The Emperor was not an enemy of the nobility as such, but he was opposed to their holding any independent political power. He was willing to accept them, stripped of such power, as the solid base of the social and political structure, the state's unpaid policemen who performed the important service of keeping the peasantry under control. To weaken their power of control, he believed, would open the gates to anarchy.

Yet the problem of how to retain the nobles' control and at the same time preserve tranquillity among the peasants was one which neither he nor his two successors could solve. He soon found that the abuses of control were so great and the peasant unrest so widespread that the police power of the nobles was often inadequate; in the first year of his reign, he was forced to deal with scattered peasant revolts in thirty-two provinces. The revolts were suppressed before they could coalesce into a general uprising like the Pugachev rebellion, but they were sufficiently threatening to cause the Emperor to attempt some correction. He asked the nobles to refrain from compelling their serfs to work on Sundays or to work more than three days a week in the landlords' fields. But, since that was a request rather than an order, it had little effect on those nobles who were accustomed to exacting excessive work from their serfs; and Paul did not dare to coerce them.

UNFAVORABLE BALANCE. The general opprobrium in which Paul is held often leads to neglect of his constructive acts. Yet his five-year reign did account for some positive contributions: new canals were constructed; the country's tariff policy was liberalized for the encouragement of foreign trade; industrial activities were increased after the discovery of coal in the Donets River basin; improvements were made in ship construction; and changes were introduced to improve the army. Whatever the Emperor may have deserved for those things, however, was disregarded in the wave of hatred inspired by his personal conduct, which became increasingly unbearable after 1798.

In the army, he made enemies by his introduction of the uncomfortable and hated Prussian uniform and Prussian training methods. The Prussian drill, with its emphasis on mechanical perfection in parade ground formations, was made obligatory. "The soldier," said Paul, "is simply a machine, stipulated by regulations." A military review before the Emperor became a time of judgment. If, at inspection, a soldier were missing a button on his gaiters or if his pigtail were inadequately powdered, the Emperor would order him flogged. Rank was no assurance of safety from his caprices, nor could one depend either upon his favor or his disfavor. A mistake by an officer at a review might bring him a period of exile in Siberia, and a bright answer to an imperial question might be rewarded by a grant of a thousand state peasants.

No one was free from his autocratic direction. St. Petersburg was put under curfew after nine in the evening. Everywhere his subjects were required to kneel when the imperial carriage passed. By his multiplied restrictions, rules, and cruelties, he created about himself a mood of uncertainty and terror. It was felt most keenly by the privileged nobility, who were often forced to endure at his hands the same kind of treatment they were accustomed to give their serfs.

CRISIS OF RESENTMENT. Paul's ill-concealed suspicions of conspiracy among the nobles led eventually to the creation of conspiracies. In 1798,

high officials at court, led by Count Pahlen, military governor of St. Petersburg, began to plan a coup by which they hoped to compel Paul to renounce
the throne in favor of Alexander. For more than two years, the absence of
opportunity and the frequent exile of key figures in the conspiracy prevented
its execution. Finally, as has been noted, Paul's turnabout in foreign policy
in 1800, coinciding as it did with the increase in his irrational brutality,
brought the conspirators to a state of desperate urgency. They asked Alexander to join them, and he did so after learning that Paul was planning to
have the Grand Duchess Catherine marry Prince Eugene of Wurtemberg
and to name the latter as successor to the throne.

On March 23, 1801, Paul, having an inkling of the plot, ordered his two
sons, Alexander and Constantine, placed under arrest in their rooms; and
the conspirators decided to act on the evening of that day. Chosen members
of their group went to the imperial residence and demanded of Paul that
he surrender the throne. According to their report, he agreed to abdicate,
but in the course of an ensuing quarrel (probably deliberately provoked
by them) he was strangled. The court and the country at large waited ex-
pectantly to see what changes would be effected by their new ruler, Alexander.

Period of quasi-liberalism: 1801-1812

ALEXANDER'S PERSONAL QUALITIES.   Alexander has been called the
last of the enlightened despots; and, if formal education could produce an
enlightened despot, he should have been a superior one. Until he was
eighteen years of age he had been tutored by Frederick La Harpe, a republican
Swiss imbued with the spirit of the French enlightenment, who had guided
him carefully through the works of Descartes, Plato, Locke, and Rousseau.
When he came to the throne, at the age of twenty-three, he was a well-
educated, handsome and affable young man; and it may have been expected
that he would show deference to his elder advisers. But he proved to be no
puppet of the conspirators who had given him the throne. His qualities did
not include acquiescence nor the inclination to follow the directives of others,
for experience had already taught him to please without following. Although
reared at the side of his grandmother, he had been permitted to visit his
parents, who lived in isolation from the court; and under that arrangement,
he had learned to ride with the hounds and run with the hares. He had earned
Catherine's praise by assiduous assimilation of La Harpe's instruction; and

Alexander I

Paul's, by displaying a love for Prussian military drill. As a consequence, it was later said of him that he was "half a citizen of Switzerland and half a Prussian corporal."

What kind of man did this training produce? Pushkin called him "a weak and sly man." Others saw him as a brooding Prometheus. Speransky's assertion that he was too weak to rule and too strong to be ruled covers many of the known facts, but no characterization satisfactorily explains the nature of his restless, secretive, inconsistent, and withal charming personality. No one knew his mind, and apparently he himself did not always know it; but, once he reached a decision, he would enforce it stubbornly and implacably. Above all, he intended to rule in his own name and to pursue his own policies; and after a few months he launched out independently on his course, leaving his early advisers in the background.

RELEASE FROM TENSION. Although Alexander was brought to the throne as a result of a palace revolution instead of a popular one, his succession was received with jubilation throughout the country. People could now forget Paul's dictatorial restrictions. The army could doff its pigtails and tight Prussian uniforms. The court and administrative officials could relax. Even the peasants were less restive than they usually were during a change of rulers. In short, the death of Paul meant a general release from tension.

Alexander's first act as Emperor was to announce that he would rule as Catherine had ruled. Soon thereafter, as has been noted, he ended hostilities with England; in addition, he restored the rights of which the nobles had been deprived, ended the ban on foreign study and the importation of foreign books, and removed the restrictions on the private printing of books. In further restitution, he released those who had been imprisoned because they had offended Paul—about 12,000 persons. The atmosphere at court and in the cities became once again that of the palmier days of Catherine II's reign; and, as an overall blessing, there came a period of peace that lasted until 1805.

Beginning his reign under such favorable conditions, Alexander could easily have chosen to follow the precepts of his beloved tutor La Harpe and tried to revolutionize Russia's political and social systems. Instead he moved cautiously. For a number of years, he talked of making fundamental changes, but he always shied away from them at the decisive moment and limited himself to reforms which left the basic institutions of the country unchanged. COMMITTEE OF FRIENDS.   After his first few months on the throne, Alexander gathered around him four old friends: Count Paul Stroganov, who had for a time been the librarian of the Jacobin Club in Paris; Nicholas Novosiltsev, a cousin of Stroganov; Prince Adam Czartoryski, a liberal and patriotic Pole; and Count Victor Kochubei, a brilliant Russian who had received much of his training in England. These four formed the unofficial Committee of Friends, which met regularly for a year—sometimes in the presence of the Emperor, sometimes without him—for the purpose of discussing, considering and investigating the broad political and social problems of Russia.

The court nobility looked upon the Committee of Friends as a group of Jacobins, ready to play hob with the regime. Actually, although its members were liberal in temper, they were quite conservative in their recommendations for practical steps. The two major problems considered by them were the establishment of a constitutional regime for Russia and the mitigation of the evils of serfdom. As for the first problem, the committee agreed that constitutionalism was desirable but that it should not be brought about at the expense of the autocratic power of the emperor. As for serfdom, it was judged an evil about which little could be done because of the inadvisability of alarming the nobility. In short, there was agreement on ends but not on means, and soon both problems were dropped from consideration. This awareness of the necessity of reforms, continually thwarted by the inability or incapacity to act decisively upon them except under the pressure of emergency, was the central tragedy of Russian political life in the nineteenth and part of the twentieth centuries.

ADMINISTRATIVE CHANGES.   The major accomplishments effected as a result of recommendations by the Committee of Friends were in the field of administration. The collegiate system, which Peter I had introduced in the departments of the central government, had not functioned well and, by 1801, existed chiefly in name only. At that time the central administration of Russia, the largest empire of Europe, was little short of chaotic; the departments were badly run and poorly organized, and only three colleges —those directing foreign affairs, army, and navy—were still functioning.

Prince Czartoryski proposed as a remedy for the situation the creation of ministries on the model of those in Western Europe, with well-defined functions, each directed by a single responsible head. That proposal was coupled with other committee recommendations behind which lay a general plan for effecting a separation of powers. According to the plan, legislative power would be vested in the emperor, who would be expected to exercise it after consultation with his ministers; the ministers, chosen by the emperor, would exercise the executive powers; and the Senate would act as the chief judicial body.

Following the recommendations of the Committee of Friends and of other advisers whom he consulted, Alexander issued on September 20, 1802, a decree and a manifesto authorizing a number of administrative changes. In place of the old colleges, eight ministries were created: foreign affairs, war, navy, interior, finance, education, justice, and commerce. In 1811 a ministry of police (later abolished) and several other executive agencies were organized. By that time the first new ministries were solidly founded, their functions and organization reasonably well established, and the authority of their heads (ministers) defined. Individually the ministers could report directly to the emperor and make recommendations. Collectively, with several other high officials, they formed the Committee of Ministers, which could make recommendations or consider common problems but could not formulate policy. The Emperor, who still considered himself the chief executive as well as chief legislator, was required neither to seek nor to wait for their approval before acting. As he interpreted his rights he might follow policies which were opposed by one minister or by the entire committee; or he might approve the policies of one minister and give him freedom to act even though opposed by all the other ministers. Nevertheless, the creation of ministries was a major advance in the history of imperial administration, removing Russia from the classification of "oriental satrapy," characterized by the ill-defined, completely unpredictable use of autocratic power by the ruler. The new ministries laid the basis for the development of an imperial bureaucracy which, while it did not limit the absolute power of the crown, performed in a reasonably regular and systematic manner the duties assigned to it.

At the same time that the ministries were created the powers of the Senate, which had been alternately active and moribund since its creation in 1711, were defined. That body, whose members were still to be imperial appointees, was now to act as the highest judicial and administrative body of the state. It was assigned the duty of examining regularly the work of the ministries and given two important rights: to remonstrate against imperial decrees which in its opinion were impracticable or contrary to existing law, and to issue decrees with the force of law—subject, of course, to imperial veto. Alexander made it quite clear, however, that he would not recognize any right that might be used in an attempt to limit or criticize him; when the Senate attempted to oppose one of his new decrees, he simply disregarded its right of remonstrance. Although the Senate, as reconstituted, could not serve as a check on the emperor, it could exercise important judicial and administrative functions insofar as he permitted.

INTERIM.   The Committee of Friends met irregularly from the middle of 1802 until the latter part of 1803, but its work as a group was over after the decree and manifesto of September, 1802, had been issued. That did not mean that Alexander had dropped completely the consideration of governmental reforms; he gave his attention to various projects up to the time of Russia's entrance into war as a member of the Third Coalition, in 1805. After that he had little time for thoughts of reform until 1808, when he was again free from war. Then he may have reasoned that some popular domestic reforms would offset the ill feeling caused by his Francophile policy after Tilsit.

A NEW ADVISER.   Alexander chose as principal adviser on his new plans Michael Speransky, generally considered the most capable statesman to serve the Russian state in the nineteenth century. Speransky, the son of a village priest, had served as professor of philosophy at the Theological Academy in St. Petersburg after his brilliant student years in ecclesiastical studies. But, his bent being toward politics, he had exchanged the academic life for that of government service; and his breadth of knowledge and keenness of mind had enabled him to rise rapidly from the position of clerk to that of right-hand man to the Minister of Interior. In 1808 the excellence of his work had come to the attention of Alexander, and by 1809 he had so risen in the Emperor's favor that he was given the post of principal adviser, a position which he held until 1812.

CONSTITUTIONAL PROJECT.   In 1809 Alexander commissioned Speransky to draw up proposals for a constitution. The problem of creating a constitutional order which would be viable for Russia suggested many questions: Could an illiterate peasantry without political traditions be given a voice in government? Was serfdom compatible with constitutionalism? If not, who would persuade the nobility to part with its privileges? Should the emperor give up his powers? If so, would he? The Committee of Friends had been unable to find satisfactory answers to these questions, but Speransky believed that, within certain limits, answers could be found. He be-lieved that it was possible to create a genuine constitutional regime which would modify but not disrupt the established political and social order and that, in time, the operation of the new political institutions necessary to such a regime would create the experience and understanding necessary for the broadening of the political base of the government and the further curtailment of legal inequalities.

In essence, the project that he worked out provided for the participa-tion of a limited electorate in the legislative and administrative processes, beginning at the cantonal level and going up to the central government. The electorate would consist of landowners and some categories of state peasants, but would exclude serfs.

To set the plan in operation, the voters would send representatives to cantonal[1] dumas, in which there would be one seat for each landowner and one for a representative of every five hundred state peasants. Each cantonal duma would choose the administrative officers of the canton and elect representatives to its district duma. Each district duma would, in turn, elect representatives to the duma of its province. And the dumas of the provinces would send delegates to the State Duma.

The plan proposed to provide a constitutional arrangement by the creation of a body of law to which the emperor and the government would be required to conform. To initiate legislation, a State Council, appointed by the emperor, would assist him in preparing new laws for proposal to the State Duma; and without its majority consent, no law could be promulgated. The Senate, to consist of members elected for life by the dumas of the provinces, would be the chief judicial body of the empire. And the various dumas would exercise substantial power in local administration.

Alexander accepted the plan as given to him by Speransky but decided to keep it secret, gradually putting into effect individual portions of it. He began at the top and, on January 13, 1810, created the State Council, nam-ing Speransky as its chief, with the title of State Secretary. The State Coun-cil (which retained its original form until 1906) became an important ad-visory body, and the Emperor submitted for its consideration many important legislative projects. That he would ever have carried out the entire Speransky plan, even if circumstances had been favorable, is doubt-ful. But circumstances were not favorable. The growing court opposition to Speransky and the outbreak of war with Napoleon in 1812 gave him

[1] A canton *(volost)* was a small administrative unit consisting of several villages.

reason to shelve the plan before carrying its recommendations any further. END OF REFORM PERIOD. Although the constitutional project itself remained secret, Speransky's humble origin and his refusal to toady to the upper nobility created the basis of ill will toward him, and his activities in other matters turned the ill will into hatred. Since he was so close to the Emperor, it was possible, if not justifiable, to ascribe all that went wrong in Russia to that "arrogant upstart Speransky." He was blamed for the economic disturbances produced by Russia's participation in the Continental System, denounced as the enemy of noble privileges, and accused of initiating the Emperor's unfortunate pro-French policy. By 1812 he had become the most hated man at court. Even the Emperor's favorite sister, Catherine, joined the anti-Speransky group. It was she who placed before Alexander the memorandum of the court historiographer, Nicholas Karamzin, attacking Speransky's ideas. That memorandum, entitled "On Ancient and Modern Russia," reminded the Emperor that the best guarantee of good government for Russia lay in a good autocrat, not in radical reforms. When the opposition finally accused Speransky of treasonable correspondence with Napoleon, Alexander could no longer ignore it. Although he knew that the accusation was false, he sacrificed Speransky in order to conciliate the nobility, whose support he needed in the coming war with France. In March, 1812, he deprived him of his offices and exiled him to Nizhnii-Novgorod. After the war the deposed favorite was rescued from his disgrace and given important posts, but he never returned to the Emperor's favor.

Period of conservatism: 1812-1825

RETREAT FROM LIBERALISM. The year 1812, which marked the end of Alexander's reform period, found Russia still an autocratic state. The only tangible results of the work of the Committee of Friends, Speransky, and others were the organization of ministries, the revitalization of the Senate, and the creation of the State Council—each of which helped to improve the bureaucratic apparatus of the state but did not modify its autocracy.

Many hypotheses have been advanced in explanation of the contrast between Alexander's liberal education and opinions and his domestic accomplishments, and of the contrast between the liberal atmosphere of his first years of rule and the reactionary tone of his last years. Some have tried to explain it by showing that in the early period of his life he was a liberal but that, because of external circumstances, he became a reactionary in his later years. It is doubtful that so facile an explanation can be upheld. Although the events of his reign may be divided so as to show a liberal period and a reactionary period, no such clearcut division can be shown in the life of the Emperor himself. He was at all times ambivalent; at one time the liberal elements in his makeup might be the stronger, at another time the reactionary; or, on occasion, both might be in evidence, as they were when he was pursuing a liberal policy in Poland and at the same time a reactionary policy in Russia. Throughout his life he remained "part citizen of Switzerland, part Prussian corporal." After 1812 the Prussian corporal in him began to dominate but not to exclude the Swiss citizen. This change toward reaction was slow and uneven, but in time it became marked.

In 1812, during the Napoleonic invasion, he became subject to profound religious disturbances and began to concentrate on a confused, mystic version of Christianity which had been part of his thinking since his early years. In 1815, it will be recalled, he established the Holy Alliance in an effort to put his religious theories into practice. Yet, after the Congress of Vienna, he showed decreasing sympathy at home for the liberal beliefs about which he had once been so eloquent—and ineffectual. Until 1820, he continued to shift from one point to another on the intellectual compass, and no one of his acts squared with another. He had no program, no fixed beliefs, no bedrock of certainty. Moody, dispirited, distant from those about him, he placed his most consistent interest in religion. He was friendly to the Quakers, to the German pietists, to English evangelists, and to the Catholics; and he admired Chateaubriand, ideologist of throne and altar. All may have contributed to his thinking, but none set its limits. One thing is certain: he came to believe that religion should form the basis of true government. But his practical expression of that belief was to be through reaction rather than through the exercise of Christian morality.

Not all of the reactionary changes in Russia after 1815 may be justly ascribed to Alexander, however. The general tone of upper-class society in Europe at that time was reactionary. Jacobin revolutionary ideology and Napoleonic imperialism had frightened Europe, and for many years after Waterloo the upper classes clung steadfastly to throne and altar as protection against a renewal of the revolutionary "plague." Russia, it is true, had not experienced the revolutionary upheavals of other European countries, but the Russian nobility which found Speransky too liberal in 1812 was soon to become well attuned to reactionary moods. The Emperor's shift to reaction did not produce reactionary nobles, but it permitted reactionary nobles and churchmen to gain the positions of influence which men such as Speransky, Czartoryski, and Kochubei had held before that time. When he began to move away from liberalism, there was a more than ample number of officials to carry out his policies and perhaps to make them even more reactionary than he intended.

CONSERVATIVE ADVISERS.   In the execution of domestic policies, Count Alexis Arakcheyev was given more and more authority, and he soon came to occupy in the Emperor's favor the position once held by Speransky. Arakcheyev was an able artillery officer who had served Paul well and who had proved himself devoted, honest, and brutal. Closely associated with him was the bigoted, obscurantist Orthodox monk Photius, who was permitted to implement the antiforeign, anti-intellectual views of the extreme reactionaries in the Russian Orthodox Church. Through those two, the Church and the army in Russia, as in the other European countries moved by the spirit of reaction to the Napoleonic period, began to regain the influence which they had previously lost.

CONSERVATISM IN EDUCATION.   The shifts in the Alexandrine policies and the intensification of the Emperor's distrust of reform are best seen in the crucial areas of Russian domestic life. His policy toward education was typical of the change.

During his first years on the throne he and his advisers had been convinced that the spread of education was desirable as a foundation for further reforms. Accordingly he had created, in 1802, the Ministry of Education, in which an important position was given to Yankovich de Mirievo, who had prepared the educational project for Catherine II. That had been followed, in 1804, by the enactment of an elaborate statute on schools, embodying in essence Catherine's plan for creating a complete state-supported and state-directed system beginning with the primary schools and extending through the universities. The changes that had been effected, though productive of improvement, had not been revolutionary. The great weakness of the statute had been its inadequate provision for elementary education. With a scarcity of primary schools, the realization of a one-class system had been impossible. Although the secondary and higher schools had been opened to all classes, the great majority of children had not been able to receive the primary education necessary for admission to secondary schools; and the upper schools had continued to serve only those children whose parents could provide private elementary instruction for them.

The advancement of education at the higher level had been more successful. In the Baltic province of Livonia the University of Dorpat, founded under Swedish rule in 1632 and closed during the Northern War, had been reopened in 1802, with German as its language of instruction. The academy at Vilna had been transformed into a university in 1803, with Polish as its language of instruction. And in 1804 universities had been opened in Kazan and Kharkov.

The major phase of educational growth under Alexander's plan had been completed by 1805. After that, war and financial difficulties had gradually slowed down expansion; and the growing tendency toward reaction had brought a decline in the quality of instruction and a change in its spirit.

In 1817 the name of the Ministry of Education was temporarily changed to Ministry of Education and Public Worship, its functions having been extended to include both educational and religious affairs. That was a basic step in the promotion of the new spirit. It was explained as an attempt to make Christian piety the basis of true education—a sharp turn from the earlier lay rationalism of the schools. Thereafter, little by little, obscurantists gained the upper hand in the educational system and began to change its character. At the University of Kazan, the majority of the professors were dismissed, most of the textbooks purged, and its administration converted into one combining the features of monastery and military barracks. Similar developments followed in other schools and universities. In St. Petersburg the Pedagogical Institute was transformed into a university in 1819, regimented and restricted according to the prevailing practice.

This reaction in education was not the direct work of Alexander, although it did reflect his spirit. It was the work of the antiforeign, anti-intellectual members of the court, bureaucracy, and Church, who were regaining the power which they had lost in his liberal days and using it to pay off scores against antipathetic persons and ideas.

CENSORSHIP.   The obscurantists gained the upper hand also in literature and journalism through the application of censorship. The practice of censorship was not new; both Catherine II and Paul had utilized it in a haphazard manner. But Alexander, in his liberal period, had not been very strict about it. In 1804 he had placed preliminary censorship in the hands of the Ministry of Education. Later a secret committee of the police had been given the right to censor publications concurrently with the Ministry of Education and to confiscate those that had been passed by preliminary censorship. Now limitations were made more stringent; the publication of any new periodical required permission from the police, and any criticism of the government or its officials was forbidden. One police official seriously proposed (without success) that criticism of actors of the Imperial Theater be forbidden. After 1820 the pressure of censorship was redoubled, and the influence of the Russian Orthodox Church in the Ministry of Education and Public Worship added to its severity. The expression of ideas that smelled of heterodoxy was dangerous, and general freedom of expression was a thing of the past.

CONFLICT OF POLICIES. For about eight years after 1812, Alexander presented the strange appearance of a ruler pursuing conservative or reactionary policies at home and liberal policies abroad. He lectured Louis XVIII on the dangers of repeating the mistakes of the Bourbons; he often opposed Metternich's tactics in Austria; and, as King of Poland, he praised constitutional government. He looked upon himself, at least in foreign affairs, as the spokesman of the true spirit of the Holy Alliance—monarchical benevolence; but it cannot be said that his attitude was in consonance with Russian foreign interests. Metternich, in contrast, had been pursuing a consistent and rational policy which took for its premise the fact that the stability of Austria required the maintenance of the political and social status quo on the continent, showing thereby a far keener appreciation of the interrelation of foreign and domestic policies.

In 1819 the rumblings of revolutionary disturbances in Europe began to turn Alexander toward Metternich's way of thinking. In 1820, while he was attending the diplomatic Congress of Troppau, in Silesia, he was informed by the somewhat gleeful Metternich of a mutiny of the Semenovsky Guards Regiment in St. Petersburg. (It was not, in fact, a mutiny but rather the peaceful complaint of the troops against the brutality of one of their officers; but the military authorities had chosen to treat it as a mutiny.) The Emperor was quite disturbed by the thought of a "revolt" at home, especially in a guards regiment; and it is probable that his alarm was intensified by the revolutions of 1820 in Naples, Spain, and Portugal. At any rate, he became convinced that it was the proper duty of Christian monarchs to put down disorder and anarchy wherever those ugly phenomena appeared. He informed Metternich that he had in the past acted mistakenly and indicated that Russia would thereafter give her support to the policy of intervention in foreign countries to suppress revolutionary outbreaks. In this fashion, the domestic and foreign policies of Russia were finally made consistent.

MILITARY COLONIES. The second period of Alexander's reign was definitely darkened by one project which he had been considering since 1810: the creation of military colonies. After 1815 he felt that Russia should maintain an army equal in size to the combined forces of Austria and Prussia in order to retain her power in European diplomacy. To avoid the economic burden of maintaining so large a standing army in the traditional way, he planned to transform the army into a kind of territorial militia. The basic feature of the plan was the conversion of designated districts into military colonies. All persons living in those districts, except peasants, were to be removed and compensated for losses in property. Then detailed regiments from the regular army were to be moved into the areas and, with the peasants already living there, formed into new military units. Members of these units were to work the land, receive military training, live under military discipline and be subject to military service in time of war. Their sons were to be educated in local military schools and taken into the ranks of the military units of the district on reaching the age of eighteen. The plan, reasoned Alexander, would not only cut the expense of maintaining an army without decreasing its size but also improve the soldier's lot.

In 1816 Arakcheyev was given the assignment of developing this system. Year after year, despite protests from the peasants and even from members of the court, the number of military colonies was increased until, in 1825, they had a total population of 750,000, including about 200,000 soldiers.

The new peasant-soldiers did not experience the satisfaction that Alexander had anticipated; rather they felt themselves and their children condemned to an unpleasant and unrewarding barracks life. Military discipline extended to every phase of their daily life. The hours of their eating, working, sleeping, and wakening were regulated by bugle calls and drum signals. Marriage without military permission was forbidden to them. Discipline was harsh, and the administrator of the system took delight in brutality. As might be expected, outbreaks were frequent; yet neither Arakcheyev nor Alexander was willing to modify the plan.

DIVIDED JUDGMENT.   In his last years Alexander cut himself off from his former friends and began to use Arakcheyev as the chief liaison between himself and the ministers. Arakcheyev and the military colonies became the symbols of black times. Photius also was arousing general resentment. Considering himself a latter-day Savonarola, called upon to denounce the evils of liberalism and rationalism which he saw about him, he hurled anathemas at evil-doers and heretics on every hand, even forced the dismissal of many prominent men—among them, his former patron, Prince A. N. Golitsyn.

Alexander, now the obscurantist and reactionary, was more popular with the upper classes than he had been as a quasi-liberal and cosmopolitan in his earlier years. Some were displeased by his excesses, by his dependence upon Arakcheyev, and by his neurotic behavior; but as long as he made secure for them what they considered the pillars of society (serfdom and aristocracy), they would offer no opposition. On the whole, the nobility had not been impressed by the idea of having their own powers extended by constitutionalism, for they saw that it might lead to an end of which they disapproved, the admission of the lower classes to power. They had judged it better to nestle closer to the autocracy and the Church, guardians of the established order, than to play with dangerous political ideas such as those that had led to Jacobinism in France and later produced the threat of revolution throughout Europe.

There were stirrings of positive discontent among a few. The intellectual activity that had begun in the second half of the eighteenth century had not disappeared under repression; in fact, the market-place of ideas had expanded with the growth of education and foreign contact. Too, the early reform projects of Alexander had fed speculation, for the discussion of Russia's problems could not be confined to the committees he created. In the salons of St. Petersburg, in the country homes of the nobility, and in the quarters of army officers, groups were considering the problems of serfdom and autocracy. Usually the leaders of the malcontents were petty noble officers who had fought with the army abroad. They had seen the changes that the revolutionary and Napoleonic epochs had produced in Western and Central Europe and had come to feel that Russia should change also, that serfdom and autocracy should be either modified or abolished. To those among them who belonged to the genteel poor of the nobility, the end of serfdom would mean little loss. To the others, it was a necessity supported by a real intellectual conviction.

After the return of the army from foreign service, many began to form discussion groups or to use the revived Masonic lodges for deliberation on political and social problems. Some formed secret political societies with definite programs showing the influence of such secret societies as the Italian Carbonari and the German Tugendbund. Only a few of the more significant of these groups can be mentioned here.

THE UNION OF WELFARE.   In 1816 about twenty men, mainly officers of the Semenovsky Guards, formed the first of the secret societies, under the name of the Union of Salvation, with the stated aim of improving political and social conditions in Russia. Among its first members was the young Colonel Paul Pestel, a firebrand who urged the organization in the most radical directions. His views, however, did not prevail; and in 1818 the organization, having changed its name to Union of Welfare, adopted a mild platform based upon co-operation with the government in progressive betterment of existing conditions. The Union of Welfare garnered about two hundred members and formed several branches. But, after the so-called revolt of the Semenovsky Guards Regiment in 1820, the government scattered its members to other regiments throughout the country. This action and the growing repression by the government caused the leaders of the organization to disband it in 1821. Formally, that was the end of the Union of Welfare, but from its ashes sprang several smaller and more militant societies.

THE SOUTHERN SOCIETY. Pestel, who had become a confirmed Jacobin, had been transferred in 1818 to Tulchin, a Ukrainian town where the southern army of Russia had its headquarters. There he became a leader of the malcontents and helped to form a branch of the Union of Welfare. That branch, refusing to disband with the parent organization in 1821, set itself up as the independent Southern Society. Its members included some of the highest officers in the region. Dominated by Pestel's views, they supported a plan for the overthrow of the monarchy by military action, the establishment of a military dictatorship to rule in the name of the people for about eight years, and finally the organization of a centralized, democratic republic.

Several of the characteristics of the Southern Society deserve attention because they were to be marks of the Russian revolutionary movement throughout the century. It was upper class in composition and had no contact with the lower classes in whose name it intended to act. It was stronger in its revolutionary ardor than in its effectiveness in organization. It advocated the establishment of a dictatorship of the revolutionary elite to make possible the transition from autocracy to democracy. And, finally, like many later revolutionary organizations, it was Great Russian in its outlook; it sought to free Russia but did not seek to free the non-Russian territories that had been conquered by Russia. This position was illustrated in Pestel's proposals on the handling of Finland and Poland: Finland should remain an integral part of Russia, while a small portion of the pre-1772 Kingdom of Poland should be permitted independence if it would accept the institutions of revolutionary Russia. Even this minor concession on the Polish question was attacked by his supporters and by another noteworthy secret group, the Northern Society.

THE NORTHERN SOCIETY. After Pestel had made unsuccessful attempts to form a branch of the Southern Society in St. Petersburg, a guards officer, Nikita Muraviev, was able to establish there in 1822 a group known as the Northern Society, differing markedly from the southern group in its program. Muraviev felt that a republic was impossible at the time and proposed instead a liberal constitutional monarchy allowing a large measure of local autonomy. According to the plan which he proposed and the Northern Society accepted, serfdom was to be abolished and all land divided, each serf receiving about five acres and the remainder being retained by the landlords (as opposed to the Southern Society's plan to expropriate the landlords).

As Pestel and his followers were in the Jacobin tradition, Muraviev and his followers were in the Girondin tradition. Both groups advocated revolutionary measures as a necessity because of the lack of any peaceful means of reform.

PROBLEM OF IRREGULAR SUCCESSION.   The most propitious time for the initiation of revolutionary action would come when the throne changed hands, and the arrangements being made for the succession after Alexander seemed fatefully inviting to such action.

Paul had thought to end the problem of the imperial succession forever, but it would not be ended. Alexander had no heir, and the next in line was his brother Grand Duke Constantine. However, Constantine had contracted a morganatic marriage with a Polish countess, and he himself felt that it was a bar to his succession (although legally it would not have stood in his way). In 1823 he signed an abdication document and a manifesto naming his brother Nicholas the heir. Alexander had three copies of these made, placed in sealed envelopes and deposited with the Holy Synod, the Senate, and the State Council; the originals were given to the Metropolitan Philaret. Thus Constantine's renunciation was kept secret from all except those to whom Alexander chose to make it known: the Dowager Empress, the Metropolitan, and Golitsyn. Nicholas had intimations that he would succeed, but he was not party to the secret; officially Constantine was still the titled heir. Why Alexander chose not to make the facts of the succession known is not certain. Some believe that he intended to abdicate the throne (he had been talking about such an act for many years) and to make the announcement at the time of his abdication.

In September, 1825, Alexander, deep in despondency, dissatisfied with himself and the world, accompanied his ailing wife to Taganrog in the hope that the climate would help to restore her health. There he contracted a fever and, on December 1, he died.

TWELVE / STRENGTHENING OF CONTROLS:

1825-1853

The internal pressure that had been evident under Paul and Alexander I was increased during the succeeding reign. To the problems of peasant discontent and governmental inefficiency was added that of national discontent among the Russian Poles. Difficulties were multiplied further by the fact that this was an age in which the power of monarchs and aristocrats was under attack in Central and Western Europe; and the autocracy and the aristocracy in Russia now had to fight against influences both from without and from within in order to conserve established powers and privileges.

It was a historical accident that gave to Russia in 1825 a ruler who found the task of handling the troubled state a congenial one.

Settlement of the succession

THE DEFERRED ACCESSION. Alexander I's arrangement for the succession created what might, under other circumstances, have passed for a comedy of errors. When Nicholas was informed of his designation as successor, he hesitated to announce himself as such because of the reported unrest among the guards regiments. Instead, he took the oath of allegiance to Constantine, thinking it best that his brother, who was then in Warsaw, should come to St. Petersburg and make known his abdication and announce the transfer of the succession. That, he hoped, would prevent any misunderstanding which might be used by the dissidents among the troops as a pretext for revolt. But Constantine, who resembled Alexander in his complexity, refused to appear and sent word that Nicholas should handle the affair. Nearly four weeks passed before the termination of the unsatisfactory, long-distance transactions between the two. Finally Nicholas ordered that, on December 26, 1825, the news of Constantine's abdication be published and the oath of allegiance to himself be administered throughout the realm.

THE DECEMBRIST REVOLT.   The confusion caused by the four-week interregnum provided the Northern Society and the Southern Society an opportunity for action against the government. The Northern Society, having learned that the government knew of their activities and was preparing to suppress them, decided on an immediate coup d'état. It was planned that the guards officers who were members of the society would enlist the support of their men in refusing to take the oath of allegiance to Nicholas and in demanding, instead, that Constantine be kept on the throne and be required to grant a constitution to Russia. It was expected that, if the guards regiments were won over, the other troops would follow.

On December 26, when the troops of St. Petersburg were called out to take the oath, the planned action was undertaken. The beginning was not heartening to the rebels, for only the Moscow Guards Regiment, several companies of the Marine Guards and scattered groups of soldiers and officers were won over. Thereupon, Prince Sergei Trubetskoi, a guards colonel who had been named to direct the revolt, lost confidence in the possibility of its success and, instead of leading the rebels, fled for safety. However, about 2,000 rebels marched to the Senate Square, took their stand and began shouting for "Constantine and the Constitution." They were joined by some workmen and serfs, but their hope lay in their chance of being joined by other regiments; and it soon faded as Nicholas surrounded the square with loyal soldiery. He tried at first to persuade the rebels to surrender peacefully; but, when persuasion failed, he used his troops against them. It was all over in a few hours and, by evening, most of the members of the Northern Society were under arrest.

In the Ukraine, there was a faint echo of the St. Petersburg events. Nicholas had been informed of the membership of the Southern Society in the Southern (Second) Army and had ordered their arrest. Pestel and other leaders had been seized; but one, Sergei Muraviev-Apostol, had escaped. Gaining the support of the Chernigov Regiment, he led it, on January 10, 1826, toward Zhitomir, where he hoped to gain the support of other military units. But the rebel regiment was intercepted by loyal troops on January 15, and that phase of the revolt was ended even before it had made a good beginning.

Nicholas was convinced that he had crushed a revolution, not a mere revolt; and he lived under the shadow of the events of December 26 (known thereafter as the Decembrist Revolt) for the rest of his life. Deeply impressed by the gravity of the situation, he dedicated himself to the task of providing lasting protection from the threat of another revolution. As a first step, he spent several months on the investigation of the antecedents of the revolt, questioning suspects as to the programs and the membership of the secret societies. One hundred and twenty-one were then brought to trial. Five, including Pestel and Muraviev-Apostol, were hanged, and the rest were sentenced to terms of hard labor, exiled to Siberia, or sent into the army ranks as privates for life.

In itself, the revolt was petty. It was poorly organized and employed the techniques of the palace revolutions of the past. Its leaders neither sought nor received any support from the general population; it was essentially a movement of young noble officers (of the 121 tried, 109 were less than thirty-five years of age) who represented neither the nobility nor the lower classes. Its importance lay in the fact that it was the beginning of organized revolutionary protest against the regime.

Revamping of bureaucracy

EMPEROR WITH A PLAN.   Nicholas I was a round peg in a round hole. In contrast to Alexander, he had no doubts about himself or his duties. As Alexander could be characterized as half Prussian corporal, Nicholas could be characterized as all Prussian corporal, having been reared in the spirit of the ordered barracks. His early education had been in the hands of tutors whose main concern was the inculcation of respect for autocracy, orthodoxy, and military discipline. Growing up under authority, he developed a deep faith in it. At twenty-nine, when he gained the throne, he was a well-integrated person with established ideas about the handling of the country he was to rule. The military barracks with each object and each person in a definite place, was to him the model for society.

BASES OF POLICY.   The material gathered during the investigations of the Decembrists provided Nicholas with a point of departure for his domestic policy. On the one hand, the investigation convinced him that the danger of revolution had been great and that, therefore, the institutions designed to curb discontent and to prevent the spread of dissidence should be strengthened. On the other hand, the investigations revealed many real

BROWN BROTHERS

Nicholas I

causes for discontent; these he wanted to correct—if their correction would not weaken the autocratic regime.

He believed in the essential justice of autocracy and felt himself equal to the task of strengthening the weak points in the autocratic scheme of Russia's government. He intended to bring good government —as he understood it—to his people; and he expected, in return, that the people trust him and obey his direction. To consult the people's wishes or to take them into his confidence was not part of his plan. His acts were not designed to please this group or that but rather to satisfy his own conscience or to meet an inescapable need. To him the ruling of Russia was an intimate operation between himself and God. When he employed advisers, it was only because he himself could not attend to everything; had it been possible, he would have directed each branch of government personally. No other emperor of Russia after 1725 ever took as active part in the administration of the country as he did.

MEN ABOUT THE EMPEROR.   The domestic problems of the state being his most urgent concern, Nicholas began at once to consider those on whom he would rely in his work with those problems. First, he removed from the government some of the obscurantist reactionaries, among them two of the most powerful of the previous reign. Arakcheyev, who had shown a desire to leave the service of the state, was encouraged to do so, although the military colonies with which his name was associated were retained in their original form until 1831. And Photius, who represented the obscurantism of the Church, was ordered to return to his monastery. Favored positions were given to men of clear-cut conservative tendencies, and a decided preference was shown for military men, in whose company Nicholas felt most congenial. General Count Alexander Benckendorff was made head of the political police; the martinet General Ivan Paskevich was given a powerful post in the army; and General Count Paul Kiselev was assigned to the peasant question. Two outstanding men were retained from the previous reign: Speransky, who by that time had learned that liberalism did not pay; and Count Yegor Kankrin, Alexander I's able Minister of Finance. THE IMPERIAL CHANCELLERY. Since Nicholas intended to keep in personal touch with the many affairs of the state, he turned first to the reorganization of the Imperial Chancellery, which before 1825 had been a relatively inconsequential body concerned only with the handling of a few minor matters of personal interest to the emperor. He changed its structure, increased its size, and specified and added to its duties. Remodeled, it consisted of four sections: the first, retaining the general duties of the old body, handled the emperor's papers; the second, created in 1826 and headed by Speransky, was in charge of the codification of the extant laws; the third, formed in 1826 and directed by Benckendorff, dealt with political police affairs; the fourth, dating from 1828, administered schools and charities in which the emperor had a direct interest. In its new form, the Imperial Chancellery acted as a kind of superministry. Regular ministries, thereafter, were permitted to handle routine administrative duties, but most functions of prime importance within their scope were transferred to the Chancellery.

CHANGING ROLE OF THE NOBILITY. Russia's bureaucracy under Nicholas I was manned, as before, largely by the nobility. Yet in the thirty years of his rule, the political position of the nobility declined, not as a result of direct assault by the throne but as a consequence of long-term developments whose effects were felt in these years. The nobles themselves had weakened their position when, after the abrogation of compulsory service, they had sloughed off the duties of administration but kept the privilege of monopolizing the higher grades of offices. In addition, the growth of bureaucracy was undermining their importance to the regime and making them more dependent than ever upon the throne. That was particularly evident in the handling of local government. Catherine II's reforms had placed administration at the district level in the hands of the local nobility, and Nicholas continued to value their work there as unpaid policemen over the serfs. Nevertheless he wished to make certain that local government conform to the policies and directives of St. Petersburg; so he introduced a greater degree of supervision of the minutiae of local administration by government officials, thus cutting into the power of the nobility.

The predominant influence of the nobles was further challenged as more men than ever before began to seek government offices and the power, prestige, and possible wealth which were the rewards of office. Increased numbers of Baltic Germans were admitted into higher government and military posts, where their presence often created problems. Although as officials they proved efficient, ambitious, and loyal to the crown, they did not become Russified. Consequently they were resented by the Russians. But the Emperor found them useful; and the roster of bureaucracy continued to feature Benckendorffs. Rennenkampfs, and Meyendorffs alongside the -ov's, -ich's, and -sky's. Other sources of officials were the new Russian universities and technical schools, which began in the 1830's to produce a supply of trained men. The graduates were mainly of noble origin; however the middle classes could not be completely excluded from higher education, and many sons of merchants and priests began to enter the bureaucracy by the diploma route. The latter were sometimes drawn by the fact that, once in the ranks of the officials, one might—but only rarely did—reach one of the four highest grades in the Table of Ranks and thereby automatically acquire the rank of hereditary noble.

BUREAUCRATIC ORGANIZATION. A centralized autocracy which set no limits to the range of its interference in the affairs of its subjects required a vast, efficient and dependable staff of civil servants. Catherine and Paul had begun the formation of a bureaucracy to meet that requirement; the administrative reforms of Alexander I had strengthened its development; and it now remained for Nicholas to bring it to full organization.

When completed according to Nicholas' specifications, bureaucracy was an intricate machine of administration. Into its hopper in St. Petersburg poured reports, summaries, complaints, and petitions; and from it poured streams of directives and orders to ministers, school inspectors, police officers, tax collectors, senators, governors, judges, heads of bureaus, government clerks, and—with the introduction of the railway and telegraph— telegraph operators and station masters. From St. Petersburg to Kamchatka, from Archangel to Odessa, the country was minutely plotted for the channeling of the interminable inflow and outflow of official papers, which at times appeared to be both the raw material and the end product of the machine.

Thousands of government employees were required to service the mammoth machine, and they were fanned out through the realm according to a definite hierarchical plan. The organization of the ranks at the upper levels was, with slight modification, that introduced through the Table of Ranks of Peter the Great. The Table established for each responsible position in the civil service and for each post of command in the armed forces a certain rank *(chin)*; and diligence, longevity or the right connections helped one to climb the ladder of the twelve ranks that existed after 1834. The names of ranks were based on the grade of an office, not on its functions. Thus the rank of Councillor of State might be held by a high official either in the Ministry of Finance or the Ministry of Interior. The Table also set up with exactitude the equivalences among officials of the civil service, the armed forces, and court and stated the honorifics which went with each rank. The rank of Privy Councillor in the civil service, for instance, was equal to that of a Lieutenant General in the army and to that of Master of the Hounds at court; and each official of that rank was addressed as "Excellency." A civil official with the rank of Actual Councillor of State was the equal of a Major General in the army; he was addressed as merely "High-born." And one with the rank of Collegiate Secretary was the equal of a midshipman in the navy; he stood near the bottom of the hierarchy, rating only the address of "Well-born." Civil servants, as well as members of the armed forces, wore uniforms with the appropriate designation of rank.

Below the officials in the civil service who had the same status as commissioned officers in the army and navy, were the numerous rank-and-file personnel, also hierarchically organized. Each inferior showed the proper deference to his superior and arrogance to his subordinate; and all, with few exceptions, treated the lower classes with disdain.

DEFECTS OF THE SYSTEM. No organization of the size and complexity of Russia's burgeoning bureaucracy could function with complete success. It is remarkable that this one could accomplish what it did. Despite its many defects, it helped to hold the sprawling, variegated empire together and to establish the imperial institutions of Russia over an area which comprised at that time nearly one-eighth of the world's land surface.

No single explanation of the defects of the bureaucratic system and its personnel will suffice, for they were the product of many interacting forces. The great expanse of the Russian land, the political immaturity and cultural diversity of its people, and the backwardness of its economy made the development of an honest and efficient civil service fulfilling the will of a centralized autocracy an almost insuperable task.

Many of the shortcomings of the system may be traced to the nature of its personnel. The mass of officials lacked training and a proper interest in their work. Peter I, it will be recalled, had sought unsuccessfully to impose education upon his service nobility; and those who followed him were slow in accomplishing that at which he had aimed, the specific preparation of men for public service. It was not until the reign of Nicholas I that the educational system, one of the chief purposes of which was to produce trained officials, began to supply some of the personnel of the civil service. Even then, trained officials were in the minority, and they were usually willing to accept the mores of the group that rewarded conformity above ability. Moreover, the absolutism at the top of the system was reproduced, with unfortunate results, at lower levels. A governor or any powerful official could safely abuse his power as long as he and his subordinates, who knew better than to go over his head, filled out the necessary reports for the central government. It is true that the Emperor, who liked to think of himself as the conscience of Russia, encouraged complaints against officials; but those who had the right of complaint (denied, of course, to serfs) soon found it unwise to exercise that right. The few who tried usually found that their complaints never reached the capital but were intercepted by the officials against whom they were informing, and that they, if they were of the lower class, could expect floggings rather than redress. There were many honest officials and some able ones, but venality and pettifogging were the rule. At all levels, those who dealt directly with the public expected tips in exchange for their services. These tips were not considered bribes but rather the normal means of putting the governmental machinery into motion. Known as "sinless revenues," they were looked upon as justified supplements to low salaries, and they entitled the giver merely to regular consideration. Special consideration was bought with bribes. Bribery and graft were common at every level of government from the court to the local police station. Government construction of railroads, for instance, was often found to be twice as expensive as private construction because of the graft of supervising officials.

In an attempt to forestall improper practices among its subordinates and to promote efficiency, the central government created an intricate system of checks on their activities and, in so doing, simply snarled the operation of the administrative machinery. The system required signatures, countersignatures, affidavits, and attestations for almost every official act. Instead of efficiency, there developed the worst features of bureaucratism: avoidance of responsibility, confusion, delay, and the accumulation of mountains of documents which hid more than they revealed. An extract on one case before the Senate covered 15,000 sheets of paper. Permission to make a minor repair in the office of so exalted a person as a governor-general might require as many as thirty days of negotiation. When Nicholas found that the system of checks was not preventing either inefficiency or corruption, he placed upon the Third Section of the Imperial Chancellery the duty of observing and reporting on the work of the bureaucracy. But even that effort proved ineffectual, for the observers soon found that life was simpler when they co-operated with the bureaucrats whom they were required to observe than when they reported unpleasant facts.

The inadequacies of the legal system also contributed to the defects of the administrative order. The courts offered no protection against the evils of bureaucracy and little protection against anything or anyone else. The law was cumbersome, antiquated, and inequitable; and respect for law was not part of the Russian tradition. Obedience to the state had been created by force and was maintained by force or the threat of force. The ordinary Russian did not look to the law or officialdom for protection. His attitude was well expressed in two of the common proverbs: "Any stick will do to beat a thief, but only a ruble will help you with an official." "The law is like an axle—you can turn it whichever way you please if you give it plenty of grease."

Neither the administrators nor those under administration in Russia had as yet developed the habits and attitudes which made the bureaucracy of Prussia so effective. The severity of the administrators was tempered by their relative inefficiency, their susceptibility to bribery, and their laxity; they had learned, moreover, to flavor their respect for laws and decrees with a measure of good-natured indifference. The people, for their part, had acquired over the centuries the skillful use of evasion.

Faults in the Civil Service were not due wholly to its enlargement during Nicholas' reign. Alexander I had admitted to one official, "I know that the majority of the administrative officials should be dismissed. . . . The army, the civil administration, everything is not as I would have it—but what can you do? You cannot do everything at once; there are no assistants. . . ." Nicholas had the necessary assistants, but he was not able to solve the problems of the system. As one of his ministers had the courage and honesty to inform him, his methods nearly drowned the work of government in paper forms. And, near the end of his reign, he admitted that the bureaucracy was not meeting his hopes.

Imposition of conformity: repression

THE BASIS OF REPRESSION.   Nicholas wanted his subjects to feel that, if they behaved as befitted their station in life, they would have his support and protection and that, if they did not behave so, they would feel his displeasure. Yet the practices of his administration emphasized the repressive rather than the protective aspects of imperial paternalism. That was inevitable because of the very nature of the Russian state, which he was determined to maintain inviolate. It was impossible to remove the basic causes of discontent without altering the nature of the state; so, in order to protect it, he was compelled to rely mainly on the negative weapon of repression.

THE THIRD SECTION.   The political policing of the country—that is, the repression of discontent and the imposition of conformity—became the business of the Third Section of the Imperial Chancellery, directed by General Benckendorff. It was carried out by a special, uniformed Gendarmerie Corps, assisted by secret agents.

In its conception, the Third Section was to be the eyes and ears of the emperor. Its gendarmes, stationed at posts throughout Russia and within the army, would observe the work of government officials and report on their delinquencies, receive complaints from the people, observe and detect political disaffection, report on the state of popular morals, keep an eye on foreigners and religious dissenters, and supervise political prisons—in short, prepare for the emperor a complete picture of the general state of mind. In actual practice, however, the section operated chiefly as political police. It failed to act as a check on the bureaucracy, but it did yeoman work in the detection and punishment of political offenses against the state and in the censorship of publications. Its powers became broad and pervasive. In defining political offense as any opposition—direct or indirect, in word or action—against the regime, it laid out for itself a wide field; and within that field, it acted as judge, jury, and executioner. It could, by its own decision (subject to review by the emperor), punish political malcontents by imprisonment, commitment to an insane asylum, exile to various parts of the empire, or enrollment in the army for the regular term of twenty-five years.

Political police had been a feature of Russian government before, but never had they been so powerful or so numerous as under Nicholas I. They were, moreover, a state within a state since their actions were subject to review neither by the courts nor by other agencies of the government. In theory, the Third Section was a part of the bureaucracy but, in fact, it was independent of it. And as long as it continued, Russia was a police state in which the rule of law was impossible. Yet neither Nicholas I nor those who came after him could dispense with the political police.

CENSORSHIP.   Censorship of publications, rigorously applied during the later years of Alexander I's reign, became even more severe after 1826. As before, several agencies of the government were given overlapping powers of censorship; and to these agencies was now added the Third Section, to investigate and send reports directly to the emperor. The censors were given the widest discretion in proscribing publications. One periodical was suspended for printing an article in which the intellectual development of Western Europe and that of Russia were compared. Another was suspended because one of its issues contained an article by Peter Chaadayev in which the development of Russian civilization was analyzed too critically. Its editor was exiled; and Chaadayev himself, a nobleman and retired guards officer, was officially declared insane and confined to his home. Such repressive practices effectively stifled open and free presentation of ideas, but they served also to encourage a growing tendency of some to present disallowed ideas in indirect ways—through philosophical speculation or learned consideration of matters seemingly remote from problems of the state but actually of timely pertinence.

Imposition of uniformity: "official nationalism"

A POSITIVE APPROACH.   Nicholas was concerned primarily with the negative aspect of opinion control, the repression of unhealthy and seditious sentiments; and the positive aspect, creation of an affirmative loyalty to the regime and its institutions, was of distinctly less importance to him. As an autocrat he had no need to concern himself about public opinion unless it appeared dangerously hostile. But the hostile ideas which were penetrating Russia at that time were sufficiently challenging to indicate the need for some affirmation of positive ideas and sentiments to offset them. Nicholas found an agreeable ideologist in Count Sergei Uvarov, Minister of Education from 1833 to 1849. Uvarov formulated for him the doctrine of "official nationalism," which remained the creed of the government until 1917. In essence, it called for the rigorous imposition of autocracy, orthodoxy, and Russian nationality. The Emperor was convinced that the infusion of that doctrine, with the aid of censorship and the political police, would save Russia from the effects of liberal and radical ideas which were shattering the political stability of Western Europe.

EDUCATION AND NATIONALISM.   Nicholas expected the educational system to serve not only as the chief disseminator of "official nationalism" but also as a regulator of the social order of the state. He disapproved of the statutes of 1786 and 1804, which had aimed at a one-class educational system, for he felt that education should be forbidden to the lower classes, to whom it would mean only the acquisition of ideas which would make them unfit for their stations in life. In 1828 his ideas were incorporated in a new statute, which aimed at a two-class system. By its provisions the organization of the school system was altered in such a way that the secondary schools were, in effect, closed to all but children of officials and nobles. They were designated as institutions for the preparation of children of the upper class for civil and military service, and their programs were planned to give particular attention to instilling in the students a deep respect for Russian civilization and an abhorrence of dangerous ideas. The secondary school curriculum was to emphasize the classic languages, which were considered admirable disciplinary subjects; but subjects which might present disturbing thoughts—logic, statistics, and even mathematics—were to be dropped or abridged in their presentation.

The universities felt the effects of the new spirit more slowly, but their time came also. In 1835 a new statute on the universities, sponsored by Uvarov, was issued. It limited, but did not abrogate, the autonomy and academic freedom of those institutions and affirmed the principle that higher education was intended to prepare upper-class children for state service. Toward the latter half of Nicholas' reign, the pressure of the government was intensified. In 1849 the enrollment in each of the six universities was limited to three hundred students exclusive of those in their schools of theology and medicine. After 1849, subjects of study were restricted; the teaching of constitutional law, metaphysics, and history of philosophy was suspended, and instruction in logic and psychology permitted only by professors of theology.

ORTHODOXY.   The strengthening of the Russian Orthodox Church was important to the development of "official nationalism" because it was one of the instruments which served the state by helping to keep the people in line. To assure its strength and pre-eminence, Nicholas set up three aims: to insure strict orthodoxy within the Church, to bring back into the organized Church those who had left it, and to encourage the conversion of the non-Orthodox to Orthodoxy.

There followed a general tightening up of discipline within the Church. The Over-Procurator of the Holy Synod was the representative of the Emperor in that aspect of the program, and his power of veto over the decisions of the Holy Synod made it possible for him to enforce the will of the state in all matters pertaining to the main activities of the Church. In order to insure orthodoxy at the lower levels, instruction in the theological academies and seminaries was purged of all elements that might encourage dissent; and village priests, whose duty it was to teach loyalty to the emperor, were encouraged to report any disaffection or heresy among their parishioners.

As a means of attaining his second aim, Nicholas began the vigorous enforcement of a rule which had previously been accepted but leniently applied: that all Russians (including, by official definition, Great Russians, White Russians, and Ukrainians) were to be considered members of the Orthodox Church, and that those who had left it should be compelled either to return or to suffer for their rejection of Orthodoxy. Of the 50 million persons listed as members of the Orthodox Church, only about 800,000, according to official records, were Old Believers and sectists. However, secret reports gathered by Nicholas' agents showed that actually the number included nearly 7 million Old Believers and 1 million sectists. Some of the Old Believers, those who included the emperor in their prayers, were considered harmless; they were left in peace but were not permitted to grow in number. On the other hand, the sectists, many of whom believed the state to be only an instrument of the devil, and those Old Believers who excluded the name of the emperor from their prayers were subjected to harsh treatment. Large numbers of them were transferred to Transcaucasia, others to Siberia. Many were sentenced to prison. However, attempted coercion and acts of persecution did not eliminate religious dissent; its growth continued, and it remained as a recurring problem for succeeding reigns.

The Uniats presented a special problem. The territory that Russia acquired from Poland in the eighteenth century contained a large number of White Russians and Ukrainians who had forsaken the Orthodox Church for the Uniat Church, a branch of the Roman Catholic Church in Poland. Since it had been the policy of the Russian government to tolerate the institutions of the newly incorporated lands, the deviation of the Uniats from Orthodoxy was not questioned until 1831, when they became involved in a revolt that had spread from the Kingdom of Poland into the territory they occupied. Thereafter, in order to eradicate Polish influence in that region, Nicholas concentrated his efforts on the reconversion of the Uniats, for he realized that their adherence to Roman Catholicism would continue to serve as a tie between them and Poland. In 1839 the bishops of the Uniat Church in Russia agreed to rejoin the Russian Orthodox Church; and in that year, with the exception of the diocese of Kholm, the Uniat Church in Russia came to an end. The reunion, not an altogether voluntary one, brought about 1.6 million Uniats into the Orthodox Church.

Nicholas accelerated not only the return of Russian dissenters but also the conversion of the non-Russians. In attempts to convert Protestants, Catholics, and Moslems, persuasion was employed. In the case of the Jews, it was found necessary to add force to persuasion in order to make even meager gains; for the background of the Jewish people of Russia was not one to dispose them toward easy assimilation.

Until 1772 the number of Jews in Russia had been negligible because the Russian rulers, regarding them as enemies of Christianity, had closed the country to them. But after the partitions of Poland, the government was forced to face the fact of having many Jews in the country, for they made up a large part of the urban population of the annexed lands. Under Polish rule, they had enjoyed great autonomy in their internal affairs and had managed to remain a distinct ethnic group, with their own language, religion, and institutions. Consequently, when they came under Russian rule, they presented a religious, cultural and economic problem. At first, the government was uncertain in its policy toward them, but by 1825 there had been issued several fundamental laws pertaining to them. By those laws, they had been permitted to remain in the annexed region or to migrate to New Russia, but forbidden to live elsewhere in Russia. Thus had been established the notorious Pale of Settlement, within which the Jews had been further restricted to the towns and cities, where they were enrolled as merchants and artisans. Within the Pale, many attempts had been made by the government to induce the Jews to adopt the language, customs, and religion of Russia. Alexander I had offered inducements in the form of bounties, land, and special privileges to converts; but few had taken advantage of his offer. Nicholas gave special attention to the problem, devoting to it about six hundred decrees and laws. He attempted to end Jewish cultural differences and to induce large-scale conversion to Russian Orthodoxy. But, having preserved their own culture and religion for centuries, the Jews did not respond to enforced assimilation. In 1827 they were made liable to service in the army, from which they and other urban groups had hitherto been exempt. Once in the army, they were subjected to both moral and physical pressure to accept the dominant faith. But neither the imposition of military service nor other methods adopted by Nicholas yielded satisfying results, and no other major attempt was ever made to solve the Jewish problem in Russia by religious conversion.

RUSSIAN NATIONALITY.   Definition of the third principle of "official nationalism," Russian nationality, did not remain constant. Nicholas preferred to interpret it as loyalty to the regime and respect for the traditions of Russia. As a rule, he did not intend that its enforcement include the imposition of Russian culture on non-Russian nationalities within the country's boundaries; but circumstances forced him to alter his intentions before the end of his reign.

Russia's early territorial expansion had usually been into lands sparsely inhabited by peoples less culturally advanced than the Russians, and in such lands assimilation had come easily because Russian colonists usually moved in and soon outnumbered the non-Russian natives. However, many of the conquests and annexations of the late eighteenth and early nineteenth centuries created different problems. At that time Russia was becoming master of many lands of denser settlement, the inhabitants of which were culturally and politically more advanced than the Russians. Since the colonization of these lands by Russians was not possible, the government faced the task of establishing a policy for handling the non-Russian peoples living there. Either it could follow the precedent established by Peter I with respect to the Baltic provinces and permit the continuation of existing institutions and practices in the newly annexed areas, or it could compel their acceptance of Russian institutions and practices. At the beginning of the nineteenth century, the problem was considered political rather than cultural. Should the government force Russian political institutions on the non-Russians under its rule? At first, no well thought-out policy was established. Action was taken as circumstances compelled action. Generally, though, the government followed a hands-off policy in regions where the native ruling class accepted Russian rule and was willing to act as agents of Russian rule; and it showed no nationalistic bias against non-Russians in those regions. How that policy was applied and how, in some cases, it evolved into a more intolerant one may be seen by a survey of its application in Russia's western border regions.

The Baltic provinces of Estonia, Livonia, and Courland remained under the administration of the Baltic German barons, no changes being made in their basic social, cultural, or political structure except the relatively minor ones imposed by Catherine II. The Grand Duchy of Finland was ruled by the Emperor as Grand Duke; and, until the end of the nineteenth century, no alteration was made in the institutions which existed there prior to annexation.

In Lithuania, White Russia and the western Ukraine[1] the Russian policy was, for many years, one of maintaining the status quo. The landowners and

---

[1] The eastern Ukraine, it will be remembered, had been slowly assimilated by Russia, its political autonomy ended, and its upper classes transformed into a Russified serf-owning nobility.

officials, mainly Poles, continued their government, using Polish as the language of administration; and the only university in the area, the University of Vilna, remained Polish. The Russian government was reasonably satisfied with that arrangement until 1831, when these regions became affected by political dissidence arising in Poland.

Congress Poland, having been granted a liberal constitution by Alexander I, remained until 1831 an autonomous state under Russian rule, maintaining its own legislature and its own army. It is true that, toward the end of his rule, Alexander had found himself in increasing disagreement with the Diet of Poland and had, on many occasions, ignored its constitution. Yet Nicholas I had felt compelled, despite his antipathy for liberalism, to rule Congress Poland in accordance with its constitution. However, the union of liberal Congress Poland and autocratic Russia was a mismating which could not last. The Polish independence movement was encouraged by the successful revolution in France in July, 1830; and, in the following November, Polish nationalists in Warsaw launched a revolt against Russian rule, demanding an independent Poland with the borders that existed before the partition of 1772. The revolt spread quickly throughout Congress Poland and into Lithuania, White Russia, and the western Ukraine. The rebels had military strength—the army of Congress Poland—but their chance of success was weakened by disagreements among their leaders, by their failure to gain mass support from all the Poles, and by the fact that Prussia and Austria were ready to aid Russia in ending a revolt which might spread to their Polish provinces. In 1831 their efforts were completely quashed by a Russian army of 150,000.

After 1831, Congress Poland practically ceased to exist as a separate political unit although, officially, it was ruled as a separate kingdom until 1863. General Paskevich, who completed the pacification of the region after the revolt, was named its viceroy and, in accordance with the wishes of the Emperor, ruled it with a heavy hand. Its constitution was abrogated and the separate Polish army and legislature were abolished. One by one Polish institutions were abolished or supplanted by those of Russia: the University of Warsaw was closed; the Russian language was introduced in administration and education; and Russian organs of local government replaced the native ones. By the end of Nicholas' reign, Congress Poland was, in actuality, a territory under military occupation by alien rulers.

In Lithuania, White Russia, and the western Ukraine, the Russian government was even harsher toward those who had sympathized with the Polish revolt. The lands of the Polish nobles who had joined the rebellion were confiscated and given to Russian nobles. The University of Vilna, a center of Polish nationalism, was closed and a university opened in Kiev as a center of Russian culture. In addition, as has been seen, the government assisted in bringing the Uniats back into the Russian Orthodox Church, thus weakening the Roman Catholic Church, which was identified with Polish aspirations. To maintain the changes, Russian officials were given strong positions in local administration, although Polish landlords who had been loyal to the Russian government retained their land and continued as officials and military officers.

Of all the problems involved in the application of the principle of "official nationalism" after 1831, those concerning the Poles under Russian rule were to prove most troublesome for the government. After the Russian state had swallowed most of Poland, it was neither able to digest it nor willing to disgorge it.

INTENSIFIED STRUGGLE AGAINST IDEAS.　The anxiety which motivated Nicholas' attempt to impose ideological uniformity on his subjects was heightened by the news of the overthrow of the French monarchy in February, 1848. He is said to have shouted, when the news was first brought to him, "Saddle your horses, gentlemen; a republic has been proclaimed in France." The spread of the revolution to Germany, Austria, and Italy deepened the fear that Russia might be next. To prevent the spread of revolutionary sentiments, the government began to tighten the censorship. Every possible means was employed to extirpate whatever seditious sentiments might still remain after twenty-three years of rigorous policing. Even censors were censored; obsequious and reactionary officials vied with one another in discovering heresies in their colleagues. Uvarov was dismissed in 1849 for an alleged lapse into liberalism. Other officials whose loyalty was impugned were dismissed without charges. In all areas of administration, governmental decrees were issued one after another to form a *cordon sanitaire* in protection of Russia against intellectual contact with revolutionary Europe.

The peasant problem

INCREASING UNREST.　At the beginning of the nineteenth century, Russia's population of 36 million included about 18 million peasants enserfed to private owners and about 13 million state peasants. In Nicholas' reign the restiveness of that submerged majority became ominous; 712 peasant uprisings—half of them serious enough to require military action—were officially recorded. It was particularly alarming to the Emperor to note that each year brought an increasing number of outbreaks. In the first ten years of his reign, the average was fourteen outbreaks a year; in the last ten years, it was thirty-five. The risings usually took the form of attacks on landlords, their bailiffs, and government officials. There occurred, in addition, many mass flights of whole villages of serfs to distant parts of the empire. Any form of peasant unrest proved difficult to handle because it usually had neither a program nor an organization, being spontaneous and direct. The suppression of an uprising in one region rarely served to discourage a new uprising in another. The reports of the Third Section, which provided the throne with a more accurate picture of popular morale than had ever been available before, made clear the ubiquity of unrest; it was no longer the stirring of a few malcontents, rather a general disturbance which could threaten the state.

EFFECT OF CHANGING ECONOMY.   Nicholas was forced into consideration of the peasant problem not only by the increasing evidences of peasant unrest but also by changes which were developing in the economic position of the nobility. During the first fifty years of the nineteenth century, the growth of the foreign market for Russian raw materials and the development of an internal market drew increasing numbers into the economic relations which characterize a money economy. And the growth of a money economy accentuated the economic differences between members of the nobility; the rich became richer and the poor became poorer. Moreover, both rich and poor were beginning to see that, in the new situation, the abolition of serfdom—on terms which the nobility would set, of course—might prove advantageous to them.

During this period, the industrialization of Western European countries and the consequent decline of their agricultural activities combined to create deficits in food, which Russia was now in a position to supply. The value of all Russian exports tripled in the first half of the century, and grain exports increased even faster; in 1800 they accounted for about 15 per cent of the value of all exports, and in 1855 for about 35 per cent. There was also a steadily growing foreign demand for livestock, livestock products, hemp, flax, and other raw materials and foods. Timber export, too, was increasing; Riga was on the way to becoming the greatest timber port of the world.

The growth of Russia's internal market was equally striking. An increasing population, a rising standard of living and the development of economic specialization resulted in a growing domestic demand for finished goods, foodstuffs, and raw materials. The growth of the domestic market is illustrated by the turnover at Russia's most important fair, that at Nizhnii-Novgorod: it quadrupled in a period of about fifteen years.

Although the primacy of agriculture remained unchallenged, the internal economy changed radically in the half-century. In the northern regions, serfs and state peasants spent more and more of their time in domestic manufacture of goods for merchant entrepreneurs; it was the heyday of Russian domestic manufacture. The factory system was still a relatively minor feature of the economy, and its growth continued to be retarded by a general lack of a large free labor force. However the number of factory workers increased from 173,000 in 1815 to 549,000 in 1858, and the proportion of free laborers grew somewhat. In the 1840's steam-driven machinery, imported from England, began to replace hand operations in the expanding cotton industry; and the manufacturing industries were soon to have the advantages of factory methods impressed upon them.

There was a demand for changed techniques in agriculture also. The growing demand for grain and livestock stimulated the desire of the landlords in the black soil areas to improve their methods of production. But in their efforts to transform their estates into large, economical agricultural units, they found themselves embarrassed by an excess of serf labor and consequently began to see the advantages of the land reforms which had taken place in the provinces of Estonia, Livonia, and Courland. There, between 1816 and 1819, the Russian government had granted the request of the Baltic German nobility that the serfs of those provinces be liberated. The freed serfs had been forbidden to leave the region in which they lived; therefore, since no land had been allotted to them, they had become a stable and cheap labor force for their former landlords. Now the nobility of Russia's most productive areas were convinced that such an arrangement would profit them also.

The landlords in the nonblack soil regions, on the other hand, were less inclined to agricultural ambitions since large scale farming was not possible on their estates. On the whole, they believed that the continuation of serfdom with its guarantee of a definite income was preferable to the uncertainties of agricultural enterprise based on hired free labor. They agreed, however, that if the emancipation of the serfs were inevitable, they would not oppose it—if they were generously indemnified for their loss of income from the serfs.

Pressure on the state and the nobility to give further thought to the peasant problem came from the increasing impoverishment of the lesser nobility. In the days of an economy based on self-sufficiency, any serf-owning noble could meet most or all of his needs from the agricultural produce, finished products and labor provided by the serfs on his land. However, the rising demand of the nobility for luxuries which could be procured only by the payment of cash and the growing tendency to market

a large part of the farm produce worked to the disadvantage of the lesser
nobility with poor land and few serfs. The nobles in that class seemed incapable of reducing their standard of living or of demonstrating the enterprise
necessary to raise their incomes. As the gap widened between the cost of
high living and the income from low production, many nobles increased the
labor and cash demands on their serfs; and when the practical upper limits of
these demands were reached, they turned to borrowing. A government loan
bank, created in 1754 to provide credit for the nobility, had, by 1855, advanced to needy nobles vast sums, for which two-thirds of all privately
owned serfs were mortgaged to the government as security. The borrowed
money had usually been employed to balance the nobles' budgets rather than
to increase agricultural productivity, and there was no reason to believe that
the borrowers would ever be able to liquidate their indebtedness under the
existing system.

DRAWBACKS TO REFORM.   The acuteness of the peasant problem was
more evident than the solution. Nicholas I and the nobility saw the question
of serfdom, not as a moral one—whether or not one man had the right to
enslave another, but as a practical one—whether or not the system of serfdom could be altered without harm to the political and economic interests of
the state and the nobility. They were seeking a cleansing fire which would
not burn them, and they could not find it. Liberation of the serfs without land
allotments would have been agreeable to many nobles, but it was disapproved
by the Emperor, who felt that the creation of an army of agricultural proletariat was socially dangerous. The other alternative, to free the serfs and
grant them land, was distasteful to the nobility as a whole and would have
brought economic ruin to many of them. Ten secret governmental committees
met and failed to hit upon any plan that would be both satisfactory to the
nobility and viable. At the end of Nicholas' reign, the government was no
closer to a solution of the serf problem than it had been in 1825.

KISELEV'S EXPERIMENT.   On the other hand, Nicholas was able to take
more effective action on the problem of the state peasants since he did not
need to consider the interests and wishes of the nobility in regard to them.
In 1837 the state peasants, responsibility for whom had been held by many
agencies of the state, were assigned to the jurisdiction of one organ: the new
Ministry of State Domains, directed by General Kiselev, in whom the Emperor placed great confidence. Kiselev, believing that a poverty-stricken
peasantry was a brake on the whole national economy, proposed to effect
improvements at least in the status of the state peasants. To that end, he
increased the size of some peasants' plots and attempted to popularize new

agricultural techniques. Some improvements resulted from his efforts, but they were partly offset by the accompanying increase of state interference in the lives of the peasants. With the intention of improving the administration of peasant affairs, Kiselev appointed government officials as chiefs of the several districts into which the state domains were divided. But the administration did not improve because, more often than not, the district chiefs employed their position and power for purposes of personal enrichment.

Even though little was accomplished toward the solution of the peasant problem during Nicholas' reign, the state had finally recognized it as an urgent problem; and a large and useful body of information and proposals had been collected by the secret committees and recorded for those to whom the problem was to be left.

Russia's long period of intellectual apprenticeship to the West was coming to an end by the middle years of the nineteenth century, and her thinkers and creators were becoming masters in their own right. The attainment of a relatively advanced intellectual status by the few served to emphasize the relative backwardness of the many. And the recognition of that backwardness could not fail to affect the direction and cast of the intellectual activity of the period.

Men of letters

POETS.   Between 1815 and 1830, Russian poetry reached a level of attainment never again equaled. The primacy of poetry during those years, known as the Golden Age of poetry, was an indication of the literary influence of the aristocracy, who then considered poetry the most desirable of literary media. The best poetry of the age was written by dandies who "deplored," but enjoyed and often reflected, the brilliant social life into which they were born. Their work, which still retained some elements of the French neoclassical poetry so popular in the early years of the century, was becoming more independent of the restrictions that neoclassicism imposed on form and content and more representative of the European romantic literary movement. It has been called the "posthumous child of the eighteenth century," neoclassical in its technical perfection and restraint but displaying something of the romantic in its verve and originality. Part of its originality may be attributed to another important change, evident not only in poetry but also in other writing of the period: the change from foreign to Russian subjects for inspiration.

Because Russian verse suffers much from translation, most of the products of the Golden Age are little known and less appreciated outside of Russia. Yet, in the space of a generation, Russia produced not only its greatest poets but also two of the great poets of world literature.

The work of Alexander Pushkin towers over all of Russian poetry. The offspring of an ancient but somewhat seedy noble family, Pushkin received an education more French than Russian; but he used the Russian language with an adeptness that revealed poetic resources not previously discovered by others. And he proved himself to be a truly national poet. He used Russian life, history, and folklore in his compositions and was, when he dared, antiautocratic in the interpretation of his subject matter. His most famous, and perhaps his most characteristic, poetic work was his narrative poem *Eugene Onegin*, in which he used a contemporary Russian type, the St. Petersburg dandy, as his central character.

Michael Lermontov, who at his best ranked close to Pushkin, appeared near the close of Russia's great poetic age. He lacked the poetic discipline of Pushkin and showed little of the latter's genius, but a small portion of his verse and much of his prose has earned him wide recognition. Of his early works, only *The Angel* (often called the best romantic lyric of the Russian language) has been judged great. Of his later works, *The Demon* received widest acclaim. Although banned during the reign of Nicholas because of its antireligious tone, it was still one of the most popular Russian poems in the latter half of the nineteenth century. All of his poetry was romantic and emotional, created on themes from Russian history and folklore.

WRITERS OF PROSE.   In the 1830's, Russian literature began to show more prosaic and serious characteristics. Many new writers—some of them now coming from the non-noble classes—understood the taste of the widened reading public for "plebeian" novels and wrote to satisfy it. Established writers, too, often chose to work on the popular prose form, fiction. Pushkin himself wrote one short novel, *The Captain's Daughter*, a story set in the time of the Pugachev revolt; and his short story *The Queen of Spades* is one of the masterpieces of Russian prose. Lermontov, also, tried his hand at a short novel, *A Hero of Our Times*, in which he drew upon his experiences as an officer in the Caucasus.

The most meritorious fiction of the period was written by Nicholas Gogol. A Russified Ukrainian, Gogol drew both on the life of his native Ukraine and on that of his adopted world of Great Russian officialdom and society for the settings and characters of his writings. He was one of the most imaginative of Russian writers and, at the same time, one of the

Alexander Pushkin, (left), Russia's first major poet; and Nicholas Gogol (right), Russia's first major novelist

country's great realists. He overrode many of the literary taboos of the time by presenting, in his stories, novels, and dramas, everyday people who had hitherto been admitted neither to the homes nor to the writings of the fashionable. In his most creative years, from 1830 to 1841, he produced two masterpieces: the unfinished novel *Dead Souls* and the drama which many have called the greatest of Russian dramas, *The Inspector General*. Both are satires on the world of Russian officialdom and nobility, and they were received as such. Yet Gogol was no enemy of the established order; he was trying in his peculiar way to preach a message of moral regeneration to his contemporaries. Although some of his work showed him to be the master of a rich and powerful prose, he wrote much that was inferior, particularly in his last years of poor physical and mental health. Nonetheless, he must be credited with opening the period of greatness in the Russian novel.

Another phase of the advance of prose was the development of literary criticism in the late 1820's. It found expression in the "thick" magazines, which featured not only literary criticism but also fiction, poetry, and essays of a general nature. The character of the criticism indicated the temper of the times; it was guided by the canons of politics as well as by those of art. The most representative critic of the period was Vissarion Belinsky, who demanded of literature that it be both useful and artistic—usefulness being judged by contribution to the advancement of the internal well-being of Russia. Since well-being, as understood by critics like Belinsky, denoted mitigation of autocracy, criticism could not avoid having a political character. Thus directed, this approach to literature, often called "civic," was to affect both the writing and evaluation of literature during the remainder of· the century.

The intelligentsia

A CLASS WITH A CAUSE.   Overlapping but not coinciding with the spheres of· the writers and scholars was that of the intelligentsia (*intelligent-siya*). The word "intelligentsia" identified for the Russians a class with no exact analogy outside of Russia, a class produced by the disparity between that country's intellectual development and its socio-political development. Intellectually Russia was a part of the nineteenth century, but socially and politically it belonged to the latter part of the seventeenth. Members of the intelligentsia sought means of erasing that disparity, being not only students of Russian society and politics but also critics and would-be reformers.

It was inevitable that a breach should open between the government and this developing class. A comparable phenomenon had appeared in eighteenth century France, where the *philosophes* had been in open conflict with the established political, social, and religious institutions. The official attitude of Russia was indicated by Uvarov, who declared that there was a need for retarding the country's intellectual development for fifty years. He understood that to preserve autocracy and serfdom required the freezing of social and political thought. Yet, despite the efforts of the Ministry of Education, the Church, and the Third Section, Russia was changing; and education was leading many minds to daring thoughts. Scholars and writers of belles-lettres seldom joined the ranks of the intelligentsia, but a surprisingly làrge number of educated Russians were, at least during parts of their lives, members of that class. Russian autocracy was able to preserve itself until 1917, but it was not able to win to the support of its ideology the leading thinkers who had identified themselves with the intelligentsia.

TYPES OF MEMBERS.   The early cadres of the intelligentsia were provided by the "repentant nobles," whose first major representative was Radishchev. Why a minority of the privileged class should come to question the institutions upon which their privileges were based is not easily explained. It can be said, at least, that most of the "repentant nobles" were young men— usually in their late teens or twenties—whose education did not fit them to accept with complacency the life of country gentleman, military officer, or government official. They were not, in most cases, revolutionaries but would-be reformers, for whom there was no place in autocratic Russia. They were, in a sense, examples of the "superfluous" men with whom later Russian literature abounded: men prevented by conscience from enjoying the lives to which they were born and yet prevented by the regime from the practical implementation of their proposed reforms.

Another outstanding group among the early intelligentsia were the "persons of various ranks." They were the ones against whom Nicholas had sought particularly to guard, the men educated above their station. As members of this group multiplied, they became an intellectual proletariat, to whom the evils of their environment were more evident than to the well born and well placed. The Church, oddly enough, contributed many to this group by allowing the growth of a kind of ecclesiastical unemployment. It made education available to the children of priests but did not have at its disposal a sufficient number of Church positions to give employment to all of them. Many of those for whom there were no posts in the Church went on to Moscow or St. Petersburg to study in the universities or to find employment as government clerks, journalistic hacks, or tutors; and there they took up the kind of life and thought by which the intelligentsia were identified. Minor officials, the educated sons of merchants and the illegitimate offspring of nobles also often joined the group of new thinkers. And it was further expanded by those from secondary schools and universities who were eternal students, never receiving a diploma or degree, never carving out a career, but depending on a family income or on odd jobs requiring a modicum of education. Many of this group were only transients among the intelligentsia; a good post with the government, a substantial income from writing, an unexpected inheritance, or a secret subsidy from the government might turn almost any of them onto the path of recognized respectability.

The chief forums for the members of the intelligentsia were the famous "circles" which began to form about the University of Moscow in the 1830's. A "circle" was a group of like-minded individuals—nobles, "persons of various ranks," and occasionally teachers, journalists, and officials—who met frequently in the rooms or homes of members for the discussion, dissection, or demolition of ideas and writings. Usually its cohesion depended on one outstanding member who dominated or led the others. The "circle," with its endless discussions over endless glasses of tea, became one of the seminal influences in Russian thought.

CURBS AND INCENTIVES.   The growth of the intelligentsia was definitely affected by the failure of the Decembrist Revolt. The elimination of the most advanced and daring political opponents of the regime and the redoubled energy of the government against any form of opposition hampered them for a time and helped to turn them from action to speculation. The hope of revolution was dimmed for many decades. On the other hand, the work of the Decembrists became the basis of a folklore and mythology. Those who had died on the scaffold or lived out their days in Siberian exile and prisons became the first saints on the revolutionary calendar, and Siberia became the region of purgatory in the cosmography of the intelligentsia. In their further development, remembrance of the heroes, saints, martyrs, and other victims of the struggle against the regime provided an emotional cement that held together the varied elements among them. They likened their cause to that of the early Christian martyrs, with one difference: whereas the early Christians looked for a new and better life in another world, the intelligentsia sought it in a changed Russia. Alexander Herzen, one of their leaders in the 1840's, summarized their position in this way:

> The heritage we received from the Decembrists was the awakened feeling of human dignity, the striving for independence, the hatred for slavery, the respect for Western Europe and for the Revolution, the faith in the possibility of an upheaval in Russia, the passionate desire to take part in it, the youth and freshness of our energies.

As the intelligentsia turned from a program of action to philosophical speculation, they entered a field held in high respect throughout Europe. At that time, the German universities were the centers of new philosophical movements, and Europeans generally looked to the German philosophers for leadership. Their influence on Russia was particularly marked. Hundreds of Russian students made their way to the universities of Berlin, Jena, and Bonn and returned to teach in Russian schools or to write in Russian journals. Many German professors took service in the universities of Russia; and Nicholas tolerated the growth of their influence because, in theory, the spirit of Metternich dominated the schools of Central Europe and surely, he thought, no evil could come from them. As the philosophies of Hegel, Kant, Schelling, and Feuerbach became the dominant ones in Russia during the 1830's and 1840's, the ideas of the French *philosophes* of the eighteenth century lost support, though they were not completely discarded.

Philosophy for the intelligentsia was more than abstruse speculation for speculation's sake; it was a social tool which, they believed, would provide the bulwark of certainty for programs of social change. The philosophy of history, especially as it was expounded by Hegel and his followers, seemed to them an admirable tool with which to prove the inevitability of almost any changes they might wish to see in Russia.

CENTRAL QUESTION.   To compress and summarize the philosophical debates and discussions of the Russian intelligentsia during this period would be impossible. It is possible, however, to state the central question with which they were occupied: What is Russia, and how must it, by the laws of its own nature, develop? They did not make a pragmatic approach to that question, declaring one way of development desirable, another undesirable. Rather, under the spell of philosophy, they felt compelled not only to find a philosophical justification for any answer they might propose but also to prove that their answer was in definite accord with the nature of things—that Russia could develop in a certain way, no other. So completely converted were they to the philosophical systems that they adhered to them long after they had lost vogue in Western Europe.

Once the great debate over the nature of Russia and its development had begun within the various "circles" of the intelligentsia, in the literary journals, and in the universities, it did not stop. Peter Chaadayev, a disciple of the Christian mystic idealism of Schelling, was one of the first to bring it into prominence. He usually expressed his beliefs and conclusions in his own salon, in the homes of friends, and in private letters not intended for publication; but in 1836 he permitted one of his letters to be published in the *Telescope* under the title "Philosophical Letter." Although it had been passed by the censor, it made a stir not only in the Third Section, as has been seen, but also among the intelligentsia themselves. Being an admirer of Roman Catholic Europe, Chaadayev found nothing positive in the past, present, or future of Orthodox Russia; he felt that Russia would have to begin again and, like a newborn child, learn what was good from other civilizations. Despite the fact that he scandalized many of the intelligentsia by his sweeping denunciations of Russian history, he became one of their revered martyrs after the government had suppressed his work and punished him. At least he had served them by heroically expressing a public opinion on the central theme of their thinking.

VIEWPOINTS.   (a) *Slavophilism.* Chaadayev considered religion the determining influence in any civilization, and he believed that Russia's choice of Byzantine Christianity had doomed Russian civilization to sterility. Other thinkers, taking the same premise, reached the opposite conclusion: that Byzantine Christianity had given to Russian civilization a vitality and meaning denied the cultural offspring of Roman Catholicism. These were the Slavophiles.

The Slavophiles, influenced by Schelling, as was Chaadayev, were at first found among student groups at the University of Moscow, but soon many mature scholars and writers were attracted to them. The most able of them was the philosopher of history and theology Alexis Khomyakov. Other leaders among them were the brothers Ivan and Peter Kireyevsky and the brothers Ivan and Constantine Aksakov. Their basic argument was that Russian civilization was internally sound and that it needed only to free itself from the alien and degenerating influences of the West which had been imposed upon the country since the reforms of Peter the Great. They believed that, in Western Europe, Roman Catholicism and the political and social institutions which surrounded it had produced a dessicated civilization based upon formal logic, cold written law, and the supremacy of a state based upon violence. They believed that Western European civilization had reached the end of its development and had nothing more to give while Slavic Orthodox Russia, on the other hand, was in its youth and was capable of a great development if it would but follow the laws of its own growth and not search for alien gods. Russian civilization, they asserted, was superior because it was based not upon scholastic logic but upon a true belief and upon the voluntary brotherly co-operation represented by such socio-political institutions as the village commune, the Assembly of the Land, and the ancient democratic assemblies of the cities, which tsarism had destroyed. The Slavophiles, who have been called conservative anarchists, saw no need for a state but accepted the institution of autocracy in an idealized form; the emperor, in their scheme of things, was simply the protector of the Russian community and, if he would express the wishes of the people and not deny them any liberty, there would be no contradiction between the true freedom of the community and autocracy.

Slavophilism appears to resemble the "official nationalism" of Uvarov; but in its essence it was opposed to the actual tyranny of the imperial regime and consequently was treated with hostility by the government. In later years many Slavophiles adapted their views to those of "official nationalism" and contributed much to the theories of Pan-Slavism. But in its inception, Slavophilism looked toward a never-never land of Russian people united by the brotherly love of the Church, working together in spontaneous and free association under the protection of a benevolent emperor. Some parts of its doctrines were found useful by both reactionaries and revolutionaries. Even Westernized Russian scholars were influenced by its respect for the Russian past to the extent that they began to treat Russian institutions and phenomena with more appreciation than they had hitherto felt.

Vissarion Belinsky (left) and Alexander Herzen (right)—two of the leading Westerners in the 1840's

(b) *Westernism.* At the same time that the Slavophiles were shaping their doctrines at the University of Moscow, another group of the intelligentsia, the Westerners, were forming their first "circles" there under the leadership of Nicholas Stankevich and Alexander Herzen. The Westerners, who rejected the viewpoint of the Slavophiles, argued that Russia had not yet reached her full development and that, in order to do so, she should emulate and learn from Western Europe. To them, Peter the Great was the hero of Russian history. They were generally rationalistic and anticlerical, finding little that was praiseworthy in either Roman Catholicism or Russian Orthodoxy.

Student-philosopher Stankevich, of a wealthy landed family, was the center of a "circle" which nourished itself on philosophy, particularly that of Hegel. His "circle," which once included the future anarchist Bakunin, confined itself to speculation and gave little thought to practical political programs.

Herzen and his "circle," on the other hand, were attracted to French utopian socialism and to political action. Their progress was interrupted when, in 1833, they enlivened a graduation party with revolutionary songs and, as a result, Herzen was arrested and exiled for six years. When he returned from exile to Moscow, he found that the intellectual scene had changed somewhat. Both the Slavophiles and the Westerners had become more tightly knit and antagonistic to each other. The Westerners, who had become more politically minded, were then under the leadership of Vissarion Belinsky.

Belinsky, whose advent signified the intellectual ascendancy of the "persons of various ranks," was the son of an impoverished military doctor. He had entered the University of Moscow in 1829 and become associated with the Stankevich "circle" there. Three years later he had been expelled from the university for writing a novel attacking serfdom. Condemned by circumstances to earn his living, he entered the field of literary journalism and, as has been noted, earned an enduring reputation as a literary critic. In that capacity he learned to adapt his language to the dictates of censorship and yet express his hatred for serfdom and autocracy; in his own words, "Nature condemned me to bark like a dog and howl like a jackal but circumstances compel me to mew like a cat and wave my tail like a fox." His acuity and partisan passion made him a leader among the Westerners, and his vigorous opposition to the Slavophiles and the representatives of official thought earned him the nickname "Vissarion Furioso." At first a Hegelian, he later rallied his crusaders under the banner of the utopian socialism of Herzen.

By the end of the forties many of the Westerners were beginning to adopt forms of socialism more extreme than those originally advocated in their "circles," and new leaders were replacing the pioneers. Herzen left Russia in 1847 and became, by choice, one of the first of Russian political émigrés. In the following year, Belinsky died of tuberculosis. In 1848, when the "circles" received news of the revolutions abroad, many of them were stirred by the desire to move from words to action. One actually proposed the organization of a revolt in Russia; it was the well established one that had been meeting every Friday since 1845 in the home of Michael Petrashevsky, a young noble follower of the French utopian socialist Fourier. It took no action, but news of its sentiments reached the police in 1849, and Petrashevsky, the young Feodor Dostoyevsky, and thirteen other members were arrested and sentenced to be shot. The government had no intention of carrying out the sentence but wished to give the young men a lesson. The commutation of the sentence to penal servitude for life was announced to the guilty ones only after they had been led to the place of execution and prepared for death.

(c) *Federalism.* The Slavophiles and the Westerners, like the Decembrists, were little concerned with the specific problems of the national minorities in Russia. But in Kiev, the center of Ukrainian culture, the problem of nationalities was keenly felt; and an assertion of Ukrainian nationalism was made through the organization there, in 1846, of a group of the Ukrainian and Great Russian intelligentsia. Known as the Brotherhood of Saints Cyril and Methodius, it was led by Taras Shevchenko, a liberated serf, who became one of the foremost figures in Ukrainian literature, and Nicholas Kostomarov, a Russian student of Ukrainian history.

The members of the Brotherhood opposed not only the subjugation of the people to autocracy but also the subjugation of the Ukrainians to the Great Russians. The change they proposed bore a resemblance (probably because of the interchange of ideas) to that proposed by the early Pan-Slavists in the Austrian Empire: the creation of a federation of liberal Slavic states including Russia, the Ukraine, Poland, Bohemia, Serbia, and Bulgaria. In their advocacy of federalism they went no further than discussion, but when their existence was reported to St. Petersburg, the government acted as if a major revolutionary conspiracy had been uncovered and, in April, 1847, took severe action against them. Kostomarov was arrested and sentenced to a term in prison to be followed by exile. Shevchenko was enrolled as a private in a disciplinary battalion and, on orders of Nicholas I, forbidden to write or to paint while in military service. The Brotherhood was ended, but the problem that had brought it into existence, the place of the Ukraine in the Russian Empire, remained in the minds of others, who would later give it voice again.

COMPARISON WITH WESTERN THINKERS.   Whereas the Western European intellectuals were generally derived from and allied with the middle classes in their drive for political power, the Russian intelligentsia formed a cohesive group in an intellectual sense but not in a legal or economic sense; they were members of a self-conscious, social-intellectual group, opposed to the government and cut off by a cultural abyss from the great mass of the Russian people in whose name they spoke. And whereas the Western European intellectuals were generally proponents of political and economic liberalism, the Russian intelligentsia on the whole were not liberals. Most of them were Westerners, but their thinking was more akin to that of Western socialism than to that of Western liberalism. They had no basic sympathy for the nascent capitalist society of Western Europe and had no wish to reproduce that society in Russia. They did wish, however, to introduce Western concepts of liberty and government and, at the same time, to achieve social justice in Russia.

Neither Russian political experience nor existing political and social conditions provided the background for genuine liberalism. Moreover, there existed no legal and peaceful means for the transformation of Russia into a constitutional state based on representative government and civil and political rights. The Decembrists had thought of a coup d'état as the instrument of transformation, but that had failed. Their successors had as yet no practical scheme for ending the autocracy. They hoped vaguely for some great upheaval which would unseat the regime, but they were not quite clear as to the kind of regime they would wish to create if that should come.

Scholars and scientists

SOCIAL SCIENTISTS. The development of the social sciences in the first half of the nineteenth century was limited by the fact that the government's general circumscription of thought prevented objective study in that field and by the fact that the intelligentsia, because of their political biases, regarded the social sciences along with philosophy as tools in the struggle with the regime rather than as areas of detached study.

However, the writing of history was encouraged by the government as long as that writing did not reflect unfavorably upon the regime. As a consequence, the collection, preservation, and publication of the raw materials of Russian history continued on a larger scale than ever before, aided by gifts from wealthy individuals, privately organized historical societies, and government agencies. Hand in hand with the undramatic but indispensable work of collecting historical materials went the task of analyzing and organizing them. Outstanding at that task was the versatile Nicholas Karamzin, who was encouraged by Alexander I to write the monumental twelve-volume *History of the Russian State*. Since he was a supporter of the regime, his history was written as an exposition on the virtues of a well-intentioned autocracy. Although it is now out of date and out of favor, it represents what was, at that time, a major advance in Russian historical scholarship. Karamzin utilized many documents which were later destroyed in the burning of Moscow, and his history is now the only source of much of the information contained in those documents.

The intellectual quarrels of the 1830's and 1840's stimulated historical investigation, particularly on the part of the Slavophiles, but did not produce anything of lasting worth. It is true that the debates over the nature of Russian history created an interest in the history of Russian institutions, but the heat of debate often exceeded the fire of scholarship. It was not until the days of Alexander II that scholars were able to consider the past of Russia with a detached attitude.

NATURAL SCIENTISTS.   Detachment from the political scene was more easily achieved in the natural sciences than in the social sciences; and the Academy of Sciences, the universities, and the learned societies trained and sponsored during this period many scientists and mathematicians of distinction. The greatest by far was Nicholas Lobachevsky, a mathematician at the University of Kazan. His non-Euclidian geometry, which he presented in 1826, was well in advance of the mathematical thinking of his time. The University of Kazan may be credited also with many other able and original workers in the natural sciences: among them, Nicholas Zinin, an organic chemist who helped to lay the foundation for the development of aniline dyes, and Alexander Savelev, who fashioned an arc lamp in 1853 to light the grounds of the university. At the Academy of Sciences, a German member, Moritz Jacobi, constructed what was probably the first electric motor and used it in 1838 to propel a small passenger boat on the Neva River.

Although the first half of the century produced many brilliant scientists, their contributions to the development of technology in industry and agriculture were slight. That was because the social and economic framework of industry and agriculture discouraged the spontaneous search for improved techniques of production, and the scientists were forced to work in isolation from the practical world to which they might have given much. The gulf between Russian science and Russian technology in the nineteenth century was but a reflection of the established gulf between the whole world of the educated and that of the masses. The government itself encouraged that isolation, fearing that the men of education might stir the peasantry to sedition; and when the government did seek technological assistance, it was not from Russian scientists and technicians but from those of Western Europe. To illustrate the government's indifference: in 1832, a Russian scientist, Paul von Schilling-Cannstadt, designed and fashioned an electro-magnetic telegraph which connected the Ministry of Communications with the Winter Palace in St. Petersburg; but his effort was ignored and it was not until 1851 that a telegraph system, based on that of Western Europe and the United States, connected Moscow and St. Petersburg.

FOURTEEN / STABILITY VERSUS EXPANSION:

1815-1856

R ussia's adherence to the Quadruple Alliance committed her to direct
participation, as one of the four major powers, in the international affairs
of Europe. And her leaders were glad to have her so committed; since Russia's
territorial and strategic interests in the West had been satisfied, they were
entirely willing to help maintain the political and geographical settlement
agreed upon at the Congress of Vienna. Russia's aggressive interests now lay
in the Near East; and as long as the implementation of her designs there did
not affect the balance of power, she could have her cake and eat it too,
protecting the status quo in the West and upsetting it in the Near East.

Maintenance of stability in Europe

ATTITUDES ON REVOLUTION.   The Quadruple Alliance provided the
basic membership of the Concert of Europe, the diplomatic system whereby
the major powers attempted by common action to maintain the stability of
Europe. In 1818 chastened and subdued Bourbon France was permitted to
join the first four powers. Together, as guarantors of the peace made at
Vienna, they were faced by an immediate problem: whether or not they
should intervene in the affairs of other countries in order to protect the
regimes established at the Congress of Vienna.

In October, 1820, representatives of the five powers met in Troppau to
consider the action to be taken with respect to the various revolts then in
progress. As has been seen, the Russian position on the question of intervention was at that time in the course of changing, and Alexander was finally

moved to accept Metternich's view that the stability of the great powers required intervention. In November, Russia, Austria, and Prussia signed a document known as the Troppau Protocol, which committed the signatories to the maintenance of the governments menaced by revolution; but England and France would not join them.

The Troppau Protocol remained for a period of over thirty years the basis of Russian collaboration with Austria and Prussia in the effort to maintain the status quo in Europe. Although there were some breaks in the spirit of collaboration, the three powers were held together by a common fear of revolution and a common adherence to the monarchical principle. Common ground for their collaboration had already been laid out in Poland, where each had a major stake. They knew that any revolutionary disturbance in one of the parts of dismembered Poland might spread to the other two parts, that any such disturbance within their own borders might inspire a Polish revolt, and that revolution anywhere might prove to be a contagion. In short, the three countries felt themselves vitally linked in a bulwark against revolution. They were particularly suspicious of France, the home of revolution. As long as the Bourbons remained on the throne, France was no threat; but the three monarchies were determined to keep a watchful eye on the health of that country.

THE GREEK REVOLUTION.   It was soon demonstrated that to state the principles of the Troppau Protocol was easier than to follow them. When the inhabitants of Greece rose against their Turkish masters in 1821, Alexander was forced to make a difficult decision. Should he adhere to the principles of counter-revolution to which the Protocol committed him, or should he support this revolution the success of which would bring what was to him a desirable end: the weakening of the Ottoman Empire? He finally decided to give no encouragement to the Greek rebels. As a result his Minister of Foreign Affairs, the Greek Giovanni Capo d'Istria, resigned and left Russia. He was succeeded by Count Karl Nesselrode, who remained in office until 1856.

Nonintervention in the Greek revolt was not in accord with what seemed to be Russia's best interests. England was covertly giving aid to the Greeks; and if they were successful, English influence in the Balkans would be increased. On the other hand, if the Ottoman Empire were successful, its control over its vassals in the Balkans would be strengthened and Russian influence there proportionately reduced. In the hope of finding some solution, Alexander suggested a meeting of the great powers. The meeting was held in St. Petersburg in 1825, but agreement on any solution proved impossible.

For a time it appeared that the stability of European diplomacy was broken. Austria opposed any support to the Greeks. Russia, however, with Nicholas at the helm after the death of Alexander, in December, 1825, accepted England's proposal to support the Greek cause; and France soon joined them. Their first joint effort was a demand that the Sultan grant an armistice to the Greeks in order to permit negotiations on a proposal for Greek autonomy. When the Sultan refused the armistice and instead sent a fleet to Greece in support of his forces, Russian, French, and English ships were dispatched to intercept it. In October, 1827, the squadrons of the three powers destroyed the Turkish fleet at Navarino Bay. Then France and England, not wishing to be drawn into war with the Ottoman Empire, washed their hands of the affair. But Russia refused to withdraw and in April, 1828, declared war on the Turks. The fighting between Russian and Turkish armies began in the Danubian principalities and spread from there to Transcaucasia. Russia was successful in both areas, and hostilities were brought to an end by the Treaty of Adrianople (September, 1829) by one provision of which the Sultan undertook to grant self-government in Greece.

Russia was then in the position of the protector of Greece, a position coveted by England. Metternich, hoping to take the problem out of the realm of controversy, proposed to England that Greece be made independent in order to eliminate further Russian interference. England approved the proposal and in 1830, a conference of the major powers in London agreed to the independence of Greece and the recognition of Russia, England, and France as the guarantors of her independence.

The Greek revolution added complexity and magnitude to the Eastern Question, transforming it into the most serious international question of the century. After the Greek revolt, the struggle of the Balkan nationalities for independence from Turkish rule became increasingly bitter and severe, thus increasing the many divisive issues brought about by the declining power of the Ottoman Empire and the conflicting interests of Russia, Austria, France and England in the Near East. However, with the establishment of Greek independence, Russian interest in that country ended—as Metternich had predicted; and Russia was content to confine her attentions to the northern Balkans.

FURTHER TESTS.　In 1830 Europe experienced a new round of revolutions; and Russia, Austria, and Prussia were once more united in their common cause, the support of the monarchical principle. Yet when Nicholas I proposed intervention in France to restore the Bourbons and in Belgium to renew the control of the King of Holland, he found his two colleagues cold to his proposal; they were more wary than he of the strong probability that England would go to war to prevent such intervention in countries facing her shores. But they gave him the most cordial support on intervention in the Kingdom of Poland to suppress the revolt which had flared up there in November, 1830.

Metternich, in particular, was anxious to insure the good will of Russia because he was seeing signs of internal disorder in Austria. In fact, there was a mutual feeling of need to reaffirm the former relationships among the monarchies. Accordingly, the monarchs and their ministers, in conferences at Münchengrätz and Berlin in 1833, renewed the general principle of the Troppau Protocol: defense of the status quo. Russia and Austria agreed further that they would consult each other before undertaking any new actions with respect to the Eastern Question. That agreement did not dispel misunderstandings between the two countries, but it mitigated them and made it possible for the tri-power understanding to operate successfully until the Crimean War.

Within fifteen years, its spirit was put to test by another wave of revolutions. The establishment of a republic in France in February, 1848, roused Nicholas to fury; and the succeeding revolutions in Austria and Prussia drove him nearly to despair, for revolution in those countries could lead to a Polish revolution. He offered assistance to both Frederick William IV, of Prussia, and Francis Joseph, of Austria. Frederick William declined the aid and was able to break the force of the revolution without assistance. Francis Joseph, on the other hand, was unable to suppress his Hungarian rebels and in 1849 accepted the Russian offer. Soon Russian troops were pouring into Hungary. General Paskevich, leading an army of 150,000 from Congress Poland, defeated the main Hungarian rebel force in short order and was able to inform Francis Joseph, "Hungary is at the feet of Your Majesty." This timely intervention by Russia gave the Hapsburg dynasty a new lease on life. It also created throughout Europe—particularly in Hungary—a fear of Russia, the "gendarme of Europe."

Nicholas was instrumental also in the restoration of the status quo in Central Europe. It was his pressure which spurred Frederick William in 1849 to end the Frankfurt Assembly and in 1850 to accept the restoration of the Germanic Confederation under Austrian leadership. Russian power in Europe seemed as high as it had been in 1815. But there was a difference: in 1815 Russia had been a liberator of Europe from Napoleon; in 1850 she was a suppressor of revolution. Public sentiment in Western Europe generally and among the liberals in Central Europe particularly had become anti-Russian.

Moreover, the gratitude of Austria and Prussia, which Nicholas accepted as his due, was tinged with the fear that he might attempt to overdo the use of Russian power in Central Europe. Nicholas and his aides, however, were confident of Russian power and influence and counted on little opposition to their foreign policies.

Crises in the Eastern Question

PROBLEMS.   (*a*) *The Straits.*   As the political power of the Ottoman Empire continued to decline during the nineteenth century and its rulers grew less capable of arresting the process of internal decay, Russia was becoming more involved in problems connected with it. One of the most vexatious of the problems and the most difficult of solution was that of the Straits. Since the time that Catherine II, in the latter part of her reign, had thrown acquisitive glances at the Straits, they had acquired extreme economic and strategic significance for Russia because of the economic growth of New Russia and because of the increase in Russia's grain export from her Black Sea ports. Although Russian commerce was legally permitted unhampered transit through the Straits, the Turks often harried or impeded it during the first decades of the century.

As Russian power on the Black Sea expanded, the strategic considerations of the Straits (the "gates to our house," as Russian statesmen called them) took on importance from both defensive and offensive points of view. If Russia were on the defensive in a war, she would want the Straits closed to foreign ships of war which might enter and attack her on the Black Sea. On the other hand, if she were on the offensive, she would want the right to send her navy through those waters. Many Russian statesmen favored outright acquisition of the Straits; but since such an act might result in a general European war, it was not pressed. Some felt that, in lieu of acquisition, a treaty might suffice, one by which the Ottoman Empire would close the Straits to non-Russian men-of-war but permit the passage of Russian men-of-war. Under no circumstances would Russia agree to domination of the Straits by a power other than herself or the Ottoman Empire.

(*b*) *The Balkans.*   Another problem over which Russia found herself at odds with the Ottoman Empire grew out of the movement of the Balkan nationalities for independence. Most of them were related to Russia by language or religion or both. The Serbs, Bulgars, Rumanians, and Greeks were mainly of the Eastern Orthodox faith and looked upon Orthodox Russia as a fellow defender against the "infidel" Turks. The Serbs and Bulgars were, in addition, Slavs and felt a degree of consanguinity with Slavic Russia. Even if Russia had not encouraged their hopes, the Balkan peoples would naturally have expected Russian support in the fight against her age-old enemy, the Sultan. The Russian rulers, however, did not neglect the encouragement of any opposition to Turkish rule, nor did they overlook any opportunity for weakening the Ottoman Empire. In spite of the fact that, since the beginning of the Greek Revolution in 1821, Russia had been officially dissociated from the Balkan nationalistic movements, she kept an alert eye on the continuing struggle of the Serbs and Rumanians for independence. She could not afford to allow another power—Austria or France, for example —to appear as their sponsors, thus diminishing Russian influence in the Balkans. Her diplomats took every care to avoid that possibility.

In the case of the Rumanians, Russian interest went quite far. Ever since the signing of the Treaty of Kutchuk-Kainardji, Russia had treated the Danubian principalities, in which the main body of the Rumanians lived, as a protectorate and had attempted to reduce Turkish control there to a minimum. And Russian influence grew perceptibly after the Treaty of Adrianople, which granted the principalities autonomy and ceded to Russia the area at the mouth of the Danube (thereby giving her control of their chief coastal region). To the other European powers it appeared that Russia was on the way to transforming her position in the principalities from that of protector to that of master.

(c) *Transcaucasia.*   In Transcaucasia also there was a trouble-breeding problem. Since the time of Peter the Great, Russia had been advancing into the Caucasus at the price of conflict with its native peoples as well as with her two rivals for influence there, Persia and the Ottoman Empire. By the end of the eighteenth century, she had begun to penetrate the region south of the Caucasus Mountains, Transcaucasia. There the ancient and weak kingdom of Georgia, divided into two dependencies—one under Turkish control, the other under Persian—had seemed ready for the taking. The eastern Georgians had sought support from Russia in their effort to gain relief from their Persian masters. Russian support, freely given, had led to armed reprisals by Persia; and in 1800 eastern Georgia had asked Russia to annex the region. The act of annexation, formally effected in 1801, and the subsequent Russian policy of extending control beyond eastern Georgia had led to war with Persia; and soon, because of these and other issues, the Ottoman Empire had also entered the fray. War with the Turks (1806–12) had been ended by the Treaty of Bucharest, by which the Sultan had given up his

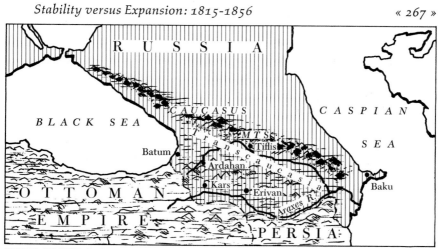

DRAWN BY EDW. A. SCHMITZ

MAP 9. The Caucasus—to 1878

claims to western Georgia, which Russia had thereupon annexed. Then Persia, by the Treaty of Gulistan (1813), had finally recognized Russian control of eastern Georgia as well as of other eastern Transcaucasian territory, including the important city of Baku.

Persia did not regard the settlement as final, however, and in 1826 again went to war with Russia. This time Russian troops penetrated Persia and advanced to within striking distance of the capital, Teheran. Again Persia agreed to peace and, by the Treaty of Turkmanchay (1828), made additional cessions and placed the Russian-Persian boundary at the Araxes (Aras) River, thereby establishing a frontier which is still maintained. While engaged with the Persians, Russia had become involved also in the war with the Ottoman Empire over Greece; and, as in nearly every Turco-Russian war, the fighting had been extended to Transcaucasia. The Treaty of Adrianople, which ended that clash in 1829, gave Russia the remaining Turkish possessions in western Transcaucasia south to, but not including, Batum. Thus, by 1829, virtually all of Transcaucasia had come into Russian possession.

Control of that region gave Russia a sizable source of wealth and brought her closer to domination of the eastern shore of the Black Sea and of the profitable trade routes through Central Asia; yet she could not feel safe about the gains there. Persia, it is true, resigned herself to the loss of her possessions and accepted Russian encouragement and support in aggressive activities against Afghanistan; but the Ottoman Empire was not reconciled to her losses,[1] nor was she pleased with Russia's evident designs on the remaining Turkish Transcaucasian areas on the Black Sea.

OPPOSITION. *(a) England.* Turkish opposition in the East was augmented by that of other opponents of Russian aims. Throughout the nineteenth century Russia and England were in open or covert conflict in the Near East, the Middle East, and the Far East, since Russian expansive policies along her southern border from the Black Sea to the Pacific Ocean threatened the English commercial, colonial, and strategic interests at the most sensitive points. Their antagonism was given an emotional coloring by the contrast between English liberalism and Russian autocracy, which led to an enduring public antipathy toward Russia in England and a profound suspicion of England in Russian officialdom.

The hostile policy of England toward Russia in the Near East dated from the beginning of British diplomatic interference in the Russo-Turkish conflict in 1791. During the reign of Nicholas I that policy hardened as both Russian and English interests in that region expanded. England's chief aim there was the prevention of the dismemberment of the Ottoman Empire by Russia, an aim born of the exigencies of England's commercial development (her exports to the Ottoman Empire increased sevenfold between 1827 and 1852). Moreover, the territory of the Sultan lay athwart important land and water routes to British India; and a weak and friendly Ottoman Empire on those routes would be better than a hostile and powerful Russia. Of particular importance, from the British point of view, were Constantinople and the Straits, keys to the important land routes; and Russia was the main threat to both. And finally, England was concerned because Russian expansion across the Caucasus and her co-operation with Persia against Afghanistan not only hurt British trade in the Middle East but also enabled Russia to menace India.

(b) France. France, also, was a potential opponent of Russian interests in the East, though not as strong a one as England. France had long since given up her paramount influence in Constantinople, but both Louis Philippe and Napoleon III wanted to restore something of France's prestige in the Near East, at least to the extent of enhancing her political, cultural, and commercial influence in Syria, Palestine, and Egypt. But French concern over the integrity of the Ottoman Empire was motivated mainly by the desire to prevent Russian expansion.

---

[1] The Turks gave secret support to the Moslem rebels of Daghestan, at the eastern end of the Caucasus Mountains, who had begun a war for political independence from the Russians in 1818. The conflict was not ended until 1859, when the rebel leader, Shamyl, was compelled to surrender.

(c) Austria. Austria gave little attention to the Eastern Question during this period, her major foreign interests being in Germany and Italy. But she could not, regardless of her friendly feelings for Russia, permit the extension of Russian control into the Balkans. The Austro-Russian agreement adopted at Münchengrätz in 1833 seemed to provide for their co-operation on the Eastern Question since it committed them to maintain the integrity of the Ottoman Empire if possible and, if that were not possible, to consult with each other before following policies which might endanger that empire's integrity. Yet Austrian and Russian policies in the Balkans remained basically antithetical.

EMERGENCE OF CONFLICT. The course of developments in the Near East after the establishment of Greek independence in 1830 intensified rather than diminished the conflicts between Russia and the other powers. In 1833 one of the Sultan's vassals, the powerful and rebellious Mehemet Ali, Pasha of Egypt, aided and encouraged by France, stood in a position to threaten Constantinople. Fearing his success, Russia offered the Sultan military assistance against him, and it was accepted with some misgivings. When the Russian fleet was dispatched to the Bosporus and a division of Russian troops landed near Constantinople, Mehemet Ali made peace with the Sultan. Thereupon Russia withdrew her ships and men and demanded her reward. It was given in the form of the Treaty of Unkiar-Skelessi (1833), which bound Russia and the Ottoman Empire to a defensive alliance for eight years and closed the Straits to foreign men-of-war.

Russian action against Mehemet Ali was an indirect blow at France, his ally. France, therefore, felt a justified animosity toward Russia. As for England, she found herself in an equivocal position: while she opposed the ambitions of Mehemet Ali, she also feared the enhancement of Russian power over the Sultan as a result of the Treaty of Unkiar-Skelessi.

Six years later the complex relationships were again tested by a new conflict between the Sultan and Mehemet Ali. When the superior strength of Mehemet Ali became evident, England proposed that both she and Russia give armed aid to the Sultan; but Russia claimed the exclusive right to "protect" the Ottoman Empire by virtue of the Treaty of Unkiar-Skelessi. This failure at agreement led to an intense diplomatic crisis between Russia and England. It was finally resolved by a compromise which permitted Russia to protect the Sultan in the Straits and Asia Minor while England limited her actions to Syria and Egypt. Under that arrangement, Mehemet Ali was once more forced to admit defeat.

The Eastern Question was now an open international squabble of such immediacy that the Concert of Europe was stirred to life to consider it.

The great powers met in London in 1840 and agreed to the Treaty of London, by which Russia, England, Prussia, and Austria bound themselves to guarantee the integrity of the Ottoman Empire. Thus the Treaty of Unkiar-Skelessi, which had made the Sultan dependent on Russia, was replaced by a multilateral treaty which would limit Russian relations with him.

In 1841 the Treaty of London was followed by the multilateral adoption of the Straits Convention, which closed the Straits to the warships of all powers except the Ottoman Empire while that country was at peace. That convention, which remained the basic international agreement concerning the Straits until after World War I, met Russian aims only halfway. It excluded the warships of other powers from the Straits and therefore from the Black Sea, and that was to the good; but it also closed the Straits to Russia's warships, and that was an ill-favor to her. For the time, however, she was forced to accept the fact that she was debarred from any unilateral action with respect to the Straits unless she was prepared to fight a combination of powers which would certainly include England.

The events of 1839-41 had brought the Russian policies of the 1830's to futility. The choice before her was either to accept the status quo in the Near East or to embark on an aggressive course. Nicholas and his advisers chose the latter, in the mistaken belief that England could be bought off. In 1844, both Nicholas and Nesselrode went to London for the purpose of convincing the British government that the Ottoman Empire was dying and that the two powers should amicably dispose of the remains. The outcome was a somewhat muddled situation. Nesselrode prepared for Nicholas and sent to the British foreign secretary a memorandum stating that, if it were foreseen in the future that the Ottoman Empire was about to crumble, the two powers would co-operate in making new arrangements for the Near East. And after that, Nicholas assumed that England would support his policies, while the English assumed that they had found a way to prevent the Emperor from taking unilateral action against the Ottoman Empire.

While Nicholas deluded himself with the belief that he had English support, English diplomacy in the Ottoman Empire was being directed toward healing "the Sick Man," giving the Sultan every encouragement to reform and strengthen his empire and to resist Russian aggression. Only unwitting self-deception on the part of Nicholas could have led him to depend on British benevolence; yet from 1844 to 1853 he and his diplomats continued to consider various projects for the dissection of the Ottoman

Empire and the establishment of Russian control of the Straits.

PALESTINE INCIDENTS. The great-power conflicts were brought to crisis in the Near East by a series of incidents which arose from discord between Roman Catholic and Eastern Orthodox clergy over the use and occupancy of the Holy Places in Palestine. The Roman Catholics claimed that the Eastern Orthodox had illegally obtained possession of the key to the main door of the Church of the Nativity in Bethlehem and had stolen the silver star of Bethlehem from the site of the birth of Jesus, about which the church had been built. In 1850 Louis Napoleon, wishing to increase Catholic support at home and sustaining himself on an old treaty by which France claimed to protect the rights of Catholics within the Ottoman Empire, began to press the Sultan to redress the grievances of the Catholics in Bethlehem. In 1852, after the French ruler had threatened to use force, the Sultan yielded and managed to have the key to the Church of the Nativity returned.

That deference to French demands was interpreted by Russia as an insult to her, the protector of the Eastern Orthodox, and she used it as an opportunity to make new demands upon the Sultan. Fortified by his misplaced confidence in Austrian and English support, Nicholas demanded not only Turkish recognition of Eastern Orthodox rights in the Holy Places (which the Sultan was readily willing to allow) but also that Russia have the right to protect all persons of the Eastern Orthodox faith in the Ottoman Empire. He knew that the latter demand, if allowed, could be used as a pretext for Russian intervention in Turkish affairs at will because incidents involving those subjects of the Sultan were constantly occurring. If the Sultan should refuse to agree, Russia (according to an explanation which Nicholas gave in an interview with the British ambassador in St. Petersburg in January, 1853) would proceed to overthrow the Sultan and divide the Ottoman Empire among the great Christian powers, reserving the major shares to Russia and England.

The British government, when informed of Russian intentions, fell into disagreement over the question of opposing Russia if she should persist in her plans. However, the British ambassador to the Sultan followed the line of stiffening the Sultan's back, encouraging him to reject the Russian claims to the right of protecting the Eastern Orthodox. With that encouragement, the Sultan felt that if war should come, England would support him; but Nicholas still believed that England would not fight. Thus both Russia and the Ottoman Empire, confirmed in their intransigency, moved on toward war.

Russian troops, under General Paskevich, were taken into the Danubian principalities in July, 1853, with the aim of bringing the Sultan to terms; and the English and French fleets were ordered into the Aegean Sea as a warning to Russia. Then European diplomacy swung into action in an effort to avoid what gave promise of being the first general European war since 1815, but no acceptable compromise could be effected. Russia had no wish to fight the European powers; yet she refused to retreat unless the Sultan recognized Russia as a protector of the Eastern Orthodox. England, although having no wish to stand idly by and see the Sultan forced into an agreement which would mean an irreparable blow to Turkish sovereignty, did not favor the prospect of war. In fact, the Sultan was the only one with a reason to be anxious to fight: he saw prospects of regaining some of the rights and territories which he had lost to Russia.

THE CRIMEAN WAR.   In October, 1853, the Ottoman Empire declared war on Russia. But the other countries still held their peace. Within a month the Russian Black Sea Fleet, under Admiral Paul Nakhimov, destroyed a Turkish fleet in Sinope Bay, on the Turkish Black Sea coast. That victory, added to Russian occupation of the Danubian principalities, convinced England and France that their intervention would be necessary. In March, 1854, after Russia had refused to evacuate the principalities, they declared war on her.

Disappointed in his confidence in England, Nicholas soon found his reliance upon Austria and Prussia also without foundation. Prussia, when asked for assistance or benevolent neutrality, declared that she could not afford to take a stand on the situation. Austria, fearing that Russia might annex the principalities, sent troops to her frontier facing those regions and, in June, demanded that Russia evacuate them. The following month Paskevich led the Russian troops back into Russia, and Austrian soldiery moved in to occupy the principalities for the duration of the war in what has been called a spirit of "malevolent neutrality."

The war, probably one of the most futile in history, might have ended at the time when Russia left the principalities but for the fact that the issues to be resolved had by then grown in number. The feeling of the English and French governments, supported by the diplomacy of Austria and Prussia, was that the time had come to set definite restraints on Russian power in the Near East.

By way of "demonstrations" intended to impress and frighten the Russian government, the Anglo-French fleets made scattered attacks on Russian territory: on islands in the Baltic and in the White Sea and on the Kamchatka Peninsula in the Pacific. However, the main plan of England and France was to localize the war and achieve a quick, though perhaps limited, victory which would compel Russia to renounce some of her rights in the Ottoman Empire. They selected the fortress and naval base of Sevastopol, on the Crimean Peninsula, as the main point of attack. In September, 1854, an Anglo-French-Turkish expeditionary force of 60,000 was landed without resistance north of Sevastopol; but divided counsels prevented an immediate allied attack, and a severe outbreak of cholera added to the delay. Thus the Russians were given time to strengthen the defenses of the city. Knowing that the wooden sailing ships of their Black Sea Fleet could not halt the steam driven vessels which the allies would bring to the attack of Sevastopol, they sank their ships in the harbor in order to prevent the entry of allied naval forces. So prepared, the Russians were able to hold the city 349 days against the allied siege.

Although the Anglo-French-Turkish forces suffered from poor organization, inadequate supplies, and miserable sanitary and medical services, the Russians were in an infinitely worse condition. Under the command of Prince Alexander S. Menshikov, they numbered 35,000 poorly trained and poorly armed regular troops and 10,000 men from the sunken ships. Their survival for so long a period was due mainly to courage and dogged endurance.

There were sufficient men (about 1 million) and supplies at the disposal of the Russian command to save Sevastopol, but the technological and administrative backwardness of Russia and the uninspired leadership of her chief officers dissipated the potential advantages. The military leaders, quite properly, detailed a large portion of the troops to the Austrian and Prussian borders, where an attack seemed probable; and those needed for action in the Crimean area were delayed by the absence of railways, the poor roads of southern Russia, and a supply organization at least two generations behind that of the allies. Men and supplies could be brought from Western Europe to that area more quickly than Russian reinforcements could be brought from Moscow. Moreover, Russian reinforcements were not started in time nor sent in adequate numbers. Here was harsh proof that the vast, lumbering Russian army, the mainspring of Nicholas' policy, could not function effectively against forces stronger than the backward Turks and Persians or the poorly armed Polish and Hungarian rebels.

On March 2, 1855, Nicholas I died, and the task of finishing the war was left to his son Alexander II. The new Emperor at once began negotiations to conclude hostilities, but he was unwilling to accede to the terms offered. Even when Sevastopol was finally taken by assault, on September 8, 1855, he still refused the allies' preliminary terms of peace. At the end of December, however, Austria threatened to enter the war unless Russia accepted the preliminary terms by January 17, 1856. Seeing the futility of further resistance, Alexander then submitted and agreed to a peace congress.

THE TREATY OF PARIS, 1856.   The peace congress was opened in Paris in February, 1856, and on March 30 the powers signed the Treaty of Paris. By its terms Russia was compelled to cede the southern part of Bessarabia as well as the area at the mouth of the Danube, and to agree to the neutralization of the Black Sea (the prohibition of warships of any power on its waters and the razing of all Russian and Turkish fortifications on its coast). She was required also to give up her claim to the right of acting as protector of the Danubian principalities and of the Eastern Orthodox subjects of the Sultan; henceforth their protection would be the duty of all the great powers. By an additional treaty (April 15, 1856) England, France, and Austria agreed to go to war against Russia if she ever violated the terms of the Treaty of Paris. The prime purpose of the provisions of the two treaties was to block Russian power in the Near East. If the provisions were respected, that would be accomplished by: (1) ending all pretexts for Russian intervention in Turkish affairs, (2) eliminating Russian naval power from the Black Sea, (3) cutting Russia off from the Danube, and (4) placing the Ottoman Empire under international protection. There was hope that the Ottoman Empire would make a recovery and thereby solve the Eastern Question—a vain hope, it proved. Russian ambitions in the Near East were held in abeyance for a generation, but during that time the Eastern Question showed more signs of survival than did the Ottoman Empire.

COLLAPSE OF THE CONCERT OF EUROPE.   The Crimean War greatly lowered Russia's position among the powers and so weakened her influence that she was unable to regain that position until 1945. The decline in influence resulted not only from loss of reputation as a military power but also from the breakup of the conservative, monarchial association of Russia, Austria and Prussia. Another outcome was the beginning of the end of the Concert of Europe, the diplomatic system which, for better or for worse, had preserved a measure of stability in Europe since 1815. It may be said that the Congress of Paris was a milestone along the road leading away from the world which both Alexander I and Nicholas I had hoped to preserve, the world of conservative monarchism.

PART 4

Russia in Transition

CHRONOLOGICAL OVERVIEW

Rulers

1855-1881	Alexander II	1894-1917	Nicholas II
1881-1894	Alexander III		

Chief Events

1860	Treaty of Peking	1905,	
1861	Emancipation of the serfs	Jan. 22	"Bloody Sunday"
1863	Revolt in Poland	Sep.	Treaty of Portsmouth
1864	Law on the Zemstvos	Oct. 30	October Manifesto
	Law on court reform	1906	First Duma
1864-1884	Annexation of Central Asia	1907	Second Duma
1866	Attempted assassination of	1907,	
	Alexander II	June 16	Issuance of new electoral law
1871	Abrogation of Black Sea	1907-1912	Third Duma
	clauses	1912-1917	Fourth Duma
1874	Law on universal military	1912, Jan.	Prague Conference of
	service		Bolsheviks
1878, Mar.	Treaty of San Stefano	1914,	
July	Treaty of Berlin	Aug.	Beginning of World War I
1881	Assassination of Alexander		Formation of Sacred Union
	II		in Duma
	Law on exceptional		Battle of Tannenberg
	measures	1915,	
1883	Formation of Emancipation	May	Austro-German break-
	of Labor Group		through in Galicia
1885	Establishment of the Land	Aug.	Formation of Progressive
	Bank for the Nobility		Bloc in Duma
1890	Revision of the Law on	1916,	
	the Zemstvos	June-Sep.	Brusilov Offensive
1892	Revision of the law con-	Dec.	Assassination of Rasputin
	cerning municipal govern-	1917,	
	ment	Mar. 8	Outbreak of March
1894	Franco-Russian Alliance		Revolution
1898	Formation of the Russian	Mar. 15	Abdication of Nicholas II
	Social Democratic Labor	Mar. 16	Announcement of forma-
	Party		tion of Provisional Govern-
1901	Combining of Socialist		ment
	Revolutionary groups into	April 16	Arrival of Lenin in
	a party		Petrograd
1903	Formation of Union of	July 16-17	July Uprising
	Emancipation	July 20	Appointment of Kerensky
	Strike movement in		as head of Provisional
	southern Russia		Government
1904, July	Assassination of Plehve	Nov. 7	Outbreak of November
			Revolution

FIFTEEN / REFORM AND REACTION: 1855-1881

The reign of Alexander II, like that of Peter the Great, coincided with a turning point in Russian social, economic, and political development. The reforms and policies of Peter had been intended to stabilize Russia as an absolutist state retaining its serf economy, and to advance it economically and militarily by whatever might be advantageously borrowed from Western Europe. But those of Alexander II took a different turn; they were intended to bring Russia into closer alignment with the monarchies of Central Europe. That would require the creation of an economy based upon free labor, the retention of political and economic superiority of the nobility, the modernization of the legal system and the admission of the populace into limited participation in administration and legislation; but it would not require any limitation of the supreme legislative and administrative power of the crown. Although Alexander II, like Peter, failed to attain all the goals that he set for himself, his reforms helped to bring about such changes that his reign may be considered the second great watershed in Russian history.

Aftermath of the Crimean War

EFFECT ON THE PEOPLE. By the time of Russia's entry into war with the Ottoman Empire in 1853, Nicholas I's suppression of public opinion had practically immobilized all opposition. But the military and administrative failures of the war helped to release them again.

The demonstrated incapacity of the Russian army, the largest and reputedly the mightiest in Europe, which had been the focus of the Russian state and the justification for a costly and oppressive government, weakened the very system of beliefs upon which the autocratic state was based. A militaristic state—and Russia was that—feeds on military victories and starves on defeats. What the Crimean War revealed was a lean prospect for such a state: the egregious errors of the army's high command, the inefficiency of its officers, the knavery of army contractors, and the backwardness of Russian military technology.

A realization of the situation gave the opponents of the regime a new and hopeful outlook. As the writer A. I. Koshelev expressed it: "It seemed as if out of a depressing, dark dungeon we were emerging if not into God's light, at least into an antechamber where we could sense refreshing air." Even the loyal officials of the Emperor expressed their criticisms with more freedom than before. And the peasants expressed theirs in their own fashion. Many of them, having accepted an unfounded rumor that voluntary enlistment in the army would be rewarded with emancipation, joined in mass uprisings when the rumor was proved to be false.

EFFECT ON LEADERS.   Alexander II extricated Russia from the Crimean War before the interior of the country had become a battlefront and before the main forces of the Russian army had engaged in fighting. Consequently, he was able to keep the domestic situation under control and to grant reforms instead of being compelled to give way before the forces which might have been unleashed if the war had been continued. He knew that he would need to effect many changes but, in 1855, he did not have a clear program of changes before him. On March 31, 1856, in a manifesto announcing the terms of the Treaty of Paris, he expressed the hope that Providence would help him to give Russia the assurance "that her internal welfare be secured and perfected; that justice and kindness prevail in her courts; that the desire for education and useful labor develop . . . , and that each man enjoy the fruits of honest labor under the protection of laws equally just for all. . . ." Although those phrases indicated more specific measures than Alexander had under consideration at the time, they were doubtless suggestions of his desire to make some kind of change in the conditions of labor (serfdom), education, and the legal system.

The Emperor's stated intentions roused great expectations among the advocates of reform and seemed to indicate that a new age was in the making. Alexander Herzen, then in exile in London, as well as many others of the radical intellectuals seemed satisfied with the implied promises. They were generally agreed that at that moment practical reforms could go no further than the abolition of serfdom, the extension of education, and the

Alexander II

relaxation of censorship; and they believed that the diffusion of education, the growth of free labor and the development of public opinion were necessary preconditions for further reform. The peasants, however, were not swayed by words which had no immediate meaning for them. Their rioting grew to such an extent and intensity that the Emperor was moved to give first thought to the peasant question. When a group of nobles, alarmed by the suggestion of serf liberation, asked him whether or not he intended to free the serfs, he stated that he had no intention of acting impulsively but that change was imperative and that "it would be better to abolish serfdom from above than wait till it will begin to liberate itself from below."

Alexander II has been called Tsar-Liberator, White Tsar, and even the Abraham Lincoln of Russia; but, actually, neither his training nor his temperament predisposed him for any of those roles. When he came to power at the age of thirty-six, he was better educated, more flexible, and more human than Nicholas had been; but he was otherwise the image of his father, drawn with less severe strokes. Like his father, he saw in himself an autocrat whose duty it was to use the power given to him by Providence. And like his father, he abhorred any movement that challenged the regime he directed. He possessed, however, the wisdom to discern what changes were unavoidable and the strength of character to see those changes through—even over the opposition of the nobility, if necessary.

Peasant reforms

CONSIDERATION AND DISCUSSION. Alexander's manifesto of March 31, 1856, opened official consideration of the problem of the peasants in general and of the serfs in particular. Yet nearly five years passed before the first major legislative enactment concerning the peasants was signed.

The delay was caused by Alexander's wish, in keeping with the policies of previous rulers, to gain the consent of the nobility before undertaking any major changes. He hoped that they, with some encouragement from the government, would work out the conditions under which the serfs might be liberated. But the nobility, even though they recognized the need for serf reform, were anxious to postpone the day of reform as long as possible and to secure themselves by the best possible terms before the dread day arrived. Consequently, there followed a five-year discussion of the problem, actually an organized delaying retreat of the conservative nobility before the offensive of the Emperor, aided by a group of liberal officials and nobles.

Formal discussion was begun in January, 1857, by committees of nobles formed in the various provinces. Proposals of the committees were forwarded to St. Petersburg, where the newly formed Private Committee of the Emperor discussed them and made recommendations. At first the work went slowly because of the dilatory tactics of the conservative nobles on the Private Committee (renamed the Main Committee in the following year), and Alexander made a personal plea that it be hurried along. In 1859 the actual drafting of legislation from the recommendations of the Main Committee was begun by a special committee, in whose work Nicholas Milyutin, Deputy Minister of Interior, acted as spokesman for the Emperor. The special committee completed its task in October, 1860, and submitted a draft of the proposed legislation for the final consideration of the Main Committee. The conservative nobles again retarded action in the Main Committee, and two months passed before the majority of the committee members agreed to the major points of the proposed act. After their agreement, the Emperor turned the project over to the State Council with the admonition that all deliberation be ended by February 27, 1861, so that emancipation might be enacted before the beginning of spring work on the farms. His words left no doubt as to what he expected of the Council: "This I desire, I demand, I command."

FINAL ACTS. The State Council voted on the proposals point by point; and, although its members disapproved some points with negative votes as high as thirty-three to eight, Alexander ordered that the act, with minor amendments, stand as drafted. In its final form the legislation consisted of seventeen articles plus special sections and was titled Act on the Emancipation of the Peasants from Serfdom. The Emperor signed it on March 3. That was followed, in 1866, by special legislation concerning the state peasants, bringing personal liberty to that group also. In addition much special and supplementary legislation was required in dealing with particular problems of emancipation.

EXTENT OF REFORMS. *(a) For the serfs.* Of the approximately 74 million inhabitants of Russia in 1861, about 1.4 million were household serfs; 21 million were serfs working on the land; and 24.7 million were state peasants. By the emancipation act the 22.4 million serfs were given their personal liberty, and the institution of serfdom was brought to an end.

The household serfs were freed but received no land. They could either remain as free, paid servants of the landowners or go where their fancy and economic needs led them. No compensation was made to the former masters for the loss of these serfs.

The emancipation of the land-working serfs was a more involved process. The law provided not only that they retain the land which they had worked for their own use but also that they could not refuse it. The purpose of that provision was to prevent the creation of a landless, agricultural proletariat such as had been created in the Baltic provinces. The landlords were not to be compensated for the loss of their serfs but were to be paid for the land either in money or in labor. One exception to that arrangement was that, if serfs and landlords agreed, they might make a settlement whereby the serfs would retain, without payment, one-quarter (known as the "beggar's quarter") of the lands allotted to them and waive any claim to the remaining three-quarters. Most of the serfs preferred to make a cash settlement. To aid those who had insufficient money to make such a settlement, the state arranged to reimburse the landlords with interest-bearing government bonds and to allow repayment by the former serfs in forty-nine yearly installments (know as "redemption dues") to the imperial treasury. By 1880, settlements had been made on 85 per cent of the land allotted to the freed serfs. Thereafter, the government ordered that immediate settlements on the remaining lands be made under the state-aid plan.

According to the plan of land division, the landlords were to retain that part of their estates which they had formerly set aside for their own use, in most cases about half. The delimitation of the plots to be transferred was no easy task; for the landlords' fields, which had often alternated with those of the serfs, must now be consolidated. In addition, it was necessary to work out rights to pastures, forests, roads, and water. If the peasants and landlords could agree on the division of the land and on the rights, settlements were simplified. But if they did not—as was often the case because the interests of the two parties by no means coincided—determination was made by special commissions appointed by the government. The interests of the landlords often prevailed in these commissions and the decisions therefore favored them. The result was that the landlords often received the more fertile and accessible portions of the arable land as well as the better arrangement with respect to pasturage, forest, and water rights. To add to the peasants' disadvantage the value of the land transferred to them was usually assessed about one-third above its true market price in order to provide the landlords with hidden compensation for lost dues and services.

Since the land allotted to the ex-serfs was in most cases insufficient for subsistence and since they were required to pay for it at inflated prices, most of them were compelled to find additional sources of income in order to feed and clothe themselves and to pay their redemption dues and taxes. So they were thrust by necessity into work as hired agricultural labor on the landlords' estates, into domestic industry, or into other supplementary employment.

The emancipation of the individual serf was further qualified by the nature of his landholding. The title to the land allotted him did not pass to him individually but to his village commune. The government, which had in the past found the commune a useful fiscal and administrative device, now saw the opportunity to continue that usefulness and to strengthen the commune as an institution of social conservatism by vesting in it the rights to the peasant land as well as the responsibility for the payment of redemption dues. Therefore the law provided that land division be made between the landlord and the village commune and that the peasant family be assigned the right and obligation to accept from the commune a portion of the land and, in return, take the responsibility for the payment of its proportionate share of the yearly redemption dues for which the commune was responsible. The law made it possible for a family to withdraw from the commune and to sell its portion of land; but, because of the complications involved in that provision, such action was not feasible.

Thus, although the emancipation act did end the serf-landlord relationship, it did not sever the peasant-commune ties. In fact, emancipation increased the jurisdiction of the commune over its members, for to it were now transferred many of the administrative and police powers which the nobles had formerly exercised. Now it was responsible to the government not only for the payment of redemption dues and taxes but also for the delivery of recruits to the army and for the maintenance of law and order on the basis of customary peasant law. No peasant could leave the locality without a passport (the use of which had been established by Peter I) from the elected officials of the commune; and if he did leave—to work in a factory, for instance—he remained a member of the commune and and was counted in the apportionment of land, taxes, and dues. The heads of the commune were still dominant in the determination of the time and order of tilling and of the crops to be planted. In short, the village commune had become a more important socio-economic-political unit than it had ever been.

The commune remained a stronghold of conservatism, agricultural backwardness and a rough kind of egalitarianism. A peasant could buy or lease land from the landlord, become a moneylender, or even establish a business; but he remained legally bound to his commune, where his status was the same as that of the other members.

(b) For state peasants. Since there were about thirty categories of state peasants, the legislation concerning their status was necessarily voluminous and complex. The most important part of it was the law issued in 1866, providing that they would receive the land which they had been working until that time. It was provided originally that they were to make annual payments on the land for an unlimited period; but in 1886 the terminal date of annual payments was set at 1931, after which the land was to be their property, free of encumbrances. Generally the state peasants did not receive the land as individuals but through the instrumentality of the commune. In effect they were, after 1866, in the same legal and economic position as the former serfs—free of personal servitude to state and landlord, yet members of a commune. However, they received larger plots of land and paid smaller redemption dues than did the former serfs.

LEGAL AND SOCIAL EFFECTS ON PEASANTS. The termination of the police powers of the landlord over the former serfs and of government officials over the former state peasants necessitated the development of new administrative organs. The village commune, as noted above, became the heart of rural administration. To supplement it, the legislation of 1861 and 1866 broadened the powers of the canton. Composed of a group of villages lying usually within an area of a nine-mile radius, the canton might include from seven hundred to five thousand persons. Its government consisted of an elder, assessors, clerk and judges—all elected by an assembly of delegates from the villages. Its court, employing customary law, exercised original jurisdiction and heard appeals from the decisions of the commune assembly. The cantonal government was also the channel for the transmission of orders from the central government; but it did not assume any significant administrative functions.

Both the village commune and the cantonal organization helped to separate the peasant from other social groups, for both bodies were exclusively peasant in composition and jurisdiction. It had been hoped that, when the emancipation act was put into effect, peasant institutions such as these would serve as schools of self-government to prepare the peasants for greater participation in government. The commune, it is true, continued to allow the peasant to participate in the control of his own affairs, but its jurisdiction as well as that of the canton was limited; for police officials and bureaucrats could interfere at will in the affairs of both.

The peasants were free; yet they remained in a class apart. Socially they were at the bottom of the hierarchy. In public places, where they were easily distinguished by their dress and manners, they were treated as trash, being allowed to use only restricted portions of public buildings and facilities. In minor civil and criminal cases, they were subject to a separate set of courts and punishments. Long after flogging had been ended for other classes, the peasants remained legally liable to corporal punishment. And even when the law did not permit, the police, landlords and village elders continued to flog them indiscriminately.

ECONOMIC EFFECTS ON PEASANTS. The reforms, which had been intended to solve the peasant problem without harming the nobility, actually led to a new peasant problem. They created a large free-peasant class unable to support itself from the product of its own land. Even if all the land had been divided among the peasants and even if it had been distributed to the individuals rather than to the communes, it is doubtful that the solution would have been immediately effective. Outdated methods of cultivation which kept down production, agrarian overpopulation, and the absence of large urban centers of employment to siphon off excess agricultural labor would have created a serious agrarian problem within a generation anyway. Emancipation had removed the evils of bondage, but it had not solved the problem of peasant livelihood. And, for that reason, it did not remove peasant bitterness. Within several months after the publication of the emancipation act, troops were required to suppress 337 peasant outbreaks.

EFFECTS ON THE NOBILITY. Emancipation of the serfs accelerated the ruin of many of the nobility in spite of the efforts made to safeguard them from untoward effects. They had been compensated for the loss of their land but not for the loss of serf labor; and, without that, many found it impossible to maintain themselves as in the past. One noble, when asked how he had been affected by the emancipation, remarked, "Formerly we kept no accounts and drank champagne; now we keep accounts and content ourselves with *kvass*" [a cheap fermented drink].

The fact is that few Russian landowners had any interest in agriculture; they simply looked upon the land as the only available source of income. The few who did have that interest settled down and became serious gentlemen farmers after the emancipation. The wealthier and more enterprising ones, particularly those in the black soil regions, introduced improved agricultural methods and machinery and, using hired labor, cultivated their land with success and profit. Among the majority, however, both capital and initiative were lacking; they let their land run down, leased it, or sold it outright. The result was impoverishment and bankruptcy for many.

Further reforms in local government

A NEW PROBLEM.   The abolition of serfdom was the first and most important of the great reforms, but progressive alteration of other aspects of Russian government and life was expected and indeed made necessary because of that first reform. It has been shown how the termination of the administrative and police powers of the nobles over the serfs required the strengthening of the commune and the extension of the cantonal organization. Now, in addition to those peasant administrative units, there was need for new units of local government embracing not only the peasantry but also the other classes.

The problem was recognized at the time of the drafting of the emancipation law and Nicholas Milyutin was placed in charge of working out new legislation for its solution. It was his belief—and Alexander II agreed with it—that local self-government should be instituted as the first step in preparation for popular participation in government. His conception included points similar to those of the Speransky project of 1809 and, like it, was never to be realized in full. Milyutin, as a result of pressure from the conservative nobility, was dismissed from his office early in 1861, and his work was taken over by the conservative Minister of Interior, Peter Valuyev, who favored the predominance of the nobility in local government. The law which Valuyev prepared and presented for the signature of the Emperor on January 13, 1864, was a compromise between his own conception and that of Milyutin.

LAW ON THE ZEMSTVOS.   The law, called the Law on the Zemstvos, provided that the people of each district (*uyezd*) elect an assembly of the Zemstvo (institution of rural self-government) on the basis of indirect and unequal suffrage. It recognized three classes of voters: landowners, wealthier townspeople, and peasants. Provision was made that each class vote separately by means of complex electoral procedures. Representation of the three classes was deliberately weighted so that the nobility might predominate. In the first Zemstvo elections about 43 per cent of the deputies elected to the district Zemstvo assemblies were nobles; 38 per cent were peasants; and about 18 per cent were from other classes, mainly urban. The law directed that each district Zemstvo be elected for a term of three years and that it meet for a ten-day period once a year under the presidency of the district marshal of the nobility. Its duties were to approve the annual budget and plans, elect an executive board every third year, and choose delegates to the Zemstvo assembly of the province in which the district lay. Each provincial Zemstvo assembly, presided over by the marshal of the nobility of the province, was also to meet once a year, consider budget and plans, and select an executive board for a three-year period. The district Zemstvo was given jurisdiction over matters pertaining to the district, and the provincial Zemstvo over such matters as concerned all the districts in the province. Neither had any jurisdiction over the cities.

These institutions, which were introduced in most of European Russia but not in the Asiatic portions, became a vital and important part of the rural life of the country. They were permitted to impose limited taxes on real estate and business enterprises, manage their own property and concern themselves with the construction and maintenance of schools, the construction of local roads and such welfare activities as the improvement and maintenance of public health, poor relief, and veterinary supervision. Their work was not subject to the supervision of any local officials representing the state except that of the governor of each province, who was empowered to judge the legality of their actions. The Zemstvos, however, were given no police power and were required to turn to the state police for assistance when needed.

Through the Zemstvos almost all classes of the population were permitted, albeit on the basis of unequal suffrage, to participate in local rural government; and through them was supplied that which Russia had so seriously lacked, popular initiative. Many of the liberal nobility and intellectuals saw in them the means for enlightenment and improvement. The Zemstvos became particularly active in the advancement of primary education among the peasants, the improvement of public health, and the development of agricultural techniques. Because their task was a formidable one progress was slow, but they did apply a much needed shock to the centuries-old inertia of the countryside. Although their drawbacks were many—the opposition of conservative nobles, nonco-operative officials and tradition-bound peasants, as well as the lack of personnel and money—their gains were soon perceptible. In 1856 there were no more than 8,000 primary schools in all of the empire; in 1880 there were 22,770. Public health and welfare had been almost wholly neglected before 1864 despite the committees appointed by Catherine II; now the Zemstvos brought doctors, nurses, medical aids and veterinaries to the peasants. Such services were not immediately provided, of course, nor were they general (large sections of Russia were without educational or medical facilities as late as 1917), but the pioneering efforts of the Zemstvos were of lasting consequence.

CHANGES IN MUNICIPAL ADMINISTRATION. Catherine II's municipal reforms of 1785 had not created a viable system of municipal government; in fact, most of the organs of government established at that time existed only on paper. Less than one-tenth of those entitled to vote in city elections exercised their franchise, and the affairs of city governments were chaotic. As early as the 1840's Nicholas Milyutin had been asked to draw up a new statute for St. Petersburg, and his recommendations had been adopted there. During Alexander II's period of reforms there were so many demands for change that the Emperor ordered the preparation of a new statute for municipal government throughout the country. The draft of it was ready for issuance in 1866, but a conservative change in the atmosphere at court resulted in its being withheld. When a new statute was finally issued, in June, 1870, it was a conservative one.

The statute of 1870 admitted to the suffrage in each city all men who paid taxes. As in the Prussian electoral system, the voters were divided into three groups, each entitled to elect the same number of delegates to the city duma: the wealthiest, a small minority, who paid one-third of the city's taxes; the less wealthy, a larger minority, who paid a second third; and the poor, the majority, who paid the remaining third. Since each group elected the same number of delegates, the first two groups, although they comprised a minority of each city's voters, elected a majority of the total number.

The delegates—numbering 250 in St. Petersburg, 180 in Moscow, and from 30 to 72 in other cities—formed the city dumas, to which they were elected for terms of four years. In St. Petersburg and in Moscow the mayor was selected by the emperor from two candidates proposed by the city duma. In other cities the municipal officers and mayor were chosen directly by the dumas, subject to the approval of the Ministry of Interior.

The jurisdiction of the municipal governments, like that of the Zemstvos, included education, social welfare, and public safety. And, like the Zemstvos, municipal governments were limited in their taxing powers and were denied control of the chief police functions, which remained under the direction of the central government. They were quite undemocratic since the non-taxpaying proletariat had no vote at all and the vote of the small property owners was dwarfed by the unequal vote given to the large holders of property. Yet, because of the fact that they were allowed much responsibility and were freed from much of the direct intervention by officials of the central government, they were able to show progressive improvement. At a time when the growth of industry and commerce was increasing the importance of cities, they were able, as a result of the authority given them by the new law, to lift their municipalities from the moribund state into which they had fallen. The large cities began to extend their primary education (Kiev, for example, increased the number of city schools sevenfold between 1870 and 1880), to improve public health and to provide other services. Their progress emphasized a fact already established by the work of the Zemstvos: that local initiative, freed from the weight of imperial bureaucracy, could accomplish much.

Legal reforms

NEW COURT SYSTEM.   In his manifesto of 1856 Alexander had implied that the courts would be reformed on the basis of equality before the law. It was generally admitted that the antiquated, corrupt, barbarous, and inequitable court system was not worth salvaging, and in 1862 work was begun on statutes creating a new one. The statutes, based on French and English practice, were published as the law of the land in 1864. They provided for open trials and the jury system, for a well-paid and independent judiciary appointed for life, and for the right to counsel. To handle the trial of petty offenses, a system of justices of the peace to be elected by the Zemstvos and city dumas was established.

EVALUATION.   The new court system, although undoubtedly a major reform, was marked by some weak features: it did not function in cases involving peasants, who remained under the jurisdiction of the communal and cantonal courts; its juries were made up of large property owners; and its juries were not permitted to function in cases of treason or violation of the press laws. Yet the courts represented some advance; they made possible and encouraged the development of an able judiciary and legal profession, and through them was introduced the principle of equality (except for peasants) before the law. Above all, they may be credited with creating the opportunity for the rule of law to develop.

Press-control reform

RELAXATION OF CENSORSHIP. Alexander recognized the necessity for the mitigation of censorship; but few officials—and least of all Alexander—believed that the termination of censorship was either possible or desirable. It was felt that some check on public opinion was necessary but that it was impossible to continue the oppressive measures which had prevailed under Nicholas. Therefore in 1865 a new set of rules was issued. As enforced, these rules relieved the severity of censorship but did not violate the fundamental principle of governmental control of opinion. Their enforcement varied, in some years being relatively mild and in others unpredictably severe; but publishers managed somehow to stem the vexations and frustrations caused by them and to serve legally the rapidly increasing reading public.

RULES ON BOOKS. Under the rules of 1865, all books of less than ten sheets in the original Russian, or of less than twenty sheets in translation, were subject to preliminary censorship. Other books published within Russia were freed of preliminary censorship before printing, but approval of the censors was required before a book could be placed on sale. Even after a book was placed on sale, the government could confiscate it or take action against the publishers. Imported books could not be sold until a special section of the post office had given its approval, and its principles of judgment varied with disquieting frequency; it might permit the importation of Karl Marx's *Capital* in one year and, in another, exclude Hobbes' *Leviathan*.

RULES ON PERIODICALS. The Minister of Interior, who was given the right to decide whether or not periodicals should be subjected to preliminary censorship, decided that the periodicals of the two capitals should have the right to choose either preliminary or punitive censorship. If a periodical chose the latter, it was allowed to publish without preliminary approval of the censors but remained liable to punitive action—reprimand, fine, imprisonment of the editor, or suspension of publication—for anything which proved offensive to the state or public order. Provincial periodicals were compelled to accept preliminary censorship, and their editors were provided with lists of the subjects concerning which discussion was forbidden by the censors. Such lists changed in length and content with the political temper of the government and the inclination of the censors.

Educational reforms

STATUTE ON PRIMARY EDUCATION.   To promote general advancement under the reforms, the repressive educational measures of Nicholas I were rescinded as soon as possible and work on educational legislation was begun. In June, 1864, a new statute on primary education appeared, showing many improvements over former laws. By its provisions Zemstvos, municipal governments, and private persons and groups were permitted to organize and conduct primary schools. The determination of educational policy in each province was placed in the hands of an educational board composed of the governor, the bishop of the Orthodox Church, the director of primary schools and two Zemstvo representatives. As has been seen, the Zemstvos began at once to encourage primary education. It was further extended by the establishment of parochial schools maintained by the Orthodox Church and subsidized by the state, schools supported by city dumas, and schools maintained directly by the state.

STATUTES ON SECONDARY AND HIGHER EDUCATION.   In 1864 there was enacted a new statute on secondary schools, one of the most important provisions of which opened such schools to children of the lower classes. Neither class nor religion might thereafter bar the entry of any applicant who could pass the matriculation examinations. The status of the universities also was liberalized by a statute published in 1863, restoring their autonomy and guaranteeing to their faculties the right to control the administration of the institutions—that is, the right to make appointments of additional faculty members and to control instruction and discipline. In addition, conditions of admission of new students were liberalized. Thus freed from outside domination, the universities entered a period of brilliant achievement which was to last for almost two decades.

AUXILIARY PROBLEMS.   The educational reforms inevitably raised the question of education for girls, who had hitherto been restricted to a few institutes and boarding schools. A movement for the emancipation of women from their inferior legal and social status was begun about this time and, in their behalf, a few timid steps were taken in the field of education.

After 1859 secondary schools for girls were opened in some of the larger cities on private initiative, but their administration was kept under government control. In 1863 courses to train girls for the profession of teaching were introduced in many of the girls' secondary schools.

This growth of interest in education and the rapid extension of facilities were viewed with misgiving by many connected with the government, for they saw the dangerous possibility that the number of critics of the regime might thereby be increased. Yet the development of education, once begun, could not easily be stopped, and the control of the educational processes remained one of the most difficult tasks which the government had to face in the next generations.

Military reforms

BASIC IMPROVEMENTS.   Although the failure of the army in the Crimean War was the starting point of the series of great reforms, the reform of the army itself was the last in the series. The task of demobilizing the wartime army was the work of several years, and the formulation of proposals for change required many more. The moving spirit behind the military reorganization was the brother of Nicholas Milyutin, Count Dmitri A. Milyutin, the Minister of War from 1861 to 1881.

At the beginning of the reorganization the army drew its enlisted men from the peasantry and the lower urban classes—all recruited for terms of twenty-five years. Discipline was tyrannical; men in the lower ranks were treated as if they were convicts, subjected to such punishments as flogging and running the gauntlet. In fact, service in the ranks was one of the punishments for offenses against the state. There was dire need of reforms.

Milyutin, who had the full support of the Emperor, sought to reorganize the army along the lines of the type then coming into approval in Western Europe: an army based on universal military service for a short period followed by enlistment in the reserves. He hoped, too, to raise the dignity of military service in the ranks and to improve the training of officers. During his first years as minister, he eliminated the employment of corporal punishment, improved and regularized the system of military justice, and reduced the term of service to sixteen years.

To improve the training of officers, Milyutin organized a system of military secondary schools to replace the cadet schools, which had offered limited training for the nobility only. In the new schools the students received both general and military education and, upon graduation, entered specialized schools where they were given officer training for the artillery, cavalry, or infantry. The nobility predominated in the new schools, but the entrance of students from other classes was possible. The guards regiments, however, remained the preserve of the nobility.

UNIVERSAL MILITARY SERVICE.   By 1874 the major step in reorganization, the introduction of universal military service, was possible; and in that year a new law replaced the former systems of recruitment with one based on such service. The law provided that each able-bodied youth, irrespective of class, was liable to six years of military service when he reached the age of twenty. Since the state did not have need of all who came of military age nor the financial capacity for training all of them, only a portion—usually about a third—of those eligible for service were actually called. Provisions for exemption from service were generous; only sons and those who were the main support of their families received exemptions. Others were granted reductions in service periods: graduates of universities were required to serve only six months; those with secondary education, two years; and graduates of primary schools, four years. Those who were not called to service were freed of further obligation except for nominal membership in the reserves. Those who were recruited served first in the standing army; then for nine years after completion of service, in the reserves; and for the next five years, in the militia.

The army reform was important not only because it improved the army itself but also because it introduced in Russia the democratic concept of the obligation of all classes to serve in the army.

Outcomes of reforms

GENERAL CHANGES.   Russia after the reforms differed substantially from pre-reform Russia, but the differences must not be ascribed solely to the effect of the reforms. The reforms themselves were made possible, and in some cases inevitable, by socio-economic changes which preceded them. Some of the developing changes were accelerated by them: the growth of an educated urban class, the extension of money relations in agriculture, and the growth of capitalist industry based on free labor. And since the reforms permitted a greater degree of popular participation in local administration than had existed since the earliest days of tsarism, they provided the framework within which legal equality of the classes might develop.

The reforms, however, were only initial steps. On the political plane, they created a dichotomy of autocracy and representative institutions existing side by side, of the arbitrary power of the imperial government operating simultaneously with the legal order of a new court system. The autocracy still retained the superior position by virtue of its exercise of arbitrary action through the bureaucracy, police, and army even while it permitted the rudimentary development of constitutionalism and representative institutions. If the state had voluntarily given up its position, Russia would have followed the paths of European political development. But as long as the state retained that position, the contradictions between the institutions introduced or strengthened by the reforms and the age-old institutions of Russian autocracy would make impossible any social or political equilibrium.

The reforms marked a change not only in the institutional development but also in the public thinking of the country. Under Nicholas' rule the legal discussion of government policy was the affair of secret committees, and public opinion was kept in check by censorship and political police. But Alexander's moves to ease the restrictions on the expression of opinion released a spontaneous development of the press, of book publishing, and of enthusiasm for education which made impossible a return to the atmosphere of the previous reign. Within three years after the beginning of reforms 1,800 book titles were under publication, as against 1,000 titles in 1855; and 66 newspapers and 156 monthlies were being published under license, as against six newspapers and nineteen monthlies ten years earlier. That increase reflected a new demand for information, growing every year as students, mainly of plebeian origin, crowded into the schools.

CHANGES IN THE INTELLIGENTSIA. When, because of the social, economic, and legal changes, the composition of the educated class was changed and its numbers multiplied, the leadership of the nobility in learning and letters was broken, and the center of gravity among the educated shifted to persons of middle-class and plebeian origin. The judicial reforms, the countrywide growth of schools, the establishment of medical, social and educational services by the Zemstvos, and the development of industrial technology led to the creation of a new class, the professionals—lawyers, teachers, doctors, and engineers; and the removal of class restrictions in the secondary and higher schools gave persons of comparatively humble origin access to the education which led to the professions and to government service.

To speak of the first years after the Crimean War as an era of good feeling would be incorrect, but certainly there was far more agreement in the expressions of public opinion than there had been before the war, more agreement indeed than there would be again until the Revolution of 1905. The imperial manifesto of 1856 created optimistic anticipation and the emancipation law encouraged hope among the various educated groups. Of course, many conservative nobles grumbled that the government was moving too fast, and some of the intellectuals murmured that the government was moving too slowly; but between the two extremes the attitude toward the government's efforts was favorable.

New currents of thought were appearing, however, among the youthful and more radical intellectuals recruited from the middle-class students (and, occasionally, noble students) in the secondary and higher schools. Radical youth was becoming impatient with those who showed themselves satisfied with the reforms. The new thinkers, having had no part in the philosophical debates of the 1840's, were laying little stress on philosophical doctrines and much on the test of utility; "natural science" and "progress" were becoming the watchwords of a new generation of intellectuals.

Herzen was a revered name until 1863, but he was an elder statesman of the intelligentsia; the youthful radicals were looking for new spokesmen. They found them in Nicholas Chernyshevsky and Nicholas Dobrolyubov. Both were well-educated sons of priests, who transferred to their politics the religious intensity of their training. They were socialist in their thinking and believed in the radical reconstruction of society. In the *Contemporary*, one of the favorite "thick" journals of the intellectuals, they attacked, in the indirect "Aesopian" language made necessary by censorship, the slowness of reform preparations. But, until the promulgation of the emancipation law of 1861, they believed that a peaceful transition to a new and better society was impossible.

The emancipation law was a sharp disappointment to them and many others of the radical youth because of its requirement of peasant payment for land received, and after its issuance an attitude of bitter opposition to the government began to appear among them. Some of them organized secret revolutionary societies, but their chief actions were confined to revolutionary manifestoes and student demonstrations. As a result of their demonstrations in St. Petersburg and Kazan in the summer and fall of 1861, some were expelled, others arrested. One of the revolutionary "circles," of which Chernyshevsky was a member, prepared revolutionary proclamations to the peasantry; but little came of their efforts since their proclamations were intercepted in manuscript form by the political police.

The young radicals lost one of their leaders in 1861, when Dobrolyubov died, at the age of twenty-five. In the following year, Chernyshevsky
was arrested and sentenced to imprisonment at hard labor, from which he
was not freed until 1883. While in prison he wrote, in the form of a novel,
a revolutionary tract on his dream of Russia's future, *What Is To Be Done*
(1863). Because of the vagaries of censorship, its publication was allowed,
and it became one of the great books of the Russian radical intelligentsia.

The attitude of the new thinkers, with their rejection of authority and
tradition, disturbed many of their elder contemporaries. One of Russia's
foremost novelists, Ivan Turgenev, described the new generation with
some acidity in his novel *Fathers and Sons*, characterizing them as nihilists.
The term *nihilist* was picked up as a badge of honor (though it had been
intended as a stigma) by the radical Dmitri Pisarev and his followers, and
became the designation of their movement for a period. From 1861 until
1866 Pisarev was the spokesman of nihilism, the leader in the propagation
of the belief that no fixed truths or standards could be established and that
no effort to hamper the free development of a personality could be justified. Strictly speaking, nihilism was not a doctrine but a negation of doctrines. It was adopted for a few years by some of the avant-garde intellectuals as a kind of self-conscious attitude and then dropped after the
death of Pisarev. Yet outside Russia—and to some extent within Russia—
the term *nihilist* continued to be used indiscriminately to designate the
later revolutionary terrorists, and it became the mistaken practice to call
all revolutionaries nihilists.

The Polish Revolt, an influence on Russian thought

REBELLION.   The Polish provinces of Russia had not escaped the general intellectual and political agitation that followed the Crimean War.
Economic distress in the cities and the countryside promoted unrest while
the prospect of reform in Russia encouraged the belief among Poles that
their country might yet be free. The moderate elements among the Polish
landowners, who hoped for political concessions from Alexander II, were
encouraged when in 1861 the Emperor began to grant Poland some measures of autonomy. However, these concessions failed to satisfy the aspirations of the more nationalistic Poles. Their goal was the restoration of an
independent Poland within the boundaries of 1772. Impatient and distrustful of Russian promises, they whipped up the fever for military action

against the oppressor. In January, 1863, the inevitable uprising took place, breaking out simultaneously against Russian garrisons in some fifteen places in Congress Poland and in Polish districts of Lithuania and White Russia. Lacking an army, the rebels could not engage in open contest with the Russian army but were compelled to resort to the tactics of guerrilla warfare.

Since Paris was the center of the Polish liberation movement, the rebels hoped for assistance from France. But France, supported by England, limited her aid to suggestions and to diplomatic protests against Russia's violation of the promises made in 1815 with respect to the Kingdom of Poland. Russia, with the solid backing of Prussia and the tardy support of Austria, rejected the protests as well as the suggestion that an international conference be called to consider the Polish situation. Thus the rebels, whose support came chiefly from the landlord and urban classes, were left to fend for themselves in a losing fight. Although the last guerrilla fighters were not defeated until April, 1865, most of the rebellious areas were pacified by mid-1864 after the execution of some 1,500 rebels and the death in fighting of 30,000 others.

CHANGED POLICY. Thereafter Russia adopted a new policy for the handling of the Polish provinces, a policy designed to Russify them and to break the economic strength of the Polish landowners, who had been the supporters of the rebellion. The ten provinces which had formed the Kingdom of Poland were given the administrative name of the Vistula Provinces and placed under the jurisdiction of a Russian governor-general, who made his headquarters in the former palace of the Polish kings. By those acts Congress Poland was officially brought to an end, although the name remained in common usage. To strengthen Russian domination every possible effort was made to eliminate evidences of Polish nationality. Russian was made the compulsory language of the schools and administration; and in 1869 the University of Warsaw, which had been closed since 1832, was reopened, with Russian as the language of instruction.

In the midst of all these offenses against the ruling class, Russia was offering conciliation to the Polish peasants. They were granted a land reform in 1864 which gave them land and freedom (at the expense of their former landlords, of course) on conditions far more favorable than those granted to Russian peasants.

EFFECT ON RUSSIAN THOUGHT. The Polish revolt was reflected in the development of Russian political thought in several ways. A few Russian radicals—most notable among them, Herzen—supported the Poles, but most Russians rallied to the government. The Polish aspirations to achieve their old boundaries roused old antagonisms, and the Polish attacks on Russian troops (in one case, against unarmed soldiers asleep in their barracks) fanned those antagonisms. Too, the attempt at diplomatic intervention by France and England provoked many to patriotic resentment. As a result, public opinion moved perceptibly to the right. Many erstwhile radicals had renounced their former beliefs after the student disturbances of 1861; and now the Polish revolt convinced an even greater number that they must support the pillar of stability, the government.

The change in the popular mood and, more particularly, the conservative reaction to the events in Poland resulted in the slow shifting of the balance of forces within the government to the right. It must be kept in mind that the Emperor, for all his claims to autocratic power, was often required to defer, even when he did not agree, to the opinions of those close about him—the most influential representatives of the nobility, army, Church, and bureaucracy. From the very beginning of the considerations of reforms there had been a tug-of-war between the conservatives and liberals in the government; and, although the competition for influence continued after 1863, the conservatives were slowly gaining advantage. Thereafter, promulgation of reforms continued at a reduced pace, while more and more officials to be entrusted with the execution of the reforms were chosen from the conservative ranks.

Conservative reaction

YOUTH UNDER DISCIPLINE. The strength of the conservatives was increased by the unsuccessful attempt of a student, Dmitri Karakozov, to assassinate the Emperor on April 16, 1866. Although no evidence could be produced—for there was none—that Karakozov had acted in the name of a revolutionary student organization, the conservatives at court made it appear that the attempt was the logical product of the revolutionary ferment which was inevitable in the type of schools set up by the educational reforms. Alexander, as frightened by this event as his father had been by the acts of the Decembrists, agreed that a spirit of dissidence had been produced in the schools and that corrective measures were in order. He made his position known through a statement that "the youth should be instructed in the spirit of the truths of religion, respect for property, and the observance of the fundamental principles of the social order."

Shortly thereafter, the liberal Minister of Education, Count Alexander Golovnin, resigned under attack and was replaced by the reactionary Count Dmitri A. Tolstoy, former Over-Procurator of the Holy Synod. Other ministers and officials who were either suspected of liberalism or who did not show enough conservative spirit were superseded by reactionaries. After these changes, particular emphasis was placed on curbing the seditious spirit in the schools and on the punishment of expressions of that spirit in cases where curbs were disregarded.

Count Tolstoy, like his forerunner Uvarov, wanted education to serve as a dike against revolution. He believed that modern studies, such as those in the natural sciences, only addled the brains of the young and made them the prey of revolutionary nonsense, and that a solid diet of Greek, Latin, and mathematics would, on the contrary, produce the solidity of temperament and tranquillity of mind that were required in educated Russians. With Alexander's support and against the opinion of the majority of the State Council, who found his proposals too harsh, Tolstoy secured the issuance of a new statute on secondary education in 1871. Under this statute the study of the classic languages was given the emphasis he sought; Latin and Greek were to occupy about two hours of each school day, while the study of the natural sciences was ended and that of history, modern languages, and literature limited. The disciplinary effect of the study of the classic tongues organized in as deadening manner as possible was augmented by the introduction of a harsh regime in the government of secondary schools.

Tolstoy's efforts were directed with equal force toward the primary schools, particularly those maintained by the Zemstvos, which were suspected of excessive liberalism. His inspectors kept a watchful eye on those schools and made sure that nothing of a liberal nature be allowed to grow in them. He attempted to reform the universities also, but there he failed. He wielded his influence wherever he could, however, and worked zealously to fulfill his duties, which he interpreted as those of a watchdog of the regime. To do that, he fought not only the free expression of opinion everywhere but also the policies of many of his colleagues.

SETBACK TO REFORMS.   The campaign to repress action and opinion actually or potentially hostile to the government weakened the positive effects of the reforms. Basic to the general weakening was the debility forced upon the new court system which had promised the beginning of the rule of law in Russia. After 1866, the government began to work out various ways by which to prevent the realization of the rule of law and to assure the continuation, side by side with the new court system, of the evils of administrative justice.

The increasingly conservative government was particularly alarmed by the courts' insufficiently severe (from the government's point of view) actions in cases involving violation of the censorship regulations and in cases concerned with offenses against government officials. Typical of the cases involving alarming "leniency" was one in which the writer of an article considered seditious by the government was acquitted by the Crown Court; and another, in which a minor clerk accused of insulting an exalted superior was freed by a court on the ground that he had been temporarily insane. Such cases placed Alexander in a dilemma; he would not rescind the court reforms nor would he tolerate leniency toward persons whom he considered enemies of the existing order. He made the fatal—but, for an autocrat, inevitable—choice of withdrawing from the jurisdiction of the regular courts more and more cases of a political nature and placing them under the jurisdiction of the political police, the gendarmerie. In 1866, press cases were taken out of the hands of the lower courts, and in 1871 preliminary investigation of political crimes was transferred to the political police. In addition, it was provided that certain categories of political offense could be punished, without court action, by a simple administrative order of exile. Later, in 1878, several categories of acts against the state were placed within the competence of military courts—that is, courts martial—operating under Article 279 of the military code, which permitted the application of the death penalty. In this fashion, Russia maintained two systems of law: one, an excellent system administered by the courts; the other, a system which provided arbitrary punishment of such offenses as the government considered political in nature.

IDEOLOGY OF CONSERVATISM. The political developments after 1863 had the effect of crystallizing and polarizing opinion. The radicals, despite— or perhaps because of—the government's repression became more radical while the conservatives became more attached to the government and to Orthodoxy. Between them, the delicate plant of liberalism was trying to sustain itself.

The intellectual conservatism of this period was not a duplication of the "official nationalism" of Nicholas I but a variation of it. Alexander II himself decreed no official ideology, but conservative leaders among the nobles, officials, and clergy began to formulate, justify, and disseminate their beliefs, thus establishing an ideology around the government. At the basis of this ideology was the conviction that Russia was beset on all sides by evil forces which should be rooted out. To accomplish that, according to the conservatives, it was imperative that definite action be taken toward certain aims: the protection of the throne and the Orthodox Church, the assurance of the domination of the Great Russian type, and the protection of the ancient Russian virtues against Western European "decadence." These were aims of frightened people, striking blindly at forces which they did not understand but which they hated and feared.

One of the most influential spokesmen of conservatism was the journalist Michael Katkov. He had begun his intellectual career as a liberal, but he became a devoted supporter of the regime after 1863. As the editor of the *Russian Messenger* and the *Moscow News* he was blessed with the means of publicizing his ideas, and his fulminations against the revolutionary spirit of the youth were eagerly read at court. Nowhere were they as effective as in the office of Count Tolstoy, many of whose educational measures were inspired by Katkov.

But if any man may be credited with the position of ideologue of Russian conservatism, he should be Nicholas Danilevsky, whose major work, *Russia and Europe* (1869), became an outstanding guide of the conservatives. In his beliefs as set forth in this book was to be found the fusion of Slavophilism, imperialism, and "official nationalism." He asserted that cultures were like animal species: they could not breed with one another. Slavic culture could not mix with a non-Slavic culture. It followed then that the Slavs, led by the Russians, should not try to Westernize themselves but should retain their Slavic purity. And the Russians, as mightiest among the Slavs, should free their weaker brothers from alien rule and create a great federation of Slavic peoples with its capital in Constantinople.[1]

Liberalism

SUPPORTERS OF LIBERALISM. Less prominent than the conservative nationalists of the right and less vocal than the radical socialists of the left were the liberals, the advocates of a political system based on representative government and the protection of the rights of individuals. Although their voices were often drowned by the roars of the conservatives and the shouts of the radicals, the liberals were numerous and influential among the educated classes.

Even though Russia lacked the broad middle classes, such as those from

---

[1] It has been suggested that Danilevsky's concept of cultures anticipated the ideas expressed half a century later by Oswald Spengler in his *Decline of the West*.

which the liberals of other European countries were drawn during the nineteenth century, elements of a middle class began to appear after the reforms.
They were drawn at first from members of the professions, and somewhat
later from small groups of urban businessmen. The old merchant class,
rooted in social conservatism, was not attracted by liberal doctrines, but some
of the later men of industry and commerce were gradually drawn to the
support of the liberals. The university and secondary school faculties (but
rarely their student bodies), the bar, and the municipal dumas also supplied
a considerable number of liberals.

THE GOAL OF LIBERALISM.   The fixed aim of Russian liberalism was the
creation of constitutional, representative government for the country—an
aim which had been given its initial public expression by the Decembrist
rebels in their call for "Constantine and a constitution." During the preparation and promulgation of the reforms in the 1860's many dared hope that
the Emperor would—to use the popular phrase of the times—"crown the
edifice" of his reforms by convoking a national assembly representing the
people. Many assemblies of liberal nobles (being the only nongovernmental
bodies permitted to address petitions directly to the emperor) openly petitioned Alexander for a national assembly. The memorial adopted by the
Moscow assembly of nobles in January, 1865, was a typical one: "Sire,
crown the political edifice which you have founded by the convocation of a
general assembly of deputies from all Russia to deliberate on the general
interests of the empire."

IMMEDIATE EFFORTS.   The "edifice" was not crowned, but hope persisted. The Zemstvos, with their wide opportunity for self-government, became an important focus of liberal activity directed toward that hope. Many
liberals, noble and middle class, began active participation in Zemstvo work
as doctors, teachers, statisticians, and agronomists. The work provided for
them not only the opportunity for constructive work among the people but
also the legal opportunity for political experience and organization. In 1878
the Zemstvo organizations of several of the provinces in southern Russia
began a co-operative effort to persuade the government to extend the personal
rights of the Russian subjects and to extend the area of self-government.
Out of this co-operation there developed shortly the Society of the Allied
Zemstvos and of Self-Government (generally called the Zemstvo Alliance),
composed of the more liberal Zemstvo leaders throughout the country.

In 1879 the government forbade the discussion of general political questions by the Zemstvo assemblies; and when their meetings were held in
secret, police action was taken against them. One active liberal among the

Zemstvo workers, Ivan Petrunkevich, was arrested and exiled. His arrest marked the beginning of a change in the operation of the liberal movement. Anxious as they were to use the legal weapons of persuasion to promote their aim of constitutionalism, some liberals saw that to avoid the repressive measures of the government they must adopt the methods of illegality which they deplored in the revolutionary movement; but most of them continued to act within the law.

The socialist movement

THE RADICAL REVIVAL.   Far to the left of the liberals there developed the youthful radical intelligentsia, mentioned earlier in the chapter, whose beliefs may be categorized as socialistic since they were generally based on the concept of the nationalization of the land and the development of co-operative means of production. In the judgment of this segment of the intelligentsia, the reforms of the Emperor were far too slight and the aspirations of the liberals were far too petty; they set their sights on a great basic change in Russian society and government.

The arrests of the revolutionaries such as Chernyshevsky, in 1862, and the conservative effects of the Polish revolt resulted at first in a temporary decline in radical activity and discussion; but in 1864 there was a revival, centered in the student bodies of the universities of Moscow and St. Petersburg, which gathered momentum as the political actions of the government became more repressive. During the decade following the revival, radical activity was largely in the field of discussion, for these were new times and new ideas were abroad.

THE EMIGRES.   Most important among the new features of the socialist movement were the émigré centers and émigré press. Herzen was the first outstanding émigré to make his influence felt after he left the country. Soon many radicals, those harassed by the government and those escaping from prison or Siberian exile, were taking up residence in foreign cities—particularly Geneva, London and Zurich—where they continued to live the life of intellectuals, formulating new and developing old doctrines which they believed would save Russia. Discussion and debate were their chief activities, and their employment often made them unwelcome to their foreign hosts. (In Switzerland, landlords of rooming houses began to advertise: "*Rooms for rent—no Russians.*") The number of émigrés was increased by Russian students who preferred the freedom of foreign universities or who, as in the case of women, sought the educational opportunities which were not obtainable in Russia. In Zurich, the most active émigré center during this period, there were some three hundred Russian students and political émigrés. In such centers the émigrés began to publish radical periodicals in Russian and to smuggle them into Russia, thus publicizing from without the ideas which they could not publicize from within.

During the decade 1864-73 the tendencies of Russian radicalism were personified in two men, Michael Bakunin and Peter Lavrov. Bakunin represented the insurrectionary tendency among the radicals, a tendency which aimed at the destruction of the existing regime by the violent action of a few leaders, to be followed by the conversion of society along completely new lines. He was a noble who had become an active intellectual in the 1840's and, in the ensuing period, had played a leading part in the radical movements of Russia and of other countries. After many arrests, he escaped from Siberian exile in 1861 and made his headquarters for a time in Locarno. He became an anarchist, convinced that the future of Russia lay in its organization on the basis of voluntary association and co-operative production free from any state organization. He argued that a violent insurrection with such an aim might be effected at any time. Many Russian intellectuals were attracted by his beliefs; and in one, the young teacher Sergei Nechayev, he found a fiery leader within Russia. Nechayev went so far as to organize a secret revolutionary group, but it was discovered by the government and broken up in 1871 by arrest and exile. Thereafter, Bakunin's influence in Russia declined, but his anarchistic and insurrectionary ideas did not die out; they were to reappear later in other groups.

Peter Lavrov and his followers, in contrast to the anarchists, were convinced that the transformation of Russia into an agrarian socialist society would be possible only after a program of propaganda and education carried out by the intellectuals among the common people. Lavrov had been a colonel of the artillery and professor of mathematics in the Military Academy before his arrest and exile because of his political opinions. In 1868-69, while still in exile, he published under a pseudonym a series of essays entitled *Historical Letters*, which became the gospel of the socialist movement known as populism *(narodnichestvo)*. He escaped from Russia in 1870 and lived for the next few years in Zurich, where the battle of words among the Bakuninists, the Lavrovists, and other groups was being energetically conducted.

POPULIST CRUSADE. In Zurich, as well as in Russia, the strength of the Populists *(Narodniks)*, of which Lavrov was the chief but not the only spokesman, grew after the appearance of the *Historical Letters*. The idea of going to the people—that is, to the peasants—with a program of propaganda and education impressed great numbers. In 1872 and 1873 student propagandists started to work in various provinces; some became teachers, some medical aides, and all attempted through their contacts with the peasants to spread the new gospel. In 1873-74 the movement to the people was strengthened by the return, on government orders, of all Russian students from Switzerland, and by the end of 1874 it had swelled into a crusade. Nearly two thousand idealistic young zealots, dressed in the clothes of peasants, descended on Russian villages throughout the empire in the expectation of an immediate acceptance by the Russian peasants. But the peasants, to whom the evangelic students appeared as exotic foreigners, were not moved. It is probable that the movement would have collapsed of itself if an alarmed government had not, by mass arrests, insured its collapse.

GROWTH OF REVOLUTIONARY ORGANIZATIONS. The failure of the idealistic movement of the Populists caused many to go over, in desperation, to the insurrectionary point of view. In 1876 there began the formal organization of revolutionary groups committed to the forceful overthrow of the government, and with it began the revolutionary activities which were to continue until they brought a definite change to the country. The first revolutionary organizations to appear were for the most part small groups of intellectuals who believed that the systematic application of terror —that is, the assassination of the worst officials of the regime—might either frighten the government into granting the demands of the revolutionaries or prepare the way for a revolution. Knowing that the oppressed and illiterate masses were not ready for mass activity, the revolutionaries made no appeal for such activity; but they believed that all would welcome the system of people's government, the popular ownership of the land, and the co-operative workshops which would be established when the government was overthrown.

THE PERIOD OF ASSASSINATION. The organization in 1876 of the group which was known as Land and Freedom marked the beginning of what may properly be called the period of assassination; from it there grew within a few years, as a result of a division among its members, a terrorist organization known as The People's Will, which at once began to throw all its energies into its self-assigned task of assassinating as many government officials as possible. Once the terror was released, its spirit infected other groups, and the government might expect it from any direction.

In February, 1878, a young girl, Vera Zasulich, wounded General F.

Trepov, chief of police in St. Petersburg. On August 16 of the same year Sergei Kravchinsky (better known by his *nom de plume* Stepniak) shot and killed the Chief of the Gendarmes, Nicholas Mezentsov, and escaped abroad. In February, 1879, the Governor-General of Kharkov was assassinated. Then attempts on the life of the Emperor were made. One of the most terrifying ones was made by a revolutionary worker engaged in repairs at the Winter Palace. He placed a charge of dynamite beneath a dining room where a dinner of state was to be held on February 17, 1880. It exploded as planned, killing or wounding a number of guards, but did not achieve its purpose; the tsar, delayed by the tardiness of his chief guest, was not even in the dining room at the time. The effort served, however, as a revelation of the opposition's reckless determination.

"Dictatorship of the heart"

NEED TO REGAIN POPULAR CONFIDENCE.   That daring attempt to assassinate the Emperor was a factor in bringing about a shift in governmental policy. Since the late 1870's the government had been aware of the fact that it was losing popular support. The establishment, under Russian auspices, of a liberal constitution in Bulgaria had emphasized the contrast between the leniency of Russian policy abroad and the severity of that practiced at home; and many Zemstvo assemblies had capitalized on that contrast by asking for privileges similar to those given the Bulgarians. Public sentiment had been further offended by the reactionary policies of Count Tolstoy; they had not proved acceptable even to the conservatives and they had not served to create among Russian students the condition of mental equipoise that had been envisaged in their design. Student disorders had, in fact, increased in scope and the growth of revolutionary sentiment among them had become clearly evident.

It was feared at court that increased repression would only alienate the moderate groups among the population; and the government seriously needed their support. Even before the attempted assassination, many high officials advised Alexander to seek by measures of political mildness to regain popular approval and thus to isolate the revolutionaries. After that incident he was willing to accept their advice and, accordingly, adopted a policy popularly known as the "dictatorship of the heart." To effect the new policy an extraordinary body with the title of Supreme Commission was immediately created; and at its head, with quasi-dictatorial powers, was placed the popular general and administrator Count Michael Loris-Melikov.

NEW POLICY IN OPERATION. For a period of six months after his appointment, on February 26, 1880, Loris-Melikov and his commission worked at their new tasks and were able, by the measures they recommended and helped to enforce, to bring about a relaxation of tension. Well-known reactionaries were removed from office—Count Tolstoy, for example, who was replaced by the more moderate Andrei Saburov. The notorious Third Section and its Corps of Gendarmes were placed under the jurisdiction of the Ministry of Interior, and Vyacheslav Plehve was placed in charge of all the police activities of that ministry. At the same time known revolutionaries were arrested and punished.

To regain popular confidence Loris-Melikov proposed that the reforms which had been effected in the earlier part of the reign be continued in full force and that, in addition, advisory bodies composed of representatives of the Zemstvos and city dumas be formed to advise and aid the government in further legislative work. These proposals, with which the Emperor concurred, were not constitutional in nature; they were simply intended to renew the rapport between government and the populace by establishing advisory bodies of a representative nature which would provide a legal channel for the expression of public opinion.

By the summer of 1880, Loris-Melikov was convinced that his commission had fulfilled its mandate, and it was brought to an end. He was then given the post of Minister of Interior, in which office he continued to act as adviser to the Emperor.

The activities of the commission, although they did not satisfy the constitutional aspirations of the liberals, were well received by them, and it appeared that a new period of good feeling was in sight. The revolutionaries, however, were not satisfied. For a few months they held the peace—in part, because of the arrest of many of their leaders; in part, because of a desire to judge the results of the "dictatorship of the heart." When the results proved far from satisfactory to them, they again adopted a policy of terror directed against the person of the Emperor. His death, they believed, would be the impulse necessary to unleash a revolution.

For several months the terrorists, members of The People's Will, attempted to assassinate Alexander II. At first they mined the streets over which the imperial carriage might pass. When these attempts failed, they decided to resort to bomb-throwing. And finally, on March 13, 1881, a bomb thrown by terrorist Ignatius Grinevitsky reached its mark; the Emperor was killed, and the terrorists had achieved what they considered an important goal.

SIXTEEN / BUTTRESSING THE AUTOCRACY:

1881-1904

After the assassination of Alexander II, the dominant groups in the ruling class, convinced that Russia was crumbling under the assault of liberalism, socialism, and other dangerous and insidious forces from the West, felt that only an uncompromising reaffirmation and application of the old principles of autocracy, orthodoxy, and Russian nationality could save the country. They had seen one European nation after another fall before the onslaught of liberalism and observed how even Germany and Austria-Hungary had been compelled to make compromises with it. In the hope of saving Russia from such a fate, they supported the two succeeding emperors, Alexander III (1881-94) and Nicholas II (1894-1917), in most of their efforts to buttress and sustain the autocracy, efforts as grandiose and costly as they were futile.

The last autocrats

ALEXANDER III.   Coming to the throne at the age of thirty-six, Alexander III proved to be a man fitted by both temperament and training to assume the role of defender of autocracy. He viewed the reforms of his father, Alexander II, with distaste and believed that the autocratic system without modification was ideal for Russia. He was vigorously supported in this belief by his chief adviser and former tutor, Constantine Pobedonostsev, the reactionary Over-Procurator of the Holy Synod from 1880 to 1905.

The new ruler, endowed with both physical and spiritual strength,

THE BETTMANN ARCHIVE

Alexander III and his wife, Maria Feodorovna

assumed his imperial duties with firm determination and deep faith in the principles he was resolved to reinforce. The problems faced by Russian autocracy during his reign, however, could not be handled by strength of will alone. Consequently, though Alexander III succeeded in repressing the revolutionary movement, he did not succeed in solving the country's problems. And when he unexpectedly died of nephritis, in November, 1894, he left his son and heir, Nicholas, a realm that was only superficially stable and calm.

NICHOLAS II.   The successor resembled his father in some respects. His education also had been supervised by Pobedonostsev, who had encouraged in him an unswerving faith in the principles of autocracy and in the divine inspiration of the imperial rule. His attitude when he came to power, at the age of twenty-six, is illustrated by his remarks to a delegation sent in January, 1895, to congratulate him on his marriage:

> I am happy to see the delegates of all social classes assembled here to express their feelings of loyalty. I believe in the sincerity of those sentiments which have always been characteristic of the Russians but I am aware that lately there have been in certain Zemstvo assemblies raised voices of certain persons who have permitted themselves to be carried away by the senseless dream of participation by Zemstvo representatives in internal government. Let all know that, in devoting all my strength on behalf of the welfare of my people, I shall defend the principles of autocracy as unswervingly as my deceased father.

In many ways, however, Nicholas II was quite unlike Alexander III. Of slight stature, soft featured, gentle, and affable, he gave the appearance of weakness rather than strength. And he was, in fact, somewhat terrified at first by the unexpected responsibility that the premature death of his father thrust upon him. Because of his initial feeling of insecurity and his apparent indecisiveness, many sought to dominate him: among them, his strong-willed wife, Alexandra, who urged him unceasingly toward stubborn adherence to the principles of autocracy.

Behind this appearance of weakness, there was a basic strength in Nicholas II that was easily missed; actually he was both resolute in matters involving his professed political principles and courageous in the face of adversity. Still, he lacked the ability to give firm and consistent direction to his ministers and, therefore, could be justly charged with permitting the development of divergent and ambiguous policies. It was unfortunate for him as well as for his country that he came to the throne at a time when Russia was about to enter a period of stress and crisis.

Beginning of reactionary control

INITIAL DECISIONS.   When the last ceremonies of mourning for the assassinated emperor were over, Alexander III was faced with the responsibility of making decisions on policy which would determine the future of the imperial regime.

First, there was the problem of dealing with the revolutionary organization whose members had participated in the conspiracy leading to the assassination. On April 15, 1881, Andrei Zhelyabov, Sophia Perovskaya, Nicholas Kibalchich, Timofei Mikhailov, and Nicholas Rysakov were executed (the actual assassin, Grinevitsky, had been fatally wounded by the explosion which had killed the emperor); and during the following year the other members of The People's Will were rounded up and imprisoned. The dispatch and severity employed in handling the cases of these enemies of the autocracy were such as to discourage for the time any activity on the part of others with revolutionary leanings.

Less immediate but more important was the problem of the reforms which Loris-Melikov had proposed and which Alexander II had approved. Among those who favored the speedy execution of them were Loris-Melikov; Minister of War Milyutin; Minister of Finance Alexander Abaza; and the Emperor's uncle, Grand Duke Constantine. Others of equal influence at court were either equivocal in their attitudes or were opposed to the reforms. Pobedonostsev led the opposition, arguing that the acceptance of them would be the first step toward constitutionalism, which, in his opinion, had corrupted Western Europe. "Russia," he asserted, "has become powerful by virtue of the autocracy . . . , by virtue of the close bonds by which the people are attached to their tsar." And the reforms, he believed, would weaken those bonds and lead ultimately to the destruction of autocratic Holy Russia. Also supporting the opposition and echoing the sentiments of Pobedonostsev was the journalist Michael Katkov with his powerful *Russian Messenger,* and *Moscow News.* Finally the Emperor himself was drawn to their side and convinced that public opinion would support a decision to abandon the reforms. Yet, he did not want to make an immediate declaration of his position; for the Loris-Melikov proposals were a legacy from his father which he could not lightly discard.

POBEDONOSTSEV'S TRIUMPH.   Alexander was urged by Pobedonostsev, however, to announce in the imperial manifesto, customarily published at the beginning of a new reign, that he would exercise firm rule in accord with the ancient principles of Russia. And when, on May 11, 1881, the imperial manifesto (in the framing of which Pobedonostsev had a major part) was published, it carried Alexander's statement:

> In the midst of our great grief God's voice commands us to stand courageously at the helm of the government, relying upon Divine Providence, with faith in the power and truth of the autocracy which, for the benefit of the people, we are called upon to strengthen and guard from any encroachments.

Constantine Pobedonostsev

The meaning of the manifesto was clear. After its publication Loris-Melikov, Milyutin, and Abaza, none of whom had been consulted in its preparation, resigned. The Loris-Melikov reforms were buried.

The resignation of the three comparatively liberal ministers was not immediately followed, as may have been hoped, by the consolidation of the government. General Count Nicholas Ignatiev, who succeeded Loris-Melikov as Minister of Interior, the most important official in the government, was a Pan-Slavist and he still held to the Slavophile belief that the ancient custom of summoning the Assembly of the Land should be revived and that the Assembly should be employed as a consultative body. That belief was his undoing; Pobedonostsev convinced the Emperor that it was simply constitutionalism in Russian dress, and Ignatiev (although he was in many ways a reactionary) was dismissed in May, 1882. The aged, reactionary Count Dmitri Tolstoy was appointed in his place, and with that appointment began a period of intensified reactionary government which was not to be mitigated until 1904.

A NEW PROGRAM. The victory of the reactionary wing at court meant the victory of a policy aimed at preserving and buttressing the autocratic regime as the only protection of Russia from the forces which had succeeded in undermining monarchical government and society in Western Europe. To strengthen the autocracy would require the rigid repression of dissenting opinion, political criticism and self-government while the power of the central government, and especially of its police, was being enhanced. The institutions which governed opinion would be required once more to mold the people to uniform specifications: Orthodox in faith, Russian in speech, and loyal in heart. And the nobility, which had of old been the good right arm of the autocracy, would be given renewed strength. An imperial manifesto issued in 1885, on the centenary of Catherine II's Charter of the Nobility, expressed the desire that

> the Russian nobles preserve the preponderance in the command of the army, in local administration and in the courts, in the propagation, by their example, of the precepts of faith and loyalty and sound principles of popular education.

It was an anachronistic plan to bail a leaking ship with the aid of a leaking pail. As long as this program was followed, there was no possibility of the peaceful accommodation of Russian institutions to the demands of new times.

GENERAL RESPONSE. Generally speaking, the public response to the government's new program was favorable. Although it involved a return to the "official nationalism" of Nicholas I, which had found limited acceptance, it had considerable support not only within the government but also throughout the country. Circumstances had prepared that support. In the bureaucracy, the army, the Russian Orthodox Church, among the conservative nobility, and even among the peasantry, the assassination of the Emperor had created a feeling of fear and anger. Undirected, that feeling had broken out in some instances with tragic results; immediately after Alexander's death, pogroms against Jews had occurred in 215 places in Russia. In other instances its intensity had been directed into organized efforts such as that of the government officials who formed the shortlived Sacred League, a prototype of later reactionary organizations, with the avowed purpose of safeguarding the regime. As patriotic and conservative elements were drawn together by a common cause, the preservation of their country, their strength became a telling factor in the development of the new program.

SPOKESMEN AND DEFENDERS. Constantine Pobedonostsev continued as the most influential spokesman of the official point of view. As such, he decried all the innovations which had appeared in Western Europe during the century, especially representative government, freedom of opinion, and the separation of Church and state. He was unmistakably emphatic about what he considered the proper foundation of government: "The confidence of the people in its rulers is founded on faith—that is, not only on identity of religious profession, but on the simple conviction that its rulers have faith themselves and rule according to it." In short, the autocratic state based on Orthodoxy could be the only genuine voice of the people.

Katkov remained, as before 1881, the most widely read of the journalistic spokesmen of conservatism and reaction. The work of other writers, also, served in the defense of reaction, but in a less direct manner. Danilevsky's *Russia and Europe* was still an intellectual inspiration to many, as were also Dostoyevsky's novels and journalistic writings, which contrasted the virtues of Orthodox Russia with the shortcomings of the decadent and atheistic West. Constantine Leontiev added to the disrespect for the decaying West through his writings, among which the most important was *By-zantium and Slavdom*. Altogether, this period's defenders of Russian society and civilization contributed little in the way of original thought; but their defensive ideology, which at its worst was characterized by a blind hatred and at its best by a deep religious faith, was typical of the thinking and expressive of the emotions which prompted the policies of the government in the generation following the death of Alexander II.

The machinery of reaction

INTENSIFIED POLICE POWER.   One of the first tasks undertaken after the beginning of the new regime was the repression of political opposition by police action. In order to provide for the rapid liquidation of the revolutionary movement, the police powers of the state were reinforced and the power of the regular courts, already enfeebled, was further limited in cases involving political offenses against the state. In August, 1881, a statute known as the Law on Exceptional Measures was enacted as an emergency step. Its original enactment was for a three-year period, but the government became so reliant upon it that it was repeatedly re-enacted until the end of the imperial regime.

The Law on Exceptional Measures invested governors and police officials with extraordinary powers in localities where, in the opinion of the authorities, political conditions required exceptional measures; and there were many such places. A locality might be designated as being under "reinforced protection"—the civil equivalent of limited martial law, or under "extraordinary protection"—the equivalent of complete martial law. The occasion for one of these designations might be a peasant riot, the anxiety of the governor, the discovery of a revolutionary organization, or any evidence of illegal political activities. When a locality had been singled out for special attention, the governor or chief of police could issue special regulations the severity of which depended upon the degree of "protection" deemed necessary to preserve security there. By those regulations they might close commercial and industrial establishments or arrest, fine, imprison, or banish persons guilty (or suspected) of political offenses or violation of security regulations. A governor of an area under "extraordinary protection" could, subject to the approval of the Ministry of Interior, banish any person from his area.

The law of 1881, supplemented by later regulations, also extended the

jurisdiction of administrative justice. Persons charged with a political offense, such as membership in an illegal organization, circulation of illegal
literature, or participation in unauthorized meetings, might still be tried
in the regular courts; but it became the practice to sentence such persons
to imprisonment or banishment to remote parts of the empire by administrative action—that is, action by administrative or police officials, subject to
the confirmation of a committee composed of representatives of the Ministries of Interior and Justice.

In some instances, persons suspected of unhealthy political thoughts
or actions might be placed under police surveillance and forbidden, while
subject to surveillance, to engage in professions such as teaching or the practice of law or medicine. In time, it was required that anyone employed in
the professions or in any work of a governmental character should hold a
certificate of political reliability, which he could obtain only from the governor's office and only after having been cleared by the police.

The campaign against revolutionary activity—which soon became a
campaign against all political opposition—increased the importance of the
police, particularly those assigned to the duty of guarding the security
of the state. Although the Third Section and the Corps of Gendarmes had
been transferred to the police department of the Ministry of Interior in
1880, there was no decrease in the importance of their political police
activities. The Corps of Gendarmes continued as a distinct body whose special duty was the safeguarding of political security. It and other sections
of the police employed a host of plainclothes detectives as well as secret
agents whose duty it was to report on sedition and political unrest. In the
cities even the janitors and owners of houses were considered by law as unpaid agents of the police and were required to report to them the comings
and goings of persons resident in the houses under their care.

CENSORSHIP.   While extraordinary police measures were being taken
to isolate and stamp out revolutionary activity, censorship was being employed with renewed zeal to eradicate revolutionary ideas. In 1882 Tolstoy
issued "temporary" regulations for the press which added to the restrictions
of the press rules issued in 1865.[1] The regulations created a special committee composed of the Over-Procurator of the Holy Synod and the Ministers of Interior, Justice and Education, whose decision could shut down
any offending press or forbid any offending editor to publish again. They
provided also that St. Petersburg and Moscow newspapers which had been

[1] Most of the "temporary" regulations issued in 1881-82 remained in force until 1906,
and some until 1917.

suspended by the censors would be required, after resumption of publication, to submit all copy for preliminary censorship no later than the evening before publication. This provision had the intended effect of causing many liberal daily newspapers which had been suspended to end their operations.

The situation elsewhere in the country was far worse; for censors outside the capitals—usually officials in the governors' offices—were allowed to make special rules, and their severity was deadening to the provincial newspapers, which were sometimes forbidden even to publish material that had appeared in the St. Petersburg press. As a consequence of the rigid regulations everywhere, the legal press of the period gave a completely distorted picture of Russian life. Occasionally a clever editor might evade the censor as did the editor of the *Riga Vestnik* when he stated in his paper:

> In today's issue it was our intention to have a leading editorial urging the Estonians to unite more closely among themselves and with the Russians, and to work with manly energy for the Fatherland; but we have not been allowed to print it.

But such evasions were exceptions to the general practice, and such daring was dangerous.

Public libraries, too, were subject to surveillance, and their circulation of books not approved by the Ministry of Public Instruction was forbidden. Among the books which they might not circulate were those of Lyell, Mill, Spencer, Renan, and Haeckel.

EDUCATION.   Tolstoy, who had once distinguished himself as Minister of Education, believed that the source of revolutionary agitation lay in the laxity of the schools; and now, as Minister of Interior, he was again in a position to encourage the elimination of that laxity and the establishment of curbs on any educational activities of which the government disapproved. Pobedonostsev also was active in his disapproval of the existing educational system, believing that universal education was pernicious and urging that all primary schools be placed under the jurisdiction of the Church. He was unable to achieve complete success for his ideas, but at his insistence a law enacted in 1884 transferred to the control of the Holy Synod a number of primary schools which had been established by the peasantry. These schools and the small number of existing primary parochial schools became the center of an expanding network of parochial schools administered by the Orthodox Church and supported in large part by the state. Thus Russia came to have two sets of competing primary schools in rural areas, the parochial schools and those maintained by the Zemstvos. The number of parochial schools grew from 4,500 in 1882 to 32,000 in 1894, but they lagged far behind the Zemstvo schools in popularity and quality, rarely teaching more than the ABC's and a few religious hymns.

Since the program of the secondary schools had been effectively shaped before 1881, the activities of the government were directed now principally toward the exclusion from them of children of socially inferior parents. In 1887 the Minister of Education, Count Ivan Delyanov, who followed the lead of Tolstoy and Pobedonostsev, instructed secondary school officials to investigate the homes of applicants for admission, to make certain that their homes possessed "all the necessary comforts for their scholarly activities"—that is, to eliminate applicants from poor homes. In the same year he ordered an increase in tuition fees in secondary schools so that "children of coachmen, servants, laundresses, small shopkeepers, and the like" should not be encouraged to rise above their station.

Tolstoy's aim to curb the universities, which had been frustrated by Alexander II, was finally achieved in 1884 through the issuance of a new university statute. By that statute the autonomy of the universities was finally broken, and full control over them was placed in the hands of the Minister of Education, who would henceforth choose professors and university administrative officers. Students were forbidden to join clubs or other organizations under penalty of immediate conscription in the army. Now government control over higher education was complete; and Katkov, many of whose ideas had been incorporated in the new regulations, could crow, "Rise, gentlemen, the government is coming, the government is returning."

THE REVITALIZED NOBILITY. To strengthen reactionary control the government undertook to bolster the economic position of the nobles and to increase their control of the Zemstvo and peasant organs of self-government.

In 1885 the Nobles' Land Bank, a governmental establishment, was set up to provide credit on easy terms to the nobility as a "means of preserving for their posterity the estates in their possession." In contrast to the bank created in 1754, it accepted land, not peasants, as security for repayment of loans. The scale of its operations may be judged from the fact that in 1904 one-third of the noble estates were mortgaged to it.

In order to give the nobles—and hence the government—closer control over peasant institutions, a new office was created in 1889, that of land captain (zemsky nachalnik). Each land captain, chosen from among the local nobility and confirmed by the Minister of Interior, was to exercise judicial and administrative control over the cantonal organization of the peasants in his canton. He was to be present at all cantonal meetings and review all of their proceedings. He was also to assume many of the judicial powers previously given to the cantonal courts: to act as judge in civil and criminal cases involving peasants, to make awards, to levy small fines and to impose terms of imprisonment up to three days. These powers, of course, gave the land captains endless opportunities for graft and for interference in peasant affairs. In fact, after 1889 self-government by the peasants deteriorated into a meaningless operation, for the elected peasant officers soon became agents of the land captain and began to display a despotic and often venal attitude toward their fellow peasants. As for the land captain himself, his loyalty was not to the peasants but to the Ministry of Interior and to the governor.

The position of the nobility in the Zemstvos was strengthened by a new statute on the Zemstvos issued in 1890, strengthening the class principle in their elections by increasing the proportion of noble representatives so that they thereafter comprised 57 per cent of the delegates elected to the district Zemstvo assemblies. In addition, the peasant assemblies were required by the new law to select twice as many candidates for Zemstvo assemblies as there were places and to submit their names to the governor, who, on the advice of the land captains, would choose the peasant delegates from among those named on the list. Thus virtually complete control of Zemstvo assemblies was placed in the hands of the nobility.

The law, at the same time, reduced the power of the Zemstvo institutions. Before 1890 the governor could veto Zemstvo acts only if they were illegal; after 1890 he was permitted to veto acts which in his opinion were contrary to the best interests of the state or the locality. Although the Zemstvos might appeal to the Senate in case of a veto, their appeals were usually denied. As a result of this arrangement, the Zemstvos spent much of their time after 1890 in conflicts with the governors.

THE CITY BUREAUCRACY.   In the government of cities the enhancement of bureaucratic power was even greater than in the Zemstvo institutions. A new statute issued in 1892 to modify the 1870 statute on city government provided that voting thereafter was to be by election districts rather than by the three-class system and that the property qualifications of voters was to be increased. By the later provision, the power of the wealthy was increased and the number of voters decreased; in St. Petersburg, for instance, the number was decreased from 21,000 to 8,000 (in a population of 1,250,000). However, just as the government did not put all its faith in the nobility in the Zemstvo institutions, so it did not trust completely the few wealthy voters in the cities. City officials were required to have the approval of the government before their confirmation in office, and their actions as well as those of the city councils were subject to the arbitrary veto of the central government.

Effect of reaction on national and religious minorities

RUSSIAN NATIONALISM.   The policies of Alexander III and Nicholas II toward the non-Russians and the non-Orthodox—policies generally grouped under the convenient label of "official Russification"—were born of a spirit that was beginning to move not only the ruling classes but many of the lower classes as well. The spirit of intolerance, chauvinism, and repression which characterized official policy after 1881 was undoubtedly inspired and sustained by the emperors and their officials, but it had a helpful amount of popular approval. Many were convinced that the growing spirit of nationalism among the non-Russian peoples of the border provinces such as Finland, the Baltic provinces, Lithuania, Congress Poland, and the Ukraine could result only in separation, and they were willing to see steps taken to prevent that result. Many sections of the Russian population had supported the official policy of Russification in Congress Poland after the revolt of 1863, and they now saw the possible need for extending that policy.

The core of the Russian Orthodox population was surrounded by a large minority of non-Russian and non-Orthodox peoples. The census of 1897, the first reliable one, showed that Russia had a population of nearly 129 million, of which 88 million were Great Russians, Ukrainians and White Russians and 41 million were non-Russians. The Poles, 9 million in number, were the largest ethnic minority; but there were in addition 11 million classified as Turco-Tatars, 6 million Finns (a category which included not only Finns but various related ethnic groups also), 5.6 million Lithuanians (probably including Letts), and nearly 5 million Jews—about half the Jews in the world.

Russian concern about those minority groups had come about as a result of the growth of Russian nationalism. In its most extreme form it was a fusion of three elements: national self-awareness, defensiveness, and intolerance.

The most positive and enduring one was national self-awareness, which had been developing for some time. Whereas in earlier periods, the focus of Russian self-awareness had been the Russian Orthodox Church, since the latter part of the eighteenth century the focus had been shifted to native language, literature, music, and scholarship. The educated Russian still regarded French as his second language, but he did not apologize for Russian culture as had the educated gentleman of the earlier years.

Defensiveness had grown particularly fast during the middle years of the century, when European antagonism toward Russian ambition in the Near East, toward Russian mistreatment of national minorities (particularly the Poles), and toward Russian autocracy in general had brought about an attitude of defense against foreign criticism. Out of this attitude had come an intensified feeling of Russian superiority and an increased distrust of foreign nations.

Intolerance, the third element in Russian nationalism, was fed by the stirrings of the non-Russian nationalities in the empire and by the growing revolutionary movement. Moved by hysterical self-deception, many saw in the non-Russian nationalities the chief danger to the integrity and security of the empire. In the first place, it was alleged, the non-Russians were seeking foreign aid for the purpose of establishing the independence of the border provinces. That allegation, except in the case of the Polish revolt of 1863, was unfounded; actually, the policy of Russification helped to inspire separatist sentiments where none had been asserted previously. In the second place, according to the extreme nationalists, the non-Russians—especially the Jews—were the source of revolutionary disturbance. And there again, by urging the policy of Russification, they helped the growth of the very evil they sought to destroy—revolutionary sentiments among the national minorities.

RUSSIFICATION. The official policy of Russification, which was revived after 1863 and broadened after 1881, was built upon the pathological fear of revolution which animated the government. It was carried forward as an urgent necessity with the avowed purpose of preserving the regime and the Empire by the elimination of cultural divergencies and the establishment of uniformity in language, beliefs, institutions and loyalty.

The Russification of Congress Poland was pressed with particular intensity after 1881. Persons of Polish origin and of the Catholic faith were prohibited from holding official positions either in Congress Poland or in the bordering regions of Lithuania, White Russia, and the Ukraine. All instruction in Polish in the primary and secondary schools—except that involved in the teaching of the catechism and of the Polish language itself—

was prohibited by law in 1885, and seven years later the use of Polish in Catholic religious instruction was likewise forbidden.

The Finns next felt the effects of the new policies. From the time of its union with Russia, in 1809, the government of the Grand Duchy of Finland had been completely distinct from that of the rest of the empire; it had enjoyed all the rights of autonomy and of representative government. Some jurists had argued that Finland was not, in fact, a part of the Russian Empire, that it was linked to Russia only by the fact that the two countries had a common ruler. In any case, it was a definite source of irritation to the Russian Government; for it was the major exception to the policy of centralization, and its liberal government made an unpleasant contrast to that of Russia. Therefore the policy of St. Petersburg was directed at assimilating Finland into the general structure of the empire. As the first step toward that end, the postal and telegraph services of the country, hitherto distinct from those of Russia, were placed under the direction of the Russian Ministry of Interior in 1890; and thereafter Russification was pushed forward relentlessly. Each step met with the opposition of the Finnish Diet, and each demonstration of opposition led to firmer action by Russia. In 1898 General Nicholas Bobrikov was appointed Governor-General of Finland; and, with the support of the Minister of War, Alexis Kuropatkin, he slashed away vigorously at its autonomous rights. He combined its armed forces with those of Russia and imposed the Russian language and Russian officials upon the Grand Duchy. In 1903 it became necessary to give Bobrikov powers generally used under martial law in order that he could quell the mounting opposition of the Finns, and thereafter he advanced the Russification program at will until his assassination, in 1904.

Although the Baltic Germans continued in high favor in the Russian bureaucracy and army until World War I, the Baltic provinces were not exempt from the sweep of Russification. The government's impelling wish to eliminate autonomous and non-Russian institutions combined with its fear of German nationalism among the Baltic Germans led to the formation of a new policy toward those provinces. The Estonians and Letts, hitherto hardly acknowledged as national minorities, were encouraged by official Russian propaganda against their German landlords; and from 1885 on, St. Petersburg sought to curb both the Lutheran Church and the German language of the Baltic upper classes. The campaign against the Lutheran Church was devoted chiefly to making its work as difficult as possible: construction of new churches without permission from the Holy

Synod was forbidden; Lutherans, especially among the Estonians and Letts, were energetically proselytized by the Russian Orthodox Church; and Lutheran attempts to reconvert the converts were punished. The attack on the German language was even more direct: all schools, except the Lutheran theological school at the University of Dorpat, were required to change their language of instruction from German to Russian; and government offices in the provinces were ordered to use only Russian in official documents.

The Russification policies were extended also to the Ukrainians. Although Ukrainian nationalism at the time of the Polish revolt was only a movement of cultural revival, it was treated as if it were part of a dangerous separatist conspiracy. To suppress it, the government forbade that any books except those in the field of belles-lettres be printed in Ukrainian after 1864. Then, in 1876, the importation of books in Ukrainian was proscribed and theatrical performances in that language were prohibited.

The activities of Russification reached out even to the millions of non-Russian peoples of the Caucasus and Central Asia who, by gradual conquest, had been brought under imperial control but not, until this time, subjected to an active program of integration. If conventional methods of enforcing the new scheme of things proved ineffectual, others were tried. When Prince Golitsyn, appointed Governor-General of the Caucasus in 1897, closed the schools conducted in the Armenian language and confiscated the property of the Armenian Church, he was faced with armed resistance and, in defense, undertook to rouse the Moslem Tatars in the Caucasus against the Armenians. Such tactics were not uncommon, nor were they considered improper in the execution of a policy to which the government attached such vital importance.

IMPOSITION OF ORTHODOXY.   Russification activities were accompanied, wherever possible, by the imposition of the Russian Orthodox faith on those who lacked it, the aim being both to Russify the non-Russians and to bring back to the Orthodox fold those Russians who had left it. The recreant Russians were subjected to the harsher treatment. Although all Russians were considered, *ipso facto*, members of the Russian Orthodox Church and were forbidden to leave the Church, it is estimated that in 1881 nearly 13 million Russians were Old Believers or members of various sects, while an unestimated number clung secretly to the forbidden Uniat Church or were members of the Roman Catholic Church.

Since most of the Old Believers outwardly conformed to the usages of the Orthodox Church and were usually tolerated by the Orthodox priests and local officials because of payment of fees to the one group and bribes to the other, they remained relatively unmolested. Russian Uniats and Catholics, however, were treated with severity; and two Russian sects, the Stundists and the Dukhobors, were rigorously persecuted. The Stundists, a sect inspired by German Baptist influence, were declared by law in 1894 to be "particularly pernicious" and were therefore denied the right of religious gathering. The Dukhobors, who had been persecuted by Nicholas I, were once more attacked by the authorities in 1895; many were then exiled to Transcaucasia, and four years later a group of more than 7,000 emigrated to Canada.

ANTISEMITISM.   The official Russian policy of antisemitism from 1881 to 1917 is often mistakenly considered one facet of the general policy of Russification; but, although official antisemitism went hand in hand with the general policy, it was in fact the obverse of Russification. It was a policy intended to isolate the Jewish population of Russia and, if possible, to end their existence.

Nicholas I had attempted to force Russification upon the Jews. And Alexander II had sought to encourage their Russification by exempting special classes of them from the legal restrictions under which the entire group lived. During his reign educational institutions had been opened freely to them, and those who had received a higher education had been permitted to reside outside the Pale of Settlement and to enter government services. Also, the privilege of residence in the interior of Russia had been granted to merchants of the first guild, specified classes of artisans, and ex-soldiers. After the Polish revolt, however, a policy of severity had begun to take shape.

After Alexander II's death, although only one Jewish girl had taken part—and a minor part at that—in the preparation of the assassination, official propaganda began to attribute the assassination and practically all other revolutionary activity to the Jews. In the middle of April, the first pogrom began in New Russia; and in the next few months there were 215 pogroms, resulting in the murder of thousands of Jews, mainly in southwestern Russia. The origin of these outbreaks is still not certain. The suspicion once held, that they were engineered by the central government, has not been confirmed; it is known, however, that local officials and military authorities either encouraged or permitted them.

The outbreaks compelled the government to reconsider its policy toward the Jewish question. Alexander III and his advisers officially deplored the massacres but in fact condoned them by insisting that the Jews had created the provocation. Official antisemitism was explained as the government's concession to popular hatred brought on by Jewish exploitation of the peasants or by Jewish participation in the revolutionary movement. After 1881 the official policy was one of dry pogrom[1] and encouragement of antisemitism. The Minister of Interior, Ignatiev, announced: "The western border [of Russia] . . . is open for the Jews. . . . Their emigration would not be subject to any restrictions." Pobedonostsev expressed the opinion that the Jewish problem would be solved only when one-third had emigrated, another third had accepted conversion to Russian Orthodoxy, and the remainder had disappeared.

The program which was followed thereafter was one of steady whittling away of the already limited Jewish rights. In May, 1882, "Temporary Regulations"—which remained in effect until 1917—prohibited Jews within the Pale from settling or acquiring real estate outside towns and cities and forbade their conducting business on Sundays. In 1887 their educational opportunities were narrowed down by the setting of low quotas for the admission of Jewish students to secondary and higher schools. Restriction followed restriction until all Jews were debarred from government service and (in practice, after 1889) from the bar, subjected to conscription (but denied in practice the opportunity to become officers), and prohibited from voting for members of the Zemstvos or of the city dumas. Thus hampered by law and harried by its capricious and brutal application, the Jews declined year by year in their economic and political position.

The Russian state in 1904

CENTRAL ADMINISTRATION.   After a survey of the twenty-three years of strenuous efforts to buttress the autocratic principle, it is interesting to see just what kind of state Russia had become by 1904. Was it a state sustained solely by that force which had upheld the official policy of repression since 1881? It has been said that no state can exist without the use of force and that no state can exist solely on the basis of force. If not force alone, then what was basic to the existence of the Russian state at the turn of the century?

The Fundamental Laws of the empire stated—without change until 1906: "To the Emperor of All the Russias belongs the supreme autocratic and unlimited power. Not only fear, but also conscience commanded by

[1] Dry pogrom is the name given to the practice of continuous harassment and intimidation, stopping short of bloodshed.

God Himself, is the basis of obedience to this power." The emperor was still the fountainhead of law and justice, supreme defender and guardian of the dogmas of the Orthodox faith, the preserver of Orthodoxy, and autocrat of all the Russias. He appointed, directly or indirectly, all the officials of the central government. And, although the State Council assisted in the work of legislation, all legislative proposals originated, in theory, from him.

Usually a proposed law was first examined by the ministry concerned and passed on to the State Council, which possessed only advisory power. Then the emperor, after hearing the opinion of the State Council, made his decision; and, if he so decided, the proposal became law. The State Council discharged also the duties of issuing administrative decrees and examining the imperial budget. The Senate fulfilled both administrative and judicial functions, supervising the work of administration, hearing complaints against administrators, and serving as the highest administrative court and the highest court of appeal in the land.

Two classes of administrative work were recognized by the government: that which dealt with the personal affairs of the emperor and other members of the imperial family and that which dealt with the broader aspects of governmental operation. The Ministry of the Imperial Court managed the affairs of court and the personal estates and properties of the imperial family, whose lands were counted in several hundred millions of acres. The Imperial Chancellery looked after promotions in the administration and handled most of the paper work of the emperor, personal as well as official. And the Imperial Chancellery for the Administration of the Institutions of the Empress Maria administered certain philanthropies and schools under the direct care of the emperor.

The chief work of central administration lay within the jurisdiction of eleven ministries: foreign affairs, war, navy, interior, justice, finance, agriculture, means of communication, education, horse breeding, and state control. The specific duties of most of the ministries are evident in their names. Four, however, were assigned broad and varied tasks not identified exactly by their names: the Ministry of Interior, the Ministry of Finance, the Ministry of Means of Communication, and the Ministry of State Control. Of these the Ministry of Interior was by far the most important. It directed police activities, censorship, postal and telegraph services, public assistance, and the special institutions of the nobility; it also supervised the organs of self-government and the governing bodies of organized and recognized religions of the empire. Since the state played an important part in the economic life of the country, the Ministry of Finance was another key department. It was responsible not only for the finances of the government, including the collection of taxes and customs and the administration of the alcohol monopoly, but also for the encouragement of industry and commerce. The Ministry of Means of Communication administered the imperial roads as well as the state railroads. The Ministry of State Control served as a general accounting office for the government.

The ministers functioned collectively as two bodies: the Council of Ministers and the Committee of Ministers. As the Council of Ministers, they were presided over by the emperor and met only at his command, considering matters of policy and exerting only such influence as was permitted them by the emperor. However, as the Committee of Ministers, which met with the chief functionaries of the State Council, they were an active body. Their task, in that capacity, was the consideration of specific administrative problems, but their decisions were still dependent upon imperial approval.

The foregoing would suggest that the emperor assigned himself much work; and he did. Nicholas II did not, of course, reach independent decisions on all matters which required his signature; but he conscientiously believed, although often mistakenly, that he made the chief decisions. Sometimes he did act independently and against the best counsel of his ministers, but more often than not he sought advice in deciding whether or not to issue a law, change a policy, or make an appointment. Frequently he made advised decisions only to reverse them later. In 1895, for example, when selecting a new Minister of Interior, he followed the advice of Pobedonostsev not to appoint Dmitri Sipyagin or Vyacheslav Plehve because one was "an imbecile" and the other "a scoundrel;" but in 1899 he gave Sipyagin the appointment, and in 1902 he chose Plehve for the post.

LOCAL ADMINISTRATION. The basic unit of administration continued to be the province, ruled by a governor acting as minor emperor. At the turn of the century Russia was divided into ninety-six provinces[1] and the separate administration of Sakhalin Island. Apart from these units were the cities of St. Petersburg, Odessa, Sevastopol, and Kertch; they were known as prefectural cities and were administered directly by the central government.

The governor of each province was the representative of the central

---

[1] Seventy-eight were classified as *gubernii* and eighteen either as *oblasty* or *provintsii*.

administration and more specifically of the Ministry of Interior. Assisted by a council, he issued necessary decrees and supervised all administrative offices and organs of self-government in his area. A province was generally divided into from eight to twelve police districts, each under the district chief-of-police *(ispravnik)*. Each police district, in turn, was subdivided into smaller units known as *stany*, under the direction of a local police officer *(stanovoi pristav)*.

The areas and functions of officials responsible to the central government often overlapped and were interlocked with those of local self-government. The city duma was subject to the close control of the representatives of the governor's office. The peasant institutions of the village commune and the canton were under the thumb of the land captain. And the Zemstvos, organized on the district and on the province level, were subject to the control of the governors.

Various forms of local government were to be found in the backward regions, in newly acquired and non-Russian regions, and in those regions presenting special problems. Nine groups of provinces, mainly frontier, were organized as governments-general, each with a governor-general serving usually as the civil head of the region and the commander of its military forces. Under such jurisdiction were Finland, Congress Poland, Lithuania, White Russia, most of the Ukraine, the Caucasus, Siberia, Turkestan, and the Central Asian steppes. The Cossack lands, which had their own Cossack administration, were under the supervision of the Ministry of War.

St. Petersburg attempted to direct or control all these organs of local government. But the aim of centralization was imperfectly realized; and the result was that local government presented the characteristics of an unplanned edifice—a wing here, a cellar there, rooms without windows, and rooms without ceilings—which constantly defied the efforts of the would-be architects to give it unity.

CEMENT OF EMPIRE.   How could this sprawling, variegated state remain intact? Force, the threat of force, and the menace of foreign attack were important factors in holding it together; but they were not the only ones. The restive peasants and national minorities might have caused disruption had not their energies been effectively diverted. As it was, various groups were balanced against one another in such a way that the state was not unduly shaken. The peasants, having had some of their demands met by the state reforms, now spent their hatred principally on the local landlords and officials. In the case of national minorities, group became pitted against group, often by accident rather than design, and the state was spared the brunt of their antagonisms. Ukrainian peasants hated the Jews and Poles; Moslems in the Caucasus hated Christians; Letts and Estonians hated the Baltic Germans; and in every case the hatred was returned in measured kind. Thus, aggressions tended to balance one another, and their continuation helped to make possible an unstable equilibrium in the empire.

Respect for power was still another factor in preserving the clumsy structure of the Russian Empire. It is true that respect for Russian power had declined at the time of the Crimean War; but some of the weaknesses had been corrected and the military power of the empire was regaining respect both at home and abroad. Internal upheavals had been quite effectively discouraged by the success with which the government had weathered many rebellions; and memories of those futile revolts, reinforced by the habit and apathy that had grown out of generations of experience in obedience, contributed to the general acceptance of things as they were. To the Russians, tsarism still seemed mighty and indestructible.

The resentment of the masses against imperial centralization presented a danger, but it also was alleviated by circumstances. The official sloth and venality which had made Russia "a despotism tempered by corruption" turned that danger to the dubious advantage of the state. As Anatole Leroy-Beaulieu stated it, "The administration's inertia or duplicity, duly paid for, paralyzed bad laws as well as good ones. The functionary sold liberty to one, tolerance to another; he sold immunity to both innocent and guilty." That situation helped for a time to keep submerged the resentment of those who had the patience, money or luck required to by-pass the laws against which they would otherwise have been more demonstrative.

In addition, many positive forces of loyalty and stability were operating to preserve the state. The patriarchal family structure continued to promote conservatism. And many traditional institutions were protected by deep-rooted attachments, such as those evidenced in the believers' loyalty to the Church, in the loyalty of the Russian Orthodox Church to the state, in Russian nationalism and in the *esprit de corps* of the bureaucracy and the army.

Perhaps the most cogent statement about the cohesion of the Russian state was that attributed to Sergei Witte:

> The world should be surprised that we have any government in Russia, not that we have an imperfect government. With many nationalities, many languages and a nation largely illiterate, the

marvel is that the country can be held together even by autocracy. Remember one thing: if the tsar's government falls, you will see absolute chaos in Russia, and it will be many a long year before you will see another government able to control the mixture that makes up the Russian nation.

SEVENTEEN / SOCIO-ECONOMIC AND

CULTURAL DEVELOPMENTS:

1855-1904

S ocio-economic and cultural developments in Russia followed a more consistent course than did the political developments after the reforms of Alexander II. The political reforms, which might have led to the transformation of the autocracy into a constitutional monarchy, became more restricted in their execution than had originally been intended and were not permitted to run their full course. On the other hand, the socio-economic and cultural changes brought about in the era of reform proved to be the forerunners of developments which marked a distinctly new age for Russia.

The economy

THE STATE'S INTERESTS. Governmental participation in economic processes during the last half of the nineteenth century was so active that the general economy cannot be examined apart from governmental policy. Two considerations prompted that participation: (1) the need to meet military requirements which kept mounting with the growth of the standing army and the refinement of military techniques and (2) the need to enhance the material prosperity of the country for political reasons.

That was an age of rapid change in the weapons of war: the breech-loading rifle was replacing the muzzle-loading musket; the cartridge was superseding ball and powder; machine guns and automatic rifles were in the process of development; the construction and design of field artillery were being revolutionized; and wooden sailing ships were being displaced by ironclad steamships. But Russia had been lagging far behind the other great powers in all of those developments as well as in communications and railroad construction (improvements in which would, of course, serve not only the armed forces but also the general economy).

The program of general governmental participation, begun under Alexander II, was greatly expanded during the reigns of Alexander III and Nicholas II, when it was definitely demonstrated that economic improvements could alleviate political discontent. By the beginning of the twentieth century the Russian Government was more directly involved in business and industry than any other government in the world, with the possible exception of the German and the Japanese. At that time nearly one-third of the annual budget was being spent on industries maintained by the government. Yet the degree of its participation cannot be gauged by the amount of its investment alone; it was literally omnipresent, granting subsidies, providing concessions and privileges, adjusting tariffs, advancing credits, and encouraging private investment. The responsibility for engineering those activities fell to four successive Ministers of Finance: Michael Reitern (1862-78); Nicholas Bunge (1881-87); Ivan Vyshnegradsky (1887-92); and Sergei Witte (1892-1903).

STATE AIDS TO ECONOMIC EXPANSION. Basic to the economic development of the country was the stabilization of the currency. At the time of Nicholas I, the ruble had been given a sound silver basis; but the inflationary effects of the Crimean War had resulted in its rapid depreciation, and the government was again faced with the problem of stabilizing it. Repeated attempts were made to return to a metallic standard, either silver or gold; but it was not until 1897 that a sound adjustment was possible. Then, thanks to the efforts of Witte, the gold standard was finally instituted. That achievement, in those days when gold was king in international trade and finance, did much to improve Russia's international fiscal position and to encourage foreign investment and trade.

Meanwhile the government was assuming still other and more direct economic responsibilities, discharging them through credit operations and encouragement of foreign and domestic investors. The State Bank, opened in 1860, served as an important source of credit and, in time, as a central bank for the first privately owned banks, which were established under the ministry of Reitern and his successors. In railroad construction the government promoted private investment and supplemented its own railroad investments by floating bond issues abroad.

The tariff policy gave additional encouragement to domestic industry and commerce. With few interruptions, Russia had always followed a protectionist policy in her tariffs. And during this period, except for a brief relaxation under Reitern, it was found expedient to continue the protectionist features not only to favor Russian industry but also to bring increased revenues to the state treasury.

An ambitious program of railway construction, begun under government encouragement after the Crimean War, was of decided advantage to the whole economy. Reitern and his associates projected and promoted work on a network of railroads which would link the agricultural regions of central Russia with Moscow, the Baltic, and the Black Sea in order primarily to facilitate the export of grain; and subsequent projects linked Siberia, the Caucasus, and Central Asia with central Russia and the seaports.

Although it cannot be said that Russia became an industrialized country during this period, the extent to which the government was able to promote industry was remarkable. In the first years of the reign of Alexander II, the rate of growth was slow; for Russian credit abroad was depressed and the immediate results of serf liberation were negative from an industrial point of view, many enterprises having thereby lost their labor force. Within a few years, however, the supply of labor from the poor peasantry began to meet the demands of new enterprises, which were at first cautiously but soon boldly established. Between 1860 and 1900 the production of pig-iron and oil grew tenfold; the extraction of coal, nearly fiftyfold. In 1860 there were hardly any corporations in Russia; in 1900 there were 1,700 engaged in industry, banking, or commerce. In 1860 there were less than 1 million persons employed in manufacturing, mining, and railroad construction and operation; and in 1900 the figure stood at 2.8 million. Such increases could not have developed without the state activities designed to force growth. One of the great handicaps would have been the lack of domestic capital for investment, a lack which continuing governmental encouragement helped to overcome by drawing surplus capital from the more industrialized countries. The rate of foreign investments in Russia grew steadily during the ministries of Reitern, Bunge, and Vyshnegradsky and mounted sharply during that of Witte.

TEXTILE INDUSTRY. The production of textiles, by this time mainly cottons, engaged nearly half of those employed in manufacture during this period, and by 1904 Russia was almost up to fourth place among the world's cotton textile producers. The chief centers of the growing industry were the Moscow, St. Petersburg, and Lodz regions. The population of Lodz grew from 32,000 in 1867 to 315,000 in 1897 and that of Ivanovo-Voznesensk, a textile center (often called the Russian Manchester) near Moscow, from 1,350 to 54,000 in the same period. Most of the textile products were marketed in Russia and in nearby countries of the Middle East, particularly Persia, where Russian and British cottons were in competition for the market.

MINING AND METALLURGY.   As the railroads and the army increased their demands for metal products, mining and metallurgy received greater attention. Exploitation of the Krivoi Rog iron ore deposits and the nearby coal deposits of the Don River and the Donets River basins, which had been under consideration since the end of the eighteenth century, was begun on an intensive scale in 1869 by a Welshman, John Hughes. Modern methods, especially that which substituted coke for charcoal in smelting, brought greater efficiency to the manufacturing processes, and the output increased accordingly. However, it was still necessary to depend in large part on foreign sources for machinery and machine tools.

OIL PRODUCTION.   The growing world demand for oil led in the 1870's to the tapping of Russia's oil resources, then among the largest in the world. Extensive production was begun with equipment installed by the Swedish industrialist Nobel and by French and English investors in and around Baku, where, between 1867 and 1897, the population grew from 14,000 to 112,000. From that beginning, Russia led the world in oil production until 1900, when the United States forged ahead of her.

FOOD INDUSTRIES.   The food industries also shared in the boom, especially those engaged in the distillation of alcohol and the production of sugar from sugar beets. In the space of ten years, from 1892 to 1902, the area sown to sugar beets was increased by 93 per cent, and the number of sugar factories rose to nearly three hundred. The population of Kiev, one of the chief centers of sugar production as well as a center of other industries, was quadrupled in the latter half of the century.

HANDICRAFT.   The new manufacturing industries did not supplant the widespread handicraft industries. Domestic textile production was, of course, seriously affected by the competition of the textile factories, but in many other fields handicraft held its own. Much of the output of the new industries was basic or producer goods, not consumer goods; consequently the peasant[1] artisan could profitably continue his traditional calling, aided greatly by the improvement in transportation and the growth of foreign trade.

As before the reforms, many peasants were their own entrepreneurs,

---

[1] The term *peasant* was applied to a person as long as he was listed on the rolls of a peasant village, and his legal status was that of a peasant whether or not he was employed on the soil.

buying the raw material, fashioning the products, and marketing them. But many were members of producer co-operatives *(artels)*, pooling their resources, buying raw materials, and selling their products in common. The Zemstvos in many regions helped *artels* with advances. At the same time the capitalist element in domestic handicraft continued to grow. Some capitalists employed methods of production which would now be characterized as "assembly line" methods; they would engage a whole peasant village for one operation in the making of certain articles, carry the partly finished articles to another village for the next operation, and so on to the completing operation.

In 1904 there were about 8 million peasants who devoted part of their time to domestic handicraft and nearly 4 million who spent all their time on such work. The range of their products was quite broad, including furniture, wooden spoons, wheels, baskets, bast and leather shoes, naval stores, linen, carpets, locks, nails, toys, harness, and dressed furs. Peasant industries were to be found, as in the past, chiefly in the nonblack soil regions, particularly in the areas of old Muscovy, near Moscow, Vladimir, Ryazan, Nizhnii-Novgorod, Yaroslavl, and Kaluga. The additional income that a peasant household received from its industry often made the difference between solvency and insolvency and, in some cases, brought relative prosperity.

The strength of domestic production was an indication that Russia was still in the pre-industrial age. In other countries, the growth of industrial manufacturing had in the main destroyed such production.

RAILROAD EXPANSION.   The expansion of the railroad system, crucial to further industrial development and to increase in grain export, was an outstanding achievement of the period. In 1855 Russia, with an area of more than 6 million square miles, had only 650 miles of railroad. During the period of Reitern's ministry nearly 14,000 miles of track were laid, mainly by private enterprise, following plans prepared by the government and aided by government subsidies and guarantees. After 1881 the government bought up most of the privately owned lines and assumed direct responsibility for most of the new construction. The largest project was the Trans-Siberian Railroad, from Chelyabinsk to Vladivostok, which was begun in 1891 and completed, unfortunately for the Russian army, only after the beginning of the war with Japan in 1904. This new line, linked to lines already built between Moscow and Chelyabinsk, provided a direct and continuous rail route of about 5,500 miles from Moscow to the Pacific. Of the other great lines constructed in this period, one connected Tashkent, in Central Asia, with Orenburg and thus with central Russia; the other ran from Tashkent to the Caspian Sea. In 1904 Russian railroads extended 39,000 miles and employed 450,000 persons; only the United States, with 213,000 miles of road, ranked above Russia in mileage. But, viewed in relation to area and population, Russia's railroad system was far behind those of other European nations. France, for example, with its far shorter distances, had in 1904 about 64 miles of railroad for each 100,000 inhabitants while Russia had only 32 miles per 100,000.

AGRARIAN DEVELOPMENTS.   While Russia's industry was experiencing a rapid transformation and expansion, her agriculture changed but little. The continuation of the village commune, which by its very nature restricted initiative, perpetuated the technological conservatism of the peasantry. By 1904 the total planted area had increased somewhat, the yield per acre had grown a bit, and the total agricultural production had mounted considerably (mainly because of increase on the large estates of nobles); but the great majority of the peasants lived and worked much as they did before 1861. On the whole, cultivation followed the old method of the strip system and the three-field cycle, and in some regions there was still in practice the even older method of continuously cropping the land until it was exhausted and then leaving it fallow for several years. Most peasants still used the horse-drawn wooden cultivator instead of the iron plow and harvested and threshed their grain by means of the sickle and the flail. By 1900 they were producing about 68 per cent of the total agricultural yield, relying mainly on the old staple crops of rye, wheat, oats, and barley. Most of what they raised was for their own families; when they sold part of their harvests, it was usually not because they had a surplus but because they required money to pay taxes, dues and debts.

Although the main features of the picture remained unchanged, here and there a few details were changing. In some regions the Zemstvos were bringing new techniques to the peasant, and in some areas agricultural specialization was advancing. Too, some of the landlords, who were responsible for practically all of the agricultural production for the market, were adopting new methods. But to speak of a revolution in Russian agriculture would be fanciful; the main source of Russian livelihood was still in a very primitive stage. The following table of harvest returns (in pounds per acre) at the beginning of the twentieth century indicates the country's comparative agricultural backwardness:

Nation	Wheat	Rye	Oats
Germany	1,109	812	1,064
United States	868	605	909
Russia	406	468	407

During the half-century under review the peasant population was increasing more rapidly than agricultural production, with the consequence that in 1904 the lot of the average agricultural peasant household was materially no better than it had been in 1861. In that period, the average acreage cultivated by a household was decreased and, to make the situation worse, the amount of farm animal power declined. Between 1870 and 1900 the number of horses for each 1,000 working male peasants fell by 30 per cent in European Russia; and by the beginning of the twentieth century, 30 per cent of the peasant families had no horses at all. Because of such conditions, the peasants, although free from the obligation to labor for or to pay dues to the landlords, found that the product of their labor was not sufficient for their elementary needs; if they fed and clothed themselves they had no surplus with which to pay redemption dues and taxes. In the nonblack soil regions, many continued to supplement their agricultural work by cottage industry or seasonal employment in the cities, and in the black soil regions some rented or bought land from the landlords at inflated rates or worked for them as laborers. Still the additional income was usually not enough to solve their problem.

As the peasants saw it, the government could reach a solution of the problem by three steps: reduction of taxes, abolition of redemption dues, and distribution of more land, preferably without payment. They saw no reason why they should be so inadequately supplied with land when the nobles still held so much. Although year after year the poorer among the hereditary nobility were selling their land (one-third of it being sold in the last quarter of the century), in 1905 the noble landlords, numbering about 116,000, held one-third as much land as the approximately 12 million peasant families. Many nobles still owned great estates of tens of thousands of acres, and an estate of 10,000 acres was not unusual. The average noble holding was 1,400 acres, and that of the peasant was about thirty acres.

The nobleman, the tax-collector, and the police official became the chief targets of peasant hatred; the noble owned the land which the peasant coveted, the police official protected the noble, and the tax collector—often the same as the police official—demanded of the peasant that which he did not have. Peasant hatred was further complicated by national factors in some areas. In White Russia, Lithuania, and the western Ukraine, most of the landlords were Polish nobles, who usually sublet their land to Jewish middlemen; and they, in turn, rented the land to the peasants. On some estates, Germans managed the lands for absentee nobles. In both cases, the peasants were dissatisfied and given to complaints against those over them, whether Poles, Jews, or Germans. In the Caucasus and the lower Volga many of the landed nobility were Russian while the discontented peasantry were non-Russian and anti-Russian. And in the Baltic provinces the German landlords were resented by the Lettish and Estonian peasants.

The government was not ignorant of the gravity of the agrarian problem. During the period of the "dictatorship of the heart" a number of proposals for improving the conditions of the peasantry were considered and, in the following years, several of them were put into effect. The Peasants Land Bank, to extend credit for the purchase of land by the peasants, was established by the government in 1883. It enabled wealthier peasants to increase their holdings, but it did comparatively little toward improving the general situation. In 1886, the poll tax on peasants, established by Peter the Great, was abolished; yet each year found large numbers in arrears on payment of other taxes and redemption dues. Numerous government commissions considered the agrarian problem, agreed on its urgency, but offered little toward its solution. By 1904 the situation had begun to resemble that of 1853; at both times the government realized the seriousness of conditions but felt helpless to effect any adequate improvement in them.

COMMERCIAL EXPANSION.   In spite of the problems and inadequacies which beset Russian agriculture during the latter half of the nineteenth century, agricultural products were still of first importance in the country's expanding commerce. It still sold chiefly agricultural products and bought manufactured goods. At the beginning of the twentieth century nearly 60 per cent of the exports were foodstuffs—mainly wheat—and about 35 per cent were raw and partly processed materials such as flax, hemp, and timber. Each year the volume and value of Russia's foreign commerce grew as the industrialization of Western Europe created a larger demand for the food products and raw materials which she could provide. The seaports reflected the growth: between 1867 and 1897 the population of Odessa expanded from 119,000 to 405,000; that of Riga from 77,000 to 283,000, that of Rostov-on-the-Don from 29,000 to 120,000; and that of Libau from 10,000 to 64,000.

Domestic commerce also grew rapidly, benefited by the greatly increased population, the development of industry, improvements in railway and water communications, and the expansion of urban centers. The meagerness of peasant demand for goods was a limiting factor, but the cumulative effect of even their slight demand for items hitherto beyond their reach—kerosene, vodka, cotton goods, boots, icons, and nails—was favorable to the increasing market. Some new marketing methods were adopted with profit, refrigeration was introduced (making possible the sale of Siberian butter in Russia and abroad) and modern stores were constructed. But side by side with the modern stores the weekly peasant fairs and the great yearly fairs continued to account for much of the commercial turnover. The fair at Nizhnii-Novgorod, held each summer, remained one of the most important because of that city's favorable location with respect to transportation and the industrial and agricultural centers of Russia. Annually it attracted as many as 130,000 buyers and sellers from all over the empire, Asia, and Europe; and its transactions often amounted to as much as $65 million.

EVALUATION OF ECONOMIC DEVELOPMENTS.   At the end of the nineteenth century, Russia was economically in the rear-guard of the European powers despite the many revolutionary improvements. Yet she was becoming part of the world economic system; she exerted little influence upon that system, but she was being more and more influenced by it. Changes in world wheat prices affected Russian agricultural prosperity; improvements in foreign agricultural production affected Russian competitive advantages in foreign trade; and disturbances in the money and industrial markets abroad were registered in the market.

In evaluating Russia's position after fifty years of industrial development, it is necessary to note that her advancement, astounding as it was, did not bring her abreast of the major European powers and the United States in most fields. Moreover, that advancement owed more to artificial stimulation by the government and to the influx of foreign capital than to the growth of domestic capital or the expansion of domestic markets. Year after year foreign capital, attracted by the promise of high dividends, government subsidies, and guarantees of capital and profits, came into the country in increasing amounts. French investors were in the van with their holdings in Russian government bonds and investments in Russian industry and banking; but the German, British, and Belgian were not far behind.

In general, Russian industry gave the appearance of a strength it did not have. Protected by high tariffs, by subsidies and guarantees, and by governmental assistance against labor demands, it could show high profits (specious indications of strength), regardless of its lack of mechanization and of labor and managerial efficiency. Without those protections, it would have been deplorably unstable. Another source of potential instability lay in the fact that only a small portion of the country was feeling the effects of industrialization. New industries were concentrated in the western part of the empire and there in only a few regions, notably the Moscow, St. Petersburg, Lodz, and Warsaw regions. Such concentration resulted in the neglect of most of the great natural resources of the country. Moreover, it led to the concentration of labor in a few key points of the empire, thereby creating possibilities of paralyzing strikes by labor in those regions. Still another brake to solid economic growth was the low standard of living of the Russian masses. The purchasing power of the peasant was slight; and if he ever bought manufactured goods, he was required to pay a higher price for them than was his German or American counterpart because high tariffs kept domestic prices of Russian manufactured goods artificially high. The comparatively small urban population, whose income was quite low, could offer little more toward increasing the market. In brief, Russia was not ready at the time to provide for industry the sound foundation it would require to make the most of the vast economic potentialities of the country's great population and incalculable natural resources.

Social conditions

GROWTH AND MOVEMENT OF POPULATION.   Since 1800 Russia had led the European countries in population, and now her lead was increasing. Although the Russian mortality rate had been higher than that in any other great power, the fertility rate had been consistently more than adequate to compensate for it, as is indicated by the following figures on population increase:

Year	Population (millions)	Year	Population (millions)
1724	13	1835	60
1796	36	1858	74
1812	41	1897	129

Generally speaking, population was densest in the western and southern parts of the empire. Congress Poland's density was 148 times greater than Siberia's, and that of the province of Kiev was 178 times greater than that of the province of Archangel. Of the entire population in 1897, 74 per cent lived in European Russia, 7 per cent in Congress Poland, 7 per cent in the Caucasus, 4 per cent in Siberia and 4 per cent in Central Asia. But people were moving, both within the empire and from it. Some of them were attracted by the new industrial and commercial centers and by the better agricultural prospects in the black soil areas and in the virgin soil areas of Siberia; others were seeking relief from oppression.

Before this period Siberia had been traditionally the involuntary home of exiles and prisoners who, with their families, numbered about 300,000 by the end of the century; and beside them there had been only native tribes and a few hard-bitten adventurers. But the land there, especially in the steppes of the western parts, looked inviting to the peasants, and they began moving in despite the fact that their emigration, in most cases, was illegal before 1889. After 1889 the government removed some of the legal restrictions on voluntary emigration to Siberia and, with the building of the Trans-Siberian Railroad, positively encouraged it. Incomplete figures show that about 28,000 peasants a year settled there during the 1880's, about 108,000 a year during the 1890's, and about 225,000 a year during the next decade.

While the peasants were continuing their voluntary movement to Siberia, others, chiefly non-Russians living within the empire, were seeking havens elsewhere to which they might escape from forced Russification, antisemitism, and poverty. Since most of them carried no passports and crossed the Russian frontier illegally, official Russian statistics on their emigration are unreliable; but from other sources, such as the immigration records of the United States (the destination of nine out of about ten of them), reasonably valid approximations may be made. Between 1880 and 1905 nearly a million Jews left, 800,000 of them entering the United States; and hundreds of thousands of Poles, Lithuanians, Letts, and Finns left for the United States and other destinations.

SOCIAL COMPOSITION. Inevitably the economic changes brought about after the reforms produced changes in the social composition of the population. In the census of 1897 each subject was legally classified, but his legal classification did not always correspond to his actual socio-economic position; he might, for instance, be an unprivileged urbanite when classified as a peasant. In spite of such discrepancies, the following, from the census, will provide a general view of the social composition:

Occupational classification	*(per cent)*	*Legal classification*	*(per cent)*
Agriculture	74.6	Peasants	77.1
Industry	9.6	Nobility	1.5
Commerce	5.8	Clergy	.5
Transport	1.6	Privileged urbanites	.5
State service	1.4	Unprivileged urbanites	10.7
Private employment	4.6	Cossacks	2.3
		Asian peoples	6.6

The urban population, as this table shows, was increasing:

Year	Number in urban centers	Per cent of entire population
1724	328,000	3
1796	1,301,000	4.1
1812	1,653,000	4.4
1851	3,482,000	7.8
1867	8,157,000	10.6
1897	16,785,000	13

The steady growth of the urban population meant a steady increase of the middle and industrial working classes. But urbanization was a slow process. Russia was still the least urbanized of the major European countries; even in Italy, over 25 per cent of the population was urban, and in Germany about 55 per cent.

URBAN CLASSES. *(a) Laborers.* The largest category in the urban population was that of laborers, including both industrial and nonindustrial workers. In the main, they were of peasant derivation and often were still legally peasants. Many of them lived in the cities part of the year on the strength of passports issued by village authorities and returned to the villages for seasonal work; others had severed all their ties with the village—either legally or otherwise—and, with their children and their children's children, were permanent urbanites.

The conditions of labor were deplorable, at first regulated only by the needs of the employer and the endurance of the workers; it was not uncommon to find even children working fifteen or more hours a day. Illegal strikes demanding improvements finally compelled the government to give some attention to the regulation of conditions. In 1882 a system of factory inspectors was installed, and restrictions were placed upon the employment of children under twelve in metal, leather, and textile factories. In 1897 the work day in factories was limited to 11 1/2 hours a day, and Sunday and holiday work was prohibited; but in 1898 a law on overtime made simple the extension of the 11 1/2 hour day. In 1903 a law was issued requiring employers to compensate workmen for injuries sustained while working, but its effectiveness was weakened by a clause freeing employers of responsibility for payment if they could prove negligence on the workman's part.

The relative indifference of the government to labor conditions, the illegality of collective economic action by labor, the fluidity of the labor market, and the low level of industrial productivity combined to keep the Russian worker on a low social and economic plane. The average workday was about twelve hours, and the average yearly wage of an adult male factory worker in 1901 was (by dollar standard) $121.00. To add to his sad plight, sanitary and safety provisions in factories and mines where he worked were primitive, and he was often subjected to beatings on slight pretexts and to searching at the end of every day's work.

Although the cost of living was low, the wages of labor did not suffice for decent existence. Adequate housing was beyond the reach of the average workman. A survey of housing in St. Petersburg in 1890 indicated the situation in a typical city: only 48 per cent of the lodgings had separate kitchens, and only 10 per cent had baths; yet the average rental was higher than the average worker's total wage. Because of such conditions, workmen were forced to concentrate in garrets and cellars or in barracks erected by the factories where they were employed.

Yet the position of the urban worker was, in most cases, better than that of his country cousin, the peasant. He ate better, was better clothed, and had superior educational and medical facilities. He joined his fellows in developing benevolent societies which offered both social and economic benefits, a modicum of monetary aid during periods of sickness and unemployment, burial services, and the stimulation of social organization. He was beginning to find it possible also to form (illegally) labor organizations for the economic and political amelioration of his conditions.

(b) The urban middle class. A striking aspect of the changing class structure is that, although nearly 17 million persons belonged to the urban category in 1897, only a small portion of them were of the middle class—merchants, manufacturers, teachers, engineers, doctors, and lawyers. That class was increasing steadily, but in relative numbers it remained small. Within it, however, distinct and solid groups were becoming defined.

Members of the professions were drawn together by both political and social ties. They generally leaned, as has been seen, toward the liberal and revolutionary movements. Then, too, the fact that they were educated encouraged their social unity in a country and age in which the educated were set apart in a nimbus of special respect. A great social distance separated them from the peasants and workers and from the higher bureaucracy and nobility, who still formed the upper class.

Those who served in such capacities as government and business clerks, salesmen, and accountants were usually ranked with the lower middle class, which was increasing in number but not in influence. Perhaps the most highly self-conscious of this group were the sales personnel and commercial travelers, who considered themselves "educated" and genteel and, therefore, much above the common man.

Another small middle-class group was made up of the newly-rich merchants, bankers, contractors, and manufacturers. Unlike the old merchants and entrepreneurs, who still lived the patriarchal life of old Russia, the newly-rich aspired to social position and high living. They read stock market quotations, speculated in grain, built summer cottages near St. Petersburg or mansions within it, occasionally sampled the waters of Baden-Baden or other fashionable spas, flashed their wealth in Switzerland, and collected art. A few of them subsidized revolutionaries, but generally members of this group were loyal to the government, which they considered their patron.

URBAN LIFE.   The few great cities of Russia reflected a variety of influences: St. Petersburg, the population of which had reached 1,267,000 in 1897, remained the most European of Russian cities; Moscow, which also had passed the million mark in population, presented an uneasy combination of Russian and Western European influences; Riga, despite Russification, remained German; Warsaw was a melange of Polish, Jewish, and Russian; and Odessa represented not only the Great Russian, Ukrainian, and Jewish elements of Russia but also the trading classes of the Near East.

Life in any one of the great cities, however, was much like that in the others. There were the theater, ballet, fine shops, gypsy restaurants, and red-light districts in proof of their modernity, but they were still sadly deficient in the municipal services necessary to safe and comfortable living. The water systems were faulty (if they existed at all), lighting was inadequate, and pavements were defective; moreover, the oligarchic and bureaucratic control of municipal government acted to restrict improvement in services. The great mass of city inhabitants had no voice in government, and the few who did have a voice often neglected the interests of the many. To cite one instance: electric trolley cars were not installed in St. Petersburg until 1908 because of the objection of the large real estate owners, who feared that improvement in transportation would strengthen the movement to the suburbs and depress rents in the city. Another limiting factor was the common Russian malady, sloth, the product of the long history of centralized autocracy which weakened initiative and inhibited activity.

As would be expected, the smaller cities of the empire showed even less progress than the large ones. Their populations might expand or contract in response to varying conditions, but otherwise they showed little change during this period.

LIFE OF THE NOBILITY. The abolition of serfdom had hastened the economic weakening of the majority of the old, established nobility, and the development of an educated non-noble class ended their leadership in education and the arts. Despite the efforts of Alexander III and Nicholas II to steady them, their decline could not be halted. But decline did not mean disappearance; the nobility were still the favorites of the state and they still held a large share of the chief wealth of Russia, land.

Although they had lost the privilege of owning serfs, they retained many other privileges as well as advantages. They dominated the Zemstvo organizations, served as land captains, held the right of corporate organization in the district and provincial assemblies of the nobility, had exclusive entry into various classes of schools, and received preference in administrative and military appointments.

Despite these privileges, after 1861 many of the nobility led a life hardly distinguishable from that of the average well-to-do urban inhabitant. They were the ones who had sold or lost their lands and the ones who, having acquired hereditary nobility by the attainment of the higher ranks in the administration or armed forces, lacked the means for lordly living.

Among those who retained their land, some were unable, without the serfs, to support themselves in the grand manner to which they had been accustomed. They lived in shabby gentility on their land and clung desperately to the symbols of their way of life—European clothes, a French governess, imported books, kennels, and stables—while they murmured sadly over the vanished days, the general decline in morality, or the drunkenness of the peasants. Yet others prospered, developing their country estates into oases of feudal magnificence among the squalid peasant villages. Some accomplished that by large-scale farming for the market. Some did it through profit from their high connections, for the days of imperial largesse were not completely gone (Alexander II alone had distributed 1,350,000 acres of land in Poland, the Caucasus, and the Urals to high court functionaries). And some augmented their fortunes by purchasing state lands, through influence, sometimes at as little as one-tenth of market value.

The upper nobility around the court managed to continue living as they had in the past. A group of perhaps one hundred families maintained a position of first preference in the government and army and, thereby, a monopoly on many high positions; decade after decade the same family names appeared in the listings of generals, ministers, senators, councillors of state, and governors. However, high position earned through service or acquired by appointment was now beginning to count as much as noble blood. The possession of an exalted title, such as General or Councillor of State, and the receipt of decorations given by the emperor, such as the Order of St. Ánne or the Order of St. Andrew, now carried as much social weight as ancient pedigree.

LIFE OF THE PEASANTS.   Many observers who saw the Russian peasants both before and after the reforms remarked on the lack of evident change in the life of this class as a result of liberation. One who visited Russia in 1854 and again in 1892 wrote:

> A change had indeed been brought by the emancipation of the serfs, but there was little outward sign of it. The muzhik [peasant] remained to all appearance, what he was before. . . . The peasants, with their sheepskin caftans, cropped hair, and stupid faces brought back the old impressions so vividly that I seemed not to have been absent a week.[1]

Outward appearances remained the same for a long time, but important underlying changes were in process. Although the average peasant village in 1904, with its two hundred inhabitants, looked little different from the village of 1861, there were differences. Village government had changed; the responsibility of the village commune was much greater than before the reforms. The joint-family was slowly breaking down into smaller units. Where there were Zemstvo institutions some medical and educational services were available. And, of great importance, the horizon of the village residents was being widened in various ways. About 28 per cent of the male peasants and 9 per cent of the female peasants in 1897 knew the rudiments of reading and writing, learned in a village or parochial school. Contacts with the nonpeasant world were increasing. The village scribe (usually a nonpeasant—perhaps a student banished from the city, a discharged government employee, or the son of a parish priest), who handled the paper work of village government, brought some new ideas. Local teachers, too, added new thoughts and new concepts from the world without. Peasants who had completed their service in the army returned somewhat better informed than when they had left. And others, who

[1] Andrew D. White, *Autobiography of Andrew Dickson White* (London: Macmillan and Co., 1905), II, 7.

Scenes from Russian peasant life

had been employed in the cities, came back to relate the wonders of that different world. Taken individually, the new contacts were not imposing, but they were of consequence because they served to broaden the general knowledge and understanding of the villagers and to fit some of them for more progressive leadership in village affairs.

Some peasants, after the liberation, were able to achieve a modest prosperity which allowed them such amenities as kerosene lamps, tea, and even samovars for the brewing of tea. A steady increase in the consumption of vodka among them indicated an increase not only in drunkenness but also in the amount of cash they were able to obtain. Some were buying ready-made cloth and occasionally ready-made boots. Yet the average standard of living among the peasants remained low and in many cases sank lower. A representative family, consisting of three married couples and their children, owned buildings and livestock valued at about $245. Its chief food was rye bread, about two pounds of which provided the main portion of an adult's daily diet. Its cash transactions for a year were as follows:

Expenditures		Income	
Firewood	$10.00	Extra earnings	$50.00
Kerosene	4.00	Sale of livestock	17.50
Clothing	45.00		
Furniture	5.00	Total	$67.50
Repairs	5.00		
Taxes	3.35		
Vodka for holidays	5.00		
Church services	2.25		
Total	$79.60		

That imbalance between expenditures and income was the great weight on the average peasant's back; if he fed and clothed himself and his family, he could not keep up his payments on dues and taxes.

Not all peasants lived on such a low scale, but few lived far above it. Although their living standard in 1904 was a notch or two above that of 1861, the margin between subsistence and starvation was a slight one; and a bad harvest might result in a famine such as struck many of the agricultural regions in 1891 and 1902. Moreover, average figures do not tell the whole story. While the economic position of the peasants in the nonblack soil regions, where industrial and other employment brought additional income, improved somewhat, that of a good portion of the peasants in the richest agricultural lands, paradoxically, declined as a result of the great increase in population and the meager opportunities for earning extra income.

Educational development

PRIMARY EDUCATION.   The educational development in the latter half of the nineteenth century was a phase of the general quickening of Russian life, but it differed from other phases in that it was more the product of popular initiative than of governmental planning and support. At the end of the century the imperial government was spending about fifty times as much on its armed forces as on education; and its contribution was only about 21 per cent of the total public expenditure on education, the remainder coming from the Zemstvos, municipalities, villages, and other sources. Moreover, the money allotted by the imperial government was given mainly to the parochial schools rather than to the Zemstvo or municipal schools. Yet, while the state contributed little, it controlled education firmly through its inspectors and directors of primary education. The Ministry of Education, by decree, set the limits of educational policy, and educational boards in every province and district carried out that policy.

In half a century the number of primary schools had grown from about 8,000 to over 78,000, and the number of pupils had increased from 450,000 to nearly 4,000,000. That increase, however, represented only a beginning quantitatively and qualitatively. The number in attendance was little more than 10 per cent of the total number between the ages of five and fifteen years. And of those admitted to the schools, most were boys (of the nearly 4 million mentioned above, only about 800,000 were girls). The quality of instruction varied greatly between city and rural districts and between region and region. Schooling in the parochial schools, the pupils in which numbered about 1,120,000 by the end of the century, was inferior to that of other primary schools. They usually offered two or three years of instruction in the elements of religion, Russian, Church Slavonic, penmanship, and arithmetic. The primary schools supervised by the Ministry of Education, which included Zemstvo, municipal and village schools, generally offered three—in a few cities, up to six—years of schooling in the same subjects as those taught in the parochial schools and, in addition, perhaps (depending upon the quality of the school) geography, Russian history, and elementary geometry. About 300,000 children of the total enrollment in primary schools were in attendance at Jewish and Moslem religious schools.

SECONDARY EDUCATION. There was a gap in the educational ladder between primary and secondary schools, for pupils finishing the ordinary primary school could not meet the entrance requirements of the secondary schools even if the paucity of those schools, their high tuition fees, and their restrictive practices had not made entrance otherwise difficult. At the beginning of the twentieth century there were about 320 secondary schools enrolling 135,000 male pupils. Some of them offered preparation leading to university admission; others offered preparation for admission to technical institutions, for commercial callings, or for government service. In addition, twenty-six cadet schools, maintained by the Ministry of War, provided secondary schooling for about 10,000 boys, mainly sons of the nobility.

HIGHER EDUCATION. Higher education showed some expansion, but its rate of growth was limited by the lack of facilities. Only three new universities were opened during this period—one in Odessa in 1864, one in Warsaw in 1869, and one in Tomsk in 1888, bringing the total number in Russia to nine. In the last quarter of the century their total enrollment rose from 6,000 to 16,500, of which the University of Moscow, still the center of learning, had the lion's share—4,400 in 1899. Ordinarily a university consisted of four schools: law, medicine, physical-mathematical studies, and historico-philological studies. Law schools attracted the largest number of students, for legal training served as the best entry into government service; they provided also popular courses in social science. Medical studies drew the next largest number, while the sciences and humanities lagged far behind in popularity. In all of them the level of instruction and scholarship was very high despite the oppressive political atmosphere which drove many scholars from Russia and made objective research and teaching difficult.

In addition to the nine universities, Russia had many specialized institutions of higher learning, some founded before the reforms and others after. Among these were the Academy of Military Medicine, the Higher Technological School of Nicholas I, the Imperial School of Law, the Lazarev Institute of Oriental Languages, and the Polytechnic Institute.

Many Russian students who were denied entrance into the higher schools because of their religious beliefs or who wanted education in a less restricted atmosphere went abroad to foreign universities, particularly those of Germany and Switzerland.

EDUCATION OF WOMEN. With the rise of feminism in Russia, educational facilities for women, particularly at the secondary level, increased noticeably. Some schools were established by private endowments; others by civic authorities, who saw in them a source of teachers for the growing number of primary schools. By 1900 there were 316 secondary schools open to girls of all classes and 64 open only to daughters of the nobility. They enrolled about 95,000. For young women who sought higher education the opportunities were quite limited. Two colleges and a medical school, all founded through private initiative in the 1870's, were the only institutions of higher learning in Russia to which women were admitted during this period.

CHURCH SCHOOLS. The Holy Synod administered, in addition to the parochial schools, a large number of schools which provided for children of the clergy general training or special preparation for the clerical life. In 1899 partial secondary education was provided tuition-free to male children of the clergy (or for a fee, to others) in 185 ecclesiastical schools, with a total enrollment of 31,000 and to female children, in sixty-nine diocesan schools, which enrolled 15,000. Sons of clergymen who wished to prepare for the church or who simply sought further free education might enter one of the fifty-five ecclesiastical seminaries after graduation from the ecclesiastical schools. The seminaries provided, in a four-year curriculum, theological preparation and the last years of regular secondary training. Any graduate of a seminary was qualified for the post of parish priest, and able graduates might be admitted to one of four ecclesiastical academies, where four years of study at the university level were provided. The fact that the four academies had only eight hundred students in 1899 indicates that few were qualified for admission, or that many lacked interest in that type of higher training.

SUMMARY OF RESULTS. The expansion of educational facilities may be viewed from either an optimistic or a pessimistic point of view. Comparing the situation at mid-century with that at the century's end, one might express amazement that so much had been accomplished; but comparing the total of Russia's achievements with those of Western European countries, one might be awed by what remained to be done. The census of 1897 revealed that 24 per cent of the population over the age of nine was literate and that two of every three literates were male. According to the same census, literacy was most unevenly distributed over the empire. It was far higher in the west than in the east; in the Baltic provinces more than 80 per cent of the population were rated as literate, and in Central Asia only 6 per cent.

The great majority of Russia's adult population could neither read nor write, and most literates could read no more than a newspaper, a romantic story, or a religious tract. Of course, the growth of literacy promised the gradual diffusion of ideas and concepts among increasing numbers of the population; but at the end of the century thought, writing, and discussion about the great problems of the country—capitalism, democracy, constitutionalism, and Slavophilism—were still confined to the small circles of the educated. Yet the diffusion was sufficient to give impetus to publication. During the fifty-year period printing establishments grew in number from about 180 to about 1,850 and the number of published titles, from about 1,830 to nearly 18,000. Religion still held first place among the subjects of printed books, 13 per cent of all titles published being in that field, while works of a literary character held second place with 12 per cent. Periodical publication, too, reflected an increased reading public; the number of periodicals published legally had grown to 944 (exclusive of those published in Finland).

Scholarship and science

POLITICAL INFLUENCE. Russian scholarship after the reforms was caught in the crossfire of political conflict. On the one hand the official ideology had little attraction for most Russian scholars; on the other hand the close governmental supervision and control of the universities, especially after 1884, limited the scope of free research and study. Consequently, there was a great difference between academic scholarship and nonacademic scholarship in almost every field; and some of the research and writing on scholarly subjects was done outside the universities by men who regarded their writings as political and social weapons. But the academic scholars, although compelled by the conditions of their employment to work within a limited range, did some remarkably good work.

HISTORICAL STUDY. Russian history, in which some of the finest academic work was done during this period, could not easily be divorced from politics, and the historian had to write with one ear cocked to the voice of the censor and the other to his scholarly conscience. Yet much work was done in bringing the materials of Russian history to light and interpreting them. The period of reforms stimulated the study of the origins of Russian institutions, and the Academy of Sciences and the several private and governmental historical and archaeological societies yearly increased the volume of data available for that study. Historians made the most of the situation.

Sergei Solovyev, who occupied the chair of Russian history at the University of Moscow, gave the study of Russian history a firm, although formidable, foundation in his 29-volume *History of Russia*, published during the years 1851-79. This work, a mine of information with little interpretation, was a starting point for subsequent historians. Upon Solovyev's death, his chair was given to his pupil Vasily Klyuchevsky, whose learning, urbane wit, and brilliance made his lecture room a mecca for Russian and foreign students. His lectures, which because of censorship were distributed only in manuscript until after 1905, still provide the best available synthesis of Russian history.[1] Among many other major figures in Russian historical writing was Paul Milyukov, a student of both Solovyev and Klyuchevsky, who divided his talents between history and politics and consequently spent much of his time between 1895 and 1905 either in prison or abroad as an exile. His principal work was *Studies in the History of Russian Culture*, published in three volumes during the years 1896-1901.
SOCIAL SCIENCES.   Little academic achievement was registered in the social sciences, which were not recognized as separate disciplines in most Russian universities but were often smuggled into the teaching of other studies. The treatment of sociology was typical; it was not studied separately until 1908, and one of the first academic sociologists, Nicholas Kareyev, was a teacher of the philosophy of history at the University of St. Petersburg. Kareyev wrote the first Russian textbook in the field, *An Introduction to Sociology*, which was published in 1897. However, Maxim Kovalevsky, whose chief interest was in the sociological study of the history of legal institutions and social change, is considered the true founder of objective sociology; and it was he who in 1908 held the first chair of sociology in Russia. The study of economics, which was recognized as a legitimate academic interest, was beset by the dogmatic debates on political issues, and little enduring work was accomplished in that field. One of the most prominent academic economists was M. I. Tugan-Baranovsky, professor of political economy at the University of St. Petersburg.
NATURAL SCIENCES.   More positive advances were made in the natural

---

[1] Vasily Klyuchevsky, *A History of Russia* (New York: Russell and Russell, 1960. Five vols.).

sciences. An adequate treatment of Russian achievements in this field would be impossible here, but the work of a few individuals may be mentioned. Dmitri Mendeleyev earned the rank of a giant in chemistry through his many contributions, of which the periodic table of elements is the best known. But even as a chemist he was not immune from political problems; he lost his post at the University of St. Petersburg because of his supporting a student movement. The distinguished biologist and discoverer of phagocytes, Elie Metchnikov, was dismissed from the University of Odessa in 1882 and forced to complete his major work abroad. Ivan Pavlov, best known for his work on conditioned reflexes, earned the Nobel prize in 1904 for his research on digestive processes. Alexander Popov, a professor at the Naval Engineering School, was an early student of the use of electromagnetic waves in communications; and in 1895, several years before Marconi's achievement, he perfected a radio-telegraphic apparatus. But he received so little encouragement from the government that the development of radio-telegraphy was left to other countries. Distinguished work was executed also in the fields of plant physiology, mathematics, physiology, engineering, and chemistry by a host of other Russian scholars, proving that there was a lode of native ability in Russia.

The government and private industry continued to make inadequate use of the work of Russian scientists and technicians, and their failure to do so was reflected adversely not only in the country's industry but also in her military technology. This was in glaring contrast to the practice in Germany, where science and technology were harnessed to the wheels of industry and utilized for the armed forces. But the Russian Government feared the possible evils of independent study more than it appreciated the advantages that it might draw from the encouragement of such study.

Letters and arts

NEW LIFE.   The creative energies of Russia burst forth abundantly in the nineteenth century. Writers and artists had become aware of the vigor and freshness of subject matter to be found in the Russian environment, and they were struggling with forms and techniques through which to interpret it. They were concerning themselves, too, with the social and political problems of the day, for they realized that in the arts and in literature there was more freedom of expression about those problems than in other media. They were profiting from the stimulating effects of new talent com-

THE BETTMANN ARCHIVE

Novelists Feodor Dostoyevsky (left) *and Ivan Turgenev* (right)

ing from the middle and sometimes the lower classes, and they were still taking inspiration from the progress of the arts and literature in Western Europe.

LETTERS.   As the pre-reform period was the age of greatness in poetry, the post-reform period was the age of greatness in the novel; and it was the novel which brought Russian literature to the attention of the world. The Russian novel of this period was generally of the realistic type, simple in language, catholic in its range of characters and moods, devoted to the depiction of the individual and his environment at the expense of plot, and concerned with contemporary subjects of social and political interest. Three writers, Ivan Turgenev, Feodor Dostoyevsky, and Leo Tolstoy, were responsible for the finest of the Russian novels. The fact that the best of their work appeared during the period 1860-1880 explains the designation of that period as the Golden Age of the Russian novel. Turgenev, himself a member of the nobility, gave a classic portrayal of the many sides of rural existence in his *Sportsman's Sketches*, which he had published at mid-century, and *A Nest of Gentlefolk*; and in his most famous work, *Fathers and Sons*, an unflattering portrayal of a nihilist, he caught the spirit of the intellectual youth of the time. No partisan in politics, Turgenev was content to express through his works merely the observations of the artist. Dostoyevsky, on the other hand, was for a time a revolutionary, but he ended his days a fervent reactionary, wholeheartedly devoted to the Russian Orthodox Church. His three most famous novels, *Crime and Punishment*, *The Idiot*, and *The Brothers Karamazov*, are intense, psychological studies with religious overtones. Tolstoy, like Dostoyevsky, experienced a great change in his life. Until 1880 he was a typical member of the cultured Russian nobility; after that he devoted himself to philosophical anarchism and a Christianity stripped of dogma and ritual—and was excommunicated from the Church for his position. His two greatest novels, *War and Peace* and *Anna Karenina* are the products of the earlier period. *War and Peace*, considered the greatest of Russian novels, provides a masterly picture of Russia during the Napoleonic Wars from the viewpoint of the nobility; and *Anna Karenina*, a glimpse of the post-reform Russia from the same viewpoint.

Tolstoy's change after 1880, the death of Dostoyevsky in 1881, and the death of Turgenev in 1883 brought to an end the period of the masters. The writers who appeared near the end of this period or followed soon thereafter may not have been great, but many of them were men of talent and artistry. Nicholas Leskov, who published his *Cathedral Folk* in 1872, was one of the few able representatives of the numerous and then popular reactionary novelists, whose heroes were usually slayers of Polish revolutionary and Russian nihilist dragons. The radical intelligentsia were better represented in the field of writing. Michael Saltykov, who wrote under the pseudonym of N. Shchedrin, gave up an influential post in the bureaucracy in 1868 to work with the intelligentsia and to write novels satirizing the vices of his time. His finest work, *The Golovlev Family*, is a fierce comment on the life of the provincial nobility. Vladimir Korolenko, one of the more endowed radical writers of fiction of the 1880's and 1890's, divided his time between literature and political causes. On account of the latter he spent several years in Siberia; but his time in exile was not lost, for his experiences during those years gave some of the best touches to his story *Makar's Dream*. Anton Chekhov left the medical profession to pursue a literary career after the appearance and heartening reception of a volume of his stories and sketches in 1886. The grandson of a serf, Chekhov ranged through all the classes of Russia in his portrayals and gently sketched the weaknesses of all. A few years later, another writer of stories, Maxim Gorky, was brought to public attention by Korolenko. Gorky was

THE BETTMANN ARCHIVE

Novelist Leo Tolstoy in his study at Yasnaya Polyana

one of the first of the proletarian literati. In his training and sympathies he was of the lower classes, which he described with much force in a collection of stories the publication of which, in 1898, set him on the road to fame.

Toward the end of the century there appeared a new literary and artistic movement, conveniently and somewhat loosely referred to as symbolism. The symbolists were affected by the neoromantic literary and artistic movement abroad, by the philosophy of Nietzsche, and by a revulsion against excessive preoccupation with social problems in art and literature. They were, on the whole, mystics in their religion and expression and ardent believers in art-for-art's-sake. Their movement united practitioners of several arts: belles-lettres, painting, ballet, and music. And, as was usual for movements in Russia, it soon had an organ for the expression of its belief—the magazine *World of Art*, founded by Sergei Diaghilev. Dmitri Merezhkovsky was the outstanding symbolist writer of the pre-1905 period, when the movement was still in its beginning stages. He began in 1893 a trilogy of novels under the collective name of *Christ and Antichrist*; the first volume of it, *The Death of the Gods*, appeared in 1896, to be followed in 1901 by *The Romance of Leonardo da Vinci* and in 1905 by *Peter and Alexis*. Out of the symbolist movement came a poetic revival the product of which is exceeded in quality only by that of the Golden Age of Russian

Anton Chekov

poetry, the age of Pushkin and Lermontov. Among the most noteworthy of the symbolist poets were Merezhkovsky's wife, Zinaida Hippius, Constantine Balmont, and (the finest of them all) Alexander Blok. The symbolist movement did not, by any means, end the popularity of other literary and artistic groups, but it had a decided effect upon Russian literary and artistic life, particularly after 1907. It may be said that the appearance of the new movement, with its emphasis on aestheticism and mysticism, was indicative of the emergence of new moods and tendencies both in the creators of literature and art and in their public.

MUSIC. Russian secular music had come into its own by the middle of the nineteenth century as a result of the successful fusion of Western European musical forms with Russian musical themes. The compositions of Michael Glinka were the first to show the style of composition that was to give Russian music a national flavor and make it famous. His two operas, *A Life for the Tsar* and *Ruslan and Lyudmila* —both composed before mid-century—are still a living part of world music.

In the latter half of the century two groups of composers guided the course of Russian music. Self-conscious dedication to the use of native Russian themes was the program of one group, leaders of the nationalist trend in music, whose center was the St. Petersburg Conservatory. Prominent in that group were Nicholas Rimsky-Korsakov, Alexander Borodin, Modest Mussorgsky, Alexander Glazunov, Michael Ippolitov-Ivanov, and Reinhold Glier. Another group, followers of Peter Ilich Tchaikovsky, promoted a romantic movement in music; their focus was the Moscow Conservatory of Music (established by the pianist Nicholas Rubinstein in 1866), where Tchaikovsky taught. An outstanding representative of this group was Sergei Rachmaninov.

The symbolist movement apparently had little effect upon music until around the turn of the century, when the compositions of Alexander Scriabin began to show the new influence.

PAINTING. While Russian literature and music were earning world recognition, nothing of comparable value was to be found in Russian painting. But Russian artists, involved in the aesthetic battles of the West and in the political struggles of their own country, were seriously seeking new principles to replace those of fading classicism in art. About 1870 a group calling themselves the Travelers announced a new creed: to emphasize realism in technique, nativism in subject matter, and social purpose in the selection and presentation of subjects. Of this group and its followers the best known are Ilya Repin and Vasily Vereshchagin. In the 1890's, when the symbolist movement was gaining headway, many artists embraced its principles; outstanding among them, the brilliant Valentin Serov and Nicholas Roerich.

BALLET. During the latter half of the century the Russian ballet, which had been firmly established under government patronage in the reign of Empress Anna, gained the reputation that it still maintains. Under the direction of Marius Petipa, who came to the Imperial Ballet from France in 1858, the classic traditions of the ballet were upheld and enhanced. At the beginning of the twentieth century the young Michael Fokine attempted to break the grip of classicism, but Petipa maintained his authority until his death, in 1910.

The Russian Orthodox Church

LACK OF CHANGE. What of the Church, so inextricably bound to the state, during this period of internal development? Its power remained great, and its hold on the minds and emotions of the great mass of believers unshaken. Yet it did not show any signs of renewed vitality. As the historian B. H. Sumner suggests, "What the church most needed, a Leo XIII, it could not produce; it was given instead a Pius IX—Pobedonostsev." Under Pobedonostsev's power the Church was forced to play its allotted role in the repressive actions of the state: the parish priest was expected to report on the political state of his parishioners, even to violate the secrets of the confessional, and to exhort obedience to the emperor; representatives of the bishop checked on the priests; the bishops found their work closely checked by lay representatives of the state; and the Holy Synod was under state control.

EVIDENCES OF DISSATISFACTION. There was some restlessness within the Church, but it was not prompted by those of high authority. Often a priest, a monk, or a religious recluse would win a wide following by his piety and fervor. Often, too, children of priests or others preparing for priesthood in the ecclesiastical seminaries renounced the careers for which they were being trained. Many who came from these ranks achieved renown as scholars—among them the historians Solovyev and Klyuchevsky. Others—among them, Joseph Stalin—turned to revolutionary movements. In the ecclesiastical seminary in Tiflis, students were frequently detected reading works forbidden to them, works such as those of Buckle, Darwin, Mill, Hugo, and Renan; and in 1893 eighty-seven of them were expelled after a student strike. Other seminaries were less turbulent; but in almost all of them, as in lay schools, many of the youth stood firm against the prevalent official beliefs.

There were some among the conscientious communicants of the Church who sought to infuse it with new life. Even among the intellectuals, although religion was rejected by many of them, there were some who sought to find a means of satisfactory adjustment to Russian Orthodoxy; but their views on Orthodoxy found little encouragement in the Church. Some of the works of the lay theologians, though banned in Russia, were published abroad to avoid ecclesiastical censorship. The official Church, however, appeared set in its ways, and the movements for internal Church reform or revivification were doomed to make little headway before 1905.

The half century which followed the Treaty of Paris witnessed the decline of Russia's influence in Europe and the expansion of her influence in Asia. Asiatic Russia, which had hitherto been a neglected and relatively unimportant part of the empire, was acquiring increasing importance, and Russian interests in non-Russian Asia were becoming more ambitious. At the same time the influence and interests of other powers were becoming so extended in Asia that Russia found her interests there in conflict not only with those of Japan but also with those of the great European powers, notably England. The enhancement of European political and economic power in Asia linked European and Asiatic international relations more and more intimately until Eurasia became, from the viewpoint of international relations, one arena.

Revival of the Eastern Question

TREATY OF PARIS RECONSIDERED. The loss of the Crimean War, it will be recalled, affected the international position of Russia in a measure which exceeded that of a military defeat alone, for it not only lowered her military prestige but also weakened her international authority. Alexander II and Alexander Gorchakov, who succeeded Nesselrode as foreign minister, were agreed that the immediate problem of Russia's foreign policy after 1856 was that of finding supporting friends to help counter-balance European enemies (among whom England and Austria were in first place) and to help in regaining the advantages lost in the Near East through the Treaty of Paris. They felt that they could count on Prussian friendship because, although Prussia had been disappointing during the Crimean War, it was to be expected that she would need Russian support in the ultimate reckoning with Austria. French friendship also seemed possible when, in September, 1857, Alexander II and Napoleon III met and discussed their common enmity toward Austria. But that possibility went by the board at the time of the Polish revolt of 1863, when Napoleon supported the Polish cause.

A definite test of Prussian friendship was made in 1870, when the time seemed propitious for Russia to assert her disapproval of the Black Sea clauses of the Treaty of Paris. As long as the freedom to maintain a fleet or erect fortifications on the Black Sea was curtailed, vigorous policy in the Near East and the Balkans was impossible, and Russia was therefore intent upon the nullification of the clauses that placed such restrictions upon her. The Franco-Prussian War of 1870-71, when Prussia was burdened by the fear of an Austrian attack, presented an opportunity that could not be overlooked. Russia offered to prevent Austrian intervention in return for a promise of Prussian diplomatic support for an attack on the Black Sea clauses, and the bargain was sealed.

In October, 1870, Gorchakov, confident of Prussian backing, announced that Russia no longer considered herself bound by the Black Sea clauses. England, of course, was outraged by such unilateral action. But Gorchakov had chosen the proper moment for action: France was beset by war; Austria-Hungary was diplomatically isolated; and Italy, engaged in seizing the city of Rome, was in no position to defend the sanctity of treaties. England, left with a choice between acquiescence or war with Russia, was grateful when Bismarck proposed a convocation of interested powers to consider the matter. In January, 1871, a conference of the great powers opened in London and, after solemnly affirming the sanctity of international treaties, agreed to the abrogation of the Black Sea clauses. Russia had taken her first daring step with impunity.

THE THREE EMPERORS LEAGUE.   Although Russia had achieved an immediate objective through the action of the London conference, it was evident that the balance of forces in Europe was still unfavorable to her. Prussia emerged from the Franco-Prussian War in the habiliment of the German Empire and in the position of the strongest continental power; and, however much Russian leaders valued German friendship, that turn of events was disquieting to them. Bismarck, on the other hand, as director of German foreign policy, was making friendly overtures to both Russia and Austria-Hungary in the hope of isolating France by preventing either a Franco-Austrian or Franco-Russian rapprochement.

It was difficult for Russia to determine a clear course at the time. The logic of power politics suggested the advantage of befriending France as a balance against Germany, but republican France was anathema to autocratic Russia. The growth of the revolutionary movement in Russia was of such concern to Alexander II and Gorchakov that they were for the time more concerned with the effect of international politics on domestic affairs than with international politics *per se.* Consequently, when Bismarck proposed a revival of the three-power understanding which had been achieved at Münchengrätz and Berlin in 1833, they were amenable and even anxious. In 1873 the emperors of Russia, Austria-Hungary, and Germany agreed to an alliance known as the Three Emperors League, providing for a mutual guarantee of the territories of the three states, common consultation on the Eastern Question, and common action against the danger of revolution. When put to test in the subsequent revival of the Eastern Question, the League proved to be an ephemeral alliance of little influence.

PAN-SLAVISM AND THE BALKANS. The delegates to the Congress of Paris in 1856 had hoped that their work would solve the Eastern Question, that the Ottoman Empire would recover from its mortal illness, that the Balkans would settle down to quiet somnolence, and that Russia would remain out of prominence. Within twenty years, however, their hopes were shown to be futile ones. Russia had freed herself of the Black Sea clauses; the Ottoman Empire was showing only increasing signs of senescence; and the Balkan peoples were putting more energy into political disturbance than ever before. The hold of the Ottoman Empire on the Balkans was becoming increasingly precarious: in autonomous Serbia and Rumania there was agitation for complete independence; among the Bulgars a sense of nationality was reawakening and, with it, the desire for national freedom; and the subject peoples in Bosnia and Herzegovina, mainly Serbs, were beginning to work for their deliverance.

The liberation movement among the Balkan Slavs evoked a strong response among many Russians. That Russians would sympathize with the struggles of the Orthodox Slavs against the "infidel" Turks was to be expected, but some carried their feelings beyond sympathy; they argued that it was the "mission" of the greatest Slavic country of all, Russia, to free her oppressed brothers in the Balkans and unite them under her aegis. Nicholas Danilevsky was one of the prominent spokesmen of this viewpoint, which became known as Pan-Slavism. General Rostislav Fadeyev, of the Russian army, was another, and his provocative book *Opinion on the East-*

ern Question (1869) won many to the cause. Even the Russian representative at Constantinople from 1864 to 1877, General Nicholas Ignatiev, was a Pan-Slavist.

The official policy of Russia was not that of Pan-Slavism, and neither Alexander II nor Gorchakov could be considered supporters of that doctrine. But, since it could be fitted into the traditional Russian policy toward the Balkans, the government did not oppose it. Many high officials, clerics, and generals were Pan-Slavists, and their influence helped to tinge the country's foreign policy after 1856 with Pan-Slavism despite the fact that the government did not officially support it.

BALKAN REVOLTS. In 1875 the Eastern Question was once more forced upon the attention of the great powers. In that year a revolt broke out in Bosnia and Herzegovina, provinces of the Ottoman Empire, and spread in the following year to its Bulgarian provinces. In suppressing the rebels the Sultan used such gratuitous brutality that Europe was roused to indignation and the diplomatic pot was set to boiling again.

Since the Treaty of Paris had made the great powers the joint guardians of the Ottoman Empire, the situation seemed to demand some joint action on their part which would, at least, prevent recurrences of such outbreaks. However, they were not of one mind as to what that action should be. Disraeli, who had become the head of the English Government in 1874, was more concerned with stopping the Russian bear than with securing concessions from the Sultan which might, while lessening the strain in the Balkans, weaken his power of resistance against Russia. The policy of Austria-Hungary wavered between the desire for annexation of Bosnia and Herzegovina and the desire to maintain normalcy. Germany, having at the time no direct interest in the Eastern Question, hoped mainly that no European war might eventuate. In Russia, the official policy was to urge international action in order to secure concessions from the Sultan; but many Pan-Slavists were working for unilateral Russian action—among them Ignatiev at Constantinople. Throughout the country, committees were formed to aid the Balkan Slavs; many individuals sent money to the rebels, and others volunteered for military service with them. Alexander, however, was reluctant to follow an overtly ambitious policy at the time because the finances of the empire were too unstable and the internal problem of political discontent was too immediate.

The events themselves helped to shape Russian policy. In July, 1876, Serbia and Montenegro (not without encouragement from Russian Pan-Slavists) declared war on the Ottoman Empire. But their small armies, of which the Serbian was led by the Russian General Michael Chernyaev, could not match those of the Sultan and were soon on the run. Seeing that the situation was becoming desperate, Russia asked for an armistice to save the Serbs and Montenegrins. The Ottoman Empire refused it—for reasons which were evident: in the first place, a palace revolution had resulted in the elevation of the warlike Abdul Hamid II to the throne in August of 1876; in the second place, the policy of Disraeli had led the new Sultan to believe that he would have English diplomatic support if he refused the Russian demand. Finally, in December, a conference of the great powers and the Sultan opened in Constantinople with the intention of settling the war with Serbia and Montenegro and of agreeing on reforms and concessions which the Sultan should make in the Balkans. But in January, 1877, it ended without agreement because of the intransigence of Abdul Hamid II, an intransigence based in part on the secret encouragement of Disraeli.

THE RUSSO-TURKISH WAR, 1877-78. While the international negotiations were in progress Russia was secretly preparing for the possibility of war in the event that the negotiations failed. Yet, even while preparations were under way, there was no official agreement on policy. Alexander II was doubtful of the wisdom of entering a conflict which might (as had the one in 1853) provoke a European war, and doubtful also of Russia's preparedness. Reitern, the Minister of Finance, insisted that the country was economically unprepared for war, and Gorchakov veered from one position to another. On the other hand, such public opinion as there was in Russia definitely favored war; so did the general sentiment at court. Those favoring it were supported by General Ignatiev's reports from Constantinople exaggerating the weakness of the Ottoman Empire and the certainty of Russian success.

As part of the preparation Russia signed a secret treaty with Austria-Hungary in January, 1877, whereby the latter promised benevolent neutrality in the event of war. In return, Russia promised not to touch Serbia or Montenegro nor to annex Constantinople and agreed that Austria-Hungary might be free to do as she pleased with Bosnia and Herzegovina. The implication of the treaty was that Russia would be free to effect territorial changes—not involving acquisition—in the Eastern Balkans in order to assure herself a preponderance of influence there.

On April 24, 1877, after having received permission from Rumania to send troops through that country, Russia declared war on the Ottoman Empire and began two offensive movements—one in the Balkans and the other from the Russo-Turkish border, in Transcaucasia. In the Balkans, the Russians, numbering about 300,000, were joined by Rumanian, Serbian, and Montenegrin troops, who looked upon the war as one of liberation; and together they met a Turkish army numbering about the same as their combined forces. In Transcaucasia the Russians used about 200,000 men against a smaller Turkish force. The German General von Moltke called the conflict a war between "the one-eyed and the blind," for both the Russians and the Turks were guilty of egregious errors. The Russian commander-in-chief, Grand Duke Nicholas Nikolaievich, had no over-all plan of attack. The army itself lacked much, for the reforms of Milyutin had not had time to eliminate the weaknesses shown during the Crimean war. Yet the ability of the junior commanders and the courage of the Russian troops and their allies, aided by the blunders of the Turkish command, enabled the attackers to drive forward. In Transcaucasia, where the terrain made fighting very difficult, they progressed slowly, and in the Balkans they moved fairly rapidly. By the end of January, 1878, they were ready to push on to Constantinople.

At the same time an international crisis was in the making. In England the war spirit was growing as the Russians approached Constantinople. Disraeli warned that England would not permit even a temporary Russian occupation of that city, and in January he dispatched an English fleet to guard the Straits. However, the Turks, regardless of England's position, capitulated when they saw the Russians at their door. On January 31, 1878, they agreed to an armistice and preliminary terms of peace, which were later confirmed in a treaty signed on March 3 at San Stefano, a town near Constantinople.

TREATY OF SAN STEFANO. By the Treaty of San Stefano, the Ottoman Empire ceded to Russia the Transcaucasian towns of Kars, Batum, and Ardahan, also the Dobrudja (which Russia would, in turn, pass on to Rumania in exchange for southern Bessarabia). Rumania, Serbia, and Montenegro were recognized as independent, and plans were made for the organization of a large, autonomous Bulgaria, stretching from the Aegean to the Black Sea and reaching as far west as Albania. Bosnia and Herzegovina were given semiautonomous status.

The treaty was not destined to go into effect unchallenged. Austria-Hungary was displeased that Russia had not provided for the cession of Bosnia and Herzegovina to her, as promised. England was opposed to all Russian gains in principle and particularly to the creation of a greater Bulgaria, which she felt would be, in effect, a Russian protectorate, en-

DRAWN BY EDW. A. SCHMITZ

MAP 10. The Near East after the Treaty of Berlin, 1878

hancing Russian might on the Aegean. Since an English fleet was lying just off Constantinople and England seemed determined to fight if not granted a hearing on her complaints, Russia had no choice but to agree to a congress of the major powers for the revision of the Treaty of San Stefano.

TREATY OF BERLIN. During June and July of 1878 the representatives of Russia, Austria-Hungary, England, France, Italy, and the Ottoman Empire conferred in Berlin and agreed upon the Treaty of Berlin, to replace that of San Stefano. The new treaty was the product of a series of compromises and deals involving England, Russia, Austria-Hungary, and the Ottoman Empire. It confirmed the independence of Serbia, Montenegro, and Rumania and the cession of Ardahan, Kars, Batum, and southern Bessarabia to Russia. It also made some important changes: Bosnia and Herzegovina were placed under the administration, but not the sovereignty, of Austria-Hungary; and Bulgaria was divided into two separate provinces (one called

Bulgaria, the other Rumelia), at the same time having her territory so reduced that she had no outlet on the Aegean.

UNSOLVED PROBLEMS.   Although for a while after the temporary settlement of the Eastern Question by the Treaty of Berlin, Russia's foreign
policy was immediately concerned with affairs elsewhere, her relations
with the great powers continued to be dominated by the Eastern Question.
The treaty of 1878 had left all the young Balkan nations dissatisfied with
the boundaries assigned to them, and their dissatisfaction was encouraged
by some of the great powers. As Serbia accepted Austrian tutelage and
hoped for Austrian backing for her ambitions and as Bulgaria was willing
to remain for some years a virtual satrapy of Russia with Russian troops
and advisers in her territory, so other Balkan states became the willing
charges of other great powers whose rival interests included their own.

For Russia the treaty was a great blow despite the territorial benefits
that it conferred. Having been forced twice in a generation to submit to
the other powers, she was now confirmed in hatred of England and suspicion of Austria-Hungary, while her confidence in Germany, from whom
expected support had not been received, was badly shaken. She felt herself
completely isolated in foreign affairs and, during the remaining years of
Alexander II's reign, did not establish any new ties with the great powers.
Alexander would have liked to renew the old bonds of friendship with Germany, but Bismarck felt that German security required first an understanding with Austria-Hungary. That was effected by the Austro-German
alliance of 1879, which remained the pivot of European diplomacy until
1918. It stipulated that, if either of the contracting powers were attacked by
Russia, the other would provide aid. In informing Alexander II of the terms
of the alliance, Emperor William I assured him that the German intent
was purely defensive; but the assurance did not mitigate the Russian lone-
liness.

REVIVAL OF THE THREE EMPERORS LEAGUE.   Both Alexander II and
William I were anxious to re-establish Russo-German friendship. Bismarck
was not averse to such an arrangement, for he saw in it the possibility of
forestalling a Franco-Russian understanding; but he insisted that Austria-
Hungary be brought into it. As a result, Russia, Germany, and Austria-
Hungary negotiated an alliance early in 1881, in effect reviving the Three
Emperors League, which had become inoperative at the time of the Russo-
Turkish War. The alliance had not been signed when Alexander II died,
in March of that year, but Alexander III agreed to the proposed terms and
gave his signature in June.

This tri-partite alliance provided that if one of the signatories were to become engaged in war with a fourth power the other signatories would follow a policy of benevolent neutrality. In addition, it included the pledge of each not to enter upon war with the Ottoman Empire or to change the status quo in the Balkans without having consulted the other two—except in two specified cases: Austria-Hungary was free to annex Bosnia and Herzegovina, and Russia might assume direction of plans to unite Bulgaria and Rumelia.

The fundamental weakness of the revived Three Emperors League lay in the fact that it attempted to reconcile the irreconcilable: Austrian and Russian interests in the Balkans. For a time the tenuous ties were maintained, but events in Bulgaria finally strained them to the breaking point. Alexander III, regarding Bulgaria as a vassal of Russia, expected its prince, Alexander of Battenberg, to respect the counsel of Russia; but neither the prince nor his advisers, despite their gratitude for Russian aid in 1877-78, were of a mind to accept a position of subordination. In 1885, without consulting Russia, they carried out a coup d'état by which the province of Rumelia was united with Bulgaria. Alexander III was so outraged by the affair that he overrode the advice of his Minister of Foreign Affairs, Nicholas Giers (who had succeeded Gorchakov in 1882), and supported a palace revolution in Bulgaria in 1886 to unseat Alexander of Battenberg. The unforeseen outcome was that the Bulgarians, still not inclined to consult Russia, chose for their new ruler Ferdinand of Saxe-Coburg, a man considered pro-German and pro-Austrian.

Russia attributed the turn of events to Austrian malevolence and to German support of it. As was to be expected under the circumstances, when the Three Emperors League reached the date of expiration, in 1887, it was not renewed. Russia was once more adrift. Many influential Russians argued that the time had come to have done with Germany and Austria-Hungary and to establish friendly relations with France, however distasteful the republican government of that country might be. France needed friends, it was pointed out, and she and Russia had no basic conflicts—certainly none in the Balkans. Katkov, who had the ear of Alexander III, urged this view and was widely supported on it. But sentiment prevailed over expediency: in 1887 Bismarck was able to salvage something of the tri-partite alliance by concluding between Russia and Germany a "reinsurance" treaty for three years, pledging each to maintain benevolent neutrality toward the other in case of attack by a third power.

When the "reinsurance" treaty expired, in 1890, Bismarck had just been dismissed, and there was no strong voice in Germany to support its renewal. The young Emperor William II showed none of William I's sentimental attachment for Russia, and the German foreign office argued that the treaty had only weakened the Austro-German alliance as well as German attempts to court English good will. Consequently, it was not renewed.

FRANCO-RUSSIAN ALLIANCE. Germany's attitude in 1890 turned Russia definitely onto a course toward which events had been leading her for some time. However sentimental and ancient the ties between the Romanovs and the Hohenzollerns, it was easily seen that they had been practically useless to Russia since 1871. Germany, during those years, had risen to a place of primacy in European diplomacy, but she had done little to prevent Russia's decline and had, contrariwise, helped to thwart Russia in the Balkans. Of the other powers, France alone had shown a growing favor for Russia. Many times during the 1880's she had demonstrated Russophile sentiments; a typical gesture had been the encouragement of French investment in Russian government bonds at a time when Germany and Russia had been engaged in a tariff war. Now, isolated and weakened, knowing herself to be at the mercy of powerful Germany, France sincerely sought the friendship of Russia.

Giers continued to insist that Russia hold fast to what remained of German friendship, but Alexander III, who looked upon Giers merely as his chief clerk in the foreign office, made his own decisions and responded more and more favorably to French importunities. Germany's failure to renew the "reinsurance" treaty in 1890, followed by her renewal of an alliance with Austria and Italy in 1891, hastened his acceptance of the French overtures. As an open gesture of good will he received a French naval squadron at Kronstadt in July, 1891 and, to the amazement of all present, rose to the playing of the French national anthem, the performance of which was then illegal in Russia. In the following month, Russia and France came to an understanding that each would consult the other in case of a threat to the peace. But France was not satisfied with such a timid measure; she wanted a military alliance. The idea was given consideration, and in 1892 a military convention was negotiated. Yet it was not until January, 1894, that the last *i* was dotted, the last *t* crossed, and the Franco-Russian Alliance became a fact. By its terms Russia was committed to go to the military aid of France if that country were attacked by Germany or by Italy with German support; and France was committed to render military aid to Russia if that country were attacked by Germany or by Austria-Hungary with German support.

The alliance marked the end of French and Russian isolation and the beginning of the division of Europe into two hostile camps. Nonetheless, the effects of the creation of the alliance on European diplomacy were rather minor during the decade which followed, for at that time the attention of the great powers was focused on Africa and the Far East rather than on Europe.

Interests in Central Asia

SLOW GROWTH OF INTEREST.   While Russia's affairs in the Near East were being maneuvered through repeated entanglements with European power politics, her affairs in Central Asia were being handled with less interference—and with less governmental concern.

For decades after Peter the Great had expressed an interest in Central Asia's possible advantages for Russia—but had done little about them—that region had remained for Russia a land of little promise and slight consequence in foreign affairs. (For that reason the early activities in Central Asia, as well as those in the Far East, have been slighted in the narrative of Russian foreign relations up to this point. It is believed that they will be more meaningful as related here in summary along with the significant activities of this period.)

When the Russians had pushed across Siberia, carrying the double-headed eagle all the way to the Pacific coast, it was inevitable that they should move south from Siberia into richer lands. At the eastern extremity of Siberia, the way south into China had been barred by the Treaty of Nerchinsk in 1689. However, in the area lying south of western Siberia and east from the Caspian Sea to the great mountain ranges—Central Asia—southern expansion was possible.

That was the region where, in the latter part of the fourteenth century, the Mongol Turcic adventurer Timur (Tamerlane) had created a great empire out of the lands of the Amu-Darya and the Syr-Darya river valleys with its capital at the fabulous city of Samarkand. After his death, in 1405, the empire had crumbled into small, warring units, and in the centuries that followed no new Timur arose to unite and strengthen them again. So, politically, Central Asia was easy prey for a powerful state. Economically, it offered little attraction for Russian colonists, for much of its area was arid and there were only a few oases and river valleys to offer the basis for settlement. But it had some compensating features: it was crossed by rich trade routes connecting Russia, Persia, India, and China, and even on its semiarid lands a pastoral economy was possible. Moreover, its people had one characteristic which kept forcing the region repeatedly upon Russian attention; they were warlike, and they were not reluctant to meet the Russians in frequent border encounters, to contest boundary lines with them or to make forays into Russian territory. The Russian Government found it necessary, therefore, to maintain frontier fortifications and to assign special officials and military personnel to the task of maintaining order on the frontier. Often ambitious governors and generals assigned to duty there found it easy to promote their careers and fortunes by independent action in Central Asia; and Russian advances in that region during the nineteenth century could more often be credited to the ambitions of such men than to policy worked out at St. Petersburg. The saying applied to England's conquering of India—that it was done "in a fit of absent-mindedness"—is applicable also to the early stages of Russia's conquest of Central Asia.

BEGINNINGS OF CONQUEST. Whenever possible, Russian governors and generals pushed the fortified frontier farther south into the lands now known as Kazakhstan, where in the eighteenth and nineteenth centuries political authority was divided among three weak, so-called states: the Great Horde, in the southern and eastern part; the Middle Horde, in the north-central; and the Little Horde, in the northwestern. It was comparatively easy for the Russians to extend their control over these lands, and by the end of the eighteenth century the Middle and Little Hordes were under Russian suzerainty.

Orenburg was the chief base for Russian expansion into Kazakhstan; and it was an energetic governor-general of Orenburg, Count Vasily Perovsky, who completed the annexation and incorporation of most of it. He built new fortresses deep in the heart of Kazakh lands and strengthened the control of Russian authority over the natives. But his sights were set on the richer lands south of Kazakhstan, where the fine valleys of the Syr-Darya and the Amu-Darya lay under the control of the Moslem emirates and khanates of Khiva, Bokhara, and Kokand. In 1839 he sent from Orenburg a small expedition of Russian Cossack and native cavalry against Khiva; but, beset by unfavorable weather, it was a failure. Undaunted by that, Perovsky in the next fourteen years extended the Russian military frontier farther south, erected new forts, and made ready for the next push against Khiva. In 1854 he executed the final phase of his plan, which resulted in the Khivan Khan's agreement to a treaty whereby he recognized the supremacy of Russia. The Khan retained his territory; but since the Russian military frontier was then at the mouth of the Syr-Darya, it was only a matter of time before the conquest would be pressed on.

EXTENDED CONQUEST. A line of fortifications which Perovsky had established from the mouth of the Syr-Darya to Verny, south of Lake Balkhash, provided the bases from which the Russians extended their efforts with greater energy in the 1860's as frequent raids by Central Asian tribesmen across the new Russian frontier provided them with occasions for renewed military action. In 1864 Colonel Michael Chernyaev, in reprisal for native attacks, began a series of military blows along the Syr-Darya, which culminated in the capture of Tashkent in the following year. From there expeditions were sent against Kokand, to the southeast. Reasonably successful, they added to Russian credit more new territory, including the city of Samarkand, taken in 1868.

The newly conquered territory of the Syr-Darya valley was incorporated by Russia as the government-general of Turkestan, with Tashkent as its capital. The able and brutal General Constantine von Kaufmann was named its governor-general and, between 1867 and 1882, he succeeded in bringing the area under control. The Emir of Bokhara accepted Russian suzerainty in 1868, and the Khan of Khiva did likewise in 1873. Three years later the remnants of the Khanate of Kokand were annexed by Russia and, as the province of Ferghana, made a part of the government-general of Turkestan. In the succeeding years, military expeditions brought under Russian control the lands west of the Amu-Darya River to the Caspian Sea. By 1884 the Russian conquest of Central Asia was complete except for the small section of the Pamir plateau, taken eleven years later; and the Russian frontier met the frontiers of Persia, China, and Afghanistan. At one point the Russian-Afghan frontier was but a few miles from British India.

GOVERNMENT. The conquest of Central Asia added vast lands and many non-Russian peoples to the Russian Empire. What is now called Kazakhstan was organized as the government-general of the Steppe Provinces, the Turgai Province, and the Ural Province; and the lands to the south and west of the vassal Emirate of Bokhara and the Khanate of Khiva were organized as the Transcaspian Province.[1] The population of this extended region of some 1.4 million square miles was about 7.7 million in 1897, of whom 90 per cent were Moslem in faith and non-Russian in cul-

---

[1] The Transcaspian Province, the Emirate of Bokhara, and the Khanate of Khiva are commonly designated as parts of the "Turkestan region."

DRAWN BY EDW. A. SCHMITZ

MAP 11. Russian Central Asia in 1895

ture. The chief ethnic groups were the Kazakh, Kirghiz, Uzbek, Tadzhik, and Turkmen peoples, predominantly illiterate and poor. The Russian Government did not attempt to Russify them but permitted continuation of existing institutions, customs, and laws. The new regions were, in effect, of colonial status. The governors-general were powers unto themselves and had at their disposal large armies to insure the tranquillity of the lands.

ECONOMIC VALUE.   The provinces in the Turkestan region, with their 5 million inhabitants, were richer and far more important than the other provinces. Their immediate economic benefit to Russia lay in their production of raw cotton; by 1905 nearly one-third of the needs of the Russian cotton industry were supplied by them.

The economic value of the region was greatly enhanced by the Trans-

caspian Railroad, begun in 1880. Its construction was started in Krasno-
vodsk, on the Caspian Sea; and following the Persian and Afghan borders,
it reached Merv in 1886, Samarkand by 1888, and Tashkent by 1905.
Another line, connecting Tashkent and Orenburg, provided a direct link
between Turkestan and central Russia. Thus laid out, the Transcaspian
Railroad not only speeded up Russian-Persian trade but also made it possible that Russian troops be easily deployed along the Persian and Afghan
borders.

POTENTIAL CONFLICTS OF INTEREST. The gradual movement into
Central Asia was not without importance in the area of Russian foreign
relations. It extended Russian territory to the border of Sinkiang (Chinese
Turkestan) and therefore caused some worry in Peking because Chinese
control of Sinkiang had never been secure, and it was feared that Russia
might be able to extend her influence to that province. In 1881, in fact,
Russia and China came near to war over Russian interference there,
but the issue was settled peaceably. Russia however maintained an economic
and political interest in western Sinkiang.

Far more significant was the effect of Russian penetration of Central
Asia upon England. The English were anxious on two scores. The annexa-
tion of Turkestan extended the Russian-Persian border and increased the
possibility of Russian economic and political influence in northern Persia.
And an even greater cause for anxiety was the unwelcome proximity of
Russia to the northwest frontier of India; only Afghanistan lay between
Russian Turkestan and northwest India, and the Emir of Afghanistan was
eager to play England off against Russia. The English remembered that
Paul I had prepared an expedition against India in 1801 and noticed with
deep concern that the Transcaspian Railroad had both strategic and eco-
nomic possibilities which were contrary to British interests.

Interests in Far Eastern Asia

EASTERN SIBERIA AND THE PACIFIC. The Treaty of Nerchinsk, which
Russia had signed with China in 1689, and which with minor modifications remained in force until 1858, had set the limits of Russia's southward
territorial expansion at the Yablonovoi Range. Since the Chinese proved
capable of holding that line, Russian activities in eastern Siberia were for
a century and a half directed northward. Motivated by prospects of fur
trade, pillage, extortion of tribute from the natives, and the spirit of ad-

venture, the Russians moved north along the Pacific coast of Siberia and then down onto the Kamchatka Peninsula. By the end of the seventeenth century they had established themselves sufficiently to construct a block-house on the peninsula, and by 1720 Russian control of the area was made secure by the establishment of regular sea connections between Okhotsk and Kamchatka.

Once in Kamchatka, the Russians were tempted to move east, north, and south from that base. In 1705 they gave their first attention to the Kurile Islands, a chain reaching south from the peninsula to the northern-most islands of Japan. Several exploratory expeditions followed. Then in 1738 Lieutenant Martin Spanberg set out from Okhotsk with an expedi-tion to explore the Kuriles and to search for a sea route to Japan. He landed on Japanese soil in 1739, was well received, and then turned back. In the succeeding years, the Russian flag was hoisted over one island after another of the Kurile chain until, in 1766, the Russians were ready to go beyond the Kuriles—to move into Yezo (Hokkaido) Island, north of the main is-land of Japan. But the Japanese, who had hitherto considered Yezo an out-post of little significance, now tightened their control over it and succeeded in halting the Russians.

From 1792 on, the Russians made sporadic attempts to open direct trade relations with Japan. They had no success until Admiral Count Yefim Putyatin led a squadron into Nagasaki in 1853 and began negotiations which culminated in the Treaty of Shimoda (1855). The treaty conferred on Russia the right to trade in Nagasaki, Shimoda, and Hakodate. In addi-tion, it awarded the northern half of the Kurile chain to Russia and the southern half to Japan and provided for joint Russo-Japanese occupation of Sakhalin Island, in which both countries had an interest.

ALASKA.   Russians had long been interested in determining whether or not northeastern Siberia and northwestern America were joined by land, as many believed. A Russian Cossack by the name of Simon Dezhnev is now believed to have crossed the Bering Straits and to have been in Alaska in 1648, but his venture received no wide notice at the time. It was probably unknown to Peter the Great, who in 1725 commissioned a Danish-born officer, Vitus Bering, to lead a naval expedition along the waters of Kam-chatka to find the point at which that peninsula joined America.

In 1728 Bering, sailing north from the Kamchatka town of Petropav-losk, reached the point now known as the Bering Strait, convinced him-self that Siberia and America were separated by water, and turned back. In 1732 a Russian geodesist, Michael Gvozdev, actually reached Alaska by ship, but no notice of his accomplishment was taken in St. Petersburg. Bering meanwhile prepared a new expedition and in 1741 sailed once more from Petropavlosk. In that year he finally landed in Alaska but turned back immediately.

Bering died from the rigors of the return voyage, but the survivors of his expedition brought back valuable furs and pelts, evidence which kindled wide interest. Russian fur traders soon descended on the Aleutian Islands and Alaska in great numbers. In their greed they overreached themselves, however; they subjected the native hunters to such indignities that a revolt broke out against them, and the Russian Government was forced to step in. The government was willing enough to do that, not only for the sake of establishing order but also to make certain that part of the profits from the fur trade should find its way into the imperial treasury.

After several methods of regulating the fur-trading activities had been tried and found inadequate, the government granted a charter to establish a trading company. The chartered organization, known as the Russian-American Company, was given a monopoly of the fur trade in Alaska, the Aleutians, the Kuriles, and other North Pacific islands and was assigned the right to administer the lands where it carried on activities. With its headquarters at Sitka, it started operations in 1799 and had soon established many trading posts. Some were set up as far afield as California, where a post named Fort Ross was established north of San Francisco in 1812 at the direction of Alexander Baranov, the energetic Russian governor of Alaska.

Russian trading activities along the Pacific Coast of North America and in the North Pacific alarmed not only the Spanish, who at the time were unable to take any effective action against them, but also the Americans and British, who had extended their interests to that part of the world. Alexander I decreed in 1821 that Russian claims on the Pacific coast of North America extended south to the fifty-first parallel. That decree, added to the Russians' insistence that they held a monopoly on trade in the North Pacific, brought sharp reaction from the United States. Secretary of State John Quincy Adams, who had been the first United States minister to St. Petersburg after the establishment of Russian-American diplomatic relations, in 1809, immediately attacked the Russian claim. While negotiations dragged on, President Monroe declared in his message to Congress in December, 1823, that the United States opposed further colonization of the Americas by European powers. After that, since the Russian stake was small and since the apparently determined United States was supported by England,

Alexander I backed down. In 1824 a treaty drawn up at St. Petersburg set the southern limit of Russian claims on the Pacific coast at 54° 40' and provided that trading and fishing in the North Pacific be open to both the United States and Russia.

The economic value of Alaska for Russia began to drop in the following years. Political misrule after the death of Governor Baranov and a shortsighted policy of unplanned hunting led to failure of plans, and the income from the region declined rapidly. Moreover, Alaska was becoming a recognized strategic handicap as well as an economic liability. When a Franco-British squadron attacked Petropavlosk (uncomfortably close to Alaska) during the Crimean War, it became evident that Russia could not hold Alaska if it were attacked. For those reasons Russia agreed in 1867 to the sale of Alaska to the United States for $7,200,000, and considered herself well disengaged from a venture which had not justified its first promises.

CHINA.   (a) Relations before 1800. After the Treaty of Nerchinsk, Russia's trade with China was conducted through the Siberian frontier post of Kyakhta, on the border of Outer Mongolia, south of Lake Baikal. Beginning in 1727 the Russians were permitted, by terms of the Treaty of Kyakhta, to conduct a caravan every three years from Kyakhta across the arid lands of Outer Mongolia to Peking. There they sold to the Chinese large quantities of furs and some Western goods and bought from them silks, porcelain, spices, and tea.

Russia was the only European nation permitted to send traders to Peking before the end of the eighteenth century, also the only European nation permitted to maintain an ecclesiastic mission there. She held that relatively favorable position because she was the northern land neighbor of China. The Chinese felt that some contact was inevitable, though they sought to keep it at a minimum. Kyakhta remained the sole port of entry for the Russians during this century, and their repeated requests for permission to enter the Amur valley were denied.

(b) Change in Chinese relations. In the first half of the nineteenth century the Russian Government began to show an increase of interest in Eastern Siberia and in Russo-Chinese relations. Michael Speransky was appointed governor-general of Siberia in 1819 and, during his brief period in office, effected many administrative changes. Among them was the division of the land into two administrative areas, Western Siberia and Eastern Siberia, each under a governor-general. This reform meant that more attention could be given to the eastern part, the encouragement of which had hitherto been subordinated to that of the more heavily colonized and richer western part. Before that division, the government had given little attention to the region east of Lake Baikal except at times when taxes and tribute were due. Occasionally exploratory expeditions had been sent there, but they had created little interest. The few Russians in the region during the eighteenth century were Cossacks, traders, adventurers, government officials, and some convicts. Now Russia was becoming concerned with the possibilities of securing entry into the Amur River valley as an advantage in the conduct of Russo-Chinese trade and in the improvement of communications with Kamchatka. The valley was in a region imperfectly known, and there was disagreement over the questions of whether or not the Amur was navigable and whether or not Sakhalin, near the mouth of the river, was an island or a peninsula. As late as 1846, an agent sent by Nicholas I came back with the report that the Amur was not navigable and that Sakhalin was a peninsula. Nesselrode, always opposed to adventurist policies, assured the Emperor that "the Amur is of no significance to Russia." Nicholas, however, would not be persuaded that the river was unimportant. England's successful war against China from 1839 to 1842 had suggested to him that Russia should look to her interests there, and in his opinion the Amur represented the first line of interest. Even if unimportant in itself, the river, he felt, should be kept from the influence or control of the British. As the agent of his personal policy he chose the energetic Nicholas Muraviev-Amursky.[1]

Appointed governor-general of Eastern Siberia in 1847, Muraviev-Amursky was instructed to improve Russo-Chinese trade through Kyakhta, extend gold production, and gain from the Chinese certain navigation rights for Russian ships on the Amur. To those tasks he brought a high degree of ability, resourcefulness, and initiative—virtues which occasionally brought him into conflict with St. Petersburg but which ultimately brought him personal glory. He was in full accord with the imperial policy in Eastern Siberia and proceeded to execute that policy as he understood it, without waiting for detailed instructions. Soon after his appointment he sent several expeditions from Petropavlosk to the Amur. Then in 1851 he established two towns, Nikolaievsk and Mariinsk, at the mouth of the Amur and began to initiate Russian activities on the river—all in reckless defiance of Russo-

---

[1] His name was originally Nicholas Muraviev, but in recognition of his work, he was made a count with the title Count Muraviev-Amursky. To distinguish him from the many Muravievs who appear in Russian history, this text will refer to him as Muraviev-Amursky.

Chinese treaties and in opposition to the wishes of his own foreign office. In the next six years he extended Russian activities on the northern side of the Amur by opening settlements and organizing an armed force of Cossacks and liberated convicts. In short, he placed Russia in *de facto* possession of the north bank.

(c) Treaties of concession. When China in 1856 became engaged in war with England and France, Russia was ready to take advantage of the situation. While representing herself as the friend of China and an opponent of the "predatory aims of perfidious Albion," she urged Chinese recognition of Russian occupation of the area north of the Amur. Then, in 1857, Alexander II decreed the organization of a new province, including the land north of the Amur. The act was, of course, in violation of legally established Chinese rights, but the Chinese were at the time in no position to insist on the letter of the law. In the following year Muraviev-Amursky succeeded in securing from the commander of the Chinese forces in the Amur region a treaty recognizing Russian possession of the north bank of the river. The treaty, which was signed at Aigun, on the southern bank, also provided (pending later negotiations) for joint Russo-Chinese occupation of the region from the Amur and Ussuri rivers to the Pacific. Technically the Treaty of Aigun had only provisional force, for it had been negotiated by men who did not possess plenipotentiary powers.

Meanwhile, the Russian diplomatic representative Admiral Putyatin was negotiating directly with the central Chinese Government in order to insure to Russia advantages similar to any which England and France might secure as a result of their war with China. In June, 1858, shortly after the conclusion of the Treaty of Aigun, he signed the Treaty of Tientsin with China. By its terms Russia gained the same rights and privileges that England and France had just won: the right to trade in various Chinese ports and to maintain a legation in Peking.

The Treaty of Tientsin was immediately followed by new complications. China not only resumed her warfare with England and France but also began to refuse implementation of her two recent treaties with Russia. The task of restoring Russian gains fell to General Nicholas Ignatiev, who had replaced Putyatin. To accomplish his ends he used tactics which earned him renown as one of the most adept intriguers among diplomats. He presented himself to the Chinese as a friend, offering helpful military advice and, at the same time, was scheming to reap a rich harvest from the Anglo-French victories against China. When Chinese military power was at its weakest, in 1860, he demanded and secured yet another treaty, the

Treaty of Peking. Signed in November, 1860, it not only confirmed the provisions of the Treaty of Aigun but also provided for the cession to Russia of the region between the Pacific and the Ussuri and Amur rivers. Thus, at little cost, Russia came into possession of an area of over 350,000 square miles and secured a boundary which placed her on the Amur and at the back door of Korea.

PLANS FOR DEVELOPMENT OF FAR EAST.   The land acquired from China in 1858 and 1860 was desolate, distant, and underpopulated (sustaining only about 15,000 inhabitants in 1860). But it was a welcome addition to Eastern Siberia, holding promise of both economic and military advantages; and Russia set about to populate and develop it. The region was divided into two provinces: the Amur Province, the administrative center of which was Blagoveshchensk, and the Maritime Province, the administrative center of which was Vladivostok, which Muraviev-Amursky had founded in 1860. Special efforts were made to increase the population of the two provinces: several Cossack settlements were transferred to the Amur and Ussuri regions; political exiles and convicts were encouraged to settle in the area; and inducements were offered to peasant settlers. However, settlement increased slowly, for the overland trip from European Russia often took as much as two years and the rewards in the bleak Far East were far from great. By 1879 the population of the two provinces had reached only 108,000, and many of those were Koreans and Chinese who had migrated north. Vladivostok was a favored location. Although its harbor was ice-bound from December to March, it was far better, more accessible and freer from ice than any other point on the eastern coast of Siberia, and those advantages hastened its growth into a military and naval center. With the opening of the Suez Canal, in 1869, sea communication between Vladivostok and Russia was speeded up; the journey to Odessa could then be made in about forty-five days.

The further development of the Russian Far East required better transportation. Muraviev-Amursky had been one of the first to see that, and he had suggested the construction of a transcontinental railroad. But his suggestion had been neglected because Russia had been concerned at the time with the construction of lines in the populous west. In 1880 government officials in the Maritime Province renewed the agitation for a railroad; and by 1890 the central government was giving serious thought to the idea, moved not only by the economic advantages of a railroad but also by a realization of its strategic importance for Russian foreign policy in the Far East. In 1891 the construction of the Trans-Siberian Railroad was approved, and its construction was begun in the west from Chelyabinsk and in the east from Vladivostok.

FAR EASTERN DIPLOMACY, 1860-94. For over thirty years after the acquisition of the Amur and Maritime provinces, Russian official interest in the Far East was secondary to her interests in Europe and Central Asia, but it was by no means neglected. In 1875 Russia reached an agreement with Japan whereby the latter gave up all claim to the island of Sakhalin in return for the cession of those Kurile Islands then in Russian possession. Sakhalin, lying at the mouth of the Amur, gave promise of great strategic and economic value to Russia, and circumstances soon made her aware of the need to work for still other points of advantage. Japan was attempting to gain preponderant influence in Korea, which bordered on the Russian Maritime Province; and Russia was roused to the particular necessity of striving for a share of influence there. In sum, however, what was done about the problem before 1894 was of relatively little consequence.

INTENSIFIED INTEREST, 1894-98. After 1894, Russian policy in the Far East turned from one of mild interest into one of intense ambition. The occasion for this turnabout was the Sino-Japanese War of 1894-95, which stirred the great powers to action by revealing the military weakness of China and the emerging power of Japan. For Russia, the war indicated two things: (1) that there was a good chance of enhancing Russian interests at the expense of China and (2) that Japan was a strong rival for the areas which Russia coveted.

One of the weapons of the great powers in China was loans, in return for each of which the bankrupt Chinese Government was expected to accede to political and economic demands. Russia did not have the capital for making such loans; but since the Franco-Russian Alliance had just been concluded, there was hope that France would provide financial backing for Russian ambition. The French interest lay in the southern provinces of China and, presumably, would not preclude co-operation with Russia elsewhere in the country.

Two other situations encouraged Russia to pursue her ambitions in the Far East at this time. One was brought about by the subsidence of her influence in the Balkans after 1887. She felt the need for a new area of concentration, and the Far East after 1894 supplied it. Another helpful situation grew out of the construction of the Trans-Siberian Railroad. It would increase Russia's military power in the Far East and enable her to play a stronger role than theretofore. Although the railroad was not conceived primarily as an aid to imperialist expansion, it was recognized as an admirable weapon for that purpose.

Russia's new orientation had the approval of Prince Alexis Lobanov-Rostovsky, who became foreign minister upon the death of Giers (in January, 1895); and Witte also, who supervised the building of the Trans-Siberian Railroad, felt that affairs were taking a proper direction. The first step on the new course was taken shortly after the signing of the Treaty of Shimonoseki, which ended the Sino-Japanese war, in April, 1895. The clause in that treaty which gave the Liaotung Peninsula to Japan was unsatisfactory to China, and she sought great-power intervention to induce Japan to rescind it. Russia, being opposed to the establishment of Japanese power in China, took the lead in persuading Japan. She was supported by two of the other powers: France, impelled by loyalty, and Germany, impelled by the desire to gain Russian favor at no cost to herself; and the three of them offered a threat sufficient to cause Japan to restore Liaotung to China. After that Russia was in a position to take advantage of China's gratitude. First, she offered a loan (the money being provided by French and Belgian bankers), and China accepted it in July, 1895. Then within a year, when Li Hung-chang, the chief minister of China, was invited to represent his country at the coronation of Nicholas II, Chinese gratitude was put to the test. Witte confronted the minister with arguments supporting Russia's need for a branch line of the Trans-Siberian Railroad across Manchuria to Vladivostok: it would appreciably shorten the distance from central Russia to Vladivostok and hasten the dispatch of Russian aid to China in case of Japanese attack. (Such a line would also enable Russia to dominate northern Manchuria, but that argument was not used with Li.) Li Hung-chang was impressed by the idea and, on June 3, 1896, he and Lobanov-Rostovsky signed on behalf of their respective countries a secret treaty, known as the Li-Lobanov Treaty. By its terms China granted Russia the right to construct a railroad across northern Manchuria, and the two countries pledged mutual aid in the event of an attack by Japan upon either of them. In the following September a public agreement between Russia and China provided for the construction of the railroad by the Chinese Eastern Railroad Company, a subsidiary of the Russo-Chinese Bank.[1] The same company was granted the right of administering the lands given as right of way to the railroad. As for final disposition of the line, it was agreed that thirty-six years after its completion China would have the option of purchasing it—a most unlikely contingency in view of Chinese bankruptcy; and eighty years after completion it would revert at no cost to China.

---

[1] This bank, established in 1895, was a private company based mainly on French capital but chartered and directed by the Russian Government.

For China the period which followed the signing of that agreement was a trying one. The great powers followed one another in demanding railroad concessions and special privileges; when one power received a concession, others would demand from China something by way of "compensation." On March 8, 1898, when Germany secured by the threat of force a 99-year lease on Kiaochow Bay, Russia demanded "compensation." She received, by two agreements signed on March 27 and May 7, 1898, a 25-year lease on the southern tip of the Liaotung peninsula with the right to construct a military and naval base at Port Arthur, open only to Russia and China, and the right to maintain a commercial port at Talien—later renamed Dalny. Russia was permitted also by these agreements to construct a railroad north from Port Arthur and Dalny (subsequently known as the South Manchurian Railroad) to connect with the Chinese Eastern Railroad, then under construction across Manchuria. Both lines were to use the Russian broad gauge of five feet rather than standard gauge, thus permitting the uninterrupted movement of rolling stock from Russian railroads into Manchuria.

GAINS IN MANCHURIA AND KOREA.   The Russo-Chinese agreements and treaties of 1896 and 1898 placed Manchuria at the mercy of Russia. The Chinese Eastern Railroad Company, in charge of constructing both the Chinese Eastern and the South Manchurian railroads, was actually an agency of the Russian Government and its policies were dominated by Witte. It interpreted so broadly the right of administration granted by the agreements that the zones through which the railroads passed were administered as if they were part of Russia. Under the guise of railroad guards, thousands of Russian troops were poured into the zones. Soon evidences of Russian influence were everywhere. Harbin, in time the administrative headquarters of the Chinese Eastern Railroad Company, took on the character of a Russian city. Throughout the zones Russians were busily exploiting the mining rights which had been included in the agreements. Particularly noticeable was the purposeful activity at Dalny and Port Arthur. Those ports, in contrast to Vladivostok, were free of ice the year round, and Russia had decided to build up Dalny as a commercial port and Port Arthur as the chief base of the Russian Pacific Fleet.

The extension of Russia's influence in Manchuria inevitably raised the question of her intentions in regard to Korea, which bordered both Manchuria and the Russian Maritime Province. Although Japan felt that, after the Sino-Japanese war of 1894-95, she had a preferred position in troubled Korea, Russia for some time showed no intention of respecting that position. However, in April, 1898, Russian and Japanese diplomats signed the Nishi-Rosen Protocol, which committed Russia to respect Japanese economic preponderence in Korea. In return, Japan was willing to respect existing Russian interests in Manchuria.

This peaceful adjustment of one conflict of interest in the Far East was followed by another in April, 1899, the Scott-Muraviev Agreement between Great Britain and Russia, staking out the respective railroad interests of the two countries in China. Many men in the Russian Foreign Office believed that their country's interests could best be served through a program of such pacific accommodations, but Nicholas II would not commit himself to a consistent policy in the Far East. Instead he agreed to mutually irreconcilable policies that ultimately resulted in war with Japan.

Most ill-advised was his Korean policy. While the foreign office attempted to operate in the spirit of the Nishi-Rosen Protocol, the Emperor was condoning activities in Korea that violated its spirit and consequently convinced Japan that Russia's real intentions were bellicose and expansionist. He became personally involved in one such activity, which developed from the so-called Yalu River scheme, devised by two former guards officers, Alexander Bezobrazov and Vladimir Vonlyarlyarsky. The scheme called for the creation of a privately held corporation, financed by the Emperor and certain members of his court, which would acquire a timber-cutting concession near the Yalu River, in northern Korea. The concession was to serve as an excuse for introducing Russian reservists, disguised as lumberjacks, into northern Korea, where they would be used later to bolster Russian interests in that area. The Emperor was drawn into this irresponsible scheme by members of the court circle—including his brother-in-law Grand Duke Alexander and Admiral Eugene Alexeyev, commander of the Russian naval forces in the Pacific as well as the Russian military forces on the Liaotung Peninsula—who approved of an expansionist policy in Korea. Since he himself had rather ambitious visions of Russia's future in the Far East, he was easily persuaded to approve the plan for the proposed organization, to be known as the East Asiatic Industrial Corporation. He gave his approval in June, 1900, but the outbreak of the Boxer Rebellion in the same month caused a temporary delay in implementing the scheme.

The Boxer Rebellion, a Chinese antiforeign uprising directed against the foreign domination of China in general and Russian actions in Manchuria in particular, marked the beginning of a new stage in Russian policy in China. Since all the other great powers sent expeditions to save their legations under attack by the Boxers in Peking, Russia could legitimately

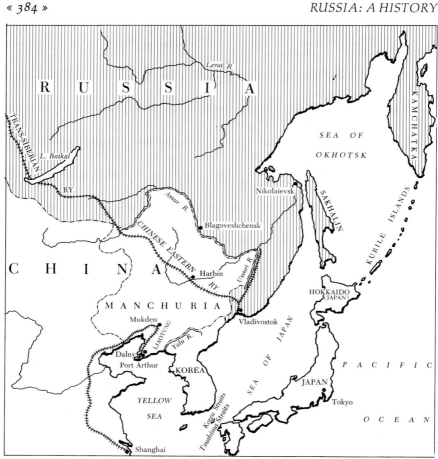

DRAWN BY EDW. A. SCHMITZ

MAP 12. Russia in the Far East, 1904

do likewise; and she used the occasion to station troops throughout Manchuria. When the rebellion was quelled, in 1901, the other powers began
to withdraw their troops, but the Russians remained in Manchuria, giving
no indication that they intended to leave.

THE APPROACH OF CONFLICT. The evidences of Russian aims in
Manchuria after the conclusion of the Sino-Japanese War were observed
by the other powers with varying reactions: France, almost the junior
partner of Russia in the Far East, continued expanding her influence in
south China and supporting Russian diplomacy in the north; Germany
was still willing to allow Russian gains if she could count on some for her-

self; but England and Japan were extremely disturbed by Russian policies. England, whose economic interest in China exceeded that of the other powers, sought to preserve the territorial integrity of China or, if that should prove impossible, to assure herself of a respectable position in what was left of the country. Japan saw her ambitions being impeded by Russian occupation of positions from which both her security and her program of expansion might be threatened. But, being only a third-rate power despite her performance in the war with China, she wanted to handle the situation by compromise if possible. In fact, both Japan and England were willing to make accommodating arrangements with Russia. The question was whether or not Russia was prepared to make bargains and keep them; and by the end of 1901, the major faction in the Japanese Government was convinced that the answer was in the negative, that no compromise with Russia was possible and that war was unavoidable. In 1902 Japan and England signed a treaty of alliance. It committed each of the signatories to neutrality if the other were involved in war with a third power; but if the third power were aided by a fourth, armed intervention was promised. In realistic terms their agreement meant that if Russia and Japan were at war, England would not interfere unless France should go to the support of Russia.

Russia had a choice of two policies: one of compromise and moderation which might leave her a preponderant influence in northern Manchuria and yet not lead to war, or one of unbridled expansion which might lead to war. The choice was not an easy one, for within the central government there was no agreement on foreign policy. Witte, key figure in economic and political expansion in Manchuria, argued for moderation. Alexis Kuropatkin, the Minister of War, was less cautious than Witte, but he too was beginning to feel that Russia was overstepping safety. Baron Roman Rosen, who in 1903 was representing Russia in Tokyo for the second time, warned against the danger of war. Count Vladimir Lamsdorff, Minister of Foreign Affairs from 1900 to 1906, took the views of Witte and Rosen. But those whose opinions counted most with Nicholas II were his new Minister of Interior, Plehve, and the men associated with the East Asiatic Industrial Corporation, who urged continued boldness, arguing that the Japanese would not be foolhardy enough to attack the greatest land power in the world.

In 1903 the key problem was that of Russian occupation of Manchuria. Faced by the Anglo-Japanese alliance, by the opposition of the United States, and by the fact that France was not prepared to give her *carte blanche*,

Russia agreed to evacuate Manchuria—but in three stages, the last to be completed by October, 1903. Had Russia fulfilled that agreement and had she refrained from taking new measures in Korea, war might have been averted. As matters were handled, the first stage of evacuation was carried out, but when the date of the second stage arrived, in April, 1903, nothing happened; Russian policy at that time was taking a fatal turn.

By spring of 1903 the Emperor was virtually ignoring the foreign office in the conduct of affairs in the Far East. Against its advice, he ordered the Russian troops still in Manchuria to remain, permitted the exploitation of the Yalu River concession to be renewed, and approved the infiltration of disguised Russian reservists in northern Korea. In August he established a new post, the Viceroyalty of the Far East, with Admiral Alexeyev as Viceroy, to deal directly with Far Eastern diplomatic problems. With that act the conduct of Russian policy in the Far East was taken completely out of the hands of the professional diplomats. Witte protested against these proceedings; and after this protest, one of a number he had made in various policy conflicts with Nicholas, he was removed from the Ministry of Finance and given the relatively inconsequential position of Chairman of the Committee of Ministers.

During 1903 Japan proposed to recognize Russian preponderance in northern Manchuria if Russia would withdraw her troops from Manchuria and recognize Japanese preponderance in Korea; but Russia was not prepared to offer any acceptable reply to the proposals. Consequently, without a declaration of war, Japan opened hostilities on the night of February 8, 1904, by a naval attack on Port Arthur, destroying at once the effectiveness of the Russian naval squadron based there.

Russo-Japanese War: 1904-1905

OUTLOOK FOR THE RUSSIANS.   When the war began Russian military leaders, supremely confident, looked condescendingly upon the Japanese, to whom they referred as *macaques* (baboons), and felt certain of an easy victory. But their judgment proved to be too optimistic. The Russian forces in the Far East were inferior to those of Japan in number and in quality. To supplement them, two army corps and four reserve divisions were dispatched from European Russia over the single-track Trans-Siberian Railroad, which was wholly inadequate for handling such a large volume of men and the matériel accompanying them. There was still a gap in the railroad at Lake Baikal, and it was necessary for the troops to cross the forty-mile expanse of the frozen lake by various means. Adding to those difficulties, the administrative and supply services of the army were as usual inadequate; both civilian morale and military morale were low; and it was difficult to stimulate any enduring patriotic feeling for the war.

All these factors worked to the advantage of the Japanese, who counted on a speedy campaign in which they could employ their immediate tactical advantage and achieve victory before Russian reinforcements could arrive. They planned first to capture the Russian naval base at Port Arthur and then, when command of the sea approaches to the Liaotung Peninsula were assured, to pour troops into the peninsula and northern Korea, from which points they could move on to engage the Russians in central Manchuria. MILITARY OPERATIONS.   By their first attack on Russia's Port Arthur squadron, completed by April 13, and their defeat of the Vladivostok squadron later in April, the Japanese greatly reduced the power of the Russians and broke their control of the sea. Thereafter, the Russians were condemned to delaying tactics, based on the expectation of sufficient reinforcement to permit the assumption of the offensive. Port Arthur, now inaccessible to relief by sea, was soon made inaccessible to relief by land also when Japanese armies, after cutting off the main Russian forces south of Mukden, landed north of the port on the Liaotung Peninsula and marched south to begin siege. After heroic resistance, Port Arthur capitulated in January, 1905.

While the siege of Port Arthur was still going on, Japanese armies hurried north toward Liaoyang; and, between August 23 and September 3, about 125,000 Japanese troops under Marquis Oyama met a Russian force of 158,000 under Kuropatkin at Liaoyang in what the Japanese hoped would be the decisive battle of the war. The Russians were defeated but were able to withdraw after administering heavy casualties to their enemy. The Japanese followed in search of a decisive battle; and in February they were once more able to engage the main body of the Russian forces, this time at Mukden, where 400,000 Japanese faced 325,000 Russians in one of the bloodiest engagements in military history. By March 10, when the Russians admitted defeat and withdrew from Mukden to retreat northward, 50,000 Japanese and 97,000 Russian casualties had been recorded.

The news of the defeat of Russia's Vladivostok and Port Arthur squadrons prompted the dispatch of the Baltic Fleet, which set sail in October, 1904, and reached Far Eastern waters late in April, 1905. When its commander, Admiral Zinovy Rozhdestvensky, learned of the fall of

Port Arthur, he decided to make for the base at Vladivostok through the dangerous Tsushima Straits. On May 27 he was met at the Straits by the Japanese fleet under Admiral Togo and, in a most unequal battle, lost or surrendered all the Russian ships with the exception of four small vessels, which succeeded in escaping and reaching Vladivostok. In that battle 4,830 Russians and 110 Japanese were killed.

CESSATION OF HOSTILITIES.   After the battle of Tsushima Straits, both countries were ready to call a halt. Japan, having failed to achieve the speedy victory on which she had counted was faced by two prospects for which she was unprepared: the heavy financial burden of an extended war and the necessity of meeting a land opposition which was growing stronger as more Russian reinforcements reached Manchuria. And the Russian Government, menaced by a revolution, was in a trying situation that could be greatly relieved by the cessation of hostilities. Although there was little prospect that the revolutionaries would succeed, their threat made necessary the retention of many troops in European Russia and might force the government to grant concessions that could be refused if its forces were concentrated. When President Theodore Roosevelt, urged by the Japanese, offered his mediation, both accepted and sent plenipotentiaries to Portsmouth, New Hampshire to negotiate peace.

TREATY OF PORTSMOUTH.   Russia was represented at Portsmouth by Witte and Baron Rosen, two whose opinions regarding Russia's Far Eastern policy had been ignored by Nicholas II at great cost to himself and his country. They were instructed to cede no territory and to accept no obligations to pay indemnities. The Japanese plenipotentiaries, Komura and Takahira, were instructed to demand both territory (all of Sakhalin and more) and indemnities. At the beginning of negotiations, it appeared that agreement was impossible. But when Roosevelt, friendly to the Japanese, suggested to them the expediency of a compromise between the extreme Japanese demands and the Russian instructions, they agreed to modify their demands; and the Treaty of Portsmouth, embodying such a compromise, was signed on September 5, 1905. By that treaty Russia renounced all interest in Korea and, in effect, recognized it as a Japanese protectorate. She gave up also her rights in the Liaotung Peninsula and ceded to Japan her rights in Port Arthur and Dalny as well as her rights on the South Manchurian Railroad from Port Arthur to Changchun. In addition she transferred to Japan the southern half of Sakhalin up to the fiftieth parallel and granted her fishing rights in the waters north of Vladivostok.

Such an outcome was not only a serious setback for Russia in the Far

East—where she lost all that she had gained since 1898 and more—but also a blow to the prestige of the government at home and in Europe generally. Her military prestige also fell considerably. Although experts realized that if the war had continued Russia might have won it, there was general agreement that her military power lay in masses of soldiery and nothing else.

NINETEEN / BACKGROUND FOR REVOLUTION:

1881-1904

During the period when the government was involved in the critical development of its affairs in the Far East, it was becoming involved also in the development of another crisis at home. In the last decade of the nineteenth century, the movement of organized protest against the established political and social order began to take on a mass character, moving from the "circles" of the intelligentsia to the streets and factories. This movement, sometimes called the "liberation movement" and sometimes the "revolutionary movement," brought into the open many issues which the government had hitherto been able to keep submerged. And as protest grew, the pressing question before the government changed from that of how to quell the opposition to that of how to preserve its own existence.

Sources of protest

INDUSTRIAL WORKERS.   The growth of protests in Russia was in great measure the consequence of the appearance of new classes, foremost among them the industrial working class. The number of industrial workers, although relatively small, was growing. Yet it was not growth so much as concentration which gave Russian labor its weight at this time. Russian industry, unlike that of most other countries in the early period of industrialization, had developed in a few large plants in which great numbers of workers were concentrated rather than in a large number of small plants. And, as has been seen, the plants were concentrated in a few regions. In the 1890's, nearly two-thirds of the metallurgical workers of the country were employed in seven establishments in the Ukraine; almost all of the oil workers were connected with the industries in Baku; textile workers were concentrated in or about Moscow, St. Petersburg, and Lodz; and the workers in the railroad repair depot in Tiflis serviced the entire railroad system of Transcaucasia. Simultaneous labor strikes in those areas could have paralyzed the country's industry and transportation.

In the early years of industrial development, the potential united strength of workers was not realized. Their first manifestations were un-organized and spontaneous and, like peasant outbreaks, directed at some single, immediate problem—usually the removal of a local grievance or the achievement of shorter hours or higher wages. Even though conditions of labor were unpleasant and the incentives for protest many, the legal prohibitions on labor organizations were serious obstacles to action. In the absence of strong organization and in the face of governmental prohibition, the workers were isolated and helpless and they acted only in desperation. The fact that most of them were peasants or only lately removed from peasant status was also a retarding factor; for a long time many felt that their roots were in the village and that factory employment was a tempo-rary phase of their lives.

With the growth of industry in the 1890's, however, changes became noticeable: the number to take permanent employment in the factories in-creased; thousands loosened their last ties with their villages; and some began to break away from old beliefs and to reject the restrictions imposed on their behavior by the Church and the patriarchal family. In addition, the first struggles in the factories had led at least a small core of the workers to see the relation between their economic problems and larger political problems; the fact that the state protected their employers—often foreign capitalists—impressed upon them the need for changing the political situa-tion in order to improve the economic.

NON-RUSSIAN NATIONALITIES.   Another source of protest against the established order was among the non-Russian nationalities of the country, upon whom Alexander III and Nicholas II had forced the program of Russifi-cation. That program, it will be recalled, had actually promoted rather than retarded nationalistic movements among the minorities, and internal social and economic changes had further stimulated them. It is obviously im-possible to make generalizations which will be valid for all the national mi-norities, with their vast range of institutions and beliefs, but a few gen-eralizations about some of the most important ones will indicate the nature of the growing protest among them.

The program of Russification, by contributing to the growth of nationalism, caused greater cohesion among the minority groups. It also provided the Russian schools in which were educated a new class of non-Russian intellectuals, many of whom either joined the Russian revolutionary
movement or became leaders of the nationalist movements among their
own peoples. Among those who attended such schools were two prominent
leaders of the revolutionary movement: Joseph Stalin, son of a poor, devout
Georgian shoemaker; and Leon Trotsky, son of an orthodox Jewish farmer.
Stalin was educated in a Russian-language theological seminary, and
Trotsky in a Russian-language secondary school.

One of the most important aspects of nationalism among many of the
minorities was the cultural revival which took place among them, as among
minorities in other European countries, during the latter half of the nineteenth century. It was of the same nature as that which had appeared among
the Great Russians during the eighteenth century—a revival involving the
rediscovery of their own cultures and the development of secular expressions of those cultures. It manifested itself in historical writing, in belles-
lettres, and in journalism. In the Ukraine, native intellectuals had some
success in their efforts to point out a Ukrainian culture distinct and different
from that of the Great Russians, but their task was made difficult by the
fact that the process of Russification had been successful among great numbers of the Ukrainian upper classes and the fact that repressive measures
had made the use of the Ukrainian language for literary and historical purposes practically impossible. However, in the Austrian province of Galicia,
with its large Ukrainian and Polish population, there was more freedom of
action, and the Galician city of Lemberg became a Ukrainian cultural center
from which books and ideas were smuggled into Russia. Lemberg became
also a center of Polish nationalism, and many leaders of the Polish cause
in Russia made their headquarters there. In Livonia and Courland the long-
forgotten Letts, touched by the nationalist awakening, began to use Lettish
on a wide scale for literary and journalistic purposes in the 1860's, breaking with the custom which had led educated Letts previously to regard
themselves as Baltic Germans or Russians. The Georgians also, feeling the
urge toward nationalism in the last decades of the century, began to produce their own secular literature, encouraged by such writers as the distinguished Ilya Chavchavadze, who helped to establish a new secular
Georgian literature. Among the Jews, Hebrew and Yiddish came into use
for secular literary purposes, and daily newspapers in Hebrew as well as
several weeklies in Yiddish appeared in St. Petersburg and Warsaw in the
1880's.

These cultural movements easily acquired political overtones, for the minorities felt the heavy hand of the Russian Government more keenly than others. At first few dared to dream of political independence from powerful Russia, but some began to talk in the 1890's of certain national rights—the right to use one's own language in education and administration and the right to exercise some political autonomy within the Russian Empire.

OTHER SOURCES. As before, dissatisfaction was pronounced also among the peasantry and the intelligentsia. These groups had no single cause of unrest, but their combined protests made up a great chorus of angry, discordant voices. And their opposition to the government was growing, not so much because the government was oppressive and inefficient as because its oppression and inefficiency stood in the way of the achievement of their ambitions and purposes. Thus the government became a target for groups which differed in beliefs and aims but agreed that a necessary precondition for the changes which they separately desired was the elimination or reform of the existing regime.

Revolutionary thinking and organization

MARXISM. After the assassination of Alexander II there had come a decline in the strength of the revolutionary movement and a loss of faith in some of its doctrines. Many were looking for a new approach to their problems, and for some of them Marxism seemed to provide it. To understand the growth of Marxist influence in Russia, four facts must be kept in mind: (1) Marxism could fill the ideological void which then existed for many disillusioned intellectuals; (2) Marxism, like various other beliefs which had preceded it in popularity, combined in itself many ingredients— a philosophy, a program of action and a belief in the inevitability of socialism; (3) Marxism could be employed to explain the growth of capitalism in Russia in such a way as to bolster the hope among revolutionary intellectuals that capitalism was paving the way to socialism; and (4) Marxism, in the words of E. H. Carr, "introduced into revolutionary theory and practice the order, method, and authority, which had hitherto been the prerogative of Governments, and thereby laid the foundations of the disciplined revolutionary state."

For a generation after 1881 the foremost theoretician and intellectual leader of Russian revolutionary Marxism was George Plekhanov, who, with other leading Populists, had left Russia after the beginning of the reaction and taken up residence in Switzerland. Although he and his followers had been disappointed in the results of the Populist movement, they had not given up their belief in socialism, and they turned easily to the doctrines of Marxian socialism, then espoused by the German Social Democratic Party. Plekhanov was convinced that the weakness of the Populist belief lay in its "utopian" character, its neglect of the political struggle against the regime, and its emphasis on the role of the peasantry. But he saw strength in "scientific" Marxian socialism, which explained the growth of capitalism and the working class and provided a political program. He believed that the working class should become the core of the revolutionary movement and that the movement itself should develop through two phases: (1) a political revolution which would substitute a constitutional regime for the autocracy; and (2)—to be possible at some indeterminate time after the further development of capitalism—a social revolution, which would place the control of means of production in the hands of the workers. To achieve these ends, he argued, it was necessary to create a separate social-democratic party of the Russian workers to be led, at least in the beginning, by the intellectuals. His beliefs, which formed the theoretical foundation for the social-democratic movement in Russia, were incorporated in three tracts: *Socialism and the Political Struggle (1883)*, *Our Differences* (1884), and *Toward the Development of the Monistic Conception of History* (1895). His followers adopted them as the immediate focus of their thinking and supplemented them by studying the works of Marx, Engels and their German and French disciples.

OTHER DOCTRINES.   Although revolutionary Marxism attracted many, it did not gain the support of all, or even of a majority, of Russian intellectuals. Other doctrines vied with it for popularity: liberalism, anarchism, populist socialism, and so many other -*ism's* that there were, according to some wits, three political beliefs for every two intellectuals. But most of the intellectuals had one thing in common, the belief in scientific materialism. They believed in "science" and "progress" as tools of human liberation and advancement, and they fed their thinking on the study of Huxley, Darwin, and Buckle. They believed that autocracy was the obstacle to "progress" and the cause of backwardness, which they proposed to overcome by the introduction of constitutionalism, representative government, and civil liberties. Most of them were agnostics or atheists and considered organized religion, as embodied in the Russian Orthodox Church, another bar to "progress." Thus Russia came to be divided into two opposing ideological factions: on one side, the regime, determined to uphold orthodoxy, autocracy, and nationalism; on the other, the intelligentsia, who, despite all internal differences, found common ground in their abhorrence of the official ideology and in the belief that Russia must free herself of the existing regime.

IMPETUS TO ORGANIZATION. During the 1880's, when the police were hunting down malcontents and dissidents, there was little organized effort among the opponents of the regime, but early in the 1890's circumstances contributed to the growth of illegal political movements. A series of great labor strikes, following in the wake of rapid industrial expansion, caught the attention of those who believed the workers' cause to be the heart of the coming revolution, and they began to convert their discussion groups into active organizations. In 1891 a famine, resulting from crop failures and bringing with it widespread death from starvation and disease in the richest agricultural regions of the country, stimulated further organization, philanthropic as well as political, among various classes. The famine, according to the opposition, was a sign of the corruption of the regime. The year 1891 was the turning point in the history of organized opposition; after that there was a rapid increase in the number of strikes, agrarian disorders and expressions of unrest among the national minorities.

THE SOCIAL-DEMOCRATIC MOVEMENT. In 1883 Plekhanov and his followers in Geneva, Switzerland, formed the first Russian Marxist or social-democratic organization; it was known as the Emancipation of Labor Group. Although it was made up of a small number of Russian intellectuals who for over a decade exercised little practical influence in Russia, it served as a great intellectual stimulus to others. It was generally true of the Russian revolutionary movement until 1905 that its stimulation came from émigrés; they were the only ones who were safe from the Russian police. In 1884 a social-democratic organization was formed in St. Petersburg, but its leaders were arrested after publishing two issues of an illegal newspaper.

During the next decade the Russian social-democratic movement, at home and abroad, was confined to the organization of small discussion groups and the attempt to gain leadership in the labor strikes. A few small workers' groups led by young social democrats began to take form during these years. Among the young leaders was one Vladimir Ilyich Ulyanov, who later took the revolutionary pseudonym of Lenin.[1] He was the son of

---

[1] The practice of adopting pseudonyms was common among Russian revolutionaries as a means of escaping police detection. In this text, pseudonyms rather than real surnames are used for those men who are better known by their pseudonyms.

George Plekhanov

a director of primary schools in the region of Simbirsk, on the Volga River, who had attained the rank of hereditary noble. Even before he became a part of the revolutionary movement, Lenin had an immediate knowledge of the consequencs of revolutionary action; his older brother had been executed in 1887 for participating in a conspiracy aimed at the life of the emperor. Already a convinced social democrat, Lenin met many of the social-democratic leaders of Europe while abroad in the first half of 1895. Among them were Plekhanov and another key figure in the Emancipation of Labor Group in Switzerland, Paul Axelrod. The germ of the idea of creating a united social-democratic party in Russia was probably incubated during discussions held by these three. On his return to Russia, Lenin, along with another young revolutionary intellectual, Julius Martov, began to unite the scattered social-democratic intellectual and workers' groups of St. Petersburg and to prepare the publication of an illegal newspaper. Their efforts were betrayed by a police agent in the group, and Lenin, Martov, and other participants were arrested and exiled to Siberia.

Social-democratic groups were being organized meanwhile in other major Russian cities and in the western non-Russian provinces. A small group of Poles formed the Social Democratic Party of Poland and Lithuania in the mid 1890's; shortly thereafter a Latvian social-democratic group made its appearance; and in 1897 a Jewish social-democratic organization known as the General Jewish Workers' League (commonly called the Bund) was established. In March, 1898, nine delegates from the social-democratic groups met secretly in the city of Minsk and established the Russian Social Democratic Labor Party, whose members are usually called SD's.

That first meeting—which may be called the First Congress of the SD's —marked the modest beginning of an organization from which was to emerge the ruling party of Russia. At the time, however, its prospects were dark; its leaders were soon arrested and the party existed only on paper for the next five years. Although its component parts continued to flourish and grow, co-operative action among them was made difficult by theoretical and organizational dispute. Many of the Social Democrats among the Letts, Jews, and Poles sought to maintain separate national organizations within the party, while many of the Russians argued for an all-inclusive party in which no distinct organization by nationality would be permitted. Another divisive issue arose from the attempt among some Western European Social Democrats to modify Marxist doctrine so as to make it more moderate and less revolutionary. In Russia this issue led to a fierce polemic between "revisionist" Marxists and "orthodox" Marxists.

The Social Democrats saw the necessity for a new congress to weld the scattered elements of the party and to formulate a common program. In July, 1903, forty-three delegates from organizations in Russia and from émigré groups met in Brussels for the Second Congress; but they soon moved on, at the request of the Belgian police, to London. In London the delegates agreed on a program which forecast a revolution to be carried through the two phases, political and social, as outlined by Plekhanov. The second phase, according to their program, would introduce the "dictatorship of the proletariat," through which the workers, controlling the political power, would effect the transition to socialism.

While there were few serious differences over the party program, there was sharp dispute over the nature of the party organization. The Bund, which wanted to maintain its separate identity and to speak for all Jewish workers, was voted down and, in consequence, left the congress and the party. An even more consequential dispute occurred over the definition of a party member. Martov and Lenin, who had completed their terms of Siberian exile and were now living abroad, were the chief disputants. Martov argued that any who were prepared to identify themselves with the party should be considered members; and Lenin, who dreamed of a tightly-knit closely-led party of professional revolutionaries, proposed that only persons who participated directly in the work of a party organization should be considered members. Lenin's proposal was defeated, but in later debates at the congress he succeeded in gaining majority support on other issues, giving him reason to assume that the majority were his followers. Thereafter, since the Russian word for majority is *bolshinstvo*, Lenin called his supporters Bolsheviks (members of the majority) and his opponents, Mensheviks (members of the minority, *menshinstvo*).

When the Second Congress closed, late in August, there was on paper a united Russian Social Democratic Labor Party—with the exception, of course, of the Bund. Within the party membership, however, the unity was superficial because there were two factions, Bolsheviks and Mensheviks, whose differences were later to widen into major disputes. Still the Second Congress marked the beginning of the party's steady growth in number and influence.

THE SOCIALIST REVOLUTIONARY PARTY.   From the ashes of the Populist groups of the 1870's a new movement grew up in the 1890's. While Plekhanov and other Marxists attacked the older Populist theories, many former adherents of those theories, particularly those who had belonged to the terrorist People's Will group, began to reform their ranks and to designate themselves as Socialist Revolutionaries (commonly called SR's). Like the Marxists, they believed in the necessity of establishing a democratic republic in Russia and in the desirability of socialist ownership of the means of production. They did not, however, accept the body of Marxian theory. They claimed that Russia should follow its natural lines of development, which were indicated by the primacy of agriculture and by the distinctive village organization of the peasantry. Whereas the SD's accorded first place to the industrial working class, the SR's gave first attention to the peasantry, among whom they were to have the larger following. The SR's proposed to solve the peasant question by dividing all the agricultural land among the peasants, who would own and work the land in common. To accelerate action, the most radical of them favored the revival of the terrorist methods employed by the ill-fated People's Will, arguing that terror might compel the emperor to call a constituent assembly which could establish a democratic republic.

It is difficult to trace the organization of the Socialist Revolutionary Party because, despite its ultimate growth, it was never as tightly organized as the Social Democratic Party. In attempts to unite all self-styled SR's several meetings were held after 1897, but it was not until the end of 1901 that all SR groups—forty-nine in number—were brought together in one party. Prominent among the leaders of the new party were Catherine Breshkovskaya, often called the "grandmother of the Russian Revolution"; Gregory Gershuni, in charge of terrorist work; and Victor Chernov, probably the ablest theoretician of the party.

The Socialist Revolutionary Party, with its rather loose organization and striking appeal, found immediate support among Russian intellectuals, particularly among students. Numerous groups were formed among those adhering to the party, and a special organization for work among the peasants, the Peasants Union, was created. For the execution of the party's terrorist aims, a separate section known as the Fighting Organization was created; its first leader was Gregory Gershuni. That section, of which there were local branches throughout Russia, made decisions as to the assassination of hated officials in the regime and assigned to certain individuals the execution of those decisions. In the plans for assassinations, the emperor was excluded, for the SR's believed that the killing of Alexander II had been a mistake. They believed, however, that the killing of other officials would spur on the revolutionary struggle and perhaps frighten the government into concessions.

THE LIBERAL MOVEMENT.   Of the many educated Russians who disapproved of the SD's and SR's and their avowedly revolutionary and necessarily illegal activities, some felt themselves compelled by prevailing conditions to incorporate in their own programs some activities which were both revolutionary and illegal. These were the liberals, who wished to see the reforms begun by Alexander II extended until representative, constitutional government should be achieved. Found in large numbers among Zemstvo workers and officials, among sections of the nobility, and in various segments of the middle class, the liberals differed greatly among themselves. Some wanted constitutionalism of the German variety; others wanted a limited monarchy on the order of England's; still other wanted a democratic republic.

The Zemstvos, offering opportunity for practical work in the fields of public education, public health, and scientific agriculture, were havens for the liberals, who believed that the enhancement of the educational and economic status of the masses was basic to the establishment of free institutions in Russia. The Ministry of Interior and the governors attempted to exclude them from Zemstvo work; but the conservative nobility, who had the power to dominate the Zemstvos, were so generally indifferent that the liberals usually won by default. The government attempted also to prohibit any national gathering of Zemstvo representatives. But after 1900 liberal members from various sections of Russia were able to gather in Moscow from time to time for private meetings, out of which grew an embryonic organization including liberals of both Zemstvo and non-Zemstvo origin. Its first major act was to establish in 1901 a newspaper, *Emancipation;* printed abroad, first in Stuttgart and later in Paris, it was smuggled into Russia and distributed. In 1903, Zemstvo members who had participated in the establishment of the newspaper co-operated with several university professors, lawyers, and other intellectuals in founding the illegal organization known as the Union of Emancipation, which took as its purpose the gaining of a democratic constitution for Russia. This organization, the kernel of the later Constitutional Democratic Party, rejected the class struggle and revolutionary action and proposed to persuade the government, by the pressure of public opinion, to grant reform. Among the leading figures of the Union of Emancipation were Peter Struve, the editor of *Emancipation,* the historian Paul Milyukov, and Ivan Petrunkevich.

The Union of Emancipation by no means represented the entire liberal movement. To the right of this organization was a respected and influential group of Zemstvo liberals who opposed a democratic constitution and abhorred the use of illegal tactics. They favored instead the tactic of persuasion, urging the Emperor to establish a true bond with his people by permitting them to advise him by means of an elective consultative assembly, such as had been envisioned by Loris-Melikov. The most prominent of these right-wing liberals was Dmitri Shipov, who served as Chairman of the Moscow Provincial Zemstvo Board.

NATIONALIST MOVEMENT. The organized oppositional movements among the national minorities were complicated by the fact that in some of them the desire for the removal of discriminatory laws and the achievement of national rights was coupled with the desire for the achievement of socialism, while in others socialism was anathema. Generally their organizations tended to mirror the divisions in the Russian political scene and to align themselves with the Russian organizations based on principles similar to their own. The alignment of the Polish Social Democrats with the Russian Social Democrats and that of Lettish liberals with Russian liberals were typical of that tendency.

The proliferation of political organizations among the national minorities was so great that even an enumeration of their names would be impossible here; the mention of a few, however, will serve as illustration. In Poland the revolutionary sentiments, which had died down after the defeat of 1863, were being revived by the 1890's, and new movements and parties were beginning to grow up. Of these the most extreme was the Polish Socialist Party, established in 1893 and led by Jozef Pilsudski. Aimed at an independent, socialist Poland it formed no ties with the Russian socialist movement but operated separately through terroristic activities against Russian officials. The Polish Social Democratic Party, on the other hand, aimed not at independence but at national rights for Poland within the boundaries of Russia. Aligned on most occasions with the Bolshevik faction of the Russian SD's, it was a training school for many later Soviet leaders, among them Felix Dzerzhinsky, who became head of the Soviet Cheka, and Karl Radek, who became a leading Soviet journalist. A third Polish party, one which had its largest following among the middle classes, was the Polish National Democratic Party, organized in 1896 and led by Roman Dmowski. Its program on the whole was liberal and its aim was Polish autonomy in a constitutional Russian state.

In Livonia and Courland, where the Letts had become politically conscious, the social-democratic movement achieved considerable strength among the workers in the first years of the century, although the Lettish Social Democratic Party was not organized until 1905. Among the Lettish middle class there was considerable support of the Russian liberal movement. In Transcaucasia, among the Georgians and Armenians, both nationalist and socialist movements were widely supported; and in Finland, the policy of Russification resulted in widespread organization of political opposition.

The Russian parties of opposition generally looked upon the national movements and parties with mixed feelings; they supported the affirmation of legal equality of all peoples in Russia, but they were not enthusiastic about nationalistic aspirations.

THE GROWING THREAT.   The numerical strength of the organized oppositional parties and groups in Russia in the first years of the twentieth century was not as threatening as the fact that among almost all ethnic and social groups a mood of opposition to the existing regime was spreading and the fact that leading figures from these groups were taking part in illegal oppositional activities. Moreover, although the various parties and groups presented a bewildering array of aims and beliefs, opposition to the government was providing a harmony of sentiment on many issues.

For the first time in Russian history, the forces of opposition were able to present at one time the three important elements of effective action: a mass base, leadership, and an ideology. Before this time there had been leaders without followers (as in the case of the Decembrist Revolt) and followers without effective leadership (as in the case of most peasant revolts). Now everything necessary for a revolution appeared to be at hand except the opportunity for action.

MOUNTING STRUGGLE.   Labor unrest was easily directed into line with the socialist movement. It was not created by the socialist leaders; it grew spontaneously out of the immediate problems of labor, aggravated by a severe industrial depression in the years 1900-1903. But the socialists did seek to lead and organize the dissatisfied workers and to recruit them for the socialist movement by convincing them that economic amelioration could come only after a change in the political structure of the country. They organized discussion groups at which workers were taught the socialist gospel; and from these groups came committees for the organization of strikes and street demonstrations or for the leading of spontaneous strike movements. In 1896 the first of a series of major strikes began when nearly 30,000 textile workers in St. Petersburg laid down their work. Those that followed showed an increase in intensity and influence. In November, 1902, a strike was begun in the railroad shops at Vladikavkaz and Rostov-on-the-Don because of the death of a girl raped by an official; and, although the incident was soon forgotten, the strike was taken up by workers throughout southern Russia. By the following summer, some 80,000 persons were out on strike. In almost all instances, the strikers, usually led by Social Democrats, demanded not only economic betterment but also the extension of civil and political rights to all the inhabitants of Russia and the summoning of a constituent assembly. Their efforts brought little improvement in labor conditions but they roused public opinion and served as an indication of the political awakening of labor. In fact, they were more than labor strikes; they were revolutionary rehearsals, gaining the support of many nonworkers and, in some instance, involving armed conflicts with regular troops and Cossacks sent to restore order.

Student activities added to the growing unrest. The government's efforts to insure docility and loyalty in the youth of the land had not been successful; secondary schools, theological seminaries, and universities were honeycombed with revolutionary groups, in which the Socialist Revolutionaries seemed to be stronger than the Social Democrats. Students not only participated in extramural revolutionary work but also often brought their activities directly to the institutions in which they were enrolled. In February, 1902, students at the University of Moscow began a demonstration within the university and barricaded themselves there against the police sent to disperse them. The fact that they were overpowered and exiled to Siberia did not deter others. At the University of Kiev about two hundred students were punished for political actions by being called up for military service, and such incidents were repeated throughout the country.

Among the peasants, also, organized revolutionary agitation began slowly to take effect as representatives of the Socialist Revolutionary Peasants Union moved into the countryside, distributing propaganda leaflets, and forming peasant groups. Even though a relatively small number were thus reached, the agitators—unlike their predecessors of the 1870's—often met with favorable reactions. The peasants did not care particularly about the problems of constitutionalism and socialism; however, they could un-

derstand the SR program of land distribution and the arguments that political change would have to come before partition. In May, 1902, peasant
outbreaks not directly inspired by the Peasants Union but showing signs
of having been influenced by revolutionary propaganda, occurred in the
provinces of Poltava and Kharkov. The estates of many local landlords
were sacked before the outbreaks were ended by the action of troops. Over
a thousand peasants were arrested, and fines amounting to $400,000 were
imposed.

Even the army, the chief bulwark of the government, was not entirely
immune to revolutionary ideas. Efforts at agitation in its ranks were at
first small in scale and rarely effective, but by 1904 the Ministry of War
was becoming alarmed by the evidence that some regiments were being affected by revolutionary propaganda.

As the revolutionary movements progressed, the scope of their propaganda and action was greatly widened. The sale and distribution of the
newspapers and leaflets of the underground press mounted rapidly. The
number of publications distributed by the Polish Socialist Party grew from
2,900 in 1895 to 177,000 in 1903. The SR organ, *Revolutionary Russia,*
first published in 1900 with an issue of 1,000 copies, soon reached 10,000;
in 1902 the SR's alone distributed 317,000 leaflets, and in 1903 over 395,-
000. As feelings were aroused, political assassinations also, for which the
SR was chiefly but not exclusively responsible, increased in number. In
February, 1901, in retaliation for the government's actions against students, a former student killed the Minister of Education, Nicholas Bogolepov.
In April of the following year, a 21-year-old student member of the SR,
Stepan Balmashev, killed the Minister of Interior, Sipyagin. And in May,
1903, a member of the SR killed the Governor of Ufa, General Nicholas
Bogdanovich, for ordering troops to fire on strikers. These terrorist acts
received an exaggerated attention because of their drama and thereby served
to create and sustain a general air of excitation. It was almost as if an underground civil war were in progress. The number of persons accused of
political crime was growing as never before: there were 919 in 1894; 1,580
in 1900; and 5,590 in 1903.

Counterattack

REPRESSION. As long as only a handful of dissidents engaged in illegal
political activity, the existing machinery of repression sufficed; but by
1900 the government found that there were too many revolutionaries and

too many persons sympathetic to the opposition to be handled by ordinary governmental techniques. Illegal political activities were being carried on under the very noses of government officials because a large portion of the population, although not necessarily revolutionary, would not co-operate with the government in the repression of opposition.

To handle the situation the repressive machinery of the political police was increased to a point not matched at the time by that of any other country in the world. The government put painstaking effort into the planting of secret agents and the employment of informers in the various circles known to be hostile, in Russian émigré colonies abroad, and among Russian students studying in foreign universities. The most notorious of these agents was Yevno Azef, the son of a Russian Jewish tailor. When recruited, he was a member of a Russian socialist student group at a German engineering school. After he had completed his studies and returned to Russia, he accepted an engineering position which the police provided for him and set about helping to organize the Socialist Revolutionary Party. When Gershuni, the first head of the Fighting Organization of the SR, was arrested, Azef succeeded to that position and helped to organize the principal assassinations that it undertook. Through agents like Azef the police were able to gather a great store of accurate information concerning the revolutionary movement. However, they did not always act on the information they received; sometimes they refrained in order to protect their agents from exposure, and sometimes they reasoned that the arrest of one group of revolutionaries would only lead to the appearance of another group, with whom the agent might not be familiar. As the state increased its dependence upon the political police, they became increasingly powerful and devious. Frequently they used agents as *provocateurs*, instructing them to stir up illegal action which the police might use as a pretext for arrest, for increasing security regulations, or for requesting larger appropriations from the government.

"POLICE SOCIALISM." Not all methods used by the government in dealing with revolutionaries were negative. Of the positive methods, one of the most striking was that proposed by Sergei Zubatov, Director of the Department of Political Police in Moscow. Having begun his career as a police informer in student revolutionary groups in the 1880's and later, in the capacity of government official, having dealt with many revolutionaries, Zubatov felt that he could devise a better scheme than the repressive ones being used for handling the growing opposition with which the state was faced. His scheme, which became known as "police socialism," provided for the organization of labor associations under the protection of police agents, these bodies to eschew any political activities and to confine themselves solely to limited economic goals. When he presented the scheme to his superior, General Dmitri Trepov, chief of the Moscow police, with the argument that it would wean the workers away from socialism, he won an influential supporter. Trepov, with the approval of the Ministry of Interior and of Grand Duke Sergei, Governor-General of Moscow, decided to give the proposal a trial. First applied in Moscow in 1900, the method was widely copied, and soon such associations existed under the protection of the police in many cities—among them, St. Petersburg and Odessa. These strange organizations proved difficult to control, and when the police-sponsored association in Odessa led a major strike in the summer of 1903, official odium fell upon the experiment in "police socialism." The scheme was officially declared a failure, and Zubatov was removed from his post and punished by banishment to a remote province.

The Zubatov plan had one aftermath of considerable consequence. An Orthodox priest, Father George Gapon, when he was serving as chaplain to prisoners in a St. Petersburg jail in 1904, heard of the plan and came to believe, quite sincerely it seems, in its basic idea: that legal, nonradical labor associations might serve as a means not only of turning workers away from revolution and sedition but also of improving their sorry lot. At his request, the St. Petersburg police granted him permission to organize the Assembly of St. Petersburg Factory Workers, the stated purpose of which was to strive for legal improvement of labor conditions and to provide a moral, God-fearing, nationalist society to engage the leisure time of workers. The organization was established in April, 1904, with Gapon as its president. The meetings of the Assembly, which opened with the singing of "God Save the Tsar" and at which liquor was forbidden, attracted only a few at first; but by the end of 1904 almost all of the labor force of St. Petersburg was giving it support. Gapon soon found himself in a difficult position: on the one hand, he was closely connected with the police, whose spies kept close watch on the organization; on the other hand, many of the leading members of the Assembly were radicals who, despite Gapon's connections, agreed to work with him if he would help to press labor demands. If he followed police instructions too closely he would lose the support of the labor leaders; if he let the leaders have their way the police would bear down upon him. This was the anomalous situation out of which was to come shortly a tragedy sufficient to shake the regime.

PLEHVE.   The key figure in the government's counterattack on the forces of dissent was Vyacheslav Plehve, a man of long experience in the police work of the Ministry of Interior. By all accounts he was able but devoid of principles and devoted to the advancement of his career at all costs. Both his training and his sympathies placed him on the side of reaction and the struggle against political opposition. When, upon the assassination of Sipyagin, in April, 1902, he was chosen by Nicholas II as the Minister of Interior, he entered upon his office with great energy and proceeded to extend its activities in every direction. On his advice, the campaign against the national minorities was heightened (particularly against the Finns, Armenians, and Jews), the Zemstvos were placed under closer control, and security regulations were tightened. With the support of the reactionaries at court, he used the power of his ministry against those officials who seemed inclined toward political reforms as well as against the revolutionaries. He was in the thick of the group who were pushing Russia to war with Japan in the expectation that a victory would clear the air of revolutionary activity. The name of Plehve came to be even more widely reviled than that of Pobedonostsev.

Under the ministry of Plehve, the antisemitic movement took on a more virulent form. He was not directly responsible for all antisemitic acts which occurred during his ministry, but he did encourage and reward many of them. One act of lasting injury to the Jews was the publication in 1903 of what was to be proven one of the most successful forgeries in modern times, *The Protocols of the Elders of Zion*. It was presented as the secret minutes of the Zionist Congress of 1897, outlining a Jewish conspiracy to gain control of the world. The document, actually prepared within the political police department, did not attract much attention at the time, but it indicated the length to which the antisemitic forces were willing to go. Of more immediate significance was an event in which Plehve had an indirect hand. It took place in the province of Bessarabia, where official protection and encouragment was given to the antisemitic movement, where only two newspapers—both reactionary and antisemitic—were permitted, and where no public meetings except those engaged in antisemitic propaganda were allowed. In Bessarabia's chief city, Kishinev, a pogrom against the Jews broke out in April, 1903, and for two days the governor—allegedly on orders from Plehve—permitted the massacre to continue unchecked. Forty-five were killed and hundreds wounded before the fury of the attack was spent and the police were ordered to restore tranquillity. In August of the same year another pogrom occurred in Gomel, in the province of Mogilev, and in that instance, troops participated in the massacre.

These events, particularly the Kishinev pogrom, increased the disfavor into which the government was falling both at home and in foreign countries, and Plehve became the target of general hatred.

THE PUBLIC AND THE GOVERNMENT.   The early enthusiasm aroused by the conflict with Japan was soon dissipated, and the war played itself out five thousand miles from central Russia while most Russians went about their ordinary affairs. Victory might have served, as Plehve perhaps hoped, to bring the people to the government; but the defeats and the evidence of general inefficiency served only to alienate. The revolutionaries and many of the liberal champions of "emancipation" capitalized on the public mood by denouncing the war as one in which the Russian people were not considered and should not, therefore, be concerned. Active evidence of the people's displeasure was seen in rioting in Congress Poland at the time of the mobilization of troops for Manchurian service and in new disturbances among the peasants in the spring of 1904.

A climax was reached on July 28, 1904. On that date, while he was driving through St. Petersburg to report to the Emperor, Plehve was killed by a bomb thrown by a student, Yegor Sazonov, acting under orders of the Fighting Organization of the SR's. The police agent Azef, who had participated in the preparation of the plot, had failed to inform his employers of it. The reasons for his failure are not yet altogether certain, but the results of it are clear: the fact that the hated Minister of Interior, symbol of "autocracy gone mad," had been purposely eliminated by one of the "people" had such an effect on both the public and the government that the Revolution of 1905 may be said to have had its actual beginning at the time of his death.

TWENTY / REVOLUTION: 1905-1907

The internal debilitation of the government and the accumulation of grievances among many classes and national groups could lead only to crisis. And the crisis came when revolutionary agitation broke into the mass violence known as the Revolution of 1905. After the subsidence of violence at the end of 1905, two years more were required to determine the results of the upheaval. Those are important years in Russia's history, for theirs is the story of what happened when the autocracy was finally tested by mass opposition with strong leadership and clearly formulated political programs.

Prelude to violence

"POLITICAL SPRING." The assassination of Plehve aroused fear at court and exultation among the opponents of the regime. Ordinarily the government would have responded to the incident by beginning a major manhunt of revolutionaries. But at the time the strength of the opposition was greater than ever before, and Russia was engaged in a losing war in the Far East. It was not possible to take the measures necessary to suppress the opposition and at the same time to put full force behind the prosecution of the war. Therefore, it seemed necessary to make some gesture of appeasement.

To that end, Nicholas II chose as the new Minister of Interior the comparatively liberal bureaucrat Prince Peter Svyatopolk-Mirsky, former Governor-General of Vilna, and allowed him to begin his duties by granting some of the milder demands then being made by the opposition. For the first time since 1881 the government seemed to be in retreat; and, to the liberals at least, its willingness to make some concessions indicated the beginning of a "political spring" which might be expected to be followed by a harvest of liberty.

Since the main activity of the liberals was in the Zemstvo organizations, they proposed to hold a public congress of Zemstvo representatives in Moscow in order to formulate a petition through which to present their political requests to the Emperor, now that a hearing for them seemed possible. Svyatopolk-Mirsky at first agreed; but, under pressure from Nicholas II, he forced them to meet privately in St. Petersburg. Their meeting, held in November 1904, was a historic one. The delegates to the congress, mainly middle-of-the-road liberals, united to formulate a petition containing eleven points—or theses (hence its popular designation as the Eleven Theses) demanding representative government and the establishment of civil and political rights for all classes and nationalities in the country. The more advanced liberals, those belonging to the Union of Emancipation, were not content with petitions but advocated the use of public pressure to gain the desired ends; and imitating the French liberals of 1848, they organized so-called "banquets"—in reality public meetings—at which demands for constitutional government were given voice. Even those meetings aroused no police action.

By the end of 1904 the government was faced with the need for more direct action. Svyatopolk-Mirsky, having undertaken to conciliate public opinion, was now finding that public opinion, insofar as it had been permitted to express itself, called for political change. Consequently, he proposed to the Emperor and his advisers that the government promise at least some civil liberties and the election of some of the State Council members. His proposals were hotly debated. Pobedonostsev, as usual, argued that no change in the autocratic system should be permitted; and in the end the proposals were watered down to meaningless promises of good intentions. On December 25, 1904, Nicholas signed an imperial decree stating that necessary reforms would be taken under consideration, but that he had no intention of altering the fundamental laws of the empire. The publication of the decree was accompanied by an official announcement that no further antigovernmental agitation would be permitted. Thus the "political spring" drew to an end, promising a very unsatisfactory harvest. The liberals were disappointed with the equivocation of the government, while many in the highest government circles disapproved of the concessions that had been made.

Father George Gapon

CONSOLIDATION OF FORCES. The end of the "political spring" reinforced the determination of the opposition to press on for political change. The Union of Emancipation took the lead, intensifying the various forms of public pressure that it had been employing and moving ahead to carry out its aim of organizing members of the professions into political unions. The Union was hopeful of unifying the entire opposition. In the preceding October it had participated, along with representatives of the SR's and many of the national minority parties, in a meeting at which a common aim, that of establishing a democratic constitutional regime, had been accepted. Now, in late December, a united front—to be sure, a loose and incomplete one—was in the making. It lacked the support of the Bolsheviks, who were suspicious of co-operation with the liberals; but it included the Mensheviks, now the dominant group in the SD Party, who were convinced of the need for co-operation in at least the first phase of the hoped-for political revolution, the creation of a democratic republic. But how could the revolution be begun? Certainly the socialist and liberal leaders did not have the following needed to initiate a mass upheaval. That lack was overcome, paradoxically, by the government itself, which inadvertently played into their hands and made such an upheaval possible.

Revolutionary outburst

"BLOODY SUNDAY." Near the end of December a spontaneous strike began at the Putilov Works, in St. Petersburg, because of the alleged discharge of some members of Father Gapon's organization. The discord spread to other establishments in the city, and over 150,000 workers were out on strike by January 20. Father Gapon was caught up by the events. He disliked the extreme radicals, but he believed that labor should receive the protection of benevolent, constitutional government. Trusting that the Emperor would respond favorably if presented with a respectful petition by his loyal and humble subjects, he took part in the preparation of such a petition. It asked for a liberal, constitutional government, the right of labor to organize, and the amelioration of labor conditions. It was to be delivered to the Emperor at the Winter Palace on Sunday, January 22, 1905, by the workers of St. Petersburg. Father Gapon informed the authorities of the plan and implored the Emperor by letter to grant the requests contained in the petition.

The situation was bizarre. Father Gapon, who abhorred the revolutionaries and was leader of the largest group of organized workers yet assembled in Russia, was opening the road to revolution. His plan was soon public knowledge, and many saw danger in it. Several eminent writers appealed to Svyatopolk-Mirsky to prevent trouble, but they were ignored. Nicholas himself remained in his winter residence, Tsarskoe Selo, fourteen miles away, while his officials carried out the task of handling Father Gapon and the petitioners.

On the designated day tens of thousands of unarmed workers accompanied by their families, singing hymns and carrying icons and portraits of the Emperor, marched in columns from various parts of the city toward the Winter Palace. As they approached the meeting place, they were intercepted by military and police detachments and ordered to halt; when they refused, they were fired upon and forcibly routed. In the square before the Winter Palace and in the main street approaching it, crowds that had gathered to witness the march and the presentation of the petition were scattered in the same manner when they ignored orders to move away from the area. Elsewhere in the city there were a few additional, but much smaller, incidents, most of them provoked by self-appointed student champions of the marchers. By nightfall, however, order had been imposed and the authority of officials and troops was generally accepted in all quarters.

The government later listed, as the casualties of the day, 96 dead and 333 wounded (34 of these dying afterwards); but the actual number was considerably higher, for hundreds of dead and wounded were carried from the scenes before they could be counted. Whatever the exact number, the harsh fact remains unaltered: the government had callously shot down unarmed men, women, and children whose only crime had been refusal to disperse. Thus Father Gapon's[1] day of hope became "Bloody Sunday," and

---

[1] Having denounced the Emperor as the arch criminal of "Bloody Sunday," Father Gapon fled from Russia shortly thereafter. He returned within the year, tried unsuccessfully to reestablish his connections with the country's revolutionary activities, and was finally marked down as a traitor by the SR's, who were responsible for his assassination, in March, 1906.

the balance was tipped toward revolution.

It was then commonly believed that Nicholas had deliberately planned the massacre. It is now evident, however, that the bloodshed was not the result of design but of bureaucratic ineptitude, which left drastic action as the only resort. The Emperor attempted to undo the damage by directing that money be given to the families of the dead and wounded and by ordering the formation of a commission to investigate the labor problem. But the effects of "Bloody Sunday" overshadowed all efforts at redress. No longer was the Emperor accepted as a divinely ordained ruler whose heart was good but whose ministers were bad. And many who had hoped that peaceful persuasion would move the government to grant reforms now began to accept violence as a necessary tool.

REVOLT.   The news of the massacre in the capital and of what appeared to be a discreditable surrender at Port Arthur combined to create a mood of revolt in nearly every social, economic, and national group. In city after city political and economic strikes broke out and members of all classes became involved. By the end of January over 400,000 workers were on strike, and during the year the number rose to over 2.7 million. More than 90 per cent of the industrial establishments experienced at least one strike during that year, and statistics indicate that each factory worker in Russia was on strike at least once during the year. The strike movement was strongest in the non-Russian provinces (Poland, Finland, the Baltic Provinces, and the Caucasus), but Central Russia and Siberia were also seriously affected. Often strikers were joined by the entire population of a city or region. Bankers, professors, and workers were to be seen side by side in protest parades calling for a constituent assembly and a democratic constitution. Shortly after "Bloody Sunday" sixteen members of the Academy of Sciences and almost the entire faculty of the University of St. Petersburg united in a declaration that freedom of learning was incompatible with the existing social order. The SR's, who had suspended the policy of terror during the "political spring," returned to it; and on February 17, 1905, Grand Duke Sergei, an uncle of the Emperor and a man noted for his harshness as Governor-General of Moscow, was killed by the Socialist Revolutionary Ivan Kalyayev.

Serious as were the disturbances of late January and February, the throne was not seriously threatened by them. The army was still loyal; the police, though powerless to deal with the strikes and demonstrations and therefore inactive, were not broken; and the administrative machinery was still holding up under the strain. By way of strengthening the government's resistance, two important new appointments were made. Trepov, noted for his energy in combatting the revolutionaries, was named Governor-General of St. Petersburg; and the conservative Alexander Bulygin was chosen to replace Svyatopolk-Mirsky as Minister of Interior.

However, it was clear to those about the Emperor that firmness alone would not stop unrest and that substantial reforms must be enacted. Nicholas, who could not perceive the gravity of the situation, shied at further concessions but agreed finally to a measure which, like so many others, was too little and too late. On March 3, he publicly announced that he was instructing Bulygin to prepare a project for an elected representative body consisting of "the most worthy person . . . to participate in the preliminary elaboration and discussion of legislative measures." Actually this was little more than the proposal made by Svyatopolk-Mirsky in December, 1904, that some of the State Council members be chosen by election.

Period of political armistice

GROUPING OF FORCES.   The project announced on March 3 failed to evoke the enthusiasm for which its promoters had hoped, but the prospect of a representative assembly, however limited, mollified some of the more moderate elements. That fact and the fact that revolutionary fervor was spending itself brought a general quieting of activity even though strikes, peasant riots, and armed clashes continued in many parts of the country. During this period of relative quiet, a revolt—the first serious one among the armed forces—occurred in the navy, where socialist propaganda had met with some success. The crew of the battleship *Potemkin*, of the Black Sea Fleet, mutinied in June, 1905, and gained control of the ship. They took it to Odessa, where a general strike was in progress and a sympathetic reception could be expected. There they issued a call to the other ships of the fleet to revolt. Only one responded, however, and the *Potemkin* mutineers, fearing imminent punishment, finally fled with the appropriated ship to a Rumanian port.

In the meantime, Bulygin and his assistants were preparing the draft of the law to create a consultative assembly. The government was easing some of its restrictive regulations. Preparations for peace with Japan were being made. Revolutionary disturbances were diminishing in frequency. In general, it seemed that both the government and the opposition were sparring for time. The government had hopes that the proposed assembly and other minor reforms would calm the public and that the revolution would flicker out. But it was not to be so; the opposition was organizing for the next round.

Tactical leadership of the opposition was held by the liberals. Liberal members of the professions were forming unions with great rapidity, among them unions of teachers, engineers, doctors, and lawyers. Once the separate unions were organized, they united in the Union of Unions, with the noted liberal Paul Milyukov as president. Several labor unions joined the Union of Unions, and it soon became the most powerful spokesman of the liberal movement. Although many socialists were to be found in the organization, its leadership was left-wing liberal, favoring the convocation of a constituent assembly on the basis of universal, equal, direct, and secret suffrage. Somewhat to the right of the Union of Unions was the central organization of the Zemstvos, which had been operating since the time of the First Zemstvo Congress. That organization, supported by representatives of the municipal dumas, demanded, if not a constituent assembly, at least a true legislative assembly elected by the entire population.

The opposition was further strengthened by the formation, for the first time in Russian history, of a broad political organization among the peasants. (The Peasants Union of the SR's had been a beginning, but it had not had a large following.) In July, a conference of peasant representatives, promoted by left-wing liberals and Socialist Revolutionaries, met in Moscow and formed the All-Russian Peasants Union. Soon thereafter it joined the Union of Unions. The peasants were interested primarily in seeing that the land belonging to the Emperor and the nobility be divided among them and that the question of partition be taken up at a constituent assembly.

BULYGIN LAW ON THE DUMA. The left-wing liberals, the socialists and others who hoped that somehow it would be possible to compel the election of a constituent assembly to write a democratic constitution were disappointed when the government finally announced, on August 19, the law for the establishment of a Duma. The law, known as the Bulygin Law on the Duma, provided that the Duma be a consultative body whose members were to be chosen indirectly by an electorate limited in such a way as to insure to the landowners the preponderance of influence. That would certainly not be a constituent assembly, not even a legislative assembly.

The question of the day for the opposition became whether or not to accept the proposed Duma as, at the least, a worth-while concession. Right-wing liberals decided to participate in the elections and to attempt to transform the new Duma into a legislative body. Left-wing liberals and socialists decided to boycott it and to press on for a constituent assembly.

THE OCTOBER STRIKE. In the early autumn of 1905, even though the force of violence had been spent, there was still widespread restiveness. The economic condition of the workers had fallen appreciably during the year, and they had become better organized and more determined. Peasant disturbances were again on the increase. And revolutionary groups, taking advantage of the restoration of autonomy to the universities at the beginning of September, were turning university lecture halls into radical meeting places immune from police raids.

But not even the most sanguine of the revolutionaries realized the extent of the subsurface discontent; and they were as amazed as the government when a strike, which began late in September among the typographical workers of Moscow, turned into a general strike. It spread from the typographers to other workers, and all were soon involved in armed clashes with the troops sent to keep order. The St. Petersburg typographers declared a sympathy strike. And before these strikes lost their force, the movement had affected the railroad workers also. They were drawn into it as a result of what proved to be a mere rumor, but their zeal was born of prolonged discontent. The rumor, which first reached and incited the employees of the Moscow-Kazan line, was that certain members of a government-sponsored congress of railroad workers, then meeting in St. Petersburg to review rules covering pension funds, had been arrested. On hearing it, the Moscow-Kazan men, with no hesitation, stopped all work on their line. And within a few days all the railroad workers of the country were on strike. Telegraphers, postal employees, bank clerks, teachers, students, and factory workers joined them, and within less than a week all organized economic activity in Russia was virtually stopped. Stores were closed, newspapers did not appear, goods and food were not moved, and newly harvested grain was left waiting for shipment. At the same time rioting spread among the peasantry. Here was the general strike for which the revolutionaries had waited, and they believed that if the force behind it could be mobilized and directed it might lead to the overthrow of the autocracy. Accordingly, revolutionary committees were formed in the strike-bound cities; and in St. Petersburg, a soviet (council) of revolutionary workers and intellectuals was organized to provide leadership.

Progress toward constitutionalism

A CHANGE IN TACTICS. At the beginning of the strike, the Emperor assumed that his troops and police could restore order; but, as the strike spread, he recognized that the country was paralyzed and that the use of force against the strikers might lead to a bloody and catastrophic war. Reluctantly he turned for advice to Count Witte,[1] who has just returned from Portsmouth. Witte, though by no means a liberal, was sufficiently flexible in his thinking to recognize the inevitable: the necessity of admitting the people to participation in the conduct of government and of establishing fundamental civil rights for all the subjects of the Emperor. With considerable misgiving, Nicholas swung around to that point of view, but he never forgave Witte for advising it.

THE OCTOBER MANIFESTO.   As a first step in the new direction, Nicholas entrusted Witte with the task of drawing up an imperial manifesto embodying the concessions agreed upon. On October 28 he received the draft from Witte; and, after two days of most painful hesitation, he signed the document (to become known as the October Manifesto) on October 30. Through it the government promised (1) to grant inviolability of person, freedom of conscience, speech and assembly, and the right to form unions; (2) to extend to all classes of the population the right to vote for the Duma, thus establishing the principle of universal suffrage; (3) to guarantee that no law be enacted without the consent of the Duma; and (4) to vest in the Duma the right to pass upon the legality of the work of the administration. Taken at its face value, the October Manifesto meant the beginning of a period of constitutional government in Russia.

It was received by the opposition as a major victory, and throughout the country the end of absolutism was celebrated by spontaneous demonstrations. In many of the large cities ecstatic crowds gathered to sing the *Marseillaise*.[2] As might be expected, there were some skeptics. One of them, a young Social Democrat, Leon Trotsky, demonstratively tore up a copy of the Manifesto before a large crowd celebrating its issuance; and many of them formed gangs to attack the celebrants. However, despite these untoward events and despite the fact that the imperial concessions did not meet the general demand for a constituent assembly, there was a general relaxation of tension. For most Russians the revolution was over.

Since the October Manifesto had promised various civil liberties, the public was insistent upon evidence that the promises were to be kept. That insistence and the threat of new strikes compelled the Emperor, within the next few weeks, to give some demonstration of good faith. He did that by

---

[1] He was given the title Count for his work at Portsmouth. Wits called him Half-Count because he had signed away half of Sakhalin.

[2] Common practice among revolutionaries throughout Europe.

granting a partial amnesty for political prisoners, the abolition of censorship and the termination of further redemption payments by the peasants after they had paid half of the dues for 1906. The abolition of censorship resulted in the mushrooming of the press, and for a few months thereafter every shade of political opinion was represented by some publication.

On the extreme right, among the reactionary officials, the hierarchy of the Orthodox Church, and the nobility, the Manifesto was taken as a humiliating capitulation to the revolutionaries. Since these reactionaries considered the revolution to have stemmed not from any genuine discontent among the people but from the malicious activities of the intellectuals and the despised national minorities, they turned their full hatred upon these groups, designating them as the enemies of Russia. Witte became another target of their hatred since it was he who had persuaded the Emperor to issue the Manifesto. They organized themselves into patriotic monarchist societies, which came to be known by their opponents as the Black Hundreds. The most important of such societies was the Union of the Russian People, under the presidency of Dr. Alexander Dubrovin. On the surface it was a patriotic organization with a most distinguished membership, including high court nobility and ministers. It had the blessing and support of Grand Duke Nicholas Nikolaievich and Peter Durnovo, the successor to Bulygin as Minister of Interior. Even Nicholas II was on occasion seen wearing the badge of the Union, which proclaimed that "the well-being of the people is based on the firm preservation of Orthodox Christianity, unrestricted Russian autocracy and nationalism." The Union's most important activities, however, were below the surface. With financial aid from officials within the Ministry of Interior and with free access to the police department's printing presses, it engaged in large scale propaganda against revolutionaries, liberals, and national minorities, especially the Jews. It operated a secret fighting organization composed of minor police agents, government employees and criminal elements, who made or stirred up armed attacks on Jews, Armenians, Poles, and Finns in particular and on intellectuals in general. It also occasionally directed the murder of outstanding figures. These underground activities were not known to all high government officials, but the Union had the support of a sufficient number of governors, ministers and police officials to be assured of immunity from action by any other officials who did learn of it.

Another reactionary group was composed of the larger landowning nobility, who were frightened by peasant outbursts as well as by the revolution as a whole. In January, 1906, a congress of the district and provincial marshals of nobility, held in Moscow, laid the basis for their organization. And in May of that year representatives of the nobility met in St. Petersburg as the First Congress of the Representatives of the Nobles Societies and formed the Council of the United Nobility to speak for them.

In addition several reactionary parties were formed, among them the Party of Rightful Order and the Monarchists-Constitutionalists, who favored the most limited interpretation of the October Manifesto and opposed any further concessions to the demands of the liberals, national minorities, and radicals.

The reactionaries of the various groups usually agreed in supporting the throne, the Church and the army and in favoring a vigorous foreign policy. They opposed new reforms, often urged the rescinding of reforms already made, and supported strict control of the national minorities. They were generally intensely antisemitic, identifying the Jews with the revolution and declaring them the root of Russia's evils. In short, the programs of these bodies were based upon the old doctrines of autocracy, orthodoxy, and Russian nationality.

The leaders of the right wing of the Zemstvo liberals who had declared themselves satisfied with the Bulygin Law, were eminently gratified by the Manifesto, which they felt granted all the reforms which might be desired. Shortly after the appearance of the Manifesto a group of them, including Alexander and Nicholas Guchkov, Michael Rodzyanko, Prince Nicholas Volkonsky, and Dmitri Shipov, organized the Union of October 17th[1] (generally known as the Octobrist Party) to support their beliefs.

The majority of the liberals, grouped about the right wing of the Union of Unions, the Union of Emancipation and the left wing of the Zemstvo organization, had organized themselves, just before the issuance of the October Manifesto, under the name of the Constitutional Democratic Party. The members of that party, who came to be known as Cadets, had originally sought a constituent assembly; but when the Manifesto was issued, they declared themselves satisfied that the liberties it guaranteed would permit the beginning of a constitutional order. They now prepared to take part in the elections to the promised Duma, hoping to transform it into a genuine parliament along English lines and to use it for the attainment of new liberties and reforms.

THREATS FROM DISSATISFIED GROUPS.   The socialists, now standing

---

[1] According to the Julian calendar, used in Russia at that time, the Manifesto was issued on October 17th. This text, as noted earlier, follows the Gregorian calendar for all dates.

apart from the liberals, wished to continue the revolutionary effort until the monarchy should be overthrown and a democratic republic established. Pondering their strategy after the issuance of the Manifesto, they concluded that there was still sufficient revolutionary unrest in the country to make possible continued revolutionary efforts. Time proved them mistaken in their assessment of the situation, but for a while events supported their renewed hopes.

There was much evidence of continued dissatisfaction. The Manifesto had not brought immediate order to Congress Poland, and unrest, strikes, and riots became so widespread there that the area was placed under martial law. In the Baltic provinces savage rioting by Lettish peasants against their German landlords became increasingly serious. In central Russia a serious peasant rebellion, on a scale not equalled since the days of Pugachev, was gathering momentum. And in the cities the workers, anxious to secure an eight-hour day and other concessions, showed signs of restiveness. The chances of trouble from these discontented groups were heightened by the fact that many had been able to procure arms during the disorganized days of 1905 and were prepared to use them.

In the armed forces, the demoralizing effect of revolutionary disturbances and the dissatisfaction with food and conditions of service made many soldiers and sailors sympathetic to revolutionary agitation. Limited, short-lived mutinies broke out in several regiments. And in the early part of November a mutiny occurred among the soldiers and sailors of the Kronstadt naval base. It was suppressed by the use of guards regiments, and some 3,000 mutineers were arrested. Following that, the sailors at the Sevastopol naval base mutinied and for a time held control of several ships lying at anchor there. Their leader, Lieutenant Peter Schmidt, hoped to gain the support of the crews of other ships in the Black Sea Fleet to strengthen the position of the mutineers. His attempt failed, however, and he and his followers were overpowered and defeated.

The plentiful evidence that the October Manifesto had not ended the revolutionary mood made the socialist leaders optimistic, and they began preparation for an armed revolt to complete the overthrow of the government. But events moved too rapidly for them. The St. Petersburg Soviet, a council of trade union and socialist representatives, called a general strike in that city on November 15 in support of the Kronstadt mutineers, demanding that they not be tried by court martial. The strike was partially successful, for the government did announce that the sailors would be tried by a regular court and not by court martial; therefore, on November 20, the strike was called off. The government, however, was taking courage, and on December 18 it arrested all members of the St. Petersburg Soviet—230 in number. That action forced the hand of the Moscow Soviet (organized in November), which felt that if it did not act its members, too, might end their usefulness in jail. Therefore the leaders—including Mensheviks, Bolsheviks, and Socialist Revolutionaries—decided on a major gamble: to call a general strike in Moscow. Knowing that many of the workers had arms and that several of the regiments stationed in the city were sympathetic to the revolutionaries, they hoped that such a strike would be transformed into an armed insurrection which would spread throughout Russia. The strike was called for December 20, and on that day most of the Moscow workers laid down their work and began to rove the city.

The government, however, was not unprepared. The Moscow regiments which were ready to join the strikers were quickly isolated by loyal troops, and by the end of a week the government's forces had been supplemented by the Semenovsky Guards from St. Petersburg. After that, the revolutionaries were able to hold out only a few days. On January 2, 1906, they capitulated, their dream of a national armed revolt shattered.

The example of Moscow was followed in only a few isolated cities, for the Moscow socialist leaders had acted without consultation with the central committees of their parties and, in doing so, had failed to get the support of the countrywide organization. There were subsequent riots and revolts in 1906 and 1907, but they were of little moment. Some socialists continued to hope for another revolutionary wave, but after the Moscow strike there was little to support their hope.

The most serious revolts being under control by the end of 1905, the government began the work of restoring general order. Troops were sent on punitive expeditions into the areas of unrest in central Russia, Siberia, the Caucasus, the Baltic Provinces, and Poland. Suspected revolutionaries and often innocent persons as well were arrested by the thousands, and hundreds were shot after summary courts-martial. Socialist leaders fled from the country, hid from the police, or found themselves in prison. The process of restoring order continued during 1906 until the authority of the government was finally re-established.

WITTE'S PROGRAM.   Meanwhile preparations for the implementation of the October Manifesto moved forward. The Emperor, having accepted Witte as his chief adviser, now placed in his hands the preparation of the new laws. He named him Chairman of the Council of Ministers—in effect premier, for hitherto the Emperor had presided over that body—and permitted him to select most of his own ministers, subject to imperial approval.

In other words, he transformed the Council of Ministers into a cabinet. In further deference to the spirit of the times, he removed his ancient mentor Pobedonostsev and other reactionary ministers from their posts. One however, Trepov, symbol of police brutality, remained at court as Nicholas' right-hand man.

Witte was neither a constitutionalist nor a liberal. But, being a realist, he believed that in order to restore internal peace it was necessary to fulfill, at least in part, the wishes of those who sought constitutional and representative government. Accordingly, he tried to achieve for Russia what Bismarck had achieved for Germany: constitutionalism which did not deprive the throne of its essential powers. To make his direction palatable he asked leading liberals to join the Council of Ministers. Some refused because he had selected the reactionary Durnovo to succeed Bulygin as Minister of Interior; others refused because he declined to sponsor certain reforms which they championed. The Premier was therefore compelled to seek colleagues among the bureaucrats, and most of those he finally selected were either unpopular or little known.

In anticipation of the election to the State Duma, Witte began negotiations for a loan from France with which to stabilize the weakened fiscal position of the government and free it from dependence upon the Duma if that body should prove balky. The government of France, then under left-wing liberal control, felt qualms of conscience about granting a loan which would only strengthen Witte's hand in dealing with the Duma; but since Russian diplomatic support was needed in the Moroccan crisis then raging, it shelved conscience and agreed to make the loan.

Of even greater concern to the Premier were the legal preparations for the State Duma. The first task was to revise the Fundamental Laws of the Russian Empire, which were based on the concept of autocracy, in order to accommodate the fact of an elected legislature. The next task was to make certain that the fundamental institutions be placed, by definition in the revised laws, outside the control of the legislature. And the final task was to draw up the laws concerning the selection and the powers of the legislature. The accomplishment of those tasks would produce a political system not unlike that then in use by Japan and Germany—an autocracy tempered by constitutionalism. When the revised Fundamental Laws were issued in April, 1906, they retained the ancient formula that the Emperor was the autocrat of all the Russias; but they also provided that no legislation could become permanently valid without the consent of the Duma, and they guaranteed fundamental civil rights.

THE PLANNED LEGISLATURE. As designed, the Duma was to be a

weak legislative body. And, to weaken it still further, a second chamber, to be known as the State Council, was planned. The latter, to serve as the upper chamber, was to be an enlargement of the body created by Alexander I and known by the same name; about half of its members were to be appointed by the Emperor, and the others were to be elected by the Orthodox Church, the nobility, the Zemstvos, the Academy of Sciences, the university professors, chambers of commerce, and trade associations. Members of the lower chamber, the Duma, were to be indirectly elected for a term of five years. Almost all adult males were to vote in the Duma elections, but their votes were to be weighted in such a way as to favor the nobility and the peasantry.

This bicameral legislature was given the right to initiate legislation but denied the right to revise the Fundamental Laws. What legislative power it had was subject to difficulty in exercise: the State Council, the composition of which was certain to be conservative, could vote down any bill passed by the Duma; and any legislation required passage by both houses and the signature of the Emperor, who had an absolute veto. In addition, Article 87 of the revised Fundamental Laws empowered the Council of Ministers, with imperial approval, to issue legislation to meet emergencies if the legislature were not in session. Such emergency legislation, however, would become inoperative if both houses denied approval of it or if it were not submitted to them within two months after their convening. The budgetary powers of the legislature, modeled on those of the Japanese Constitution of 1889, actually nullified the essential power of a legislature, the power of the purse. Certain sections of the budget might not be considered by the legislature at all; and in the event of disagreement between the upper and lower chambers over a proposed budget, the government was free to select the estimates of either house or to proceed on the basis of the previous budget. Ministers could be interpellated by the legislature on the legality of their acts; but since ministers were responsible to the emperor alone, the legislature could do no more than criticize.

STATUS OF THE EMPEROR.   The emperor retained his executive authority, with complete power of appointment and removal of administrative officers. His appointments included also about half of the members of the State Council and all the members of the Senate, which retained its traditional duties. He could issue administrative decrees without legislative approval if such decrees did not violate existing law. He commanded the army and navy and had the exclusive right to declare war and to sign and ratify treaties. He could proclaim a state of emergency in any part of the empire, such a proclamation meaning—as it had since 1881—the suspension of all legal guarantees. And he retained the direction of the judiciary and the Russian Orthodox Church. It cannot be denied that the emperor's prerogatives were powerful ones, but it should be borne in mind that these prerogatives were now defined by fundamental law, and even the emperor could not legally alter that without legislative consent.

The First State Duma

ELECTIONS. On December 24, 1905, the law concerning elections to the Duma was issued, and the dates for the elections were thereafter set for the months of March and April. They were to be the first national elections in Russian history. The several socialist parties decided not to participate in the elections; and, fearing that acceptance of the Duma and participation in elections to it would divert the attention of the populace from the preparation of another revolutionary outburst, they called upon everyone to boycott both the elections and the Duma. The field was left to the Cadets, the Octobrists, the middle-class nationalist parties, the parties of the extreme right, and some newly organized political groups.

The election campaign was bitterly fought, for it was not only a struggle to secure votes but also an opportunity for each political party to propagandize its aims. The Cadets, now at the height of their prestige, were the most energetic in the campaigning. Their candidates promised to transform the Duma into a genuine parliament and to fight for the establishment of equality for all nationalities and religions, complete civil and political rights, suffrage (direct, secret and equal) for both men and women, agrarian reform, and liberal labor legislation. Their efforts paid off. When the election returns were in, it was clear that the opposition would hold the majority of seats in the Duma. Party affiliations of deputies were somewhat indefinite at first, but they soon became more distinctly defined. Of the 497 seats, about 178 were occupied by Cadets; 94 by members of the Labor Group, representing radical peasant sentiment; 32 by Polish nationalists; 17 by Social Democrats (who at the last moment had decided to enter the campaign in some areas); 44 by Octobrists and members of right-wing parties; and the remainder, by deputies who belonged to minor political groups or who did not affiliate themselves with any party or group.

THE SESSION. The first meeting of the Duma[1] opened on May 10, 1906,

---

[1] The State Council met at the same time as the Duma; but since it was so unrepresentative in composition and conservative in tone, it received little notice. The limelight was on the Duma.

under rather unfavorable circumstances. The strength of the opposition, which had been apparent even in the first stages of the elections, had shocked the Emperor; and he had quite unjustly blamed Count Witte for it. Witte, opposed at court by the reactionaries and in public by the liberals and socialists, had offered his resignation, and the Emperor had accepted it on April 29. He had been replaced as Chairman of the Council of Ministers by the ineffectual Ivan Goremykin, and a new cabinet had been formed, including Peter Stolypin as Minister of Interior and Alexander Izvolsky as Minister of Foreign Affairs. It was a conservative cabinet on the whole and its chairman hoped that the Duma would be a complacent body which would consider only matters laid before it by the government. However, the majority of the deputies expected to act on their own, initiating laws on agrarian reform and on civil and political rights. They hoped, too, to compel acceptance of the principle of ministerial responsibility—that is, that the cabinet have the confidence of the majority of the Duma. There was no evident basis for co-operation between government and Duma.

Nicholas II, who in 1895 had denounced the "senseless dreams" of those who sought a national assembly, opened the first session of the Duma at the Winter Palace. The deputies then withdrew to the Tauride Palace, where the regular business began and their oppositional mood expressed itself immediately through demands for reforms. Goremykin made it clear that the proposed reforms could not be considered; and more than two weeks passed before the government submitted the first business to the Duma— a bill to establish a laundry at the University of Dorpat.

During the remainder of the short-lived First Duma no genuine legislative business was conducted; instead impassioned attacks on the abuses of the government were delivered, commissions were set up to prepare reforms, and votes were taken on declarations of censure and "no confidence" against the cabinet. The government, for its part, tried to ignore the Duma, for it was unwilling to take either of the two steps possible to break the stalemate. If the cabinet had recognized the wishes of the majority of the Duma, it would have been in effect accepting the principle of ministerial responsibility; and neither Nicholas nor his ministers were prepared to allow that step. On the other hand, the Duma could have been dissolved and, in accordance with existing law, new elections held; but since that action would be likely to result in serious disturbances in the country, the government was reluctant to risk it.

DISSOLUTION. The activities of the Duma, however, compelled the government to act. One of its appointed commissions was preparing the draft of a bill providing for radical agrarian reform, and the government wanted to prevent consideration of such a bill. In addition, the Duma had undertaken to investigate the activities of local government officials in connection with an anti-Jewish pogrom in Bialystok which had taken eighty-eight lives early in June. In defense against its excessive zeal, the government decided to dissolve the Duma. Goremykin hesitated to take the responsibility for enforcing the decision, and Stolypin was appointed to replace him as Premier. Stolypin gave no preliminary notice of the planned dissolution but set about to strengthen the military forces in the capital and throughout the country against the possibility of rioting which might follow it. When the deputies arrived at the Tauride Palace on July 22, they found the doors closed. Then they were informed of the dissolution.

Between two dumas

RENEWAL OF REACTION. To protest the dissolution, the socialists proposed a call to revolt; but the Cadets, who had adopted the policy of using only peaceful means of opposition, refused to agree. To express their dissent, most of the Cadet deputies, joined by members of several other party groups of the Duma, made the short journey from St. Petersburg to Vyborg, in Finland; and there, safe from the police of the capital, they issued the Vyborg Appeal to the people of Russia, urging them to refuse to pay taxes or serve in the army until the government had announced the date for the election of another Duma. This call to passive resistance had little success, and its promoters were deprived of their electoral rights, some of them sentenced to short terms in prison.

The people had become apathetic to new calls to action; and the government, led by the forceful Stolypin, was ready to handle the few outbreaks which occurred after the dissolution of the Duma. Among the peasants, who had hoped for legislative action on the agrarian question, new rioting started but speedily died down. Toward the end of July brief revolts broke out also among the sailors at Kronstadt and at the naval fortress of Sveaborg, in Finland. At the time of these revolts, representatives of the Social Democrats, the Socialist Revolutionaries, the Polish Socialist Party, and the Labor Group, meeting in St. Petersburg, felt obliged to issue a call to a new general strike. But both the ill-timed strike, called at the end of July, and the naval revolts ended in failure. Stolypin, in reprisal, ordered the establishment of field courts-martial to take summary action against revolutionaries; and before the summer of 1906 ended, some five hundred persons had been executed.

While the revolutionary threat was waning, a new reactionary wave was rising. The Council of the United Nobility called upon the Emperor either to end the Duma or to alter the suffrage to insure a conservative majority in it. At the same time, the Union of the Russian People began operating freely. Before the opening of the First Duma, it had published the names of forty-three men, headed by Count Witte and including the leaders of the Cadets, whom it considered fit for extermination. Two of them were now assassinated by agents of the Union, both Cadet deputies in the First Duma: Gregory Iollos, a Jew, and Michael Herzenstein, a converted Jew. Meanwhile gangs of the Black Hundreds organized attacks throughout Russia with impunity.

THE GOVERNMENT'S RESPONSE. Stolypin, who had shown both energy and determination in his earlier career as an official, did not want to go as far as most reactionaries then counseled. With one hand he sought to quell all revolutionary disturbances; with the other, he aimed to carry out such meaures as would wean the masses away from the opposition. As the most pressing cause of unrest, he recognized the peasant dissatisfaction, which had not been quieted by the promise of termination of redemption payments and which still expressed itself through continued appeals for more land. At the height of the revolution there had been some sentiment at court for granting to the peasants part of the lands of the nobility, but by 1906 the extreme fear which had motivated that sentiment had been dispelled. Still, it was recognized that something must be done to calm peasant unrest.

For several years high government officials had felt that the village commune, which had once been extolled as the institution to preserve peasant conservatism, was an evil. They believed that if the peasants could think of their land as private property and could buy and sell the land hitherto held in common by the commune, a class of prosperous peasant proprietors would emerge from the ranks of the peasantry and that such a class would be a conservative one, cherishing its property and opposing the rebellious poorer peasants. Stolypin, agreeing with that point of view, reasoned that if the government could now issue an agrarian law welcomed by the peasants, the government and not the Duma would receive credit. Moreover, the Duma would be likely to oppose the government project, thus placing itself in a bad light with the peasants. Therefore, using the authority granted by Article 87—to issue emergency legislation while the

Duma was not in session—Stolypin issued several laws respecting the peasants. Among them the most important was that of November 22, 1906, permitting a peasant to acquire title to his allotment of village communal land, to consolidate his strips of land into one parcel, and to sell or devise such land. It was a revolutionary arrangement, threatening to end a system of land tenure which had existed for centuries. When it was put into effect, the peasant was further favored by a series of edicts ending many of his legal disabilities.

The Second State Duma

ELECTIONS. By dissolving the First Duma, bringing the revolutionaries to heel, and issuing agrarian laws calculated to gain peasant sympathy, Stolypin had gained the initiative for the government. The next steps in his program were to insure the election of a new Duma dominated by deputies from the moderate and conservative political parties and to bring the leaders of those parties into the cabinet, thus achieving a working relationship between the government and the Duma. He endeavored to persuade the leaders of the Octobrist Party to enter the cabinet, but all refused because he would not promise to make concessions to their party. Consequently, since the Cadets were too far to the left for his taste, and the parties of the extreme right were too unpopular except at court, he had to content himself with the continuation of the existing cabinet.

He failed also to influence the elections to the Second Duma, although every method, except the direct use of force or fraud, was employed to insure the election of deputies acceptable to the government. Parties to the left of the Octobrists were deprived of the ordinary tools of election campaigning: their newspapers were suspended, their meetings forbidden, and often their leaders were arrested. Thousands of voters suspected of radical tendencies were deprived of the suffrage. And the Holy Synod of the Orthodox Church urged its priests to prevail upon the populace to vote for conservative candidates.

When the elections were held, they revealed that, while the revolutionary spirit had ebbed, the spirit of opposition was still pervasive; the voters sent to the Second Duma an overwhelming majority of deputies in opposition to the government. In the First Duma opposition deputies held about 69 per cent of the seats; in the Second Duma their number was only slightly decreased. Except for the 63 representing the extreme rightist group and

34 representing the Octobrists, the deputies were either oppositional or unaffiliated with any party. Of the major parties, the Cadets won 123 seats (a decrease from their number in the First Duma); the Labor Group, 97 (an increase); the Polish nationalists, 39; and the socialists, who had decided to enter this campaign, 83[1]. The failure of the government was further emphasized by the fact that of thirteen Orthodox clergymen elected to the Duma ten were of the opposition, including one adherent of the Socialist Revolutionaries.

THE SECOND DUMA IN SESSION.   When the Second State Duma opened, on March 5, 1907, Stolypin was caught between two fires. At court, in the Council of the United Nobility and among the rightist groups, the cry was for dissolution of the Duma and alteration of the electoral law to insure the election of a conservative majority. Stolypin believed that the execution of such proposals would only create worse difficulties for the government; yet he knew that he could not get the co-operation of the majority of the Duma without agreeing to legislation considered unacceptable by the government. He had to resign himself to a hostile Duma, but he announced to it, "You will not intimidate us."

The opposition groups in the Duma, resolved to push the consideration of reform legislation, worked diligently to set up commissions to consider and prepare bills on the governmental budget and legislation on local government, compulsory education, civil rights and agrarian reform. Yet a great portion of their time was spent in their unending fight with Stolypin and in debates with the extreme rightists in the chamber.

As the session continued, agitation for the dissolution of the Duma grew. In April a congress of the organized nobility and the patriotic societies petitioned the Emperor to dismiss it. The conservative nobility were particularly disturbed by the agrarian legislation under consideration, fearing that new peasant outbreaks might be stimulated by it. Stolypin, too, was disturbed, for he was required to submit to the Duma within two months after its opening the agrarian laws which had been promulgated under Article 87, and the Duma was certain to refuse approval of some sections of those laws. It would also certainly vote against several sections of the budget presented by the government. Dissolution seemed unavoidable.

DISSOLUTION.   The occasion for dissolution arose from the efforts of

---

[1] Paul Milyukov, *Histoire de Russie* (Paris: Librairie Ernest Leroux, 1933) III, 1148. Other sources give somewhat different figures because party affiliations of some deputies were not clearly defined and because party affiliations shifted during the session. Milyukov's figures, however, give a fair approximation of the political composition of the Second Duma.

the Social Democrats to spread revolutionary propaganda among the troops, in which efforts several of the SD deputies were involved. On June 14, Stolypin demanded of the Duma that it agree to the expulsion of the SD deputies, thus depriving them of their parliamentary immunity and permitting the government to take action against them. The Duma refused to act before being given an opportunity to examine the matter. As a result, on June 16, 1907, an imperial manifesto was issued, declaring that since the Duma did not represent the people and since it had harbored enemies of the state, it was dissolved. The manifesto further declared that new elections were to be held on September 14 and that the Third Duma would convene on November 14. At the same time the government issued a new electoral law, altering the basis of suffrage and representation in such a way as to cut the representation of Russian workers and peasants and of non-Russian peoples.

The end of a period

SIGNIFICANCE OF JUNE 16. The promulgation of the electoral law of June 16 without the consent of the Duma was clearly an unconstitutional act and consequently was labeled by the opposition as a coup d'état. Some designate this act as the end of the Revolution of 1905, for it marked the regaining by the government of the authority it had begun to lose after the death of Plehve. Actually the revolution did not end on any particular day. It began to die down in December 1905; and June 16, 1907, may be taken, for purposes of convenience in periodization, as the date on which its momentum was obstructed with official finality.

GENERAL ESTIMATE. The results of the revolution satisfied few. The demand for a democratic, constitutional government had not been met. Civil and political rights had been gained in theory, but the practice of the government had limited the exercise of those rights. Labor had gained some of its demands—shorter hours, higher wages, and the right to organize—but it was far from satisfied. The peasants had reached an improved legal position, but they had not gained the land for which they had agitated. Whether or not the Stolypin agrarian laws would mitigate discontent remained to be seen. The national minorities generally found little gratification in the results of the revolution. The autonomy of Finland had been restored in November, 1905, but elsewhere national minorities had received scanty concessions.

For their part, the members of the ruling class regarded the effects of the revolution with displeasure. Many of the noble landowners who had flirted with liberalism now turned reactionary for fear that any further change would deprive them of their lands. Nicholas himself was ill-pleased with the reforms which he had granted; yet, despite the urgings of his wife and many of the court nobility, he was prepared—at least, after June 16, 1907—to accept the status quo. He and his advisers knew that any attempt to turn the clock back by withdrawing the reforms which had been granted might result in a new revolution; and they did not care to invite that.

TWENTY-ONE / BETWEEN REVOLUTION AND
WAR: 1907-1914

The seven years which passed between the dissolution of the Second Duma and the outbreak of World War I were part fat and part lean years for Russia. The government was confronted with the need for overcoming the difficulties created by the war with Japan and by the Revolution of 1905. At the same time, it had before it the opportunity of continuing the cultural and economic progress interrupted by war and revolution and of extending representative government and civic freedom. The outcome depended upon whether or not the necessary leadership could be provided to guide the country out of its difficulties into a period of peaceful domestic progress, and whether or not the discontented classes and groups would accept what was provided.

Political evolution

RIGHTS UNDER INTERPRETATION. The promises of the October Manifesto, taken at the time to mark the beginning of a constitutional period for Russia, were only partly fulfilled in the years following its issuance. The governmental action of June 16, 1907, and subsequent actions demonstrated that the government was not prepared to live within the rules which it had set if those rules proved too confining. Yet it was not prepared to dispense with them altogether. As a consequence, the country entered a period of political transition, retaining many characteristics of autocracy while taking on the characteristics of a limited constitutionalism. The government after 1907 has been aptly called "a bureaucracy slightly tempered by constitutionalism."

The civic freedoms which Nicholas II had promised in the Manifesto were, in practice, subjected to various curtailments. The provisions of the Law on Exceptional Measures, issued in 1881, remained in force; and from time to time large areas of the country were placed under reinforced or extraordinary protection, governors and police being thereby permitted to suspend the guarantees of ordinary law. Administrative justice was continued also; and since its use allowed the imposition of punishment and imprisonment without due process of law, the "inviolability of person" which had been promised was made meaningless.

It was now possible to publish newspapers without securing special permission from the authorities and to publish without preliminary censorship. However, an editor was held responsible for what he printed and was subject to imprisonment, fine, or suspension of his paper for such practices as criticizing the emperor or government officials or making reference to forbidden subjects. In regions under reinforced or extraordinary protection the press was, of course, completely subject to the whims of the authorities. All in all, publishing remained such a hazardous profession that many publishers found it convenient to hire bogus editors whose only function was to assume legal responsibility for what was printed and to go to jail when necessary. Yet the vagaries of press control were such that many shades of political opinion and ideas which had been uttered previously only in private could now manage to find expression. The illegal Bolshevik organization, for instance, was able to establish a legal newspaper, *Pravda* (Truth), which despite forty police raids continued publication until July, 1914.

Political party organizations were now so limited that only the Octobrist Party and the parties of the extreme right were permitted legal existence. Others existed, often published legal newspapers, and elected representatives to the Duma; but in law their organizations were forbidden. On the other hand, the right of labor to organize was recognized in law but strictly circumscribed in practice. In short, the various liberties enumerated in the October Manifesto were realized only in small part although the people did have a theoretical claim on them.

THE THIRD DUMA. The Third Duma, which convened in November, 1907, was the first to live out its allotted five years. The period of its duration is often called "the period of the Stolypin reaction." Premier Stolypin did indeed rule with a strong hand during that time, but that the result of his rule was actual reaction is questionable. He did not attempt to return the country to pre-1905 conditions but rather to regain and maintain governmental control, tolerating the Duma but guarding against its interference with the execution of governmental policy.

That the Third Duma be a properly subservient one was foreordained by the electoral law of June 16, 1907. That law, one of the most complicated ever devised by man, was intended to exclude from the suffrage those who might vote for opposition candidates. To accomplish that it violated the promise of universal suffrage by reducing the electorate and making representation even more unequal than before. It favored the upper classes over the lower, declaring the vote of a landowner equal to that of about 260 peasants or 540 workers. It also favored areas inhabited by Russians. To illustrate: the province of Tambov, with 3 million inhabitants, mainly Russians, was allowed twelve deputies; Transcaucasia, with about 6 million inhabitants, mainly non-Russians, was allowed only seven deputies, one of whom was to be a Russian; and Congress Poland's representation was reduced from 37 to 14 deputies, two of whom were to be Russians. The restrictions of the new law were further increased by the continuance of the old system of indirect elections, by which each socio-economic group voted separately for electors who, in turn, formed an electoral college in each province for the election of deputies to the State Duma.

In application, it justified the hopes which its drafters placed in it; of the deputies elected to the Third Duma, about 300 could be generally counted on to vote with the government. These included 153 Octobrists (the largest single group) and about 150 from various scattered right wing groups, whose political philosophy was, in many cases, that of the Union of the Russian People. The Cadets elected 54 deputies; the Labor Group, 13; the Social Democrats, 20. The remainder represented small nationalist groups or were not affiliated with any group or party.

The Octobrist group, led by A. Guchkov, became the pivotal one. With its support and that of the extreme right Stolypin could command a majority. He was offered that support by Guchkov and his followers (mainly conservative landlords) in return for the promise that he would follow constitutional principles. It was a bargain in his favor: he was assured of a majority in the Duma but needed to give little in return. He began at once to use his advantage to push through measures for the government. The first was a bill designed to restrict the autonomy of Finland (which had been restored in 1905) by depriving the Finnish legislature of its jurisdiction over matters relating to taxation, military regulations, tariffs, and civil rights. Although the bill was in violation of the Finnish constitution, it was passed by both the Duma and the State Council. Stolypin had

similar success with the agrarian laws which he had issued in 1906 under
Article 87; they also were approved, with a few changes, by both chambers.
However Guchkov was of no mind to serve merely as a tool of the Premier;
he wanted to gain, by the policy of co-operation with the government, some
measure of power for the Duma itself. For one thing, he and the Octobrists,
with the support of the opposition, sought to increase the share of the Duma
in formulating the imperial budget, a large portion of which—including
the sections on the army and navy—was not even subject to discussion by
the Duma. When the Cadets began to vote with the Octobrists on budgetary
matters, toward the end of 1909, Stolypin was placed in a difficult position.
Facing the loss of the supporting majority on which he had depended, he
began to form a new coalition of the extreme right wing parties and the
right wing of the Octobrists, which was breaking away from the leadership
of Guchkov. This core of votes, to which were added the votes of a scatter-
ing of other deputies, enabled him to maintain his majority at decisive
moments.

The final break between Stolypin and Guchkov was brought about by
the Premier's proposal for the introduction of Zemstvo institutions into
several western provinces of mixed Russian, Polish, and Jewish population
where there had been no Zemstvos. The bill, which excluded Jews from the
franchise and discriminated in outrageous fashion against the Poles in fixing
representation, was aimed at strengthening the position of the Russians
in these areas. The opposition and the left-wing Octobrists, under Guchkov,
balked at its provisions, and the bill was passed by the Duma in June, 1910,
by only a slender margin. Stolypin himself was far from pleased with the
situation in which he found himself: attacked by the Duma as a reactionary
and by the State Council as a radical. When the upper house refused, in
March, 1911, to pass the bill, arguing that it was against the interests of
the nobility, he resigned. At the insistence of the Emperor, however, he
resumed his office and reclaimed his power by proroguing the Duma and
the State Council and issuing the law on the Zemstvos under authority
granted by Article 87. Guchkov, who had been elected president of the
Duma in the preceding year, thereupon resigned his post in protest against
the Premier's arbitrary action.

Stolypin did not live to complete his program. In September, 1911,
while attending a performance in the municipal theater of Kiev, he was
killed by a revolutionary who had once served the secret police. Count
Vladimir Kokovtsev was selected to replace him as Premier. Although not
as strong as his predecessor, Kokovtsev followed the same policies, hewing

to a line which was too conservative for the Octobrists and too liberal for the Black Hundreds.

THE FOURTH DUMA, 1912-1917. Kokovtsev, lacking confidence in the Octobrists, made an effort, when the term of the Third Duma had come to an end and elections for the Fourth Duma were in preparation, to assure the election of a majority of deputies by the parties and groups to the right of the Octobrists. The effort did not come off with complete success. The voters returned 185 deputies of the extreme right, 98 Octobrists and 150 from the opposition.[1] The returns made the Premier dependent on the Octobrists for a majority—a fact which they used to advantage, voting on some occasions with the government, on others against it.

Although Kokovtsev was usually able to muster a majority for his proposals, he found the Fourth Duma a trial, for the opposition employed every opportunity to attack government proposals and policy. Even the deputies supporting the government grew restive and critical because of the scant respect paid the Duma, especially by those at court. The Emperor often deliberately slighted it—as on the occasion of the 1912 celebration of the centenary of the Battle of Borodino, when no places were assigned for deputies. The Empress constantly urged her husband to dispense with it altogether, and for a time he did entertain the notion of stripping it of its slight legislative power. Ill feeling between the government and the Duma was further increased by disagreement over the character and worth of Gregory Rasputin, who had become a power at court by 1912. Rasputin, a peasant who set himself up as a holy man, had been brought to the attention of the Empress Alexandra in 1905 as a wonder-worker who could cure the heir apparent, her infant son Alexis, of hemophilia. She had fallen under his influence and would believe no evil of him even when reports of the "holy man's" immoral life were brought to her from every side. The Emperor, too, had supported him by silencing or ignoring the critics. Having his position at court thus firmly established, Rasputin had used it to influence the policies of the Orthodox Church; and many, including the Over-Procurator of the Holy Synod, had found it expedient or desirable to remain on good terms with him. In 1912 criticism of Rasputin was voiced in the Duma; and its president, Rodzyanko, undertook to advise Nicholas to rid himself of the "holy man." The advice was ignored. But criticism continued; and when Nicholas dismissed Count Kokovtsev

---

[1] Among the opposition were thirteen Social Democrats—seven Mensheviks and six Bolsheviks. The leading Bolshevik deputy was Roman Malinovsky, a Russified Pole, who, it was revealed after 1917, had long been a police agent.

Nicholas II with Empress Alexandra and family

as premier in January, 1914—allegedly for agitating against Rasputin— and appointed the aged and reactionary Goremykin to that position, the opposition became more vocal. The activities of Rasputin were only one cause of irritation in the Duma; others were added day by day, and the outlook for co-operation with the government became progressively gloomier.

Neither the Fourth Duma nor its predecessors achieved much that was of immediately evident or tangible worth. That body's power in the determination of governmental policy was still negligible, its role in legislation slight. A summary of its work between 1907 and 1912 will serve to illustrate that fact: in those five years the Duma was responsible for the initiation of only 34 of the 2,197 bills enacted; the others, with the exception of two bills initiated by the State Council, were submitted by the Council of Ministers. Moreover, the Duma had grown more palpably unrepresentative of the people. Yet one positive achievement had been made; it had provided a forum for criticism of the government and had made possible legislative experience for a people long accustomed to exclusion from participation in government.

TREATMENT OF NATIONAL MINORITIES.   During the period 1907 to 1914 the national minorities within the empire became more self-conscious and more ambitious for recognition of their right to the use of their own languages in education and administration and their right to administrative autonomy. And the government had only exacerbated their feelings by pursuing a policy of Great Russian chauvinism. It is true that some of the oppressive policies of the government toward non-Russians were mitigated after 1905; but real concessions were few, and often what was given with the right hand was taken away with the left (as in the case of Finland, mentioned above). The continuation of the policy of Russification after 1905 and the clear indication in the new electoral law that non-Russians were to be regarded as second-class subjects helped to aggravate the already serious discontent. Matters were made still worse by the fact that there was no single official policy with respect to the national minorities. Many of the chief officials, although concurring in the policy of Russification and repression of the non-Russians, opposed the excesses committed during these years by the Black Hundreds. Yet those bands continued to have sufficient support and encouragement—often official—to operate freely. Having no proof to the contrary, the non-Russians believed that the Black Hundreds represented the conscious policy of the government as a whole.

DECLINE OF REVOLUTIONARY MOVEMENT.   For the revolutionaries the period after 1907 was one of declining power and influence. The force of unrest upon which the socialists had staked so much had begun to ebb after the failure of the Moscow general strike, in December, 1905, and it receded rapidly after the dissolution of the Second Duma. When the government finally demonstrated its ability to maintain the initiative in the face of revolutionary unrest, few except the most diehard revolutionaries had the faith or courage to continue the struggle. The government's measures of repression further enhanced their weakness by forcing their leaders underground, into prisons or into exile, suspending the publication of their newspapers, and making organized activity generally difficult. And, when a former police official revealed, early in 1909, that Azef and numerous other revolutionaries were police agents, the confidence of many revolutionaries in themselves and in their work was badly shaken. Thereafter most of their organizations declined until they became almost moribund.

Another debilitating process at work within the thinning revolutionary ranks was the division of opinion. It has been seen that the Revolution of 1905 divided the ranks of the opposition, many erstwhile liberals becoming reactionaries or conservatives and others refusing to support any further revolutionary actions. Thereafter revolutionary opposition was supported mainly by the scattered and weakened socialists, and even they could not agree among themselves as to the nature of the methods they should employ to achieve their ends. Some believed that they should utilize fully the tools which were legal—the press, trade unions, and election campaigns —and that illegal methods should be eschewed; others believed in using legal methods as far as possible, supplementing them, if necessary, by illegal ones; and still others judged any use of legal methods to be a sign of weakness. Tactical differences such as these and personal differences among the leaders themselves produced a multitude of cleavages. The Polish Socialist Party, the Polish Social Democratic Party, the Socialist Revolutionary Party, and the Bolshevik and Menshevik factions of the SD's —all were torn by internal conflicts and divisions.

The most important disturbances occurred within the ranks of the SD's. At a congress in Stockholm, in April, 1906, a superficial unity was restored to the party when the Mensheviks and the Bolsheviks patched up their differences; but as soon as the congress was over, the quarrels began anew. Lenin, leader of the Bolsheviks, was neither willing nor able to compromise with those who differed from him. He believed that another opportunity for revolution would come in Russia and that the Social Democratic Party, as he conceived the party, should be ready at that time to serve as the general staff for the struggle. He argued that it was better to have a small, well-knit party than a large, heterogeneous debating society. In theory a single party existed until 1918, but in fact the Bolsheviks formed themselves into a separate party at a conference called by Lenin in Prague in January, 1912. That conference announced that it alone spoke for the SD's. It elected its own Central Committee;[1] and on May 5, it printed the first issue of its new party organ, *Pravda*. The Bolsheviks thereafter considered themselves the true Social Democrats, while the Mensheviks—who were themselves split into several factions—maintained in theory that there was still only one Social Democratic Party, consisting of all factions.

[1] The Central Committee soon thereafter added to its membership the name of the revolutionary Georgian, Joseph Stalin.

Despite the differences among the many socialist factions, there still existed among them a core of common belief. All felt that another revolution would be required before a bourgeois democratic republic could be established. But the final revolution out of which a socialist society would emerge was, in the opinion of most socialists, still quite distant.

The pall which had enveloped the revolutionary movement began to lift in 1911. An important index of the rise and fall of the movement was always the incidence of labor strikes. In 1905, about 2,750,000 workers had gone on strike; in 1906, the number had fallen to 1 million; in 1910, it was 46,000. Then in 1911 the number rose again—to 105,000. The new strike movement was chiefly economic in nature, but it began to take on a political character also as a result of an incident in the gold fields along the Lena River, in Siberia. There, in February, 1912, a strike broke out and spread rapidly. In the following April a procession of strikers was fired upon by troops, and over five hundred workers were killed or wounded. The response to the killings was a series of sympathy strikes throughout Russia, and the movement kept increasing from that time until 1914. Some of the strikes were for economic gains; others were purely political in nature, begun as demonstrations of the strikers' opposition to the regime. In 1913, more than 1 million workers laid down their work, and in the first six months of 1914 the strike roll rose to 1,425,000. To add to the gravity of the situation, labor unrest was accompanied by a resurgence of peasant riots after 1910.

It appeared that a repetition of the revolutionary disturbances of 1905 was in the making. But much had happened in the intervening decade to make this a different kind of disturbance. The community of purpose which had served the opposition in 1905 had been lost. The liberals and socialists had gone into opposite camps. Intellectuals still provided the chief revolutionary leadership, but the rank-and-file revolutionaries came now from the growing labor class and, in small part, from the peasants rather than from the youthful intelligentsia. Storm signals were evident, but their meaning could not be interpreted by comparison with the past.

Economic development

GROWTH OF CAPITALISM. The ability of the regime to regain its political authority was closely connected with the development of the economy. War and revolution had given it a set-back; but as the strike movement declined between 1905 and 1911, as normal economic activities were resumed and as foreign and domestic confidence in the stability of the regime was strengthened, industry entered a period of prosperity which lasted until the eve of World War I.

This economic acceleration was fed by foreign as well as by domestic resources. By 1914 French investors owned 21.9 per cent of the stock of the major privately-owned banks in Russia; German investors, 17.7 per cent; and English investors, 3 per cent. About one-third of the capital of mining and manufacturing corporations was that of foreign investors— chiefly French, English, German, and Belgian. And much of the remaining industrial capital was provided by foreign loans to the Russian Government. In 1914 about 48 per cent of the government bonds were held abroad; and, of those, French citizens held about 80 per cent. The extent of the French investments at that time is indicated by the fact that about one-quarter of the total French income from long-term investments abroad came from Russia.

During this time there was also a decided increase in the contribution of Russian capital, both private and governmental, for the further development of industry and banking. Men of wealth, hitherto restrained by traditional timidity and the inadequacy of their fortunes, grew bolder as prosperity appeared; many became titans of industry and finance. Once engaged in large scale business, the financiers began to realize the value of capitalist organization and began working toward the concentration of control in industry and toward the establishment of trade associations. The factory owners among them had begun early in the century to form monopolistic combinations to regulate production and marketing. In 1902 a syndicate for the sale of metal products had been formed under the name of Prodamet, and by 1908 it controlled about 70 per cent of such sales. The example of Prodamet was now followed in many other branches of industry with the result that control was concentrated in a few hands and that cutthroat competition was slowly eliminated. At the same time, the organization of trade associations developed. The owners and operators in the various industries formed regional trade associations for the consideration of common problems; and these associations, in turn, formed national associations; and from the latter grew interindustrial associations comparable to the American National Association of Manufacturers and the United States Chamber of Commerce. Their central organization, the Council of the Conference of Representatives of Industry and Commerce, met frequently and exerted great influence on the government. Individuals, also, often controlled wide interests. Alexis Putilov built up a veritable industrial empire through his interests in metallurgical enterprises, shipbuilding, armament, banking, and the Chinese Eastern Railroad.

Many ministers and members of the imperial family were connected with industry and banking and were personally friendly to industrial and banking interests. The government as a whole continued its policy of favoring industry, banking, and commerce; and it remained industry's best customer.

Thus financed and supported, Russian industry showed phenomenal gains. Between 1909 and 1913 the production of pig iron increased by 59 per cent; iron and steel, 50 per cent; coal, about 40 per cent; and coke, 60 per cent. Industrial growth was accompanied by the development of mechanization and the introduction of the latest technological innovations. Still, with all these advantages and improvements, Russia continued to drift behind the advanced industrial nations of the world. A few comparisons for the year 1913 will indicate her position:

Country	Coal	Pig-iron	Electricity produced per capita	Cotton utilized per capita
	(in millions of tons)			
Russia	36	4.6	14 kw.-hrs.	6.8 lbs.
United States	517	31.5	175.6	30.8
Germany	190	16.8	———	———
Great Britain	287	10.3	———	41.8
France	40	5.2	———	———

When one takes into consideration the fact that Russia had a far larger population than that of any other major power, her relative economic position appears even worse. The impressive growth of industry could not obscure the fact that the country remained, economically speaking, comparatively poor, backward, and rural.

AGRARIAN ADVANCES.   The major changes in the agrarian situation after the Revolution of 1905 grew out of the reforms associated with the name of Stolypin. Although they bore his name, these reforms should not be credited solely to him; they represented the considered policy of the government and a number of the nobility, who had concluded that the pressing danger of agrarian unrest could be avoided by decreasing some of the disabilities of the peasants and by fostering the development of a class of conservative peasant proprietors. Stolypin vigorously undertook the task of setting the major reforms into motion.

It will be recalled that in November, 1905, the government had removed one source of peasant complaint by declaring that peasants would be no longer liable to redemption dues after the payment of half of the dues for 1906. In the same month it had ended, in those villages where it still existed, the principle of joint responsibility of the members of the village commune for taxes and other obligations which had previously been assessed on the commune as a whole. However, the most important measure initiated in those years was the law of November 22, 1906 (known as the Stolypin Law), which the premier had issued under the authority granted by Article 87 and which was finally passed, in June, 1910, by the Duma and the State Council. By its provisions peasants could, under conditions varying with the landholding practices in their villages, acquire title to the strips of communal land to which they had a right and consolidate such strips into unified parcels of land.

The sponsors of the Stolypin Law had visualized a peasantry transformed by its provisions; but transformation came slowly, for the power of custom and tradition in the village commune was not easily overcome. The law appealed mainly to the more energetic and prosperous among the peasants, who saw in it an opportunity to enhance their positions. Between 1907 and the end of 1915, when the operation of the law was suspended, about 24 per cent of the peasant households were granted their allotments as personal property. In the same period about 10 per cent of all peasant households changed their holdings into unified plots similiar to the farms of Western Europe and the United States. To that extent the law initiated a process of fundamental change even though it did not alter the face of peasant Russia completely. The change weakened the village commune, but it remained a powerful force and continued to play its time-honored role.

Other measures, operating along with the Stolypin Law, opened still other opportunities to the peasants. In November, 1905, the government had announced that the Peasants Land Bank would extend its aid by buying land from nobles, the government, and members of the imperial family and by selling it on credit to peasants willing and able to increase their holdings. Peasant acceptance of this aid tended to increase the economic cleavage in the villages; well-to-do peasants acquired more land, but poorer peasants often lost their land. As a result three major groups soon became distinguishable: (1) the wealthy peasants, or kulaks,[1] who often leased land to poorer peasants or hired them as laborers, (2) the middle peasants, and (3)

---

[1] *Kulak*, a Russian term meaning *fist*, was applied to wealthy peasants because they were known as tight-fisted money lenders.

the poor peasants, who lost all or most of their land and became agricultural proletarians.

The government's policy after 1905, in contrast to its earlier policy, not only permitted but actually encouraged co-operative movements among the peasants in order to raise the economic level of that group. Many co-operatives for the purchase and use of agricultural machinery and for marketing were established. More popular, however, were the co-operative savings and credit associations. By 1914 such associations had enrolled 8 million peasants, who were thereby enabled to weather bad times and to purchase needed machinery and farm supplies.

Unquestionably the average peasant was living more comfortably in 1914 than he had been in 1905; and a few, by peasant standards at least, were prosperous. The Stolypin reforms, increased Zemstvo activities, expansion of the foreign and domestic market for agricultural products, and developments in agricultural techniques—all contributed to the general improvement. Yet agrarian tensions were far from relieved. The rural population continued to grow rapidly, and the great majority of peasants were still land hungry and miserably poor. They looked with undiminished appetite at the lands of the nobility, the government, and the monasteries.

Cultural growth

EDUCATION. Stolypin's period in office marked the beginning of a concerted effort to deal positively with another problem, that of illiteracy. Previously neither the Church nor the state had made much headway in the promotion of education for the masses; in fact, the initiative in expanding general education had usually come from other sources. But after 1905 the government became more concerned about the encouragement of general primary education. In 1908 a bill to establish free and universal primary education was passed by both legislative chambers; the government approved it and laid out a program, promising the allocation of increasing sums of money for schools to be administered by the Zemstvos, the Church, municipalities, and the state. At that time 37 per cent of the children of school age were receiving schooling, and plans were made to increase that to 100 per cent by 1920. The government did not give sufficient financial support to the project to maintain the planned rate of growth; yet by 1914 the number of primary schools had increased by 50 per cent over 1908, and about half the children of school age were in school.

Most of the schools offered three-year programs in which pupils acquired the minimum skills of reading and writing. In 1914 it was anticipated that another ten years of uninterrupted growth would be required before primary schooling would be available for all children of school age.

The rate of progress in secondary and higher education, although not as rapid as that in primary education, was nonetheless considerable in this period. As a result of the extension of educational autonomy during the revolution, the quality of instruction at those levels was greatly improved. And the number privileged to study beyond the primary schools was increasing: by 1914 the secondary school enrollment had risen to 764,000, and that of universities and higher technical and professional schools to 112,000. One new university was opened, at Saratov, in 1909, bringing the total to ten.

INTELLECTUAL LIFE.   The successes and failures of the revolution and the events which followed it altered the outlook of Russian intellectuals. Political differences among some of them became sharper, as has been noted. Some, disappointed in the revolution and pessimistic about the future, became indifferent both to political and to social problems. Of these many turned to the advancement of careers or the amassing of fortunes, and others turned to the cultivation of art for art's sake. Whereas, before the revolution most intellectuals, despite theoretical differences, had so much in common that they formed a recognizable class, now their cohesion was beginning to weaken.

The symbolist movement, which met the aesthetic and emotional needs of an increasing number of educated persons, began to dominate the scene, reflecting itself in literature as well as in the fine arts. It achieved its greatest triumphs in the medium best suited to its aims, poetry. Balmont and Blok continued their work, and Andrei Bely joined them as one of the leaders. After 1910 the symbolists began to divide into new aesthetic groups, among them the "acmeists" and the "futurists"; and each, like corresponding groups in Western Europe, considered itself more "advanced" than any other and became disdainful of the traditional canons of art and language.

In the field of prose, writing of social significance continued to hold a strong position, much of it influenced by Maxim Gorky, who had achieved such success at home and abroad that he was now able to help other writers. Gorky had won great fame as a dramatist with the play *The Lower Depths* (1902), portraying the lowest strata of Russian society. And his novels, one of the best of which was *The Mother* (1907), increased his fame. Being sympathetic to the Bolsheviks, he helped to publish the works of a number of writers whose viewpoints were close to the left. Although most of those he sponsored left no mark on literature, three did outstanding work: Alexander Kuprin, who satirized the Russian army in several novels and short stories, the most compelling of which was the novel *The Bracelet of Garnets;* Leonid Andreyev, who gained an enviable but not a lasting reputation with his realistic dramas and such stories as *The Seven That Were Hanged;* and Ivan Bunin, whose worth is still recognized in such works as his novel *The Village.*

The fine arts of the period gave evidence of definite change. The Russian ballet particularly, in which were fused many of the arts, began to improve as the hold of tradition was slowly broken by the work of Michael Fokine and Sergei Diaghilev. Diaghilev brought together for the ballet the best of the country's talent—composers like Igor Stravinsky, painters and scenarists such as Alexander Benois, and dancers of the quality of Anna Pavlova and Vaslav Nijinsky. Through their efforts the Russian ballet achieved a vitality unsurpassed in preceding years.

Foreign affairs

FORMATION OF TRIPLE ENTENTE. While the government was recovering its strength at home after the revolution, it was seeking to recover also its position abroad after the inglorious defeat by Japan. But its foreign policy was complicated by the fact that the European powers were becoming divided into hostile camps. Russia's most constant friend was France, and the Franco-Russian Alliance was the point of departure for the government's diplomatic thinking. When France in 1904 had come to an understanding with England which prepared the way for common diplomatic action against Germany, Russia had been faced by a dilemma. Should her foreign policy be based exclusively on the Franco-Russian Alliance—which now implied friendship with England, or should it be aimed at salvaging whatever was possible from the former friendship with Germany? Tradition and sympathy supported friendship with Germany as did also the fact that each country provided a valuable market for the other. Yet German policy had on the whole been opposed to Russian interests for more than a generation, particularly in favoring Austro-Hungarian interests above those of Russia in the Balkans. In addition, since 1903 Germany had been taking an undesirably lively interest in the Ottoman Empire. After weighing the pros and cons, the Russian foreign office decided to continue using the French alliance as the core of Russian foreign policy. France in turn sought not only to strengthen her alliance with Russia but also to bring Russia closer to England, her new-found friend.

Anglo-Russian understanding required rapprochement of some kind between Russia and England's friend Japan; and the Russian Government, which had accepted its check in the Far East as a fact and was now turning once more to the advancement of interests in the Balkans and the Middle East, was prepared to come to terms with that country. Consequently, on July 30, 1907, Russia and Japan signed a convention whereby southern Manchuria was acknowledged as a Japanese sphere of influence, and northern Manchuria as a Russia sphere. It was essentially a recognition of the status quo and an affirmation by Russia that the policies which had led to war in 1904 would not be renewed. A fruitful area of expansion still remained for Russia in northern Manchuria, in the regions served by the Chinese Eastern Railroad.

There remained three other areas in which the conflicting interests of Russia and England had to be considered—Afghanistan, Persia, and Tibet. Each had a position to defend in those areas: England felt that her control of India demanded predominance of influence in Afghanistan; Russia wanted to expand her economic and political influence in Persia; and both regarded influence in Tibet as a matter of strategic importance in Central Asian affairs. The matter was finally resolved on August 31, 1907, when the two countries signed the Anglo-Russian Convention, covering the three disputed areas. The convention represented mutual concessions. Both powers agreed to refrain from seeking influence in Tibet. Russia recognized Afghanistan as an English sphere of influence and promised to conduct her relations in that area through England. Northern Persia was accepted as a zone of Russian political and economic influence; southern Persia, as a British zone; and the rest of Persia, as a neutral zone in which both powers were free to seek economic advantage. That arrangement completed the establishment of the Triple Entente of Russia, France, and England.

The Anglo-Russian Convention was but one of the influences on the easing up of Anglo-Russian hostility at this time. England had come to view Russian interest in the Straits with less misgivings than in the past because the development of the Suez Canal as a major link in the lifeline to India had lessened the strategic importance of those waters for her. Her fear of the Russian threat elsewhere in the Near East had been overshadowed since 1870 by concern about the growth of German interest in that region. And her general antipathy for Russia had been mitigated since the establishment of a Duma and the liberalization of Russian institutions. In short, she was beginning to feel that the Russian bear was perhaps not such a bad fellow after all—at least, not as bad as the German Junker. As for Russia, she felt that the Anglo-Russian Convention was desirable; if for no other reason, because it assured her that England would now not go so far in checking Russian interests as in the past.

RENEWAL OF BALKAN QUESTION.   At the turn of the century Austria-Hungary and Russia had agreed to maintain the status quo in the Balkans, but after 1905 both powers experienced a change of heart. In 1906, Alois Aerenthal, who was strong in his belief that Austrian interests should be pushed in the Balkans, succeeded to the office of Austrian foreign minister; and Alexander Izvolsky, who held a similar belief on behalf of Russia, had received the portfolio of Russian foreign affairs. With them a new period of Austro-Russian rivalry was begun. Serbia, already an area of contention, became an important pawn in that rivalry. Austria-Hungary had been particularly concerned since the overthrow in 1903 of the pro-Austrian Obrenovitch dynasty in Serbia and the installation, in its stead, of the pro-Russian Karageorgevitch dynasty. That Serbia should seek and gain Russian support was a possibility which Austria-Hungary could not tolerate, for she felt that the several million Southern Slavs living in the Austrian Empire would be readily susceptible to the influence and propaganda of a strengthened Serbian nationalism. Aerenthal began trying to devise ways of restoring Austrian influence in Serbia, while Izvolsky assumed a jealous guardianship of Russia's advantages. They had not long to wait before events brought their competition in Serbia, as well as in other parts of the Balkans, into the open.

The political temperature in the Balkans was raised appreciably by the Young Turk revolt of 1908. Disturbances in the Ottoman Empire had for generations stimulated ambitions in other powers, and this one was no exception. The Balkan nations began to think of it as an opportunity for expelling the Ottoman Empire completely from the peninsula. Austria-Hungary saw it as an opportunity for formally annexing Bosnia and Herzegovina, which she had occupied since 1878. And Russia interpreted it as a chance for renewing her efforts for the opening of the Straits to Russian warships. Neither country lost any time in promoting its aims. In September, 1908, Izvolsky and Aerenthal concluded an agreement by which Russia would support Austrian attempts to arrange for the annexation of the two provinces and by which Austria-Hungary would support a Russian attempt to secure revision of the Straits Convention. Three weeks later Austria annexed

Bosnia and Herzegovina. Her act enraged Serbia, who had hoped to gain the provinces, largely Serb in population, for herself; in fact, Serbia was in a mood to go to war if she could be assured of Russian help. The Russian spirit also was strong for war, but the situation required careful consideration. According to Izvolsky, Austria-Hungary was guilty of a breach of faith; he interpreted the agreement of September, 1908, as implying that she would not take unilateral action with respect to Bosnia and Herzegovina but would, with Russian support, present the problem of annexation before an international body for consideration. Yet the prospect of war in defense of that position was not inviting to Russia. Her army was in no condition for war; and on the diplomatic front Austria-Hungary had the advantage of strong German support. Consequently, the crisis ended without war. Serbian hatred of Austria-Hungary, however, remained fever high, and there appeared to be no method short of war to resolve Austro-Serbian antagonism. Austro-Russian relations, too, remained strained, and Serbia continued to be their diplomatic battlefield. Izvolsky lost face through what was considered an unsatisfactory position on the matter and in 1910 was replaced by Sergei Sazonov.

Sazonov set to work to bring the Balkan states together with the aim, of course, of strengthening Russian and ultimately weakening Austrian and Turkish influence over them. With his encouragement a network of alliances was formed among the Balkan states. These alliances, in which were included Serbia, Bulgaria, Greece, and Montenegro, constituted the Balkan League. Late in 1912 the League declared war on the Ottoman Empire and was so successful that in the spring of 1913 the Sultan agreed to renounce almost all of his territories in Europe. But when the members of the League began working out the division of those territories, Austria-Hungary interposed to forbid their assigning to Serbia an outlet to the Adriatic. Serbia's attempt to make up for that loss at Bulgaria's expense led to a second war, one in which Bulgaria's former allies and Rumania as well were aligned against her. Bulgaria was defeated and came out of the war with little to show for her effort, while the victorious states gained the major share of the former Turkish holdings.

For Russia the two Balkan wars brought mixed results. Bulgaria drew close to Austria-Hungary and Germany; so did the Ottoman Empire, out of resentment for Russia's part in the Balkan wars. And Austria-Hungary was more hostile than before, being now more disturbed than ever about the gain in Russian influence. On the other hand, Serbia and Montenegro remained close to Russia, and Rumania was turning to her for support of

Rumanian irredentist hopes of gaining Transylvania from Austria-Hungary. But Russia was by no means comfortable in her position. If her influence continued to predominate in Serbia and if—as seemed probable—she could depend on Rumania, she could control all of the northern Balkans. However, if Serbia should fall under Austrian control and if Bulgaria should remain friendly toward Austria-Hungary and Germany, Russian influence would be brought to a virtual end in the Balkan Peninsula.

RUSSO-GERMAN RIVALRY IN THE OTTOMAN EMPIRE. Whereas in the Balkans, Russia faced Austria-Hungary, in the Ottoman Empire she faced Germany. Bismarck's belief that Germany had no major interest in the Ottoman Empire had come to be disregarded, and about the turn of the century Germany had begun to extend her political and economic interests there. Not at all loath to play the major predatory powers off against one another, the Sultan had accepted German advances even to the extent of granting a concession to German financiers for a projected railroad from Constantinople to Bagdad. Russia, being experienced in the political uses to which a railroad might be put by a great power in a weaker country, sensed danger and at first opposed the implementation of the concession. However, Sazonov, who was disposed to improve Russo-German relations, agreed in November, 1910, to drop Russian objections to the railroad in return for German recognition of the Russian sphere in northern Persia.

Russia's alarm was renewed when, late in 1913, the Sultan engaged a German military mission to modernize the Turkish army and appointed the German General Liman von Sanders to head the Turkish troops garrisoned in Constantinople. Russia, supported by France and England, protested the appointment with considerable force, and Constantinople responded by relieving von Sanders of his command but granting him the post of Inspector-General of the entire Turkish army. Such incidents as that indicated to Russia that, although the Ottoman Empire had not yet signed an alliance with Germany, the understanding between them was definite and threatening.

ON THE EVE OF WAR. Russian interests ranged across two continents in 1914, their vital center lying between Persia and the Adriatic Sea. From the position of the foreign office it appeared that Russia could not afford any further impairment of her interests in the Balkans, most important of which was her interest in Serbia, whose cause was enveloped in Pan-Slav sentiment. Russia could not afford to let her little Serbian brother down— that would be not only immoral but also impolitic.

The Austro-Russian and the Russo-German conflict in the Near East could not be dissociated from the general European tension in the second decade of the century, when events were calling for a tightening up of alliances and an acceleration of preparation for the war which none wanted but all anticipated. The existing alliances were all defensive in their terms, leaving open the question of whether or not allies would support one another in case of an offensive war. Austria-Hungary felt that Germany would support her if she should find it necessary to take offensive measures against Russian-supported Serbia. Russia was not certain that she would have French support in case of offensive action in the Balkans; but her confidence was bolstered by the fact that France had offered no major objections to her actions there and could therefore, presumably, be counted on for support if Russia were the attacker. Still, France had not explicitly affirmed such a commitment, and she had offered a few protests at impetuous actions of which she had not been given prior notice. As for French support in case of action against Germany, Russia felt confident of that. Serbia felt assured of her position, convinced that if she were compelled to fight Austria-Hungary, Russia would send aid; she had the assurance of the Emperor himself, who had informed the Serbian Premier Nicholas Pashich in January, 1914, "For Serbia, we shall do everything."

THE OUTBREAK OF WAR.   The test came for all on June 28, 1914, when the heir to the Austro-Hungarian throne was assassinated in Sarajevo by a member of a Serbian secret society. Austria-Hungary, believing that the moment had come to settle affairs, began the preparation of an ultimatum to Serbia, which if accepted would make that country a subordinate of hers and which if rejected would provide a proper pretext for war. She was not certain that Russia would fight to save Serbia; but she felt certain that if Russia fought, so would Germany.

On July 23, the 48-hour Austrian ultimatum was delivered to Serbia. Russia advised the Serbian ruler to agree to all demands which he could but to make no concessions which would impair Serbian sovereignty. In answer to the ultimatum, on July 25, Serbia agreed to all but a few of its demands. Two days later she was assured by Nicholas II that if all efforts to avoid war failed, Russia "would not remain indifferent to the fate of Serbia." Then, on July 28, Austria-Hungary, considering the reply unacceptable, declared war on Serbia. On the same day, the Russian Council of Ministers, meeting with the Emperor, decided to mobilize part of the Russian army near the Austrian border. The order for partial mobilization, published on July 28, was properly interpreted as a threat to Austria-Hungary, a threat which could be averted only by Austrian cessation of hostilities. France assured Russia of support on her position.

The initiative meanwhile was passing from the hands of the diplomats, whose job it was to prevent war, to those of the military, whose job it was to wage war. If war must come, argued the military, the side that mobilized first would have a great advantage. Because of the partial mobilization of the Russians, the German General Staff urgently requested that the Kaiser order mobilization, even while he was urging Vienna to show moderation. In St. Petersburg, the Russian generals urged that general mobilization be ordered; but the Emperor hesitated, hoping that a last-minute compromise with Austria-Hungary would be possible. On July 30, however, at the request of the Minister of War, Vladimir Sukhomlinov, and the Chief of Staff, Nicholas Yanushkevich, he consented to see Sazonov and hear his position on the matter. The Foreign Minister assured him that war was inevitable. It was, he said, being "thrust upon Russia and Europe by the ill-will of the enemy, determined to increase their power by enslaving our natural Allies in the Balkans, destroying our influence, and reducing Russia to a pitiful dependence upon the arbitrary will of the Central Powers." Nicholas recognized the logic of this argument and, on the following day, published the order calling the reservists to the army. The justification of this act is still debated; some argue that in ordering general mobilization Russia was choosing an all-out war, and others argue that having exhausted all opportunities to settle the Austro-Serbian conflict without war, she had no choice but to do as she did. The consequences of the act, however, were clear even at that time: Germany would also order general mobilization, and the possibility of avoiding war would be further reduced.

On July 31, two hours after the publication of the Russian order for general mobilization, Germany declared "a state of war emergency" and in a few hours dispatched an ultimatum to Russia, demanding a halt in military preparations within twelve hours; otherwise, Germany would proceed to general mobilization. Russia did not submit, and on August 1 Germany went beyond mobilization and declared war. Three days later Austria-Hungary followed Germany's example. On August 3, Germany declared war on France. On August 4, England entered the war against Germany. World War I had begun.[1]

[1] Once the fighting had begun, the original combatants were joined by other states: chief among them, the Ottoman Empire (October, 1914) and Bulgaria (1915), which entered on the side of Germany and Austria-Hungary; and Japan (August 23, 1914), Italy (1915), Rumania (1916), and the United States (1917), which entered on the side of England, France, and Russia. The opposing sides came to be known respectively as the Central Powers and the Entente (or the Allies).

TWENTY-TWO / PARTICIPATION IN WORLD
WAR I: 1914-1917

Foreign Minister Sazonov had informed the Emperor in December, 1912, that Russia could not be ready for war before 1915. But war came in 1914; and, ready or not, the country had so much at stake that it could not afford to quibble. Having failed the tests of the Crimean War and the war with Japan, it needed to make a strong showing in this one for the sake of morale at home and diplomatic advantage abroad. Moreover, there was the urgency of protecting the new Russian economy, dependent to so large an extent upon the capital and the trade of France and Great Britain.

War was a precarious undertaking in 1914 because of the uncertainty of such vital factors as the civilian support, the adequacy of the armed forces, and the resilience of the economy; but to avoid it would have been to invite other and more fearful uncertainties. Ironically, the outcome was more catastrophic than any which had been thought possible.

Diplomatic considerations

ALTERED APPROACH.   At the opening of the war, the statesmen of the great powers thought of it in traditional terms: it would be continued until one side should admit defeat and accept conditions advantageous to the other; its conclusion would not bring the extinction of any of the powers but a modification of their relationships. Consequently they began looking ahead to the day of reckoning. On September 5, 1914, Russia, England and France signed the Treaty of London, by which each country was pledged not to sign a separate peace. At the time, they felt that the consideration of specific postwar problems could be postponed until after victory. But it soon became evident that military and diplomatic problems could not be separated. In order to secure the adherence of Italy to the Allied side, for instance, many territorial prizes had to be offered; then other nations interested in the same prizes demanded compensations, and additional diplomatic problems were presented. Since such maneuverings were unavoidable, diplomacy was accepted as a necessary adjunct of military planning. Russia, for her part, had a broad and ambitious program to plan, one which had been in the making throughout her history.

THE POLISH PROBLEM.   Poland could be expected to present a special problem since some of the Polish people were under Russian rule, some under the rule of the Central Powers. In fact, it became a problem as soon as hostilities opened. Before Russia had taken any step to invite the good will of the Poles, Austria-Hungary permitted Jozef Pilsudski, who had been residing in Galicia, to organize the Polish Legion to fight the Russians. The Russian Council of Ministers wanted to make an immediate affirmative declaration to the Poles; and, on August 14, Grand Duke Nicholas Nikolaievich, Supreme Commander-in-Chief of the Russian army, issued to them an appeal framed by the Council of Ministers, promising that after the war all of Poland (including Prussian and Austrian Poland) would be united under Russian rule and granted freedom of language, religion, and local administration. The appeal gained no response among the Austrian and Prussian Poles, who continued to fight for their respective states; and it roused little enthusiasm among the Russian Poles, who, while loyal to Russia had little faith in her promises. Essentially, it was not a promise to warm the hearts of those who hoped for independence. The émigré Poles in Paris were soon hammering away at the thesis that an Allied victory should bring the liberation of Poland from Russia, urging England and France to prevail upon Russia to promise that. Russia, however, would not permit any discussion of the question by the Allies. Meanwhile, Germany and Austria-Hungary were attempting to exploit the latent ill will of the Russian Poles toward Russia by promising the creation out of Russian Poland of a constitutional monarchy under a German or Austrian ruler.

Sazonov, who realized that the Polish question could be a stormy one unless the Poles were conciliated, urged on Nicholas the necessity of promising without delay or equivocation the restoration of independent Poland, united to Russia by a personal union under the Romanovs, who would retain authority in Poland only over questions affecting both states. But he had little support at court. It soon became clear to all except the government that, even if Russia should be one of the victors in the war, she would be beset with an unresolved Polish problem.

SLAVDOM.   Since Russia's propaganda presented the war as a struggle to rescue the Slavs—including Czechs, Slovaks, Serbs, and Poles—from oppression, she was in a position to exploit their restiveness in Austria-Hungary and Germany. Although the Poles were not very amenable, the Czechs, Slovaks, and Serbs within the Austro-Hungarian Empire were encouragingly responsive. They did not admire the Russian form of government, but they needed Russian aid in gaining their freedom.

Among the Slavs outside of those two countries success was uneven. The Serbs of Serbia, for whose sake Russia had allegedly entered the war, were distant and could not be given aid when they most needed it. Those in Bulgaria ignored the call of Slavdom, and their country joined the Central Powers.

THE ANCIENT DREAM.   In August, 1914, although the Ottoman Empire had secretly signed a treaty of alliance with Germany (August 2, 1914), there was still a remote possibility that it might join the Allies—for a price. On August 5, Enver Pasha, Minister of War and one of the triumvirate which dominated the Turkish Government, began to sound out Russian willingness to promise the return of western Thrace and the Aegean islands to the Ottoman Empire in return for a Turco-Russian alliance; but the Russian Government made no active response to his offer. To accept it at the price demanded would be impolitic, for the whole question was too closely tied to the problem of securing for the Allies the support of the Balkan states. Furthermore, it seemed doubtful that the Russophobe Enver Pasha was sincere in his offer. In any event, nothing came of the discussions; and, in October, 1914, the Ottoman Empire entered the war on the side of the Central Powers.

Turkish adherence to the Central Powers, although a military loss to the Allies, was a political gain for Russia because it provided a kind of justification for her further pursuit of ambitions at the expense of the Ottoman Empire. It revived the ancient dream, both within the government and among the people, of placing the double-headed eagle over Constantinople. Sazonov, authorized by the government to discuss the possibility of Russian annexation of the Straits and Constantinople, overcame the Allies' disinclination to discuss the matter by offering them Russian aid in their annexation of other portions of the Empire. He could do that because the diplomatic scene had changed much since Nicholas I had proposed the partition of the Ottoman Empire in 1853; now England and France did not regard Russian presence at the Straits with so great concern. Moreover, they were very anxious to keep Russia in the war and were therefore more agreeable to Russian wishes than they would have been in peacetime. In March, 1915, England agreed to support Russian acquisition of Constantinople and the Straits, and a month later the French gave their assent. France agreed also to Russian annexation of Turkish Armenia and part of Turkish Kurdistan. In return for these concessions, Russia not only promised to lend her weight to the fulfillment of French and English territorial ambitions in the Ottoman Empire but also agreed to the transformation of the neutral zone in Persia into a British zone. The texts of these agreements were secret, but it was public knowledge in Russia that victory would bring a realization of the ancient dream with respect to Constantinople and the Straits.

Period of the Sacred Union

WAR SPIRIT.   In 1914 the great majority of the Russian people seemed to look upon the war with approval, and the news that Germany and Austria-Hungary had declared war on Russia led them to great demonstrations of patriotic fervor. They were ready to fight in what they took to be a just war of defense against militaristic Germany and against Austria-Hungary, the oppressor of Slavic Serbia. The liberals and radicals believed that a war in alliance with liberal England and France against the conservative and militaristic Central Powers would help ultimately to bring liberal reforms to Russia. Even the socialists, with few exceptions, were caught up by the fever of war although, until its actual outbreak, they had denounced wars in general; and in Paris, Plekhanov, still the high priest of Russian Social Democracy, began to rally Russian volunteers for service with the French army. Only the Bolsheviks, a few Mensheviks, and a few Socialist Revolutionaries opposed the war.

The strength of the war spirit was demonstrated at the special session of the Duma called for August 8, when deputies representing almost all groups—extreme rightists as well as Cadets—and including Great Russians, Ukrainians, Poles, Lithuanians, Moslems and Jews, expressed their approval of the government's action. Milyukov stated the view of the erstwhile opposition and that of most informed Russians when he said on the floor of the Duma:

> We are fighting to deliver our fatherland from foreign invasion, to liberate Europe and Slavdom from German hegemony. . . . In this struggle we are united: we do not make any conditions, we de-

mand nothing, we simply place in the balance of war our firm will
to conquer.

Only the small Social Democratic group[1] in the Duma refused to lend its
support to the war. The other deputies united to form the Sacred Union, by
which all political differences were put aside and a platform of unconditional support of the government in the war was accepted. The spirit of
the Sacred Union pervaded the country. From all sides came expressions
of support for the government and declarations of the wish to give all possible aid. The actions of the municipal governments and the Zemstvos
were typical: in August they formed, respectively, the All-Russian Union
of Cities and the All-Russian Union of Zemstvos for the purpose of establishing and operating military hospitals and maintaining rest stations for
the troops.

WAR ECONOMY.   The Russian economy was better keyed to war in 1914
than it had been in 1904. The booming basic industries could supply a large
part of the needs of the army, and Russia's allies could be counted on to
supply some matériel. Furthermore, the present military front was much
closer to the bases of supply than the 1904 front had been.

However, Russia—and this was true of the other powers as well—
was not prepared for an extended war. Military thinking had assumed that
even a general war would be decided in a matter of weeks or, at the most,
months. For that reason no serious planning for the transition of industry
from a peace to a war footing had been undertaken by the government. The
treasury had not been put into condition to sustain the burden of a lengthy
and costly war. And the railroad system had not been adequately developed
for the task of moving men and matériel in war. France had loaned Russia
money to extend her railroad system in Poland for the purpose of facilitat-
ing rapid mobilization of troops for an attack on Germany, but little attention had been given to the long-range problems of transportation. There
was not even sufficient rolling stock to utilize existing lines to capacity. Nor
had there been proper preparation for the maintenance of supply lines from
the outside world. Russia might have foreseen that, in the event of war,
she would be cut off from the use of the Baltic ports and her western land
frontiers, that she would lose the use of the Black Sea if the Turks should
enter the war against her, and consequently that she might need to depend
upon the use of the ancient sea route by way of the White Sea. Yet Arch-

----

[1] Of that group the Bolsheviks were soon arrested, and the Mensheviks later recanted
their opposition.

angel, poorly developed and useless during half the year because of ice, remained the only White Sea port of any consequence; and it had only a narrow-gauge railroad connection with the interior. Logic might have suggested the development of ice-free Murmansk, but hardly anything had been done there. In short, the Russian economy was ill prepared for anything but a short, victorious war.

MILITARY PREPARATIONS.   Experiences in the Russo-Japanese War had impressed the Russian military leaders with many of the shortcomings of the army, and in the decade following that war they had attempted to overcome them. But time had proved too short and resources too few. They had managed, between 1905 and 1914, to improve the quality of military training and the technical equipment of the troops somewhat; but despite these advances, the quality of the Russian armed forces in 1914 was lower than that of the forces of the other major powers with the exception of Austria-Hungary. The Russian army suffered by comparison on every count: the General Staff was poorly organized and manned; intelligence organization was ineffectual; there was a dearth of trained commissioned and noncommissioned officers; technical equipment was inferior and inadequate; and supply and medical services were rudimentary.

Russia's major advantage lay in a seemingly inexhaustible supply of manpower. However a large proportion of the youth of military age had received no military training at all, and the others were poorly trained. In 1914 the standing army numbered 1,423,000 and the reserves 3 million. During the war more than 15 million men were called to the colors, but only a small portion of that number received anything like satisfactory training.

PLANS OF WAR.   The Franco-Russian military plans, which had been based on the probability of a war with Germany and Austria-Hungary, assumed that Germany would use the main body of her troops against France first. If this were the case, Russia's role would be to relieve the pressure on France by compelling Germany to retain five or six army corps in the east to meet a Russian offensive of 800,000 men directed at either East Prussia or Posen by the sixteenth day after Russian mobilization. This was a major commitment for Russia since it required that there be no hitches in her mobilization and, more important, it required the immediate risk of most of her trained troops. Operations on the Austro-Russian front were not included in the joint plan. It was assumed that Austria-Hungary would direct her major effort against Russia, and the General Staff had planned an offensive against her to coincide with the Russian attack on

Germany. The fact that these two phases of the offensive—the one against Germany, the other against Austria-Hungary—were not carefully co-ordinated led to the ultimate impairment of Russia's effectiveness in the war. MILITARY OPERATIONS, 1914. Following the order of general mobilization and the declaration of war, France appealed for immediate action; and Grand Duke Nicholas responded by deploying his troops, according to plan, on two major fronts: the northwestern front, facing East Prussia; and the southwestern front, facing Austrian Galicia.

On the northwestern front the First Army, under General Rennenkampf, and the Second Army, under General Samsonov, prepared to take the offensive. August 17 was fixed as the date on which Rennenkampf was to enter East Prussia from the east; and Samsonov, moving north from Warsaw, was to cross the boundary two days later. They were expected to defeat the German forces in East Prussia, prevent the Germans from receiving assistance from the west, and effect a junction between the two Russian armies. Rennenkampf was victorious in his first meetings with the Germans, and Berlin became alarmed about the prospect in East Prussia. Therefore the German General Staff, under von Moltke, decided to strengthen the area by sending reinforcements and by placing the retired General von Hindenburg in command there. The Germans, even then, were numerically inferior to the Russians; but they had superior knowledge of the marshy and lake-strewn terrain of the region as well as superior officers, intelligence organization, and artillery. In addition, von Hindenburg knew of a long-standing enmity between Samsonov and Rennenkampf, dating from a fist-fight between the two at the Mukden railroad station in 1904, which he thought he could use to advantage. He took the risk of neglecting Rennenkampf and concentrating the German attack on Samsonov near Tannenberg,[1] trusting that Rennenkampf would not hasten to aid his hated colleague. Between August 23 and 30, the Germans encircled and cut up Samsonov's army, killing or taking prisoner the major part of his men; and Samsonov, seeing his army thus virtually destroyed, committed suicide. Rennenkampf, meanwhile, dawdled unconscionably, as had been predicted. His failure to support Samsonov prompted a German officer later to say that, "if the battle of Waterloo was won on the playing fields of Eton, the battle of Tannenberg was lost on the railway platform at Mukden." After Tannenberg, von Hin-

---

[1] Although serious fighting occurred near other villages also, the Germans called the engagement the Battle of Tannenberg, when it proved successful, in order to erase the stigma of the defeat of the Teutonic Knights by the Poles and Lithuanians at Tannenberg in 1410.

denburg was free to turn against Rennenkampf, who, after severe setbacks, was compelled to retire from East Prussia in mid-September.

Although the Russian offensive had failed and Russia had suffered a disastrous defeat, the ultimate purpose of the offensive had been gained: Germany had been forced to weaken her forces in France. As a result, the French had been able to stop the Germans at the Marne, thus frustrating their plan, which had assumed a quick victory over France and a subsequent concentration on the Russian front. Thereafter, Germany was compelled not only to divide her armies between the Western and Eastern Fronts but also to support the Austro-Hungarian army against Russia.

On Russia's southwestern front, the story was more favorable for her. Austria-Hungary, having reached the decision to fight Russia, reduced her forces on the Serbian front, giving Serbia a temporary respite, and concentrated the main body of her army—about 1 million strong—in Galicia for an offensive thrust into Russian Poland. Her forces succeeded in entering Russian Poland before the Russians were able to launch a successful counterattack; but on September 3 the Russians entered Lemberg, the chief city of Galicia, and in the next few weeks forced the Austro-Hungarians into disorderly retreat along most of the front. This was the first major victory of the Allies over the Central Powers. By mid-September almost all of western Galicia was in Russian hands.[1]

The French command then pressed Grand Duke Nicholas to open a new offensive from western Russian Poland into Germany, and he was inclined to comply. But von Hindenburg forestalled that move by an offensive directed against Warsaw, partly for the relief of the Austro-Hungarians in Galicia. His forces reached the outskirts of Warsaw, but the Russians held fast, and on October 20 the Germans began to retreat. However, Russian pursuit was so delayed by the slow regrouping of forces that the Germans were able to re-form their lines and, in the latter part of November, launch a new attack—this time on Lodz. That attack was frustrated also; and, with the onset of winter, there followed a period of relative quiet on the northwestern front.

AUSTRO-GERMAN BREAKTHROUGH, 1915. Von Hindenburg's efforts had not been successful in relieving the Austro-Hungarians; and General Ivanov, commander of Russia's southwestern front, sought to take advantage of that fact by resuming the offensive in the winter of 1914 in order to prevent the enemy from regaining strength. He hoped that the

---

[1] The Russians entered Galicia as "liberators" of the Poles and Ukrainians there, but they created only ill will by the harassing of the Roman Catholics and Uniats among them.

Russians, who were already approaching the Carpathians, would be able in the next year to cross the mountains into the Hungarian plain and force Hungary out of the war. The Austro-Hungarians received reinforcements from the German army, and fighting was resumed in Galicia. The hilly terrain and the wintry weather made combat difficult and costly for both sides, but the Russians managed to advance slowly. In March, 1915, several units crossed the Carpathians into Hungary, and in the same month the key Galician fortress of Przemysl surrendered with 120,000 men. It was a heartening period for Russia. By that time the entry of Italy into the war on the side of the Allies was imminent; and if she should attack Austria-Hungary from the south, the Russian offensive would be aided by the consequent division of the enemy's forces.

Von Falkenhayn, who had replaced von Moltke as Chief of the German General Staff in September, 1914, wished to direct the principal emphasis of the 1915 campaign against the English and French armies on the Western Front, but the situation of Austria-Hungary was too critical to be ignored completely. The Austrian High Command and many of the German generals wanted to make an all-out effort on the Eastern Front, believing that success there might turn the tide to victory. Von Falkenhayn, however, favored a limited effort which would relieve Austria-Hungary but would not prevent the delivering of a major blow in the west if the occasion for it arose. It was finally decided to transfer a German army from the west to reinforce the Austro-Hungarians, to place the combined forces under the brilliant German General von Mackensen, and to attempt a breakthrough in the region of the Dunajec River in western Galicia. In April, von Mackensen moved into position under the unseeing eyes of the Russians, whose lines were only about two miles away. He had seasoned troops, an immense advantage in artillery, and a generally superior organization with which to meet the Russian force. On May 1, 1915, he began his attack with such overpowering vigor that he was able to smash through the Russian lines and force a disorganized retreat. In May alone he took 153,000 prisoners, and by the end of June he had thrust the Russians almost completely out of Galicia.

The German High Command was then faced with the question of whether or not to push on from Galicia into southern Russia. Since their strategy demanded priority for the Western Front, a drive into southern Russia, although offering possibilities of success, was ruled out on the grounds that it might tie up too many German troops. Russian Poland, where the Russians held a salient position, was selected instead as the next goal of the Austro-German effort. A victory there would insure the Central Powers against Russia's being able to resume offensive warfare for some time and would permit the Germans to transfer their best troops elsewhere. During the summer of 1915 a German force from East Prussia struck south into Poland while Austrian and German troops moved north from Galicia. Kholm and Lublin fell to them on July 31 and Warsaw on August 4. Grand Duke Nicholas, convinced that the Russian defeat in Galicia had made Russian Poland indefensible, had already decided to retreat until he could fight more effectively. Accordingly, retreating with skill and in good order, he gave up all of Russian Poland and part of Lithuania; and by the end of August he had established a line running roughly through Riga, Vilna, Pinsk, and Tarnopol. Von Falkenhayn was content to accept this line, and in the fall of 1915 he ordered his generals to stabilize the front and disengage themselves from any further major fighting in the region. Confident that the Russians could not resume the offensive, he then transferred his best troops for action on other fronts.

During the campaign of 1915 about 2 million Russian troops lost their lives, were wounded, or were taken prisoner. It was a grave defeat for Russia, but the skill of Grand Duke Nicholas had kept it from being stark disaster. Nonetheless, he was made the scapegoat. Nicholas II decided, against the advice of his ministers, to remove him from the post of Supreme Commander and to take the post himself. On September 5, the Emperor arrived at the Russian General Headquarters, at Mogilev—to which it had been transferred from Baranovichi, in Poland—and assumed his new role as war chief.

TURKISH SUCCESSES.　　To the Russian losses on the Eastern Front were added others, incurred at the hands of the Ottoman Empire. In November, 1914, the Turks, under Enver Pasha, struck their first blow at Russia in Transcaucasia. At that time Russia called on her allies for a diversionary attack on Constantinople but found that she was able to repulse the Turkish forces without that aid. On the Black Sea, however, Turkish ships, reinforced by two German cruisers, nullified the power of Russia's Black Sea Fleet. England and France meanwhile even after Enver's setback, were giving serious thought to an attack on the Turkish capital; they saw that such an attack, if successful, would not only relieve the Russians by opening the Straits to supply ships but also change appreciably the strategic situation in the eastern Mediterranean. They began their effort by a joint naval-military attack on the Dardanelles in March, 1915. Russia hoped to assist their campaign later by sending a task force from Odessa; but the campaign in

Galicia forced the diversion of her Odessa troops to the Galician front. The Dardanelles campaign failed, and in the fall of 1915 England and France withdrew their forces. To add to the despair of the Allies in that area, the Serbian army was defeated in September, 1915; and with that, the Straits and most of the Balkans were in the hands of the Central Powers.

Disruption of the Sacred Union

ECONOMIC DEBILITY.   As the war continued, the inability of the Russian economy to support an extended conflict became more and more apparent. The entry of the Ottoman Empire into the war cut Russian foreign trade almost to the point of disappearance; one estimate shows that exports declined by 98 per cent, and imports by 95 per cent. Reduced imports and inadequate domestic production resulted in a shortage in arms and munitions which became acute by the spring of 1915. Replacement troops sent to the front were often without rifles (in some regiments, as many as one-third of the men) and were forced to equip themselves with rifles taken from the casualties. Many artillery batteries could not reply to enemy fire at all; others were restricted to a daily ration of four shells per gun. In some sectors, infantrymen, with no support from their own artillery, advanced with only the cold steel of bayonets to employ against the enemy. One general is reported to have said during the summer fighting of 1915, "Today our artillery and our infantry are mute, and the army is drowning in its own blood." The front suffered also from faulty transportation and distribution of supplies. With Poland, Russia lost her best railroads and thereafter had to place an excessive load on the remaining ones. And transportation over those was so mismanaged that critical maldistribution resulted. The fighting forces took the consequences: some regiments lacked boots, others had too many; food rotted in some areas of the front while troops in others were on short rations; and military hospitals often ran short of bandages and medicine.

The production shortage on the home front was a result of the failure to prepare and execute policies necessary for an efficient wartime economy. During the first year of fighting 5 million men were called up with little or no regard to their role in the economy; skilled workers from armament plants and peasants from the farming areas were drafted indiscriminately, jeopardizing industrial and agricultural production. Conversion of industry to war purposes was similarly retrograde. Some plants already in war pro-

duction were swamped with war orders; others, engaged in civilian production, were left idle because of lack of raw materials, shortage of labor,
or absence of orders.

WEAKENING OF THE SACRED UNION. Great as were the weaknesses
on the military and home fronts by the spring of 1915, the government
displayed little awareness of them. Nicholas II showed no greater ability as a
leader in 1915 than he had shown in 1905. His ministers were, for the
most part, inept and reactionary. The 67-year-old Minister of War, Vladimir
Sukhomlinov, refused for a long time to inform the French and British of
munitions shortages. The 76-year-old Premier, Ivan Goremykin, described
by a colleague as "a weak old man, capable at best of petty, childish tricks,
avidly clinging to power, or, rather, to those material goods which power
brought him," did nothing to promote improvements in conditions. The
reactionary Minister of Interior, Nicholas Maklakov, was more concerned
with the possibility of subversive actions by the unions of Zemstvos and
cities than with the very real assistance they were giving to the country in
its emergency. Ivan Shcheglovitov, the Minister of Justice, was more energetic in his friendship toward the Black Hundreds than in his support of
the country's general interests. These were not the men to keep the public
confidence which had been so freely given to the government at the war's
opening.

Yet the spokesmen of public opinion, the leaders within the Duma, and
the moving spirits of the unions of Zemstvos and cities were willing to
continue full co-operation in the war effort, encouraging the people to do
likewise. The government, however, preferred to dispense as much as
possible with the proffered aid. The Duma had been summoned to a one-
day session on August 8, 1914, and then dismissed until, in conformity
with the law requiring that it meet once a year, it was summoned once more
on February 9, 1915, for a three-day session. The bulk of the legislation
during the war was issued by the government under the powers of Article
87. A large portion of western Russia had been entirely removed from
civilian authority as a result of a law issued at the beginning of the war,
placing in the hands of the military the control of areas considered "military
zones"—interpreted broadly to include not only the front but also large
areas adjacent to it.

It appeared that the government intended to limit the people to the
traditional roles of working, fighting, and paying taxes. But the spokesmen of public opinion were not prepared to continue their acceptance of
this limitation indefinitely. After the meeting of the Duma in 1914, the

deputies who lived in Petrograd[1] organized the Provisional Committee for War Relief, under the leadership of the Duma president, Michael Rodzyanko; and, as the defects of the government became more visible, it took on an increasingly political character. The unions of Zemstvos and cities, also, began considering political problems in the course of their work. For some time these organizations held themselves in restraint out of respect for the spirit of the Sacred Union, avoiding criticism of the government, hoping that faults would be righted. But their discontent began to be openly expressed after a revelation made in March, 1915. At that time Colonel Sergei Myasoyedov, whose friendship with Sukhomlinov had enabled him to hold high military office while transmitting vital information to the enemy, was brought to justice and hanged. The case of Myasoyedov, for whose loyalty Sukhomlinov had publicly vouched as late as February, stirred public opinion deeply. And worse was to come with the Austro-German offensive of May, 1915; it was not the defeat alone which roused public opinion but the knowledge, often garbled by the public, that blunders of the government and the military had helped make defeat possible. Rising prices and increasing evidence of economic disorganization added to the irritation. And it was further aggravated by the badly executed military policy in regard to portions of the civilian population (particularly Jews and Poles) of the territories to be given up to the enemy. They were forced, sometimes with extreme brutality, to flee to the interior of Russia; and, joining the tens of thousands of voluntary refugees, bringing the total number to at least 3 million, they streamed into Russian cities behind the lines, carrying poverty, disease, and despair with them. The already burdened public began to feel that they could bear no more.

INITIAL CONCESSIONS. When Nicholas II was at last made aware of the extent of criticism and of the economic difficulties of the government, he was faced with a choice: to continue business as usual, courting public opposition, or to take steps to increase public participation in the affairs of the home front. As a gesture toward righting matters, he agreed to a proposal made by Rodzyanko—and vigorously opposed by Sukhomlinov, Maklakov, and Shcheglovitov—that joint committees made up of members chosen by the government, industry, and banking be created to aid in solving the munitions shortage and in dealing with other economic problems. The reactionary ministers were forced out of office. Sukhomilov was replaced by General Alexis Polivanov; Shcheglovitov, by Alexander

[1] To remove the Germanic ending from its name, St. Petersburg had been renamed Petrograd at the beginning of the war.

Khvostov; and Maklakov, by Prince Nicholas Shcherbatov. Sazonov, who had opposed Sukhomlinov, remained Minister of Foreign Affairs. The new Council of Ministers was more popular and less tainted with reaction than the old, but its composition did not inspire the public confidence for which Nicholas had hoped.

In June, 1915, the Emperor, with the approval of the Council of Ministers, began to implement the proposals of Rodzyanko by creating a Special Council to co-ordinate the supply of munitions and other matériel to the army. Headed by the Minister of War and composed of representatives of the government, the Duma, and industrial and public organizations, it was given extraordinary powers in both industry and transportation. Subsequently other Special Councils were created for transport, fuel, food, defense, and refugees.

THE PROGRESSIVE BLOC. As the next step toward regaining public support, the government called a new session of the Duma for August 1, 1915. Despite the predominance of conservatives and reactionaries in it, that body showed none of the earlier agreeableness of spirit when it met. The majority of the deputies, dissatisfied with the composition of the Council of Ministers (particularly with Goremykin) and alarmed at the unfavorable news arriving daily from the front, declared their conviction that victory could not be won unless the government permitted the full co-operation of the people. That co-operation, in their opinion, could be gained only through improvement in internal administration and the formation of a Council of Ministers "enjoying the confidence of the people." Their sessions were filled with speeches arraigning the misdeeds of one official or another.

The Cadets chose this time to organize the opposition. They succeeded in forming the Progressive Bloc, which included most of the deputies except those of the extreme right and left and which gained much support, even in the State Council. The Progressive Bloc demanded (1) ministerial responsibility, (2) extension of local self-government, (3) the curbing of military interference in civilian affairs, (4) the granting of autonomy for Poland, (5) removal of legal disabilities on the Jews, (6) termination of religious persecution, (7) a general amnesty for persons accused of political and religious crimes, and (8) the re-establishment of the trade unions, which had been curbed at the beginning of the war.

A majority of the Council of Ministers favored coming to some terms with the recrudescent opposition in the legislature, but Goremykin was opposed; and he had the support of the Emperor, the Empress, the Council of the United Nobility and the court. His position prevailed, and on September 16, the Duma was prorogued. The Sacred Union was manifestly at an end.

GOVERNMENT WITHOUT LEADERSHIP. The Emperor and those who had advised him to suspend the sessions of the Duma believed that it was using a national emergency to further its own aims; and that was true enough. Yet the fact that a conservative and hitherto complacent Duma should act in such fashion was sufficient to give the monarch pause; it was bald evidence of the growing distance between government and people.

The suspension came in the midst of a serious domestic situation. The strike movement, which had virtually come to an end after the opening of the war, had picked up strength in the spring. In addition, the growing dislocation of the economy had resulted in food shortages in many cities— not because there was no food but because of disorganized transportation and supply; and in April food riots had begun in the two capitals, sometimes taking the form (with the encouragement of the police) of attacks on stores owned by persons with German or other foreign names. But popular unrest could not be thus diverted indefinitely. The closing of the Duma occasioned an increase of strikes with clearly political character and also brought protests from most public organizations. Fortunately for the government, although the rift between it and the public was growing, there was as yet no pronounced defeatist mood. The exalted mood of August, 1914, was gone, but there was still support for continued participation in the war.

Official acts helped finally to dissipate the remnants of loyalty. Nicholas' decision to assume the command of the Russian forces, a decision made against the advice of both the army and the government, had most unfortunate consequences. The Emperor was nowise qualified as a general, and he was mistaken in his belief that his presence at the front would serve as an inspiration to the troops and to the country at large. Even though he had demonstrated limited ability as a ruler, he would have been more useful on the home front than on the military: his absence deprived the country of what little unity it had and inaugurated a period of critical weakness.

When Nicholas left for Mogilev, the chief authority, in effect, fell to Empress Alexandra; and that change could only aggravate an unpromising situation. Daughter of the Grand Duke of Hesse and granddaughter of Queen Victoria, Alexandra had taken very seriously her position as Empress, becoming a devotee of the Orthodox Church and a firm believer in autocracy. In the estimation of an ill-disposed public, she had become an

*Gregory Rasputin (seated) with Prince Putyatin (right) and Colonel Loman,
Commandant of the Tsarskoe Selo Palace*

unreasonable reactionary, a religious fanatic, and a generally harmful influence in the government. Now that influence was to be a more direct one: new acts or appointments would still require the Emperor's assent, but the Empress would be in a position not only to pass on to him, as background for official judgment, stories and opinions based on misinformation but also to initiate and promote plans of her own. As she informed the British ambassador, "The Tsar unfortunately is weak; but I am not, and I intend to be firm." The outlook was bad, and it was to become worse, for Rasputin now emerged into his brief span of power. The Empress had never lost her faith in the "holy man," but he had been kept on the fringes of politics until September, 1915, and on occasion, his presumption had been openly defied. It is reported that when he offered to go to the front to bless the troops, Grand Duke Nicholas had wired, "Come and be hanged!" But now his position was changed; he stood beside the Empress in her new power. As Alexandra despised all officials who showed either independence or any spirit of liberalism, so Rasputin despised all who would not bend to his will; but whether or not he had any ambitions beyond the advancement of his own fortunes and the satisfaction of his carnal appetite is still a moot question. It appears that he entertained some vague hopes of improving the peasant lot, although there was little in his actions to indicate any program directed to that end. Before the war, he had opposed involvement; and many Russians believed, without foundation, that he and the German-born Empress were working for the enemy. Whatever his position, he now had the ear of the Empress; and every self-seeker at court, in the government, and in the Church sought favors from him and gave favors in return.

The fifteen months from September, 1915, to December, 1916, during which Rasputin rode high, were months of degradation for the government. One by one, men offensive either to the Empress or to Rasputin were forced out of office. Goremykin, reactionary though he was, fell out of favor and was replaced by Rasputin's tool Boris Stürmer, more reactionary and even less competent than Goremykin. Sazonov, who had the confidence of the Allies, was ejected; and for a time Stürmer held the portfolio of Foreign Affairs as well as that of Premier. As time went on the replacement of ministers became so rapid that the period has been called one of "ministerial leapfrog." Confidence in the government diminished both at home and abroad. The throne was losing its power as a unifying symbol; and the Empress was becoming for many, including commanding generals in the army, an object of vilification, blamed for all troubles, real or fancied.

ALLEVIATION OF MUNITIONS SHORTAGE. Meanwhile the plans already laid were being carried out to supply Russia's military needs. The Special Councils, aided by the War Industries Committee (created at the same time as the Councils to act as a superior co-ordinating body), registered considerable success in raising production of war materials. The War Industries Committee, which operated through twenty-eight local committees, had adopted the suggestion of its chairman, Alexander Guchkov, that representatives of labor be added to the committees in order to improve morale. The Bolsheviks attempted to persuade the workers to boycott the election of labor representatives but were generally unsuccessful. Domestic energy was further accelerated by the arrival of English and French technical advisers to give assistance on production problems.

It was, of course, very important for the Allies that Russia be able to utilize her still abundant manpower on the Eastern Front. To aid her, England and France increased their shipments of matériel, and the United States and Japan sent additional supplies. But utilizing the aid was still a problem for Russia. Archangel and Vladivostok, the two chief ports of entry, could not handle the volume of freight which arrived; and often precious cannons and rifles rusted at the wharves for lack of transport to the interior. Completion of the railroad to Murmansk was speeded up in 1916 with the use of conscript Russian and prisoner-of-war labor, but it was not ready for use until early in 1917.

Despite these handicaps some supplies were getting through, and by early 1916 the munitions crisis was passing and the army had new reserves of matériel. At the same time the older classes of the reserve were called up, and the training of new men was being improved. The Russian army appeared ready for a new drive.

THE BRUSILOV OFFENSIVE. Since the late summer of 1915 the Eastern Front had been relatively inactive. The Germans felt that the Russians were exhausted and, in the belief that the major decision of war would be made on the Western Front, they were preparing for the attack on Verdun. Austria was planning an attack on Italy, in Trentino. And the Allies, for their part, were planning a combined offensive for the summer of 1916. As her share in it, Russia had pledged, at the Allied military conference at Chantilly, in December, 1915, a major offensive to be begun on or before June 15, 1916.

In May, 1916, the Austro-Hungarians began their attack on Trentino with such success that the King of Italy appealed to Russia for a diversionary attack. Without dropping the plan for a June offensive, the Rus-

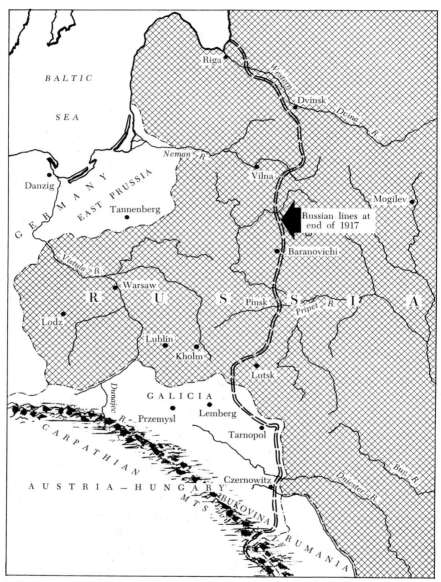

MAP 13. The Eastern Front

sians agreed to aid Italy; and General Alexis Brusilov was given the assignment of conducting a limited offensive. In the first days of June, he gave orders to attack along a 300-mile line from Lutsk to Bukovina. His preparatory artillery attack proved amazingly successful; the Austro-Hungarian troops who received the blow were in poor morale and broke over a wide area, permitting rapid Russian infiltration.[1] This early success of the Brusilov offensive proved so gratifying to Emperor Nicholas' Chief of Staff, General Michael Alexeyev, that he shelved the plan for a later offensive and ordered an extension of the line of attack and the commitment of a larger number of troops than had originally been assigned to Brusilov's effort. The Germans, once more compelled to stiffen the back of the Austro-Hungarians, transferred fifteen German divisions from the Western to the Eastern Front during the struggle. Fighting continued until the end of September but, although Brusilov took 450,000 prisoners, he was not able to extend his first gains. His army had, by that time, been bled dry of men and matériel.

After Brusilov's initial success, Rumania entered the war. She had been wavering between war and peace for many months; France had tried to overcome her hesitation while Russia, politically antipathetic to her and convinced of her military weakness, had argued that Rumania neutral was worth more than Rumania belligerent. But in the summer of 1916 France insisted that Rumanian aid was needed to help relieve pressure on the Allies along the Somme. Russia, represented by the bungling Stürmer, agreed and, when Rumania began to haggle over terms, bullied her into an immediate decision. Late in August the ill-prepared Rumanians, with little support from Russia, declared war and advanced into Transylvania. Again the Germans rushed aid to Austria-Hungary and, by December, 1916, had pushed into Bucharest.

Thus the fighting on the Eastern Front during 1916 ended in disaster for Rumania and in a stalemate along the Russian lines. But it had brought relief to the Allies, for the Eastern fighting had taken the attention of eighty-three divisions of the enemy. The Russian army, however, was left in a torpor from which it could not recover. Yet the Russian military leaders, displaying the same generosity and lack of prudence that had characterized them since 1914, agreed in September, 1916, to prepare a new offensive for the spring of 1917 to coincide with an Allied offensive on the Western Front.

[1] Many of these troops were Czechs, Slovaks, and Serbs, who had no wish to fight for the Habsburg Empire and deserted in great numbers to the Russians.

On the eve of revolution

MILITARY EXHAUSTION.   During the period between August, 1914, and the end of 1916, Russia had called to service more than 13 million men; and of these nearly 2 million had been killed and 4 million wounded, the Brusilov offensive alone having cost nearly a million casualties.[1] Proportionally Russia had not drawn as heavily on her manpower as had France, but she had felt the strain more severely. Her best troops had been used up, and the cadres of commissioned and noncommissioned officers had been so depleted that the problem of adequate leadership was even more serious than the shortage of reliable manpower for the ranks.

Still, the Russian army might have continued to be of some service if its morale had held. It is impossible to assess accurately the state of mind of the Russian army at the end of 1916, but scattered evidence indicates that there was an increasing apathy among the troops. Those near the rear, particularly, were beginning to show the effects of the growing disturbance on the home front. Desertions and failures to report for mobilization increased. Because of food shortages in the rear, many troops spent their time on foraging expeditions instead of on duty. Rumors that the Empress was a German agent and complaints that England and France were bleeding Russia spread and took hold. In October, 1916, two regiments of the Petrograd garrison which were called out to suppress a strike joined the strikers and fired on the police instead, necessitating the summoning of Cossacks to restore order.

Early in February, 1917, an Allied mission visited Petrograd to complete preparations for the promised spring offensive, persuaded itself in spite of evidence that the Russians would hold, and optimistically went home—two weeks before the revolution broke out.

ECONOMIC CRISIS.   By the winter of 1916 the economic pinch was being felt everywhere in Russia. The government had been covering most of its war costs by loans, totaling over $21 billion, of which more than $4 billion were borrowed abroad. In addition it had begun to print paper money which could not be converted to gold and which, therefore, declined in real value. Those efforts were accompanied by a slow but steady fall in the national income and a steady increase in the portion of the income devoted to military needs. The common man began seriously to feel the effects of all this in 1916. By the end of that year the cost of living had

---

[1] These figures are only estimates, for available statistics on Russian casualties during World War I are not reliable.

risen by nearly 300 per cent over that of 1914 while wages had increased by less than 100 per cent. The urban-dweller consequently found himself unable to maintain even a meager standard of living.

Food shortages were widespread, resulting not only from the breakdown in the system of distribution but also from forces at work in the countryside. In the first year of the war the agricultural production had held up; but the loss of Poland, the conscription of peasant labor, and the requisition of horses for the cavalry and cattle for the feeding of troops caused a decided decrease in the volume of production. As compensation for this decrease, however, there was a virtual cessation of food exports from Russia. The real problem was to get the food from the field to the consumer. The peasants became increasingly reluctant to sell grain to the government, which had practically ended free trade in grain and sought to buy it at prices fixed without consideration of the fall in the value of money. Transportation difficulties had increased also. Railroads were required to carry in 1916 nearly twice the volume of goods they had carried in 1913—and that with depleted and obsolescent rolling stock.

The government's attempts to overcome the difficulties in distribution were energetic but insufficient. It accumulated limited stocks of food and goods but turned distribution over to local authorities who, while often conscientious, were also often inefficient. No systematic policy of rationing and price control was put into effect, and long queues formed in the cities to compete for inadequate supplies at more than adequate prices. Rumors of corruption and theft by officials—often justified—were common, and queues often turned into angry, window-smashing mobs.

RENEWAL OF RESTIVENESS. Military and economic exhaustion in themselves did not produce the revolution, although they did help to bring about the mood for it. Other countries at this time were able to maintain internal stability under worse conditions than those in Russia; and Russia herself had ridden out worse storms during the Time of Troubles and the period of the Napoleonic invasion. But in 1916 the bonds which had previously held the people in check—throne, Church, and tradition—were losing their binding powers. It was a situation that had been in the making since the Revolution of 1905. The government's power of recuperation from that outbreak had tided it over till 1914, when the war temporarily rallied the people to its support. Now the old restiveness was returning, supplemented by additional complaints and aggravated by widespread suffering. Convinced of the futility of dependence upon the government, the people were ready to resort to bolder measures than ever before. No symptom of the general restiveness was more ominous than the continued strike movement. At the end of 1915 strikes affected 539,000 workers, a number that grew to 961,000 in 1916.

In Russian Turkestan and in the Steppe Provinces restiveness produced revolt in 1916. The occasion was the government's order for the conscription of the Moslem natives (hitherto exempt from military service) for labor service at the front. Most of the rebels were subdued within a few months by Russian troops, but a few were still fighting when the revolution came. Although the revolt had little effect on the spirit of interior Russia, where the censorship prevented the spread of information about it, it may be called the first spark of the actual fire of revolution.

PREPARATION FOR REVOLT. The decline of morale in 1916 was not the work of the revolutionaries, but it helped to condition minds for the reception of revolutionary agitation and propaganda which were under preparation by a small antiwar group, the Bolsheviks.

Lenin, the acknowledged leader of the Bolsheviks, had been in Galicia, close to the Russian border, when the war broke out. Arrested there by the Austrian police as an enemy alien, he was permitted to leave for neutral Switzerland, where he spent the next years planning Bolshevik strategy. In September, 1914, he prepared a statement known as the *Seven Theses on the War*, presenting the essentials of Bolshevik policy for the war. The *Seven Theses* denounced the international organization of the socialists, the Socialist International, for failing to rally its members against the war and declared that the task of Social Democrats everywhere was to transform the war into a revolution directed at the rulers of each country. In September, 1915, antiwar socialists from several countries gathered at Zimmerwald, in Switzerland, to unite their efforts. The Russians included the Bolsheviks Lenin and Zinoviev, the Mensheviks Martov and Axelrod, Leon Trotsky (who stood somewhere between the antiwar Mensheviks and the Bolsheviks), and representatives of the extremist antiwar wing of the SR's. A future Bolshevik leader, Karl Radek, represented the Polish SD's. Lenin wanted the conference to agree that the immediate task was to turn the war into a civil, revolutionary war, but the majority voted for less drastic action. Denouncing the war as imperialist, they called upon the workers of Europe to struggle for immediate peace "without indemnities and without annexations," a peace which would permit each nationality to determine its own government. Before adjournment, the representatives at the conference formed the Zimmerwald Union, an informal organization to permit continued collaboration among the left wing, antiwar groups.

DISCONTENT AT COURT. The disaffection among the people at large was matched by a feeling of desperation among the leaders in Russian public life. While the Emperor remained at Mogilev, the government drifted without purpose or leadership under the ministrations of the Empress and Rasputin. In other countries powerful leaders like Clemenceau and Lloyd George were rallying their wavering peoples, but in Russia a succession of bumbling and often irresponsible ministers involved themselves in court intrigues and did virtually nothing about the country's most imminent dangers, defeat and revolution.

At the beginning of November, 1916, a new session of the Duma opened with members in a rebellious mood. Milyukov led the attack of the Progressive Bloc; in a ringing speech, he enumerated the mistakes, errors, and crimes of the government, tagging each accusation with the question, "Is this stupidity or treason?" He was seconded by other deputies of both the right and the left. Premier Stürmer, who was suspected of pro-German tendencies, was the target of the open attack, but it was clear that the words of abuse were meant also for the Empress. The government responded ambivalently; it prohibited publication of the denunciatory speeches made in the Duma but permitted Stürmer to resign in the face of attack. Neither gesture was successful. The prohibited speeches were illegally reproduced and circulated in millions of copies throughout the country, providing further material for the discontented. And the removal of Stürmer did nothing to allay the anger of the Duma, since his successor as premier, the ineffectual Alexander Trepov, had neither its respect nor its confidence. Moreover, Trepov retained as Minister of Interior the much reviled Alexander Protopopov, who was known to be under Rasputin's influence. Relations between Trepov and the Duma speedily reached a critical point, and on December 30 he prorogued that body until late in January, 1917.

The following morning the public learned that Rasputin had been assassinated. The deed had been done during the night by the Emperor's cousin Grand Duke Dmitri, Prince Felix Yusupov, and the reactionary Duma member Vladimir Purishkevich, in the hope that his death would result in a change in governmental policy. The news was generally received with joy, but the Empress was prostrate. The Emperor, despite his wife's feelings, refrained from punishing the murderers, knowing that such action would be impolitic at the time. Rasputin's death actually did little to improve the situation. The Empress, supported by the reactionary element at court, continued to dominate her weak-willed husband. And the changes which were made were far from conciliatory. Trepov, weak as he was, found himself unwanted at court and was forced to resign at the end of December. In his place was put the 66-year-old Prince Nicholas Golitsyn, who had little to recommend him except the favor of the Empress. One of his first acts was to postpone, at the Emperor's behest, the new meeting of the Duma from January 25 to February 27, an act which stirred up further resentment against the government.

These and other unfortunate occurrences opened the new year with intimations of disaster. Disaffection in the army and among the civilians was now being regularly reported by the secret police. Many generals and high officials were considering plans for a coup which would replace Nicholas by one of the grand dukes. At a New Year's reception in the Winter Palace, Rodzyanko courageously informed the Emperor, who had returned from Mogilev for a visit, of the state of chaos in the government and of the widening lack of confidence. Sir George Buchanan, the British ambassador, ignoring protocol, warned Nicholas a few days later that the government was losing the support of the people and the Duma. Several members of the imperial family expressed similar sentiments in a joint letter to their exalted relative. Yet Nicholas, disregarding the many signs of a revolution from below and of a coup d'état from above, calmly planned to return to army headquarters, apparently convinced that matters would take care of themselves.

TWENTY-THREE / THE REVOLUTION OF 1917

I t is significant that the three major periods of change after 1800—those beginning in 1861, 1905, and 1917—were the aftermaths of military reversals. Just as the military misfortunes suffered betfeen 1914 and 1917 were far greater than those experienced between 1853 and 1856 and between 1904 and 1905, so the changes which began in 1917 were far greater than those which began in 1861 and 1905.

The Revolution of 1917 was, in fact, the most radical event in more than a thousand years of Russian history and the greatest political and social upheaval in modern times. It was the first successful mass effort to transform the entire society and government of Russia by the use of force, which Karl Marx had called the midwife of new societies. One of the big problems which the Russian people had to face, even while the revolution was in progress, was just what form the changes were to take. Some hoped that their country would follow the example of Western countries and become a liberal, democratic state; others placed the achievement of social and economic justice above civil and political liberties. To resolve that problem required much planning and activity beyond that which made possible the overthrow of the imperial dynasty.

Political phase of the revolution

RECOGNITION OF THREAT. By the beginning of 1917 many officials were becoming fearful of immediate trouble. They saw that the increase in the number of food riots and strikes in Petrograd, with its 400,000 factory workers, was about to reach serious proportions; and that the opening of the Duma, scheduled for February 27, might be the signal for increased disturbances. At last, they began to take steps to forestall an outbreak. Protopopov, hoping to weaken organized labor, ordered the arrest of the labor delegates on the War Industries Committee. The Petrograd garrison was brought up to a strength of 160,000 men. Police, Cossacks, and other troops were prepared for action. Protopopov questioned the reliability of some of the troops; but he was assured by General Khabalov, Commander of the Petrograd Military District, that the men would "do their duty" when called upon. Still the Minister was so apprehensive about the whole situation that he urged the Emperor to defer his trip to Mogilev. Nicholas refused to do so; but when he left, on March 7, he promised to make his stay a short one and to return within ten days.

When the Duma opened, the expected riots did not materialize. But the dangers remained: the Petrograd populace, their mood exacerbated by the government's security measures, continued restive; and the spirit of the deputies was one of turbulent opposition.

OUTBREAK.   On March 8 restiveness gave way to popular demonstrations which marked that day as the first of the revolutionary outburst. Great crowds were brought onto the streets of Petrograd by three events: a scheduled Woman's Day celebration organized by the socialists, food rioting, and a lockout of workers by the management of the Putilov Works as a result of a wage dispute. Gradually the various crowds coalesced in angry demonstrations against the government. They were beginning to realize their oneness of purpose.

On the following day the street crowds were swelled by nearly 200,000 strikers who had come out in sympathy with the Putilov workers. But there was still little violence. The crowds had formed in the workers' Vyborg district of the city, and the police were able to prevent their moving toward the government offices and the Tauride Palace, where the Duma was meeting. The mood was like that of 1905: crowds sang the *Marseillaise*, intoned curses on the autocracy, and demanded bread and freedom. On March 10 the number of strikers increased, students left the universities to join the crowds, and municipal services began to close down. The next day, on orders from the Emperor, troops were used in several areas to disperse the crowds. At the same time the government decided that the Duma should be dissolved. Seeing the turn of events, Rodzyanko sent Nicholas II a warning that danger could be avoided only if the government made a conciliatory move. But the Emperor was unconvinced that there was an emergency, as his statement to an aide indicated: "This fat Rodzyanko has written me some nonsense, to which I will not even reply."

ARMED SUPPORT. A critical point of the revolution was reached on March 12, the day on which the Duma was to be dissolved. On the evening of the previous day the men of the training detachment of the Volynsky Regiment, which had been employed against the crowds, had decided to refuse to attack them again. Now, disregarding the orders of their officers to disperse the crowds, they marched off to join the demonstrators in the Vyborg district and, on the way, persuaded other regiments to join them. Such an act was possible because most of the troops in Petrograd were untrained men, fresh from civilian life and at heart sympathetic with the crowds. Even the guards regiments were composed of green youths, for the original complements had been sent to the front. It was a situation favorable to the success of the revolution. After the Volynsky Regiment had gone over to the revolutionaries, General Khabalov found that he had no reliable troops; and on the following day he quietly stole away. The government no longer had any armed strength in the capital.

Meanwhile the Duma had listened to the order of dissolution and closed its session on the morning of the 12th. Its members, however, after learning of the collapse of the military in the city, remained in the Tauride Palace and elected a committee, known as the Temporary Committee, to aid in the restoration of order. And during these tumultuous events another organization of importance was formed; the labor delegates of the War Industries Committee, left-wing Duma deputies, members of labor organizations, and representatives of the rebel troops met in the Tauride Palace and, following the tradition of 1905, formed the Soviet of Workers' and Soldiers' Deputies, to give organizational expression to the wishes of the Petrograd crowds.

Unchallenged, the crowds now surged through the streets, breaking into prisons, releasing the inmates and replacing them by government ministers and police officials. The Emperor, finally realizing the extent of the lawlessness and the possibility of its spreading, ordered fresh troops to march on the city. The fresh troops came—and fraternized with the rebels. After March 15 no further attempts were made to send troops. The conflict had cost about 1,300 casualties on both sides.

Petrograd in 1917, like Paris in 1789, was the weathervane of the revolution. The rest of the country followed its example as soon as the news of its activities could spread. Everywhere, the garrisons went over to the revolution, and officials and officers prudently left the scene if they could. Authority in the various cities was taken over, with little violence, by self-appointed committees of revolutionaries, in which soldiers were predominant.

FORMATION OF THE PROVISIONAL GOVERNMENT. As matters

stood, there was no single authority in Russia. At the front the discipline of the army held, but in the cities the imperial authority had disappeared. In Petrograd the Temporary Committee had a measure of legal and moral authority while the Soviet had behind it the physical authority of armed masses.

From the moment of its creation the Petrograd Soviet acted as if it possessed governmental authority and began to publish orders in its organ, the newspaper *Izvestia* (News); yet it did not want the responsibility inherent in political power. Its Executive Committee, in which the left-wing Mensheviks held the balance of power, believed that this was the long-awaited bourgeois revolution, whose function was to create a democratic, capitalist republic. And the task of implementing the revolution, it believed, should be left to the liberal non-Socialist parties represented in the Duma, while the Soviet should stand to one side, acting as "the watchdog of the revolution" but not entering any government which would be formed. The Bolshevik minority in the Executive Committee demanded the creation of a revolutionary provisional government led by socialists, but they had little influence.

The Temporary Committee was thus in a position to take the political initiative in forming a new government. Its members realized, however, that it could not go far without the support of the Petrograd Soviet. Milyukov, acting for the Committee, arrived at a working agreement with the Soviet whereby the Temporary Committee would form the Provisional Government, in which the Soviet would not participate. According to the agreement, the Provisional Government was to exercise executive authority until an elected constituent assembly could decide on the permanent form of government to be established. It would immediately establish full civil liberty, provide for the election of local administrative bodies, and abolish all legal restriction based on class, nationality, or religion. And since the power of the Soviet depended in large part on its support by the revolutionary troops in the capital, Milyukov agreed that they be neither disarmed nor sent out of the city. No agreement was reached on the further prosecution of the war nor on agrarian reforms, and full discussion of those problems was postponed.

The Temporary Committee was now free to act, not only because of the agreement with the Soviet but also because of the disappearance of the Council of Ministers; Prince Golitsyn had resigned during the revolt, and the other ministers had departed without a formal farewell. On March 16 the assumption of office by the Provisional Government was announced.

The members of the new government, selected by the Temporary Committee, were representative of the Progressive Bloc. They included Prince George Lvov, leader of the Union of Zemstvos, as Premier; Alexander Guchkov, as Minister of War and Navy; Paul Milyukov, as Minister of Foreign Affairs; and Alexander Kerensky, as Minister of Justice. Kerensky, leader of the Labor Group in the Fourth Duma, member of the right wing of the SR's, and Vice-Chairman of the Petrograd Soviet, was the only socialist in the government; the Soviet permitted him to enter for the purpose of handling liaison.

END OF THE IMPERIAL DYNASTY.   There still remained the question of what to do about the Emperor. Nicholas, like an actor offstage waiting for his cue, was at Pskov, en route from Mogilev. He had no understanding of the situation in the capital and believed that he had but to make a few concessions to regain popularity. However, even the most ardent monarchists were convinced that the monarchy could be saved only by Nicholas' abdication. And that was the recommendation of the Temporary Committee. On March 15, after being told that his generals counselled abdication, the Emperor agreed to the recommendation and signed the act of abdication, transferring the throne to his brother, Grand Duke Michael. He agreed also to the appointment of Prince Lvov as Premier.

Grand Duke Michael, aware of the dangerous antimonarchical sentiment in Petrograd, refused to accept the crown; and on March 16 both his renunciation and the abdication of Nicholas were published. A week later the Provisional Government, under pressure from the Petrograd Soviet, placed Nicholas and his family under arrest, with the intention of permitting them to leave later for England, where they had been offered asylum. Russia was still technically a monarchy—but without a monarch. The Romanov dynasty, which had assumed power under a Michael, had now lost that power through another Michael.

The Provisional Government on trial

STATUS OF THE NEW GOVERNMENT.   The legality of the Provisional Government was based on the Emperor's agreement to Prince Lvov's appointment as Premier and strengthened by the fact that the army commanders took the oath of loyalty to it. And that legality was further confirmed by the immediate diplomatic recognition accorded it by the United States, England, France, and Italy. It was, nonetheless, a revolutionary government; it had promised reforms which, according to the Fundamental Laws of Russia, could not be effected without the consent of the Duma, the State Council, and the Emperor. From its inception it was in an anomalous position: although it had been brought into being by revolution, its members represented middle-class liberalism. On the whole, they favored the establishment of a democratic, constitutional monarchy and the vigorous continuation of the war. But they opposed any social revolution even while recognizing the fact that the workers and peasants must be given consideration.

Whatever authority the Provisional Government had was largely moral authority. The imperial administration and the police had disappeared; the troops in the rear had shaken off discipline, and that of the troops at the front was uncertain. From the beginning the stability of the new government depended upon its relationship with the soviets—in Petrograd and elsewhere in the country, for they represented the masses. Even the soviets were far from stable, depending as they did upon the revolutionary soldiers and armed civilians whose mood was far more militant than that of the government and often more militant than that of the soviets. Yet the government could take some comfort from the fact that the soviets did promise their support—albeit with a noticeable lack of warmth.

It was Alexander Kerensky's role to preserve harmony between the Provisional Government and the Petrograd Soviet. He received that role not only because he was the only socialist in the government and an officer of the Soviet but also because he was personally suited to it. The other members of the government did not have so much to recommend them to the people. Many were suspect as members of the wealthy or conservative classes: for example, Guchkov was an industrialist; Prince Lvov was an aristocrat; and Milyukov, once considered a radical, was now looked upon as a conservative, the country's mood having shifted far to the left of him. Kerensky, however, was more widely acceptable; and his eloquence, however sentimental and turgid it may appear in retrospect, was perfectly suited to the excited mood of the time.

INITIAL REFORMS.   The government's task was three-fold: the execution of the reforms that had been promised, the re-establishment of order and authority on the home front, and the preparation for the combined military offensive which had been promised at Chantilly at the end of 1916. It was a formidable program, the most pressing part of which was the execution of the reforms.

By the end of April the government had fulfilled with admirable dispatch its promises of domestic reforms. In summary, they present an impressive catalog of adjusted wrongs. A general amnesty was declared for all persons convicted of political and religious offenses. Political émigrés were invited to return home as free men. All restrictive legislation with respect to non-Russians and non-Orthodox was abolished. Class privileges were ended. The death penalty was abolished. The Constitution of Finland was restored. The Poles were informed that the government favored the creation of an independent Poland (including all regions in which Poles were a majority), which would be joined to Russia only by a voluntary military union. The eight-hour day for factories was instituted. Civil liberties were promulgated. Local officials were replaced by Zemstvo officials until local elections could take place. The promise of the early election of a constituent assembly was published, and the peasants were promised that the agrarian question would be considered by that assembly.

A liberal, democratic regime had come into existence. Prince Lvov declared, "We should consider ourselves the happiest of men for our generation finds itself in the happiest period of Russian history."

HAZARDS TO BE OVERCOME.   The promulgation of fundamental liberties and the removal of onerous restrictions were well received by most sections of the Russian population. The extreme right disappeared momentarily from the political scene, and liberals and socialists moved for a while in a spirit of good will generated by the victory over the autocracy. But there was still no genuine internal peace. The roots of unrest were many, and they reached out to sources which could not be quickly eradicated.

The success of the Provisional Government and its ability to fulfill Russia's promises to the Allies depended upon its establishment of a firm administration and its restoration of the economy. To attain those ends, it needed solid backing; it needed the assurance that all, without exception, would accept the status quo, postpone further demands, submit to authority, and work without question and without food if necessary. Even if that assurance were gained, extraordinarily good fortune would be required to re-establish financial stability, unsnarl the railroads, secure necessary raw materials and food supplies, and get needed munitions from the Allies. But the situation around the government was far from favorable to such undertakings. Guchkov summarized its position when he declared,

> The Provisional Government possesses no real power and its orders
> are executed only in so far as this is permitted by the Soviet of
> Workers' and Soldiers' Deputies, which holds in its hands the most

important elements of actual power, such as troops, railroads, postal and telegraph service.

In the provinces the authority of the government was nominal not only because the soviets in many cities looked to the Petrograd Soviet for leadership rather than to the government but also because the local officials
designated by the Provisional Government proved too conservative for
the masses.

Another factor working against the development of administrative authority was the resurgence of nationalism in the non-Russian border regions, where the revolution released movements for immediate attainment
of national rights. In most cases, the movements were not for independence
but for political autonomy in a Russian federal state. In Latvia, Georgia,
and the Ukraine, nationalist groups took over the local administration
and began to press Petrograd for recognition of their national rights; and
their example was widely followed.

Administrative difficulties were matched by economic difficulties. The
war economy required much state control, and the weakening of that control negated the wisest economic policies formulated in Petrograd; decrees
alone could not move locomotives nor bring grain to the market. The
government needed particularly the co-operation of labor and peasant organizations, but that was not forthcoming.

The factory workers were radical, hungry and impatient with delays.
They expected immediate benefits from the revolution—shorter hours, improvement in living standards, and an enhanced status for their unions.
The trade union movement blossomed rapidly after March 8 as did also
conflicts between capital and labor. Strikes for higher wages, for closed
shops, minimum wages, and vacations with pay were met in many cases
by lockouts. This struggle between labor and capital, the continued shortages of raw materials, and the decline of labor discipline and employer confidence resulted in a rapid drop in industrial production.

In the countryside the situation was equally grave. Usually the peasants had followed the news of the revolution by revamping their cantonal
and village committees or electing new ones, which ignored or obeyed the
representatives of the Provisional Government as their fancy dictated. That,
of course, added difficulties to the government's task of collecting grain
to feed the cities and the army; and on March 25 it was forced, in order
to insure a full supply of grain, to declare the grain trade a state monopoly
and to order that grain be sold only to government representatives at fixed
prices. The peasants, having already felt the painful effect of the "scissors"

—the disparity between high prices for manufactured goods and low, fixed prices for grain—would not be coerced. Many either held back their grain or sold it on the black market, thus helping to reduce the legal supply. The government's grain policy was not the only prod to peasant discontent; an even stronger one was the peasants' desire to appropriate the landlords' fields. Being restless and of no mind to wait for the constituent assembly's consideration of redistribution, they began to take direct action. At first they burned a few manor houses and drove out or killed a few landowners and managers; but once the example was set, the practice increased with alarming rapidity. The government's policy of wait-and-see was no longer of any avail.

LOSS OF ARMED SUPPORT.   While the most feverish activities of the Provisional Government were being directed toward preparations for the new offensive, the army, which was to execute the offensive, was visibly melting away. This was hardly surprising, since the success of the revolution had been assured by the collapse of army discipline in the rear; but it presented the government with another embarrassing problem.

The focal point of the military breakdown was Petrograd, where 160,000 soldiers had successfully defied their superiors and refused to acknowledge military authority. In order to retain the backing of the Petrograd garrison for the cause of the revolution, the Petrograd Soviet issued on March 14 its famous "Order Number 1," which virtually ended military discipline in that garrison. Its provisions reversed the entire system of disciplinary control: units were to elect committees to control the issue of arms and serve as grievance boards; troops were to obey only those government orders which were not in conflict with orders of the Soviet; and traditional signs of respect for officers were to be curtailed in some cases, abolished in others. In short, officers would be deprived of any real authority over the troops, and the authority of the government was to be limited. "Order Number 1" and other declarations of the Soviet, although intended only for the Petrograd garrison, were followed throughout the army. Soldiers elected committees which carried on endless debates with the officers; they refused to submit to customary discipline; and often they paid off old scores by disobedience, insults, beatings, and occasionally by lynchings. After the issuance of "Order Number 1," neither the government nor the military command felt capable of taking the necessary steps to restore discipline, knowing that such steps could quickly promote wholesale mutiny; instead, in April, they accepted the inevitable by sanctioning the election of soldiers' committees. Such committees, for which both enlisted men and officers were permitted to vote, were formed in all units. Some were dominated by revolutionaries, but many proved more conservative than the men whom they represented and acted as restraints on violence. In any case, the over-all discipline was almost broken.

The disintegration of the army was further hastened by the nationalist movement. Caught up by the spirit of that movement, national units began to form throughout the army as Poles, Letts, Georgians, Armenians, and Ukrainians left their regular units to join soldiers of their respective nationalities in the formation of new ones. These national units were extremely responsive to the demands of their peoples and increasingly apathetic to orders from Petrograd.

Finally, the army was beset by a wave of desertion. The soldiers were tired of fighting and even of service, and the decline in discipline made desertion easy for them. The agrarian movement also accounted for many desertions, for soldiers were anxious to get home and share in the anticipated division of landlord lands. The records show that Russia had an army of 6.9 million men in the first part of 1917; of that number it is estimated that more than 2 million deserted—or, as some of them put it, "demobilized themselves"—during the year.

HARDENING OF POLITICAL DIFFERENCES. Among the first acts of the Provisional Government were the opening of political prisons and the summoning home of political exiles. Soon a jubilant procession had begun. Out of a Moscow prison came the Polish pro-Bolshevik Felix Dzerzhinsky; from Siberia, the Bolsheviks Stalin and Leon Kamenev; from Western Europe, Kropotkin, Plekhanov, and Breshkovskaya; and from America, Trotsky and Nicholas Bukharin. In Switzerland Russian socialist émigrés made preparations to return, but found themselves frustrated by the refusal of Anglo-French authorities to permit transit through Allied territory. Among them, Lenin, anxious to get to the scene of action as soon as possible, discussed his problem with the Germans; and they, thinking that as a dangerous agitator he might weaken the war spirit in Russia, agreed to permit passage to him, his wife, Karl Radek, Gregory Zinoviev, and a group of non-Bolsheviks through Germany to Sweden. From Sweden, Lenin went immediately to Petrograd, where, upon his arrival on April 16, 1917, large crowds welcomed him in a reception demonstrating the still powerful spirit of the revolution. Nicholas Chkheidze, the Menshevik Chairman of the Petrograd Soviet, in making the welcoming speech, expressed the hope that Lenin would join in the common task of "protecting" the revolution.

Chkheidze's hope was a timely one, for the unity of purpose behind the revolution was weak and daily growing weaker. The leaders of the several political groups could not or would not agree on either the nature or the purpose of the revolution.

The liberals, among whom the Cadets were most prominent, believed that the establishment of a democratic political regime, the enactment of moderate labor legislation, and the distribution of the landowners' lands among the peasants on the basis of adequate compensation to the former owners represented the full measure of what the revolution should bring. The Cadets had been monarchists; but after the abdication of Nicholas their party congress, meeting in Petrograd at the end of March, 1917, accepted the idea of a republic. With respect to the war, they argued for complete co-operation with the other Allies.

The right Socialist Revolutionaries and right Mensheviks were the moderates of the period. Like the Cadets, these two factions sought to establish a common front for the completion of the war and believed that the execution of fundamental reforms other than those establishing civil and political liberty should be postponed until a more suitable time—preferably after the ending of the war, certainly after the meeting of the constituent assembly.

The left wings of the Socialist Revolutionaries and Mensheviks, which in the early part of 1917 spoke for the largest number of peasants, soldiers, and workers, considered the revolution in progress a bourgeois one, which they would support but not lead. They gave their somewhat doubtful blessings to the Provisional Government and assumed the position of watchful critics who could use their powerful mass support to prevent its backsliding. Like many socialists throughout the world they agitated for an early termination of the war and a settlement assuring "peace without indemnities and annexations, on the basis of self-determination," but they opposed immediate Russian withdrawal.

The position of the Bolsheviks before Lenin's return, a position shared by some extreme SR's, has already been stated. Lenin's arrival brought a stiffening in their attitudes and program. His study of the lessons of the Revolution of 1905, the World War, and the first events of the Revolution of 1917 in the light of his conception of Marxism had brought him to a point of view which was to influence the further course of the revolution. He was convinced that capitalistic society throughout the world had reached its final stage, imperialism, out of which had grown the World War, a struggle between competing alliances of imperialist states for the redivision of the world. The war, in his opinion, would bring a worldwide revolution, led by Marxian socialists and effected by the workers in alliance with the poorer peasants. As for the March Revolution, he asserted that it was only the first stage of the revolution—the bourgeois stage. It would be followed by a second stage—the transfer of power from the Provisional Government to the soviets, who represented the workers, poorer peasants, and soldiers; and the soviets would answer the immediate mass demand for "peace, bread, and freedom." This second stage of the revolution would not immediately bring about socialism but would bring certain advances: confiscation of all landed estates; nationalization of all lands and their distribution among the peasants; nationalization of all banks; and abolition of the bureaucracy, police, and army (to be replaced by elected officials and a people's militia).

According to his plan, it would be the function of the Bolsheviks to lead in the transition to the second stage by gaining a majority in the soviets and then ousting the Provisional Government. To achieve this task the Bolsheviks should cut the still tenuous links with the Menshevik Social Democrats and, to make the separation more absolute, change the name of their party from the Russian Social Democratic Labor Party (Bolsheviks) to the Russian Communist Party. He believed that this party could, by proper leadership and propaganda, win a majority in the soviets and proceed with the program he outlined. He believed, further, that the extension of the revolution in Russia would be accompanied by social revolutions in other countries, leading ultimately to the worldwide victory of socialism.

Lenin's views were the subject of much controversy among the Bolsheviks after his return; but at a conference of Bolshevik leaders, meeting in the latter part of April and the early part of May, his position was accepted.[1] The Bolsheviks were then ready to take up the task of destroying the Provisional Government. Most non-Bolsheviks were inclined to ridicule the uncompromising, fanatical Lenin, who, with his small band of followers, seemed to be baying at the moon. Actually he was assessing the mood of the masses more accurately than were any of his opponents, and he was therefore better prepared to use it to advantage.

MAY CRISIS. The Provisional Government's determination to continue the war brought it to its first major crisis. Urged by France and England to take a strong stand for war until victory and harried by the Petrograd Soviet and by socialists throughout the country to support a negotiated peace "without annexations and without indemnities," the Provisional Gov-

---

[1] The Bolsheviks did not change the name of their party at this time; that remained to be done later, in March, 1918.

ernment sought to satisfy both the Allies and the socialists. As a gesture of appeasement to the Soviet, it issued on April 22, a statement to the Russian people, which, while avoiding the explicit assurance that Russia had no desire to annex foreign territory, asserted that it was not the aim of "free Russia to dominate other peoples." The Soviet then demanded that the government relay this statement to the Allied governments as an indication of Russia's anti-imperialist sentiments, and that was done on May 1. But at Milyukov's insistence and with the consent of the government, an explanatory note was attached to the statement, declaring that Russia would carry out all her obligations to her allies. When the text of the explanatory note was published two days later, there was a cloudburst of anger upon the government, for the note was taken correctly to mean that Russia expected to abide by the agreements to partition the Ottoman Empire. Socialist speakers denounced Milyukov and his alleged imperialism, and crowds of armed soldiers demonstrated before the Marinsky Palace, the governmental headquarters. The Provisional Government, aware of its instability in the face of popular opposition against which it could not use armed force even if it wished (since the soldiers of Petrograd took orders, if at all, from the Soviet), decided to reorganize itself and strengthen its position by including representatives of the Soviet.

The Executive Committee of the Petrograd Soviet agreed to end the policy of abstention from the government and accept the proffered offices. Milyukov and Guchkov resigned, and five socialists were added to the Provisional Government, among them the leading SR, Victor Chernov, as Minister of Agriculture, and the prominent Menshevik Iraklii Tsereteli, as Minister of Posts and Telegraphs. In this cabinet, formed on May 19, Lvov remained as Premier, and Kerensky became Minister of War and Navy. With six socialists and ten nonsocialists (including four Cadets), the new cabinet was heterogeneous, but its inclusion of the representatives from the Soviet seemed to promise greater co-operation from that body. Its socialist members were instructed by the Soviet to push for a peace without indemnities and annexation but, at the same time, to support preparations for the coming offensive.

JULY OFFENSIVE. The preparation for a new military offensive, in view of the breakdown of discipline, was futile; but it had become a matter of honor, a gesture in defense of the position of the government at home and abroad. Kerensky, aspiring to the role of a latter-day Danton, "the organizer of victory," sought to infuse a fighting spirit into the civilians and the troops with his fiery oratory. And although few generals believed that the army was ready, a special force of 200,000 picked troops was sent to the southwestern front for an attack on the demoralized Austro-Hungarians. On July 1 they began the attack near the Dniester River. The first assaults were successful, but they took a great toll of the best men left in the army; and when German reserves appeared, the remaining Russians fled without a semblance of order. The Germans did not push on because their High Command was preparing for and already participating in more important actions elsewhere and felt confident that there was little to fear from the crumbling Russian army. For tactical reasons, however, they undertook to capture Riga, and on September 3 they were successful. The much publicized offensives thus ended in failure and proved what was already clear to many—that the army could not be restored to fighting trim. Within Russia the failure, of course, added fuel to the opposition.

JULY CRISIS.   The preparations for the offensive not only failed to rouse support for the government but also failed to divert attention from political problems. Within the Provisional Government, the socialists and nonsocialists had failed at co-operation and were moving farther and farther apart. The socialist members were the source of disharmony; torn between the satisfaction of the radical demands of their followers and the maintenance of harmony with their nonsocialist colleagues, they achieved neither aim.

Meanwhile the authority of the soviets had continued to grow. The Petrograd Soviet, a mammoth deliberative body af about 3,000 delegates elected by the workers and soldiers of the city, had become the nerve center of soviets throughout the country. And the number was steadily growing; at an All-Russian Conference of Soviets in Petrograd on April 11, delegates from 138 local soviets had been present in addition to those from numerous army units. To provide proper leadership and direction for so many units the Petrograd Soviet had found that its large Executive Committee was too cumbersome and, in April, had formed an inner bureau of twenty-four members to perform the major executive work.

The Bolsheviks' efforts at gaining leadership in the soviets were at first far from successful. At the first Congress of Soviets, which opened in Petrograd on June 16, only 105 of the delegates were Bolsheviks while 248 were Mensheviks and 285 were SR's. However, the Bolsheviks with their extreme program were best able to capitalize on popular discontent, and their influence among factory workers and troops grew daily. One of the greatest dangers to their success lay in the fact that in many cities— and particularly in Petrograd—the organized workers and troops were on edge, armed and angry, anxious for positive action; and they were liable to break into violence if unwisely handled. The Bolsheviks' task was to gain leadership of these turbulent masses without setting off premature explosions or what Lenin called "playing at insurrections."

In July, after the reverses at the front, the Provisional Government, unable to give purposeful leadership, was fast losing its grip. The domestic situation was heavy with danger. Neither the leaders of the soviets nor the Bolsheviks wanted a popular outburst, but it came anyway. It began with a new crisis within the Provisional Government, when its four Cadet ministers resigned, on July 15, after learning that their socialist colleagues had agreed to some of the Ukrainian nationists' demands for autonomy. The resignation of the Cadets practically ended the coalition of the non-socialists and the socialists; and, while the socialists sought to repair the break, armed demonstrators in Petrograd demanded that it be made permanent and that the soviets take over governmental authority. Then, when the government ordered the recall to the front of the forty-year-old soldiers who had been furloughed to work on the farms, there were intimations of violence in some of the Petrograd regiments and elsewhere. On July 16, several military units in Petrograd decided to make an armed demonstration. And on the next day, ignoring the attempts of the Bolshevik leaders to prevent them, the restless soldiers, joined by 20,000 Kronstadt sailors and thousands of workers, marched on governmental and Soviet headquarters, demanding that the soviets assume power. Although there was no actual fighting at the time, there was much random shooting and looting.

The Bolshevik leadership was in a quandary: if they washed their hands of the demonstration, they might lose their hold on the crowds; and if they assumed leadership of a movement which would probably end in failure, they might be isolated and crushed. They finally decided on assuming leadership in the hope of ending the outbreak quickly. Once they had taken charge, many feared a repetition of the March Revolution. However, the fury of the armed crowds began to subside even before the Provisional Government could make its first countereffort, the release on July 17 of documents (later proven false) purporting to prove that Lenin and other Bolshevik leaders were German agents paid to foment an insurrection.[1] Still the documents served some purpose; their release hastened the calm-

---

[1] See George F. Kennan, "The Sisson Documents," *Journal of Modern History*, June 1956, 130-54.
  Though the documents released by the Provisional Government were false, there is other evidence, substantial and dependable, that Lenin accepted aid from the Germans. See Zbynek Zeman, ed., *Germany and the Revolution in Russia, 1915-1918* (London: Oxford University Press, 1958).

ing of the demonstrators and convinced the Preobrozhensky Guards Regiment that it should move against the crowds. When the last armed demonstrators dispersed to their factories and barracks, the government ordered the arrest of Lenin and other leaders. To evade arrest Lenin crossed the border into Finland, where he remained in hiding for several months.

That demonstration, known as the July Uprising, seemed to make an end of Bolshevik influence since the Bolsheviks were then tarred both as German agents and as irresponsible insurrectionaries. It served also as a spur to the Provisional Government. Hitherto dominated by a fear of seeming to disregard civil liberties and by an anxiety to refrain from violence of any kind, it now began to show more determination. Its immediate problem was to form a new coalition supported by the soviets as well as by the nonsocialists and yet capable of pursuing a co-operative and firm policy. Kerensky, who at the moment had both his usual audacity and a measure of popularity, decided to become Premier. He forced the rather weak Lvov out of office and, on August 7, formed a new coalition in which he assigned to himself the posts of Premier and of Minister of War and Navy. The Cadets were persuaded again to take four posts in the government, and moderate SR's and Mensheviks took the majority of the remaining ones. The Executive Committee of the Petrograd Soviet gave its support to the new coalition on the condition that the government take immediate action on the land question, hold elections for a constituent assembly within two months, and propose an inter-Allied conference on war aims. Kerensky and most of his associates, however, thought mainly in terms of restoring morale in preparation for new military efforts.

THE MOSCOW STATE CONFERENCE. Kerensky's enthusiasm created an illusion of bright prospects for the new coalition, but there was actually little to affirm it. Although the July Uprising had started a temporary popular trend to the right, the forces of disruption were still powerful. The SR and Menshevik leaders tried to keep their followers in hand, but the pressure on them was inexorable: they knew that they could not continue to support the Provisional Government much longer without losing their influence. On the other hand, the nonsocialist supporters of the coalition demanded greater firmness on the part of the government in restoring military discipline and in bringing labor unrest to an end; and army officers, industrialists, landlords and others were even more vigorous in urging firmness.

The government had the choice of moving to the left by ending the war and undertaking immediate agrarian and labor reforms or moving to the right by taking firm action against disorder and unrest. But, incapable of either choice, it simply made gestures in each direction. In the direction of firmness, it took punitive action against the Bolsheviks, restored the death penalty in the army and ordered workers (who gave little heed) to turn in their arms. In the direction of conciliation, Kerensky summoned a State Conference of representatives of all sections of the population, except the Bolsheviks, to meet in Moscow. In response to the summons, more than two thousand delegates from former Dumas, the soviets, trade unions, chambers of commerce, and co-operatives met in Moscow from August 25 to August 28. Kerensky made impassioned, if somewhat unconvincing, speeches to them, calling for unity. But there was no unity, rather a clear division of sentiment. When General Lavr Kornilov, the recently appointed Commander-in-Chief of the Army, spoke before the Conference in denunciation of the existing anarchy and disorder at the front and in the rear, he was cheered by the right while the left remained pointedly silent. And such evidence of disunity was repeated as speech followed speech for three days. The Bolsheviks, who were not at the conference, accentuated the discord by using their influence to call a one-day general strike in Moscow while the conference was in session.

KORNILOV'S ATTEMPTED COUP.   Following the Moscow State Conference, General Kornilov became the hero of the right. Army officers in despair over the collapse of the army, as well as all who deplored the power of the socialists, saw in him a possible savior of order as they conceived of it. He was not a monarchist; he simply wished to see the Provisional Government free of dependence upon the Soviet and powerful enough to restore order, renew the production of war matériel, and prepare the army for new battles. Among his advisers, however, were many who hoped to overthrow the Provisional Government and replace it with a right-wing government.

Politically inexperienced, he mistakenly believed that Kerensky was sympathetic to his aims and, therefore, began to prepare a military coup which would place Petrograd in the hands of reliable troops and make possible the changes he sought. He gathered several units of Cossacks and a unit of 1,500 Moslem cavalrymen (known as the Savage Division) for an attack on Petrograd, to be executed on September 9 with the aid of sympathetic officers inside the city. His plan was to disperse the Soviet, hang the Bolshevik leaders, and recast the government in such a way as to place supreme civil and military direction in his hands, reserving the Ministry of Justice for Kerensky. On September 8, Kerensky, in a telephone conversation with him, learned details of the plans and slyly promised his support. However the next morning, having informed his colleagues of the plot, Kerensky asked for and received full power to remove Kornilov and disrupt his plans.

When informed of his dismissal, Kornilov ignored it, as did most of his officers. The march on Petrograd began as planned. Immediately the Bolsheviks, Mensheviks, and SR's in the Petrograd Soviet formed a temporarily united front and began to organize the defense against the coup, while the masses and the revolutionary troops fell into line to help. With this support Kerensky's position improved immeasurably. While troops and armed workers in and around Petrograd prepared to meet the attack, he instructed railroad workers and telegraph operators along Kornilov's route from Mogilev to commit acts of sabotage to delay the approach. At the same time, Kornilov was discovering that he had a superfluity of sympathetic generals and a pitiful paucity of sympathetic troops. He felt that he could rely on a few of the Cossack regiments and the Savage Division, originally prepared for the attack; but his judgment proved wrong, for he was not taking into account one unusual type of weapon they were to encounter. The Savage Division, led by Prince Bagration, was within forty miles of the city by September 10, but, finding that rails leading to Petrograd had been torn up, was forced to stop at that point. And there the unexpected weapon appeared—propaganda. A Moslem delegation, including the grandson of the rebel Shamyl, had been sent by the Petrograd Soviet to argue their co-religionists out of further action. Their effort was successful, as was a similar effort with the Cossack divisions. Kornilov was thus effectively halted, and his attempted coup ended on September 12. Kerensky himself then assumed the post of Commander-in-Chief; and Kornilov, Denikin, and other generals were arrested.

Social phase of the Revolution

WEAKENING OF CONTROL.   The attempted coup of Kornilov drove the wedges of disunity deeper. The right was now discredited and Kerensky was forced to rely more and more on the soviets, while the masses who supported the soviets were constantly moving to the left. The country was rapidly passing out of control.

Among the peasants the demand for confiscation of the landlords' lands began more frequently to break out of the bounds of discussions and manifestoes. During 1917, there were 5,782 officially recorded instances of agrarian outbreaks, half of which took place in central Russia and the Volga region, where hatred of the landlords was greatest. They took expression in the stealing of grain from the landlords' fields, illegal cutting of timber, burning of manor houses, and occasional murders. The SR's, whose agrarian program was most attractive to them, succeeded in gaining and maintaining leadership among the peasants as they grew away from dependence on their communal and cantonal assemblies alone and formed Soviets of Peasants' Deputies. In May their soviets had sent 1,115 delegates—chiefly SR's— to a Congress of Soviets of Peasant Deputies in Petrograd, where they had demanded that all land belonging to landlords, the state, and the Church be divided among the peasants. The predominantly SR executive committee elected by the Congress soon found that it could not lead, but only follow, the unchecked agrarian movement sweeping through the land—a movement strengthened now by returning peasant soldiers. The government did little; in order to preserve the coalition with the nonsocialist elements it was dilatory about agrarian reform although the SR Minister of Agriculture, Victor Chernov, stressed the urgency of action. In September the violence and number of agrarian outbreaks began to increase, and in October nearly as many attacks on manor houses and landlords took place as in the previous eight months.

Of all the elements in the population, labor was the best organized, most radical, and most susceptible to Bolshevik persuasion. The trade unions grew steadily in membership—from nearly 1.5 million in July to more than 2 million in October. Their central organization, the All-Russian Trade Union Council, was divided among Bolsheviks, Mensheviks, and Socialist Revolutionaries; but the factory committees were dominated by Bolsheviks. During the summer and autumn of 1917 a small-scale civil war was waged in the factories; strikes, accompanied by violence, were again on the increase, and management replied to them by lockouts or temporary closing of plants. Often factory committees refused to permit the closing of plants and assumed the responsibility of management themselves. In many factories unpopular engineers and managers were removed from the premises on wheelbarrows; and in a few, owners and managers were killed. The workers were angry and desperate, and as each month passed they became better armed and more willing to use their arms. They were preparing themselves to demand not only improved economic conditions and a share in factory management but also a government entirely prolabor in its sympathies.

In the army and navy, cases of desertion and disobedience increased in frequency after the July offensive, and still more after the Kornilov affair, which intensified the hatred and suspicion of officers by enlisted men. The unruly troops now saw in their officers not only personal enemies but also traitors to the revolution and allies of the landlords. Although the Bolsheviks were not responsible for the rebellious mood of the soldiers and sailors, they did capitalize on it. The Military Organization of the Bolshevik Party, created for the purpose of organizing the armed forces, gained much support in the military committees of the troops, particularly in Petrograd and Kronstadt.

THE DEMOCRATIC CONFERENCE. The Cadet ministers had again resigned at the time of the Kornilov affair, and Kerensky was once more compelled to re-form the government. In the hope of getting an expression of general support for a new coalition, he called representatives of various soviets, trade unions, co-operatives, Zemstvos, and city governments to meet in Petrograd. About twelve hundred responded, making up the Democratic Conference of September 27. But that body behaved equivocally, barely approving the principle of coalition and voting an objection to the inclusion of the then unpopular Cadets. Kerensky went ahead, however, without a mandate from the Democratic Conference, and on October 8 formed a new government, including two Cadets. Then, to gain popular favor, he announced the establishment of a republic.

But the Democratic Conference was not a futile gathering. It made one request which brought action: that a body be formed to represent organized opinion and guide the government until the convening of a constituent assembly, the elections for which had again been postponed. After extended negotiations between Kerensky and various political leaders, it was agreed that such a body be formed. It was to consist of 37 socialist delegates and 156 nonsocialists, to be known collectively as the Council of the Republic. The Council was formed as planned and met in Petrograd on October 20. Its meetings were expected to continue for six weeks, at the end of which the constituent assembly was to be convened. Although the members of the Council included some of the most prominent men of the day, they did not concern themselves with the immediately pressing problems but spent their time in fruitless discussions on the restoration of morale in the army, apparently oblivious of the fact that a new revolution was in the making for their country.

BOLSHEVIK PREPARATIONS. Events were playing into the hands of the Bolsheviks as they continued their plans for the eventual overthrow of the Provisional Government. The July Uprising and the denunciation of

Lenin as a German agent were no more than a tactical defeat for them. They still stood with the masses in the demand for "peace, land, and bread," whereas the Provisional Government and the Mensheviks and Socialist Revolutionaries who were unwilling to break with it were showing less recognition of the popular demand. For that reason the Bolsheviks were drawing an increasing following: in February they had been able to count at most 30,000 party members; in July, 240,000.

At the end of July, with Lenin in hiding but still directing affairs, the Sixth Congress of the Russian Social Democratic Labor Party (Bolsheviks) met secretly in Petrograd.[1] Even without Lenin, it was an imposing gathering of men who were to make Russian history; and during its sessions, yet another potential leader was added to the Bolshevik Party—Leon Trotsky, who had cut his ties with the left-wing Mensheviks.

The chief task of the Sixth Congress was the determination of future strategy. The delegates, following Lenin's guidance from afar, agreed that the peaceful transfer of political power from the Provisional Government to the soviets, which had been envisaged in April, was no longer possible and that only an armed uprising of workers and poorer peasants, properly timed, could accomplish the task. It was assumed that the successful rising would be accompanied or followed by socialist-led revolutions in Europe. Some delegates—Bukharin, for example—were of the opinion that if there were no successful socialist revolutions in Western Europe, the task of establishing a socialist society in Russia could not be undertaken even if the Bolshevik-led uprising were successful. Others, notably Stalin, maintained that the socialist transformation of Russia could take place even if Western Europe did not go socialist. But all agreed that the *ultimate* success of the socialist revolution in Russia was dependent on similar success in Western Europe.

As a result of the decisions reached at the Sixth Congress, the Bolsheviks were embarked on preparations for an insurrection against the Provisional Government. Their leaders intended to begin action when they had secured a sufficiently large following in the soviets and when the weakness of the Provisional Government had become so marked that the uprising would be likely to succeed. And because of domestic developments during the late summer—peasant disturbances, labor unrest, the Kornilov episode, and the continuing state of crisis in the Provisional Government—they were

---

[1] Because there had been no congresses of the R.S.D.L.P. since the fifth, held in 1907, this was, by Bolshevik reckoning, the sixth, inasmuch as they regarded themselves as representing the true R.S.D.L.P.

optimistic about the nearness of that time. During August and September they succeeded in drawing away the following of the Mensheviks and Socialist Revolutionaries in the major cities and in the armed forces. Those parties were weakened not only by internal divisions but also by their inability to promise satisfaction of the immediate demands of their followers. They were losing members to the Bolsheviks also because they (with the exception of the extreme left wing, led by Maria Spiridonova) were not willing to oust the Provisional Government in favor of the soviets. On September 13 the majority of the Petrograd Soviet for the first time voted in favor of a Bolshevik resolution, thereby disowning the Menshevik-Socialist Revolutionary leadership. Soon thereafter its control passed into Bolshevik hands, and Leon Trotsky was elected its Chairman. On September 18 the Bolsheviks gained control also of the Moscow Soviet. Control of those two soviets was particularly important, for the country as a whole was strongly influenced by examples set in the two capitals. Thereafter in city after city the majority of the soviets passed to the Bolsheviks. And all the while their following was growing steadily in the army and in the Baltic Fleet. In Petrograd, where the Soviet virtually directed the large garrison, it established on October 13 the Military Revolutionary Committee, the ostensible purpose of which was to mobilize the Petrograd troops in the event of a possible German attack from Riga; and Trotsky was chosen chairman of it. The Military Revolutionary Committee was of great potential value to the Soviet, for the Petrograd troops were more willing to obey its orders than those of the government.

Early in October Lenin returned to Petrograd, and on October 23 he and eleven members of the party's Central Committee met secretly to make one of the most fateful decisions of modern times. Lenin impassionately demanded that an early date be set for the armed uprising, arguing that the popular mood might shift away from the Bolsheviks if they took no action. His position was supported by all of those present except two, Kamenev and Zinoviev. It was then decided that the Bolshevik Central Committee should make immediate preparations. And, in order to permit rapid decisions to be made in the events to come, the gathering agreed to the formation of an inner Political Bureau (generally called Politburo) of seven men: Lenin, Trotsky, Stalin, Kamenev, Zinoviev, Gregory Sokolnikov, and Andrei Bubnov. The next weeks were filled with hurried and far from secret preparations. In Petrograd, Trotsky's Military Revolutionary Committee found that it could count not only on the support of the troops but also on that of nearly 20,000 armed factory workers who had formed units known as Red Guards. Some Bolshevik leaders felt confident that the All-Russian Congress of Soviets, which was to meet on November 7 in Petrograd, would have before it the accomplished fact of a successful overthrow of the Provisional Government.

THE NOVEMBER REVOLUTION. The Provisional Government finally decided on November 5 to break the strength of the Bolsheviks by closing their newspapers, arresting their leaders, dissolving the Military Revolutionary Committee and bringing reliable troops to Petrograd. On the next day it actually took its first step in counteraction by closing several Bolshevik newspapers. In reply, the Military Revolutionary Committee began calling troops onto the streets. Seeing that, Kerensky appeared at a meeting of the Council of the Republic, then in session, and demanded a vote of unconditional confidence. He received instead a Council resolution criticizing the Bolsheviks and demanding that the Provisional Government undertake immediate agrarian reform and begin negotiations with the Allies to end the war.

While Kerensky and the Council of the Republic were discussing resolutions of confidence, the Bolshevik leaders assembled at the Smolny Institute and put the last touches to their plan for action. They decided to begin by having detachments of Kronstadt sailors and Red Guards make an assault on the Winter Palace (where Kerensky had his headquarters) while other forces took control of postal, telegraph, and railroad services and of the chief buildings of the city. In Moscow, armed attack was to take place simultaneously with that in Petrograd.

On the morning of November 7 the revolution began in Petrograd. Sailors from Kronstadt, regiments from the Petrograd garrison, and Red Guards moved into action. Before noon the Winter Palace was under attack, and the chief railroad stations, the telephone and telegraph buildings, and the State Bank were in the hands of the insurgents. Kerensky, in the hope of summoning loyal troops from the front, managed to escape in an automobile of the United States Embassy. Many other members of the government were seized, and the Council of the Republic was dispersed by armed units. By the afternoon the whole city, with the exception of the Winter Palace, had been taken by the rebels with hardly any bloodshed. Within the Winter Palace were the remaining members of the Provisional Government, defended by a handful of loyal troops, including a woman's battalion which had been formed within the past year. After lengthy but futile negotiations with the defenders, the rebels finally opened fire and, with little effort, took that building also.

Late in the evening the Second All-Russian Congress of Soviets of Workers' and Soldiers' Deputies opened at the Smolny Institute and began proceedings to deal with the fact of a successful armed uprising. The Military Revolutionary Committee had already issued a statement to the country that the Provisional Government had been overthrown.

But Petrograd was not yet quiet. The anti-Bolshevik forces, led by moderate Mensheviks and SR's, were busy. They immediately created the Committee for the Salvation of the Country and the Revolution, which declared itself the heir to the Provisional Government and undertook to create a new government. On November 10 came the first evidence of Kerensky's meager success at bringing relief troops; a detachment of 700 Cossacks under General Peter Krasnov took Tsarskoye Selo, and attempted to enter Petrograd. On the following day their attempt was aided by an anti-Bolshevik rising within the city. But Krasnov's men were easily driven back, and the rising failed. Kerensky's effort to rouse the front commanders to march on Petrograd in support of Krasnov also failed. Several refused to obey him, and those who were willing were disobeyed by their men. On November 15 Krasnov's Cossacks gave up the futile battle, and he himself was placed under arrest. Kerensky, who had been with him at the last moment, escaped under the disguise of a sailor.

Elsewhere in the country the Bolsheviks and their supporters were able to seize power with little fighting except in a few places. In Moscow, on November 7, the Kremlin and many other strategic points passed to Bolshevik hands, but the anti-Bolsheviks offered considerable opposition. They fought on until November 16 when, overpowered and outnumbered, they surrendered. In a few places the opposition was more effective: in Tiflis, the Georgian Mensheviks gained and kept control; in Kiev, Ukrainian nationalists used the disturbance as an opportunity to begin preparations for the establishment of the Ukrainian Republic; and the Don, Kuban, and Orenburg Cossacks successfully opposed the Bolsheviks in their regions. Elsewhere, however, the transfer of power to the Bolsheviks moved rapidly, and in most cities authority was taken over at once by Bolshevik-led soviets.

One of the most serious problems confronting the Bolsheviks at first was that of the troops at the front, who could easily smother the revolution if they chose to obey their commanders. But, with the exception of Krasnov's unit, they remained inactive while the tide of Bolshevik power moved westward from Petrograd to the front. General Nicholas Dukhonin, the acting Commander-in-Chief, ordered the troops to attack the capital, but his orders were not executed. Taking advantage of his position, the Bolshevik leaders ordered him to begin peace negotiations with the Germans and, when he refused, dismissed him and sent the Bolshevik Ensign Nicholas Krylenko to take over his command. Krylenko's journey to army headquarters, at Mogilev, was a promenade; one general after another submitted to him or escaped when it became clear that the troops would not oppose him: Dukhonin gallantly remained at Mogilev. On December 3 Krylenko and his men arrived at his quarters and seized him. He was immediately lynched by unruly troops, in defiance of Krylenko's orders. The army was now under Bolshevik control, and its command was soon completely reorganized with Krylenko as Commander-in-Chief.

By the end of December the Bolsheviks were in nominal control throughout the land except in Georgia, in the western Ukraine, and in some of the Cossack lands. They had succeeded not because they had the positive support of the majority of the people but rather because the majority had lost confidence in the Provisional Government and would not fight for it; in short, the Bolsheviks were strong because their opponents were weak. With a numerous following in the major cities and in the army, they had successfully struck at a decisive moment and had been able to take the leadership because the people in large part approved of their immediate program of peace, bread, and land. Few knew what the long-range program of the Bolsheviks was, but for a time their immediate program sufficed. Whether or not they would succeed where the Provisional Government had failed was to depend upon their ability to provide immediate satisfaction of the demands of the majority of the Russian people.

PART V

Communist Russia

CHRONOLOGICAL OVERVIEW

1917
Nov. 8 Assumption of power
by Congress of Soviets
Nov. 8 Decree on land
1918
Mar. Treaty of Brest-Litovsk
May Beginning of Civil War
July Adoption of the Con-
stitution of the R.S.F.S.R.
1919
Mar. Formation of Com-
munist International
1920
Nov. End of major do-
mestic warfare
1921
Mar. Treaty of Riga
Introduction of New
Economic Policy
1922
April Election of Stalin as
General Secretary of party
Central Committee
Oct. 25 Entry of Reds into
Vladivostok
Dec. 30 Establishment of the
USSR
1924
Jan. 21 Death of Lenin
Jan. 31 Ratification of the
Constitution of the USSR
1927
Nov. Expulsion of Trotsky
from the Communist
Party
1928
Oct. 1 Beginning of First
Five-Year Plan
1929 Intensification of anti-
religious drive

1929-1930 Intensive drive for
collectivization
1932-1933 Famine in the Ukraine
and North Caucasus
1934
Sep. Russian entry into
League of Nations
Dec. Assassination of
Sergei Kirov
1935
May Franco-Soviet Treaty
of Mutual Assistance
1936
Dec. Adoption of new constitution of the USSR
1936-1939 Period of trials and
purges
1939
Aug. 23 Soviet-German Pact
of Non-aggression
Nov. Annexation of eastern
Poland
1939 Nov. Soviet-Finnish War
1940, Mar.
1940
Aug. Annexation of Lithuania,
Latvia and Estonia
1941
May Election of Stalin as
Premier of the USSR
June 22 German invasion of
Russia
1942, Aug. Battle of Stalingrad
1943, Feb.
1943
May Dissolution of Communist
International
1945
Feb. Crimea (Yalta) Conference

May 7	Unconditional surrender of Germany			first secretary of party Central Committee
Aug. 8	Declaration of war on Japan		**1955**	
Sep. 2	Japanese surrender		May	Warsaw Pact
1947			**1956**	
Feb.	Peace treaties with Italy, Hungary, Rumania, Bulgaria and Finland		Feb.	Twentieth Party Congress
			Apr.	Dissolution of Cominform
Sep.	Creation of Communist Information Bureau		Oct.	Hungarian uprising
1948			**1957**	
June	Expulsion of Yugoslavia from Cominform		Oct.	Launching of first space satellite, *Sputnik*
1949			**1961**	
Apr.	North Atlantic Pact		Apr.	Launching of first manned space satellite
1950			Oct.	Twenty-second Party Congress
June	Outbreak of Korean hostilities		**1963**	
1952			Aug.	Treaty banning above-ground nuclear tests
Oct.	Nineteenth Party Congress		**1964**	
1953			Oct.	Fall of Khrushchev
Mar. 5	Death of Stalin		**1966**	
Sep.	Election of Khrushchev as		Mar.-Apr.	Twenty-third Party Congress

We have defeated the bourgeoisie, but it is not yet destroyed and not even completely subjugated. We must, therefore, resort to a new and higher form of the struggle with the bourgeoisie, we must turn from the very simple problem of continuing the expropriation of the capitalists to the more complex and difficult problem—the problem of creating conditions under which the bourgeoisie can neither exist nor come into existence again. It is clear that this problem is infinitely more important and that we shall have no Socialism until it is solved.

LENIN (1918)

The Bolshevik program

SOCIAL BLUEPRINT.   The Bolshevik leaders of 1917 believed that, being the faithful followers of Karl Marx, they were acting as the agents of history, whose course only Marx had predicted accurately. They were convinced that capitalist society had entered a period of general crisis which would culminate everywhere in the establishment of a new society. And what would the nature of the new society be? Marx once stated that he was not prepared to "write a duodecimo edition of the new Jerusalem," for only the most general features could be indicated in advance, and the details of the new order would have to be worked out after the destruction of the capitalist system. To fill in some of the details became the self-imposed task of Lenin during the summer of 1917, while he was in hiding from the Provisional Government. The results were published in a brief pamphlet entitled *State and Revolution.*

Lenin's reasoning in that treatise is developed on the premise that the state is the organized coercive power of the ruling class, represented by the army, the police, and the bureaucracy. As his argument proceeds from that premise, his plan for the new society emerges, step by step. First, since every state is the organ of the ruling class, a capitalist state—whatever its political form may be—is the organ of the capitalist class and its allies; and to establish socialism, the initial step must be a violent one by which the armed proletariat overthrows the capitalist class. Following that overthrow, there must come a long transitional period during which the proletariat must retain the state as a weapon of coercion in order to destroy the old ruling class and the machinery of their rule. During this period (known as the period of the dictatorship of the proletariat) the workers, acting as the leaders of the exploited masses, must so transform society that the need for the state will be gradually lessened and it will begin to "wither away."

That transformation will be effected in several stages. In the first stage all factories, banks, machines, and land will be socially owned; the exploitation of workers will be ended; and labor, required of all, will be rewarded by payment proportional to the quantity and quality of work. During this first stage of the dictatorship of the proletariat, some private production may be permitted, but it will gradually be transformed. Only when all production, industrial and agricultural, is socialized will it be possible to speak of the existence of *socialism*. Finally, at some future date when all men have learned to rule themselves and willingly give society their best efforts without thought of reward, and when the economy will be so productive as to satisfy the needs of all, the final stage, that of *communism*, will be achieved. Then men will be rewarded not on the basis of what they produce but on the basis of what they need. When that stage is reached, the state, no longer necessary, will have "withered away," and the period of the dictatorship of the proletariat will come to an end.

MASS PARTICIPATION.   Lenin's remark that "every cook must learn to administer the state" was a concise expression of the goal he expected the dictatorship of the proletariat to attain. According to his plan, the state machinery was to be placed in the hands of the proletariat in order that they might become experienced through participation in administration and the maintenance of public order. The soviets which had sprung up spontaneously in 1917 seemed to him excellent devices through which to provide this mass participation. The country was to have the aspect of a vast office-workshop-farm the administration of which was to be in the hands of the masses. The old bureaucracy was to be replaced by "officials, without exception, elected and subject to recall *at any time*, their salaries reduced to the level of ordinary workmen's wages."

PARTY PARTICIPATION.   Although Lenin believed in mass participation in government, he did not believe in liberal democracy. The limits of freedom would be determined by the goals of the new society, and the people would be guided into acceptance of those goals. Before 1917 he said little on the subject of such guidance, but what he said indicated that the true Marxist party—presumably the Bolshevik Party—would be expected to assume the task of leadership. In *State and Revolution* he made this definite statement:

> By educating the workers' party, Marxism educates the vanguard of the proletariat which is capable of assuming power and *of leading the whole people* to Socialism, of directing and organizing the new order, of being the teacher, guide and leader of all the toilers and exploited in the task of building up their social life. . . .

Certainly Lenin and his colleagues, believing that they were endowed with the Truth, did not conceive of themselves as the passive instruments of the revolution but rather as its leaders. It is clear, too, that they would not hesitate to disregard the expressed will of the majority if they believed the majority to be mistaken. Even Plekhanov, more moderate than Lenin, stated in 1903, on the question of democratic rights during the period of the dictatorship of the proletariat:

> Each democratic principle should not be considered individually in the abstract, but in its relationship to that principle which may be called the basic principle of democracy—*salus populi, suprema lex.* Translated into revolutionary language it means that the good of the revolution is the highest law. And, if for the good of the revolution, it were necessary temporarily to limit one or another of the principles of democracy, then it would be criminal to hesitate. . . . And it is necessary to consider the continuance of parliaments from this point of view. If the people, in the grip of revolutionary enthusiasm, were to elect a very excellent parliament. . . . , then we should try to transform it into a Long Parliament; but if the elections should turn out unfavorably, then it would be necessary for us to disperse it, not after two years but, if possible, after two weeks.[1]

---

[1] Quoted in V. Vaganyan, *G. V. Plekhanov* (Moscow: State Publishing House, 1924), 367-368.

SUMMARY. The beliefs which the Bolshevik leaders consciously entertained in November, 1917, when they offered the political power over Russia to the Second Congress of Soviets, may be briefly summarized as follows: The goal of historical development is the Heavenly City of communism on earth. When it has been reached there will be no exploiters and no exploited; all men will live as brothers without external compulsion or coercion, working for the common good and living a full life, both materially and spiritually. The attainment of this goal may, and probably will, require several generations, but success is certain since the political and economic power of the old ruling classes has been broken and power is now in the hands of a class capable of creating a communist society. To achieve the goal of peace and plenty for all will require the use of force, but the end justifies the use of harsh means.

Formation of the Soviet Government

READY-MADE FOUNDATION. One of the first needs of the Bolsheviks after their coup d'état of November 7 was an organization to administer their program, and they lost no time in forming it. Late on the evening of that day the delegates to the Second All-Russian Congress of Soviets of Workers' and Soldiers' Deputies gave a majority approval to the Bolshevik seizure of power and thus provided them with a foundation upon which to build a government structure. Such approval was to be expected since, of the 650 delegates to the Congress, 390 were Bolsheviks and about one hundred were left Socialist Revolutionaries, willing to co-operate with the Bolsheviks. The minority delegates, right SR's and Mensheviks, had no course but to register their protest and leave the meeting.

THE SOVNARKOM. The Bolsheviks, who clearly dominated the deliberations of the Congress, proceeded to direct the remaining delegates toward the establishment of a new government and the enactment of revolutionary legislation. On November 8 the Congress confirmed the creation of a cabinet, composed exclusively of Bolsheviks. The left SR's had refused to enter the cabinet unless it represented a coalition of all socialist parties—a condition rejected by Lenin. Members of the new cabinet were to be called "people's commissars" rather than "ministers" since the latter term was too suggestive of tsarist terminology, and the cabinet as a whole was to be known as the Council of People's Commissars, a designation contracted in Russian to *Sovnarkom* (from *Soviet Narodnikh Komissarov*). Prominent

SOVFOTO

Vladimir Lenin and Joseph Stalin (1922)

among the members confirmed by the Congress were Lenin, as Premier of the Sovnarkom; Alexis Rykov, as People's Commissar of Internal Affairs; Trotsky, as People's Commissar of Foreign Affairs; Anatol Lunacharsky, as People's Commissar of Education; and Stalin, as People's Commissar of Nationalities.

CENTRAL EXECUTIVE COMMITTEE.   The Congress then elected a Central Executive Committee (C.E.C.), consisting at first of 101 members, including 62 Bolsheviks, 29 left SR's, and ten representatives of other parties, to act in the name of the Congress when it was not in session. In theory, sovereign power was vested in the Congress of Soviets, which delegated legislative authority to the C.E.C. and executive authority to the Sovnarkom. But as practice established their functions, the Sovnarkom exercised both executive and legislative authority; the Central Executive Committee enacted legislation either on its own initiative or at the request of the Sovnarkom; and the Congress itself, although its designated functions were similar to those of Western European parliamentary bodies, actually did little beyond confirming what was done by the Sovnarkom or by the C.E.C. Real power lay in the hands of the Sovnarkom, and behind it stood the Bolshevik Party.

First steps of the Soviet Government

SHARING WITH THE PEASANTS.   Having gained power by force, the Bolsheviks did not concern themselves now with legal niceties. They did, however, concern themselves with the strategy of power. Since they had formed the new government through the Second Congress of Soviets, representing only workers and soldiers, they still lacked the support of the peasants, without which the authority of the new government would be limited. Therefore when the All-Russian Congress of Peasants' Soviets was held in Petrograd in mid-November, Lenin set about to gain its support. The fact that the left SR's dominated that body made the task simple, and on November 27, the Congress of Peasants' Soviets agreed to fuse with the Congress of Workers' and Soldiers' Soviets and to accept the offer of 108 seats in the Central Executive Committee. At this time also the left SR's reconsidered the question of entering the Sovnarkom and accepted three offices in it.

THE CONSTITUENT ASSEMBLY.   There still remained the problem of the long promised and long deferred constituent assembly. Since the overthrow of the imperial regime in March, 1917, most Russians had assumed that the final determination of the form of their government would be made by such an assembly, freely elected. The Provisional Government had, before its overthrow, finally set the date of elections for November 25; and the Bolsheviks, who had been the loudest in demanding elections, felt compelled to go through with the plan. The election returns showed that 25 per cent of the voters had supported the Bolsheviks, 62 per cent the other socialist parties, and 13 per cent the conservative and liberal parties. The Constituent Assembly opened in Petrograd on January 18, 1918, with the Bolshevik and left SR delegates in the minority.

Lenin had maintained, even before the elections, that the Second Congress of Soviets reflected the real will of the people and that the duty of the Constituent Assembly would be to recognize the authority of the Congress of Soviets and then quietly dissolve. The majority of the delegates to the Constituent Assembly, however, refused to hand over their mandate to the Soviet Government as requested and, in so doing, doomed the Assembly. Early on the morning of January 19, the pro-Bolshevik guard entered the meeting hall and, complaining that the "guard is tired," instructed the delegates to close the meeting. They had no choice but to comply. Later that day the C.E.C. of the Congress of Soviets issued a decree "officially" dissolving the Constituent Assembly.

BOLSHEVISM SUPREME.   The dissolution passed with little incident, for the country was weary and the new Soviet Government was strong and determined. Although foreign governments withheld their recognition of the Soviet regime, it was clear by the end of January, 1918, that there was no organized force in Russia capable of challenging the Soviet power. It was clear also that Soviet power meant Bolshevik power.

Many Bolsheviks wanted to form a coalition with the other socialist parties, but Lenin insisted that the Bolsheviks alone must control the government. He had approved of admitting a few left SR's into the Sovnarkom because they commanded wide support among the peasantry, but he could not countenance the compromises which would be required if Bolsheviks and moderate socialists were to co-operate. It was clear after the dissolution of the Constituent Assembly that a one-party system was in the making in Russia.

REVOLUTIONARY LEGISLATION.   Neither before nor after the meeting of the Constituent Assembly did the Soviet Government think of itself as a caretaker government, dependent upon the mandate of the people. Its leaders felt that the coup d'état was mandate sufficient and, from their first day in power, they moved rapidly to carry out the program of "smashing the old state machinery" and enacting revolutionary legislation. Decrees and laws issued thick and fast from the Congress of Soviets, the C.E.C., and the Sovnarkom. The meeting of the Constituent Assembly was to them but a minor incident which neither halted nor altered their activities. A survey of those activities will indicate their relentless progress.

One of the first acts of the Bolshevik leaders was aimed at satisfying the peasant demand for land. Taking a leaf from the agrarian program of the left SR's, Lenin had proposed on November 8, 1917, and the Congress of Soviets had accepted, a decree on land. This decree, the most radical approach to the agrarian question ever undertaken in Russia, provided that all land owned by landlords, the crown, the churches and the monasteries, together with all livestock and implements on such land, be transferred without compensation to the former owners into the temporary custody of peasant land committees and peasant soviets until the meeting of the Constituent Assembly. It forbade the use of hired labor in the cultivation of the land, also the sale, mortgaging or leasing of land. Title to the land was to be vested in the state, but the use of it would be given in perpetuity to the peasants. After the dispersal of the Constituent Assembly, there was no longer any need to speak of temporary custody of the expropriated land by land committees and soviets, and the peasants proceeded to divide land, livestock, and implements among themselves.

Another urgent task of the Soviet Government was to make basic changes necessary to the operation of the dictatorship of the proletariat. During November and December it went far toward discharging that task. It abolished all existing titles and legal class distinctions and placed all Russians in the category of "citizens." It introduced the principle of egalitarianism in the army by a decree abolishing all ranks and titles, vesting full control in elected committees of soldiers, and providing that all positions of command be filled by election. It abolished the existing court system and instituted in its place elected tribunals to be known as "people's courts," designed to administer class justice. It completed the dissolution—begun by the Provisional Government—of the old police organization and assigned the task of policing to local units, the Workers' Militia, under the authority of the local soviets. And in order to combat anti-government acts, it established a body with extraordinary powers comparable to those of the old political police and gave it the mouth-filling name of the All-Russian Extraordinary Commission to Combat Counter-Revolution and Sabotage (later contracted, from the Russian name, to *Cheka*). It was placed under the command of the Bolshevik leader Felix Dzerzhinsky.

The problem of nationalization required another series of far-reaching changes, but within six months the government had achieved its chief aims in that direction. Its intention was not to introduce complete nationalization of the economy at once but to nationalize key sectors of the economy, apply some egalitarian principles in economic life, and place all private enterprise under governmental or workers' control. The eight-hour day was approved at once. Shortly after that, by the Decree on Workers' Control, workers in all establishments were given a large share in management, including determination of prices and production; and all were to be represented in local Councils of Workers' Control and in the All-Russian Council of Workers' Control. Then the Supreme Council of National Economy—later to become the directing organ of the economy—was created. Privately

owned railroads and merchant vessels were nationalized, and foreign trade
was declared a state monopoly. All banks were nationalized and placed under the authority of the State Bank. All bonds of the Imperial and Provisional governments and all financial obligations to foreign individuals
and governments were repudiated. Transactions in stocks and bonds as
well as payment of interest on bonds and dividends on stocks were suspended. Inheritance of property was abolished and it was decreed that
property should pass to the state upon the death of its owner. The outcome
of all this economic legislation was not social ownership of the means of
production but the curtailment or abolition of the traditional forms and
activities of private enterprise and the introduction of the principle that men
should be rewarded only for their own toil.

Another group of decrees sought to alter the traditional cultural patterns of Russia. The most important of these was the decree of February 5,
1918, pertaining to the relationship between Church and state. It abolished
all ties between Church and state, proclaimed complete freedom of worship
insofar as it did not "violate public order," and ended all discriminatory
legislation based upon religion. It forbade the Church to own property of
any kind and declared the property hitherto owned by it nationalized and
subject to use for religious purposes only by privately organized groups of
laymen upon application to the government. It prohibited all religious
instruction in the schools but allowed for private religious instruction. And
it declared the registration of births and marriages an exclusive function
of the state. Not only did the new government seek to make all family
affairs exclusively civil matters but it also sought to introduce complete
equality of the sexes in the eyes of the law. On December 31, 1917, it decreed the legality of automatic divorce at the wish of both parties to a marriage and of divorce by court action upon application by one partner.

In two other decrees the government followed the precedent of Peter
the Great: on January 3, 1918, it stripped the Russian alphabet of several
of its archaic letters, and on February 7 it introduced the Gregorian calendar
of the West, thus eliminating the thirteen-day discrepancy which had
existed between the Russian and Western calendars.

THE NATIONALITY QUESTION.   In its handling of the national minorities within the Russian boundaries the Soviet Government was faced not
only with theoretical problems but also with immediate, practical ones, for
many of those minorities were seeking either independence or autonomy.
In theory, the government conceded the right of nationalities to secede but
hoped to prevent secession. It did not want to hasten the disintegration of

the former Russian Empire into independent national states but rather to create a multinational state based upon the legal and cultural equality of all the nationalities within it. Its Declaration of the Rights of the Peoples of Russia, published on November 15, asserted the complete equality of all nationalities in Russia, the right of full cultural self-development of each, and the right of secession.

Problems of secession arose immediately. The Finnish movement for independence was so powerful that the Sovnarkom was compelled, in December, to recognize the independence of Finland. In other areas where the Bolsheviks had a foothold, they made a determined effort to discourage secession. In Lithuania and the Baltic Provinces of Estonia and Latvia,[1] the struggle between Bolshevik and anti-Bolshevik forces aided by German troops continued for some time. In the Ukraine the anti-Bolshevik Ukrainian nationalists announced the establishment of the independent Ukrainian Peoples Republic in January, 1918, but its jurisdiction was limited by the fact that a large part of the Ukraine was actually under Soviet control. Transcaucasia, on the other hand, although dominated by anti-Bolsheviks, aimed not at secession from Russia but at autonomy in a non-Bolshevik Russia. Thus national and political questions were inextricably intermingled. The problem of Russia's border provinces was not to be settled for many years to come.

FIRST EFFORTS TO BRING PEACE.   Problems did not present themselves singly to the Soviet Government. The problem of bringing about the promised peace had been under extended consideration at the same time as those mentioned above. On November 8, 1917, Lenin proposed and the Congress of Soviets accepted a decree on peace, suggesting to the belligerent governments that they immediately agree to an armistice and begin negotiations to establish a peace without annexations and indemnities. He hoped that the publication of the decree would rouse the masses in other belligerent nations to demand that their governments end the war. There were, in fact, peace movements in England, France, and Germany, but they were of little consequence. The Allies, waiting for the arrival of troops from the United States (which had entered the war in April, 1917), were greatly disturbed by Soviet Russia's move to end the war; but Germany, preparing for what she hoped would be the final offensive on the Western Front, was anxious to see Russia out of the war so that the German troops then on the Eastern Front could be safely transferred to the Western Front.

---

[1] Latvia had been formed from the former provinces of Courland and Livonia.

Because the Central Powers were prepared to discuss peace, the Soviet Government opened negotiations with them on December 3 at Brest-Litovsk. Twelve days later an armistice was signed. However, the Soviet delegates, led by Adolf Joffe, and those of the Central Powers, led by the German General Max von Hoffman, could not agree on the basis of peace negotiations; the Russians demanded peace without annexations and indemnities, and the Germans demanded both territory and indemnities. After negotiations had been twice suspended because of deadlock, Trotsky, People's Commissar of Foreign Affairs, offered a formula of "no peace, no war," implying that Russia would neither sign peace nor continue fighting. It was soon put to test: General von Hoffman ended the armistice on February 18 and ordered a German advance along the Eastern Front.

The remnants of the Russian army could offer little resistance, and the Germans were soon in the vicinity of Petrograd. The Bolshevik leaders knew that their forces could not hold unless the Allies were willing to provide assistance, and their pleas for assistance had been ignored. Lenin argued that there was no alternative except acceptance of the terms offered; any sacrifice of territory was justified if it would give the Soviet Government a breathing space. It was not a popular argument; however, on February 23, it gained the support of the Central Committee of the Bolshevik Party—but only by a vote of seven to four, with four abstaining. On the next day it received a favorable, though slim, vote from the C.E.C. of the Congress of Soviets. TREATY OF BREST-LITOVSK. Negotiations were resumed, and on March 3, the Soviet Government signed the Treaty of Brest-Litovsk with the Central Powers. The Fourth Congress of Soviets ratified the treaty on March 14.

By the terms of that treaty the Soviet Government agreed to recognize the independence of Georgia and the Ukraine and reaffirm her recognition of Finland's independence; to leave Poland, Lithuania, Latvia, and Estonia to the disposition of Germany and Austria-Hungary; and to hand over Kars, Ardahan, and Batum to the Ottoman Empire. The territory of Russia was thereby reduced by 1,267,000 square miles and her population by 62 million. Included in that loss were 32 per cent of her arable lands, 26 per cent of her railroads, about 33 per cent of her factories, and 75 per cent of her coal and iron mines. It was a sad end to Russia's participation in a war in which 2 million Russian soldiers had lost their lives, over 4 million had been wounded, and nearly 2.5 million had been taken prisoner. UNEASY PEACE. Although it appears clear now that Russia could not have fought any longer, her withdrawal from the war drew disfavor from many sources. Lenin was accused by his opponents of selling Russia's birthright to the enemy, and the old charge that he was a German agent gained greater currency. The left Socialist Revolutionaries withdrew from the Sovnarkom and began to move toward the side of the still loosely organized opposition. And the Allied governments, which had hitherto opposed intervention in Russia, began to accept the idea.

On March 6, 1918, Lenin made his report to the Seventh Congress of the Bolshevik Party, which opened with delegates representing 145,000 Party members.[1] He stressed the fact that the peace treaty provided a respite during which the Soviet regime must prepare itself for new tests of strength. Speaking at a time when the Germans seemed to be in sight of victory on the Western Front and German troops were still in the Ukraine, Lithuania, and the Baltic Provinces, he felt sure that the fate of Russia would be determined by Germany. As he judged the situation, if the German left-wing socialists, led by Karl Liebknecht, should bring about the expected revolution, Soviet Russia would be saved and could join hands with Soviet Germany. But he feared that Russia would be doomed if the German revolution did not come. He apparently did not expect an Allied victory and believed that a victorious Germany, if untouched by revolution, would move east into Russia. In any case, he argued, Soviet Russia might soon have to fight— either against a monarchist Germany or alongside a Soviet Germany— and the government should therefore begin at once to revitalize the army and put every effort into restoring order and discipline throughout the country.

The Constitution

DEFINITION OF STATUS.   While the Soviet Government had been moving from decree to decree, establishing new institutions, abolishing old ones, and handling foreign relations, it had been operating without a constitution. In April, 1918, the C.E.C. appointed a committee to draft one. Their draft of the Fundamental Laws—or Constitution—was presented to and ratified by the Fifth Congress of Soviets on July 10. This constitution, upon the principles of which the government of Russia was to be based until 1936, declared Russia "a republic of Soviets of workers', soldiers', and peasants' deputies" and gave it the name of the Russian Socialist Federated Soviet Republic (R.S.F.S.R.).

---

[1] There were 270,000 Party members at the time, but it was not possible to send representatives from all areas in time to participate in the Congress.

PROVISIONS OF CONSTITUTION.   The text of the Constitution opened
not with the traditional declaration of the rights of man but with the "Declaration of the Rights of the Toiling and Exploited Peoples." It stated that
the object of the Soviet Government was to establish socialism not only in
Russia but also in all countries, that Russia was in the transition period
of "the dictatorship of the urban and rural proletariat and the poorest peasantry," and that its aim was "the complete suppression of the bourgeoisie,
the abolition of exploitation of man by man. . . ."

The body of the Constitution gave definite form to those principles on
which the new government was to continue. The principle of compulsory
labor, that he who does not work shall not eat, was set forth. The previous
decrees on nationalization, workers' control, and renunciation of government debts were reaffirmed. Civil rights were guaranteed in a limited fashion, including "freedom of religious and antireligious propaganda," freedom
of assembly, organization and press for the workers and peasants, and the
right of workers and poorer peasants to have free education.

The political organization sketched by the Constitution was based upon
the existing Soviet structure. All authority was declared to be derived from
the local (urban and rural) soviets, the delegates to which were to be elected
through open voting by all persons of both sexes over eighteen years of age
with the exception of clergymen, members of the Romanov family, former
police agents and high officials, private business men, commercial representatives, the insane, and the criminal. Votes, however, were still to be
"weighted"; urban citizens were to be represented on the basis of one delegate for every 25,000 *voters*, and rural citizens by one delegate for every
125,000 *inhabitants*. Since there were about two inhabitants for every voter
in rural areas, the actual ratio was about five to two in favor of the urban
residents, an acknowledgment of the greater reliance placed upon their
loyalty to the regime. Above the local soviets was to be a hierarchy of congresses of soviets, one for each of the administrative units: the canton, the
district, the province and the region. Delegates to these were to be elected
indirectly; that is, each body elected from its members those to represent it
in the next higher body, and so on to the top. The hierachy was to culminate
in the All-Russian Congress of Soviets.

As for the central organization of the government, the Constitution
merely summarized what had been created by the Soviet Government; the
All-Russian Congress of Soviets was to be the chief legislative body of the
republic; between its sessions its work was to be carried on by the All-Russian Central Executive Committee, elected by it; and the Sovnarkom, with

eighteen People's Commissars, was to be chosen by the C.E.C. to serve as the chief administrative organ.

The Communist Party

POSITION IN REGIME.   The Soviet Constitution omitted mention of the most important element in the new regime, the party which had brought it into being and which was to remain its heart and brain. In March, 1918, the name of that party was changed from R.S.D.L.P. (Bolsheviks) to the Russian Communist Party (Bolsheviks), but its principles were unaltered. A resolution adopted by its Eighth Congress, meeting in March, 1919, thus summarized the purposes which had guided it in its relation to the regime up to that date and which continued to guide it thereafter:

> The Communist Party sets as its goal the achievement of de-cisive influence and complete leadership in all organizations of the workers: in trade unions, co-operatives, village communes etc. The Communist Party strives especially to establish its program and its complete leadership in the . . . Soviets. . . . The Party at-tempts to guide the activity of the Soviets, but not to replace them.

MEMBERSHIP.   According to Communist theory, the supremacy of the party was not to be founded on force alone but rather on a combination of leadership, example, persuasion, and compulsion. The party was to be a well-knit, highly disciplined body, limited in membership to persons— preferably of working class or poor peasant origin—schooled in Commu-nist beliefs and able and willing to undertake any task required by the party, however dangerous or disagreeable. Members were expected to lead, to teach, and to serve as examples. Any member who attempted to use his position for purposes of self-enrichment or who abused his powers or who disobeyed the directives of the party was to be expelled. Most of the party leaders in the beginning led austere lives with few material comforts and great responsibilities. Some abused their positions, but they were usually punished; a few were shot.

EXTENSION OF CONTROL.   By the summer of 1918 the Communists controlled the chief posts not only in the government but also in the army, the trade unions and other influential organizations. Their authority among the masses centered in Communist nuclei in these organizations. Most of the city soviets had Communist majorities, and the local officials were usual-ly selected from among Communist Party members. In the village soviets the Communist position was weaker, but nonetheless effective. Election in local soviets was by show of hands, and few had the temerity to vote against the nominees of the Communists. Thus small Communist groups in each area, supported by a core of militant nonparty followers, were able to determine the real base of the Soviet Government in its first years and to secure majorities in the higher bodies of the government. At the Fifth Congress of the Soviets, in July, 1918, 66 per cent of the 1,164 delegates were Communists.

During the first year of the Soviet regime, centralization of control in both state and party developed rapidly. The central government tended to restrict the authority of the lower administrative and legislative bodies; and within the central government, the Sovnarkom was becoming the dominant organ. In the party, the process was even further advanced, with the grip of the Central Committee on lower party organs growing ever tighter. Since the work of the central government was directed, both in matters of policy and personnel, by the Central Committee, it was becoming evident that the dictatorship of the proletariat was in fact the dictatorship of the party, and more specifically the dictatorship of the Central Committee.

PROBLEM OF GOVERNMENT PERSONNEL.   Although the Communists occupied the key positions, from highest to lowest, in the government, they lacked experienced personnel for the actual governmental operations. It was easy enough to speak of "smashing the old state machinery," but it was difficult to get the new state machinery in running order without the assistance of experienced men. Most of the old governmental personnel refused to serve the new government and, of those who continued to serve, many were of the most doubtful loyalty. The problem is illustrated by the experience of Trotsky when he assumed the office of Commissar of Foreign Affairs. He called a meeting of the staff of the old Ministry of Foreign Affairs and asked those who were prepared to serve the new Soviet Government to step to the left. A few stepped to the left. He then informed the others that the building was surrounded by troops, demanded that they give up their keys and papers, and then ordered them out of the building. But Trotsky was left with the problem of finding satisfactory replacements for those he ordered away—as were other Soviet officials on like occasions. Everywhere it became necessary to rely on untrained Communists to fill important positions and to act as a check on the personnel carried over from the old regime. Communists whose previous experience had been confined to scholastic disputations and underground agitation were forced to become overnight experts in foreign affairs, banking, railroad management, and foreign trade. Often they were shuttled from one field of activity to another as new problems arose; a man might one day be the chief of the archives in a people's commissariat in Petrograd and the next day be ordered to Omsk, in Siberia, to direct food distribution. These Communists sent out by the government to administrative posts in various parts of the country, generally known by the generic name of "commissars" and usually distinguished by the leather jackets they affected, served as the "eyes" and "ears" of the Party.

"BELTS AND LEVERS."   In defining the position of the Communist Party, Lenin once used a striking figure of speech, later elaborated by Stalin, which has remained active in the vocabulary of Communist ideology; it designated the party as the "guiding force" and the soviets, the trade unions, and other mass organizations as the "belts and levers" for the transmission of guidance and instruction from the party to the masses. In other words, the nonparty masses would learn the new doctrines and acquire experience through mass participation, guided by party members in one form of activity or another. It was anticipated that the indoctrination of the masses would be increasingly effective and that, finally, greater participation in the determination of policy by the nonparty masses would be possible. Until that time—and it was assumed to be far removed—the chief tasks of the masses were to learn Communist doctrines and to participate in the establishment of a new order in accordance with policy determined from above.

Although the leaders of the Communist Party admitted the necessity of using force against the old ruling classes and against opponents of the regime, from whatever class they might be derived, they realized that no state can exist on force alone. They believed that the Soviet regime needed at least the active support of the majority of the working class and of a significant minority of the peasantry, buttressed by a majority of their class who would passively accept the new order. They did not plan to allow the masses a major role in determining policy, but they did plan for mass participation in the execution of policy.

To the loyal masses was assigned still another privilege, that of expressing "self-criticism." It was expected that this "self-criticism" would become the gyroscope of the new system. Lenin and his associates agreed that any system could become stultified and bureaucratic if those who led were not subject to criticism from below. But that criticism was to be exercised within proper bounds: it should not touch upon the goals of the system, only upon the means employed in attaining those goals. Thus limited, merciless "self-criticism" was encouraged in every organization in the Soviet state—the soviets, the army, the trade unions, the schools, the co-operatives, and the Communist Party. Periodically, any citizen was free to speak his mind about the manner in which policy was carried out, to enumerate the faults of officials and to point out shortcomings in the operations of institutions; and periodically, the work of each member of the Communist Party was reviewed at meetings open to nonparty members, who were permitted to speak on the merits or shortcomings of the members. In this fashion, Lenin believed, the Communist leaders would win the confidence of the masses and would be aided in avoiding or correcting errors in policy or administration.

TWENTY-FIVE / THE CIVIL WAR. 1918-1921

The establishment of the Soviet regime in Russia was an event of international concern, for the Communists hoped and the outside world feared that what had happened in Russia would be the prelude to world revolution. The Communists were as determined to safeguard the new regime as their opponents were to destroy it; and both groups were inspired by the belief that their cause involved not only the fate of Russia but also that of the world. The first clash came within Russia itself, when the issues born of the domestic and international aspects of the Bolshevik revolution led to a gory civil war.

Soviet regime on the defensive

THE BREATHING SPACE.   The breathing space bought at the enormous price of the Treaty of Brest-Litovsk proved to be a troubled one. The peasants on the whole were prepared to accept the new regime, which had given them land, if they were permitted to live without further disturbance of their mores and traditional institutions. But the former upper classes, the middle class, most of the intelligentsia, the liberals, and the non-Communist socialists were hostile to it. In the face of their opposition, the Communists would have had difficulty in bringing about their proposed social, political, and cultural transformation even under the best of circumstances; and they were beginning their task under circumstances far from the best.

A basic drawback to their undertaking was the fact that they had inherited a faltering economy. To the economic losses sustained through the Treaty of Brest-Litovsk were added those which stemmed directly from the November Revolution. The traditional drives necessary to the functioning of a money economy were fast declining. Factory owners, deprived of raw materials and harassed by the interference of workers' committees and the new government, could not maintain even the low production levels of the recent past. Labor did little to improve the situation: the workers, conscious of their new position in society, concerned themselves more with bringing employers, managers, and officials to heel than with the problems of production. And while production and commerce flagged, the peasants added to the general plight by continuing to refuse grain to the cities in exchange for paper money which would buy little at the prevailing inflated prices. The grain shortage was the more acute because the loss of the rich Ukrainian granary had cut deeply into the potential supply of the country.

The government was anxious to restore the flow of both goods and food, but food was the more immediate necessity. Rations were growing shorter in the cities, and political disaffection among the urban proletariat could be expected if the decline were not arrested. In desperation the government adopted the policy of wresting surplus grain from the kulaks and pitting the poor peasants and city workers against them. On May 9, 1918, the Central Executive Committee declared that trade in grain was a state monopoly and ordered the sale to the government at fixed prices of all grain not required for personal use or for seed. A month later it decreed the creation of Committees of the Poor, consisting of poor peasants and agricultural proletarians, to execute the grain policy, to collect and distribute goods and food in the rural areas, and to seize—by force if necessary—surplus grain hidden by the wealthier peasants. These committees, often aided by armed detachments of urban workers, became the agents of the government in the battle for food. They were abolished in November, 1918, but their functions were then taken over by the village soviets, in which the poorer peasants predominated. The food policy, which was maintained with little change until 1921, insured at least a minimum of grain for the cities; but it was politically expensive to the government, resulting as it did in the alienation of the wealthier and middle peasants and in bitter class warfare in the villages.

STIRRINGS OF THE OPPOSITION.   At the time that the Soviet Government was seeking to gain strength, its opponents were doing likewise. Large-scale, organized opposition had disappeared by the end of 1917, but latent opposition was widespread and needed only a strong, purposeful leadership to muster it for an active armed struggle. Potential sources of such leadership were the former ruling classes, led by the old army officers, and the anti-Communist socialist and liberal parties.

The old army officers were the first to regroup their forces. In December, 1917, General Kornilov and several other generals—chief among them, Denikin, who had been arrested with him, in September—escaped from jail and took refuge in the territory of the Don Cossacks. There they joined the former Chief of Staff, Alexeyev, who had begun the organization of the anti-Soviet Volunteer Army. This group at first attracted mainly officers and, in January, 1918, numbered no more than 3,000 men; but it consisted of the best trained soldiers in Russia and was to prove the most formidable of anti-Bolshevik armies. Denikin assumed its command in April, after Kornilov had been killed in a skirmish. But the Volunteer Army was not to strike the first blow against the regime; that was to come from what seemed, at the time, a less likely source—an army unit made up of Czechoslovaks.

THE FIRST BLOW.   Early in the World War the Imperial Government had organized the Czechoslovak Brigade, consisting of Czechs and Slovaks living in Russia; and after March, 1917, the Provisional Government had allowed some 30,000 Czechoslovak prisoners of war to join it for service on the Eastern Front. With the Treaty of Brest-Litovsk, of course, that front disappeared, and the unit asked permission to join the Allies on the Western Front. Permission granted, they found that the only unobstructed route out of Russia to that destination was by way of Vladivostok, and in March, 1918, they entrained for the long journey eastward across Siberia.

Although generally left-wing in sympathy, the Czechoslovaks were for the most part anti-Communist and distrustful of the government's sincerity in allowing this venture. On the other hand, the government distrusted them, suspecting them of conspiring with counter-revolutionary forces within Russia. So great was the tension created by this mutual distrust that a minor incident on May 14 (a riot involving a group of returning Hungarian war prisoners and the Czechoslovaks, near Chelyabinsk) was sufficient to create a crisis. On May 20, the Soviet Government ordered the Czechoslovaks—now strung out over the Trans-Siberian Railroad from the Volga to Vladivostok—to give up their arms. When they refused, Trotsky, who had become the People's Commissar for War, ordered that they be forcibly disarmed and detained. But the Soviet officials along the route were not strong enough to carry out the order, lacking proper support from those under their authority, many of whom were anti-Communist. The result was that the armed and inflamed Czechoslovaks, about 35,000 in number, were easily able to resist the authorities and, with the aid of local anti-Communist groups, to capture city after city along their route: Chelyabinsk on

May 26, Tomsk on May 31, Omsk on June 7, Samara on June 8, and Vladivostok on June 29.

ALLIED INTERVENTION.   The Czechoslovak successes had an electrifying effect on the Allies, particularly France, under whose tactical command the Czechoslovak troops had been placed. Even before that time the Allies had been greatly disturbed by the Russian Government's falling into the hands of a party which opposed all the fundamental beliefs of Western society and by the succeeding withdrawal from the war and renunciation of government debts. And, although all Allied strength was needed to meet the German threat on the Western Front, many Allied statesmen and generals had privately urged armed intervention to oust the Communists, a policy that had at first received little encouragement from their governments. However, the Allied attitude toward intervention had altered somewhat at the time of the Soviet decision to discontinue fighting, for it seemed then that the Germans could break the Russian lines and capture the military stores that the Allies had brought to Murmansk and Archangel in 1917 for Russian use. Consequently British troops, followed by French and American detachments, had been landed in Murmansk in March and, somewhat later, in Archangel. About the same time, Allied troops had been landed in Vladivostok to guard the Allied military stores from the alleged —and, as it turned out, nonexistent—danger from German and Austrian prisoners in Siberia, purportedly being released by the Soviet Government for use against the Allies. These troop landings had not been directed toward intervention in the internal affairs of Russia, but many in England and France at that time favored intervention; and Japan, her eyes fixed on eastern Siberia, was most anxious.

The Czechoslovak victories decided the issue. The fact that so small a force could win battles so easily was interpreted by the Allies as meaning that the Communists were weak and were opposed by a majority of Russians. It seemed logical to them to expect that the anti-Communists would rise up against their new masters if Allied troops were present on Russian soil with moral and material assistance and, consequently, to expect that the venture would be quickly successful at little cost in men, money, and time. The first step toward actual intervention was taken at the end of May, when the French ordered the Czechoslovak troops to abandon their plan for leaving Russia and to complete the task, already begun, of gaining complete control of the Trans-Siberian Railroad. On July 2, the Allied Supreme War Council adopted the policy of armed intervention and laid out a plan whereby additional Allied troops would land at Vladivostok and move westward to give support to the Czechoslovaks and the anti-Com-

The Moscow Kremlin, seen from the southern bank of the Moscow River. The wall, sixty-five feet in height and a mile and a quarter in circumference, was built during the reign of Ivan III. Within it, from the view, are seen (at left) the Great Kremlin Palace, erected during the reign of Nicholas I; (at right) the dominating Bell Tower of Ivan the Great, constructed in the sixteenth century; and (in the center, left to right) the Cathedral of the Annunciation (in which tsars were baptized and married), the Archangel Cathedral (in which tsars before Peter I were buried), and the fifteenth-century Cathedral of the Assumption.

munist Russians. Within a year 7,000 troops of the American Expeditionary Force, under General Graves, 72,000 Japanese, and small French, British, and Italian detachments landed at Vladivostok. At last, the internal opposition to the Soviet Government had a powerful backing.

WITHDRAWAL OF LAST SUPPORT. Another stimulus to civil war came from the left SR's. Although they had opposed the acceptance of the Treaty of Brest-Litovsk in March as a humiliating capitulation to Germany, they had not completely broken with the Communists at that time. However, at the Fifth Congress of Soviets, which opened in Moscow[1] on July 4, their 269 delegates openly opposed not only the peace but also

---

[1] The seat of government had been moved from Petrograd to Moscow in March, 1918, when it appeared that the Germans might advance on Petrograd. The transfer, at first considered temporary, was later made permanent.

the Communist policy of rousing class warfare in the villages through the Committees of the Poor. When their proposals to remedy the situation were outvoted by the Communist majority—as was to be expected—they broke with the Communists and began to concentrate their energies on their own program. Their immediate aims were to terminate the Treaty of Brest-Litovsk and to oust the Communists from control of the Soviet Government. On July 6, two left-wing SR's assassinated the German Ambassador, Count William von Mirbach, in the expectation that Germany would attack in retribution and that Russia would be compelled to fight once more. Later in the day, some of them made armed attacks upon Communists at a few points in Moscow, but their badly organized effort availed little. The government rounded up most of the conspirators and shot several of the leaders. Thereafter the left-wing SR's became an underground party, united with other socialist, liberal and conservative groups in opposition to the Communists. The Soviet Government was now a one-party government, faced on all sides by hostile political organizations.[1]

Fratricidal conflict

REDS *V.* WHITES.   Civil war was the inevitable result of the desperation brought on, both for the government and its opponents, by the combination of food shortages, rural class warfare, the isolation of the Communists, and Allied intervention. In fact, it might be said to have begun already—with the Czechoslovak outburst. Now it broke in fury throughout the country. The opposing forces in the strife were known as the Reds, defending the government, and the Whites (or White Guards), bent on its destruction. The Reds had the advantage of interior position, even at the most perilous moments controlling central Russia; and their opponents had the advantage of access to the seas and thereby access to foreign aid.

TERRORISTIC WARFARE.   Their conflict proved to be the bloodiest scourge experienced in Russia since the Time of Troubles. It was a primitive and savage war in which passions ran high and the rules of organized fighting were disregarded. Guerrilla fighting and banditry, the concomitants of the breakdown of order, were common. Fighting raged simultaneously on

---

[1] Although non-Communist parties were in fact treated as outlaw because of their opposition to the regime, limited activities by some Mensheviks and SR's were permitted until 1922. Thereafter, although no law was passed to that effect, activity in non-Communist political organizations was treated as counter-revolutionary.

many fronts, and the fronts themselves were ill defined; at times Reds might be fighting behind the White lines and vice-versa. Moreover, the fronts shifted frequently; Kiev changed hands nineteen times and many other cities nearly as many. But the worst of all the extraordinary practices was the use of terror by both sides.

The Red instrument of terror, the Cheka, which called itself the "unsheathed avenging sword of the Revolution," followed the principle that it is better to punish ten innocent persons than to permit one guilty person to escape. In the first months of its existence, it had limited its activities mainly to rounding up active opponents of the regime, but after the July rising of the SR's, it began to execute opponents summarily. This practice was intensified after August 30, when left SR's assassinated the Petrograd Cheka chief, Michael Uritsky, and attempted to assassinate Lenin. Five hundred persons, including four tsarist ministers, were shot in retaliation for those acts. In the next three years thousands of persons charged with espionage, desertion, and counter-revolution fell before Cheka firing squads.

The Whites equaled or exceeded their opponents in the use of terror; the paths of their armies were lined with gallows and open graves. Most of the White forces were fiercely antisemitic, and their progress through regions inhabited by Jews was marked by pogroms more bloody than those of 1881.

Introduction of War Communism

SHIFT OF EMPHASIS.   The beginning of the Civil War put an end to the Communist hope of a period of internal peace during which the economy could be restored and the gradual transition to socialism achieved. Instead the government leaders were faced with the urgent task of supplying the needs of a war economy. They undertook to accomplish it by a system of complete governmental control and direction of economic life, giving preference to the workers above other urban classes and to the poor and middle peasants above the kulaks. The system was known as War Communism. EXTENSION OF GOVERNMENT CONTROL.   In operation, War Communism involved the requisitioning from the peasants of all surplus foods at fixed prices, the nationalization of almost all industry, the general imposition of the duty to work, and the devaluation of money.

After the outbreak of fighting the system of grain collection imposed in May, 1918, was extended and made more stringent. Other phases of

War Communism were developed as they became necessary to the operation of the new regime and its continuance under emergencies of war. Further nationalization of industry became necessary because of the conflict, in those industries still privately owned, between workers' control and the interests of the owners. Since the virtual abolition of the profit system, the owners had no incentive to maintain production, and the government was compelled either to restore owner-control and the profit principle or to nationalize all industry. It chose nationalization, that being in line with its fundamental ideology. On June 28, 1918, the major industries —iron, steel, chemical, textile, and oil—were nationalized without compensation to owners and placed under the direction of the Supreme Council of the National Economy. The policy of nationalization culminated on December 29, 1920, with the nationalization of all establishments employing more than ten workers as well as those employing more than five workers and utilizing mechanical power. The management of the individual enterprises was at first entrusted to workers' committees; but when they proved ineffectual, it was turned over to individual managers. Lacking trained personnel, the Supreme Council often permitted the installation of former managers and owners in responsible positions but arranged to have their work checked by Communists.

As the need for labor grew greater, the principle that all who expected to eat should work was translated into actuality. In December, 1918, it was decreed that all between the ages of sixteen and fifty were required to work. At first no effort was made to limit the choice of work; later, however, persons with special technical skills were mobilized and compelled to accept any work assigned to them. Finally, on January 29, 1920, all labor was declared subject to mobilization.

The war emergency helped also to speed government action on the handling of trade; in November, 1918, all internal trade was nationalized. After that, articles for individual consumption were purchased by the government and distributed by government-owned stores, co-operatives, and special distributing centers. Distribution was controlled by a system of rationing which favored soldiers and industrial workers. The holders of ration books, whose number reached about 35 million in 1920, were divided into classes with varying rations; at one time, for example, industrial workers, soldiers, and children were allowed 35 pounds of bread a month and persons who did not work for a living only twelve pounds. Peasants, on the whole, did not come under the rationing system since they were expected to supply their own food needs, but occasionally manufactured goods were distributed among them under a special system. This government-controlled distribution virtually dispensed with money and, by early 1921, money was no longer used in payment for rationed articles, rationed housing, postal and telegraph services, medicine, and newspapers. Workers received such goods and services in return for their labor. It is estimated that at the beginning of 1921 about 93 per cent of the wages of workers was paid in kind.

Although money came to be of less and less importance as a medium of exchange, the government printing presses turned out more and more of it. The amount in circulation in 1917 was already of inflationary proportions; but three years later the total was twenty-two times as great and, at the beginning of 1921, over one hundred times as great as in 1917. This rise in the amount of money and the fall in production caused a spiraling inflation. By 1920 the value of the ruble was so decreased that an item which would have cost one ruble in 1913 brought 2,420 rubles. The result was that, as money lost its value, exchange gradually took on the aspects of barter.

The Red Army

THE NEED. The army which the Soviet Government inherited was a shell. Most of the officers and men of the regular army had left it and there remained only a disorganized mass of soldiery of doubtful military value. The Red Guards, the armed formations of factory workers which had helped the Bolsheviks to power, were incapable of coping with an organized enemy force. The need for a strong army was early acknowledged by the Soviet leaders, but they were compelled to proceed slowly in view of the general apathy among the population for further fighting or military service.

THE FORMATION. On January 28, 1918, the Sovnarkom decreed the formation of a new army to be known as the Workers' and Peasants' Red Army (usually shortened to Red Army), to be recruited by voluntary methods and organized under the direction of the People's Commissariat of War. In the next five months about 100,000 volunteers joined the Red Army, but the number was inadequate and the need was becoming more pressing. In June the government began conscription, in the chief cities, of workers and peasants between the ages of eighteen and forty; and on July 29, the Sovnarkom decreed universal military service throughout the R.S.F.S.R. By August 1, the Red Army had been increased to 300,000 men.

Leon Trotsky

By January, 1920, it numbered over 5 million, although probably no more than 60,000 were ever fighting at any one time.

The summer of 1918 was critical; it was clear that if the Whites could strike quickly the poorly organized and equipped Red Army could be smashed. Therefore Trotsky and other members of the government worked feverishly to strengthen what they had. The election of officers, which had been decreed in December, was abolished. Sterner discipline was introduced throughout the army. All former officers of the tsarist army were ordered to report for service or risk imprisonment, and about 50,000 of them obeyed the order. But since their loyalty was suspect, it was necessary to devise means to keep them in check: their families were held as hostages, to be shot if the officers were recreant to duty; and political commissars, members of the Communist Party, were appointed to every unit for the purpose of checking on the work of the officers and carrying on political propaganda among the troops. As quickly as possible, sometimes after courses of no more than two months, new officers of unquestioned political loyalty were sent to relieve the old ones of command duties.

Civil War in progress

EARLY OPPOSITION GAINS.   By July the White resistance to the Soviet regime was well under way. Most of Siberia was in the hands of the Czechoslovaks and their supporters. The Far North was under anti-Communist control as a result of aid provided by the Allies. The Ukraine, most of White Russia, the Baltic provinces, Transcaucasia, and Russian Turkestan were held by anti-Communist forces. In the northern Caucasus, the Volunteer Army, supported by the Kuban and Don Cossacks, was holding its own against the forces loyal to the regime.

The Whites, it is true, had not yet succeeded in assembling large, organized forces, and Allied troops had been of no great assistance to them. On the other hand, the Red Army had yet to show its ability to fight, and the Soviet Government felt far from secure.

FIRST TESTS OF THE RED ARMY. The first direct threat to the government itself came from the east after the Czechoslovak capture of Samara. A group of Socialist Revolutionaries who had been members of the Constituent Assembly organized themselves in Samara as the Committee of Members of the Constituent Assembly, proclaimed themselves the nucleus of a new Russian government, and began organizing a military force known as the People's Army. The Allies encouraged them with the promise of aid, and they took their first action by striking westward with the aim of effecting a junction with Allied troops which were to move southward from Murmansk and Archangel. They took Ufa on July 4 and Kazan on July 6.[1] Then they met unpredicted resistance. Trotsky had whipped some of the Red units into fighting shape and now gave them their first test, against the People's Army. Their achievement was heartening; they recaptured Kazan on September 10 and Samara on October 8. These victories gave the Communists some confidence in their position. They had given the Whites their first major setback, had driven them east from the upper Volga and had eliminated the possibility of a junction between the Whites in Siberia and the Allies in the Far North.

But they still faced an adverse situation in the lower Volga region. On June 22, Denikin and his Volunteer Army had begun a new offensive in the northern Caucasus. And, although apparently inferior to the forces made up of local partisans and volunteers of the local soviets, they had been able to gain victory after victory because of their better training and because of the support they received from the large anti-Communist population there. On August 26 they took Novorossisk, a port on the Black Sea, thus gaining access to the sea and to foreign supplies. At about the same time Denikin's ally, General Krasnov, newly elected ataman of the Don Cossacks, was clearing the Don region of Communists and seeking to

[1] Paradoxically, the anti-Communist successes brought doom to the imperial family. Nicholas II had been offered asylum by the British Government but, as a result of opposition by British labor, the offer had been withdrawn; and when the Bolsheviks seized power, he and his family were being held prisoners in Tobolsk, Siberia. Under orders from Moscow, they had been moved on April 26 from Tobolsk to Yekaterinburg, in the Urals. Now, with the approach of anti-Communist forces and the possibility that Nicholas might be freed by them, the local soviet of Yekaterinburg decided that Nicholas and his family should be executed. On July 16, the Emperor, the Empress, and their children and retainers were shot and their bodies completely destroyed.

strengthen his position by gaining control of the railroad from Novorossisk to Tsaritsyn. If he should succeed, he could join his forces with the Czechoslovak units and the People's Army on the middle Volga. Consequently, Tsaritsyn became a point of great strategic importance to the Reds. By mid-August, Krasnov was in position to attack that city on three sides. But Stalin and a young partisan commander, Klimenty Voroshilov, directed its defense so well that it was able to hold out until the summer of 1919. Thus Krasnov's chance of a junction with the Czechoslovaks and the People's Army, which had by that time been driven back into Siberia, was thwarted, and the Red Army was proved capable of turning the tide.

EXTENSION OF ALLIED INTERVENTION.   The collapse of the Central Powers in 1918, ending with the German-Allied armistice of November 11, immediately altered the nature of the Civil War. The Allies could no longer employ the German danger as a justification for intervention and were compelled either to support intervention openly or to abandon their efforts. Woodrow Wilson and Lloyd George were anxious to find, if possible, a peaceful solution to the Russian problem; but most of the other Allied leaders, particularly Winston Churchill and Georges Clemenceau, favored open and energetic intervention. However, the Allies were in no position to make war; their troops were war-weary, and it seemed hardly proper that those who were promising each nation the right to decide its own fate should try overtly to prevent one from doing so. The policy they finally decided upon resulted in muddled and disastrous action.

England, France, the United States, Italy, and Japan agreed to support intervention. As events worked out, England and France handled the major activities in the West, and Japan handled those in the East. An Anglo-French military convention provided that, in the Black Sea and Caucasus area, French operations would be confined to Bessarabia, the Ukraine, and the Crimea; and British operations to Transcaucasia. Upon the opening of the Baltic after the signing of the armistice, the British sent arms into Estonia. And, at the end of November, the French and British co-operated in the sending of ships into Novorossisk with arms and advice for Denikin.[1] Following that, the French landed a division in Odessa, and the British moved some of their troops from Persia to Batum and Baku, where British corporations had strong financial interests in the oilfields.

Woodrow Wilson and Lloyd George, still seeking a peaceful solution between the Reds and the Whites, proposed in January, 1919, that the So-

[1] During the course of the Civil War, Denikin received about $500 million in aid from the British.

viet Government and the various White forces in Russia send delegates to a conference for the purpose of arranging terms on which to end hostilities. The Soviet Government replied favorably to the proposal, but the anti-Communists refused to have any dealings with the Communists. So the entire idea was abandoned and the Allies, whose leaders were then assembled in Paris for the conference, decided to push their intervention plans. They set as their aims the providing of material aid to the Whites and the sponsoring of the formation of a unified White government which would assume power once the Soviet Government was overthrown, and they ordered an immediate economic blockade of the territory under Soviet control.

THE KOLCHAK GOVERNMENT.   When considering the formation of a unified White government, the Allies were forced to look in many directions. In the South, Denikin and Krasnov represented the strength of the opposition; in Estonia, General Nicholas Yudenich commanded a small White force; and in the Far North, General Eugene Miller was the chief figure in a temporary government set up by the anti-Communists and supported by Allied troops. In Siberia various anti-Communist forces competed for command. In September, 1918, at the insistence of the French and Czechs, the Samara Committee and other White groups had met at Ufa and created a united anti-Communist government in the form of a five-man Directory, declared by them to be the heir of the Provisional Government. But the Directory, composed of representatives of both the left and the right wing of the anti-Communists, had satisfied no one—least of all, the former military officers, who wanted a strong, conservative White government. As a result, intrigue had developed. Admiral Alexander Kolchak, Minister of War in the cabinet formed by the Directory, had become the leader of the conservative faction, which in mid-November, by a successful coup d'état directed against the socialist members of the Directory, had displaced that body and set up another government. He himself had been invested with dictatorial civil and military power and the titles of Supreme Ruler and Commander-in-Chief. With British support, he had been able to establish his authority in Siberia east to Lake Baikal. East of that point, however, the predatory Cossack ataman Semenov had been strong enough, with Japanese aid, virtually to ignore Kolchak.

The Allies, believing that Kolchak represented the ablest of the anti-Communist force, regarded his government as the nucleus of the future government of Russia and planned that it should be the body to summon a Constituent Assembly upon the overthrow of the Soviet regime. Denikin, Yudenich, and other White leaders, in deference to Allied wishes, acknowledged Kolchak's supremacy. The Allies felt confident that the overthrow of the Communists would come in 1919.

Kolchak took the offensive early in 1919. He directed three armies, of about 120,000 men, westward across the Urals in an attempt to take Moscow. Opposed by inferior forces, his armies moved rapidly, retaking Ufa from the Reds on March 13 and moving on to threaten Samara and Kazan in April. It appeared likely that he might reach Moscow. But his weaknesses soon showed up: few of his troops were trained, and he could command little support among the Siberian peasants, who were then being won back by Communist influence. At the end of April, he reached his high-water mark. Then the Red Army began to batter his weakened forces. He lost Ufa on June 9 and was soon forced back across the mountains. At the end of July his forces faced the Reds in pitched battle near Chelyabinsk and lost. Retreating to Omsk, they made another stand, only to lose that city also, on November 14. Such ill fortune was too much for his then broken armies, and most of his men deserted him and went over to the Reds. In despair he named General Denikin the successor to his titles in January, 1920, and fled eastward to seek refuge with the Allies. Some of his former friends, however, turned him over to the Reds, who executed him on February 7. Siberia west of Lake Baikal was then in Soviet hands, but the territory east of that lake was still under the power of White forces and Allied units.

THREATS FROM NORTH AND SOUTH.   While the Reds were concentrating their major efforts against the Kolchak forces they were not neglecting vigilance and activity elsewhere. This war of many fronts was a conglomeration of fighting, not a series of battles. In the Ukraine the Reds were struggling with the Ukrainian nationalists under the leadership of Petlyura. In the western Ukraine, Poles were fighting Ukrainians. On the Black Sea coast, Communist Russians and Ukrainian nationalists were struggling against the French occupiers. And everywhere guerrilla leaders were joining forces with whatever group they found for the moment to their liking.

The most formidable threat from the south came when, in May, 1919, Denikin went on the march. His forces, the name of which had been changed to the Armed Forces of South Russia, took Kharkov and Tsaritsyn at the end of June and Kiev on August 30. By the middle of October, he was in Orel, 250 miles south of Moscow.

During the time of Denikin's advance to Orel, General Yudenich, with an army of about 20,000 based in Estonia, had planned a desperate attack on Petrograd. His plan, of which his British advisers approved, was motivated in part by the desire to aid Denikin by a diversionary move. On October 11, he began his drive from Estonia, hoping to cut the railroad communications between Petrograd and the outside. Five days later, he was thirty miles from Petrograd and had cut all but the Petrograd-Moscow line. The Soviet Government, unable to spare troops from the southern front, contemplated for a time the abandonment of the city. However, Trotsky rallied the local Red forces and maintained a successful defense. Since he could not break through the Red lines and was too weak to undertake a siege, Yudenich began a retreat. In the middle of November he was back in Estonia, where the remnants of his army broke up.

The repulse of Yudenich lessened Denikin's chances; his southern successes might have been extended if some of the Red troops facing him had been diverted. As it was, his forces, spread out along a 700 mile front and weakened after much fighting, were not equal to those the Reds were able to muster against them. Moreover, the civilian population at his rear, outraged by the wild behavior of his men and the reactionary character of his officers, were a menace to him. On October 20, he was forced out of Orel and, four days later, out of Voronezh. By the end of the year the remnants of his armies were falling back toward the once hospitable Don region, where he hoped to regroup them. But he had lost the confidence of many of his own officers and of his Cossack allies also, and the results of his efforts were discouraging. At the end of March, 1920, with the aid of British ships he evacuated about 35,000 men to the Crimea and expected to make a stand there. Instead, finally convinced that the hostility among his officers was sufficient to offset his effectiveness as a leader, he named General Baron Peter Wrangel his successor as commander, on April 4, and left the country.

WHITE COLLAPSE.   General Wrangel faced an impossible task. Among the major drawbacks to his continuing the fight was the fact that he lacked the Allies' support, which had strengthened his predecessors. The French, menaced by mutiny in their fleet in the Black Sea and unsuccessful in their promotion of the anti-Communist cause in south Russia, had recalled most of their forces from the Black Sea area in April, 1919. The British had abandoned their positions in Transcaucasia and Central Asia in the summer of 1919. In September and October the Allied detachment in the Far North had been withdrawn, and General Miller had given up the struggle in the early part of 1920. In January, 1920, the Allied Supreme Council had ended the blockade against Soviet Russia. Now all the Allies, except the Japanese, were out of Siberia.

The British advised Wrangel to end the fighting and evacuate his troops, but he refused the advice, courageously proposing to fight on although hope of success was slight. And, against heavy odds, his forces held out in the Crimea until November. By that time he saw that the only alternative to annihilation was evacuation, and he ordered his men to leave. About 135,000 refugees—civilian and military—were transported by French vessels to Constantinople to begin the life of émigrés. With the collapse of Wrangel's army, the last major White force was dispersed. But the fighting in Russia was not yet over.

Border settlements

IN THE WESTERN PROVINCES.   In the former western border provinces of Russia there had been established anti-Communist governments which had, with the blessing of the Allies, participated in or supported the struggle against the Communists. However, in February, 1920, after the Allies had become convinced that the Communists could not be dislodged from Russia and that the exhausted Soviet Government was sincerely anxious for peace, they informed Russia's western neighbors that they would receive no further aid in the struggle and advised them to establish peaceful relations. In February the R.S.F.S.R. signed a treaty of peace with Estonia, recognizing her independence; and similar treaties were signed with Lithuania in July, with Latvia in August, and with Finland in October.

Negotiations with the new state of Poland proved more difficult. At the Paris Peace Conference of 1919, the eastern frontiers of Poland had been left undecided since the establishment of a frontier would have involved Russia, not represented at the conference. The conferees had, however, included in the text of the Treaty of Versailles the proposal for a tentative Russo-Polish frontier (commonly known as the Curzon Line), laid out in such a way that the majority to the east of it would be non-Poles, and the majority to the west of it, Poles. The Polish Government, with aspirations fixed on regaining the Polish frontiers of 1772, rejected the Curzon Line as a basis for discussion and asked that Soviet Russia turn over to Poland all lands west of the old frontier. The Soviet Government offered a compromise, which was rejected. The Poles thereupon concluded an agreement with refugee Ukrainian nationalist Petlyura, which stipulated that he would help to rouse the Ukrainians in support of the Poles against the Soviet Government in return for Polish support of the establishment of an independent Ukraine.

In April, 1920, the fledgling Polish army advanced into the Ukraine and, by May 8, had reached Kiev. However, the great Ukrainian revolt did not materialize; and the Red Army was soon able to take the offensive with such success that, by August, it was threatening Warsaw. The Reds, having thus turned the tables, believed themselves capable of destroying the Polish army and creating a Soviet Poland. But the Polish army, strengthened by a French military mission led by General Weygand, rallied and drove them back in defeat. Finally, in October, the Soviet Government and Poland agreed to an armistice and, on March 18, 1921, signed a treaty of peace at Riga. The Treaty of Riga created a frontier which ran between the Curzon Line and the Russo-Polish border of 1772. About 4.5 million White Russians, Ukrainians, and Great Russians were thus placed under Polish rule.

IN TRANSCAUCASIA.   Although Soviet Russia was not strong enough to have her way in the establishment of her western frontiers, she was more nearly successful in Transcaucasia, where three anti-Communist republics —Georgia, Armenia, and Azerbaidzhan—had been created during the Civil War. The withdrawal of British forces from Transcaucasia in 1919 and the defeat of Denikin in 1920 laid the region open to the Reds. In April an invading Red force, aided by local Communists, gained control of Azerbaidzhan. Armenia was the next to fall, when her government, involved in a losing war with Turkey, was compelled to ask for Soviet military aid and pay for it with her independence. Georgia, ruled by a Menshevik government, was the last; Soviet troops entered Georgian territory in February, 1921, and forced capitulation. Each of the conquered republics became a Soviet socialist republic, nominally independent but, in fact, closely subordinate to the R.S.F.S.R. in military, diplomatic and economic affairs.

One of the first problems in Soviet-controlled Transcaucasia was the termination of hostilities with Turkey. The revolutionary government of Mustapha Kemal, then involved in a war to free Turkey from European control, was prepared to make peace; and a treaty of "amity and brotherhood" between Turkey and the R.S.F.S.R. was signed on March 18, 1921. By its terms Turkey was to keep Kars and Ardahan (as stipulated in the defunct Treaty of Brest-Litovsk), but Batum was to remain under Georgia's administration. On October 13, 1921, the three Transcaucasian republics signed a treaty of peace with Turkey, recognizing the new frontiers.

The return of peace to the region was followed by a period of integration of the three Soviet republics. In the first part of 1922 the railroad lines and the postal, telegraph, telephone, and radio systems of the three governments were placed under unified administrations. The federation of the three republics was another logical step toward integration; and it was taken on March 12, when the Transcaucasian Socialist Federated Soviet Republic was created by treaty.

IN CENTRAL ASIA.   The establishment of Soviet power in Russian Central Asia was determined largely by the events in the main theaters of the Civil War. During the early part of the war most of the area—except Tashkent—was in anti-Communist hands, but British withdrawal in June, 1919, and the defeat of Kolchak in Siberia exposed it to penetration by the Communists. By the end of the following year they had succeeded in taking from the opposition the two former protectorates of Russia, Khiva and Bokhara, as well as the old province of Turkestan. In Khiva they overthrew the Khan and established the People's Republic of Khorezm, and in Bokhara they replaced the government of the Emir by the People's Republic of Bokhara. Heavy fighting in the latter region continued even after the establishment of its new government. Enver Pasha, who had visions of a new Moslem empire in Central Asia, led the anti-Communist rebels until his final defeat, in June, 1922.

Neither Khorezm nor Bokhara adopted the constitution of the R.S.F.S.R. in full; both continued to recognize full property rights, freedom of religion, and the due process of law. Perhaps Moscow felt that the process of political and social transformation in these fanatically Moslem regions should be permitted to move more slowly than elsewhere. Turkestan was treated differently, being annexed to the R.S.F.S.R. but given a limited autonomy.

IN THE FAR EAST.   The establishment of Soviet power in eastern Siberia was not completed until two years after the death of Kolchak. After his fall, Siberia west of Lake Baikal was incorporated into the R.S.F.S.R., while the Cossack Semenov, aided by the Japanese, still struggled to hold that portion east of Lake Baikal. Thereafter the Reds continued to push the opposition forces farther and farther east until, in April, 1920, they considered the regained territory large enough to have an established government. From it they created the Far Eastern Republic. The new republic did not follow the Soviet pattern and did not proclaim the dictatorship of the proletariat—a deviation due to the strength of its non-Communist elements, whose principles were closer to those of the socialists than those of the Communists. At that time the socialists were strong in eastern Siberia and, although willing to co-operate with the R.S.F.S.R., they were not willing to be absorbed into it. Moscow was for the time being content to accept the existence of the independent Far Eastern Republic since it supported the Soviet foreign policy, which in eastern Siberia was aimed at the expulsion of the Japanese, and served as a buffer state between the R.S.F.S.R. and Japan.

In October the forces of the Far Eastern Republic, still pursuing Semenov and his ally, entered Chita, from which Semenov barely escaped to the protection of the Japanese.[1] The Japanese withdrew to the coast of eastern Siberia and showed the greatest reluctance to depart from it when urged by the Far Eastern Republic. And they continued to mark time there until the United States, opposed to any extension of Japanese power in Siberia, added a strong voice of protest. Finally, in the latter part of 1922 they began to remove their troops from Siberia. Behind them followed the troops of the Far Eastern Republic, who systematically defeated the White forces that had been maintained under the Japanese aegis. On October 25, 1922, the task was completed when the soldiers of the Far Eastern Republic entered Vladivostok. With that, Moscow's need for a buffer state ceased to exist, and the Communists, who had gained a majority in the government of the Republic, voted in November to end its separate existence and to amalgamate it with the R.S.F.S.R.

Vladivostok was the last center of White resistance. With its acquisition by the Far Eastern Republic, the drawn-out and consuming Civil War came to an end.

Evaluation of Communist victory

FAILURE OF WORLD REVOLUTION. Lenin had hoped that by the time victory came in Russia it would be accompanied by socialist revolutions abroad under the leadership of Communist parties united in a new international organization. In March, 1919, his dream of a new International had been realized when representatives of the Russian Communist Party, together with delegates from nineteen foreign parties and groups, had met in Moscow to form the Communist (or Third) International.[2] The non-Russian delegates to this founding session of the Communist International had represented in the main the left wings of socialist parties which were then very small groups. But the meeting had made up in enthusiasm what it lacked in strength and had confidently called the world proletariat to the final struggle against capitalism.

[1] He was captured by the Red Army in 1945 and executed.
[2] The First International, an international association of socialist and anarchist groups, was formed in 1864 and expired in 1876. The Second International, consisting of socialist and labor parties, was founded in 1889.

The call had been feebly answered. For a time, however, it had appeared that some countries would go Communist. A large portion of the Italian Socialist Party had shown sympathy to the Communist cause and carried out revolutionary actions, but the prospect of its promoting a revolution had soon vanished. In Germany, the hopes for a social revolution had been extinguished after the failure of a short-lived rising in Berlin and the elimination within weeks of a Bavarian Soviet. In Hungary the Communists had actually gained political power and established a Hungarian Soviet Republic in March, 1919, under the leadership of Bela Kun, but the republic had soon collapsed. Lenin and the Russian Communists had continued to hope that new revolutions were in the offing, but by the spring of 1921, their optimism had waned.

Thus the Civil War in Russia, in a broad sense, ended in a stalemate: the Allied effort to destroy Russian Communism had failed, and the Russian Communist effort to rouse world revolution had failed. It appeared that Soviet Russia and the non-Communist world would be compelled to live in peace for a while. The Russian Communists, however, looked upon the cessation of hostilities not as peace but as an armistice which could not long endure. They believed that either the enemies of Soviet Russia would open a new attack on her when the opportunity arose or a new wave of revolutions would deluge the capitalist world. But for the time being they accepted for Soviet Russia the new "breathing space," during which she could continue the work of creating a new society.

POLITICAL LOSS AND GAIN.   The advantages that brought victory to the Reds were more directly political than military. The Communists were able to draw military strength from the Russian populace because they could show evidence of their intention and ability to guarantee to the people the fruits of the revolution. The Whites, on the other hand, showed less and less evidence, as the war progressed, that they intended to support the changes brought about by the revolution; consequently they could not command the faith necessary to bring them the popular backing needed for military victory.

A large part of the Russian population was anti-Communist, ready to welcome another regime if it were able to give assurance against the loss of what had been gained by the revolution. But when leaders for such an alternate regime failed to appear, the people could only hold to what they had. The Soviet regime had already given them a sense of equality which they had never experienced before. The power of the old ruling classes was broken, and they were at the bottom of the social heap. The peasant had his long-wished-for land and freedom from the hated landowners and officials. The urban worker, though actually not living as well as he had before the revolution, was satisfied for the time being to see former palaces and mansions being turned into workers' apartments, to know that the former upper classes were given smaller rations than he, and to have the assurance that his former employer or foreman had no further power over him. All of that the Communists (the Reds) had been bringing to the people while the Whites had been moving farther away from them.

During the course of the war, more and more power among the White forces passed from the hands of the anti-Communist liberals and socialists to the conservatives and reactionaries, among whom former officers and landowners predominated. Although no White generals considered it expedient to proclaim as their goal the re-establishment of the old regime, their conduct and actions too often created the impression that they were fighting under the old imperial eagle. And, to their everlasting discredit in the minds of the peasants, the major White leaders did not accept the peasant division of the land as permanent. Moreover, most of them were Great Russian nationalists, and as such they alienated also the national minorities. Denikin's slogan, "Russia shall be great, united, undivided," turned against him the Ukrainians and other minorities who were more concerned with the achievement of national freedom than with the continuation of an undivided Russia. It is true that the White leaders promised the creation of a constitutional government, but the activities they permitted indicated that their liberal statements were thin camouflage for reactionary sentiments. White military victories were generally followed by pogroms, looting, and political repression which repulsed popular sympathy.

POPULATION LOSSES.   The cost of the Communist victory, in terms of lives and property, can never be accurately stated. Red and White Terror took thousands of lives, the actual fighting took far more, and hunger and disease took more than bayonets, bullets, and hangman's nooses combined. It is estimated that World War I, the Revolution, and the Civil War together left Russia with a population deficit of about 28 million. On the basis of normal growth, the population should have been 175 million in 1926, when the first postwar census was taken. Instead only 147 million were counted.

About a million of those lost as a result of the Revolution and the Civil War were emigrants, including nobles, industrialists, tsarist officials, army officers, intellectuals, professionals, and many persons from the lower classes. The exodus reached many countries; but France, Czechoslovakia, the Kingdom of the Serbs, Croats and Slovenes (now Yugoslavia), and China received most of the emigrants. The Soviet Government felt well rid of most of those who left, but it could ill afford to lose the talents of the thousands of doctors, lawyers, teachers, scientists, and writers who preferred not to live under Communist rule.

RESULTS OF WAR COMMUNISM. War Communism, which surpassed even Peter the Great's gargantuan efforts at economic control and regulation, has been called the greatest failure in history. Yet for a space of two and a half years the economy under its pressure did manage to sustain the war-burdened country, albeit at the lowest possible level. The system of grain requisitioning met the food needs of at least the favored urban groups; industry supplied at least the minimum needs of the Red Army; and the systems of distribution and transportation continued to function in some way. Furthermore, without the drastic marshaling of the meager material resources of the land the Communists might not have won the Civil War.

Some of the economic hardships experienced by the country during the Civil War Years were unavoidable and should not be charged against War Communism. World War I had already resulted in a sharp decline in Russia's imports, and the blockade cut her off almost completely from essential industrial raw materials, industrial and agricultural machinery and manufactured goods for consumer use. The value of imports fell from $400 million in 1917 to $30 million in 1918, and to a low of $1.5 million in 1919. It must be remembered, too, that during the Civil War many of the most valuable territories of Russia were outside the area of Soviet control. The Donets Basin, previously the source of 75 per cent of Russia's iron ore and 60 per cent of her pig iron, was in White hands during a large part of the war. The opposition blocked access to other needed supplies also: the cotton of Russian Turkestan, the manufactured goods and raw materials of Poland and the Baltic provinces, and the grain of southern Russia. Even the distribution of the scant available supplies was made difficult in 1918 and 1919 by the fact that some 60 per cent of the Russian railway system was outside Soviet-held territory.

The system of War Communism aggravated some of the unavoidable difficulties. It actually cut potential supply by removing the normal incentives of a money economy and by the prodigious use of compulsion. Robbed of their former motivation for work, the producers, as has been seen, often let their output decline. Often, too, driven by privation, they turned their attention from work to the desperate search for means to sustain life. In further complication of a bad situation, governmental control and centralized administration resulted in the creation of a Behemoth pyramidal bureaucracy, whose activities prompted the lament that what had been achieved in Russia was not the "dictatorship of the proletariat" but rather the "dictatorship of the secretariat." Inefficiency, inexperience and red tape transformed what had been the simplest economic processes into monumental operations. The distribution of salt in a city might require weeks of preliminary paper work in governmental agencies. Bureaucratism made actual shortages seem even worse than they were; often freight cars, the number of which was perilously low, stood empty on sidings as a result of interoffice squabbles or oversight. Such faulty operations proved more easily instituted than reformed.

Under those conditions, the decline of capital goods through normal deterioration, misuse and abuse, lack of replacement, and military losses was catastrophic. Between January, 1917, and December, 1919, the number of freight cars in usable condition fell from about 515,000 to about 205,000, and the number of locomotives in operation from about 15,000 to 4,000. In industry there was a corresponding loss in equipment, with little or no replacement. As a result, in 1920 the production of iron ore was down to 1.6 per cent of what it had been in 1913, pig iron to 2.4 per cent, cotton goods to 5 per cent, and manufactured consumer goods as a whole to about 13 per cent.

The deterioration of agricultural production was not as marked as that of industrial production, but it was nonetheless alarming. Warfare, the division of large estates, and the lack of agricultural machinery and artificial fertilizers contributed to the lessening of the farm output. In addition, the requisition policy of the government and the near uselessness of the money given in exchange for grain discouraged peasants from producing any more than they needed for themselves or could sell or barter on the black market. In 1920 the yield in crops was a little more than 50 per cent of the yield in 1913.

The inability of the Russian economic system under War Communism to satisfy the basic material needs of the population stimulated the use of illegal methods by peasants and workers to meet their needs, regardless of the prohibitions on private trade. In the cities the black market flourished; and in the rural areas, illicit private trading. Workers often stole manufactured goods from the factories in which they worked to exchange for food which the peasants, old adepts at outwitting officials, had hidden from government purchasing agencies. It is estimated that in 1920 nearly one-third of the gross agricultural production of the country was illegally hidden by the peasants. Sometimes they exchanged their withheld products for manufactured goods or other articles of value; sometimes they illegally distilled alcoholic liquor from their grain and sold or exchanged it. Such practices made economic life in reality far different from that decreed by the government.

Although there was little actual famine before 1921, many died before their time from disease and malnutrition; and life for the majority of the remaining ones was transformed into a primitive search for food. Between 1917 and 1921 nearly one-third of the urban population left the cities for the farms, where they could find some food. Moscow and Petrograd lost more than half of their populations in this fashion. Russia was expending her human as well as economic capital at a dangerous rate.

As 1920 drew to an end and the Communists, feeling that victory was practically assured, began to consider postwar problems, the question arose as to whether or not, with the return of domestic peace, the system of War Communism should be modified and a more gradual method of attaining socialism be adopted. Many believed War Communism ideally suited to peacetime purposes; others felt that some modification of its features would be required. However, the men in power showed no inclination to relax the extreme controls. In fact, new and more severe controls were imposed in the first two months of 1921. It required a major crisis to convince the government that the continuation of War Communism would threaten the political stability of the regime.

In the winter of 1920-21 grumbling, discontent, and even open revolt were on the increase. Within the Communist Party itself opposition to existing policies was gathering strength. The worst rumblings, however, came from the countryside, where the combined effects of a bad harvest and the continuation of grain requisitions brought on numerous peasant riots, particularly against food collectors. The greatest unrest was in the Tambov regions, where a former Socialist Revolutionary, Antonov, had been leading a band of anti-Communist peasant guerrillas since 1919. By the beginning of 1921 he had the entire region up in arms. Although the government was able, without much difficulty, to crush the revolts by force, there were clear indications that discontent was still spreading.

The tension in the countryside soon reached out to one of Russia's traditional danger spots, the Kronstadt naval base, where the sailors at that time were chiefly of peasant origin. Their discontent with governmental policy expressed itself in revolt on March 1, 1921. At first their revolt was a bloodless affair in which the sailors, taking possession of the land forts and the ships at the base, demanded that the government ease the pressure on the peasants, permit free re-election of all soviets by secret ballot, and grant civil liberties to all workers' and peasants' political organizations. The government ignored the demands and ordered the unconditional surrender of the mutinous sailors. When they refused to surrender, government troops made an attack on the naval base, reaching it by crossing on the ice of the frozen Neva River. The rebels held out until March 17.

The meaning of the Kronstadt revolt was not lost on the Communist leaders, assembled for the Tenth Congress of the Communist Party, which opened in Moscow on March 8. It was clear that War Communism, if continued in all its severity, would deprive them of the fruits of their political victory. They opposed, of course, any such political concessions as those demanded by the Kronstadt sailors, but they agreed to the necessity of making some economic concessions in order to save their political power. Lenin, who could reverse himself in midfield when necessity demanded, proposed that instead of requisitioning surplus grain the government fix taxes in kind, giving the peasant freedom to dispose of his surplus-after-taxes through private trade channels. This concession was necessary, he said, in order to restore the alliance between workers and peasants, without which the regime could not endure. His proposal, which was adopted by the Congress and later translated into law, marked the beginning of the end of War Communism and the beginning of a new period to be known as that of the New Economic Policy.

TWENTY-SIX / RECOVERY AND ADJUSTMENT

UNDER THE NEP

The New Economic Policy (NEP), adopted in March, 1921, was a tactical retreat for the leaders of Soviet Russia, but it did not signify—as many thought at the time—an abandonment of the original Communist goals. It was rather a calculated relaxation of policy in the economic field, designed to safeguard internal political stability and to encourage economic recovery so that a new drive for the attainment of Communist economic goals might be safely undertaken later. During its operation, Russia was not only recovering her economic vitality but she was also continuing the social transformation begun in 1917 and making internal and external adjustments necessary to the Communist political scheme.

Economic developments

"ORGANIZED RETREAT."   Lenin and his associates were ready to admit, by March, 1921, that the Soviet Government had gone too far in its economic regimentation, that it had committed many blunders which should be rectified. As Lenin put it, the Revolution had "tried to take the citadel of capitalism by a frontal attack" and had failed. It was therefore necessary to adopt other tactics—in short, to permit the partial reintroduction of capitalism into Russia and to adopt new policies to correct the mistakes made in the highly centralized and bureaucratic administration of the nationalized industries. To facilitate such tactics the NEP was adopted.

Lenin himself called the NEP a retreat, an organized retreat for the purpose of preparing a new attack on the citadel of capitalism and establishing socialism in all phases of economic life in Russia. He interpreted it as a necessity for a period of recovery during which the Communist Party and the Soviet Government would retain the political and economic "commanding heights" of a one-party government, state control of foreign trade, credit, and large-scale industry. From that position, he believed that the party and the government could hold the "capitalist" sector of the economy in check and ultimately eliminate it.

In addition to serving immediate economic ends, the NEP was expected to serve also one of the basic needs of the Communist program: the overcoming of the Russian people's general ignorance of elementary business and administrative practices. Lenin told his followers in March, 1922, "We have eighteen People's Commissariats. Of these, at least fifteen are absolutely no good." And unless the Communists learned to do business, he declared, the Soviet regime would not survive.

THE PEASANTS AND THE NEP.   As long as the Soviet Government had adhered to the policies of War Communism, it had burdened the peasants grievously by the practice which Lenin euphemistically called "borrowing from the peasants," requisitioning their surplus grain. But the adoption of the proposal to substitute a tax in kind for requisitioning gave them a promise of relief. The new tax, a percentage of the peasant's agricultural production above his own needs, was to be announced in advance of harvest in order that he might judge the surplus he would have, once he had paid the tax, to dispose of as he chose. In conception, this tax policy was a political one, designed to lessen peasant antagonism; but, once adopted, it had widening effects of an economic nature. Since the peasant could legally dispose of his surplus-after-taxes in any way he wished, it became necessary to legalize private trade once more. Private trade, in turn, required a return to the use of money as the primary basis of exchange; it also made necessary the partial revival of private manufacturing for profit since the nationalized industries were not yet capable of supplying the goods required by the peasants. In addition, the new policy proved an active stimulation to the recovery of agriculture. From the very first, the peasants were encouraged to produce as much as possible in order to realize greater gain. Still further inducements came in 1922, when they were permitted to lease land for short periods from other peasants; and in 1925, when they were granted the right to hire labor.

INDUSTRY AND THE NEP.   In December, 1921, the government[1] de-

---

[1] Reference is made here to the government of the R.S.F.S.R. The other Soviet republics of the time followed its policies with little deviation.

creed that industrial establishments employing fewer than twenty persons would either be returned to their former owners or be leased to private individuals or co-operatives. The enterprises thus denationalized were chiefly small workshops, employing only about one-eighth of the total of the industrial labor force. All other industry remained nationalized. However, in order to attract foreign capital, the government permitted the leasing of some nationalized enterprises to foreign capitalists, usually for periods of twenty-five years, and the letting of contracts to foreign firms for technical aid. The number of such leases and contracts—commonly called concessions—was small, about 163.

One of the most important changes in industry made under the NEP was the decentralization of nationalized industry with a view to encouraging the development of more businesslike methods of operation and the reduction of excessive red tape. To overcome the inefficiency of the cumbersome, centralized organization which placed control over the purchase of raw materials, production schedules, disposition of manufactured goods, and accounting in the hands of central bureaus in Moscow, the state-owned industries were grouped in smaller compact associations known as trusts, with a large degree of autonomy in operation. Thereafter they were encouraged to improve efficiency, to balance their accounts, and to pay for themselves.

PRIVATE ENTERPRISE AND THE NEP.   The most outstanding concession which the NEP made to private enterprise was the legalization of private domestic trade. By the end of 1922, three-quarters of the entire retail turnover was in private hands. Wholesale domestic trade and foreign trade, however, remained under state control. Despite the limited revival permitted, the government held private enterprise at a distinct disadvantage by retaining control over taxation, credit, and the most important raw materials. Moreover, the enterpreneur was treated politically as a second-class citizen, subject to discrimination in education, the army, and government service. Private enterprise existed only on sufferance, and its existence could be terminated at any time.

FISCAL STABILIZATION.   As money again became the chief medium of exchange, it was found necessary to undertake the stabilization of the monetary system. The task was a difficult one, complicated by an unbalanced government budget, the deterioration of credit facilities, and widespread poverty. However, by 1924, after a series of preparatory measures the government was ready to put basic fiscal reforms into operation. In February of that year a new issue of paper rubles based on gold was au-

An example of inflation: the 100,000-ruble note pictured above was almost worthless when issued, in 1921; a note of the same denomination issued in 1913 was worth approximately 50,000 American gold dollars.

thorized, and in March the redemption of earlier issues of paper money for the new was ordered. Holders of rubles of the 1923 issue were given one new ruble in return for 50,000 of the old, and holders of rubles of earlier issues were given one new ruble for 50 million old ones. Stability was further aided by the revamping of the tax structure and the termination, after July, 1924, of the practice of printing money to cover government deficits.

HANDICAP. Economic recovery was handicapped in the first years of the NEP by the after-effects of war and revolution, the most serious of which was famine. Reduction in cultivated area and lack of agricultural equipment had, as has been seen, cut agricultural production seriously by 1921, and the breakdown of the machinery of distribution had added to the food deficit in many areas. Under the circumstances the threshold to famine was easily crossed when droughts caused crop failures along the Volga, in the Urals, in the Kuban region and in portions of the Ukraine. It is estimated that, during the years 1921 and 1922, 33 million persons were starving in Russia and that 5 million died of starvation and disease. But by the end of 1922 the famine-stricken regions were being relieved by improving crops and by foreign aid. The United States was particularly generous in providing medical aid and food through the American Relief Administration, under Herbert Hoover; at the height of its activity, in the summer of 1922, it was distributing food to 10 million Russians.

RECOVERY.   The revival of incentives to produce and sell, improvement in governmental efficiency, and the traditional Russian powers of recuperation helped Soviet Russia along the road to economic recovery. Generally speaking, recovery meant the attainment of prewar levels of production. By the end of 1927, agriculture and much of large-scale industry had attained those levels, and the real earnings of industrial workers had reached —and in some cases, exceeded—them. In some industries recovery was unavoidably delayed; the mining and processing of iron ore, the main centers for which were in the regions most seriously affected by the Civil War, were still considerably short of prewar standards. On the whole, however, Russia had recovered her economic strength by 1927.

Political developments

THE NATIONALITY PROBLEM.   Although, as a result of the Revolution, many non-Russians—Poles, Lithuanians, Letts, Finns, Jews, and Estonians—passed to the jurisdiction of other states, there remained a large non-Russian population under the jurisdiction of the Soviet Government.

Basic Russian stock (Great Russian, Ukrainian, and White Russian) accounted for about 77 per cent of the population; yet the non-Russians inhabited a major part of the Soviet area. The Communist policy toward the nationality problem thus presented was based on the Declaration of the Rights of the Peoples of Russia, issued in November, 1917, declaring legal equality, the right of cultural development and the right of self-determination among all nationalities. Following that policy, the regime faced the task of satisfying the national aspirations of the Russians and the non-Russians while maintaining a highly centralized government. At the same time, it was under obligation to assure national, racial, and religious equality while transforming peoples at various stages of historical and cultural development into Soviet citizens. Considering the diversity and size of the groups concerned, that was no easy task.

The following table, based on the first census after the Revolution, indicates the relative size of the major ethnic groups in the country:

| | | Per cent of total |
Ethnic group	Number	population
Great Russian	77,791,124	52.9
Ukrainian	31,194,976	21.2
White Russian	4,738,923	3.2
Kazakh	3,968,289	2.6
Uzbek	3,904,622	2.6
Volga Tatar	2,916,536	1.9
Jewish	2,680,823	1.8
Finnic (Volga-Ural region)	2,658,700	1.8
Georgian	1,821,184	1.2
Azerbaidzhan	1,706,605	1.2
Armenian	1,567,568	1.1
Tadzhik	978,680	.7
Turkmen	763,940	.5
Others	10,335,945	7.3
Total	147,027,915	

From its beginning, the Soviet Government had actively fostered the development of non-Russian cultures, thus reversing the tsarist policy of Russification. The termination of tsarist restrictions on the use of non-Russian languages and the initiation of Soviet approval of their use resulted at once in their extensive employment in the press, literature, schools, and administration. For many of the backward peoples it was necessary to create alphabets, since their languages had never before been reduced to written form, and in many regions schools in the native tongue were now established for the first time in history.

As for the right of national self-determination, the Soviet regime upheld it in theory but discouraged it in practice, offering as a substitute the right of quasi-independent and quasi-autonomous national organization. This substitute was justified on the grounds that it encouraged the cultural development of the minorities and fulfilled the letter—if not the spirit—of the right of self-determination. Quasi-independent national organization was at first given to the largest and most developed nationalities: the Great Russians, Ukrainians, White Russians, Georgians, Armenians, and Azerbaidzhani. The first of the Soviet republics formed after the Revolution was, as has been seen, the R.S.F.S.R., primarily Great Russian in composition.

Immediately after it, the Communists created the Ukrainian Socialist Soviet Republic, in the area in which the Ukrainians predominated, and the White Russian S.S.R., in the region where the White Russians were dominant. Then in 1922, the Transcaucasian S.F.S.R. was established. These four republics were theoretically independent states, each having its own army and foreign office and being bound to the others only by treaties of friendship and alliance. Actually they operated as one. In each there was one party, the Communist Party, and in each the basic political structure was the same. Their leadership was assumed by the government of the R.S.F.S.R., and decisions adopted by its governing bodies were for the most part either applied directly in the other republics or were copied by the governing bodies.

The national minorities within the four republics were given so-called political autonomy. Where the minority was relatively small in number, an autonomous region was created; where it was large, an autonomous republic was created. In the R.S.F.S.R. alone, thirteen autonomous republics and fifteen autonomous regions were established between 1918 and 1927. Notable among these were the Volga German Socialist Soviet Autonomous Region (later elevated to the status of an autonomous republic), whose population consisted chiefly of Germans descended from the immigrants whom Catherine II had invited to Russia; the Bashkir Autonomous Socialist Soviet Republic; and the Tatar A.S.S.R. Autonomous regions and republics differed from ordinary political subdivisions only in detail. Each, it is true, was permitted the dignity of its own Congress of Soviets, its Central Executive Committee, and its Council of People's Commissars. But the competence of these bodies was very limited and no deviations from the policies laid down in Moscow were permitted. Consequently, autonomy existed in form rather than substance and actually implied only the right to employ the native tongue of the area as the official language of government and education.

ESTABLISHMENT OF THE USSR.   As early as 1919 the Soviet republics then in existence had recognized the need for some arrangement to facilitate the co-ordination of their policies, and the C.E.C. of the R.S.F.S.R. had established a commission to consider the means for forming a closer union among them. But not until 1922, with Soviet power firmly established, were active steps taken toward the formation of such a union. At that time the party adopted Stalin's suggestion that a federal union of the four republics be created, and within a few months the necessary preparations were made. On December 26, 1922, Stalin submitted a resolution to the

Tenth Congress of Soviets of the R.S.F.S.R., calling for the creation of a federal union to be known as the Union of Socialist Soviet Republics (hereafter referred to as the USSR). The resolution was adopted and, since the other three republics had already indicated their desire for union and since their representatives were then in Moscow, the whole process of unification was completed in four days. A commission of representatives of the four republics prepared a declaration of union and a treaty of union. The treaty was ratified on December 30, 1922, by an assembly of delegates from the republics, sitting in Moscow as the First Congress of Soviets of the USSR. GOVERNMENT OF THE USSR.   Within six months after the formation of the USSR a constitution, based upon the Constitution of the R.S.F.S.R., had been prepared for the new state. It declared the USSR to be a federal republic comprising four union republics voluntarily united, with its capital at Moscow. Promulgated on July 6, 1923, it was ratified by the Second Congress of Soviets of the USSR on January 31, 1924.

The Constitution of 1924 left civil rights and suffrage qualifications practically as they had been under the individual constitutions of the republics. But in matters pertaining directly to the operation of the union, innovations were necessary. The Constitution gave the federal government exclusive jurisdiction over foreign affairs, the army and navy, foreign trade, means of communication, and postal and telegraph services; to the federal government and the governments of the union republics it gave concurrent powers over the national economy, food, labor, inspection, finance, political police, and justice. All powers not exclusively delegated to the federal government nor prohibited to the union republics were reserved to the union republics. In appearance, the powers of the individual republics were broad, but actually the government of the USSR was highly centralized since the Communist Party—although ignored in the Constitution of 1924 —dominated the governmental agencies and executed a single policy.

The Constitution named as the chief organs of the federal government the All-Union Congress of Soviets, the All-Union Central Executive Committee, the All-Union Presidium, and the All-Union Council of People's Commissars—or Sovnarkom. (Hereafter mention of Congress of Soviets, Central Executive Committee, Presidium, and Sovnarkom should be taken to refer to the All-Union organs of the federal government unless otherwise indicated.)

The Congress of Soviets, indirectly elected on the basis of one deputy for each 25,000 urban *voters* and one deputy for each 125,000 rural *inhabitants*, was declared to be the chief source of legal authority. This body, made up of about 2,000 deputies, met briefly (usually for a week) once a year until 1927 and biennially thereafter. The Congress elected a bicameral Central Executive Committee (C.E.C.) of about 750 members, who met ordinarily three times a year to conduct legislative business. The C.E.C., itself an unwieldy body, chose a Presidium of twenty-seven members, who exercised the powers of the C.E.C. when it was not in session. In operation, the Congress of Soviets was only an elaborate mass meeting which did little but hear speeches and reports and elect the members of the C.E.C.; the latter fulfilled most of the legislative functions ordinarily associated with a parliamentary body, issued decrees, and approved or disapproved decisions of the Sovnarkom and the union republics.

The chief admininstrative and executive body of the USSR was the Sovnarkom, appointed by the C.E.C. and consisting originally of ten People's Commissars, each in charge of one department of government, and chairmen of several important commissions. Individually the members of the Sovnarkom directed the work of their departments, and collectively they formed the counterpart of the cabinets of Western countries. The duties of the body were to formulate policies on general governmental matters, make appointments of higher administrative officials, and submit budgetary and financial proposals to the Presidium and the C.E.C. Since the Constitution drew no sharp line between legislative and executive functions, the Sovnarkom was permitted also to issue decrees with the force of law, subject to confirmation by the C.E.C. The chairmanship of the Sovnarkom[1] was designed to be an office similar to that of the Western premier or prime minister. The chairman of the Presidium of the C.E.C.[2] was considered chief of state for formal occasions, such as diplomatic receptions.

GOVERNMENT OF INDIVIDUAL REPUBLICS.   Each of the union republics revised its constitution to accommodate its membership in the USSR, but no essential changes were made. Each still had its hierarchy of soviets leading from the village and city soviets to its Congress of Soviets, and each had its Central Executive Committee, Presidium, and Sovnarkom. Coordination between the federal and union governments in matters of concurrent jurisdiction was achieved through federal representation in the Sovnarkoms of the individual republics. And co-ordination in matters reserved to the union republics was usually achieved by the simple expedient of accepting the leadership of the R.S.F.S.R.

---

[1] From 1924 to 1930, this office was held by Alexis Rykov; from 1930 to 1941, by Vyacheslav Molotov. In 1941 it passed to Joseph Stalin.
[2] Michael Kalinin held this position until 1936, when it was abolished.

EXPANSION OF THE UNION. The Soviet Republics of Bokhara and Khorezm, in Central Asia, did not immediately enter the USSR after its formation but were tied to it by treaties and agreements. In 1924 Moscow began pressing them to apply for admission to the union and they did so. At the same time, it was proposed to divide the territories of Bokhara, Khorezm, and Turkestan (which was then a part of the R.S.F.S.R.) along ethnic lines. Finally two republics were so formed and admitted to the USSR in May, 1925: the Uzbek Soviet Socialist Republic, in the eastern part of the territory, and the Turkmen S.S.R. in the western. In 1929 the portion of the Uzbek S.S.R. inhabited by the Tadzhik peoples was split off and admitted to the USSR as the seventh republic.

Of the seven republics making up the USSR in 1929, the R.S.F.S.R., with a population of over 100 million, was clearly the most important. It was followed by the Ukrainian S.S.R. with 29 million inhabitants; the Transcaucasian S.F.S.R., with 5.8 million; the White Russian S.S.R., with 5 million; the Uzbek S.S.R., with 4.4 million; the Turkmen S.S.R., with 992,000; and the Tadzhik S.S.R., with 827,000.

Creating the new Soviet citizen

FOUNDATION FOR A NEW ORDER. Soviet leaders realized that the new state could function successfully only if its citizens would accept a life outlook totally different from that of old Russia. They expected that at least a generation would be required—perhaps many generations—before the ideal Soviet man would emerge. And they knew that the creation of that ideal would require a planned use of education, persuasion and coercion. Their plan was that every Soviet citizen be taught, from the kindergarten to old age, to believe in and act according to the Communist philosophy. No one was to be exempt from the duty of teaching that philosophy; every party member and every writer, actor, scientist, scholar, teacher, and official—whether a Communist or not—was expected to teach it. The Communist Party, with its control of all media of communication and all the organs of persuasion and coercion, set the patterns to be followed. Since the Communist philosophy embraced all phenomena of life, there was no matter on which there was not an official Communist point of view, known as the "party line," to be followed by all engaged in the task of persuasion and education.

Against those who would not be persuaded of the truths of Communism, the party was prepared to use its reserve weapon, coercion. Lenin's view was that the Soviet state was based on a balance between persuasion and coercion; and the Communist Party fell in line with the belief that, although the use of coercion was undesirable, it was necessary as long as remnants of the old ruling class and vestiges of the old mentality remained. As it was applied, coercion varied in stringency according to the case: a student antagonistic to the regime would find the doors of higher educational institutions closed to him; a writer unsympathetic to the government would be denied the right to publish; and those who overtly opposed the government might face jail, a labor camp, or a firing squad.

Dealing with political opponents was the duty of the political police. At first, each of the republics had its own political police—the Cheka. In February, 1922, however, the Cheka was reorganized, restricted somewhat in the extent of its powers, and given a new name, the GPU (from the initials of its name in Russian, *Gosudarstvennoe Politicheskoe Upravlenie*, or State Political Administration). The GPU was entrusted with the combatting of counter-revolutionary acts and espionage within the country and with the conduct of Soviet espionage abroad. It could turn a culprit over to the regular courts for trial or it could imprison or exile him by simple administrative action, but it could impose the death sentence only with the approval of the highest governmental authorities. The chief subjects of the attention of the GPU were priests, former tsarist officials, and members of underground organizations; but anyone whose actions might be construed as being opposed to the Communist state had cause to fear that body. Over the GPU organizations was the federal political police organization known as the OGPU (from the initials of its name in Russian, *Obedinenoe* [Unified] *Gosudarstvennoe Politicheskoe Upravlenie*). Felix Dzerzhinsky became the first head of the OGPU when it was established in November, 1923; and after his death, in 1926, Vyacheslav Menzhinsky was appointed to the office.

EDUCATING THE NEW GENERATION.   The new regime undertook the double task of liquidating the cultural backwardness of Russia and of rearing a new Communist generation by reforming the educational system of the country. Important as it was to educate and re-educate the adult population, the greatest emphasis was to be placed on gaining and training the youth in order to insure loyal and efficient workers, technicians, managers, and teachers to perform the tasks of the new society.

In order that children might be properly trained to achieve that end it was deemed necessary to isolate them as much as possible from the influences of the old regime. The first steps toward educational reform were in the realm of legislation rather than practice, for a backward school system and a teaching force which was generally hostile to the new regime made the task a difficult one. The steps taken by the R.S.F.S.R. were typical: in the first part of 1918 it had forbidden all religious instruction in governmental and private schools and had placed almost all schools under the supervision of the People's Commissariat of Education. That body, under the direction of Anatol Lunacharsky from 1917 to 1929, attempted to apply an entirely new set of educational principles. Emphasizing the predominant position of the workers and poorer peasants, it gave the children of those classes preference in admission to secondary and higher schools and denied or limited admission to the children of the former higher classes. Inexperienced but enthusiastic in policy-making, it condemned the old concepts of formal discipline both in subject matter and in student-teacher relations and introduced new methods of instruction, many of them inspired by the theories of John Dewey. One of its decrees abolished the practices of standing for recitations, memorization of homework, and curtsying to teachers. Pupils, even the youngest, were permitted a wide range of self-government.

Having been neglected during the Civil War, schools were in a discouraging state in 1921; the primary school attendance was lower than it had been in 1914 and continued to fall until 1923, while the decline in secondary school attendance was even greater. The economic and political recovery of the country after 1921, however, made it possible to speed up educational expansion. Between 1923 and 1928, attendance in the primary schools rose from 3,210,000 to 12 million, and that in secondary schools rose proportionately. It was hoped that primary schooling at least would be available for all by 1934.

The training of the new generation was not left to the schools alone. To help in the task three mass children's and youth organizations were established through the efforts of the party. The Union of Communist Youth (generally known as the Komsomol, the contraction of its Russian name) had been established in 1918 for youths between the ages of fourteen and twenty-three. From an initial membership of 20,000 it grew to an organization of 2 million by 1928, enrolling about 7 per cent of the population in its age group. It served the party's purpose by teaching the Communist doctrine and serving as a center of Communist influence in the schools, the army, the factories, and on the farms. Under the auspices of the Komsomol, organizations for younger groups were formed. The first one of the kind, for children between ten and sixteen years of age, was organized in 1922 by members of the Komsomol in Moscow. Known as the Children's Communist Organization of Young Pioneers, it grew to a membership of nearly 2 million by 1926. A third organization, led by Komsomols and Young Pioneers, was that of the Little Octobrists, for children between eight and eleven years of age. Its membership was about 274,000 in 1926. Other organizations for children and youth were forbidden; and the Komsomols, Young Pioneers, and Little Octobrists were encouraged in every way as junior partners of the adult Communists.

HIGHER EDUCATION. The first efforts of the Soviet regime to introduce the Communist principles into the institutions of higher learning resulted in a decline in the standards of those institutions. The faculties of the universties and of other higher educational institutions were on the whole cool or hostile toward the plans for integrating their programs into the new Soviet system. Some recalcitrant professors fled; others were dismissed or arrested, and a few submitted. Thus the whole of higher education was subjected to a period of contention and turmoil during the time required for placing organizational control into the hands of Communist personnel. Even when that control was established, the quality of work lagged because the new personnel was too often more distinguished for party loyalty than for academic attainment.

The accomplishments of the various institutions were further curtailed by the introduction of the Marxian viewpoint into instruction and research and by the practice of favoring workers and peasants in admission of students, often without proper regard for qualifications. Whereas in 1914 about 57 per cent of the university students in Russia were children of nobles, merchants, priests, and officials, in 1928 about 77 per cent were workers or peasants or children of workers or peasants—most of them with inadequate preparation for the work previously expected of university students. To restore standards was to be a slow and laborious process.

EDUCATION OF THE ADULT GENERATION. It was a clearly recognized fact that formal education alone could not meet the educational needs of the new society. Special education was needed for the millions of illiterate adults who were such an important part of that society, for as long as they remained illiterate the process of Communist indoctrination would lag and the program of training skilled personnel for the industrialized economy would falter. To meet the need, the government established a system of adult educational centers. They dotted the country with schools for illiterates and semiliterates, factory schools, night schools, army schools, schools for peasants, and village reading rooms. Through such facilities about 7 million adults were taught the rudiments of reading and writing during the years 1917-28. Yet about 49 per cent of the population over the age of nine was illiterate in 1928. The government set 1934 as the year by which illiteracy would be eliminated, but even then the goal was not attained.

POLITICAL EDUCATION THROUGH PARTICIPATION. A number of mass organizations, some already in existence before the Revolution and others created subsequently, served as supplementary schools of communism. Chief among these were the village and city soviets, the trade unions, and the organizations of the co-operative movement.

The village and city soviets, which were intended to draw the people into mass participation in government through the activities of voting and holding office, had suffered an early setback in the discharge of their duties. The elections had been frequent during the first year of the Soviet regime but, once the Civil War had begun, the practice of electing deputies to the soviets had been abandoned except in the major cities. Regular and general elections were resumed in 1921, but the candidates for office were named from above; as a consequence, interest in the elections was low. Finally, in 1924, when attendance at election meetings was so slight that the election results were nullified, it was decided that thereafter nominations should be made only by the voters and that the party should content itself with the use of persuasion to secure the election of candidates suitable to it. The elections of 1925 and 1926 were the first genuine elections with open nominations since 1918, and the results were heartening: over 45 per cent of the rural and 60 per cent of the urban voters cast their votes. Each year thereafter the percentage of participation increased.

The activities of the village and city soviets were of particular importance in the Communist scheme not only because they provided opportunity for the practice of citizenship but also because they provided a link between the Communists and the non-Communist masses. The percentage of soviet deputies who were not members of the Communist Party was great (as late as 1927, about 87 per cent of the members of the village soviets being non-Communists). They were not, of course, anti-Communists, since the controlling position of the party made the election of avowed anti-Communists well-nigh impossible. But the fact remained that of the nearly one million members of the soviets of all kinds in the USSR a large number were non-Communists working in co-operation with the controlling party and representing the interests of many who, by evidence of their votes, approved of that co-operation.

The trade unions represented an equally important link, for in them, as in the soviets, Communists and non-Communists worked together for their common good—even though the Communists managed to provide the direction of policy. The unions had suffered, as had the soviets, during the Civil War because membership had been made compulsory at that time and the election of officers suspended. But after 1922, when membership was once more made voluntary, they made a rapid recovery. In 1928 about 10 million persons were trade unionists—90 per cent of all who received wages or salaries. Individually the organizations followed the plan of the industrial rather than of the craft union. In addition to industrial workers, they included office workers, government employees, and almost all professionals. The several unions were affiliated with one another in a vast organization at the apex of which was the All-Union Central Council of Trade Unions. Although the trade unions ostensibly represented the interests of their members, the efficacy of such representation was limited by the fact that the unions were expected to act as subordinate allies of the government, the chief employer in the country. There were left to them only those functions through which they could best serve both themselves and their employer: the development of labor discipline, the provision of various benefits, the promotion of productivity, and the education of their members. Their educational activities were many in number, carried on through special schools, workers' clubs, reading circles, libraries, special film showings, and factory newspapers. In their every organized effort, the Communist point of view received special stress. Even their social and athletic activities were expected to show political discretion; in workers' clubs, for example, activities considered "bourgeois"—such as card-playing, drinking, and dancing to jazz music—were banned (although, in fact, not always avoided).

The largest but least integrated of these mass organizations which served to advance political education through participation were the co-operative societies. These societies, which had a membership of 15 million as early as 1917, had come under the control of the government by 1920. Thereafter the government gave serious attention to encouraging their growth, for it recognized the benefits to be derived from consumers' co-operatives as aids in retail distribution and from agricultural co-operatives as effective means for breaking down the individualistic habits of the peasantry. In 1928, the various co-operatives included some 25 million share-holders, representing about 50 per cent of the peasants and 60 per cent of the industrial and office workers of the country. In addition to functioning as an approved part of the Soviet economic system, they functioned also as schools of Communism, directing their organizational activities in such a way that the participants might learn and practice the duties of Soviet citizenship.

RE-CREATION OF THE FAMILY. The first Soviet legislation on the family, it will be recalled, was designed to relieve the family of reliance upon religious sanctions and to establish equality of the sexes. Radical as they were, those early measures failed to satisfy all Communist theoreticians; a few extremists believed that the family was an outmoded institution, and many believed that it required at least some further redesigning. However there was a prevailing belief that nothing should be done to destroy the monogamous family based on love and the mutual compatibility of the two partners. It was generally conceded, nevertheless, that the economic and educational functions of the family should be assumed by the community and that the woman should have a role equal to that of the man in the economy and society.

The R.S.F.S.R., as usual, took the lead in advancing reforms by adopting new legislation to supplement the 1917 and 1918 decrees on marriage. In November, 1920, it legalized the performance of abortions, at the same time denouncing abortion as an evil which would in time be eradicated. And in November, 1926, after a period of extended discussion, it adopted a code of laws on marriage and the family which served as a model for similar codes in the other union republics. The code recognized all marriages as valid—whether legally effected or not—and granted equality of rights to both legitimate and illegitimate children. It provided that either party to a marriage might end the union by the simple act of registering the divorce at a government registration office; and it assured absolute legal equality of husband and wife, even declaring that each was entitled to alimony.

In order to make equality of the sexes effective and to relieve women of the traditional household duties so that they could work outside the home, the government undertook a variety of actions: it prohibited, in employment practices, all discrimination on the basis of sex; it guaranteed to every employed woman a vacation with pay both before and after bearing a child; it established nurseries in factories and on collective farms; and it set up communal kitchens and laundries in the cities. Such provisions had been carried so far by 1929 that one sanguine writer was prompted to predict that by 1942, "vast factory-like kitchens, in numbers sufficient to serve the entire population must supersede home cooking" and that the day would come when there would be no "need or reason for the separate life of separate families in isolated flats and little houses. . . ."

The new concepts of marriage and family took root slowly. As a whole, they were more readily accepted in the cities than in the rural areas. Among the Moslem peoples of the USSR particularly they were at first viewed with great disfavor. Nonetheless, women began to take an important part in political life, the economy, the professions and the schools. The resulting effects on the stability of the family were not as unsettling as some had expected. The countrywide ratio of marriages to divorces was about four to one in 1927, when the ratio for the United States was about six to one. The greatest family instability at the time was recorded in Moscow, Leningrad (formerly Petrograd), and other major cities. Moscow's record of about thirteen marriages to ten divorces was typical of such cities.

CONFLICT WITH RELIGION.   In the attempt to mold a new generation, conflict with organized religion could not be avoided, for Communism's philosophy of life was at variance with the philosophy offered by religion. The original Communist policy toward religion was based on the argument that religious beliefs would ultimately die if subjected to proper discouragement. The Soviet Government attempted to speed the process by the separation of Church and state, the prohibition of organized religious instruction of the young, the restriction of organized religion to the narrowest functions of the performance of religious rites, and the systematic antireligious instruction of both young and old.

But the Orthodox clergy had been forehanded enough to take steps for the strengthening of the Church before the Provisional Government had been overthrown. After the March Revolution, they had begun a movement—already considered before 1917—to revivify the Church by the restoration of the office of Patriarch, which had been abolished by Peter the Great. The Council of the Orthodox Church, meeting in Moscow on August 28, 1917, had agreed to the restoration. And on November 18, while fighting was in progress, they had elected Tikhon, the Metropolitan of Moscow, as the first Patriarch to hold office in Russia since 1700. The new Patriarch, confronted by the new Soviet Government, had immediately asserted his position by denouncing its decree on the separation of Church and state and by anathematizing those responsible for it. With that the struggle between the Orthodox Church and the government had begun. The outbreak of the Civil War had intensified that struggle. The Orthodox clergy, as well as many of the clergy of all faiths, had accepted the White forces as the champions of a government which would restore religion to its former status in Russia and had therefore given them their blessings and support. The Reds, on the other hand, had been clearly identified as enemies, subjecting the clergy as they did to the Red Terror, imprisonment, or exile. The final victory of the Reds left the Church in a precarious position; and that position became more precarious after November, 1921, when a convention of monarchists and reactionary émigré Russian bishops, priests, and laymen, meeting abroad, demanded redoubled efforts to oust the Communist Government. Tikhon was accused by the government, apparently with some justice, of supporting the monarchists, and in 1922 a new series of attacks on the Church was begun. As a result many of the clergy were executed, and the Patriarch was arrested in May as a monarchist. While awaiting trial, Tikhon decided to make his peace with the regime. In June, 1923, he offered, if freed, to end his opposition to the government and to dissociate himself from the anti-Soviet movements. His offer was accepted and he was released. The government had gained an advantage which it followed up by refusing, when Tikhon died, in April 1925, to permit the election of a successor.

Thereafter, it continued sedulously to spread its antireligious propaganda through all the channels at its command—the schools, the press, the party, and the mass organizations. In 1925 an organization exclusively devoted to the antireligious campaign, the Union of Militant Atheists, was founded and placed under the direction of Emelyan Yaroslavsky. Although it did not have a rapid growth (its membership being 128,000 in 1928), it was an active organization, sponsoring antireligious activity throughout the country and engaging in the publication of many books and periodicals. Its chief organ, the *Atheist*, had a wide distribution.

The efficacy of the antireligious campaign, which combined the teaching of a materialistic-scientific view of life with overt attacks on religion, is difficult to evaluate. A large number, already indifferent to religious observance, fell away from the various organized faiths; many formerly religious adults broke with their beliefs; and a large proportion of the youth educated by the new society were growing up with no religious beliefs. Nonetheless, old beliefs persisted among many of the adults, particularly among the peasants, who kept their icons in their time-honored places and carried on their acts of piety with little change. It was a situation which satisfied neither the antireligious nor the religious; the former felt that the process of weaning the people away from religion was proceeding too slowly, while the latter felt that it was proceeding too rapidly. Still, the Communists had cause for optimism: through this part of their program, as through other parts, a gradual but definite transformation was being made throughout the country. The habits and beliefs of 147 million people could not be altered in a decade, but it was evident that they were being altered at a rate probably never before equaled.

By 1927 a *modus vivendi* was established between the government and the Church. After promising to refrain from hostility toward the government, the Church was permitted to establish a temporary Patriarchal Holy Synod and to maintain an ecclesiastical administration. But the arrangement did not bring peace to the Orthodox Church. Like other organized faiths, it continued to suffer from severe limitations on its activities, frequent arrests of its priests, and the closing of many of its buildings.

Redirection of culture

THE NEW APPROACH.   The Communists' general position on culture was clear. They declared that in a class society culture could be only the reflection of the views of the ruling class and held, therefore, that under the dictatorship of the proletariat it should reflect the views of the proletariat and further their interests; none engaged in the furtherance of Russian culture could "stand outside the class struggle." But their position on the application of that theory to specific problems was, for a decade or more, far from clear or coherent. Extremists among them believed that all ties with the arts and sciences of Russia's past should be cut, while moderates held that the best of the past should be retained and made to serve in a new direction.

It was a trying period for those engaged in cultural pursuits. In the first years of the regime, the number of the country's active intellectuals, artists, scholars, and scientists was greatly decreased. Some were killed during the Civil War, many emigrated, and many who remained in Russia either would not or could not accommodate themselves to the new outlook.

LITERATURE.   The best writers of prerevolutionary Russia, with few exceptions, disappeared from the literary activity of their homeland at the end of the Revolution. Maxim Gorky was one of the exceptions. He overcame his first disapproval of the Communist rule to the extent of offering his services as a friend and counselor of young Russian writers seeking to become proletarian authors. Since he was of proletarian origin and since his works had demonstrated his sympathy with the masses, the Soviet Government was glad to accept his services. In the early years of the regime, when the State Publishing House published only works of value as literary propaganda and when private publication was practically impossible, many young authors were dependent upon Gorky and the employment he could find for them as translators, assistants in the theaters, or lecturers. Gorky himself did little creative writing after 1917 except for his powerful tetralogy *The Life of Klim Samgin* (1927-36), set in the period 1880-1917.

Adverse conditions in the early years of new rule and during the Civil War did not completely stifle literary growth. There was a temporary decline in prose writing, but poetry kept up its vigor. Since many of the conservative poets were out of line with Communism, it is not surprising that their places were pre-empted immediately after the Revolution by those who had been out of line with the old regime—the extremists, particularly the symbolists and the futurists. The government was willing to support and encourage these extremists as allies in the cultural rehabilitation of the country as long as they would keep their places in the new scheme of things and produce literature of a proletarian appeal.

Individually, some of them did outstanding work. Among these were the symbolist Alexander Blok, whose work is well represented by *The Twelve* (1918), a great poem of the Revolution, utilizing the coarse diction and the rhythm of a workers' song; Sergei Yesenin, a peasant imaginist poet, whose *Pugachev* (1922) is excellent evidence of his proletarian leanings; and the futurist Vladimir Mayakovsky, whose satire *150,000,000* (1920) is typical of his poetic attacks on the bourgeois world.

But, as a whole, the extremists failed to live up to the specifications set by the government. They grouped themselves according to their particular theories, and group fought group for the monopoly of the literary field. Moreover, the newness of their approach and the obscurities of their style did not always appeal to the people in general. Their tendency to draw into sympathetic groups that struggled ambitiously for strength and prominence caused Lenin to suspect them of aiming at independence from state direction and obscured for him the virtues both of their proletarianism and of their poetic excellence. His incomplete acceptance of them resulted in the publication on December 1, 1920, of a decree by the Central Committee, declaring that all cultural organizations thereafter, regardless of nature, might operate only under the direction of the Commissariat of Education.

After 1921, however, with the easing of restraints under the NEP, the literary scene began to change as writers were gradually admitted to more liberal treatment. In line with its relaxation of restraints in other fields, the Politburo passed a resolution in July, 1924, granting all writers relative freedom in their work if they were willing only to declare their belief in the basic principles of the new society. The following years, as non-Communist writers entered the field and all writers were inspired by the new freedom, there came about a shift of emphasis from poetry to prose and a great increase in literary output. Writers chose their themes generally from that part of their country's history in which they had been or were then involved—the Revolution, the Civil War, the period of the NEP—and they treated those themes realistically.

The most impressive Soviet work on a historical theme, begun in this period and completed in 1940, is *The Silent Don* (first volume published in 1928), by Michael Sholokhov. Other works representative of the able literary treatment given to the Revolution and the Civil War are *A Bare Year*, by Boris Pilnyak; *The Armored Train*, by Vsevolod Ivanov; *Chapaev*, by Dmitri Furmanov; and *Red Cavalry*, by Isaak Babel. And two outstanding examples of the fiction expressive of the strains and stresses of the NEP period are *Cement*, by Feodor Gladkov, and *Three Pairs of Silk Stockings*, by Pantaleimon Romanov. Those were all serious works, marked by the purposeful manner which the government expected of writers. There was not much relief from the pervasive seriousness of the period, but now and again a little humor broke through, usually satirical humor such as that which characterized *The Little Golden Calf*, by Ilya Ilf and Eugene Petrov, and the sketches and short stories of Michael Zoshchenko.

From a literary viewpoint, the government had no reason to regret the moderation admitted under the NEP. It resulted in better national-themed literature and wider reading by the people—two results highly desirable in the program for the development of proletarian culture.

MUSIC. Music was threatened by the same intellectual maelstrom in which literature was caught. Many musicians had chosen to leave the country when they saw the coming of evil days for themselves and their art—among them, Stravinsky, Grechaninov, and Rachmaninov. In the first years after the Revolution, their fears of catastrophe for Russian music seemed to be borne out; composers with a daring disregard for classic traditions subjected the country to an orgy of modern music which neither interested nor intrigued the general public, and experimentation in some cases became so fantastic as to repulse music lovers.

But the urge toward novelty soon spent itself and, after 1921, older musicians such as Alexander Glazunov, Nicholas Myaskovsky, and Michael Ippolitov-Ivanov were able, as teachers and composers, to pick up and transmit the musical traditions of Russia. At the conservatories of Leningrad, Moscow, and Kiev they and others were permitted to train a new generation of musicians, who were to make their mark in the 1930's.

ART. Among the active artists who remained in Russia after the Revolution, mostly young men, the break with tradition was even more extreme than among the writers and composers. A group known as LEF (for Left Front), led by such men as Punin and Sternberg, gained the favor of the party and, with it, material advantages which gave them ample room for experimentation. Denouncing "pictures" as "a form of bourgeois aesthetics," declaring "irreconcilable war on art" as a concept, they attempted to bring the work of painters, sculptors, and architects to the masses by employing the most advanced techniques of abstract art. In their zeal to reach the masses they worked feverishly, splashing their colors at random, often on city walls and buildings, even employing cartoon and caricature to serve their purposes.

By the middle 1920's the influence of LEF began to wane as it became evident that the people at large could not understand its strange and, to them, often grotesque work. The party therefore began to favor the artists belonging to AKHRR (the Association of Artists of Revolutionary Russia) who believed that art must be "understood' by the masses. Far from rejecting representational arts, as had the LEF, the members of AKHRR reduced representation to the level of photography, producing such works as Brodsky's *The Second Congress of the Communist International*, which completely sacrificed artistry to detail. Neither the members of LEF nor AKHRR produced work of lasting value, but both organizations helped widen the audience for art by expanding the facilities of museum and art galleries and awakening in the lower classes an interest in the graphic arts.

THEATER AND FILM. The most noteworthy artistic achievements of the 1920's were made by the theater and the film. Both had been readily recognized by the government as important media for mass propaganda, for their messages could transcend the barriers of illiteracy and limited education. And both, fortunately, had attracted men of rare gifts, who understood the value of artistic experimentation and were therefore not adverse to breaking with old forms and manners if the break could be turned to the advancement of their art.

The theater, which had been consistently strong since the middle of the eighteenth century, continued to flourish during the grimmest days of the Civil War; and many of its directors and producers were ready, when peace came, to help the theater take its place in the new design of Russian life. Constantine Stanislavsky and Vladimir Nemirovich-Danchenko, directors of the Moscow Art Theater, had supported the Soviet Government from its beginning and had therefore suffered no break in the progress of their work. Now with new talent, new plans, and almost complete freedom they were able to conceive and execute dramatic productions which drew international respect. The "Stanislavsky method," employing realism and ensemble acting, was so enthusiastically accepted in other countries that many who might otherwise have remained uninterested in the new Russia, began to take an interest.

Two others prominent among those who helped to advance the Russian theater during this period were Vsevolod Meyerhold and Alexander Tairov. Meyerhold, once a follower of Stanislavsky, discarded the master's approach and developed what he termed a "biomechanical" approach which, though artistically commendable, finally caused him to lose support of the government. Tairov, who had organized the Chamber Theater in Moscow in 1914, brought still other vitalizing innovations to the theater—particularly in stagecraft—and was able, for a few years, to add to its popularity and growth while satisfying both his artistic integrity and the Soviet Government.

The film industry had been encouraged by the Communist leaders since the first months of 1918, but it was not until 1926 that the Soviet film achieved artistic success. In that year *Potemkin,* directed by Sergei Eisenstein, and *Mother,* directed by Vsevolod Pudovkin, were released and acclaimed at once as definite contributions to their field. Eisenstein had been influenced by the American film and had been able to choose and stress just those features that were needed to make his productions best for Russia. He directed attention to the masses rather than the individual and was thus able to express the message of his productions in broad terms. Pudovkin employed similar techniques with striking success. The work of these two directors was well received not only in Russia but also in other countries; and, of even greater importance, it was approved by their closest critic, the government.

SCIENCE AND SCHOLARSHIP.   In line with Marxian socialism, the government was anxious to promote both the natural and the social sciences as aids to the reforming of society and as means of providing substitutes for what they considered the mystical and impractical conceptions represented by religion.

The scientific research facilities of the several universities and of the venerable Academy of Sciences were expanded as soon as possible after the Revolution. The Academy of Sciences of the Ukrainian S.S.R. was founded in 1920. In addition, a number of purely Communist institutions and organizations were established—in part, as an expression of distrust toward the intellectuals of the old regime who remained in the general institutions of learning and, in part, as a sincere effort to provide broader opportunities for a greater number of Russian students and scholars. Among them were the Communist Academy, created in 1918 as the chief institution for the study of Communist theory; the Marx-Engels (now Marx-Engels-Lenin) Institute, opened in 1920 as a center for the editing and publishing of the Marxist classics; the Institute of Red Professors, organized in 1921; and the Association of Marxist Historians, founded in 1925.

Because of the nature of the use to which the natural sciences and social sciences were to be put, there was great differentiation in the freedom accorded to scholars in the two fields. The natural scientists were given more latitude, for no particular aspect of their work was offensive to the principles of Marxism. Theirs was the task of exploring the structure and function of the universe, and their work was required for a practical and immediately useful purpose; it was to provide the technical basis for the economic stability necessary to the progress of the new society. The relative freedom allowed them did not, however, result in the kind of stimulated activity witnessed among the writers, musicians, and artists; their work did not lend itself to novel experimentation and "modern" approach. Progress depended upon the leadership of those elder scientists who had remained in Russia and were willing to continue their work under the new regime. Outstanding among those who continued their work and thereby, to the satisfaction of the government, helped to prepare the way for the industrial and agricultural revolution which was to come with the Five-Year Plans, were the physiologist Ivan Pavlov (who refused to declare himself for the new regime but whose work was acceptable to it); the physicists Abram Joffe, Sergei Vavilov, Peter Kapitsa, and Leonid Mandelshtam; and the chemists Nicholas Kurnakov and Vladimir Vernadsky.

The social scientists, in contrast to the natural scientists, were limited by the fact that the doctrines of Marxism-Leninism provided ready-made answers to many fundamental questions within the scope of their studies, and those answers might be neither ignored nor analyzed. Economists and sociologists in particular were required to hew close to official doctrine. Historians, too, were greatly affected, being required to rewrite general as well as Russian history in the Marxist manner. The dean of Communist historians was Michael Pokrovsky, who had been an eminent Marxist historian before the Revolution. Under his influence, the study and teaching of history were completely revamped. History as a formal subject practically disappeared from the schools, to be replaced by general social studies. Russian history was taught and studied from a rigidly formal Marxist viewpoint, almost all of its earlier content except that which could be shown to be of revolutionary value having been condemned and rejected. The Soviet citizen was to be taught to think of himself not as a product of the Russian past but as the heir to all progressive and revolutionary movements in the world. So restrained, most of the historical writing of the period was of little merit. Pokrovsky and others, however, did creditable work in improving old archival collections and organizing new collections which were to aid later historians.

International relations during the NEP

SOVIET POSITION.   During the period of the NEP, foreign affairs presented problems as important to the continuance of the Soviet regime as those presented by domestic affairs. Having withdrawn from the World War in 1917, Russia had not been included in the peace conferences; now she was an outsider, looked upon by most of the world as a weak, third-rate power and a dangerous source of revolutionary infection. Between her and the non-Communist world there was a feeling of mutual distrust and antagonism. Yet it was generally conceded that she and other nations must find some means of accommodation to one another, however distasteful it might be.

The very nature of the Soviet Government's foreign policy made the approach to such accommodation a devious one. It was a policy determined in large part by the forced acceptance of the fact that the "capitalist" world had entered upon a period of temporary stability and the fact that the hoped-for world revolution had yet to be brought about. The Soviet leaders believed that the temporary stability of the great powers would of necessity break down eventually in new wars, including probably a new attempt at intervention in Russia, and that world revolution would be made possible. Until that time, they intended to direct the foreign policy of the USSR toward two ends: the preservation and strengthening of the Soviet state and the promotion of revolutionary movements abroad.

To readjust Russian foreign relations under that policy became the task of the Commissariat of Foreign Affairs, headed by George Chicherin, a member of the Russian aristocracy who had been trained in the tsarist foreign office and had later become a Bolshevik, and his chief aide, Vice-Commissar Maxim Litvinov, a Russian Jew who had joined the Bolsheviks as a youth. Considering the preservation and strengthening of the Soviet Union the more urgent of the foreign policy aims, they emphasized the maintenance of peace, in order that the regime might continue uninterrupted its program of internal stabilization; the gaining of friends for Soviet Russia among the dissatisfied, small or weak nations who would be willing to accept her as an ally or as a champion of their cause against the stronger powers; and the re-establishment of commercial and diplomatic relations with all powers. Since the Commissariat of Foreign Affairs had denounced the Treaty of Versailles, it could easily and logically declare the USSR in alignment with the revisionist powers, notably Germany and Turkey. And since the Soviet Government had denounced the aggressive policies of the tsarist regime and renounced all special privileges which tsarist Russia had acquired in China, Persia, and Turkey, it stood *ipso facto* in alignment with those and other countries which might have cause to fear "imperialism."

While the government was subscribing to a program of peace and good will in furtherance of one of its objectives, it appeared, at the same time, to be vitiating its own efforts by the pursuance of its other objective—the promotion of revolutionary movements—in the very countries whose good will was being sought. The Comintern (Communist International), headed by Gregory Zinoviev, was responsible for the immediate emphasis on the second objective. Yet it was not solely to blame for the anomalous position in which the government found itself. Technically the Commissariat of Foreign Affairs and the Comintern were separate bodies, but both were working for the same ultimate ends. The difficulty lay in the fact that the Commissariat recognized as its first objective the preservation and strengthening of the Soviet state, while the Comintern recognized no objective above the advancement of the international revolutionary movement. Inevitably, progress toward the re-establishment of Soviet foreign relations was often impeded by this dual emphasis.

PARTIAL ESCAPE FROM ISOLATION. Progress toward the establishment of commercial and diplomatic relations with the rest of the world was negligible during the first years of the new regime. The four Baltic states had officially recognized Soviet Russia in 1920; and Poland, Turkey, and Afghanistan had done likewise in 1921. Germany and Sweden, while still refusing diplomatic recognition, had established commercial intercourse with her in 1920. Negotiations for the resumption of normal relations with Great Britain had begun as early as May, 1920, but Soviet refusal to accept responsibility for the debts of the previous Russian governments had hindered their successful conclusion. That refusal had hindered negotiations with other creditor nations as well. Finally, in March, 1921, an Anglo-Soviet agreement for the resumption of commercial—but not diplomatic—relations was reached, and similar agreements with other European nations followed. The United States, however, remained adamant and would have no official dealings of any kind with Soviet Russia.

It was evident that some compromise would have to be offered if any progress were to be made toward the complete re-establishment of relations with the powers. And since Russia could ill afford to forego much longer the benefits of foreign trade and foreign trade credits, she offered to make a slight concession: while still not recognizing any obligation to pay the disavowed debts, she would agree to pay them in part in return for foreign loans. That offer was considered at an international economic and monetary conference held at Genoa in April, 1922, the first to which Soviet Russia had been invited; but the question of Russian debts and obligations was not settled then—nor, in fact, at any subsequent time.

However, during the course of that conference, one advantage was gained by Soviet Russia; she signed her first treaty for the resumption of diplomatic relations with a major power, Germany. By that treaty, signed at Rapallo, near Genoa, on April 16, 1922 (and known as the Treaty of Rapallo), the two powers not only established diplomatic relations between themselves but also renounced financial claims upon each other. For both of them, pariahs in the society of nations, the treaty was of far-reaching importance; it forced the other powers, which were anxious to prevent a Russo-German entente, to a more conciliatory attitude toward them. One of its first advantages to Soviet Russia lay in the fact that it accelerated the process of diplomatic recognition. England granted her full recognition in February, 1924, and later in that year full recognition was accorded by Italy, Norway, Austria, Greece, Sweden, China, Denmark, Mexico, and France. Then, on January 10, 1925, diplomatic and commercial relations with Japan were established by a treaty which reaffirmed the provisions of the Treaty of Portsmouth.

These gains, however, by no means restored Russia to her former position in the European state system. French foreign policy, which for a decade was to determine the tone of European diplomacy, was still dedicated to the isolation and weakening of the USSR; and most of the states bordering on or in proximity to it, all violently anti-Communist, aligned themselves with France. Moreover, many of the minor European nations—Spain, Portugal, The Netherlands, Belgium, Switzerland, Czechoslovakia, Yugoslavia, Bulgaria, Hungary, and Rumania[1]—withheld their recognition. Exclusion from the League of Nations and other international organizations further emphasized the fact that the USSR was still relatively isolated. Much more bolstering was required before the new state could stand with the strength of the old Russian Empire.

EFFORTS TOWARD PEACE AND SECURITY. The military and material weakness of the new state and the need for a very long period of security during which to develop the new socialist society led the Soviet Government to a sincere effort to maintain peace for the country and to establish assurance that, if the peace should be broken elsewhere, Russia would be kept free of the resulting conflict.

As the Soviet leaders appraised existing conditions, there was no organization nor alliance upon which the Russian plans for peace and security could be safely based. They did not regard the League of Nations as an instrument for the preservation of general security but rather as "a mere mask to conceal from the broad masses the aggressive aims of the imperialist policy of certain Great Powers or their vassals." The prewar basis of Russian security, the Franco-Russian Alliance, was gone, and France was now hostile. Even Germany, a possible ally, was attempting to remain in the good graces of both Russia and France. The best chances for Soviet security, therefore, lay in active efforts to insure peace with neighboring countries and to play off the powers against one another.

In furtherance of her peace policy Russia began a movement for disarmament and for arrangement of nonaggression pacts with neighboring states. Although she did not anticipate anything like success in her striving for general disarmament, she hoped at least to secure the reduction of armaments and fortifications in the countries on her frontiers. In December, 1922, at the invitation of Litvinov, representatives of Poland, Latvia, Estonia, and Finland met in Moscow to discuss disarmament. At that time Litvinov proposed that the Red Army, which had already been cut from its peak strength of 5 million to 800,000, be further cut to 200,000; that the other powers

---

[1] Rumania was willing to recognize Soviet Russia but refused to discuss the former Russian province of Bessarabia, which she had occupied in 1918 and later formally annexed. Soviet Russia refused to recognize Rumanian annexation of the province; so the resumption of normal relations between the two countries was delayed until 1934.

present agree to reduce their armies by the same ratio; and that a demilitarized zone be created at the frontier between Russia and the four other states represented. The proposal failed of acceptance, and the foreign office was forced to look elsewhere to find sympathy for the disarmament campaign.

In January, 1926, despite Soviet disrespect for the League of Nations, Chicherin accepted the League's invitation to participate in the work of its commission for the preparation of a general disarmament conference. Litvinov, who was assuming ever greater responsibilities in the Commissariat of Foreign Affairs as Chicherin showed signs of failing health, represented the USSR on the preparatory commission and became, in the eyes of the Western world, the spokesman of Soviet foreign policy. He produced a sensation in February, 1928, when he submitted a proposal for complete and rapid disarmanent of all nations, to be guaranteed by a permanent system of international inspection. But the proposal did not receive any serious attention from the other powers; they believed that Litvinov had produced the plan, knowing that it would fail, in the hope of scoring a propaganda victory for the Soviet Union.

Soviet attempts to gain security through a series of nonaggression pacts met with greater success—on paper, at least. A nonaggression treaty with Turkey, agreed to on December 17, 1925, was followed by similar treaties with Germany, Afghanistan, Lithuania, and Persia. The treaties provided that the signatories would not commit acts of aggression against each other and would not support hostile or aggressive actions by any third power. In 1928, the USSR became a signatory of the Kellogg-Briand Pact for the renunciation of war as an instrument of national policy, and her leaders were encouraged to believe that some headway was being made toward temporary security.

DIPLOMATIC SETBACKS IN EUROPE. While Russia was having to accept half-gains from her efforts to make peaceful adjustments with her neighbors, she was being ill-favored by the general trend of European diplomacy.

The Treaty of Rapallo had provided her with an alignment in which she could not have complete confidence since Germany was so desirous of rapprochement with England and France and the mitigation of the terms of Versailles. As it was, however, she gained some advantages beyond the initial one of increased strength for bargaining with the other powers: her trade with Germany grew, German technical specialists came to Russia as industrial advisers, and German army officers came to help in the organization and training of the Red Army—also to gain military experience forbidden them in Germany under the Treaty of Versailles. But, at the same time, Germany was holding herself in readiness to take any advantage offered her by the West. And when, in 1925, she became a party to the Locarno Pacts, Moscow feared that she was pledging herself to an anti-Soviet bloc. That fear was somewhat allayed, however, by Germany's agreement in 1926 (after an irritating delay in her admission to the League of Nations) to another treaty with the Soviet Union. This treaty pledged each to refrain from supporting any aggressive move by a third power against the other. It gave them at least a tenuous extension of friendship.

There remained the possibility of that which Soviet Russia most feared, a hostile combination led by France and Great Britain. Her relations with those countries were definitely unfavorable. Her negotiations with France on the question of Russian debts had been frequent and fruitless, and in 1927 they broke down altogether. France, as the pivot of a postwar European diplomatic system aimed at containing both the Soviet Union and Germany, had become, in Russian estimation, the source and fount of anti-Soviet diplomacy.

Relations were even worse with Great Britain, now looking with particular distaste upon the world-revolution aspect of the Soviet foreign policy. In Asia, Britain's position as the chief colonial power was threatened by Communist support of the anti-imperialist native movements; and, at home, she was further beset by Communist participation in domestic politics. The USSR was recognized by the British Labor Government in 1924, but in the same year the Labor Government was displaced by the bitterly anti-Soviet Conservatives. The victory of the Conservatives was made possible in part by the pre-election publication of a letter allegedly written by Zinoviev (but later declared a forgery) outlining tactics to be followed by the British Communists in preparing a revolution. Once in power, the Conservatives began an active fight against the Communists. One of the most damaging bits of evidence against them was revealed during the British General Strike of 1926, when it was shown that the Soviet trade unions had contributed about $5 million to the support of the strike. The period of bad feeling reached a climax in a British police raid, in May, 1927, on the Soviet Trade Building in London and on the premises of Arcos Ltd., a company engaged in Anglo-Soviet trade. The British Government, claiming to have discovered by the raid that those were centers of Soviet espionage and propaganda, severed diplomatic relations with the USSR on May 26. Moscow could only cry "capitalist intrigue" and humbly begin negotiations again.

Added to the setbacks in Soviet foreign relations in 1927 was the assassination, in June, of the Soviet Minister to Warsaw, Peter Voikov, under circumstances which led Moscow to feel that the Polish Government, then headed by fiery Marshal Pilsudski, was responsible. It seemed possible that Poland, with the support of England and France, might be preparing for another war with Russia. Though feelings ran high for a time, the tension finally passed without war. The USSR was left to her friendless peace— again a virtual cipher in European diplomatic affairs.

ACTIVITIES IN NEAR AND MIDDLE EAST. Whereas Soviet Russia was having difficulties in entering European activities, she was moving into Asiatic activities without delay. In the Near and Middle East conditions seemed favorable to the operation of that part of her foreign policy which she was finding definitely ineffectual in Europe: the promotion and expansion of the Communist revolution. Revolutionary movements in those areas, directed chiefly at great-power control, had been spreading since World War I, and they needed outside support. To give them that support would serve Russia's purpose perfectly; she might gain allies and potential recruits for the future world federation of Soviet republics and, at the same time, she would be helping to weaken the great powers, particularly England.

Mustapha Kemal's young, revolutionary Turkish Republic was engaged in a war to oust Greece from the Turkish territory she had received by provision of the Treaty of Sèvres, and Moscow was glad to abet the effort. Following the Turco-Soviet treaty of March, 1921, whereby Moscow renounced the tsarist aggressive policy toward Turkey, sufficient Russian assistance was given to the Turkish Republic to make possible the ousting of the Greeks in 1922. The outcome had both a positive and a negative aspect for Soviet Russia. The defeat she had helped inflict upon Greece served also as a setback for England and France, since they had supported Greece; that pleased her. On the other hand, Mustapha Kemal's government did not repay its debt as expected, by accepting Communism; that was a disappointment. Equally disappointing was the Turkish failure to support Russian interests in the Straits when that old question was brought up again late in 1922 at the Lausanne Conference to consider revision of the Treaty of Sèvres. After that, Turco-Soviet relations remained friendly, but little more than that. Turkey, like Germany, hesitated to alienate the great powers by aligning herself too closely with Soviet Russia.

The Turkish experience was repeated in other Asiatic countries. Soviet assistance made it possible for Persia to defy Great Britain by refusing to ratify an Anglo-Persian agreement signed in August, 1919, making Persia a virtual protectorate of Great Britain. Then Russia and Persia negotiated a treaty, ratified in December, 1921, by which Russia renounced all rights and privileges in Persia acquired under the tsarist regime and was given, in return, the right to send troops into Persia if a third power were to use Persian soil as a base for war on Russia. Yet Persia was not ready to take the next step, to accept Communism, and thus Russia was again denied the full realization of her aim. Afghanistan, likewise, accepted Soviet Russia's aid to offset English pressure but failed to support her hope of advancing Communism through that region.

ACTIVITIES IN THE FAR EAST. At the beginning of the NEP period, Russia's influence in the Far East was almost nil. But her new foreign policy led her to a re-entry into the affairs of that region just as it led her into the affairs of the Near and Middle East. In the interest of world communism, she could easily take up the cause of the natives in their postwar movements to rid Eastern Asia of foreign control.

Japan proved to be an arid field; her government was strong enough to prevent the growth of Communism and to hold against the general disturbances which were spreading in the East. She had reluctantly quit Siberia and had established diplomatic relations with the USSR in 1925, but thereafter she stood fast. As far as the Asiatic mainland was concerned, her policy was temporarily nonaggressive, and she contented herself with looking over the sights of silent guns at Russian activities in Outer Mongolia and China.

In Outer Mongolia, Russia was able to pursue her policy with gratifying success. That region had been prominent in her interests as early as the eighteenth century, for it was so situated as to be an ideal buffer between Siberia and China and to provide an important link in a trade route from Siberia to China. In 1921 the Red Army helped the Mongols to create a revolutionary government in Outer Mongolia with political and economic policies patterned after those of Soviet Russia; and the new government, under the name of the Mongolian People's Republic, declared itself independent of China. In 1924, Moscow agreed, for diplomatic reasons, to recognize Chinese sovereignty over Outer Mongolia, but that recognition was only a gesture. Actually the Chinese Government could not make use of its formal rights in the region because the Mongolian People's Republic continued to be dominated by Moscow.

Russian influence in Outer Mongolia was of minor significance in comparison to the influence which would be gained if Communist plans for

China could be carried through. And in China the outlook seemed favorable. The revolutionary Kuomintang party of Sun Yat-sen was in revolt against the shadowy government of the Chinese Republic. Its policy was in large part anti-imperialist, aimed at freeing China from control by the great powers; and Sun Yat-sen, although opposed to the establishment of Communism in China, believed that Soviet Russia, as an opponent of the great powers, would be a useful ally to the Kuomintang. Moscow was entirely willing to deal with the revolutionaries and proceeded to do so, even while carrying on successful negotiations with the official Chinese Government for the establishment of diplomatic relations. In 1923 the Soviet diplomatic emissary Adolf Joffe came to an understanding with Sun Yat-sen whereby Russia agreed to aid the Kuomintang in unifying China and freeing her from foreign control but not to impose the Communist system on her. This understanding was followed by four years of Kuomintang co-operation with the Comintern and the Chinese Communist Party. The Soviet Government disclaimed any official connection with the revolutionary activities of the Kuomintang, but its connection was nonetheless real and vital. Through Michael Borodin, chief Soviet adviser to the Kuomintang, and the Red Army General Vasily Blücher (known in China under the pseudonym of Galen), and hundreds of other political and military advisers, the Kuomintang received not only the arms and money but also the skills and techniques which enabled it to carry out a revolution.

The Chinese Revolution, which began in the southern part of the country in 1924, attracted wide attention in the USSR and became the cause of a major conflict between Trotsky and Stalin. Trotsky wanted to turn the revolution toward immediate Communist goals while Stalin argued, with success, for the acceptance of the revolution as a nationalist movement which had not yet reached the Communist stage.

Nor was there complete accord among the Chinese revolutionary leaders. The middle-class elements of the Kuomintang, under the leadership of General Chiang Kai-shek, feared the ultimate result of the alliance with the Russian and Chinese Communists and favored the establishment of friendly relations with England and the other powers against whose Chinese interests the revolution was initially directed. On April 11, 1927, Chiang Kai-shek's troops disarmed the Chinese Communists in Shanghai, and that act was followed by others of an anti-Communist nature which finally culminated in the complete breakdown of the Kuomintang relations with Russia. Blücher, Borodin, and the other Soviet advisers returned to

Moscow, and the Chinese Communists became the opposition to the Kuomintang.

Meanwhile the government of the Chinese Republic, in Peking, was turning against the Soviet Government, which had been supporting the revolution and, at the same time, seeking to maintain "correct" relations with Peking. On April 6, 1927, it raided one of the buildings adjoining the Soviet Embassy, arrested several Russian employees and Chinese Communists, and seized documents establishing the fact of Soviet relations with the Kuomintang. Four days later Litvinov announced the severance of diplomatic relations with Peking, and by the end of the year Soviet consular representatives had been expelled from all parts of China except Manchuria. This rebuff, coming just when Russia was failing in her efforts with the Kuomintang, meant complete political defeat for her in China. But she still had an important economic interest in that country—the Chinese Eastern Railroad.

The Sino-Soviet treaty of 1924 establishing diplomatic relations between the two countries had provided that the formerly Russian-owned Chinese Eastern Railroad in Manchuria be jointly managed by China and the USSR until 1956, when it would revert to China. But the Kuomintang, having established its control over all of China, began in 1928 to seek means of ousting Russia from the joint management. In May, 1929, Chinese authorities raided the Soviet consulate in Harbin, claiming that it was the center of Comintern propaganda, and in July they arrested and deported the Soviet officials connected with the management of the Chinese Eastern. As a result, feelings between the two countries became so strained and conflict seemed so imminent that fellow signatories of the Kellogg-Briand Pact warned them against breaking their pledge to keep the peace. Both responded shortly that they were not seeking war. But their preparations continued. In November, Soviet armed forces made several limited but effective land and air attacks on Manchuria, and the Chinese Government quickly asked for negotiations. By a protocol signed in December, the *status quo ante* was restored with respect to the railroad and the maintenance of Soviet consulates in Manchuria. That was followed by a conference in Moscow for the purpose of repairing the breach between China and the Soviet Union. But its efforts were fruitless. Although the antagonism between the two countries took on a quieter tone thereafter, their diplomatic relations were not re-established until 1932.

The struggle for Lenin's mantle

THE RISE OF CONFLICT.   During the last years of Lenin's life, sharp conflicts of opinion and personality appeared among the leaders of the Communist Party. Of those conflicts the one between Trotsky and Stalin overshadowed all the others and produced results of lasting influence not only
upon the history of Russia but also upon the history of the world.

Trotsky at that time was widely known as a powerful speaker, a brilliant writer and an inspiring leader, and he was expected by many to be
the successor to Lenin's position. Stalin was hardly known outside the Soviet Union, but he was a man of considerable consequence within the party.
His strength lay in an organizational ability and a quiet, unrelenting determination which had helped him steadily to increase his power. In 1921
he was the People's Commissar of Nationalities, the People's Commissar
of the Workers' and Peasants' Inspection, and a member of the Politburo.[1]

Stalin was clearly first among the members of the Politburo in the understanding and direction of the organizational work of the party. His position was further strengthened when, in April, 1922, he was named to the
office of General Secretary of the Central Committee of the party. That
new office (created in March, 1922) was not intended to carry with it the
titular leadership of the party but was designed rather as an administrative
position for the co-ordination of the various branches, offices, and committees, whose steadily growing organizational machinery was almost as
formidable as that of the government. However, it became an office of immense power; and, as General Secretary, Stalin added to his influence by
bringing into the office many of his closest supporters, notable among them
Vyacheslav Molotov and Lazar Kaganovich.

Lenin was aware of the conflict among the Communist leaders and became increasingly disquieted about the future of the party as his health
began to fail in 1922. His fears of a split within the party were expressed
in a letter dated December 25, 1922, and supplemented by a postscript of
January 4, 1923. In that letter, made public by Trotsky after Lenin's death
and generally known as "Lenin's Will," he gave his estimation of the two

---

[1] The Politburo established in October, 1917, had not been intended as a permanent
body and functioned but for a short time. In March, 1919, at the Eighth Party Congress,
it had been decided to establish once more a Politburo, this time consisting of five members, to be elected by and responsible to the Central Committee. The function of the
Politburo was to "make decisions on questions not permitting of delay." It soon began
to act as the chief policy making body of the Party and to overshadow the Central
Committee.

WIDE WORLD

Chief Soviet leaders in 1925: (left to right) Stalin, Rykov, Kamenev, and Zinoviev

principal figures in the party controversy. He characterized Trotsky as "the most able man in the present Central Committee" but noted that he was possessed by a "too far-reaching self-confidence." He characterized Stalin as a man who "has concentrated enormous power in his hands" although he was "too rude" and probably without "sufficient caution" to use the power wisely. And he proposed that, in order to prevent an intraparty split, Stalin be replaced as General Secretary by a man having Stalin's virtues but lacking his vices.

TUG OF WAR.   By that time, however, circumstances leading toward a split had gone beyond easy correction. In the Politburo of 1923 (composed of Lenin, Trotsky, Stalin, Kamenev, Bukharin, Zinoviev, and Tomsky) the greatest power, aside from Lenin's, was concentrated in the hands of Stalin, Zinoviev, and Kamenev. Working in concert, they were able to isolate Trotsky and minimize the effectiveness of his efforts. His position was further weakened by an incident at the time of Lenin's death, on January 21, 1924. Away from Moscow, recovering from an illness, Trotsky could not attend the funeral ceremonies. As a result, Stalin acted as the chief spokesman of the party and the government at the ceremonies and appeared to be assuming the position of Lenin's heir. Although he made no overt declaration of his position, many were impressed by the appearance.

After Lenin's death, the personal and doctrinal conflicts within the party were intensified. It is difficult to distinguish between personal and doctrinal differences in the activities of men for whom doctrine is the breath of life, but a review of the struggle which followed clearly indicates that both were involved. No one openly admitted that the struggle was concerned with succession to party leadership; each man and his followers simply maintained that they were defending the orthodox version of Leninism against others who were departing from it.

Trotsky and Stalin refrained from attacking each other directly but worked circuitously to that end. In the autumn of 1924 Trotsky, in his essay *The Lessons of October,* accused Zinoviev and Kamenev of having been less than revolutionary in 1917. They defended themselves, with Stalin's support, and turned the situation against Trotsky. Together the three were able to force his resignation from the important post of People's Commissar of War. Thereafter the issues became more clearly defined. Trotsky began energetically to emphasize and develop further his doctrine of "permanent revolution," already postulated before 1914, which declared that the socialist revolution in backward Russia could not be successful unless the base of revolution were continuously expanded. Stalin, on the other hand, took the position that, according to Lenin, socialism could be established "in one country [Russia] alone by that country's unaided strength." He was in no wise rejecting the Communists' ultimate aim of world revolution but merely asserting his belief that socialism in Russia need not wait on the success of world revolution, the time of which no one could predict. In fact, the main difference between his position and Trotsky's was one of strategy and tactics, not of doctrine. Trotsky, who would assign priority to the support of revolutionary possibilities abroad, found much to criticize in the tactics of those who did not support his views. He blamed Zinoviev, for instance, for not pushing the Comintern's revolutionary activities in Germany in 1923, when he believed that country ripe for revolution. And he blamed Stalin's timidity for the lack of Communist success in China. On such problems, arguments begat arguments until all members of the party were involved, but there could be no resolution of them until the main issue should come to a vote. That happened in December, 1925, when the Fourteenth Party Congress voted by overwhelming majority to adopt Stalin's program for "socialism in one country."

VICTORY OF STALIN. General Secretary Stalin was now in a controlling, though not entirely secure, position in the party. His victory at the congress was, in part, the expression of the desire among Russian Communists for concentration on domestic progress rather than foreign adventure and, in part, the result of his own quiet but effective use of the party apparatus to place his supporters in commanding positions. At the time, few realized how great his power had become and how he intended to use it.

After the Fourteenth Congress, the opposing groups in the struggle took firmer stands, and some prominent party men openly shifted their support from one leader to the other. Kamenev and Zinoviev, who had veered toward Trotsky's position at the time of the Congress, joined him in 1926 to form a bloc against Stalin in the Politburo; and Stalin joined hands with Bukharin, Tomsky, and Rykov. In the same year, majority support in the Politburo was assured to Stalin by the election to that body of Voroshilov, Kalinin, and Molotov—each a defender of Stalin's view.

Trotsky, Kamenev, and Zinoviev soon began to agitate actively against the dominant group; and, in so doing, they became guilty of a grievous sin from the point of view of the party, which condemned the formation of factions and demanded rigid submission of all members to party decisions. As a result, Zinoviev was expelled from the Politburo in the summer of 1926; and Trotsky, in the following October. Thereafter, a peaceful solution of the intraparty conflicts seemed almost beyond hope. The leaders of the minority, having despaired of getting a hearing of their case within the organization, took it to the public, thus laying themselves open again to the charge of violating party discipline. During the celebration of the Revolution on November 7, 1927, Trotsky and Zinoviev capped their previous acts by organizing their own demonstration. A week later the two were expelled from the party. Then, at the Fifteenth Congress, in December, 1927, Kamenev and some seventy-five other leading members of the opposition were likewise expelled for improper activities within the party.

The chief struggle was virtually over by the end of 1927. By that time Stalin's control of the party—and, therefore, of the state—was quite established, although the extent of his control was not immediately apparent. It became apparent, however, as the purging of the supporters of the opposition was continued. Some of them, notably the early expellees Zinoviev,

Kamenev, and their lieutenants, publicly repented of their oppositional activities and were re-admitted to the party. Trotsky, however, remained un-
repentant. In January, 1928, he was exiled to Alma Ata, in Soviet Central
Asia; but he still refused to abstain from political activity. Finally, a year
later, he was deported from the USSR. Then Stalin turned his attention to
his erstwhile friends Bukharin, Rykov, and Tomsky, who in his opinion
were not giving adequate support to his plans for speeding up socialization; and their political fortunes soon began to fail. Bukharin was expelled
from the Politburo; Rykov was expelled from the party and replaced as
premier by Molotov; and Tomsky was removed from his position as chairman of the Soviet trade unions.

Although Zinoviev, Kamenev, Bukharin, Rykov, and their many followers remained free men and occupied responsible positions for the next
few years, they were completely removed from positions of power. Those
positions were passing to a new generation of Communists, chief among
them Molotov, Voroshilov, Kalinin, Kuibyshev, Kaganovich, Kirov, Andreyev, Mikoyan, and Ordzhonikidze. They were, with few exceptions,
men of a younger generation, little known in the early years of the regime.
They were less akin to the old Russian intellectuals than their predecessors
had been, and they were free of the foreign cultural influences which had
affected many of the former during the early period of frequent political
exile. Moreover, they were dependent on, and subordinate to Stalin.

The establishment of Stalinist control and the acceptance of the doctrine of "socialism in one country" in the USSR were paralleled in the
Comintern and in the Communist parties throughout the world. Everywhere,
during the years 1927-29, alleged party heretics—whether left or right
deviationists—were removed from positions of control, and men completely
responsive to the new leadership of the Communist Party of the Soviet
Union were installed. Such reformation, of course, did not end opposition;
it merely pushed opposition beyond official party bounds. The new political émigrés from the USSR joined forces with the disaffected Communists abroad in organizing an opposition which they characterized as "more
Leninist" than Stalin's followers. Even within the USSR, remnants of the
opposition, although professing their loyalty to Stalin, secretly maintained
contact with the opposition abroad.

By 1929 Stalin was being called the dictator of Russia. Officially he
was only the General Secretary of the Communist Party and a member of
the Politburo; he had occupied no governmental post of any consequence
since 1923, when the Commissariat of Nationalities was abolished. Yet he

was able to dominate the government by controlling the party through his supporting majority in the Politburo.

THE NEW SOVIET COMMUNISM.   Trotsky declared that Stalin's victory marked the "9th of Thermidor of the Russian Revolution," thus figuratively comparing it to the coup that had ended the Jacobin power during the French Revolution and led to a gradual abandonment of many of the aims of the revolution. He was correct in his implication that a new period in the development of Soviet Communism was beginning, but he was mistaken in implying that the consequences of his own downfall were analogous to those following the Jacobins' reverses.

The consequences in this instance were determined by factors and conditions peculiar to this time and place: (1) the kind of political and social system that had already evolved in Russia, a system administered by a party committed to public ownership both of the means of production and of the land, and to the acceptance of Marxism-Leninism as the unquestionable truth; (2) the concentration of power in the hands of Stalin and his supporters, men predisposed towards the destruction of intraparty democracy; (3) the party's acceptance, without adequate regard for the spiritual and material costs, of the rapid industrialization of Russia as a primary goal; and (4) the Russian historical traditions.

TWENTY-SEVEN / THE SECOND DRIVE FOR
SOVIET SOCIALISM: 1928-1932

What Soviet leaders called the second drive for socialism in Russia was begun in 1928. Some of its aims resembled those set for the first drive, during the period of War Communism; but its execution was a more thoroughly planned one and its success, therefore, a more likely one. In this drive the Soviet people found themselves involved by the decision of the Communist leaders in a great, concentrated effort to convert their individualistic, agrarian economy into a socialistic, industrial one in the space of a few years. It was an effort which demanded of them not only strain and sacrifice but also the subordination of their individual interests to the common interest as it was defined by their leaders. It was the greatest effort ever undertaken to direct all the energies of a nation into a definitely planned economy.

The initial phase of the effort, known as the First Five-Year Plan, was a crucial test of the ability of the Communist leaders to carry out the greatest of their party's tasks, the industrialization of Russia on a socialist basis. To facilitate its execution, they laid out their campaign with careful consideration for hazards and advantages, aiming at a precision of operation comparable to that of a well-planned military operation. In fact, the activities under the First Five-Year Plan had enough in common with military operations that its designers felt justified in referring to its different aspects as "fronts"—the agricultural front, the industrial front, and so on. Establishing those fronts, mapping their strategy, and synchronizing their activities engaged every effort of the Soviet Government during the period 1928-1932.

Conception and organization of the First Five-Year Plan

RENEWAL OF ADVANCE.   Lenin had made it clear in 1921 that the NEP was to be but a temporary retreat from the policy of socialist transformation of the country and that, as soon as it was feasible, a new, concerted effort would be begun to renew the advance. There was difficulty, however, in determining when, under what conditions, and with what immediate aims it should be begun. Those were questions that had received much attention in the intraparty debates of the middle 1920's. One group, the rightists, led by Bukharin, had held that the rate of industrial growth should be moderate, considerable emphasis being given to light industry (manufacturing consumer goods), and that it would have to be supported by a prosperous, still largely individualized, and favorably treated peasantry. The opposing group, the leftists, led by Trotsky, had argued for a rapid rate of industrialization with major emphasis on heavy industry (manufacturing producer goods), part of the financial support for which would have to be extracted from the peasantry by various means. And the Fourteenth Congress, although it declared in favor of a renewed drive for industrialization, did not take a definite position with respect to the opposing views. Even the Fifteenth Congress, which approved the basic directives for an industrialization plan, did not decide whether the working policies of the plan should be rightist or leftist.

It was only in the course of translating the general terms of policy into specific ones that the decision was made. That task was begun in 1926 by the State Planning Commission, working under the direct supervision of the Sovnarkom and the guidance of policy determined by the Politburo. Two years later it presented the final draft of the program for beginning the industrialization of the USSR, the First Five-Year Plan. By joint decree of the Sovnarkom and the Central Committee of the Party, the program was to go into operation on October 1, 1928, and was to be completed by September 30, 1933. This plan was based on the leftist position—an ironical situation, since the chief leftist was now an outcast, and the implementation of the plan was to be directed by his foremost opponent, Stalin.

MAIN OBJECTIVES.   The plan was an elaborate and detailed instrument (in six volumes, after revision) in which the State Planning Commission, allowing for unforeseen circumstances, indicated both the maximum and minimum attainments expected from its operation. The immensity of their conception may be judged from the maximum figures on the main objectives of the plan—which were the ones actually used.

The remnants of private industrial enterprise were to be eliminated, and nationalized industry was to be so expanded that it could provide the basic needs of an industrialized and mechanized economy. Industrial production was to be increased, during the five-year period, about 236 per cent; to support that production electrical power was to be increased about 600 per cent; and coal, iron, and oil were to be produced in sufficient quantities to supply the expanding needs. Such rapid advances would, of course, necessitate greatly increased investments on the part of the government. That fact was recognized by the planners, who provided that, by 1933, investments in industry, particularly large-scale industry, and electrification should be five times the total capital invested in industry in 1913. One lack in this ambitious program was to be railroad lines. That, too, was recognized by the planners, but they believed that extensive building would be impossible until a later date and, therefore, provided for the laying of only about 10,000 miles of new lines during this first planned period. The productivity of agricultural labor was to be increased through the wider use of machinery and the improvement of techniques. In addition, the socialization of agricultural production was to be encouraged in the hope that, by 1933, at least one-fourth of the peasant households would be working on collective farms.

In order to insure that those industrial and agricultural achievements should benefit the country as intended, it was necessary that they serve also a corollary function: to supply a modernized army capable of protecting the country from foreign attacks. The maintenance of peace had never been more important to Soviet Russia than it was to be during these crucial five years.

Without exception, it was necessary that every phase of Russian life be adjusted to the new plan. The concessions made during the period of the NEP in the cultural, political, and economic fields were now reviewed and, in most instances, rescinded. All efforts had to be of single and concentrated purpose if the plan were to succeed; to allow deviation would have been both wasteful and dangerous. The fulfillment of a plan so broadly conceived would have required, under ordinary conditions, the work of a generation. But the USSR expected to fulfill it in five years.

REQUISITES FOR SUCCESS.   The success of the Five-Year Plan depended upon the accuracy of a number of assumptions underlying the computations made by the planners and upon the efficient operation of the administrative machinery of government and party.

Some of the basic assumptions were: (1) that the increase in industrial and agricultural productivity could be brought about immediately without a long transition period, (2) that there would be no major crop failures, (3) that there would be a rapid expansion of foreign trade, (4) that there would be a long period of relative peace, permitting a maximum of uninterrupted work within the country and a minimum of military expenditures, and (5) that Soviet Russia would be able to carry out the plan by her own unaided strength.

The assumption that Russia could carry the burden of the plan by her unaided strength was of basic importance, and its realization would require that the government prove itself capable of doing what appeared to many to be the impossible. The Communist leaders would have been loath to invite foreign investment and thereby to make political and economic concessions to capitalism. And they knew that they could not expect the favor of long-term, large-scale loans from abroad, such as those which had been extended to tsarist Russia. Therefore domestic capital, to be derived in large part from the increased productivity of industrial and agricultural labor, would have to be sufficient. The major portion of the receipts from the expected increase would have to be turned into additional investments, and the volume and value of exports would have to increase to the point that income from them would make possible the purchasing of needed industrial equipment from abroad and the hiring of foreign industrial specialists. That scheme, of course, would be likely to put more emphasis on balancing the state's books than upon improving the condition of those whose labor was to make it possible. According to the plan, the laborers standard of living would be raised somewhat, but it would still remain so low as to preclude most amenities and many necessities.

Only a large and elaborately organized administrative arrangement could be expected to put the Five-Year Plan into operation and to direct it, and the organization of the Soviet Government was a good base for such an arrangement. The Communist Party, through the Politburo, was to make major policy decisions. The State Planning Commission, with divisions throughout the country, was to collect data and estimates from all branches of the economy and, on the basis of policy laid down by the Politburo and the government, prepare quarterly and yearly estimates for each industry and each region. Periodically it was to assemble data on actual achievements in order that comparisons might be made between performance and plan.

Since, ultimately, the success of the plan depended upon the effectiveness with which the planned tasks were performed, the government revitalized existing programs of education, propaganda, and compulsion and initiated new ones in order to prepare everyone for the part expected of him. Every Soviet citizen was to be convinced of the importance of the plan; he was to believe that all depended upon its success and that the postponement of individual material benefits was both necessary and desirable. Each was to believe it his duty to give to the best of his ability, regarding the fulfillment of his part in the plan as a moral obligation. Shirking, malingering, and pilfering were to be considered as criminal offenses. No person was to stand aside from participation in the plan; writers, teachers, painters, and musicians were to consider the proper use of their skills as important to the plan as the workers' and peasants' use of their skills. In short, the execution of the plan was to be accepted by everyone as an "all-out" effort.

The industrial front

PROVISION OF NEEDED SKILLS.   The construction, development, and operation of industry called for more skilled workmen, engineers, specialists, and managers than Russia had; and a great effort was made to supply them while new enterprises were being put into operation and old ones expanded. Special factory apprentice schools were set up and, under adverse conditions, were able to turn out about 450,000 skilled workers in four years. The enrollment in technical courses in universities and in specialized higher schools was increased at a dizzying rate; in the technical schools alone, the number of students rose from 208,000 in 1928 to 745,000 in 1932. Such acceleration, necessarily at the cost of educational standards, made it possible to train tens of thousands of engineers, chemists, managers, and statisticians; but with their lack in thoroughness of training and in experience, they were insufficient for the tasks set by the plan. Moreover, in the first years of its operation, the number of specialists demanded was greater than the number in supply. The need was met in part by the willingness of foreign specialists to come to Russia to work. Many came from the United States, Germany, Great Britain, France, and other countries. Some were drawn by their admiration for the Soviet Union, some by the promised adventure of taking part in such a daring enterprise, and others by the lure of high salaries. In addition, many American and other foreign industrial corporations contracted to provide technical assistance by sending to the USSR squads of engineers and technicians to supervise the construction of new plants and the installation of new equipment.

INCENTIVES AND CONTROLS.   The problem of incentives in any society lacking the profit motive is a difficult one, and in Russia it was complicated by the fact that a centralized, bureaucratic control of the economy had worked against the development in the individual of a responsible attitude toward work. But every means of persuasion and compulsion available to the government was employed now in an effort to create incentive. To supplement the propaganda which reiterated the theme that each citizen was a partner in the Five-Year Plan, various new devices were employed to emphasize the social nature of all work. "Socialist competition" was introduced, and department was urged to compete against department, factory against factory, in an effort to win group honors. The personnel of successful factories were expected to encourage the personnel of less successful ones, and trained workers were expected to aid and advise those with less skill. But social incentives were not enough. The Communist leaders had realized for some time that generations must pass before the individual would devote himself to the common good without thought of individual reward. From the first months of the regime, the principle of payment for work on the basis of quantity and quality had been accepted and employed in many industries, although many leaders believed in the principle of equality of wages. After 1928, piece-work wages became more common and more alluring; workers were paid progressively higher rates for production above normal standards, and managers and directors received bonuses if their plants exceeded scheduled production. Most party members, by this time, had been relieved of the necessity of turning over to the party all earnings in excess of about $120 per month; and now they, as well as nonparty workers, were encouraged to strive for the larger gains.

In handling those who would not be persuaded to work diligently and honestly, compulsion was used. New concepts of crimes against the state and the economy were evolved, and punishments were made drastic. Sentences ranging up to twenty years might be imposed on those found guilty of actions impairing production or discipline, the severest of them being imposed for deliberate reduction of production, considered wrecking or *sabotage* (a term used very loosely in those hectic days). Theft of state-owned property, considered one of the greatest offenses, could be punished by death.

LABOR FORCE. At a time when other countries, suffering from the world depression, were faced with a surplus of labor, Russia was beset by a labor shortage. Her pool of unemployed workers, numbering about a million in 1928, was exhausted by 1930. Workers thereafter were recruited from women and youths who had not been previously employed and from the surplus rural population. There was an evergrowing need for them; in large industry alone, the number of workers required grew from 2,691,000 to 5,153,000 during this five-year period.

The enhanced labor force was numerically sufficient for the needs of industry, but a high rate of labor turnover, absenteeism, low productivity, the insufficiency of skilled workers, and the geographical maldistribution of workers still produced labor shortages. After 1930, when the average factory job was found to pass through three hands in the course of the year, excessive turnover was recognized as one of the greatest impediments to the creation of a dependable labor force. But the other impediments were serious also. Labor was the mainspring of a machine which was operating on a fixed schedule; to keep it in order was of prime importance. At first every effort was made to improve the quality of the workers and of their workmanship, but the habits of generations kept their stubborn hold. Finally it became necessary, if the goals of the Five-Year Plan were to be reached, to subordinate quality to quantity, which could be forced. The result was that the number of laborers was continually increased in order to make up for the individual's low rate of production. Yet various schemes were employed to get the greatest possible production from them. The three-shift day and the "continuous week" (a schedule which disregarded Sundays and assigned workers to overlapping periods of four or five days of work, followed by a day of rest) were adopted in order that no time would be lost. "Shock brigades" of good workers were transported here and there to help keep production up to schedule in delinquent plants. Such measures, supplemented by the continued efforts to create incentive and enforce controls, produced the desired result: the goals were reached. Of course, the expense was great, but as to whether or not it was too great only time would make it possible to judge.

NEW CONSTRUCTION.   In the field of its major emphasis, basic industry, the Five-Year Plan called for the expansion and modernization of old plants, the establishment of new plants, and the development of formerly neglected natural resources in backward regions. The carrying out of those projects resulted in the development of the eastern regions of Russia, particularly those east of the Urals, at a more rapid rate than the western. Thus the center of Soviet industry was shifted during this period to the east, where it has since remained.

One of the most ambitious developments in the east was the Ural-Kuznetsk combine, planned to increase the supply of coal and iron, which had hitherto depended chiefly upon operations in the Donets River Basin and the Krivoi Rog region, both in the southeastern Ukraine. New operations, leading toward the combine, were begun in 1930 in the hardly touched iron ore reserves of the Magnitogorsk region (in the Urals) and in the Kuznetsk coal-fields (in south-central Siberia), which were believed to hold a third of Russia's coal reserves, although accounting for only 3 per cent of the total output. The plan was to co-ordinate the operations of the two regions in this way: part of the Kuznetsk coal would be transported by rail 1,400 miles to Magnitogorsk, where it would be used in smelting part of that region's iron ore; and the iron ore in excess of what could be processed in the Magnitogorsk foundries would be taken, on the return rail trip, to the newly constructed foundries of the Kuznetsk Basin. The combine was not working to planned capacity at the end of the five-year period, but it had begun to supply much of the needed coal, pig iron, and steel. In European Russia, the most important construction was the Dnieper River Power Station, the work on which was supervised by an American, Colonel Hugh Cooper. That station, the largest of its kind in Europe, was designed primarily to supply electricity for use in the Donets Basin. Outstanding among other new construction projects were the tractor plant in Stalingrad (formerly Tsaritsyn), the automobile plants in Moscow and Gorky (formerly Nizhnii-Novgorod), and the Turkestan-Siberian Railroad, running between Kazakhstan and western Siberia and connecting the cotton producing regions of Central Asia with the grain areas of Siberia.

GENERAL ATTAINMENT. At practically all points along the industrial front the objectives of the Five-Year Plan were achieved; at some points, with additional gains beyond those planned. A few figures will illustrate how effectively planning, concentration and pressure changed the industrial scene in the allotted five years. More than 1,500 industrial plants were constructed and with their production the total industrial output of Russia was more than doubled. The production of machinery was nearly quadrupled and that of electrical equipment quintupled. The output of coal, pig iron, and oil increased more than 150 per cent; that of electric power, nearly 250 per cent. The production of automobiles was advanced to twenty-four times that of 1928; the production of tractors, to fifty times that of 1928. With such advances, the USSR was well on its way toward industrialization.

The agricultural front

AGRARIAN RUSSIA IN 1928. At the beginning of the Five-Year Plan the Russian economy was primarily agricultural, and Russian society was primarily rural, about 82 per cent of the population being classified as rural and about 75 per cent depending upon agriculture for income and sustenance. Moreover, as will be recalled, the agrarian part of the population had consistently resisted changes in the techniques of their work and in the organization of their community life. The movement toward the withdrawal from the village commune and the consolidation of strips into single, unified farms had not gone far since the days of Stolypin. Only about one peasant household in ten owned a consolidated farm, and most of them were in the western Ukraine.

However, a few changes had been brought about by 1928, the most striking of them having been effected in 1917 and 1918, when the old landlords were dispossessed and their lands distributed among the peasants. About 20 per cent had thus been added to the total of peasant holdings. Yet the average holding had not been increased by the same measure since many peasants who had previously held little or no land had been given allotments during the partitions, and many large peasant households had been split into smaller units. As a result of these efforts at equalization, there were more than 25.5 million peasant households in the USSR in 1928, whereas there had been about 16.5 million at the beginning of the Revolution.

The efforts of the government to improve agricultural techniques had brought little change. About 5,000 imported tractors had been distributed to co-operatives, and on state-owned farms (sovkhozes, farms on state lands not yet distributed) an attempt had been made to introduce and develop new techniques as an example to all peasants. But the new tools and methods had not become popular, and production had increased only slightly. Reliable figures are not available, but a safe estimate is that the average Russian peasant's production per acre in 1928 was only about one-sixth of that of the average American farmer. Another government effort, to encourage the organization of collective farms (kolkhozes), had met with the same indifference on the part of the peasants. Three types of collective farms had been organized: the commune (not to be confused with the village commune), in which the members worked the land in common and shared common quarters and meals; the artel, in which the members pooled land and machinery, worked collectively, divided the crop, but retained separate homes and gardens; and the society for joint cultivation, the members of which worked their land jointly (though they did not pool it) and divided the crop on the basis of the size of the holdings of each member. But none of the types had attracted many members. At the beginning of the Five-Year Plan not more than 35,000 collective farms, including about 420,000 peasant households, had been organized.

Whereas the peasants had not been impressed by advanced techniques nor collective farming, the most ambitious of them had been impressed by the individual possibilities they could see in the new freedom to hire labor and lease land; and they had made good use of that freedom. Those who had been able to improve their lot and increase their incomes by leasing land and hiring labor had often become the local middlemen and money-lenders and had consequently come to be known by the old designation *kulak*. On the eve of the Five-Year Plan about 5 per cent of the rural population belonged to this new class of kulaks. By Western standards the average kulak was a man of very modest means—just a peasant who owned tools, machinery, farm buildings, and livestock worth about $400 and who hired labor for a period of more than seventy-five days of the year. But in the village economy he was rich. He leased equipment or animals to poorer peasants, rented land, speculated with grain, or loaned money at high rates. In short, the kulak was a person of power in the rural economy.

SOCIALISM *V.* INDIVIDUALISM.　Beginning operations on the agricultural front in 1928 required some caution because of the Soviet Government's previous handling of the agrarian problem. In order to achieve power in 1917 the Communists had been compelled to support the individualistic desire of the peasants for more land; and to retain their power in 1921, they had made many new concessions to individualism in order to eradicate the resentment which War Communism had aroused. But now, to carry out the program of Soviet socialism to which the government was committed, it was necessary to take measures counter to individualism.

The problem had both a political and an economic side. From the political point of view, collectivization was necessary in order to end peasant individualism, to convert peasants into socialist producers and proper citizens of the Soviet state, and to end class differentation among them. From the economic point of view, it was necessary to increase productivity so that fewer hands could produce more food and industrial raw materials, thus providing for the needs of an increasing urban population and releasing farm labor for industry. Solving the problem required giving simultaneous consideration to both of its aspects.

The economic success of the Five-Year Plan demanded that immediate attention be given to ways and means for increasing productivity. Despite the slight increase in agricultural production, much less produce was being offered to domestic and foreign markets in 1928 than had been offered fifteen years earlier. In 1928 only 8,080,000 tons of grain were marketed as against 21,310,000 tons in 1913. The decline had come about because the peasants were now living better and consuming more than they had when working for the landlords, who had often deprived them in order to increase the amount to be marketed. How could the situation be handled now so as to achieve both the political and the economic ends of Soviet socialism?

It was evident to the designers of the Five-Year Plan that, in order to increase production most economically, the size of the farming units needed to be enlarged so that waste might be eliminated and mechanization might be utilized to best advantage. But they would not urge the development of large-scale individual farms, for in a socialist scheme such development would have been politically unacceptable. There remained for them, then, two alternatives: to expand the state farms at the expense of individual holdings or to increase the number of collective farms. Since the first would have been unwise at the time because it would have caused general antagonism among the peasants, they chose the latter, which they thought could be handled with less friction. They planned also to increase the production of the state farms, but the main emphasis was to be placed on increase through collectivization. To make it more attractive, they provided that collective farms should be favored in the allocation of agricultural machinery and government credit.

PROMOTION BY PRESSURE.   When the time came to start the drive for collectivization, the agricultural front was in a state of unfavorable disorganization. The trouble had started in the previous year when the government, unable to purchase sufficient grain, had laid the blame upon the kulaks, who held about 40 per cent of the marketable grain and refused to sell it at goverment prices. Believing that their refusal was prompted by their opposition to the proposed changes in agricultural policy which would benefit principally the poorer peasants, the Fifteenth Congress of the Party had voted to use stern measures in dealing with them. That was the beginning of a policy of harshness toward the kulaks which created what actually amounted to class warfare in the villages. During 1928 emergency measures were taken to seize the withheld grain of the kulaks, and poorer peasants were urged to inform authorities about hidden supplies and promised one-quarter of the confiscated grain as a reward for information. So encouraged, many of them, aided by officials, worked off their spite against richer neighbors. And the kulaks, resenting compulsion, often forcibly resisted it. The more rebellious of them were deprived of their property and sentenced to periods of service in labor camps or forced to move to other regions where, without property, they were left to begin a new life as best they could. The struggle lasted until the end of the year, when the government, having collected a temporarily sufficient stock of grain, ended the emergency confiscation and relaxed the pressure on the kulaks.

It was against this background that the drive for collectivization began at the end of 1928. The First Five-Year Plan provided that collectivization be a gradual development, individual farming continuing to be the general practice while about a fourth of the peasant households were being drawn into the use of co-operative methods. The intention was to make collective farming and co-operative efforts more attractive than they had proved to be in the past, not to force them upon the countryside. The planners felt that this kind of gradual development would be consistent with the traditional alliance between the proletariat and the poor and middle peasantry, for which the party professed great concern.

Reality, however, proved to be quite different from the plan. In the summer of 1929 the party and government, claiming that the kulaks were again withholding grain, ordered the complete elimination of the kulak class. And there was carried out, during that year and part of the next, a brutal process known as "dekulakization," directed toward that end. Peasants classified as kulaks—and the term was used more loosely than ever before—were expelled from their holdings without compensation. Some of the less affluent among them were assigned inferior land elsewhere in the area where they were living; the more affluent, together with their families, were deported to distant and unattractive parts of the country; those deemed to be "counter-revolutionary"—that is, opposed to the government's policy in the villages—were arrested by the OGPU and sentenced to terms in labor camps. Such measures, reminiscent of the draconic methods of Ivan IV and Peter the Great, were effective in dekulakizing an estimated 15 per cent of the peasantry.

A few months after the beginning of dekulakization, the tempo of collectivization was officially accelerated. On January 5, 1930, the party changed the modest goals set in the original plan, and called for complete collectivization of all peasant holdings in the North Caucasus and the Volga regions by the spring of 1931; in other regions, by 1932 or 1933. Thereupon every conceivable method of agitation and persuasion was put into use in the effort to reach the new goals. The very poor among the peasants, being both easily impressed by the inducements and intimidated by the firm promptings of party and government representatives, took the lead in the movement into the collectives; but others held back. Where the less stringent methods failed to bring the desired results, compulsion was used: in regions where the majority of peasants agreed to join a collective farm, the minority were required to join also. And any show of resistance was met by threats of force. Thus, by March 1930, 55 per cent of all peasant households had been brought into collectives—a number far in excess of the goals set by the party itself.

The simultaneous execution of the policies of dekulakization and rapid collectivization in the first months of 1930 gave rise among the peasants to a mood of resentment similar to that of early 1921, when the party had been forced to alter its policy in regard to them. To those affected, it seemed that official policy was now being directed not only against the kulaks but also against the majority of other peasants. And it was evident that the situation was growing into a threat to the avowedly all-important alliance of the proletariat with the poor and middle peasantry. What lay behind the frenetic policy that produced these results is not clear. However, regardless of what impelled the leaders to push collectivization so rapidly and harshly and to use such a heavy hand in dealing with the peasantry, it did not lead them to press on when conditions became threatening. They were not willing to risk chaos. And by the beginning of March, 1930, it seemed that the countryside was close to that state.

The time had come to take stock of the situation. Collectivization was almost out of hand, and it was not adequately serving its purpose in the over-all plan for Soviet Russia. Because mechanization of the farms had not progressed as fast as their organization, old methods were still being widely employed and production was lagging. The limited number of available machines could not make up for the great number of agricultural workers who had left the rural areas—those who had gone to the urban centers to escape collectivization or to improve their lot by industrial work and those who had been driven away, the kulaks (the most capable and industrious of the peasants). Nor could any amount of planning overcome immediately the operational deficiencies caused by the general disorganization and the unwilling and inefficient work of the many peasants who had reluctantly accepted the forced change in their lives. Moreover, it was understood that a disgruntled peasantry could become a formidable obstacle to the country's planned progress if not properly handled. A change in tactics was imperative; and on March 2, 1930, Stalin released a letter entitled "Dizzy with Success," calling for a check to the rapid pace of collectivization and denouncing the use of threats or coercion to force peasants into collectives. This was the signal to the government and the party to relax the pressure. Peasants who wished were thereupon permitted to withdraw, with their land and stock, from the collective farms. Many took advantage of the permission; whereas on March 1 there had been about 14 million peasant households in these farms, by May 1 the number had dropped to 5 million, representing about 24 per cent of all households.[1]

NEW COLLECTIVIZATION TACTICS. The reduction of pressure for collectivization did not mean the abandonment of the drive. The goals set by the Communist Party in the winter of 1929-30 were reaffirmed; only the methods for achievement were altered. Thereafter greater attention was paid to the improvement of the existing collective farms in the hope that both their production and their attraction might be increased.

The advantages given to the collective farms, in comparison to those allowed to private farms, placed them in a greatly superior economic position. They received preferential treatment in taxation, in credit allowances and in the distribution of manufactured goods. In addition, they had the continued advantage of access to the machine-tractor stations. The establishment of those stations had grown out of an experiment in the Odessa region during the period 1927-29. There government-owned agricultural machines operated by technicians had been used to cultivate and harvest peasant crops in return for payment in kind, and the arrangement had proved very economical. In June 1929, the government began the organization of machine-tractor stations (known as MTS's) throughout the country. At first the ownership of the machines in the stations was vested in the peasants, who made installment payments on them; and noncollectivized peasants were allowed to share along with the collectivized ones. In 1932, however, ownership was transferred to the government, and noncollectivized peasants were no longer permitted to use the services of the stations.

In respect to the organization of the collectives, new rules were adopted after March, 1930. The peasants were assured that their homes, small garden plots, dairy cattle and poultry for family use, and small tools (which had formerly been treated as common property on many collective farms) would thereafter be exempt from collectivization. This allowance, assuring a limited individual economy, made collective farming less objectionable

---

[1] One of the by-products of the collectivization drive was the ultimate dissolution of the ancient village commune in Russia. It began when the R.S.F.S.R. decreed on July 30, 1930, that the village commune be dissolved in every village where more than 75 per cent of the households were collectivized and that its powers and duties be taken over by village soviets.

Collective farm homes with private plots

Collective farmers at an exhibition in Moscow

to many. And that fact, plus renewed pressure by the government, started another increase in the enrollment in collective farms. By the end of 1932, more than 14 million peasant households, more than 50 per cent of the total, were again pledged to collectivization.

FIRST RESULTS.   The transformation of individual peasants into collective farmers has been called the "second revolution," the first being that of 1917. Certainly it brought a revolutionary change in the relationship of the peasants to the land and to one another. More than half of them had been collectivized, and the "socialist sector" of agriculture (as the Soviet leaders called it) was definitely on the increase while the "nonsocialist sector" was on the decline. Peasant households, once individual units on small farms averaging about fifteen acres, were now grouped on collectives averaging 1,190 acres and comprising 78 households each.

However those advances toward the goals had not brought with them the expected increase in production nor the hoped-for acceptance of socialism by the peasantry. There had been a number of drawbacks. In the first place, the collectivized peasants had not yet adjusted themselves to the mores of collectivization and often neglected the group interests to favor their own. In the second place, the tools of production had been insufficient through much of the period. As has been stated, farm mechanization did not keep pace with collectivization; and the lack of machine power was made doubly serious by the added lack of animal power, caused by the slaughter of many horses and oxen (about 25 per cent of the total) during the period of kulak suppression. And finally, a great deficit in meat and dairy products had developed, since many rich peasants had chosen to kill all their livestock—not just the horses and oxen—rather than turn them over to the collective pool; by 1932 there was a 50 per cent loss in the number of goats and sheep and a 33 per cent loss in the number of cattle. Those conditions, added to crop failures in 1931 and 1932, helped to bring about serious famine in parts of the Ukraine and the North Caucasus in the winter of 1932-33. Such was the gloomy culmination of the first planned operations on the agricultural front. The situation was still indecisive; a strong, satisfactory position had yet to be established.

The commercial front

NEW AIMS.   Harnessing domestic and foreign trade to the Five-Year Plan required the reversal of certain domestic policies and the establishment of favorable economic relations with countries in whose diplomacy the

USSR was still ill-favored. Planned production throughout the country demanded planned distribution of goods; and that, in turn, necessitated the elimination of private trade, which had been revived in 1921. Abroad, arrangements had to be made to insure the import of those goods and services demanded by the plan and to establish markets for the Russian agricultural products and industrial raw materials with which payment was to be made for the imports.

ELIMINATION OF THE NEP MAN.   The first to feel the weight of the new commercial policy was the private trader, the NEP man, as he was called. With the initiation of the plan, co-operative and state-owned stores were established in great numbers, and the privately owned stores were forced out of business. Unequal advantages and confiscatory taxation made competition economically impossible for the private trader, and the government was able to take over the distributive system with little effort and no fear of effective resistance.

RATIONING.   Two outgrowths of the drive for industrialization made rationing necessary: the decline in the supply of consumer goods, resulting from the shift of emphasis to heavy industry and the insufficiency of the amount of food which the decreasing rural population could supply for the increasing urban population. Inflation and unfair distribution could be averted only by a strict system of allocation according to plan. The system adopted was one of direct rationing to individuals on the basis of their service in the promotion of the plan. The industrial workers, of course, were favored with higher quotas than other urban workers, but all were assured of at least minimum subsistence at low prices.

At first, only bread was rationed, but it soon became necessary to include all food and practically all goods on ration lists. Even then there were shortages. Bread was generally in supply, but stores were often bare of eggs, cheese and meat for long periods. Manufactured consumer goods were even scarcer, and suffering from lack of clothing and housing facilities was widespread.

FOREIGN TRADE.   During the period of the First Five-Year Plan the foreign commerce of Soviet Russia was governed by her necessity to import machines to make machines; in those years producer goods accounted for nearly 90 per cent of the value of her imports, while consumer goods accounted for less than 8 per cent. Her foreign purchases of machine tools, machinery, tractors, electrical equipment, iron, steel, cotton, wool, chemical products, and rubber made her one of the foremost importers of industrial goods. She bought over 20 per cent of all machinery exported in the world, her purchases including about 80 per cent of the British machine tool exports and, in one year (1931), over 25 per cent of the American industrial and electrical equipment exports.

The cost of these imported goods and of imported technical assistance was met with the traditional products of Russian export, agricultural produce and industrial raw materials. Despite the fact that Russia's share in the world export of wheat fell to 15 per cent in 1930 (having been 25 per cent before World War I), agricultural products constituted 40 per cent of the value of her exports in 1931, a peak year of her foreign trade. The remaining 60 per cent was made up chiefly of industrial raw materials, such as timber, oil, manganese, and coal. Thus the pattern of an agricultural economy was maintained in foreign trade, although an industrial economy was being rapidly developed.

The political-cultural front

THE IRRESISTIBLE FORCE.   After 1928 the political and cultural aspects of Soviet life were virtually merged. All individuals and institutions were centrally directed and compulsively bound to one effort: to create and strengthen the beliefs, habits, attitudes, and disciplines which, when combined, would produce nationwide loyalty to the aims of the Five-Year Plan.

The Communist Party, of course, led the way; and even it was revamped to insure agreement with the new aims. At the time of the Fifteenth Congress, the party had 887,233 members and 348,957 candidate members,[1] but the new leaders were not sure of their unanimous loyalty. Therefore the congress was followed by a period of reregistration (popularly known as a purge) of all party members, during the course of which "Trotskyites," other "deviationists," and persons with poor party records of one kind or another were expelled. Then came a new period of careful recruitment. Although many who sought to join could not meet the party standards, the increase in membership was large; in July, 1930, the number of members and candidate members was almost 2 million, and two years later it was about 2.5 million.

The increasing of party solidarity and the clarification of party inten-

---

[1] A candidate member was one whose application for membership had been accepted but who was yet required to pass through a period of candidacy (ranging from six months to two years, depending upon his class origins), during which he would study and perform certain directed activities.

tions served to accentuate the opposition, which grew rapidly and won a strong following, even including some from the highest circles of the renovated party. Opposition, as now defined, meant any disagreement with, or any failure in support of, the Five-Year Plan. The plan was supreme and, although its fulfillment would demand severities and sacrifices, it was to be carried forward. Stalin, in an address before a conference of industrial managers in February, 1931, stated the situation thus:

> It is sometimes asked whether it is not possible to slow down the tempo a bit, to put a check on the movement. No, comrades, it is not possible! The tempo must not be reduced! . . .
>
> We are fifty or a hundred years behind the advanced countries. We must make good this distance in ten years. Either we do it, or they crush us. . . .

That had been the sentiment of Stalin and his followers from the beginning of the drive for industrialization, and in their interpretation any form of opposition to it was a criminal offense against the state. To emphasize the seriousness of such offenses, to forestall others, and to prove to the people that the state was vigilant in the protection of their interests, opponents were speedily brought to trial and condemned, sometimes with melodramatic effects. For a while the trials followed one another in a steady stream. The most important ones involved accusations of groups: in May, 1928, sixty engineers were tried for sabotage; in March, 1930, a group of alleged Ukrainian separatists; in December, 1930, eight men led by Professor Leonid Ramzin, who confessed to the organization of an "Industrial Party" which planned, allegedly with French assistance, to overthrow the Soviet regime; in March, 1931, a number of Soviet officials and former Mensheviks, accused of conspiring, in co-operation with socialist parties abroad, against the government; and in October, 1932, several leading Communists, accused of counter-revolutionary conspiracy. By such trials the government and party made gains in their political battle: they were able to point out to the people that Russian interests were being protected against men who were conspiring with foreign enemies (though there are serious doubts as to the veracity of the confessions to such charges), and they were able for a time to discourage political opposition.

All agencies of the government and party were employed in dealing with opposition but the most important of them was the OGPU. Despite the earlier belief on the part of the Soviet leaders that the need for a political police would disappear with the stabilization of the regime, the OGPU continued to grow in significance and became a powerful weapon in the struggle to impose conformity. Through a network of informers—many of them party members—in government offices, factories, schools, military units, collective farms, and state farms, it kept watch on the opinions and activities of all Soviet citizens. Any act which could be construed as being of a hostile political character could land its author in the offices of the OGPU and might result in trial before a regular court or in detention, without benefit of trial, in one of the labor camps of the OGPU.

RENEWED ATTACK ON RELIGION. Overt antagonism to the regime was only one form of opposition recognized by the Communists; there was another, which they interpreted as equally dangerous, deep in the cultural life of the people—their religion. The limited tolerance they had shown toward religion came to an end in 1929, and a new drive was begun to eradicate religious activity and belief. The spirit of the drive is illustrated by this statement from *Izvestia*, the official government newspaper: "Religious ideology is one of the chief obstacles in the path of a socialist reconstruction of the country. Religion and socialism are incompatible."

In 1929 the constitutions of the R.S.F.S.R. and some of the other Soviet republics, which had previously permitted "freedom of religious and of antireligious propaganda," were amended to permit "freedom of *religious belief* and of antireligious propaganda." The change in wording was slight, but the limitation implied was great: religious groups no longer had the *freedom of propaganda*. With the constitutional amendment came also a number of legislative restrictions on organized religion. It was denied the right to promote nonreligious activities, such as the organization of charities and study groups. It was strictly limited in the training of clergy and in the establishment of regional religious organizations. Its publication of religious literature was sharply curtailed; no religious periodical was permitted to appear between 1929 and 1943. And even the use of ecclesiastical buildings was limited. Churches, synagogues, and mosques might be used for religious purposes only if an organized body in a locality applied for and received permission. In 1929 more than 1,400 churches and monasteries were closed or put to other than religious uses.

By restraints on the training of young men to replenish the clerical ranks, the government hoped soon to reduce the clergy to an inadequate number of declining old men with no successors. And the promise of such results was in evidence as early as 1930, when about half of the clergymen of the country were over fifty years of age while less than one out of twenty was under thirty years of age. At the same time, by antireligious propa-

CARTIER-BRESSON

*Typical scene in Russian church in Soviet period, the communicants
predominantly middle-aged women*

ganda, particularly among the youth of the country, the government hoped
to reduce the religious laity. If both hopes were fulfilled, the aging clergy
and laity could be expected gradually to pass away, leaving no organization to represent religion.

While religious activity and growth were being subjected to a policy
of attrition, antireligious propaganda and activity were receiving not only
complete freedom but also active encouragement and support from the
government and party. In the schools antireligious instruction was given
greater emphasis than ever before. In the country at large, the Union of
Militant Atheists—membership in which had grown to 2.5 million by Feb-

ruary, 1930—worked diligently and effectively to encourage and direct antireligious manifestations. In many cities and on many collective farms organized mass-meetings demanded the closing of churches or the removal of church-bells to be used for metal in industry. Mass petitions were responsible for the closing of many of the churches and monasteries, and such petitions often included requests that the buildings be put to use as museums, theaters or clubs. Workers and peasants were encouraged to remove all religious vestiges from their homes, and in many cities workers burned their icons in public ceremonies. Not only religious beliefs and symbols but religious habits also were included in the program of eradication. Crossing oneself, saying grace, making references to the deity—all were discouraged and derided as habits from the unenlightened past. One of the most radical steps taken to eliminate religious habits was the introduction, noted earlier, of the "continuous" week, which disregarded Sunday, the traditional day of rest and worship. Surface evidence seemed to indicate that the old Holy Russia of pious peasants and innumerable churches was fast disappearing. In many of the new cities growing up as a result of industrialization there was not a single church, and the number of people attending services was dropping throughout the country. Yet there remained a solid core of believers, mainly of the older generation but including also some young people who refused to accept the new beliefs. Their number was not great enough, however, to stay the progress of the antireligious drive. When the drive reached the peak of its intensity in 1929-30, the Soviet leaders were satisfied with the prospect—that within a few years organized religion would have disappeared entirely from Russia.

GENERAL EDUCATION AND INDOCTRINATION. General education, of course, provided the basic approach to the task of displacing the old culture and instilling the new. However, reforms in Russia's educational system had begun so late and its inadequacies had been so extensive that, at the beginning of the First Five-Year Plan, the system was far from ready to take over its proper share of the responsibility for training the new generation. Although facilities were increased as rapidly as possible at all levels, education lagged behind other fields in supplying the needs of the new society. But Soviet leaders did not allow it to fall to a subordinate place in their plans. Stalin, in a statement to the Sixteenth Party Congress, meeting in June, 1930, said, "The chief task now is the transition to compulsory primary education. I say 'chief' because this transition would mean the decisive step in the cultural revolution." At the end of 1932 it was reported that the school system had developed to the point of being able to accommodate all children between the ages of eight and eleven, and that compulsory four-year primary education was at last achieved. The leaders wanted a school system which could assure for all children a full primary education in the then basic seven-year school, but that could not be accomplished in five years. Seven-year schools in adequate number and with adequate staffs were provided in the large cities of the R.S.F.S.R.; elsewhere the four-year school, where some knowledge of the three R's and a few political slogans were taught, remained the source of what formal education most children received.

Intensification in the general education program was accompanied by intensification in the program of retraining and indoctrinating the masses. It became virtually compulsory that everyone practice his citizenship duties by participating in the election of members to the soviets and by demonstrating an interest in the work of the soviets. The government continued to use the party organization, the press, the radio, mass organizations, and adult education organizations in the effort to accelerate the transformation of all people within the Russian borders into good Soviet citizens. The increase in party membership, mentioned above, was matched by increases in the mass organizations. By 1932, the membership of the Komsomol was over 3 million, that of the Young Pioneers about 5 million, and that of the trade unions about 17 million. Mass participation was expanded also through civilian defense organizations, in which were taught various skills which would be useful in the case of attack: flying, parachute jumping, skiing, shooting, and defense against air and chemical warfare. All defense organizations were united in the Osoaviakhim (the contraction of the Russian name for the Union of Societies for Co-operation in the Defense of the Aeronautical-Chemical Construction of the USSR), membership in which totaled over 5 million in 1932. The Osoaviakhim not only taught military skills to its members but also helped in the technical training of workers in the aviation and chemical industries. In total, the efforts of these various organizations, combined with those of radio and press, touched the life of every Soviet citizen and insured the penetration of Communist ideology into every home.

THE CREATIVE ARTS.   The program of education and indoctrination demanded the planned and concentrated effort not only of organized groups but of individuals also. Writers, musicians, and artists were now forced to abandon the limited freedom extended to them under the NEP and to use their talents exclusively for the expression of ideas profitable to the

Five-Year Plan. Writers were placed under the virtual dictatorship of RAPP (abbreviation of the Russian words for Russian Association of Proletarian Writers), a body representing the government and the party, which determined acceptable literary themes and judged the propriety of all creative writing. Under its direction, writers visited construction projects and collective farms and, from the material and ideas received there, produced a spate of novels and short stories—most of them devoid of literary merit—about the achievements of the Five-Year Plan. Only a few novels of the period rose above the level of mediocre propaganda, among them Boris Pilnyak's *The Volga Flows to the Caspian*, Valentin Katayev's *Time Forward!*, and Michael Sholokhov's *Seeds of Tomorrow*, probably the best novel of the period. The other creative arts suffered from the same regimentation as that applied to literature. The standards for music were set by RAPM (abbreviation of the Russian words for Russian Association of Proletarian Musicians) and those for painting, by RAPKH (abbreviation of the Russian words for Russian Association of Proletarian Artists). This rigid determination of artistic standards by small groups of party members, whose aim was to force the production of "proletarian" art at any cost, and the consequent sterility of the arts under the Five-Year Plan led to such criticism that the Central Committee felt the necessity for change. In April, 1932, it decreed the dissolution of RAPP, RAPM and RAPKH and ordered the formation of one society for each of the arts which would include all professional practitioners of the arts, whether or not they were party members. Thereafter, although the general aims were not altered, creative artists were not so directly subject to unprofessional direction but were "persuaded" to find their own way to "proletarian" art through the Union of Soviet Writers, the Union of Soviet Musicians and the Union of Soviet Artists.

International relations: 1928-1932

CONTINUATION OF PEACE POLICY. The guiding motive of Soviet foreign policy during the years of the NEP, the avoidance of war, was reinforced after 1928, since the successful execution of the Five-Year Plan was possible only if Russia remained at peace. On the surface, the Soviet peace policy appeared little different from that of other states, but Moscow was willing to pay a higher price in order to avoid war or the threat of war.[1] Included in that price were the acceptance of a secondary role in the areas where Russia had traditionally maintained a great interest and the acceptance of a second-rate position for the USSR among the powers.

The defensive nature of Soviet policy was evident in the extent of the country's military preparations. Following the end of the Civil War, the size of the armed forces was rapidly reduced. By 1924 there were only 562,000 men in the standing forces of the Red Army and Navy combined, and that number was not increased again until 1934. Although military service was in theory a general obligation, only a small number of the young men eligible for service were enlisted. The forces were held at the smallest number considered consistent with security against attack; they were certainly not large enough nor sufficiently trained and equipped for offensive operations against the superior forces of France and her allies, in whom the Soviet Government saw the principal threat.

The Commissariat of Foreign Affairs, under the direction of Chicherin and Litvinov (after Chicherin's retirement, in July, 1930), applied the peace policy by promoting the idea of world disarmament, by playing a prominent part in negotiating nonaggression treaties, and by attempting to establish normal diplomatic relations with all the powers. Soviet delegates figured prominently in the disarmament talks held in Geneva under the auspices of the League of Nations until those talks ended in complete failure in 1934. And nonaggression pacts were concluded with Finland, Latvia, Estonia, France, and Poland in 1932. However, Soviet Russia's efforts toward establishing diplomatic relations with the many powers with which she did not have ties were less successful. Normal relations with England were restored in November, 1929; but the United States continued to refuse recognition, and Mexico broke diplomatic relations in 1930, leaving Uruguay as the only nation in the New World to have diplomatic ties with the USSR.

The Communist International also helped to support the peace policy. Its Sixth Congress, meeting in Moscow during the summer of 1928, acknowledged acceptance of Soviet leadership and picked up the routine of its purposeful business. Superficially the Sixth Congress seemed to follow the tradition of laying principal stress on world revolution; its manifesto cried,

---

[1] The Soviet attacks in Manchuria in 1929 to prevent expulsion from affairs connected with the Chinese Eastern Railroad may seem an exception to that statement. Actually, though, they were no more than border skirmishes and did not entail the possibility of war either with China or with other powers.

> The Sixth Congress of the Communist International . . . appeals
> to you from Moscow, the Red capital of the new world, to prepare
> yourself for a struggle against the ever more insolent forces of
> capitalism. . . . Long live the proletarian world revolution.

But, in sober reality, it concentrated not on the possibility of a new wave
of revolutions but on strategy for thwarting any attack on the Soviet Union. It
accepted "Defense of the Soviet Union" as the principal motif of Communist
propaganda throughout the world and decided upon the tactics to be employed everywhere against anti-Soviet policy and against militarism. At
the same time, it laid plans for the strengthening of the Communist parties
and Communist-led organizations, whose duty it would be, if war against
the Soviet Union should break out, to lead revolutionary attacks on the governments of their native countries. Again, the Commissariat of Foreign
Affairs and the Comintern were seeking the same ends but by different
means. And again the tactics of the Comintern were of such nature as
to hinder the efforts of the Commissariat, for they would make it appear
that Communist Russia was professing to seek peace and, at the same time,
promoting sedition.

That peace was actually maintained could be credited neither to the
efforts of the Commissariat of Foreign Affairs nor to those of the Comintern. As long as international affairs were dominated by the "status quo
powers"—primarily France, England, and the United States—the world
remained at peace because those countries wanted it so. France, named by
Stalin in July, 1930, as "the most aggressive and militarist country of all
aggressive and militarist countries of the world," was feared by Moscow
as the center of active anti-Soviet designs, but the fears were unfounded
at that time. It is true that France—as well as England and the United States
—was hostile to the Soviet Union; but none was preparing war, for all had
more to gain by preserving the status quo. Therefore the USSR had her
period of peace. But it was not a wholly untroubled one.

SHADOW OF WAR.   A serious disturbance of peace came in September,
1931, when Japan invaded Manchuria and thereby aroused the immediate
concern of Soviet Russia for her interest in the Chinese Eastern Railroad
and in the security of the Soviet Far East. The invasion placed Russia in
a difficult situation; she realized that she could not handle Japan with impunity as she had handled China, by show of arms, in the contest over the
same issue in 1929. Yet she was not willing to risk involvement in war.

At first the Chinese Eastern Railroad was not seriously involved in
Japan's actions; she merely occupied the railroad zone, moving troops in

and, despite promises, refusing to withdraw them. But, after she had transformed Manchuria into the Japanese puppet empire of Manchukuo, in February, 1932, she replaced the nationalist Chinese colleagues of the Russians in the railroad administration by Chinese who were pro-Japanese; and it became evident that the Russians were to be harried out. After that the USSR was forced to choose a position: to try to continue her participation in the administration of the railroad by peaceful means, to try to force a fair readjustment, or to liquidate her interest in the railroad. She chose the last because it involved the least risk. On May 2, 1933, Litvinov informed the Japanese ambassador to Moscow that the Soviet Union would sell its interest in the railroad to Japan or Manchukuo, and the Japanese later agreed to purchase it at a price of $47,804,000.

By that arrangement Moscow gained an extension of peace but not a release from danger. The Japanese militarists who were responsible for the attack on Manchuria regarded the USSR as an obstacle to Japanese expansion and assumed that a conflict was inevitable. The Soviet Government realized that but, believing the situation not immediately threatening, was still unwilling to use force or to collaborate with the other powers (China, England, and the United States) opposed to Japanese expansion. Instead, it adopted a policy of watchful neutrality, refusing even to participate in the work of the Lytton Commission, formed by the League of Nations in April, 1932, to investigate the events in Manchuria. The refusal was probably motivated by a desire to show no hostility toward Japan. And the same desire prompted repeated offers by the USSR, beginning with one made by Litvinov on December 31, 1931, to sign a nonaggression pact with Japan; all were rejected.

Inevitably the events in Manchuria drew the Soviet Union and China closer, and in December, 1932, their governments finally arranged a resumption of diplomatic relations. Moscow, however, made it clear that the resumption of relations with China was not to be interpreted as an anti-Japanese action.

Although the USSR did not want to show hostility toward Japan, she did want to show evidence of strength. She intended to demonstrate by the clearest evidence known to international relations, armed force, that any attack on the Soviet Far East would result in war. After the invasion of Manchuria she began preparations to defend not only her Far Eastern territories—those east of Lake Baikal and those bordering on Mongolia, Manchuria and Korea—but also Outer Mongolia, which was in fact a Soviet protectorate. Soviet troops were transferred from the west to reinforce those in eastern Siberia, and Blücher was placed in command of them with instructions to build up a strong Red Army. At the same time heavy investments were made in the Soviet Far East in order to create an industrial base for the maintenance of the defensive army. Soviet Russia had been forced to a recognition of the source of the greatest threat to her peace.

The First Five-Year Plan in perspective

OVERFULFILLMENT.   Early in the period of the First Five-Year Plan, the Soviet leaders, having decided to accelerate the tempo of the planned economic growth, called for the completion of the five-year program in four years; later they extended the time to four and one-quarter years. On December 31, 1932, it was declared successfully completed and, therefore, overfulfilled because completion came nine months ahead of the original schedule. That meant much to the leaders, for they felt that the Soviet system itself had depended upon the success of the plan. Failure would have meant loss of prestige for the government both at home and abroad, the indefinite postponement of the creation of an industrialized socialist economy, the loss of domestic stability, and consequently the weakening of the country, already precariously situated in a hostile world. Overfulfillment, on the other hand, was interpreted as meaning that Soviet Russia was at last a solidly established state, capable of well-nigh miraculous feats and justified in setting herself up as an authority on the theoretical and practical problems of the confused and downtrodden throughout the world.
GENERAL ACHIEVEMENTS.   The Soviet claim of success is substantially true, although it must be accepted with some reservations. Certainly the planned operations in basic industry were even more successful than anticipated, as illustrated by figures given earlier in the chapter. Industry made commendable gains in every area, and the aim of producing machinery and electrical power and equipment in quantities sufficient to maintain the continued progress of an industrialized economy was amply realized.

Socialization also, as important to the plan as industrialization, was advanced in like degree. In 1928, that part of the economy which the government called the socialized sector (including state-owned industry and transportation, foreign and domestic commerce, and both state and collective farms) accounted for less than 50 per cent of the national income; in 1932 it accounted for 87 per cent. By that time all industry, transportation and commerce had been brought into the socialized sector, and nearly 80 per cent of the cultivated area belonged to state and collective farms.

There had been only two periods of comparable economic growth in Russian history: the period of Peter the Great and that of Sergei Witte's ministry. The growth during the First Five-Year Plan, however, far overshadows that of the earlier periods; and it is all the more impressive because it represents a generation of normal economic expansion effected in less than five years by the use of the relatively new and untried techniques of a planned economy, without the aid of foreign capital.

SHORTCOMINGS OF THE PLAN.   Citing only the figures of production, construction, and socialization as evidence of the success of the plan could result in distorted conclusions. Absolute success depended upon more than material evidence. It demanded, first of all, harmonious operation and coordination throughout the program, and those were not achieved. Mechanization did not keep pace with collectivization; wages did not keep up with rising living costs; housing facilities did not increase as fast as urban populations; school facilities could not be developed as fast as plans for expanding education; indoctrination could not prepare the peasants fast enough to make them receptive to the changes forced upon them; dictatorial methods produced bad results in the field of creative arts; inadequacies in transportation hindered proper distribution; and the urge to stifle political opposition led the government to waste precious time in purging and policing.

Moreover, the execution of the plan was marked by irregularities, because the assumptions made by the planners were not borne out. It was assumed that there would be no crop failure during the period, but there were poor harvests in 1931 and 1932. It was assumed that a high level of foreign trade would be maintained, but the world depression of 1929 resulted not only in a drop in demand for Soviet exports but also in a faster fall in the prices paid for agricultural products and raw materials offered for sale by Russia than in the prices paid by Russia for the manufactured goods imported. It was assumed that international conditions would permit a relatively low military expenditure, but the Japanese invasion of Manchuria necessitated a rapid increase in governmental outlay on military preparations. It was assumed that labor productivity would rise rapidly as a result of better training and the introduction of more and better machinery, but productivity did not rise as rapidly as anticipated and consequently production costs greatly exceeded the original estimates and quality fell far below what was expected. It is to the credit of the organizers and promoters of the Five-Year Plan that such drawbacks did not disrupt it altogether. Yet they must not be overlooked in judging the actual success of the plan.

HUMAN GAINS AND SACRIFICES.   It will never be possible to make a complete human balance sheet of the First Five-Year Plan, but a few debits and credits may be noted. On the whole, the average Soviet citizen was living more poorly in 1932 than he had been in 1928. Those who agreed with the viewpoint of the regime, however, accepted in good faith the promise that the development of basic industry would soon result in an increase in the standard of living for all. Indeed, many social gains were already in evidence. Most workers were on a seven-hour day, and urban workers had the satisfaction of knowing that they would profit by the established plans for social security through old-age pensions, medical care, paid vacations, and maternity care. In addition, there was work for all and opportunity for most. The apparently limitless demand for trained personnel in industry, agriculture, and education made it possible for one to rise rapidly in the Soviet world if he had the ability and determination to fit himself for advancement. And for many there was the added reward which came with participation in an effort embodying the characteristics of a crusade.

Against those credits certain debits must be balanced. Everyone was affected by the personal restrictions accompanying the demand for conformity; freedom of discussion diminished steadily, and the cost of opposition grew. And it cannot be forgotten that execution of the plan involved ruthlessness to individuals; about 15 per cent of the peasants were uprooted and harshly dealt with; other peasants were hurried into new life patterns; entrepreneurs were forced out of business; creative artists were made to abandon freedom of expression; and many were separated from their cultural and religious heritage. In short, individualism had been severely curbed, and what the leaders called socialism had yet to be proved as a satisfactory substitute.

TOWARD A SECOND FIVE-YEAR PLAN.   Even before the First Five-Year Plan was declared completed, the Soviet leaders began preparations for a second plan. In designing the second one, they took into consideration many of the mistakes made during the first phase and allowed for changes to correct them. But they retained the essential premise of the first, the possibility of organizing an entire economy by plan; and its essential goal, the creation of an industrialized Russia.

TWENTY-EIGHT / THE USSR: PROSPECTS AND

PROBLEMS: 1933-1939

I n the period between the completion of the First Five-Year Plan and the beginning of the Second World War, few changes were made in Soviet goals. The Second Five-Year Plan, covering the years 1933-37 inclusive, and the Third Five-Year Plan, designed for the years 1938-42 but not completed because of the outbreak of war, led the country nearer to the realization of those goals. But the programs of the new plans did not require the speed and ruthless compulsion which had marked the first. For a short time, life became somewhat more comfortable for the Russian people, and they began to realize a few of the advantages of the country's economic improvement. During this period, too, revolutionary extremism was toned down; some links with the Russian past were restored, and the emphasis shifted from revolutionary ardor to respectability.

Soviet leaders declared that the country was developing according to the prescriptions of Lenin as interpreted by his faithful disciple Stalin: socialism was being realized, and communism would be achieved in the foreseeable future. But was this the case? Societies never develop quite as their leaders wish; and Soviet society, even with the unparalleled concentration of power in the hands of a few, was no exception. At the end of the First Five-Year Plan, it was evident that there was a disparity between the leaders' interpretation of socialism at that time and their interpretation in 1917. In the earlier instance, they held that socialism would be achieved when, capitalist society having given way, the means of production and distribution of goods were controlled by the producers—that is, workers and peasants; but by 1933, they were publicly emphasizing the abolition of capitalism and ignoring the question of control. They had, in fact, come around to the acceptance of control by a self-perpetuating group dominated by one man, Stalin. And any future re-defining of socialism might be expected to depend upon whether this group would hold steady, intensify, or relinquish its control.

Six-year continuance of planned economy

THE REVISED PROGRAM. Although the second and third plans represented no deviation from the aim to socialize all production and to develop Soviet industry until it surpassed that of all other industrial countries, they allowed a gradual slackening in the rate of industrial development and a slight decrease in investment in capital goods. Whereas the first plan required a yearly increase of 21 per cent in industrial development, the second provided for an increase of about 16 per cent, and the third, for an increase of a little less than 12 per cent. And whereas nearly 25 per cent of the national income was set aside for capital investment in 1933, the new plans provided that such investment take somewhat less than 20 per cent by 1937.

The emphasis on expansion of industry and mining in the Soviet Far East, Western Siberia, and Central Asia was continued, with the added aim of providing national security supplementing that of economic development. It had long been a recognized fact that the concentration of production in European Russia was a source of military weakness, that if Russia were attacked from the west and should lose her European industries to the enemy, her army would be without an industrial base. Therefore it was important to create an industrial base east of the Urals which would be reasonably safe from attack. Hence the development of Central Asia. Then, since the Central Asian supply base would be too far removed from the Far East to support a defense against a possible Japanese attack in that area and since the central Siberian region was disadvantageous for the development of a base, it was necessary to develop the Soviet Far East so that it also could supply the needs of an army. Of course, an eastern army supported by a Far Eastern base would be just as vulnerable as a western army supported by a western base, but that arrangement was the best possible at the time. And it had advantages to offset its disadvantages: a show of force would deter Japan, and the general development of the area would add materially to Soviet Russia's economic growth. The latter advantage alone would have justified the continuation of the Far Eastern enterprises. However, as the activities of the new plans progressed, the importance of military considerations grew. The revival of German militarism and the extension of Japanese aggressive policies in the middle 1930's caused the Soviet leaders to devote more and more production to military needs and to think in terms of the possibility of war in the very near future. Between 1932 and 1939 annual military expenditures increased thirty-fold, and the proportion of the expanding governmental budget devoted to such expenditures grew from 5 per cent to 25 per cent.

In the Ural region and Siberia the completion of projects begun under the first plan and the progression of new projects caused an unprecedented increase in urban population—from 3 million in 1926 to 9 million in 1939. The cities in the region of the Ural-Kuznetsk combine, still under active construction, grew in proportion to the project. Magnitogorsk, the center of the Ural end of the combine, had been begun in 1931 as a collection of tents and huts housing the workers who set up the furnaces and rolling mills to process the local iron ore; by 1939 it had become a city of 146,000. At the other end of the combine, in the Kuznetsk Coal Basin, the city of Stalinsk (formerly known as Kuznetsk) grew in population to 170,000, forty times its population in 1926. New cities sprang up also. Typical of them were Karaganda, established during the period of the Second Plan and developed into a city of 166,000 by 1939; and Komsomolsk, founded by a group of 4,000 enthusiastic Komsomol members in 1932 and developed into a ship- and machine-building city of 71,000 by 1939.

Collectivization, well on its way at the end of the first plan, was virtually completed by the end of the second; 93.5 per cent of all peasant households were in collective farms by July, 1938. Furthermore, by that time, collective farming had been more uniformly and satisfactorily organized. Observation of the different types of collectives had led the government to the conclusion that the *artel* type was the most desirable, and in February, 1935, a model *artel* charter was adopted and recommended to all collectives. The charter provided that the title to the land pooled in a collective farm be vested in the state but that members be granted use of the land in perpetuity without payment of rent. Each household was allowed, for individual use and profit, its dwelling, household goods, and minor tools in addition to some land—an acre or less. The management of a collective farm was theoretically the joint responsibility of all its members over sixteen years of age. They met in assembly and elected a chairman and a farm board, who were supposed to act for them. However, since the chairman was usually nominated by the Party and since the farm was obliged by the terms of the charter to conduct its operations according to plans worked out by the government, the members actually had little part in management. The kinds of crops they would plant and the acreage they should devote to each crop were predetermined by plan, and they were required to sell stipulated quantities of their crops, amounting on the average to 15 per cent of the total yield, to the government at fixed prices.

In revolutionizing the agricultural economy through collectivization, the government found it necessary also to revolutionize the thinking of the peasants, to change it from an individualistic to a socialistic pattern. That change came more easily to the Russian peasants than it would have to agrarian groups in Western Europe or the United States because they had been affected by a degree of socialization in the village commune. However, as has been seen, the peasants had a strong attachment for private property. And now there were added obstacles to their acceptance of socialism: their passivity and hostility toward the government and its ideology. Recognizing those obstacles, the government tried to overcome them by education, persuasion, and coercion through the schools, radio, press, movies, mass organization, and the political police. The machine tractor stations—or MTS's—were also brought into use in the ideological campaign. They were capable of a wide influence because of the importance they had gained in the new system of agriculture. In 1938, employing 1,403,000 persons in 5,800 units throughout the country, they were providing the plowing service for 71.5 per cent of the farm lands, as against 1 per cent in 1928; and 95 per cent of the threshing service, as against 1.3 per cent in 1928. Therefore, their power of coercion, through the withholding of services, was great, even though they seldom exercised it. Their chief activities in the promotion of education and ideology were carried on through contacts between their personnel and the collective farmers. In January, 1933, the Communist Party began the organization of a political department in every MTS in the country, detailing 17,000 party members to the task. In the political departments they were to be jacks-of-all-trades—agitators, agronomists, organizers, and the givers of advice, threats and encouragement. If a collective farm failed to reach its quota, it was the duty of the political department to discover and correct the source of the failure. If there was a need for political education among the collective farmers—and there usually was—it was the duty of the political department to provide it.

The government also made a special effort to increase party membership among the collective farmers. However, after particularly active recruiting, peasants (mainly collective farmers) accounted for only 28 per cent of the membership in 1934, although peasants still made up the majority of the population. In 1939 the primary party organizations (groups of three or more party members) existed in only 5 per cent of the collective farms, and about 50 per cent of such farms had neither a party nor a Komsomol organization.

NEW UNDERTAKINGS.   The Second and Third Five-Year Plans included some undertakings that had been omitted from the first even though their importance to the industrialization of Russia had been recognized from the beginning. One was the provision of more adequate transportation facilities through the construction of new waterways, roads, railroads, and airlines and through the extension of old ones. A number of canals were built to facilitate the use of natural waterways. Two of the most important were the 141-mile Baltic-White Sea Canal, built to aid the economic expansion of Soviet Karelia by shortening (from 2,840 miles to 674 miles) the water route from Archangel to Leningrad; and the 80-mile Moscow-Volga Canal, which served to make navigable the waters between the Volga and the Moscow rivers and to increase the water supply to Moscow. Construction of automobile roads was undertaken also to give access to some of the new centers of industry not reached by either navigable waterways or railroads. Although few such roads were constructed, they were of great importance to the regions they served. The one connecting the Trans-Siberian Railroad (at a point near Chita) with Yakutsk (in northern Siberia) reduced the journey between the two points from about twenty days to two, and others provided similar advantages to other out-of-the-way places. The most noteworthy growth in the Soviet transportation system was that of civil aviation. Since airlines were less costly and more efficient than railroads or automobile roads in regions where distances were great and the population small, they were established as the sole means of communication with many such regions, bringing the inhabitants directly from the age of cart and sled to that of the airplane. In 1933 Russia had 21,580 miles of regular airlines; by 1939, she had almost 100,000 miles, which carried about twenty times as much freight as her lines had carried in 1933. Comparatively little new railroad construction was undertaken before 1939, only enough to bring the total mileage to about 59,000 miles, an increase of about 23,000 miles over the 1913 mileage.[1] But much was done toward the reorganization and modernization of existing lines. During this period, the Trans-Siberian

---

[1] The 1913 mileage in that part of Russia which remained under the USSR

Railroad was completely double-tracked in order to increase its utility for both military and economic purposes. And a new branch of the Trans-Siberian was constructed to Sovetskaya Gavan, on the Pacific, opposite Sakhalin Island.

Another undertaking, not newly conceived but newly emphasized under the second and third plans, was that of tapping the resources (timber, minerals, fish, and furs) of the regions north of the Arctic Circle. The chief problem in the undertaking was the establishment of a dependable northern sea route connecting the mouths of the great Siberian rivers—the Ob, Yenisei, Lena, and Kolyma, which flow into the Arctic—with Archangel and Murmansk and, if possible, with Vladivostok. The obstacles to this latter-day search for the Northeast Passage were great, for navigation in the Arctic was possible only during a part of the summer. Some efforts had been made to establish such a northern sea route as early as 1921; but systematic, large-scale efforts began with a series of expeditions in 1932 and 1933. In 1934 the icebreaker *Litke* accomplished the feat of sailing from Vladivostok to Murmansk in one season; and by the next year, the combined efforts of navigators, meteorologists, and engineers had developed means whereby regular commercial navigation could be carried on over that route during the summer seasons. Two new ports north of the Arctic Circle were opened: Igarka, on the Yenisei, and Tiksi Bay, near the mouth of the Lena River. Much of the work required to open those ports and to provide for inland transportation to them was done by prisoners from Soviet labor camps. Thereafter vessels from Murmansk could carry goods and equipment to the half-million inhabitants of the Siberian Arctic and pick up their export goods from such points as Tiksi Bay.

NEW SLOGAN.   Among the changes undertaken to correct or avoid the mistakes and weaknesses of the First Five-Year Plan, one of far reaching effect was introduced by these words of Stalin: "Formerly we used to say, 'Technique decides everything,' now this slogan must be replaced by a new slogan, 'Personnel decides everything.'"

The application of that slogan was felt throughout the Soviet system. The intelligentsia, that group which by Soviet interpretation included professionals, government officials, military officers, technicians, and the higher white-collar workers, recognized a definite improvement in their status as a result of it. When the First Five-Year Plan had been initiated their number was made up principally of men trained in tsarist schools or abroad, and they suffered from Soviet disapproval of their "bourgeois" derivation. They were given rations inferior to those of workers, their children were discriminated against by the admission policies of educational institutions, their professional work was hindered by interference from the Communist Party and trade union representatives, and they were forced consistently to bear the blame for mishaps and deficiencies in production. But when Soviet-trained men began to appear in their ranks, even as early as 1931, the status of the intelligentsia began to advance, partly because they were then considered a "safer" group politically and partly because Soviet leaders recognized the fact that their low morale threatened production. Before long, discriminatory practices against them were ended and they were accorded more favorable treatment than workers, receiving better housing and salaries and being allowed greater independence in their work. Thereafter their professional competence was given just recognition, and their authority over their work was subjected to less interference. Some saw in this change the danger of the emergence of a new elite, a privileged professional class; but since it was profitable to the immediate Soviet plans, the policy remained in force.

The labor personnel—i.e., the workers—likewise felt the influence of the new slogan. They were the focus of an intensified effort to improve the quality of production by increasing rewards and incentives. More attention was given to the encouragement of "socialist competition," and it was made more attractive by the introduction, in December, 1938, of a series of medals and awards. If a worker proved worthy of the highest of these, the award of the Order of Lenin, he was given also the title Hero of Socialist Labor, carrying with it the highest honor of the USSR. Individual incentives were combined with social incentives, and exemplary achievements brought not only honors but material rewards as well. Despite the fact that many Old Bolsheviks still insisted that inequality in wages was contrary to socialist principles, the Soviet leaders believed that unequal wages were necessary as incentive to both the skilled and the unskilled. So workers continued to be paid on the basis of quantity and quality, the differentiation in their wages and salaries growing sharper as the second and third plans progressed. The most striking example of the combination of social and individual incentives was provided by the Stakhanov movement. It was begun after the miner Alexis Stakhanov was able, on August 30, 1935, by the use of improved techniques to cut 102 tons of coal in a six-hour shift and thus earn a month's normal wages for a day's work. The government and party made a hero of him and worked up a mass movement among workers to emulate him. Those who did so, called Stakhanovites, received both honors and monetary rewards.

Domestic economic situation in 1939

INDUSTRY AND AGRICULTURE. The year 1939 is a good point from which to review the accomplishments of the drive to transform the economy of the country. The programs outlined in the first three plans were as near completion then as they were to be for some time; when that year ended, the economy was being converted to purposes of war and many of the planned objectives had been dropped. Statistics are available for accomplishments to that date or to years near it, and by comparing them with statistics available for earlier years, it is possible to indicate the actual progress of the first three plans.

Soviet Russia was approaching her goal in industrialization: "to overtake and surpass the most advanced capitalist countries." Before World War I, her industrial production had trailed behind that of the United States, Great Britain, Germany, and France, but by 1939 it had surpassed that of Great Britain and France and was nearing that of Germany. The following production figures give some measure of the increase:

Product	1913[1]	1928	1938
Pig iron (million tons)	4.2	3.3	14.6
Steel (million tons)	4.2	4.3	18
Rolled steel (million tons)	3.6	3.4	13.3
Electricity (billion kilowatt hrs.)	2	5	39
Railroad locomotives	418	478	1626
Tractors		1,200	80,000[2]
Motor vehicles		700	211,000

The monetary value of industrial production, according to Soviet statistics,[3] increased more than seven-fold between 1928 and 1939.

The growth in agricultural production was not so satisfactory. Of course, the plans had not provided for an agricultural increase commensurate with

[1] The figures for 1913 represent production in that territory of the Russian Empire which was later included in the USSR.

[2] The figure for 1937 is used here, that for 1938 being unavailable.

[3] Non-Soviet economists have seriously questioned the validity of certain Soviet statistics and particularly of Soviet indices. There is general agreement on the judgment that the indices are too high, but not on how they are to be corrected. For a clear discussion of the problem, see Robert W. Campbell, *Soviet Economic Power* (Cambridge: Houghton Mifflin Co., 1960), 28-48.

the industrial increase, but results did not measure up even to the goals set by the plans. The untoward effects of collectivization, discussed in the preceding chapter, were not overcome to any satisfactory degree until after 1935, and then it was too late to reach the anticipated level of productivity before the coming of the economic disturbances of 1939. However, there were encouraging advances. Between 1928 and 1939 the total acreage under cultivation increased 21 per cent while the farm population declined about 5 per cent. That was a gain in the planned direction: toward the production of more with less human labor. In addition, the nature of cultivation had improved. Large tracts, cultivated more efficiently with the use of machines were accounting for greater production per acre. And, with direction from agrarian experts, farmers were beginning to diversify their crops, thereby giving a better balance to the country's agricultural economy. Grain remained the chief crop, but the percentage of land sown to grain was decreasing while the percentage used for cotton, vegetables, grasses, and fodder was on the increase.

Although, through planned change, the USSR had achieved a high degree of industrialization by 1939 and the position of agriculture in the national economy had declined, the country had not become primarily industrial. Rather it had reached a reasonable balance as the occupational distribution of its population had been changed in this way:

Occupational field	Percentage of population (approx.)	
	1926	1939
Agriculture	77.5	55
Industry	10	25
Public administration and social service	3	10

THE HUMAN FACTOR.   In 1937 Molotov made the official declaration that socialism had been achieved in the Soviet Union—i.e., that classes, in the Marxist sense, had disappeared. The great majority were by that time engaged in so-called socialized activity: about 35 per cent of the working population were employed in state-owned enterprises, and 55 per cent were members of collective farms. The rest were mainly self-employed peasants, and their number was steadily decreasing. No one remained in the category of capitalist. This situation supported Molotov's declaration if the official definition now equated socialism with the complete abolition of capitalist enterprise and the virtual elimination of individual enterprise, but not if it recognized the original requirement that the socialized activity replacing capitalist enterprise be controlled by workers and peasants.

Moreover, socialization thus far had not raised the general welfare of the people as rapidly as it had raised the economy of the country and, therefore, could not be said to have fulfilled the promises of the leaders. The basic cause of this shortcoming lay in the urgency with which the material ends of the plan were pursued. Although social and individual incentives were drawing more effort from the workers and although they were accommodating themselves somewhat to great changes in their traditional work habits, their productivity remained low, far lower than the planners had anticipated. And as long as it remained so, the standard of living likewise remained low. The three plans required the investment of a large portion of the national income in heavy industry, but the second and third plans provided an increase in the proportion to be used for consumer wants. Had productivity been higher, that amount might have been sufficient to raise living standards adequately, and certainly prices would have been lower. As it was, prices remained high, and the average Soviet citizen could not yet live comfortably on his earnings.

To make a fair comparison between the living standard of the average Soviet worker and that of an average worker in the Western countries, one must take into consideration, among many things, the fact that the computation of "wages" was different for the two. The Soviet worker was considered to have two types of wages: an "individual wage" and a "socialized wage." The first was his actual cash earning; the second, his earning in social services, which were financed in part by money deducted from his individual wages. The "individual wage" is known to have been comparatively very low. It could provide the worker with food of a coarse and simple nature and with housing which, by Western standards, was not adequate for comfort; his family lived in one room, oftentimes sharing cooking and toilet facilities with four or five other families. But it could buy him little else in a market where the price of a pair of shoes was equal to about two weeks' wages and the price of a suit to about two months' wages. Yet he had his "socialized wage," providing him access to social services such as unemployment insurance, medical care, education, entertainment, and old-age pensions—all hitherto available to only a few. The increase in the availability of some of those services under the three plans is shown by these statistics:

Social services	1928	1939
Students in elementary and secondary schools	12,068,000	31,517,000
Students in higher schools	177,000	603,000
Public libraries	28,900	77,600
Books in public libraries	72,200,000	146,700,000
Movie houses	9,700	30,900
Hospital beds	247,000	672,000
Doctors	63,000	110,000

The economic conditions growing out of the three five-year plans brought change to the people *en masse* as well as individually. The census of 1939 showed a population of 170 million (an increase of 23 million over that of 1926), which, according to population experts, was lower by 5.5 million than it would have been if growth in population had been normal. Certainly economic conditions had not been entirely responsible for that lack of growth, but they had been definitely involved in it. The national economy had not been keyed to the proper handling of the famine and near-famine conditions which brought the heavy population losses to the Ukraine, the North Caucasus and Kazakhstan in the thirties. Growth in population was adversely affected also by the decline in the birth rate resulting from the economic emancipation of women and the laxity toward divorce and abortions in the early thirties. In 1939 both the birth and the death rates in Russia, although lower than in the past, were still higher than in most of the European countries.

The great movements of population from country to city and from the west to the east were, as has been explained, a direct outcome of change of emphasis in the national economy. By 1939, the urban population had grown to 55 million, more than twice that of 1926; and the rural population had fallen from 120 million to 114 million. During the same period, the number of cities with populations over 200,000 increased from twelve to 39. And the largest ones of them grew phenomenally: Moscow, from 2 million to over 4 million; and Leningrad, (formerly Petrograd) from 1,690,-000 to 3,190,000. The movement from west to east is illustrated by the fact that while the population of European Russia grew about 11 per cent during this period, that of Central Asia (the Kirghiz, Kazakh, Uzbek, Tadzhik and Turkmen republics) expanded by 38 per cent, Siberia as a whole by about 31 per cent, and the Soviet Far East by 88 per cent.

Social and cultural changes

RETURN TO SOCIAL STABILITY. Activities on the economic fronts were progressing smoothly enough during the years of the second and third plans to allow the Soviet leaders time to consider the conditions of the country's social and cultural institutions, which had been deeply shaken by the extreme revolutionary measures of the earlier years.

The compulsion to change old attitudes and institutions and to create new ones was giving way to the necessity to improve and stabilize. Some of the early changes had not proved satisfactory; others had not followed the general progress. Now an inventory was needed. As the people became settled and adapted themselves to the economic changes in their lives, they began giving more attention to their home and community life, seeking adjustments and thereby making it necessary that the government watch and handle developments carefully in order to give them the proper political direction. Another factor influencing the government to turn renewed attention to social direction was the fact the USSR was now facing the possibility of war. War would demand men; consequently, steps were to be taken to increase the birth rate. And war would demand discipline; consequently, the family and the school as well as the army were to be directed toward the development of discipline.

The Soviet press led the way to an appreciation of the need for social stability at the family level by pointing out the high rate of divorce, the frequency of abortions, and the general instability of family life. On June 27, 1936, the government issued a new decree on the family, thereby amending some of its earlier revolutionary concessions. The decree forbade abortions except for reasons of health and made divorces somewhat more difficult by imposing divorce fees, requiring that both parties be present to record a divorce, and increasing alimony payments. To encourage childbearing, it stipulated that the government expand its maternity homes and kindergartens, increase financial allowances to mothers, and provide particularly large allowances to mothers with six or more children. Thereafter emphasis was placed on the maintenance of the family as an intrinsic social unit responsible for the care and rearing of children. Within the family, relations were changed also. Greater responsibility was placed upon the father, whose duty was now, in the words of *Pravda*, "to prepare good Soviet citizens. . . ." And the child, said the Komsomol, "must respect and love his parents, even if they are old-fashioned and do not like the Komsomol."

There were complaints about the schools also. As a result of the use of so-called progressive methods, children were learning little except vague political phrases, and the authority of the teacher was being virtually ignored. A partial return to former practices, begun in 1931, was now speeded up. Traditional methods, including the assignment of homework and the administering of formal examinations, were reintroduced, and the emphasis on political indoctrination was partly supplanted by emphasis on the formal subject matter of history, arithmetic, geography, and native and foreign language. Those changes were accompanied by an increase in the disciplinary powers of the teacher through the abolition of the system of self-government of pupils in the first four years and the restriction of its operation in the higher grades. The duty of the schools was now more definitely defined: they were to lay a firm foundation of knowledge and introduce the young to the discipline necessary to their future Soviet usefulness.

Another reversal of policy involved the reintroduction of ranks, titles, and academic degrees, which had been abolished in the days of egalitarian fervor. Realizing the incentive value of special designations, the government began to allow their use again for the purpose of making certain callings more sought after. In September, 1935, ranks were reintroduced in the army and navy; and commanding personnel (the term *officer* was taboo), hitherto designated simply as commanders, were given traditional ranks ranging from lieutenant to brigadier. A new title, Marshal of the Soviet Union, was created, and the Red Army Commanders Voroshilov, Tukhachevsky, Budenny, Yegorov, and Blücher were immediately designated as Marshals. In the academic world also ranks and degrees were reintroduced. Then the government went even further, creating entirely new titles—such as Hero of Socialist Labor, Distinguished Scientific Worker, and Distinguished People's Artist—to be awarded for meritorious work. Prestige was again to be as well marked as in the days of the tsars.

Religion received the last and least consideration in the social readjustment program. Even then there was no evidence of change in the essential Communist attitude toward religion; the change was only in the methods of the antireligious campaign. Since it was seen that many still clung to religious beliefs, tactics calculated to shock or directly antagonize the religious were dropped. The mass closing of churches and burning of icons was stopped, and in 1936 the disenfranchisement of the clergy was ended.

While specific steps were being taken to establish social stability, there was a general relaxation of restrictions against social attitudes, customs, and habits hitherto condemned as "bourgeois." The Bolshevik of 1917, although consecrated to the happiness of mankind, disclaimed "selfish" interest in such things as home comforts, personal finery, adornment, and politically unproductive social entertainment. Stalin's simple military tunic set the tone of masculine dress. Most Communist leaders eschewed ties, business suits and felt hats, and their wives would have been perilously out of fashion in evening dresses. But, by the middle 1930's, "nonproletarian" interests and styles were returning, and disapproval was being withdrawn. Soon attention to dress and deportment was being encouraged as evidence of "culture." The Second Five-Year Plan included lipsticks, women's clothing with some degree of style, and household appliances on the production lists. Jazz became more acceptable and the ban on ballroom dancing was lifted. The evidence indicated either that the Soviet leaders had redefined the word "bourgeois" or that they were granting it more respectability.

SOVIET PATRIOTISM.   In the beginning, Soviet loyalty was directed toward international communism, represented, for the time being only, by the Soviet regime and the Communist Party in Russia. The Red Army man took his oath to give himself "for the liberation of toiling mankind" throughout the world. The national anthem of the USSR was the *Internationale*, the traditional hymn of international socialism and communism. And the motto of the Soviet press was "WORKERS OF THE WORLD, UNITE!" Russian nationalism—or any form of nationalism—was taboo in the USSR. School children studied the history of the class struggle in Russia but not the history of Russia as such. Teachers and writers who praised Kutuzov, Suvorov, or any of the other Russian heroes of the past were liable to punishment through the loss of their positions or otherwise.

However, the gradual stabilization of society, the approaching threat of war, and the lessening of the prospect of world revolution led in the 1930's to a re-examination of the bases of loyalty. It was then apparent that the USSR might be, for an indefinite period, the only soviet socialist state in the world, and it was apparent, too, that she might soon be at war. It was time to ask: Would the abstract cause of international communism have any real appeal to the Soviet citizen under test either in war or peace? There was no reason to believe that it would. His loyalty needed to be fixed on something tangible and enduring. The USSR was tangible; the individual could think of it in terms of his family, his home, his city. And it was enduring; it had a future, a present and a past which could be traced back for at least a millennium. But to make loyalty to that past a part of the loyalty of the Soviet citizen required a new interpretation of Soviet ideology; hitherto the past had been relegated to the limbo of evil and disregarded ex-

Moscow, Old and New. In foreground: *southern end of Red Square: Cathedral of St. Basil, begun in 1554 (in honor of taking of Kazan) and completed in 1679; near its main entrance, statue of Minin and Pozharsky.*
In background: *Moscow River and buildings constructed during the Soviet period.*

cept as a source of horrible examples. That difficulty was resolved, however, by the formulation of a new conception, that of "Soviet patriotism." The first step toward its introduction was the issuance of a decree by the government and party on May 16, 1934, in which the existing state of historical instruction in the schools was thus denounced:

> Instead of learning *civic* history in a vivid and interesting way, by presentation of the most important events and facts in chronological sequence and with characterization of historical personalities, the students are given abstract definitions of social and economic structures.

The decree demanded the preparation of new textbooks in history which would eliminate the faults mentioned, and it ordered the reestablishment of the schools of history in the universities of Moscow and Leningrad.

The new textbooks, prepared under the close supervision of Stalin and other high party leaders, presented the new interpretation of the past upon which Soviet patriotism was to be based. Through them the student was to see the USSR as the culmination of a long process of historical development and to understand that, while the Soviet regime was the best and only regime suitable for Russia, it had been made possible because the leaders and the people of Russia—non-Russians as well as Russians—had established, preserved and enhanced the Russian state in the preceding millennium. Many institutions of the Russian past which were now undesirable or destructive, according to the new texts, had been of positive value in the past; Christianity, for example, had helped to civilize Russia, and tsarist absolutism had helped to protect her from destruction. Now the USSR was the heir and guardian of the best in the Russian past, and the Soviet citizen was privileged to protect it—with his life if necessary.

This new interpretation, this Soviet patriotism, was not confined to history textbooks but was expounded in the daily press, in novels, plays, and motion pictures. Every expression of it, of course, had to be made with cautious consideration. Many historical characters were being shifted from the role of villain to that of hero, and even contemporary ones were subject to shift; so it was well to know the exact position, in honor or dishonor, of anyone whose name was mentioned. Lenin, as father of the revolution, remained the greatest of heroes, and Stalin was considered his chief disciple. History, as rewritten, proved that Stalin had always been at Lenin's right hand. As the 1930's progressed, idolization of Stalin grew; he was given credit for all major Soviet achievements, and to him was ascribed incredible ability in all spheres of life. His picture, beside that of Lenin, was omnipresent. Cities, villages, locomotives, canals, and factories were named for him. Other Soviet leaders received homage, too, but in conspicuously lesser degree. At the same time, there was publicized a great catalog of villains, headed by Trotsky and including also other Soviet leaders who had fallen from grace. To these were ascribed all errors and evil deeds.

SOCIALIST REALISM.   In a meeting of Soviet writers on October 26, 1932, Stalin suggested that they should employ the methods of "socialist realism" in their work and, by that suggestion, started a new trend not only in literature but in the other arts as well. The meaning of socialist realism was expounded lengthily at the First All-Union Congress of Soviet Writers held in 1934 and thereafter became the subject of wide critical discussion. The writer or artist following the requirements of socialist realism looked upon his calling primarily as a means of educating the people both in the values of Soviet society and in general cultural values, and he created for a mass audience in a simple, realistic manner calculated to produce both understanding and belief.

Socialist realism permitted a greater latitude in the choice of subject and method than had been permitted during the period of the First Five-Year Plan. It demanded less emphasis on "proletarian" subject matter and encouraged greater emphasis on the historical past. Nonetheless, the writer or artist, by Western standards, was seriously limited by it. All creative work was expected to contribute to the Soviet socialist society by stressing its values, and art for art's sake and pre-occupation with esoteric problems of form and technique were forbidden. Yet the successful creative artist had one comforting assurance: his work would be received by a mass audience the like of which was unknown outside of Russia.

On the whole, the artistic work of this period was superior to that of the preceding one, but no men of the stature of Leo Tolstoy or Peter Tchaikovsky appeared. In the field of fiction the works of Michael Sholokhov, Alexis Tolstoy, and Nicholas Ostrovsky were outstanding. Sholokhov continued his work on *The Silent Don;* Tolstoy, considered the dean of Soviet writers after the death of Gorky, in 1936, set a new trend in historical fiction by his sympathetic portrayal of an imperialist figure in *Peter I;* and Ostrovsky made an effective presentation of Soviet life in his novel *How the Steel Was Tempered.* Five composers accounted for a great part of the musical work of the period: Dmitri Shostakovich, composing for the symphony orchestra, opera and ballet; Nicholas Myaskovsky, considered the finest of Soviet symphonic composers and teachers; Sergei Prokofiev, who returned to the Soviet Union in 1933 after an absence of many years and took up a simple style for the interpretation of national themes; Aram Khatchaturian, a native of Soviet Armenia, who composed chamber and symphonic music; and Ivan Dzerzhinsky, who composed operas based on Sholokhov's *Seeds of Tomorrow* and *The Silent Don.* In the graphic arts the emphasis on socialist realism produced many competent but few distinguished works. The artists usually took as subjects the Soviet leaders, past and present, and scenes from Soviet history. Among the most popular of them were the sculptor Sergei Merkurov and the painters Alexander Gerasimov and Igor Grabar.

GENERAL EDUCATION. The restoration of traditional subject matter and methods of pedagogy was followed by the allotment of an increased budget for the training of teachers and the opening of new schools. However, the Second Five-Year Plan fell short of its aims for education, the provision of seven-year schools for all children, and in 1937 about half of the children had access only to compulsory four-year schools. The Third Five-Year Plan renewed the aim of providing a minimum of seven-year schooling for all and added another, that of providing ten-year schooling in all cities and in some rural areas. And again achievements were short of the goals. However, by 1939, much had been done toward liquidating illiteracy. More than 81 per cent of the people over the age of nine were literate—a great gain over 1926, when 51 per cent were literate, and over 1897, when 24 per cent were literate. Women had made a particularly striking advance: whereas only 37 per cent of them had been literate in 1926, about 72.6 per cent were literate in 1939. But the greatest gains were among the backward peoples of Central Asia; in the Tadzhik S.S.R., the most backward area of the USSR, the percentage of literacy had increased from 3.7 in 1926 to 71.7 in 1939.

SCIENCE AND SCHOLARSHIP. There was a great expansion of scholarly and scientific activity during the period 1933-39. The Academy of Sciences of the USSR, parent body of the major scholarly and scientific bodies of the country, increased yearly in size and scope. By 1939 it was directing the work of some 3,000 scientists and 80 institutes and was working closely with more than 1,000 other scientific bodies. It provided the same type of service for science and scholarship that the State Planning Commission provided for economic affairs: it planned work, allocated funds for research, and published the results of research. On the whole, the scholarly and scientific work done during this period, in comparison with the past, was greater in volume and superior in quality. As in all fields of Soviet endeavor, such work was limited somewhat by Communist ideology; but as long as the scholar or scientist did not offend Communist orthodoxy and as long as he applied himself to the advancement of those studies considered worthwhile, he was afforded unparalleled facilities for his work and was assured of great economic security. Within this mixed environment of opportunity and limited freedom, many were able to carry on serious and productive work.

The most productive work was in the field of applied science, the importance of which was paramount in the conduct of the Five-Year Plans, but pure sciences were not neglected. Of the prominent Soviet scientists, Alexis Favorsky was working on the problems of synthetic rubber production; Nicholas Vavilov, on the development of plants suitable to the various climates of the USSR; Peter Kapitsa, on various physical problems; and Abram Alikhanov, on cosmic rays. Others were carrying on research in fields ranging from public health to atomic energy.

The social sciences and the humanities were still restricted by the point of view of the party; but the degree of party interference was somewhat less than before, and it was possible to conduct and complete considerable research in those fields. Following the death of Michael Pokrovsky, in 1932, and his posthumous castigation by party authorities, the study of history, restored to its full status as an independent discipline, began to show signs of vigor. Important advances were made also in the study of the various languages of the Soviet Union and of the archaeology and paleontology of the country.

The Constitution of 1936

POLITICAL READINESS.   According to the Communist leaders their program of evolutionary political progress—from the dictatorship of the proletariat to socialism and finally to communism—was well on its way by 1934. They declared that socialism, the second stage of progress, had been achieved, since production in industry and agriculture was then on a socialistic basis and since the basic principle of socialism, "from each according to his ability, to each according to his work," was in effect. That was true, they said, despite the fact that progress in the first stage had been retarded, that the dictatorship of the proletariat had not yet ended and that the state had not yet "withered away." That retardation, as they saw it, resulted from no fault in the program; it was the inevitable result of "capitalist encirclement." As long as the USSR was encircled by hostile capitalist powers intent on the subversion of Soviet efforts, the basic features of the dictatorship of the proletariat (party control and a strong state) would of necessity be continued. In fact, according to Stalin, the USSR might be compelled to retain those features even after it had reached the stage of communism. Now, however, it was time to make some changes in the political structure of the state in recognition of the developments to date.

One of the changes was the break-up, in July, 1934, of the OGPU and the transfer of its component units to the newly created All-Union People's Commissariat of Internal Affairs, or NKVD (for *Narodnyi Komissariat Vnutrennikh Del*). The NKVD, headed by Henry Yagoda, assumed direction of the regular police (known as the militia), the fire protection services, several other activities, and the units of the former OGPU. Although the NKVD was the heir of the old OGPU, its powers were more limited; it was permitted to impose administrative exile or imprisonment for terms up to five years only and was required to refer to regular courts all political cases involving sentences of more than five years. The differences between the powers of the new NKVD and the former OGPU were not great, but they indicated a gradual relaxing of political police power. Further evidence of a tendency toward relaxation came with a governmental decree in July, 1935, which granted amnesty to a large number of persons under punishment for anticollectivization activities.

Meanwhile throughout the country tension was being eased by the general economic improvements which were bringing more real wages, food, and goods to everyone. By a decree of the Sovnarkom the rationing of many foods was ended on January 1, 1935, and within a year all rationing of food and goods was ended. Generally, the people were being given some reason to agree with Stalin's declaration that "life has grown better, life has grown merrier."

PREPARATION OF CONSTITUTION. To climax and give formal recognition to changes which had occurred during the period since the Constitution of 1924 came into force, the Seventh All-Union Congress of Soviets in February, 1935, instructed the Central Executive Committee to have the draft of a new constitution prepared. The C.E.C. appointed a Constitutional Commission, with Stalin as chairman, to prepare the draft. It was published in June, 1936, and the public was invited to discuss it. Thousands of suggestions for amending the draft were made, but only a few minor suggestions (mainly for verbal changes) were incorporated in the final draft, which was approved by the Eighth All-Union Congress of the Soviets on December 5, 1936.

BASIC FEATURES. The Constitution of 1936 differed from the Constitution of 1924 in only a few points and did not make any radical alteration

in the Soviet system of government. One of the chief differences was embodied in Article 134 of the new Constitution, which stated that henceforth
all elections were to be conducted "on the basis of universal, direct, and
equal suffrage by secret ballot," and in Article 135, which provided that
"all citizens of the USSR who have reached the age of eighteen, irrespective
of race or nationality, religion, educational and residential qualifications,
social origin, property status or past activities, have the right to vote in
the election of deputies and to be elected. . . ." Those articles placed all
people on an equal footing and restored the vote to all who had previously
been disenfranchised. Article 134 also terminated the practice of voting by
show of hands, the unequal weighting of votes in favor of the urban worker, and the indirect election of deputies to the higher soviets.

Two conditions already recognized were given legal form in the new
Constitution. Its bill of rights guaranteed the right to employment, leisure,
social insurance, and free education. And Article 126 stated that the Communist Party "is the core of all organizations of the working people, both
public and state." Another condition already existing, the de-emphasis of
the world revolutionary aspect of Soviet thinking, was recognized by an
omission; the new Constitution did not state, as had the Constitution of
1918 and the Constitution of 1924, that the Soviet state was the nucleus of
the future Worldwide Socialist Soviet Republic.[1]

The formal organization of the USSR was defined as a federal union of
eleven union republics, voluntarily united.[2] The supreme legislative authority in each union republic was to be a directly elected, unicameral Supreme
Soviet, which would choose a Presidium, to carry on its chief legislative
functions between sessions, and a Council of People's Commissars, to serve
as the chief administrative and executive body of the union republic.

The form of the federal legislature was changed by the provision that,
instead of the cumbersome All-Union Congress of Soviets, the C.E.C. and
the Presidium, there would be only two bodies: the bicameral Supreme Soviet, popularly elected for four years, and the Presidium chosen by the
Supreme Soviet for the same period. The two chambers of the Supreme
Soviet would be the Soviet of the Union, representing the people on the
basis of population with one deputy for each 300,000 persons, and the So-

---

[1] By 1936 it had become customary to write "Soviet Socialist" rather than "Socialist
Soviet."

[2] The number was raised to eleven by dissolving the Transcaucasian S.F.S.R., raising
Georgia, Armenia, and Azerbaidzhan to the status of union republics, and promoting
the Kazakh and Kirghiz Autonomous S.S.R.'s to union republics.

viet of Nationalities, representing the various nationalities with twenty-five deputies for each union republic, eleven for each autonomous republic, five for each autonomous region, and one for each national area. The federal government was to exercise exclusive jurisdiction over affairs of general concern, such as foreign affairs, matters relating to war and peace, coinage, foreign trade, preparation of the economic plan, and preparation of the budgets for all governmental agencies. All rights not reserved to the federal government nor prohibited to the union republics were reserved to or shared by the union republics. Functions under the exclusive jurisdiction of the federal government were to be carried out by All-Union People's Commissariats of the USSR (each within its special sphere—such as defense, foreign affairs, foreign trade, and railroads); and functions shared by the federal government and the union republics were to be carried out by the Union-Republican People's Commissariats of the USSR (dealing with such matters as agriculture, justice, and health) in conjunction with corresponding Union-Republican People's Commissariats in each of the union republics. Finally, the functions reserved to the union republics, such as the administration of the school system, were to be exercised by bodies known as Republican People's Commissariats.

The basic characteristic of the Soviet Government, one-party dictatorship, remained unchanged. The following statement, made by Stalin in presenting the draft of the Constitution, summarizes the party's attitude toward that dictatorship:

> I must admit that the draft of the new Constitution does preserve the regime of the dictatorship of the working class, just as it also preserves unchanged the present leading position of the Communist Party of the USSR. Several parties can exist only in a society in which there are antagonistic classes. . . . In the USSR there are only two classes, workers and peasants, whose interests—far from being mutually hostile—are, on the contrary, friendly. Hence there is no ground in the USSR for the existence of several parties, and consequently for freedom for these parties. In the USSR there is ground only for one party, the Communist Party. . . .

SOVIET DEMOCRACY.   Soviet leaders spoke of the new Constitution not as the most democratic but as the only democratic constitution in the world. Their interpretation, of course, rested upon a use of the term *democracy* quite different from that current in other countries. True democracy, they contended, required that the interests of the masses be expressed by the government and party and that every individual be assured the means of realizing his abilities; and only in Russia were those requirements met. They saw no reason to qualify their position simply because freedom of speech, press, assembly and organization, as conceived in the Western world, did not exist in Russia.

The first election under the new Constitution took place on December 12, 1937. On that day over 96 per cent of the more than 93,500,000 persons eligible to vote cast their secret ballots for deputies to the Supreme Soviet of the USSR. It was an election without contest. Some had expected that there would be several candidates for each seat in the Supreme Soviet, but on election day the voters received a ballot with the name of only one candidate for each seat; they could vote either *yes* or *no*. Although several nominees had been proposed in each electoral district during the period of nomination, the local party organizations had chosen those to be recognized as candidates for office, and the others had withdrawn. Of the voters who went to the polls, 98 per cent voted *yes* for the selected candidates. Thus a hand-picked Supreme Soviet was elected by the process of Soviet democracy, and a precedent was set for subsequent elections under the new Constitution of the USSR.

The Great Purge: 1936-1939

RENEWAL OF REPRESSION.   The abolition of the OGPU and the adoption of the new constitution gave promise of a relief from political pressure, but the promise was not fulfilled. At the very time that the encouraging measures were being carried into effect, there was an official turn toward increased repression. This turn became immediately evident at the time of the assassination of Sergei Kirov, by Leonid Nikolayev, in December, 1934. Kirov had ranked second to Stalin in prestige and influence and was thought by many to be opposed to his associate's harsher policies. Some believed that Stalin, in resentment of such opposition, arranged for the assassination; but evidence is still insufficient to support any conclusive judgment. At the time, this deed, the first assassination of a leading party member since 1918, was treated by Stalin as a blow against himself and the Soviet state. The criminal code was immediately amended to deny the right of appeal and representation by counsel to persons accused of terroristic acts against government officials. Then the government, after an investigation, announced that the assassination of Kirov was the work of a counter-revolutionary group led by followers of Zinoviev and financed by foreign agents. In January, 1935, Nikolayev and scores of persons accused of being associated with him in the plot to kill Kirov were executed, and Zinoviev and Kamenev were imprisoned on the charge of having encouraged the conspiracy.

THE TRIALS.   During the following eighteen months an intensive investigation, particularly of former followers of Trotsky, Zinoviev, Kamenev, Rykov, and Bukharin, was carried out by the NKVD. Many arrests and executions took place, but the country at large was not greatly disturbed. Many former members of the left and right opposition in the party were still in responsible, although not primary, positions; Bukharin, for example, was editor of *Izvestia*, organ of the government, and Rykov was People's Commissar of Communications.

In 1936, however, the relative calm was broken and the political troubles became publicized. In August of that year Zinoviev, Kamenev, and fourteen other important persons were charged, in public trial, with conspiring, in collusion with the exiled Trotsky, to overthrow the government with aid from German sources. The accused, having pleaded guilty and confessed in fulsome detail, were sentenced to death and, according to official report, shot. In January 1937, a group of seventeen were tried publicly on similar charges. Among them were Karl Radek, leading party journalist; George Pyatakov, a noted party leader; and Gregory Sokolnikov, former People's Commissar of Finance. They likewise confessed, and thirteen of them were sentenced to death while four, including Radek and Sokolnikov, were sent to prison. In May and June the purge reached into army personnel. Yan Gamarnik, chief of the political administration of the Red Army, committed suicide after having been accused of anti-Soviet conspiracy. Robert Eidemann was deprived of his position as Chairman of Osoaviakhim. A number of leading army commanders, including the popular Marshal Tukhachevsky, were deprived of their command positions on the western frontier. Then came an official announcement that Marshal Tukhachevsky, Eidemann, and six other leading army commanders had been tried secretly on the charge of "habitual and base betrayal of military secrets to a certain hostile Fascist power and working as spies to compass the downfall of the Soviet state and to restore capitalism," and that they had been found guilty and executed. Six months later occurred the execution of seven noted party leaders, the experienced diplomat Leo Karakhan among them. The last and most important of the trials took place in March, 1938, when Rykov, Buk-

harin, Yagoda, and eighteen other highly placed defendants were tried
on the then commonplace charges of treason and espionage. All confessed.
Three were sentenced to prison, and eighteen—including Rykov, Bukharin,
and Yagoda—were sentenced to death.

THE GENERAL SWEEP.   These trials represented a small part of the extensive purge. While they were going on, the party was expelling members
by the tens of thousands, and the NKVD was carrying out mass arrests of
even greater numbers. The initiative for the great purge came from Stalin
and his close associates, but its tempo and atmosphere were soon affected
by mass hysteria. Officials as well as humble citizens, anxious to prove their
loyalty or motivated by fear, hatred, cowardice, or ambition, took part in
a rapidly increasing movement of denunciation. They denounced neighbors,
fellow-workers, superiors, subordinates, and even close relatives, knowing
that likely they would be arrested and condemned as "enemies of the people."

Whether or not a given individual fell victim to the purge was often
a matter of chance, but the record indicates that it was directed primarily
against certain persons in the party, industry, the government, the army,
and the intelligentsia. They were the "Old Bolsheviks," former members of
opposition groups in the party, former members of other parties, persons
of foreign birth or with ties abroad, and national minorities such as the
Ukrainians, White Russians, Jews, Armenians, and Georgians. The accusations against individuals, usually based on flimsy or fabricated evidence and
generally supported by confessions obtained under duress, ranged from
sabotage to treasonable conspiracy against the government. Many of the
accused were shot, but more were imprisoned and condemned without trial
to labor camps or exile in remote parts of Siberia, Central Asia, or the
north of European Russia.

The full extent of the purge is not known, for the Soviet Government
has never made complete figures available; but some statistics are known.
Seventy-eight of the 139 members and candidates (those not having the
right to vote) of the Party's Central Committee were shot, and 1108 of
the 1966 who had been delegates to the Party Congress in 1934 were arrested. In the army, the sweep of the purge included three of its five marshals, thirteen of its fifteen commanders of armies, sixty-two of its eighty
corps commanders, and 110 of its 195 divisional commanders. Of the
eighteen members of the Council of People's Commissars, fourteen were
among the purge victims. A complete listing would probably show that
the majority of those in responsible positions were removed from office

and imprisoned, and to those must be added the great number who were of lower station but equally unfortunate in their fate.

RECESSION OF HYSTERIA.   The hunt for alleged traitors, spies, wreckers, saboteurs, and counter-revolutionaries reached its high point in 1937. By that time fear and hysteria were undermining all forms of organized life. Factory managers were afraid to make decisions lest they be accused of "wrecking" if the decisions proved ineffective; officials mistrusted their subordinates as informers; and subordinates dared not be too friendly with superiors, who might be arrested at any time. Naturally such a situation worked against industrial production. And that fact apparently brought the government to a realization of the danger of continuing the purge with such intensity. In 1938, steps were taken to stop indiscriminate purging. Many who had conducted purges against innocent persons were themselves purged; and the chief of the purgers, Nicholas Yezhov,[1] head of the NKVD, was removed from office and, presumably, shot. A great slackening of the purge followed, and by March, 1939, it was over. Yezhov's successor, Lavrenti Beria, in co-operation with other leaders, undid some of the evil by releasing thousands of innocent persons from prison and labor camps and restoring them to their previous positions, reinstating many expelled party members, and allowing many exiles to return home. But complete restoration was not made by any means. Thousands were dead; and tens of thousands, although once more free men, were broken in spirit and body. In addition, many persons, low and high (Marshal Blücher, for example), had disappeared from their homes—some having been shot, others sent to labor camps without the right of correspondence. The very names of those who disappeared were obliterated by the eradication of any mention of them (if they were of such importance as to be mentioned) in history and reference books, and by the removal of their books (if they had written any) from the public libraries.

EFFECT ON PARTY LEADERSHIP.   The purge removed a great number of leading Soviet figures from public life. Hardest hit were the Old Bolsheviks, the men who had joined the party in the early days; both the Society of Old Bolsheviks and the Society of Ex-convicts were dissolved in 1935. The outcome was a great change in the composition of party leadership: whereas four out of five delegates to the party congress in 1934 had joined the party in 1920 or earlier, only one out of five delegates to the

---

[1] Because of the prominence of Yezhov's part in the purges, Russians call this period the *Yezhovshchina*.

congress in 1939 could make that claim. In short, most of the men who had helped to make the revolution and establish the regime had been removed from public life to make way for younger men reared under the Soviet regime.

A MOOT QUESTION.   What is the explanation of the purge? If the official explanation given by the Soviet Government at the time is accepted, the holocaust of expulsions, arrests, and executions was the only possible means of dealing with a great conspiracy, directed or led by Trotsky, Zinoviev, Kamenev, and Bukharin and aided by the majority of the responsible leaders of the party, government, and army, who for nearly a generation had been acting as spies and agents of foreign countries with the aim of overthrowing the Soviet system. Even if the existence of a conspiracy were admitted, it would still be a matter of wonder that the majority of the trusted leaders of the Soviet Union should have been spies and traitors. But it is quite evident that the allegation of a conspiracy was without foundation and that the men who confessed were accepting guilt for crimes they had not committed. Why they confessed as they did, in open court, is a puzzle. The facts surrounding the assassination of Kirov are far from clear. And even less evident is the motivation of those who directed the purge: Stalin and his lieutenants—among them, Kaganovich, Mikoyan, Molotov, Voroshilov, Zhdanov, Beria, Nikita Khrushchev, and George Malenkov.

The purge cannot be properly explained because many of the facts connected with it are not known and may never be known.[1] Still, more than a dozen widely differing and serious explanations have been suggested. Some interpret the purge as an expression of Stalin's blood lust; others feel that those who were punished were actually guilty of acts endangering the security of the Soviet Government. And somewhere between those extreme views the truth lies hidden. One is tempted to dismiss the problem of the meaning of the purge as insoluble, but it is such an important episode in the history of Soviet Russia that it cannot be so lightly dismissed.

This purge was the repudiation of a position the Bolsheviks had taken as a result of their study of the French Revolution; they had promised themselves that the Russian Revolution, unlike the French, would not "devour its own children." Hitherto this position had been maintained: party mem-

---

[1] The special report made by Nikita Khrushchev to the 20th Congress of the Communist Party, on February 24 and 25, 1956, was the first official revelation of some of the important facts, but his report ignored much that must be known before reasonably certain conclusions can be reached. For the text of his report, see the *New York Times*, June 5, 1956.

bers had been expelled, sometimes imprisoned or exiled, but not executed. Now the party was killing its own—in fact, the very men who had led the revolution. That Stalin and his associates should resort to such measures, which might provide a precedent for their own executions and which certainly were producing instability in the country, suggests that they were either desperate or reckless.

It is probable that several factors lay behind the purge. It may be that Stalin, following the general rule of dictators, was seeking an ever-increasing concentration of power in himself, whatever the danger involved. It may be that the tensions produced by forced industrialization and collectivization were such that it was felt necessary to find scapegoats for all the hardships experienced by the people and, at the same time, permit the continuation of the tension-producing policies. It may be that the ones who were purged were expected to use the disturbances of the next war to unseat Stalin and set aside his policies. It is also possible that some of those who were purged were even then seeking to remove Stalin—not in order to restore capitalism, as charged, but in order to return to Communist policies that Stalin had abandoned (many Communists in Russia and abroad were convinced that Stalin had subverted the original aims of the revolution).

Necessarily the explanations of the purge are in the realm of speculation; the consequences, in contrast, can be clearly established. Those who had been, or might still be, in opposition to the line for which Stalin stood in the party were removed or silenced. When the party chief spoke thereafter of the Communist Party as being "monolithic," he meant that there was no longer any room for dissent or faction, that the party was firmly united and animated by a common will—he did not allude, of course, to the fact that it was primarily his will, adopted by others under compulsion. In the "monolithic" party, as well as in other Soviet institutions, the last vestiges of free debate and open disagreement were now gone; the party now expected unanimous support of all decisions handed down from above and a reverence for Stalin that verged on idolatry.

On the surface it was made to appear that the Soviet people were one in mind and heart, but the appearance was produced at the cost of continued coercion and exhortation. The many who had suffered directly or indirectly from the purge could hardly be expected to fall willingly into line with the regime. And the Soviet leaders were left with a fear and suspicion of renewed opposition.

As a result, the coercive nature of the regime became hardened into a fixed pattern characterized by the demand for complete loyalty from Soviet citizens and the punishment of disloyalty, minute or great, with rigorous severity. That led to the extension of the political police functions of the NKVD, the complete domination of the party by the Politburo, and the increasing control of the Politburo by one man, Stalin. At the same time, the government was impelled to complete the process of isolating the Soviet people from the outside world. Foreign workers and technicians were required to assume Soviet citizenship or to leave the country. Travel to and within the Soviet Union by foreigners became increasingly difficult. Soviet citizens found it expedient to end any foreign contacts they might still have. Publication of official information by the government became more and more restricted; by 1938 the publication of exact statistics concerning the Soviet economy was virtually ended, and later even the publication of the Moscow telephone directory was discontinued. The "iron curtain" had been lowered.

EFFECT ON INTERNATIONAL POSITION.   The Great Purge had significant consequences for the USSR both as the center of world Communism and as a member of the family of nations. Although Moscow could not coerce Communists abroad as easily as those in Russia, it succeeded in making non-Soviet Communist parties as "monolithic" as the Soviet one. It started with the purging of foreign Communists in the Comintern headquarters; many of them were imprisoned without public trial and a few (among them, Bela Kun) were shot. As a result, the Comintern became an even more submissive instrument of Moscow than it had ever been.

Soon thereafter, it had expelled from foreign Communist parties all those deemed guilty of lack of faith in Moscow. Some parties—that of France, for instance—lost comparatively little strength in the process. Some, on the other hand, were virtually destroyed: on orders from the Comintern, all members but one, Joseph Broz Tito, were removed from the Central Committee of the Yugoslav Communist Party; and the entire Polish Communist Party was dissolved on the charge that it was dominated by "enemy" agents. Still others were gravely weakened by the defection of members who could not reconcile the purges with the avowed Communist aim of "liberating mankind."

Among the world powers, the general distaste for the Soviet scheme was increased by the arrests and executions. And the decimation of the commands of the Red army and navy weakened confidence in Russian military strength at a time when several powers (see pp. 655-57) were considering the USSR as a possible friend and participant in plans for collective security against the growing threat of Nazism.

Problems of national security

THE NAZI THREAT. It will be recalled that, before the Japanese descent upon Manchuria in 1931, Soviet Russia had looked upon France and Great Britain as the chief threats to her security and upon Poland as a minor one and that, after that incident, she had switched her attention to militaristic Japan. After the Nazi victory in Germany in the first months of 1933, however, an even more formidable threat began to take shape. At first, Moscow failed to see any particular reason for fearing Nazi Germany. German National Socialism seemed simply the ultimate expression of a "decadent capitalism" and Germany appeared neither better nor worse than France or Great Britain. Hitler, it is true, made destruction of Communism in Germany one of his main objectives and German acquisition of the Ukraine one of his dreams; consequently his regime was repugnant to the Soviet Government. But Soviet policy was not guided by likes nor dislikes, rather by considerations of rational interest. It did not oppose the maintenance of normal relations with anti-Communist Fascist Italy, seeing no threat to Soviet security from that source; and, if Nazi Germany were prepared to continue the foreign policy of Weimar Germany, it would not oppose friendly relations with her.

That hope of mutual accommodation soon gave way to uneasiness, however, as Moscow began to realize that Germany's policy was actually anti-Soviet and that her objectives were a threat to the peace of Europe. Other powers also became uneasy, and there was a general feeling that old animosities should be overlooked in an effort to solidify an opposition to the Nazi threat.

EFFORTS TOWARD COLLECTIVE SECURITY. The change in the international political temper began to be converted to action in November, 1933, by the resumption of Russian-American diplomatic relations and the subsequent appointment of William G. Bullitt as the first United States Ambassador to the Soviet Union and of Alexander Troyanovsky as the first Soviet Ambassador to the United States. That was followed by resumption of friendly relations between Russia and France. After a series of talks in the spring of 1934, Litvinov and the French Foreign Minister, Louis Barthou, agreed on arrangements for Franco-Russian collaboration to strengthen European security against Germany. The arrangements were to include Soviet entry into the League of Nations (since the League represented the chief instrument of collective security), Soviet collaboration with the allies of France in the East, a Franco-Soviet alliance and, if possible, a pact for

Eastern Europe, resembling that of Locarno for Western Europe, to guarantee existing frontiers.

Following the Barthou-Litvinov talks, action was rapid. In June, 1934, two members of the French-supported Little Entente, Czechoslovakia and Rumania, established diplomatic relations with the USSR. However, Yugoslavia, the third member of the Little Entente, stubbornly refused to extend recognition at that time. Her refusal was ostensibly based on her moral objection to regicides, but it was probably influenced also by the fact that she had more to fear from Italy than from Germany and was not anxious to offend Germany gratuitously. Meanwhile, improvements were developing in the hitherto cool Anglo-Soviet relations. Although Great Britain avoided formal commitments toward the USSR, she approved the development of Franco-Soviet friendship and backed the successful efforts of France to secure the admission of Russia, in September, 1934, to the League of Nations with a permanent seat in the Council of the League.

Formal efforts to establish a pact to guarantee existing frontiers in Eastern Europe (popularly known as an Eastern Locarno Pact) and a Franco-Soviet alliance were begun in June, 1934. The plan for an Eastern Locarno was that the USSR, Germany, Poland, Czechoslovakia, Finland, and the Baltic States guarantee existing frontiers and pledge mutual assistance in the event of an unprovoked attack upon one signatory either by another signatory or by a nonsignatory. Germany, whose eastern aspirations the pact was intended to contain, refused to adhere to it; and Poland, suspicious of the Soviet Union and desirous of maintaining good relations with Germany, also refused. Consequently the plan failed.

The consummation of a Franco-Soviet understanding was delayed by the death of Barthou in October, 1934. His successor, Pierre Laval, was more interested in a Franco-Italian understanding to offset Germany than in one with Russia. Nevertheless he continued—though not wholeheartedly —the negotiations begun by Barthou; and on May 2, 1935, the Franco-Soviet Treaty of Mutual Assistance was signed. This treaty provided that either signatory would give aid if the other should become the object of unprovoked attack by a *European* power. Two weeks later, on May 16, a Treaty of Mutual Assistance between the USSR and Czechoslovakia was signed. Its provisions were similar to those of the Franco-Soviet treaty with one exception: that the obligation to render aid would exist only if France also were to aid the signatory under attack. The next logical step was to arrange for a treaty between the Soviet Union and Poland or Rumania since Soviet power could not be used against Germany, the obvious but unspecified nation against whom all these arrangements were directed, unless the Red Army could cross Poland or Rumania to attack Germany in support of Czechoslovakia or France. But both Poland and Rumania refused proposals for such a treaty, thereby weakening the proposed security system. Another weakness was the failure to implement the Franco-Soviet treaty by specific military agreements like those which had accompanied the Franco-Russian Alliance of 1894. Apparently both the government and the military leaders of France had cooled toward the Franco-Soviet pact and, despite reciprocal visits by French and Soviet military missions in 1935 and 1936, no military agreements were reached.

THE "POPULAR FRONT" FOR SECURITY.   As the Soviet foreign policy changed to accommodate the need for security, so did the world Communist movement. The Communist parties in France and Spain began altering their policies in 1934; and the Seventh Congress of the Communist International, meeting in Moscow from July 25 to August 25, 1935, adopted a changed policy for all Communist parties. Generally referred to as the "popular front" policy, it was based upon the recognition that the chief danger of war—that is, war against the USSR—came from governments labeled by Russia as Fascist, particularly Germany; and that the Communist antiwar crusade must now be directed specifically against fascism. To that end, every party was to form a "popular front"—sometimes called a "people's front"—with socialist, labor and liberal parties and groups in its country to combat fascism within that country and to support a foreign policy directed against the Fascist countries.

Translated into practical terms, the decision of the Seventh Congress meant that the Communist parties would co-operate with anti-Fascist parties and with any government following a foreign policy which coincided with that of the USSR. In countries where the "popular front" was possible, the Communist parties were to tone down their international revolutionary programs and concentrate on finding points of common interest with non-Communist, anti-Fascist parties—such interests as the preservation of national independence or of "bourgeois democracy." In brief, the Communists of the "popular front" were to become less radical, less oppositional, more nationalistic, and, from the point of view of foreign governments, more respectable.

SIGNIFICANCE OF CHANGED POLICY.   To the Soviet Commissariat of Foreign Affairs, the new program of the Communist parties was important because its execution would help rouse opinion in the non-Fascist countries to oppose the aggressive policies of such countries as Germany. Russia was not interested in fighting fascism *per se* but in opposing those Fascist countries which presented a military threat to her. That was made clear by Stalin in his report to the Seventeenth Congress of the Soviet Communist Party in January, 1934:

> Some German politicians say that the Soviet Union now has an orientation toward France and Poland, that from an opponent of the Treaty of Versailles the USSR has become its supporter, that this change is to be explained by the establishment of a Fascist regime in Germany. That is not true. Of course, we are far from enthusiastic about the Fascist regime in Germany. But fascism is not the issue here, if only for the reason that fascism in Italy, for instance, has not prevented the USSR from establishing the best relations with that country. Nor is it a question of any alleged change in our attitude toward the Treaty of Versailles. It is not for us, who have experienced the shame of the Brest-Litovsk peace, to sing the praises of the Treaty of Versailles. We merely do not agree to the world being flung into the abyss of a new war on account of this treaty. The same must be said concerning the alleged re-orientation of the USSR. We never had any orientation toward Germany nor have we any orientation toward Poland and France. Our orientation has been and is toward the Soviet Union and only the Soviet Union. And if the interests of the USSR demand a rapprochement with these or those countries which are not interested in breaking the peace, we shall act without any wavering.

That policy helped to lead the USSR out of isolation and to bring her more consideration from other countries than she had known since November, 1917. Yet it did little to relieve mutual distrust; Russian leaders did not abandon the belief that France and Great Britain were anti-Soviet, nor did all the leaders in foreign governments trust or even want Soviet friendship.

The USSR would have been glad to extend the policy of collective security to Asiatic as well as to European affairs, but at the time no great power felt its interests so menaced by the rise of Japan as to warrant security arrangements with Soviet Russia to forestall trouble from that quarter.

DRAWBACKS TO COLLECTIVE SECURITY.   Even in Europe, collective security was based on shifting sands. Since French foreign policy depended in very large measure upon that of Britain, the strength and meaning of the Franco-Soviet Treaty of Mutual Assistance were determined by British views of foreign affairs. And Great Britain had assumed no definite commitments toward the USSR. The British Government welcomed the improvement in its own and French relations with Moscow, but it did not consider them of prime importance in European affairs. Of greater importance was its policy (since called appeasement) which aimed at preventing an understanding between Italy and Germany by making concessions to each. Moreover, there were many in the British Government who felt that of the two evils, Germany and Russia, the greater was Russia. In both Great Britain and France there was the fear that friendship with Russia would lead to the strengthening of Communism in all countries—a fear which was given some substance by the election victories of the "popular front" in Spain and France in 1936. Moreover, the French interest in Soviet friendship had waned after the Polish and Rumanian refusals to permit the transit of Soviet troops in the event of war. And, finally, there was a declaration by Hitler, the adroit Führer of Germany, to be considered: that he would come to terms with France and Great Britain only if the Soviet Union were excluded from the negotiations. As a result of this uneasy combination of interests and fears, English and French diplomacy followed an erratic course during the years between 1935 and 1939, gradually alienating Russia as it sought to satisfy Germany and Italy with small favors wherever possible.

Collective security received its first positive setback through the failure of the League of Nations to take effective action against Italian aggression in Ethiopia in 1935 and 1936 and through the subsequent efforts of England and France to keep Italy in the League by securing League acceptance of her annexation of Ethiopia, a step vigorously opposed by Russia. After that, other setbacks followed.

The German remilitarization of the Rhineland, unopposed by Great Britain and France, was particularly alarming to Russia since it indicated what she considered a dangerous lack of will on the part of those two countries to stand up to Hitler and since it lessened the value of her alliance with France, whose military security was thereby seriously weakened.

The Spanish Civil War, beginning in July, 1936, with a rebellion led by General Francisco Franco, strained collective security still more. When it began, Russia was concerned about the fact that the revolt had been made possible by German and Italian military assistance, and she was politically sympathetic with the Republican government, which was directed by a "popular front" cabinet; but she apparently did not intend to become involved. In August, she agreed to the French proposal for the formation of an international committee to insure nonintervention by foreign governments; and in September, Soviet delegates, together with delegates from twenty-five other countries, formed the Nonintervention Committee. But the situation, as far as Germany and Italy (both members of the Committee) were concerned, did not change; they continued their aid to Franco. Russia denounced their violation of the nonintervention agreement and, early in October, declared that if they continued their aid, she would not be bound to nonintervention. When they still persisted, the Soviet Government decided to counter their activity by aiding the Republican Government, expecting, no doubt, that France and Great Britain would soon do the same. Officially Russia gave aid in the form of food, war matériel, and military and political advisers. Unofficially she gave further aid by permitting the recruiting of men from non-Russian Communist refugees in the USSR (among them, Joseph Broz Tito) for service in the International Brigade in Spain. On October 28, Soviet tanks went into action in Spain, and on November 8, the International Brigade, including volunteers from Russia as well as from many other countries, appeared outside Madrid.

After three months of participation, however, the Soviet Government began to restrict its direct assistance. Soviet military personnel, variously estimated at between 700 and 2,000 in number, were gradually withdrawn, and other Soviet aid declined. It is probable that the government realized the danger in trying to give adequate support to Republican Spain at a time when that support might result in a war with Germany or encourage Japan to attack in the East. For the remainder of the Spanish Civil War, Moscow limited itself mainly to denouncing the ineffectiveness of the Nonintervention Committee and giving verbal encouragement to the Republican Government.

All the while, Soviet misgivings were increasing. Great Britain and France, although the dominant powers in the Nonintervention Committee, had not used their positions to make it effective; in fact, Great Britain seemed to consider Franco's followers less objectionable than their Spanish opponents. And because of the general ineffectiveness of the nonintervention agreement, Germany and Italy had drawn together, at the same time helping to create in Spain a regime dependent upon them. In October, 1936, finding so many interests in common, they formed an entente known as the Rome-Berlin Axis. And they continued to strengthen their friendship with Japan. In November, Germany and Japan signed the Agreement against the Third International—better known as the Anti-Comintern Pact—which was ostensibly directed against Communism as an organized movement. Italy added her adherence to the Pact in November, 1937, and thereafter other countries in the Axis orbit did likewise. Actually the Anti-Comintern

Pact was a cover for the formation of diplomatic agreements against the USSR, and Moscow recognized it as such.

Russia's alarm over the growing strength of the Axis powers was matched by her alarm over the growing tendency of Great Britain and France to offer them appeasements and to ignore her. In 1936 and 1937 she renewed her efforts to supplement the Franco-Soviet Treaty of 1935 by military agreements, but France chose to ignore her efforts. That Great Britain also chose to ignore her was made evident by the declaration of the British Prime Minister, Neville Chamberlain, on February 21, 1938, that "the peace of Europe must depend on the attitude of the four major Powers of Europe: Germany, Italy, France, and ourselves."

Germany, apparently confident that there would be no British or French opposition, annexed Austria in March, 1938, and immediately thereafter began a propaganda campaign against Czechoslovakia. Believing that the next crisis would involve Czechoslovakia, the Soviet Government declared that Russia would give assistance to that country if France would aid also. In addition, it proposed that Great Britain, France, the United States and the USSR confer on steps to meet the new crisis. The proposal was not acted upon, and Russia was ignored in the further development of the crisis, which ended in Czechoslovak capitulation to Hitler's demands in September, 1938. The resolution of the Czechoslovak crisis was, in all probability, the turning point in Russia's foreign policy. She had lost confidence in the French and British will to stop further German expansion.

As the hope of collective security against the German threat waned, so also did the hope for continued security in the East. Japan, renewing her expansionist policy in 1937 by beginning an unofficial but nonetheless bloody war against China, had become a positive threat. Russia increased her Far Eastern armies to 400,000 as a precaution against the possibility that the 300,000 Japanese troops in Manchukuo and Korea be directed against Soviet territory, and Japan decided not to risk war with her. Nevertheless some of the Japanese generals tested the Russian temper by provoking local border conflicts with Soviet troops. Of these conflicts, two were on a large scale. In July, 1938, Japanese troops attempted to seize Changkufeng Hill, a Soviet stronghold south of Vladivostok, claiming that it was legally Japanese. After several weeks of major fighting there, the Japanese were defeated and the claim was dropped. Then in the summer of 1939 there was an even bloodier engagement between Japanese troops and combined Soviet and Outer Mongolian soldiers on the Manchukuan-Outer Mongolian border; it likewise ended in Japanese defeat. Russian strength, for the time being, had been convincingly demonstrated.

As she strengthened her Far Eastern defenses, Russia also sought to bolster up China since that country was engaging about a million Japanese troops which could be used against the USSR in case of a Chinese collapse. But to give much aid to China was to risk provoking Japan; so Russia limited herself to sending some military advisers and barely enough matériel to keep China from defeat. She tried to interest Great Britain, France and the United States in increasing their aid to China, but those countries, like Russia, were seeking to avoid embroilment in Far Eastern troubles at the time.

TWENTY-NINE / THE USSR AND WORLD WAR II:

1939-1945

Soviet Russia could no more escape involvement in the great-power conflict which began in 1939 than tsarist Russia could have escaped involvement in the 1914 conflict. However, the forces drawing her into participation in the disordered affairs of Europe in 1939 were different, and her state of preparedness was different. Whether or not she was ready for war, which Lenin had called the all-round test of a nation's material and spiritual strength, was not certain. Only war itself could provide answers to the critical questions: Had the Five-Year Plans given Russia the material strength to sustain a war? Had the Communist program of political and social transformation developed in the peoples of Russia the devotion and unity required by a government at war?

Collapse of collective security

BID AND COUNTERBID.   Convinced of the futility of dependence upon collective security, Soviet leaders began considering other means for safeguarding the USSR. Stalin gave a hint of the new direction in their thinking when, in his report to the Eighteenth Congress of the Communist Party, in March, 1939, he asserted that Great Britain and France had abandoned collective security not out of weakness but out of a wish to see Russia at war with Germany. He added that the Soviet Union was determined to maintain "peaceful, close, and friendly relations with all neighboring countries" which sought such relations and that she would not permit herself "to be drawn into conflicts by warmongers who are accustomed to have others pull the chestnuts out of the fire for them." This was a diplomatic way of saying that Russia now felt free to come to terms with Germany.

However, Russia was drawn once more to the side of Great Britain and France in March, 1939, when the three countries joined in a denunciation of the German division of Czechoslovakia into the protectorate of Bohemia and the puppet state of Slovakia. Still another attempt at tripartite action was made when Germany began to make territorial demands of Poland and to assume a hostile attitude toward Rumania. But, from the beginning, such action seemed hopeless; French and British views on its direction were too divergent from those of the USSR. Great Britain and France proposed a three-power declaration in which the signatories would announce their readiness to aid one another if one or more of them were compelled to fight Germany as a result of German attack on Poland or Rumania. The Russian proposal was of broader scope. It included a binding three-power alliance whereby the signatories would guarantee the integrity not only of Poland and Rumania but also of all other states on the western border of Russia from the Black Sea to the Baltic Sea, a commitment on the part of each power to aid the others if they went to war with Germany, and a specific outline of the nature of the military assistance to be given in the event of such a war. The British Government was not prepared to accept such a proposal, and the French Government reluctantly followed the British lead. There were various reasons for Britain's attitude. She apparently hoped that a peaceful settlement with Germany might yet be possible and felt that, while a tripartite *declaration* might bring that country to terms, a tight *alliance* might frighten her into considering Great Britain an implacable foe. In addition, such an alliance would offend Poland, a country which feared Soviet aid as much as a German attack; and since the British leaders rated Soviet military strength below that of Poland, they were more inclined to offend Moscow than Warsaw. Finally, neither Great Britain nor France wished to be committed to war in defense of Finland, Estonia, and Latvia, the border states which Russia proposed to place under three-power guarantee.

Since Russia did not consider the proposed three-power declaration satisfactory evidence of the sincerity of Great Britain and France and since their attitude toward the proposal for an alliance seemed negative, she felt free to proceed independently. Therefore while the negotiations on tripartite action were dragging along, Russia began to put out secret feelers to Germany. On April 17, the government informed Berlin that it wanted friendly relations; and on May 3, Litvinov, the spokesman for collective security, was replaced by Molotov as Commissar of Foreign Affairs—a move which

Berlin could easily interpret as a sign of Soviet displeasure with England and France and as an invitation for Germany to court Russia. This change in attitude was heartening to Germany, for she was determined to secure territorial concessions from Poland—by negotiations if possible, by war if necessary—and she needed the assurance that, if Great Britain and France should oppose her, they would not have Soviet assistance. After Litvinov's removal, Berlin began to press Moscow to state the terms for an improvement of Soviet-German relations. But Moscow, waiting for the outcome of negotiations with London and Paris, simply kept German hopes alive and postponed any definite statement.

In the late spring and early summer, Germany adopted an increasingly belligerent attitude toward Poland; and Great Britain and France, awakened to the immediate seriousness of the situation, began more energetic efforts to come to terms with Russia. For weeks their efforts yielded only proposals and counterproposals. Finally, early in August, they sent military missions to Moscow for discussions with a Soviet military mission headed by Marshal Voroshilov. Even then little progress was made. The greatest difficulty before the conferees was Russia's insistence that any military agreement include provision for the use of Soviet troops in Poland in the case of war with Germany. On August 14, Voroshilov stated positively that, without that, tripartite military action could not be arranged. The British and French tried to persuade Poland to agree to the Soviet demand, but they were unsuccessful. Recognizing the stalemate, Voroshilov suggested on August 21 that the military talks be adjourned. His suggestion was accepted, and the last effort for collective security was concluded.

BARGAINING WITH GERMANY. In the middle of August, Germany, having already decided to attack Poland before the end of the month, renewed her pleas to Russia by offering to send Foreign Minister Joachim von Ribbentrop to Moscow by plane with full powers to negotiate a settlement satisfactory to Russia. On August 19, apparently convinced that the Poles would not change their position, Moscow informed Berlin that Ribbentrop would be received. He arrived in Moscow on August 23 and, before the day was over, he and Molotov had concluded the Treaty of Nonaggression and a secret protocol.

The Treaty of Nonaggression, valid for ten years, provided that neither party would commit an act of aggression against the other and that, if one signatory were to go to war with a third power, the other signatory would not provide aid of any kind to that power. The secret protocol provided for future territorial arrangements: (1) that Finland, Estonia, Latvia, and that part of Poland east of the line formed by the Narev, Vistula, and San rivers be considered Soviet spheres of influence; (2) that the part of Poland lying west of that line be considered a German sphere of influence; (3) that the further existence of Poland as an independent state be considered later; and (4) that Germany acknowledge Soviet interest in Bessarabia. In nondiplomatic terms, the treaty together with the protocol meant that Russia would not fight Germany over Poland, that she would give Germany a free hand in western Poland, and that she would be permitted, in return, to take political and economic advantages in the specified areas without fear of German opposition. They represented a bargain between enemies, each of whom gained by it. Germany gained through the assurance that she would not face a Soviet attack from the east. Of course, she paid for that assurance by granting concessions to a power whom she expected ultimately to fight, but she was now confident that she could choose the time of the conflict since Russia was too weak to begin an offensive war. For her part, Russia, unable to believe that Great Britain and France really wanted to stop Germany, felt that she was making the best of a bad situation. At least, the bargain freed her for the time being from the fear of involvement in war and, at the same time, increased her power in eastern Europe. It was to be expected that Germany would be strengthened by the extension of her controls over western Poland; yet there was still the possibility—on which Russia did not count very heavily—that Great Britain and France would fight Germany over Poland and thereby wear her down. It was a gamble, but the Soviet leaders felt compelled to take it.

When the signing of the Treaty of Nonaggression was announced, on August 24, the hopes of Great Britain and France for three-power action were ended. But the two powers remained firm in their decision to support Poland. On September 1, Germany began her attack on Poland, and two days later Great Britain and France declared war on Germany. The Second World War had begun.

Developments in the Soviet defense position

EASY GAINS.   The Soviet Union, in a neutral position, was now able to realize the promises made by Germany in the secret protocol. On September 17, after the German army had virtually destroyed the Polish forces in western Poland, the Red Army marched into eastern Poland, allegedly to save the Ukrainians and the White Russians in that area from an uncertain fate, and moved westward to the Narev-Vistula-San line, taking captive hundreds of thousands of Polish troops. The Polish Government fled the country and delegated authority to representatives in London to set up the Polish Government-in-Exile, leaving Russia and Germany free to carry out their plans for Poland's future. Ribbentrop and Molotov met in Moscow on September 28 and signed a treaty, assigning the disposition of western Poland to Germany and that of eastern Poland to Russia. The treaty extended the German sphere in Poland, however, to a line somewhat east of the Narev-Vistula-San line, which had been set in the first secret protocol. And in return for that extension Germany, in a second secret protocol, now recognized Lithuania as within the Soviet sphere.

By those arrangements, an area of some 70,000 square miles of Poland was placed at Soviet disposal. Of the 13 million inhabitants in that area, less than 40 per cent were Poles; the remainder were Ukrainians, White Russians, Great Russians, Jews, Lithuanians, and Germans. The Soviet authorities hurriedly arranged for the election of the Ukrainian People's Assembly in the southern part of the newly acquired territory and of the White Russian People's Assembly in the northern part. After the elections, it was announced that over 90 per cent of the voters had voted for pro-Soviet candidates; but there is every reason to believe that the elections were fraudulent. The two assemblies asked for union with the USSR and, on November 1, the northern portion of the territory was incorporated into the White Russian S.S.R. and the southern portion into the Ukrainian S.S.R.

Russia next turned to the Baltic countries and demanded of them treaties of mutual assistance providing for military aid in the event of aggression or the menace of aggression by outside powers, the maintenance of Soviet land and air contingents in those countries, and the lease of naval bases (by Estonia and Latvia) to Russia. Having no choice, the little countries signed such treaties, thus placing themselves at the mercy of the USSR. Estonia signed on September 29, Latvia on October 5, and Lithuania on October 10.

WAR WITH FINLAND.　Finland was more resistant to Soviet demands than were her Baltic neighbors. When she was asked by Russia, in October, 1939, to accept a mutual assistance treaty similar to the ones signed by Estonia and Latvia, she refused. Russia then offered to bargain: if Finland would lease territory at the mouth of the Gulf of Finland for use as a Soviet naval base and cede the region above Leningrad, she could have in return a portion of Soviet Karelia. Finland declined the offer. But the Soviet Union was determined. On November 29, she severed relations with Finland and, without a declaration of war, sent land and air forces into Finnish territory on the following day. Simultaneously, the Finnish Communist Otto Kuusi-nen organized a puppet government, which the Soviet Government promptly recognized as the government of Finland and with which it signed a treaty of mutual assistance. Moscow hoped that the Finns would accept the Ku-usinen government, but they did not; the authority of the new government never extended beyond the bayonets of the Red Army. Russia was compelled to fight in order to gain her ends.

The Soviet-Finnish war quickly reduced Soviet standing abroad and aroused adverse opinion throughout the world. The League of Nations, act-ing with an energy it had not shown toward Japan, Italy, or Germany, ex-pelled the USSR in December. The United States declared a moral embargo on her and prohibited the shipment of strategic materials to her. England and France prepared to send a military expedition to Finland and another to at-tack the Soviet Caucasus. But their preparations were too late.

In February, 1940, after a winter of difficult fighting, the Red Army be-gan an offensive which drove the Finnish Government to the acceptance of defeat. On March 12, it accepted a treaty of peace whereby Finland made cessions highly profitable to the USSR. She ceded territory to the north, south and west of Lake Ladoga, placing that lake entirely within Soviet terri-tory and moving the Finnish-Soviet border about seventy-five miles farther from Leningrad than it had been. She ceded also some territory in the north and granted a thirty-year lease on the Hangoe Peninsula, at the mouth of the Gulf of Finland, for use as a Soviet naval base. With the lease on the Hangoe Penninsula, Soviet control of the Baltic approaches to the USSR was complete. Most of the territory taken from Finland was added to the Karelian Autonomous S.S.R., which, at the end of March, was raised to the status of a union republic and renamed the Karelo-Finnish S.S.R.

TIGHTENING THE OUTER DEFENSES.   In the spring of 1940 the satis-faction which the Soviet leaders felt about the events of the past six months suddenly gave way to alarm. In April the Germans seized Norway and Den-mark. A month later, they broke into The Low Countries, forced the British to withdraw their troops from the continent, and pushed into France. Italy, with the courage of certainty, declared war on France and Great Britain. And, on June 22, France signed an armistice with Germany and withdrew from the war.

The defeat of France was a great blow to Russia; her position was changed thereby from one of apparent strength to one of unmistakable weakness. Germany and her lesser partner Italy now directly or indirectly controlled all of Western and Central Europe and a substantial part of the coastal areas of Northern Europe. If they could successfully invade England, Russia's position would be even worse, for then she would fear a concerted attack by Germany and Italy from the west and by Japan from the east. Otherwise, Germany and Italy could now be expected to begin extending their power in the Baltic and in the Balkans. Russia might have taken the offensive, but she was neither willing nor able to do that at the time. She decided rather to concentrate on strengthening her position as best she could without risking war.

The first step was to make control of Lithuania, Latvia, and Estonia complete. To that end, the Soviet Government, in the middle of June, sent each of the three countries an ultimatum demanding that they form governments acceptable to Moscow. They complied by forming left-wing governments; and, in the following month, each held parliamentary elections in which only pro-Communist candidates were permitted to stand for office. The newly elected parliaments immediately asked for admission to the Soviet Union, and Lithuania, Latvia, and Estonia were admitted as union republics in August.

In the meantime, Moscow had been engaged also in strengthening the southern frontier. As early as March, 1940, Rumania had been asked to give up Bessarabia, but she had refused. In June the Soviet request was strengthened by the marching of Soviet troops to the Soviet-Rumanian border. Molotov informed Berlin that Russia now wanted not only Bessarabia but also the Rumanian province of Bukovina. Berlin demurred at the addition of all of Bukovina to Soviet claims but compromised by agreeing to the inclusion of the northern part of it. On June 26, Moscow gave Rumania twenty-four hours in which to cede the areas in question; and Rumania, informed by Berlin that she would not receive German backing if she resisted, acquiesced. Thereupon northern Bukovina and the portions of Bessarabia inhabited by Ukrainians were added to the Ukrainian S.S.R.; and the remaining portions of Bessarabia, together with the Moldavian Autonomous S.S.R. (hitherto part of the Ukraine), were formed into a union republic with the name of the Moldavian S.S.R. The union republics were now sixteen in number.[1]

Elsewhere in Europe, Soviet attempts to gain new and to maintain old positions were not so successful. Yugoslavia, hoping to remain outside the German orbit, was the only country to seek Soviet friendship, and her over-

[1] In 1956, the Karelo-Finnish S.S.R. was reduced from the status of a union republic to that of an autonomous republic and incorporated into the R.S.F.S.R., the number of union republics being thereby reduced to fifteen.

tures were warmly received. However, the strength of the German-dominated Axis was increased by the extension of German influence over Finland, Rumania, and Hungary. Bulgaria, still vacillating between Moscow and Berlin, was leaning toward the German side.

STRENGTHENING THE HOME FRONT.   Even before the fall of France, the Soviet home front was being put into readiness for the war which was felt to be imminent. The strength of the Red Army had been greatly increased by the calling-up of new classes of recruits and by the extension of terms of service for those already in the army. The war with Finland had revealed many military weaknesses, and steps had been taken to remedy them. Marshal Semyon Timoshenko had replaced Voroshilov as Commissar of Defense. The authority of regular army officers had been increased and that of the political commissars, whose function was the supervision of political training in the army, had been reduced. The ranks of "General" and "Admiral" had been re-established. After the fall of France, military preparations were again speeded up. More and more men were called into service until, by the end of 1940, more than 5 million, according to estimate, were in the armed forces. In addition, to provide a source of reserves, the physical and military training of all civilians, from school children to graybeards, was intensified.

At the same time, every possible means was being employed to increase production, which was already largely devoted to military needs. A decree issued in June, 1940, restored the eight-hour day and provided for only one day of rest in seven instead of one day in six—and, as a gesture toward favoring the religious, that day of rest was placed on Sunday. Departure from one's job without permission and tardiness in arriving to work were made crimes. Later the government decreed that all industrial workers, technicians, and engineers were subject to transfer from one place to another at the government's will. And, to increase the labor force, it began to divert youths from school to industry by requiring tuition payments for schooling after the first seven years and by introducing the system of State Labor Reserves, whereby about 1 million boys at the age of fourteen (girls were later included) were drafted annually for two years of vocational training in special schools, to be followed by four years of work in the vocation to which they were assigned by the government.

ATTEMPTED NEGOTIATIONS WITH GERMANY.   There had been no overt demonstration of enmity between Germany and Russia up to this time, but it was evident to both countries and to the world at large that tension between them was growing. Neither wanted the other to grow any stronger; yet neither wanted open conflict with the other. Germany took the initiative in seeking a new basis for mutual understanding by inviting Molotov to Berlin on November 12 for a two-day review, with Ribbentrop and Hitler, of the state of Nazi-Soviet relations. Ribbentrop and Hitler, desirous of directing Soviet interests away from the Balkans, offered to support Soviet interests in the Middle East and to bring the USSR into the Axis coalition, which had been strengthened by an Italo-German-Japanese alliance in September, 1940. But Molotov insisted that there should be an understanding on the Balkan situation and on many other matters before there could be talk of an alliance. Since no such understanding could be reached, Molotov returned to Moscow to confer with Stalin and the other members of the Politburo. It appears that the Soviet leaders did not give serious consideration to the German proposals but wished to prolong negotiations until they could determine German aims. On November 26, Molotov informed the German ambassador to Moscow, Count von der Schulenberg, that Russia would join the Axis powers if Germany would withdraw the troops which she had been sending into Finland since September, if she would recognize Bulgaria and Persia as part of the Soviet sphere, and if she would support Soviet efforts to lease a military and naval base near the Straits. As was to be expected, the demands with respect to Bulgaria and the Straits were unacceptable to Germany; therefore negotiations for a new, general Soviet-German agreement were ended by mutual consent. The situation was analogous to that which existed between Russia and France between 1809 and 1812, when Napoleon refused to accept Russian claims in the Near East, since they conflicted with his, and thus ended the uneasy Franco-Russian collaboration.

The breaking of restraints

THE GERMAN DECISION.   That Hitler was not relying upon a favorable turn in relations with Russia but was convinced that war with her was inevitable is indicated by his planning prior to the November negotiations. Four months earlier, on July 21, 1940, he had directed his advisers to formulate plans for an attack on Russia. Apparently the decision to invite what German generals dreaded, a two-front war, was motivated in part by the belief that the defeat of Britain could not be realized as long as Soviet military power presented a potential threat to Germany and in part by the danger of the friction developing in the Balkan and Baltic areas. The preliminary plans stated the chief objectives as the speedy destruction of Russian military power in a campaign that would probably open in May, 1941, and be brought to a victorious conclusion before late October. The abortive negotiations with Molotov, no doubt, strengthened Hitler's determination to fight; and on December 18, 1940, he issued his most fateful order, Directive No. 21, instructing his generals to begin "preparations to crush *Soviet Russia in a lightning campaign* even before the termination of hostilities with Great Britain. . . ."To continued objections from his advisers, Hitler replied that his decision could not be changed; and to Soviet inquiries about the large numbers of German troops near the Russian border, the reply was that they were only in training.

FINAL PEACE EFFORTS.   While Germany prepared to fight, Russia sought to save what she could in the Balkans without the use of force. She began by trying, through diplomatic effort, to keep Bulgaria from joining the Axis, but she failed there; on March 1, 1941, Bulgaria joined the Axis and opened her doors to German troops. Berlin then demanded that Yugoslavia join the Axis, and Belgrade agreed. However, on March 27, a successful revolt in that country, inspired in part by the hope that Moscow would support an anti-German government, placed in power a new government committed to resistance to German demands. Russia signed a treaty with the new government on April 6, promising friendship but not military assistance. Since Russia would not give military aid, the treaty was of little avail when Germany attacked Yugoslavia a few hours after its signing. But the treaty was another clear sign of Soviet opposition to German expansion in the Balkans, and Hitler became more determined than ever to attack Russia. The Yugoslav crisis, however, caused him to postpone the date of attack from May 15 to June 22.

In the meantime Japan, planning a blow at Singapore, was trying to make certain of Soviet neutrality in the event that her action resulted in an Anglo-Japanese war. Therefore, she asked the Soviet Government to join her in a nonaggression pact and to sell her northern Sakhalin. Germany, being anxious for a quick Japanese attack on Great Britain in the Far East, did not oppose a Japanese understanding with Russia, but she did caution Japan against going too far, since war between Germany and Russia was so near. Moscow would not agree to a nonaggression pact nor to the sale of northern Sakhalin but offered to join in a treaty of neutrality instead. The Treaty of Neutrality, valid for five years, was signed on April 13, Japan and Russia each agreeing to observe neutrality if the other should be involved in war. At the time, the treaty benefited both parties: Moscow had been seeking such a treaty since 1933 to lessen the fear of a Japanese attack in the event of military involvement in the West, and Japan needed the assurance that she could move south without fear of a Soviet attack.

With the situation as it was in Europe, Moscow decided that the best course was to continue seeking peace and, at the same time, to prepare for war. So, while troop concentrations near the western frontier were being increased, Soviet diplomacy was directed toward friendliness with Germany. Within the government a significant change was made: on May 6, Stalin, who had not held an important governmental position in eighteen years, took over from Molotov the position of Premier. It seems likely that this move was motivated by Stalin's desire to maintain peace and his conviction that the times required his openly taking the helm.

THE END OF PEACE.   The Soviet Government was aware of German troop movements west of the Soviet frontier but refused to believe warnings from both the English and the American governments that Germany would attack on June 22. As late as June 21, Molotov asked Count von der Schulenberg why Germany was "dissatisfied with the Soviet Government." On the following day war came. At 4 a.m. on June 22, Ribbentrop informed Vladimir Dekanozov, the Soviet Ambassador in Berlin, that, in view of the concentration of Soviet troops on Germany's eastern frontier, she was declaring war on the USSR; and within the hour, German troops and planes crossed the Soviet frontier. On the same day Italy and Rumania declared war on the USSR; and Slovakia, Finland, and Hungary followed suit on June 23, 25, and 27 respectively.

Adjustment to war

NEW INTERNATIONAL POSITION.   Russia at war against Germany came into a new position in relation to the anti-Axis powers. Within a few hours after the news of the German attack was received, Winston Churchill, the British Prime Minister, stated in a radio broadcast: "We are resolved to destroy Hitler and every vestige of the Nazi regime. We will give whatever help we can to Russia and the Russian people. . . . The Russian danger is our danger. . . ." On June 23, the United States, not yet at war, announced that any struggle against Germany, even by Russia, was to the benefit of American "defense and security" and promised to extend full aid to the USSR. And on the same day the Polish Government-in-Exile announced from London that it wished to resume diplomatic relations with the USSR.

APPEALS TO SOVIET PEOPLE.   The Soviet leaders lost no time in appealing to the people in the name of the cause to which their loyalty and strength
were to be called. Every Soviet radio station, on the day of the attack, broadcast Molotov's words:

> The government calls upon you, citizens of the Soviet Union,
> to rally still more closely around our glorious Bolshevik Party, around
> our Soviet Government, around our great leader, Comrade Stalin.
> Ours is a righteous cause. The enemy will be defeated. Victory will
> be ours.

Stalin's first public exhortation was broadcast on July 3, when the people were in full realization of the painful actuality of the war. In it he defined the struggle as a war of liberation in which the Soviet people were
joined with those of Europe and America for "independence, for democratic
liberties." He justified the Russo-German pact of August, 1939, as a means
by which Russia had gained a year and a half of additional time for military
preparation. And he urged the necessity of everyone's joining in certain
activities of irregular warfare: the formation of guerrilla units to fight and
harry the advancing enemy, and the execution of the "scorched earth" policy
in retreat—the destruction of all machinery, means of transportation and
fuel, the driving away of all cattle and the turning over of all grain to the
government for removal to the rear.

Even the Church, the strength of which had not previously been recognized by the government, was urged to co-operate in mobilizing sentiment for the support of the war. It responded loyally, acting Patriarch Sergei
calling upon all the Orthodox to defend the fatherland and bestowing his
blessings upon the defenders of the country. In September the government
suspended the publication of the two chief antireligious periodicals, the
Atheist and *Anti-Religion;* and in November, 1942, the acting Patriarch
gave his blessing to atheist Stalin, whom he called the "divinely anointed
leader of our armed and cultural forces."

ADMINISTRATIVE CHANGE.   As one of the measures to insure the efficient prosecution of the war, the Presidium of the Supreme Soviet decreed,
on June 30, the formation of an omnipotent body to be known as the State
Committee of Defense, with Stalin as chairman and with an original membership consisting of Molotov, Voroshilov, Beria, and George Malenkov,
one of Stalin's closest assistants.[1] The State Committee of Defense was

---

[1] Voroshilov was later replaced by Nicholas Bulganin; and Lazar Kaganovich, Nicholas
Voznesensky, and Anastas Mikoyan were added.

actually a modified version of the Politburo. Its members were either at the time of appointment members of the Politburo or were subsequently elected to membership in that body. The Politburo continued during the war to make the major decisions on policy while the State Committee of Defense exercised complete power in the direction and co-ordination of civilian and military organizations without recourse to normal legislative and executive procedure.

At the same time that authority was being concentrated in the State Committee of Defense, administrative power was being concentrated in the hands of Stalin, who was named Defense Commissar and Commander-in-Chief of the Red Army in July, 1941. He now held the supreme offices of the party, the government, and the army.

PERSONNEL AND MATERIEL.   At the beginning of the war, manpower was mobilized rapidly. In June, 1941, most of the young men between the ages of eighteen and twenty-two were already in the armed forces, which then numbered about 6 million. As soon as fighting began, men between the ages of twenty-three and thirty-six were mobilized; and later, all between seventeen and fifty-five. In September, all civilian males from sixteen to fifty years of age were ordered to take short courses of military training in anticipation of guerrilla or street fighting. All who did not fight were expected to work at tasks connected with the war and to work harder than ever before. Each worker was made subject to a requirement (generally imposed) of three overtime hours daily, and all vacations were cancelled. In February, 1942, it was decreed that all civilian male urban inhabitants from sixteen to fifty-five years of age and all urban female inhabitants from sixteen to forty-five were subject to mobilization for war industries. And in April all those who were not engaged in industry or transportation were made subject to mobilization for harvest or planting in the rural areas.

Many inhabitants of western Russia whose loyalty or political support was suspect were removed to new places of residence in the interior. Previous to this time, between 1939 and 1941, over a million Poles, Lithuanians, Latvians, and Estonians had been removed from this area for political reasons; and in September, 1941, the German Volga Autonomous S.S.R. was abolished and its 400,000 German inhabitants were resettled in other parts of the country.

Fewer emergency economic controls of a major kind were needed in the USSR, of course, than in countries where private enterprise was allowed. It was necessary to reintroduce rationing, however. And it was necessary to impose direction in the evacuation of people and machinery from the regions threatened by the Germans. During the course of the war, an estimated 12 million persons either fled or were evacuated from the fighting zones to the eastern parts of European Russia, western Siberia, and Central Asia. Impressive mass transfer of factories, machinery, research institutes, and even movie studios from the war zones to the east was carried out also. There were inevitable losses and confusion in the process, but amazing accomplishments were recorded; one airplane factory, for example, was in productive operation a month after its removal to a new site.

Soviet strength under test: June, 1941 to March, 1943

THE PLANS. The German plan was to destroy the Red Army in the western parts of European Russia within about three months by a three-pronged offensive aimed toward Leningrad, Moscow, and Rostov. "The ultimate objective of the operation," Hitler stated in his directive, "is to establish a defense line against Asiatic Russia from a line running approximately from the Volga River to Archangel." So great was the German assurance of the success of their projected operations that they had planned also the disposition of the gains from it. Once the defense line was established, all of the conquered territory—with the exception of some sections in Karelia (to be given to Finland) and southern Russia between the Bug and the Dniester (to be given to Rumania)—was to be held under German dominion, serving as an agricultural colony. Success of the German plan was predicated on *immediate* numerical superiority in manpower, the dependability of a confident and battle-tried army with equipment superior to that of the Russians, and a more productive industrial base, including almost all of Central and Western Europe. Although Hitler did not share the low opinion of the Red Army that many non-Russian observers held, he rated its capacity lower than that of his forces. Moreover, he was confident that large groups of the Soviet population would welcome the Germans and even assist them in their advance.

Soviet plans were based on defensive tactics. Retreat was considered as a last resort, but the expectation was that the Germans would be stopped in western European Russia.

INITIAL LOSSES. Because Stalin refused to credit warnings about the impending attack, the German onslaught caught the Russians off guard. The 180 divisions of the Red Army were not all deployed for immediate execution of the defense plans and those which were so deployed had not been alerted. Moreover, despite careful screening, there were many men among them who had no wish to fight for the regime. As a result there was at first little resistance by Soviet units; many fled in panic and others surrendered *en masse*. The 175 German and other Axis divisions moved forward rapidly. Within a few weeks Russia had lost all the territory she had gained since 1939: Brest-Litovsk, Kaunas, Vilna, and Libau fell before the end of June; and Riga, Lvov, Vitebsk and Kishinev were lost during July. The Red Army began to slow down the German drive by the middle of July but could not stop it. On all fronts—the northern, under the command of Voroshilov; the central, under Timoshenko; and the southern, under Budenny—the Russian forces gradually gave way. On the central front, Smolensk, the gateway to Moscow, was lost in July. In the south, Krivoi Rog, the iron ore center, fell in August; in the next two months Odessa, Kiev, and Kharkov were taken; and in November, Rostov was captured, then regained. In the north, the drive against Leningrad rolled on, the Finns moving down the Karelian Isthmus and the Germans pushing eastward from Estonia. On September 2, the Germans were twenty miles from Leningrad, beginning what was to be a two-year siege of that city.

THE BATTLE OF MOSCOW.　　On October 2, the Battle of Moscow—which some have called the most important battle of the war—began. The next day, Hitler announced, somewhat prematurely, that "Russia is already broken and will never rise again." For two weeks the Germans pushed their offensive against that city and, by mid-October, reached their high point with the capture of Mozhaisk, sixty miles west of Moscow, and Kalinin, about a hundred miles to the northwest, on the main railroad line to Leningrad. At that time Moscow seemed doomed. Foreign embassies and Soviet governmental agencies in the city were evacuated to Kuibyshev; women and children who were not employed in war industries were removed to places of safety; and preparations for street fighting were made. Before the Germans could break through, however, the Red troops under Gregory Zhukov, who had replaced Timoshenko, rallied and began to hold them—at some points, to turn them back. Early in December the Germans, feeling the effects of cold weather and unable to advance their lines, announced that the offensive would be suspended for the winter. The Russians, however, undertook a counteroffensive on all fronts and, around Moscow, were able to push the enemy back. By the end of February it was clear that the Russians had won the Battle of Moscow. The cost had been great in men and matériel both to the Russians and to the Germans, but to the Russians the gain was worth the price.

The loss of the Battle of Moscow was the first major setback to Germany in land fighting since 1939. And she was now faced with an unpleasant prospect: having realized none of her major objectives in Russia, she could look forward to a long conflict in which Russian manpower and geographical position would count heavily against her.

NEW GERMAN OFFENSIVE.   In the spring of 1942 the Germans undertook a second offensive, which Hitler declared would bring victory by September. Its aim was to divest Russia of critical supplies. The chief objective was the capture of Soviet oil resources in Transcaucasia. A secondary objective was the seizure or, at a minimum, the destruction by artillery fire of the key industrial and transportation center, Stalingrad. Following that plan, the Germans pushed on rapidly until they had advanced their front about 300 miles. Sevastopol fell to them in July after eight months of resistance, and three weeks later Rostov fell, opening the way to the Caucasus. By forcing their way along the Black Sea coast in the Caucasus, they reached the environs of Ordzhonikidze, deep in the mountains, in September. Meanwhile, farther north, the main drive was carried relentlessly eastward until, in the last week of August, the Germans were at Stalingrad. Soviet determination to hold that city at all costs made the Battle of Stalingrad one of the bloodiest of the war. Even when the Germans had captured most of the city and its key points after lengthy street fighting, the Russians would not surrender it.

SOVIET COUNTEROFFENSIVE.   For Russia, the turning point of the war came on November 19, 1942, when the Red Army began a long-planned counteroffensive both at Stalingrad and at Ordzhonikidze.

At Stalingrad the offensive took the form of a pincer movement: one army striking from north of that city was to meet another from the south at Kalach, west of Stalingrad. Within five days the pincer movement was completed and the German Sixth Army of 330,000 men, under General Friedrich Paulus, was caught. Hitler, promising relief (which never arrived), ordered the army to fight on to the last man. At the beginning of February, 1943, however, Paulus (now a field marshal) surrendered with the remnants of his army, about 90,000 men.

The forces in the counteroffensive at Ordzhonikidze were successful also. And after they had cleared the Germans from the Caucasus, they moved on to Rostov, meeting there, in mid-February, the Soviet armies which had pushed westward from Stalingrad. Thereafter an offensive along a 200-mile front was undertaken to clear the Ukraine. But, by the middle of March, strong German resistance and the spring thaw had combined to bring the Soviet advance to a halt along a line midway between the Donets and Dnieper Rivers. At the same time, Soviet offensive movements on the central and northern fronts were slowing down. Then, for a period of about three months, there was little movement on any front, neither side being able to recover its momentum until troops and supplies were renewed.

Russia under occupation

THE GERMAN PROGRAM.   The relaxation of the strain on the fighting fronts did nothing to ease the strain elsewhere. The occupied areas, in particular, were suffering increasingly. In the first year of the war, the Germans and their allies had occupied about 580,000 square miles of Soviet territory with a peacetime population of about 85 million persons. Finland was permitted to occupy the areas which had been lost to Russia in 1940 and that part of Soviet Karelia taken during the war. Rumania was permitted to reannex Bessarabia and northern Bukovina, to occupy the Soviet area between the Dniester and the lower Bug, and to administer the latter under the name of Transnistria. The remainder of occupied Russia was administered by the Germans, and it was in that area that the hardships of occupation were most rigorous.

The German-occupied lands were placed under the jurisdiction of Alfred Rosenberg, head of the Ministry for the Territories Occupied in the East. And their immediate administration was handled by two branches of that ministry: the Reichskommissariat Ostland, serving from headquarters in Riga, with jurisdiction over White Russia, Lithuania, Latvia, and Estonia; and the Reichskommissariat Ukraine, with headquarters in Rowne. The administration was concerned primarily with policing the occupied territory, using its manpower in the service of the German war machine and cultivating anti-Soviet sentiments among its inhabitants. The first two objectives took precedence and made the achievement of the third one difficult.

Greatest emphasis was laid on the recruitment of laborers for work on the farms, in the factories and in the semimilitary organizations in Western Europe. At first, laborers were urged to volunteer for the work; but when the number of volunteers proved inadequate, compulsion was employed. Of the 8 million foreign civilian workers and prisoners of war serving Germany in 1944, more than half were from Soviet territory. These Eastern

DRAWN BY EDW. A. SCHMITZ

MAP 14. The USSR under Axis Occupation

Workers, as the Germans called them, were forced to serve under conditions of near-slavery and subjected to the brutal treatment which the Germans felt due to the "inferior" Slavs.

German efforts to win the favor of the people of the conquered areas were at first well received by the anti-Soviet elements of the population, who felt that the Nazis were less to be hated than the Communists. Many in the Baltic countries, the Ukraine, and White Russia and many among the Moslems of the Crimea and the Caucasus, out of hatred for the Soviet regime, collaborated with the invaders. And among the prisoners of war in Germany, General Andrei Vlasov, who had been taken prisoner 1942, was able to organize a "Russian Army of Liberation" with the avowed purpose of liberating Russia from Bolshevism. But his forces were kept quite small (only two divisions were activated) and never saw action on the Russian front because Berlin suspected that Vlasov was anti-German as well as anti-Bolshevik.

Those who looked to the Germans for improvement in their status were disappointed. They soon understood that the Germans intended to be masters of the occupied areas and not liberators, as they professed themselves to be. The collective farmers who had anticipated a return to individual farming were disillusioned when the Germans not only retained the system of collective farming but also placed the farms under German management and began exploiting the farmers.

The harshest phase of the occupation program was that which involved the practice of genocide. Considering the Slavs to be an inferior race whose leaders should be exterminated and whose masses should be callously treated, the Germans killed, out of hand, all they could apprehend of those who were thought to be Communists, those who supported the Soviet Government by participating in guerrilla fighting, and those who were found guilty of failure to inform the occupation authorities of anti-German activities. In addition, they carried out mass killings from time to time for purposes of coercion. The Jews were singled out for complete extermination. Before the opening of hostilities the Soviet Government had evacuated small numbers of Russian Jews to Central Asia, but the majority of them fell under the occupation rule; and about 2.5 million of them were destroyed by the Germans. Russians, Ukrainians and other civilians also were ruthlessly treated; about 1.5 million of them died as a direct result of the German occupation.

NATIVE RESISTANCE.   The occupation forces themselves were subjected to as much ruthless treatment as was within the power of the Russian guerrilla fighters to impose upon them. They harried the invaders extensively and incessantly, aided and often led by Soviet troops who had either filtered through the German lines or been dropped by parachute. Arms and communication equipment were dropped to them by Soviet planes, were captured from the enemy, or, in some cases, bought from the Rumanians in Transnistria or other venal enemy troops. What they lacked in numbers the guerrillas made up by such tenacity and ferocity that they were able to engage a disproportionate number of the occupation forces.

Relations with Allies

AMBIVALENT ALLIES.   Although the German attack had brought Russia what several years of negotiations had failed to bring, some support and co-operation from the anti-German coalition, there still remained suspicions and troubled thinking on both sides. From the beginning the allies-for-convenience had struggled with irreconcilable points of view and disagreements on procedure, for the differences which had separated the USSR from the Western European countries and the United States before the war had not disappeared; they were simply being subordinated for the time being to the interest in achieving a common military objective, the defeat of Germany.

England, as has been noted, was the first to offer friendship to Russia. On July 12, 1941, an Anglo-Soviet agreement was signed, committing each power to give the other full aid in the war against Germany and not to "negotiate nor conclude an armistice or treaty of peace except by mutual agreement." And in December, British Foreign Secretary Eden went to Moscow to discuss with Stalin their countries' war and peace aims. They agreed on the necessity of completing the defeat of Germany and making the revival of her military power impossible. In the discussion of peace settlements, Stalin asked for British recognition of the Soviet borders of June 22, 1941, the weakening of Germany by the creation of an independent Austria, the possible creation of an independent Rhineland and an independent Bavaria, and the cession of East Prussia to Poland—as replacement for the eastern territories Poland had lost to Russia. In return for British support of those wishes, Russia was willing to support the British acquisition of bases in Western Europe. Prime Minister Churchill was agreeable to such arrangements for the postwar period, but the United States Government was so opposed to the making of territorial commitments in advance of the peace negotiations that he dropped the consideration of them. The Eden-Stalin proposals for the prosecution of the war, however, were approved by both the Russian and the British governments. That was followed by a more binding step when, in May, 1942, Molotov went to London to complete the negotiations for a formal treaty of alliance which had been considered during Eden's visit. On May 26, the treaty was signed, reaffirming the agreement of July 12, 1941, and establishing an Anglo-Soviet alliance against Germany for a period of twenty years. Each party agreed to give the other full economic and military assistance and promised not to join any coalition directed against the other.

From London, Molotov went on to Washington, where he conferred with American and British representatives on the possibility of creating a second front against Germany by the landing of English and American troops in Western Europe during the summer of 1942. After the conference, the United States Government issued a statement asserting that "a full understanding was reached with respect to the urgent tasks of creating a second front in Europe in 1942." Molotov regarded that statement as a promise, but Washington and London interpreted it as no more than an indication of intention. By late summer of 1942 England and the United States had decided that the opening of a second front was not feasible and that it should be postponed. The news of that decision had a chilling effect on the Russians; and when Churchill, regarded by the Russians as bitterly anti-Soviet, made his first call on Stalin, in August, Stalin received him with the accusation that the postponement of the second front was an indication of the British willingness to let the Russians bear an unfairly large part of the human cost of the war.

Regardless of the lack of mutual confidence among them, the fact remained that the further prosecution of the war and the preparation for peace rested primarily on the Big Three: the United States, Great Britain, and the USSR. By this time, the number of states arrayed against the Axis was impressive, but the main strength lay in those three. In August, 1941, President Roosevelt and Prime Minister Churchill had issued a joint statement of peace aims, known as the Atlantic Charter, setting forth their countries' desire for a world in which nations could live in peace, freedom, and prosperity; and a month later the principles of the Atlantic Charter had been approved by the USSR, the Free French, Australia, Canada, New Zealand, the Union of South Africa, and the governments-in-exile of Belgium, Czechoslovakia, Greece, Luxemburg, The Netherlands, Norway, Poland, and Yugoslavia. Then, in January, 1942, all the powers which had approved of the Atlantic Charter had signed the Declaration of the United Nations, by which they agreed to fight on together until the defeat of Germany and to carry through the principles of the Atlantic Charter when the war was over. Thereafter any power entering the struggle against the Axis might join the United Nations by signing that declaration.

MATERIAL AID.   Even though aid through a second front was delayed, Russia was receiving very valuable aid of a different kind from her allies: a direct supply of foodstuffs and military and industrial equipment. At the end of September, 1941, an Anglo-American mission had gone to Moscow to map out a supply program. And on October 1, the American, British and Soviet representatives had set their signatures to the First Moscow Protocol, providing for Soviet purchase of goods and equipment from the United States and England. In November, after Congressional approval had been granted, President Roosevelt had made war materials available to the USSR without payment, under the terms of the American Lend-Lease Act. That action had been formalized by a Soviet-American mutual aid agreement, signed on June 11, 1942, by which the United States promised to supply Russia "with such defense articles, defense services, and defense information as the President of the United States shall authorize to be transferred or provided," and Russia had agreed to "provide such articles, services, facilities, or information as it may be in a position to supply."

American and British supplies were sent to Russia chiefly by way of Murmansk and Iran. Although Murmansk was the closest port of entry, it was the most dangerous since shipping to that point was exposed to German attack; about one-fourth of the American and British shipping en route to Murmansk during the spring and summer of 1942 was sunk. The route through Iran was longer but safer. Even that route had its hazards, however: a pro-Axis government in Iran, which had to be overthrown by the allies, and inadequate railroads and truck roads from the Persian Gulf to the Soviet border, finally made usable by American and British engineers. By March, 1943, that route was comparatively safe and fast, and thereafter it became the chief supply route to Russia.

POLISH RELATIONS.   The most controversial problem plaguing Russia's relations with her allies during the war was that of the settlement of affairs with Poland. The fortunes of war had brought the Polish Government-in-Exile to the side of the Soviet Union in 1941, but the traditional antagonisms of the two countries were not thereby erased. The Polish representatives wanted Russia to promise the restoration of eastern Poland, annexed in 1939.

Russia had no intention of making that restoration, but she was willing to support Polish acquisition of East Prussia if the Poles would renounce claims to their former eastern territories. Although the prospect of acquiring East Prussia was agreeable to the Polish Government, it would not accept it as compensation for the eastern territories. The differences on that question seemed irreconcilable.

Nonetheless a Soviet-Polish agreement was signed on July 30, 1941, setting forth certain points on which the two governments would cooperate: (1) the restoration of diplomatic relations between the two countries, (2) the release of all Polish soldiers taken prisoner in September, 1939, and of all Polish civilians under detention in Russia, and (3) the annulment of the treaty of 1939 concerning the Soviet-German division of Poland. That agreement left the Poles free to argue that the *status quo ante* 1939 would be restored; and the Russians, to argue that their claim to the eastern Polish territories rested not on the treaty of 1939 but on the elections held there in October, 1939.

In conformity with that agreement and later ones, the Soviet Government granted release to Polish prisoners in the USSR and made provisions for the organization of a Polish army in Russia. But from the beginning, there was ill-feeling about both actions. As for the prisoners released, they did not include, according to a Polish complaint (denied by the Soviet Government), 10,000 Polish officers who had been taken in 1939. As for the Polish army, the Russians insisted that it should be hurriedly prepared for front-line service, while the Poles insisted that its preparation was delayed by Russia's failure to provide sufficient equipment for it. Finally, the Polish Government asked and was given permission to evacuate its troops from the USSR to Iran. The evacuation was practically completed by the end of 1942.

The tenuous Soviet-Polish rapprochement came to a definite end on April 15, 1943, when the German radio announced the finding of a mass grave in the Katyn Forest, near Smolensk, containing the bodies of about 10,000 Polish officers who had, according to evidence, been killed by the Russians in 1940. When the Germans offered to have an inquiry made at Katyn by the International Red Cross, the Polish Government responded favorably. Meanwhile, Moscow was busy providing evidence that the 10,000 officers had been in a camp which the Red Army had been compelled to abandon in the retreat of 1941 and that they had been killed by the Germans. At last, on April 25, 1943, the Soviet Government severed diplomatic relations with the Polish Government-in-Exile, claiming that its action in accepting the German offer capped a series of anti-Soviet actions which made further friendly relations impossible.

Victorious campaigns: 1943-1945

"END OF THE BEGINNING." In July, 1943, the military future of the United Nations began to look favorable. On the Eastern Front, the Red Army had shown itself capable of halting and even of turning back the German forces. And in the West, the Anglo-American forces had activated their plans to break through the German-controlled land approaches to Europe. American and British troops had landed in North Africa in November, 1942, and defeated the Italo-German forces there in May, 1943. Then, in July, the landing of American, British, and Canadian soldiers in Sicily was accomplished, marking a point in the progress of the war which Winston Churchill declared was not the "beginning of the end" but the "end of the beginning." Now the allies were in a position to begin an attack through Italy while they finished preparations for a northern invasion and Russia held the main German forces on the Eastern Front.

FROM KURSK TO BERLIN. Before the allied attack could get under way, the Germans began their last major offensive in Russia, on July 5—this time to eliminate the Soviet salient west of Kursk. The Russians were ready for it, having superiority now in land forces, air forces and matériel. By August that superiority was clearly evident as the Red Army began to push forward in what proved to be a lengthy and costly—but triumphal—march to Berlin. Military morale was high, fed by reports of the successful Anglo-American invasion operations in Sicily and Italy. By the end of the year the Red Army had entered White Russia and had taken the Ukrainian territory east of the Dnieper—in many places, had crossed the Dnieper. The fighting, unabated during the winter months, was particularly intense in the Leningrad sector, where the Red troops finally forced the Germans, on January 27, 1944, to lift their long-drawn-out siege of Leningrad. In the next two months the Red Army crossed the pre-1939 borders of the USSR into Poland and Rumania before the Germans were able to slow them down.

Meanwhile, at the Moscow Conference, in October, 1943, Molotov, Eden, Hull, and their military advisers had agreed on the advisability of opening the Second Front with a cross-channel invasion in May, 1944, and beginning simultaneously an intensive Red Army offensive to prevent the

Germans from transferring more than fifteen divisions from the Eastern Front to France in the first two months of the invasion. Near the end of November, at a conference in Teheran, Stalin, Roosevelt, and Churchill made the final plans for the combined action.

The long awaited Second Front was opened by the landing of American and British forces in Normandy on June 6, 1944, unfavorable weather conditions having made the landing impossible in May. Then, while the American and British forces fought on through France, where they were joined by the French Forces of the Interior (an underground resistance organization), and finally broke over the German frontier, a new Soviet offensive was launched on the Eastern Front. In the middle of June, Red Army operations were directed toward Lithuania, Latvia, and Estonia and up the Karelian Isthmus—to force Finland out of the war. And in August another push was directed against Rumania.

Rumania, like the other minor Axis countries, hoped to save herself from going down with Germany; therefore, after disarming the German troops within her borders, she signed an armistice with Russia, the United States and Great Britain on August 23, 1944. She also agreed to declare war on Germany at once—and did so on the following day. Then Finland asked for an armistice and, on September 4, after preliminary conditions had been agreed upon, signed one with Russia and Great Britain (the United States had not declared war on Finland). Bulgaria found herself in a peculiar position. As a member of the Axis she had declared war on Great Britain and the United States but had maintained neutrality toward Russia. Now, after Rumania had joined the anti-German coalition and after British troops had landed in Greece in August, she sought desperately for an armistice with Great Britain and the United States. To forestall such an armistice, which would permit the British troops then in Greece to occupy Bulgaria, Russia declared war on Bulgaria on September 5. It proved to be one of the shortest wars in history; on September 9, Bulgaria surrendered to Russia.

Then the swiftly moving Soviet armies crossed Yugoslavia, where they joined forces with the Yugoslav Partisans, under Tito. Together, they swept the country and were able to free Belgrade on October 20. While that was being accomplished, other Soviet armies approached Hungary, whose government was considering the Soviet warning that it had little time to disengage itself from the German embrace. Admiral Horthy, Regent of Hungary, sent emissaries to negotiate with the Russians; but, in the middle of October, before the negotiations were complete, a strong German force, aided by Hungarian Nazis, succeeded in overthrowing Horthy's government and in establishing a new one, dedicated to war to the end. The result was a struggle which made a shambles of the country, for the desperate Germans fought the Russians for every inch of Hungarian soil.

By the end of December the American, British, and French forces in the west were in good position, having rallied after the heavy American losses in the Battle of the Bulge, and were ready for another great joint-offensive effort at the beginning of 1945. As they drove on into Germany, the Red Army in mid-January began a new offensive on a front extending from the Neman River to the Carpathians, its three major goals being Vienna, Prague, and Berlin.

Between the Red Army and Vienna there was still most of Hungary. Within that country, on January 20, a hastily formed anti-Nazi government signed an armistice terminating hostilities between Hungary and Russia, but the Germans still occupied much of the country. Budapest finally fell to the Red Army in February, and two months later Hungary was free of Germans. Then, on April 13, Marshal Feodor Tolbukhin's troops took Vienna, bringing one major phase of the Russian offensive to an end.

The drive to Prague went more slowly. In April, the Red Army entered Bratislava, the chief city of Slovakia, but Prague held out for more than a month longer.

The bulk of the Russian forces were meanwhile moving on to Germany through Poland. In the middle of January, Warsaw was freed of the Germans. By the end of March, Gdynia and Danzig had fallen. And early in April, Russian armies crossed the Oder and began to converge on Berlin. They began their attack, from a line ten miles from the city, on April 19 and continued it for two weeks against dogged German resistance. Elsewhere the allies were moving in with relentless progress. On April 25, advance units of American and Russian forces met at Torgau, on the Elbe River, near Leipzig. Four days later American and British forces in the Italian invasion forced the unconditional surrender of the German divisions in Italy. On April 30, while the Germans were making their last desperate effort to hold Berlin in street fighting against Red troops, the men of Marshal Zhukov's armies were able to place the Soviet flag atop the German Reichstag building. And on May 2, after the last street fighting had ended and Hitler had committed suicide, massed cannon in Moscow roared out a victory salute.

Five days later, in Reims, General Jodl signed on behalf of the German High Command the document of unconditional surrender to the Soviet High Command and the Allied Expeditionary Forces. On May 8 the ceremony of surrender was repeated in Berlin.

FROM BERLIN TO THE *U.S.S. MISSOURI.*   While celebrating the victory over Germany, most of the United Nations were still seriously pursuing war in another quarter, the Far East. There the United States, China, Great Britain, and others of the United Nations, after more than three years of intensive operations against Japan, had weakened her to the point that her defeat was almost in sight. But it appeared that the cost in men and time which would yet be required to complete it would be great. The United States and Great Britain felt that the cost could be greatly reduced and the end of the war hastened by Soviet aid. Although the USSR had maintained a considerable Far Eastern force, amounting to about thirty divisions, against the possibility of a Japanese attack during her involvement in Europe, the Soviet High Command had not felt that it could divert either more men or more supplies to that region until the defeat of Germany. However, as early as October 30, 1943, Stalin had informed Cordell Hull that Russia intended to join in the war on Japan after the German defeat; and a year later, during a conference in Moscow with Churchill and General John Deane, the chief of the American Military Mission in Russia, he had stated his willingness to attack Japan three months after the termination of hostilities with Germany. (Three months were necessary to transfer additional divisions to the Soviet Far East and to create, with prior American assistance, a sufficient reserve of supplies for an offensive.) Later, at a meeting of Stalin, Roosevelt, and Churchill at Yalta, in February, 1945, Stalin, after securing many political concessions, had reaffirmed the Soviet intention to join forces against Japan. That had been followed, on April 5, 1945, by the Soviet Government's informing Tokyo that it was denouncing the five-year Treaty of Neutrality, signed in April, 1941.

After the German surrender, the movement of Soviet troops to the Far East began. It was hoped at the time that an American invasion of Japan, planned for November, 1945, might be accompanied by an advance of the Soviet Far Eastern forces into Manchuria and China to engage and defeat the Japanese armies on the mainland. However, the American release of an atom bomb on Hiroshima, on August 6, opened the prospect that Japan would capitulate without an invasion of the Japanese islands. On August 8, three months after the German surrender in Berlin, the Soviet Government declared war on Japan; and the next day Soviet armies, under the command of Marshal Alexander Vasilevsky, invaded Manchuria. Shortly thereafter Soviet marines, with naval support, landed in northern Korea, while other Soviet forces invaded the Japanese half of Sakhalin, the Kurile Islands, and Port Arthur.

The Japanese Government, seeing the country driven beyond endurance by nearly four years of war with the United Nations and recognizing, after the atomic bombing, the virtual inevitability of destruction, capitulated and accepted the surrender terms of the United Nations on August 14. Organized fighting, however, continued in Manchuria until August 23, when Stalin announced the complete surrender of the Japanese Kwantung Army in Manchuria. On September 2, a Soviet representative took part in the formal Japanese surrender to the United Nations aboard the *U.S.S. Missouri.*

Preparations for peace

THE WAR CONFERENCES.   Prosecution of the war and preparations for the peace had required many conferences of the Soviet Union, the United States, and Great Britain and many conferences of all the United Nations before the end of the Second World War. The most important of those were the Moscow Conference, of October, 1943 (attended by Molotov, Eden, and Hull); the Teheran Conference of November, 1943 (attended by Stalin, Roosevelt, and Churchill); the Dumbarton Oaks Conference, in Washington, D.C., of August-September, 1944 (attended by representatives of the United States, Great Britain, the USSR, and China); the Moscow Conference, of October, 1944 (between Churchill and Stalin); the Yalta Conference, of February, 1945 (attended by Stalin, Churchill, and Roosevelt); the San Francisco Conference, of April, 1945 (attended by representatives of the signatories of the United Nations Charter); and the Potsdam Conference, of July-August, 1945 (attended by Stalin, Truman, Churchill, and Attlee).

PLANS FOR POSTWAR INTERNATIONAL CO-OPERATION AND ORGANIZATION.   Planning for Soviet-Western co-operation in the postwar world was made difficult not only by the fact that the USSR was the heir to a traditional policy of Russian aggression but also by the fact that the USSR was the center of the worldwide Communist movement which had for its object the overthrow of established governments in other countries. One of these difficulties seemed to be eradicated when, on May 22, 1943, the Executive Committee of the Communist International, meeting in Moscow, decided to dissolve the Comintern, thus apparently freeing the Communist parties of the world from its direction and control. The end of the Comintern was less world-shaking in 1943 than it might have been in earlier years since it had been for some time a moribund organization. Nonetheless it was received by Russia's allies as an indication that she was dissociating herself from the worldwide Communist movement and preparing to enter into whole-hearted co-operation with the United Nations.

Even more indicative of the possibility of postwar co-operation was the Soviet leaders' unequivocal willingness to assist with plans for a new international organization for peace and security to replace the discredited League of Nations. The drafting of plans for such an organization, to be known as the United Nations Organization (later designated as the United Nations or the UN), was begun at the Dumbarton Oaks Conference, where agreement was reached in all fundamentals of the organization except the voting procedure in its executive body. At that conference, the Big Three agreed that each of the major powers would have the right to veto any action of the organization involving the use of force or sanctions, but they could not agree on methods of voting. The United States and Great Britain argued that if a major power were a party to a dispute, that power should not be permitted to vote on it. Russia, fearing that the new organization might be used against her, argued that a major power should be permitted to vote on a dispute to which it was a party and that it should be able to use the veto power in such a vote. A less important source of disagreement at the conference was the Soviet proposal that each of the sixteen union republics in the USSR be given membership in the United Nations Organization.

Those two problems were settled at the Yalta Conference, when American compromise proposals were accepted by Churchill and Stalin. It was agreed that in the Security Council of the proposed organization each of the five major powers (the United States, England, the USSR, France, and China) would have the power of veto on substantive matters; that meant that the Security Council could not recommend, without the consent of all five powers, any means of settlement—whether pacific or forcible—in any dispute, not even in a dispute involving one of the five major powers. And with respect to the proposed admission of the sixteen republics, it was agreed that only the White Russian and Ukrainian republics would be admitted. Those matters decided, a general conference of representatives of the United Nations countries convened in San Francisco in April, 1945, and formed the United Nations Organization.

SETTLEMENT OF WESTERN FRONTIERS. One of the most disturbing tasks which faced the Big Three in their wartime planning for postwar settlements was that of finding an amicable solution of the problems involved in the establishment of Russia's western frontiers. Once more, the Polish Question arose, this time involving not only the fixing of the postwar Polish-Soviet boundary but also a decision on the status of the Polish Government-in-Exile. Since the work of clearing the Germans from Polish territory would fall to the Red Army and since the Soviet Union, after April, 1943, did not recognize the Polish Government-in-Exile, the Soviet Government felt that it was in a position not only to decide the new Polish-Soviet boundary but also to install another Polish government. Washington and London, recognizing the danger in such high-handedness, began negotiations to reconcile the Polish Government-in-Exile with the Soviet Government. But even while the negotiations were in progress, Moscow decided to sponsor the formation of a new Polish government. The first step toward that end was taken in July, 1944, when, with Soviet blessing, the left-wing Poles of the Polish underground and the pro-Soviet Poles in the USSR organized the Polish Committee of National Liberation, to assume the administration of Polish territory liberated by the Red Army. Six months later, the Polish Committee of National Liberation declared itself the Provisional Government of Poland; and on January 5, 1945, it was recognized by Moscow.

The United States and Britain, confronted with this *fait accompli*, were in a quandary: they considered themselves morally obligated to the Polish Government-in-Exile; yet they felt compelled to maintain friendship with the USSR, now recognizing the Polish Provisional Government. At the Yalta Conference, they resolved the problem by gaining Soviet agreement to a compromise whereby the Polish Provisional Government would be enlarged to include some representatives of the Polish Government-in-Exile and free elections would be held at the earliest possible time to determine the permanent form of government in Poland. It was also agreed at Yalta that the Polish-Soviet boundary would be that of June 22, 1941, with little modification, and that Poland should receive the German territory east of the Oder River as well as most of East Prussia—except Koenigsberg, to which Russia aspired.

It was necessary also to make decisions on the other western frontiers of Russia. The British and American governments decided in 1943 that little could be done to alter Russia's determination to set them where they had been in 1941; and subsequent developments bore out their decision. The armistice signed by Finland in 1944 provided for the re-establishment, with minor changes, of the Soviet-Finnish frontier of 1940. The armistice which Rumania signed with the Big Three provided for the return of Bessarabia and northern Bukovina to the USSR. And Latvia, Estonia, and Lithuania were reincorporated into the USSR after those areas had been cleared of Germans in 1944-45.

DIVISION OF INFLUENCE IN THE BALKANS AND CENTRAL EUROPE.

As the war in Europe neared its end, the prospect of Soviet predominance in the Balkans and Central Europe grew. Throughout those regions, except in Greece, the task of clearing out the Germans fell to the Red Army; and where the Red Army entered, Soviet influence followed.

Great Britain was particularly concerned with the prospective growth of Soviet influence but could do little to halt it. London had recognized since December, 1943, when the Czechoslovak Government-in-Exile had signed a twenty-year treaty known as the Treaty of Friendship, Mutual Assistance and Postwar Collaboration with the USSR, that Czechoslovakia would look to Moscow rather than to London in the future. It was recognized also that there was little chance of preventing Moscow's using the presence of Red troops in Rumania, Bulgaria, and Hungary for the extension of influence in those countries. In Yugoslavia, where the Communist-led Partisans opposed the return of the pro-British Yugoslav Government-in-Exile, British influence was slight but of some promise. In Greece, the advantage lay definitely with Great Britain; the British forces had landed in Greece in 1944, and the Greek Government-in-Exile favored Britain. But, even there, a strong Communist-led partisan movement opposed the Greek Government-in-Exile and hence its sponsor, Great Britain.

On a visit to Moscow in October, 1944, Churchill made the best possible bargain with Stalin on the division of influence: during the first months after hostilities, Great Britain was to recognize preponderant Soviet influence in Bulgaria, Rumania, and Hungary; Russia was to recognize preponderant British influence in Greece; and the two powers were to share influence in Yugoslavia.

Several months later, at the Yalta Conference, Roosevelt, Churchill, and Stalin agreed to the establishment by the Yugoslav Partisans of a government including a few members of the Government-in-Exile. They agreed also to the formation, in the countries freed from German and Italian rule, of provisional governments representing "all democratic elements in the population" and pledged to early and free elections. This agreement seemed to contradict the one made by Churchill and Stalin in October, for there was no certainty that free elections in the countries where Soviet influence had been recognized would produce governments amenable to Soviet influence. The Russians, however, chose to believe that the Yalta agreement did not supersede the earlier agreement.

During the remaining months of the war, the struggle for influence worked itself out in the Russian favor. In Bulgaria, Rumania, and Hungary, provisional governments heavily weighted with Communist and pro-Soviet members were formed under the eye of the Red Army. In Czechoslovakia, several key cabinet posts were given to Communists. In Albania, to which the outside world paid little attention, native partisans formed a pro-Communist, pro-Soviet government. And the British share of influence in Yugoslavia grew smaller daily as the provisional government, led by the Communist Joseph Tito, pushed former adherents of the defunct Government-in-Exile out of power. Only in Greece did Great Britain retain her influence, and even there it was menaced by an armed conflict between the leftists and the rightists, which began in December, 1944, and continued beyond the end of the war.

DISPOSITION OF GERMANY. The disposition of Germany, with which two great wars had been waged in one generation, was another responsibility of the Big Three. They agreed that it was necessary to prevent Germany's ever becoming a military power again and that, to accomplish that end, it would be necessary to disarm and de-Nazify the country and to occupy it for an extended period. But how should Germany be occupied? If Russia alone were to occupy it, it would fall under Soviet influence; if Great Britain and the United States were to perform the task, they might transform it into an anti-Soviet buffer state. The only satisfactory arrangement would be one designed to do three things: (1) prevent Germany from becoming a recurring danger to the peace, (2) prevent either Russia or England and the United States from securing preponderant influence in Germany, and (3) preclude the possibility that Germany might regain her power by playing on East-West rivalries.

After many conferences the Big Three reached agreement, by 1945, on what was then thought to be a workable arrangement: Austria was to be restored as an independent state; Poland was to administer several German territories; Russia was to annex Koenigsberg; and the remainder of Germany was to be divided into four zones, each to be placed for an indefinite period under the control of one of four occupying powers—the United States, Great Britain, the USSR, and France (whose inclusion was a gesture of international courtesy). The occupying powers were to aim at the complete demilitarization and de-Nazification of Germany in preparation for the eventual formation of a democratic German government and were to co-ordinate their work through an Allied Control Council for Germany, consisting of representatives of the four powers. It was further agreed that Germany be compelled to make reparations for the damage done to the United Nations, such reparations to be in the form of capital equipment, goods, and labor. The amount of reparations to be paid was not definitely set, but a tentative amount was suggested: $20 billion (in kind)—half of which was to go to the USSR.

PLANS FOR THE FAR EAST. As long as Russia maintained neutrality with respect to the war in the Pacific, her postwar intentions in that region could not be discussed. But, after 1944, when Soviet plans to enter the war had been officially stated, the powers were compelled to consider her intentions. At the Yalta Conference, Stalin asked for a number of concessions in return for Soviet entry, and Roosevelt and Churchill, feeling that Soviet aid was imperative, were willing to grant them. Most important among them were the preservation of the status quo in Outer Mongolia, the return of southern Sakhalin to Russia, the cession of the Kurile Islands to Russia, the lease of Port Arthur from China for a Russian naval base, and the joint Sino-Soviet administration of the Chinese Eastern and South Manchurian Railroads. Roosevelt undertook the task of gaining China's assent to the arrangements in which that country would be involved. And his efforts were rewarded by the conclusion of a number of Sino-Soviet agreements and the Treaty of Alliance (signed on August 14, 1945), a thirty-year arrangement for the co-operation of China and the USSR against Japan. The agreements provided for a thirty-year lease of Port Arthur to Russia, the operation of the Chinese Eastern and South Manchurian Railroads for a period of thirty years by a joint Sino-Soviet company to be known as the Chinese Changchun Railroad Company, and a plebiscite in Outer Mongolia to determine whether or not its inhabitants wished to be independent of China.

Concerning Korea, the Big Three agreed only on the principle that Korea was to be an independent state; but it was suggested that, during the period of transition to independence, it should be subject to some kind of international control. Since, at the time of the Japanese surrender, Soviet troops were in northern Korea and American troops in southern Korea, an arrangement was made for the Red Army to accept the surrender of Japanese troops north of the 38th parallel and for the Americans to accept the surrender of those south of that parallel.

As for Japan, the Big Three agreed that the country be occupied for an indefinite period, during which it would be transformed into a pacific, democratic state. The United States proposed that the occupation be under American auspices and that the supreme commander of the occupation forces be an American, General Douglas MacArthur. Moscow proposed, in August, 1945, that there be two supreme commanders, General MacArthur and Marshal Vasilevsky, but the suggestion was summarily rejected by Washington and hastily withdrawn by Moscow.

Developments on the home front: 1942-1945

THE ECONOMY. During the war Russia mobilized about 22 million men and maintained the strength of the armed forces at a level of about 12.5 million from late 1942 until the end of hostilities. To supply the needs of so many fighting men for four years and to provide the necessities for the home front, the economy was greatly strained. The major part of the country's regular labor force was taken to replenish the military, and the resources of the occupied areas became unavailable when most needed; yet production had to be increased. The initial efforts to mobilize for economic service all able-bodied persons not in military service were intensified as the war progressed, and the factories and farms of the unoccupied parts of the country were pushed to the last iota of their capacity. The main weight of the industrial effort was borne by Asiatic Russia, where established industries, industries evacuated from occupied regions, and industries established during the war were in full-time production. They supplied most of Russia's average annual production of 30,000 tanks and self-propelled guns, 40,000 planes, 450,000 machine guns, and 5 million rifles and tommy guns. They supplied some civilian needs also, but only up to the barest minimum.

Although the economy was far better equipped to supply military and civilian needs during the Second World War than it had been during the First World War, it could not meet all basic requirements. Supplies from Russia's allies, primarily the United States—at first purchased and later secured under Lend-Lease—helped to make up many deficiencies. During the course of the war, the Soviet Union received, under Lend-Lease, American goods valued at about $11 billion. Of all items so received, the most important were motor vehicles—478,899 of them, almost half of all motor vehicles used on the Soviet front.

Foodstuffs were supplied by careful planning, intensive work, and governed distribution. The early loss of rich agricultural regions to Germany and the Nazi occupation of the northern Caucasus during the 1942 harvest introduced the Russians to food shortages which they had difficulty in overcoming. But the people responded to the emergency, making up in part for the loss of land and for the loss of the agricultural laborers being drawn into industry and the armed forces by working harder and existing on less. There were still shortages, but they were partly relieved by the shipment of fats and oils, canned meats, and dried fruits and vegetables from the United States.

Consumer goods provided by domestic production and Lend-Lease kept the people alive but at the lowest level of subsistence. Yet workers and peasants received more money than before the war; the workers were paid for their overtime work• and the peasants were permitted to sell much of their produce at inflated prices in the open market. As a result, the number of rubles in circulation was increasing just when available goods for purchase were decreasing. To throttle inflationary tendencies, the government siphoned a large part of the surplus rubles back into the treasury of the state by increasing income taxes and by floating large government loans to which almost all citizens felt obligated to subscribe. Any remaining rubles were laid aside by the population against the time when consumer goods would again be available on the market.

PATRIOTISM AND MORALE.   The need for rallying the people behind the war effort resulted in the reinforcement of the practices, already introduced before the war, aiming at the creation of a new focus of loyalty, the Soviet Fatherland. All forms of appeal were employed to whip up love of fatherland and hatred of the enemy. The heroes of Old Russia—Alexander Nevsky, Dmitri Donskoi, Kuzma Minin, Dmitri Pozharsky, Bogdan Khmelnitsky, Alexander Suvorov, and Michael Kutuzov—were now extolled as examples for emulation. Their struggles against foreign invaders—Germans, Poles, Tatars, and Frenchmen—were presented as models for the contemporary struggle against the German invaders. At the same time a number of new medals and orders—such as the Order of Kutuzov, the Order of Suvorov, and the Order of Bogdan Khmelnitsky—were created and awarded with great liberality for military service. The pre-1917 custom of designating crack units as guards units was revived. And special stress was placed upon improving the esprit de corps of the commanding personnel. In 1943 the term *officer* was reintroduced to replace the term *commander;* the pre-1917 shoulder boards for officers were restored; and officers' clubs, orderlies, and all the trappings of an officer corps reintroduced. Fraternization between officers and men, once the rule of the Red Army, was discouraged, and special codes of behavior and discipline for officers were formulated. At the same time sharp distinctions in rank in many civilian activities, particularly the diplomatic and railroad services, were introduced, evidently for the purpose of creating a professional élan among responsible personnel.

Religion, also, continued to be employed in bolstering wartime morale. The loyal support given by the Orthodox Church was repaid when the prelates of the Church were permitted, in September, 1943, to elect a patriarch to fill the office vacant since 1925 and to elect a Holy Synod to act as the governing body of the Church. Acting Patriarch Sergei was selected as Patriarch of Moscow and All Russia, and on September 12 he was enthroned with all the pomp of ancient services. Thereafter many concessions were made to the Russian Orthodox Church; it was permitted to publish a periodical, publish religious books, open theological schools, give religious instruction to children, and perform religious services outside the church buildings. Other religious groups—Protestants, Jews, and Moslems—received similar concessions. This relaxation of pressure did not indicate that the state and party had changed their basic position on religion; it indicated only their acceptance of the necessity of granting concessions in order to promote internal harmony at that time.

An act as striking as the election of a patriarch was the replacement, in December, 1943, of the *Internationale* as the national Soviet anthem by a new one, *The Hymn of the Soviet Union*.[1] Thereafter, instead of the sweeping words of the old song, " 'Tis the final conflict, let each stand in his place/ The International Soviet shall be the human race," the people sang, "Unbreakable union of freeborn Republics/Great Russia has welded forever to stand." The theme had changed from one of proletarian internationalism to one of Soviet nationalism.

In February, 1944, the government took another step calculated to strengthen popular support of the state. At a special session of the Supreme Soviet, Molotov proposed that each of the sixteen union republics be permitted to engage in foreign relations and to maintain separate military formations, subject to the general direction of the federal government. His proposal was accepted, and, during the following eighteen months, the sixteen republics established their people's commissariats of foreign affairs and began to engage in relations with foreign countries. Two of them, White Russia and the Ukraine, sent representatives to the United Nations. (For reasons which are not yet clear, no steps were taken to create the proposed separate military formations.) These reforms were not intended to lead to the formation of sixteen independent foreign offices and sixteen independent armies; they were intended merely to permit the republics to enjoy a wider semblance of federalism than they had heretofore. In substance, control of foreign relations and military affairs of the USSR remained, as before, in the Kremlin.

The foregoing concessions of the ruling party to the people apparently did not indicate that the party was relaxing its hold nor that, once the war

---

[1] The *Internationale* remained the official song of the Communist Party.

was over, the regime would become milder. It appears now that they were calculated concessions, as the NEP concessions had been, to hold the people's support in time of need. It is true that, during the war there were fewer references to Marxism-Leninism and more to Russian patriotism than before and that there were liberal concessions to religion and to traditional Russian nationalism. But the Communist Party at no time during the war gave up its position of dominance either at the front or in the rear, and its leaders continued to rule both the party and the country. Indeed, as early as 1944 the emphasis on Marxism-Leninism was beginning to reappear, indicating that the lines of Soviet development mapped out before the war would be followed after its conclusion.

The cost of war

HUMAN LOSSES. Four years of war were paid for by heavy losses in men and property, the full extent of which is still not known. In March, 1946, Stalin stated that 7 million Soviet citizens had lost their lives either in battle or as a result of occupation, but he did not cite the number wounded or taken prisoner. Seven million dead is probably a conservative figure; but, accepting this number, experts have estimated that at least 3 million of them died in combat or as a result of combat, that 2.5 million of them were Soviet civilian Jews killed by the Germans, and that 1.5 million of them were other Soviet civilians killed by the Germans. And estimates place the number of Red Army troops taken prisoner somewhere between 3 and 4 million. There is no way of knowing or estimating how many were seriously wounded or crippled for life.

MATERIAL LOSSES. The material losses suffered by Russia were almost as staggering as the human losses. The official Soviet figures show that $128 billion in damage was done to property, including the destruction of 1,700 towns, 70,000 villages and hamlets, 31,000 factories, 84,000 schools, and 40,000 miles of railroad track, in addition to the loss of 7 million horses, 17 million head of cattle and 20 million hogs. That represented about one-fourth of all Soviet property. At war's end, Russia faced a back-breaking task of reconstruction.

The USSR in 1945 gave the appearance of being in a highly favorable and comfortable position: the Soviet system had survived the stresses of an extensive and horrible war, and the country was now a member of a powerful victorious coalition. On the whole, the prospects for domestic tranquillity and international stability seemed good. The reality of the following years, however, bore out these appearances only to a limited degree. Peace among the great powers was preserved, but it was a fitful and feverish peace, accompanied by unsettling tension within the USSR.

Perspectives

"LESSONS" OF THE WAR. At the end of hostilities, Stalin and his lieutenants publicly declared themselves satisfied with the results that had been achieved. According to them, the Soviet system had "successfully passed the ordeal in the fire of war," thereby proving its qualities of strength and endurance. As for the future, the goal was as before: to overtake and surpass economically the most advanced capitalist countries. To achieve this goal, they said, the USSR required "a lengthy period of peace and ensured security," which would entail the preservation of amicable relations with the United Nations as well as the maintenance of a strong military establishment.

These statements concealed more than they revealed of the lessons that the Soviet leaders had actually drawn from the war. Their real conclusions were determined at secret deliberations among themselves, and these were not shared with the public. In fact, so little direct information about those deliberations has ever been made publicly available that outsiders have been left to infer Soviet intentions from Soviet actions. And, because action is usually an imperfect realization of intention, inference educed in this way can be no more than a substitute for conclusive knowledge.

FOREIGN POLICY.   In making their decisions concerning future foreign policy, the Soviet leaders were undoubtedly influenced by a number of changes that had been wrought in their country's international status. Not since the end of the Napoleonic Wars had Russia been in a position as strong as that she enjoyed in 1945. Her armies were spread from Korea to Germany. The two major threats to her security were removed—at least for the time being. From prewar weakness, isolation, and ostracism, she had risen to a position of strength, acceptance, and prestige. Moreover, she had achieved certain important advantages: recognition as one of the Big Three, a powerful position in the United Nations, preponderant influence in Eastern Europe, gains in the Far East, Anglo-American support for changes in the administration of the Straits and for oil concessions in northern Iran, and a decisive voice in the making of the peace.

Since Russia's position was such a favorable one, it seemed that she would have more to gain from helping to preserve the peace than from doing anything that might provoke war. This was, in fact, the professed view of the Soviet leaders; but, in their interpretation, it was subject to certain unstated reservations based on their conception of future international relations. They believed that peace, though desirable, could not be considered a permanent condition as long as most of the world was "capitalist." In their view, capitalism had fallen into a state of general crisis, which would continue to produce wars and revolutions. And, since the "capitalist world" was thus unstable, there was no wisdom in basing Soviet security exclusively, or even primarily, on co-operation with the "capitalist" allies. Moreover, the opportunities to extend Soviet power, particularly in Eastern and Central Europe, should be taken while the Red Army was still in those areas, for such opportunities might not be repeated in the foreseeable future. These conditions were, to them, acceptable arguments for following policies repugnant to the allies. On the other hand, they understood that it would be disastrous if, in the pursuit of advantage, the USSR should drive the United States or Great Britain into war; therefore advantage must be sought in areas that the allies did not regard as vital to their own security.

Soviet foreign policy, thus interpreted, was quite a complex policy, the product of what one social scientist has termed "the interplay of utopianism and cynical realism." Despite its complexity, the government expected through its application to insure Soviet security and to expand Soviet power and Communist influence. These were ends to be attained by the considered use of certain instruments: (1) the economic and military strength of the USSR, (2) the new zones of Soviet influence, (3) the support that would be forthcoming from the world Communist movement, (4) the Big Three, and (5) the United Nations organization.

Since, in the pursuit of its goals, the Soviet Government would inevitably encounter some incompatibles, it would be necessary to determine priorities. Was the friendship of the United States more important than the extension of Soviet power in Eastern Europe? Were reparations more important than the good will of the German people? Was the Greek Communist movement more important than amicable relations with Great Britain? Because of the need to resolve such problems, Moscow could expect to be compelled sometimes to jeopardize the attainment of one goal in order to realize another.

DOMESTIC POLICY.   In reaching decisions with respect to domestic policy, the leaders undoubtedly considered the evidences of disaffection that showed up among the people during the war. And they were undoubtedly aware of pressures for modifications in the system: for slowing the tempo of industrialization, extending religious and intellectual freedom, and increasing the opportunities for cultural contacts with the outside world. They had yielded to some of these pressures during the war but it was now evident that they had no intention of making any substantive changes in the Soviet system. Their decision at this point may not have been a unanimous one: a suggestion that it was not so is to be seen in the assertion of Nikita Khrushchev, in July, 1963, that if Stalin had "departed ten years sooner from the leadership," the Soviet people would have been better off. Nevertheless, Soviet domestic policy after the war appears to have been dictated by the official determination to continue as before. To maintain the usual course meant rapid industrialization, with continued emphasis on heavy industry, much of it devoted to meeting the country's military needs; and it meant the maintenance of one-party government, the police state, cultural isolation from the outside world, and a thin veneer of democracy over the reality of a dictatorship that had come to be, in essence, "Stalinolatry."

Foreign affairs

PEACE SETTLEMENTS.   The making of the peace was the first major test of the USSR's ability to work in harmony with her allies. And the test was a taxing one, even though the Big Three had already agreed to postpone the difficult task of making peace with Germany, Japan, and Austria.

The immediate objective was to make treaties of peace with Italy and the lesser Axis states—that is, Bulgaria, Rumania, Hungary, and Finland. It had been agreed at Potsdam that the foreign ministers of the five major powers, acting as the Council of Foreign Ministers, would prepare drafts of such treaties and submit them to a conference of the anti-Axis powers. The first session of this council showed the USSR at odds with her allies. One obstacle to amity was a matter of mood: the Soviet diplomats tended to be suspicious and inflexible, often making major issues of minor ones. Another was a matter of power. The USSR urged that Trieste be turned over to pro-Soviet Yugoslavia, but the other states objected, knowing that such an arrangement would give Russia a foothold on the Adriatic. The USSR, in turn, opposed the suggestion that Great Britain administer the former Italian colonies in trust for the United Nations, thereby enhancing British power in the Mediterranean. When it became obvious that these issues could not be settled within a reasonable time, they were tabled for future action by the United Nations, and the treaty drafts were completed. They were submitted to a peace conference meeting in Paris from July to October, 1946; and, after editing, they were signed in Paris on February 10, 1947.

By the provisions of those treaties, the USSR was to receive $100 million in reparations from Italy, $200 million from Hungary, and $300 million each from Rumania and Finland. Two of the treaties included also territorial clauses. Rumania agreed to the restoration of the Soviet-Rumanian border as it had been set in June, 1940, when Rumania had ceded Bessarabia and northern Bukovina. Finland reaffirmed the territorial cessions made to the USSR in 1940 and made one more cession, the province of Petsamo; in addition, she agreed to grant the USSR a fifty-year lease on Porkkala, near Helsinki, for use as a naval base (this, instead of Hangoe). Each of the treaties included an agreement that the defeated country would dissolve all Fascist and Nazi organizations within its borders and guarantee free and representative government. In return, the USSR agreed to withdraw Soviet troops from those countries occupied during the war—Bulgaria, Hungary, Rumania—within ninety days after the treaties with them became effective.

Poland had already agreed (by treaty, August 16, 1945) to the restoration, with minor modifications, of the Soviet-Polish border as it was after the Soviet occupation of eastern Poland in 1939; and Lithuania, Latvia, and Estonia had been reincorporated into the USSR in 1944 without benefit of international agreement. Thus, by 1947, Soviet Russia had regained her 1941 boundaries in Europe.

But Soviet gains were not limited to the re-establishment of prewar boundaries. They included also a number of other territories and privileges acquired through various arrangements:

1) The government of Czechoslovakia, submitting to Soviet persuasion, ceded the province of Carpatho-Ukraine to the USSR on June 29, 1945. This area of 5,500 square miles, the population of which was culturally akin to the Ukrainians, was incorporated in the Ukrainian S.S.R.

2) In accordance with the Yalta and Potsdam agreements, the USSR assumed administration over the city of Koenigsberg and its environs (renaming the city Kaliningrad), the Kurile Islands, and southern Sakhalin, pending formal confirmation of the cession of those areas by peace treaties with Germany and Japan.

3) Acting on the terms of the Soviet-Chinese agreements of August, 1945, the USSR transformed Port Arthur into a Soviet naval base and entered into joint administration, with China, of the Chinese Eastern and South Manchurian Railroads, united under the name of the Chinese Changchun Railroad.

4) Also in accordance with the Soviet-Chinese agreements, a plebiscite was held in the Mongolian People's Republic on the question of whether or not its people wished to be independent of China. The vote was overwhelmingly in favor of independence, and the Mongolian People's Republic became legally an independent state—in reality, a Soviet sphere of influence.

5) The former Chinese region of Tuva, where a pro-Soviet government had long been in existence, was annexed to the USSR during the war—a fact made known by the Soviet press at the end of hostilities with Japan.

All in all, the territorial arrangements after 1939 added to Russia about 260,000 square miles and 23 million people and went far toward restoring what she had lost in earlier years. All the territory which she had lost in Europe between 1917 and 1921, with the exception of Congress Poland and Finland, was restored. And in Asia, having regained the Kuriles (which she had renounced in 1875) and all the territory and privileges surrendered to Japan in 1905, she lacked only the Transcaucasian provinces of Kars and Ardahan, which had been ceded to Turkey in 1918. In addition to those restorations, she now had some territory that had never before been under Russian control—Tuva, Carpatho-Ukraine, and Koenigsberg. Also, she had satisfied some long-standing ambitions: the regaining of access to the Baltic Sea and control of the Gulf of Finland.

EXTENSION OF SOVIET INFLUENCE AND POWER. As soon as possible, Russia began to use her new world position to advantage, Soviet diplomacy speaking now in a loud and confident voice. In some instances, the ensuing actions were reminiscent of tsarist Russia; in others, truly typical of a Communist state.

Following its limited concessions to religion, the Soviet Government sought to use the Russian Orthodox Church for its own ends. It encouraged the church to re-establish hegemony over Russian Orthodox adherents abroad and to strengthen the Russian position in the Eastern Orthodox Church. Many of the Russian Orthodox abroad, stoutly anti-Soviet rejected all overtures, but here and there parishes and dioceses placed themselves under the Patriarch of Moscow. The Russian Orthodox monks in Jerusalem had already given him their allegiance in 1944; and now the Orthodox leaders in Albania, Bulgaria, and Rumania accepted his direction.

The USSR capitalized also on the strong emotional response that its role had evoked among the Slavic peoples during the war, when it had wooed them by the argument that theirs was a common fight against the Teuton. The All-Slav Committee, organized in Moscow in 1941, served as a basis for postwar efforts to rally Slavs throughout the world to support Russia. The results were mixed: many Slavs remained both anti-Russian and anti-Communist, but some accepted the idea that Russia was the bastion of Slavdom. Some émigrés, interpreting the appeals as an indication that Communism was giving way to nationalism, returned to Russia in the first years after the war.

In Iran and Turkey, Russia began an effort to regain the position that she had lost after 1917 and had foresworn as "imperialistic." As early as 1944, Moscow had begun to press Iran for oil concessions under circumstances indicating political as well as economic aims. When Iran temporized, waiting for the promised evacuation of all foreign troops from her territory, the presence of Russian troops was used to promote pro-Soviet political movements in the northern part of the country. Soviet demands on Turkey, first set forth in March, 1945, and repeated in greater detail in August, 1946, included the return of Kars and Ardahan and the revision of the Montreux Convention, which dealt with the Straits, in such a manner as to place Russia on equal terms with Turkey in the administration of the Straits.

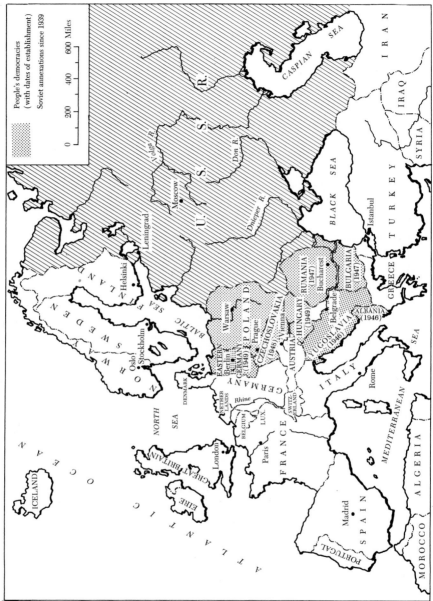

MAP 15. *The Growth of Communist Power in Europe*

In Eastern Germany, Russia was not limited to requests or demands; she simply ordered. For the administration of their zone, the Russians created the Soviet Military Administration, under the command of Marshal Gregory Zhukov until April, 1946, when he was succeeded by Marshal Vasily Sokolovsky. It attempted to achieve two disparate objectives: the extraction of full reparations from the Germans and the gaining of their political support. To achieve the first aim, the Russians dismantled many industrial plants and shipped them to the USSR, took a large part of current German industrial production for Soviet use, and put German prisoners of war to work at reconstruction in the USSR. The total of reparations taken is not known, but some notion of the amount may be gained from the fact that in Thuringia about 60 per cent of current industrial production during the first years after the war were taken for reparations and occupation costs. Although the Germans had borne down even more heavily on the Russians when they had the chance, that fact did not prevent them from bitterly disliking the Soviet reparations policy. To achieve the second aim in Eastern Germany, the Soviet Military Administration sought to bring about political changes that would assure effective Communist control and to introduce economic changes calculated to win friends. Positions of trust and responsibility were given freely to two groups: German Communists and German officers who, after capture by the Russians, had agreed to co-operate with them. Political parties were permitted but were so circumscribed as to make them instruments of Soviet policy: all legal parties were required to act in coalition under Communist leadership. Communist power was further enhanced when, in February, 1946, the Social Democratic leaders in the Soviet zone were persuaded to unite with the Communists in a new party, the Socialist Unity Party, thereby giving the Communists the Social Democratic strength and eliminating the latter as a separate political force.

The most spectacular growth of Soviet power and influence occurred in Eastern Europe. As has been noted, the Big Three recognized that friendly governments in Eastern Europe were necessary to Russia's security; and, in 1944, Russia began to shape the desired political developments in Finland, Poland, Czechoslovakia, Hungary, Rumania Bulgaria, Albania, and Yugoslavia. The instruments for determining policy varied. As defeated powers, Hungary, Rumania, and Bulgaria were to be occupied by Soviet troops until the conclusion of peace treaties. Finland was not occupied but was made subject to the orders of the Allied Control Council, which was actually dominated by the USSR. The government of Poland, which had been created under the aegis of the USSR, followed Moscow's lead and was buttressed by Red Army troops, who remained in Poland to guard the lines of communication between Germany and Russia. Czechoslovakia had voluntarily allied herself with Russia, and several strategic positions in her first postwar cabinet were held by Communists. In Albania and Yugoslavia, wartime developments had already placed Communists in power. In each of these states, except Finland,[1] the first two postwar years saw the establishment of Communist control and the subordination of national policy to that of Moscow. The pace of developments varied, and the means employed varied from country to country. In some (e.g., Yugoslavia) the changing situation was received at first with the approval of very large minorities; in others (e.g., Hungary), with the approval of insignificant minorities. In a few instances the threat of force was used, as in Rumania, where Soviet representative Vyshinsky, in March, 1945, compelled King Michael to appoint a premier acceptable to the Russians. Sometimes less evident measures were employed, but the general line of development was the same: the political parties that were sanctioned either chose, or were required, to act in coalition, and the Communists sooner or later gained control. As in Eastern Germany, the Communist and Social Democratic Parties fused in most of the countries. Communists generally took the lead in the ministries of interior and justice, using them to achieve command over the instruments of police power; and elections, for the most part, were organized so as to confirm those in power. As their influence increased, the Communists began to push their opponents out of political life and to put into effect radical policies such as the nationalization of large enterprises and distribution of large estates among the poorer peasants. The result was that the seven states were more than friendly to the Soviet Government; they were so nearly subordinate to it that they came to be known in the West as "satellite" states.

GROWTH OF DIPLOMATIC CONFLICT.   Between 1945 and 1947 Big Three unity gave way to deepening animosity between the USSR on the one hand and the United States and Great Britain on the other. The conduct of Soviet foreign policy in the early postwar period was marked by an uncompromising, arrogant, suspicious, and often insulting manner. Though not new, this manner made negotiations with Russia difficult and weakened the good will that she had gained abroad during the war. As the issues between Russia and her wartime friends became sharper, the atmosphere in which negotiations were conducted became more and more disturbed. The

---

[1] If Russia had treated Finland with severity, neighboring Sweden would probably have abandoned her neutrality and joined the Western bloc against the USSR.

fact of enhanced Communist Russian power aroused many, particularly in the United States, for some felt that it was too high a price to have paid to insure victory. On the other hand, Soviet leaders continued to suspect the capitalist powers of the basest motives and to feel certain of the eventual breakdown of capitalist economy. As mutual hostility grew, each side became more confirmed in its fears and suspicions.

On matters considered during the first two years of peace, Russia disagreed with Great Britain and the United States more often than she agreed. Many of the divisive issues involved genuine conflicts of interests; but some were factitious, being used by Russia for bargaining purposes only, and others were the product of hostility and distrust.

The sharpest conflict arose over Germany, where most was at stake. The Allied Control Council, which had been formed for the purpose of establishing economic unity among the four occupied zones and building political unity upon that, soon showed itself unable to fulfill its purposes. It could operate only on the basis of unanimity, a condition made impossible by the Soviet opposition to the policy of the other occupying powers and their opposition to Soviet policy. And as long as that body was ineffectual in its work, the Council of Foreign Ministers, though it met frequently, could not accomplish its task of making a peace treaty with Germany. As time passed, the Soviet zone became more closely tied to Russia, and the possibility of German unification became more remote.

Co-operation in Germany was hindered by three issues of major significance:

1) Russia insisted that $10 billion (the figure suggested by her at Yalta) be considered the definite amount of reparations to be paid by Germany in capital, current production, and labor. The other powers refused to accept that figure as definite and, basing themselves on the Potsdam agreement, argued for reparation payments in capital only.

2) Russia demanded that the Ruhr, the industrial heart of Germany, located in the British zone, be placed under four-power control; the others rejected that demand.

3) Russia held that the German territory placed under Polish administration by the Potsdam agreement should be considered as irrevocably Polish; the other powers held that the arrangement was provisional, to be maintained only until a peace treaty with Germany could be signed.

Perhaps even more important was an issue that was not formulated: whether or not Germany would be used to tip the scales in favor of the

West or of Russia. The USSR wanted to make certain that any government of a unified Germany be at least friendly—and probably subservient—to Moscow, and it would oppose any arrangement for unification that did not insure such a government. Maintenance of Soviet control in Eastern Germany was therefore an advantage to be carefully guarded.

In trying to draft the treaty of peace for Austria, the occupying powers —the USSR against the three others—reached an impasse that was not to be broken for ten years. Disagreement arose from two overt issues: the definition of what constituted the former German assets in Austria, which had been awarded to Russia by the Potsdam agreement; and Yugoslavia's claim (favored by Russia) to parts of Austrian Carinthia and Styria. On those points, conference after conference ended in deadlock. It was suspected that Russia wanted to delay the making of a peace treaty in order to use the need for maintenance of communications between Russia and the Soviet zone in Austria as an excuse for keeping troops in Rumania and Hungary. Moreover, the prospect of a treaty might be useful in bargaining on other matters.

Tension and dispute were common all along the perimeter of the Soviet empire, and opposition to Soviet tactics sometimes prompted appeals to what was beginning to be called the Anglo-American bloc. In January, 1946, Iran complained to the Security Council of the United Nations against Soviet interference in her affairs. The Soviet delegate to the council used his veto (setting a precedent for frequent use of the veto on behalf of the USSR) to block action on the issue, but the USSR subsequently evacuated its troops from that area. In the fall of 1946, Soviet demands on Turkey (already noted) touched off a diplomatic disturbance that ended with Turkish refusal to accede to Russian wishes and clear evidence that Washington and London favored Ankara rather than Moscow. And, at the end of 1946, when the Greek Government brought before the Security Council the accusation that the Soviet satellites Yugoslavia, Bulgaria, and Albania were giving aid to the rebels who had been engaged in civil war with the British-backed government since 1944, the Soviet delegate again used the veto, to prevent action against the satellites.

Soviet policy in Eastern Europe brought on acrimonious disputes when Great Britain and the United States denounced the USSR for ignoring the British and American representatives on the Allied Control Councils in Bulgaria, Rumania, and Hungary; for violating the Yalta and Potsdam agreements to permit free elections in Poland, Bulgaria, Rumania, and Hungary; for taking a high-handed attitude toward foreign property rights in Eastern Europe; and for denying outsiders access to the satellite countries. But denunciations were simply countered with denunciations. By the end of 1946 it was evident that, by Soviet interpretation, "friendly" states were those subservient to Moscow and hostile to the West.

Tension in Europe was matched by tension in the Far East. In 1946, the USSR and the United States, the joint occupying powers in Korea, began negotiations for the establishment of an independent Korean government, but their efforts broke down over Soviet proposals intended to guarantee a government oriented toward Moscow. In contrast to the stalemate in Korea was the checkmate of Russia in Japan. As the chief occupying power in Japan, the United States proposed to have the decisive voice in dealing with the defeated country; and Soviet protests, combined with those of other countries, resulted only in superficial changes in the machinery for formulating occupation policy. American influence was not limited by the changes.

The differences between Soviet and Anglo-American policies became a serious handicap to the work of the United Nations. The irreconcilability of those differences was plainly demonstrated when the question of international control of the atomic bomb was being considered. On the basis of an offer made by the United States to share its secret of atomic bomb production, the United Nations established the Atomic Energy Commission early in 1946 to prepare a plan whereby the use of atomic energy might be outlawed for military purposes but made available to all for peaceful purposes. The American delegation on the commission was soon standing in complete opposition to the Soviet delegation, for the United States proposed to release its secret only after the establishment of an international inspection and supervisory authority capable of detecting the preparation of atomic weapons, while the USSR insisted that the United States destroy its atomic bombs and that thereafter the United Nations establish an international authority with limited inspection rights. The Russians, then engaged in developing their own atomic weapons, stood fast in their opposition to any arrangement permitting international inspectors free access to their territory. The United States would not throw away its advantage without assurance against misuse of the atomic bomb. And there the matter rested.

Thus, within less than two years after the end of hostilities, the hope for Big Three unity had been virtually dispelled. In consequence, the making of the peace was unfinished; the United Nations was unable to fulfill its most important functions; and Russia held the assurance of future bargaining power by virtue of her position in Eastern Germany, Eastern Austria, and Northern Korea.

OPEN ADMISSION OF DISUNITY.   After the signing of the peace treaties with the former German allies, in February, 1947, the Big Three abandoned even the pretense of partnership. And there was no assurance that the impasse to which their dealings had brought them could be peacefully overcome.

The determination to resolve the unresolved was growing more urgent in the West. And there was now a greater inclination toward the frankness that marked the words of Winston Churchill spoken in 1946:

> From Stettin in the Baltic to Trieste in the Adriatic, an iron curtain has descended across the Continent. Behind that curtain lie all the capitals of the ancient states of central and eastern Europe . . . and all are subject, in one form or another, not only to Soviet influence but to a very high and in some cases increasing measure of control from Moscow. . . .
>
> Whatever conclusions may be drawn from these facts—and facts they are—this is certainly not the liberated Europe we fought to build up. Nor is it one which contains the essentials of permanent peace. . . .
>
> I do not believe that Soviet Russia desires war. What they desire is the fruits of war and the indefinite expansion of their powers and doctrines. . . .
>
> What is needed is a settlement, and the longer this is delayed, the more difficult it will be and the greater our dangers.
>
> From what I have seen of our Russian friends and allies during the war, I am convinced that there is nothing they admire so much as strength, and there is nothing for which they have less respect than for weakness, especially military weakness.
>
> For that reason the old doctrine of a balance of power is unsound. We cannot afford, if we can help it, to work on narrow margins, offering temptations to a trial of strength.[1]

In March, 1947, the United States openly took the initiative by adopting the Truman Doctrine, which called for "containment" of Russia—i.e., the prevention of further extension of Soviet power. The "containment" was to be effected through the provision of military and economic support

---

[1] *New York Times,* March 6, 1946, p. 4.

to those countries on the periphery of the Soviet zone of influence that were directly or indirectly menaced by the USSR. Behind the plan was the belief that internal forces were at work in Russia to weaken the Soviet system and that, while Russia was being prevented from expanding, time would serve as an ally to the United States. The Truman Doctrine, which resulted in aid to Greece, Turkey, China, and Iran, was a direct admission of the existence of two opposing blocs in the world—one led by the USSR, the other led by the United States—and an explicit expression of the generally accepted conviction that the differences between Russia and the West could not be settled by negotiation alone. After its enunciation, the powers of the two hostile blocs began to assert their position more emphatically.

During the remaining months of 1947 the line of division became more incisive. First, the political coalition between Communists and non-Communists came to an end in France and Italy. Then there came a shift in the policy of Communist Parties throughout the Western countries from one of professed co-operation with the governments to one of open opposition.

The changing atmosphere was demonstrated by the revival, in truncated form, of the Communist International. The new organization was formed at the end of September, 1947, by representatives of the Communist and Workers' Parties (in some countries the Communist Party was designated as the Workers' Party) of the USSR, Yugoslavia, Bulgaria, Rumania, Hungary, Poland, Czechoslovakia, France, and Italy, meeting in Poland. There, after they had denounced the United States as an "imperialist" country aiming to dominate the world and having already divided the world into two camps, they set up the Communist Information Bureau. That body, commonly known as the Cominform was organized as a committee of representatives of the nine parties.[1] Its headquarters was established, largely for purposes of camouflage, in Belgrade rather than in Moscow, where the power lay. From Belgrade the Cominform was to serve the parties by organizing and co-ordinating their work and publishing a periodical *(For a Lasting Peace, for a People's Democracy)* to express the Communist point of view.

The dissolution of the Big Three took on economic as well as political forms. In the summer of 1947, as an aid to the European countries in their efforts to meet their postwar economic problems, the United States proposed the Marshall Plan, the purpose of which was European economic rehabilitation by intra-European co-operation bolstered by American economic aid.

---

[1] The Cominform was dissolved in April, 1956.

Although it was stated that the Marshall Plan was intended to weaken Communist influence in Europe by promoting political stability through economic rehabilitation, Washington invited the USSR and her satellites to participate in the plan, and several of the satellites were willing. However, on orders from Moscow, all members of the Soviet bloc rejected the invitation, claiming that the plan was only a move to impose American domination on Europe, and it was adopted only by those countries in the non-Soviet bloc. Russia countered the Marshall Plan by one of her own (called the Molotov Plan by the non-Soviet) for accelerating the integration of the satellite economies with that of the USSR.

By the end of 1947, the "cold war," as the conflict of words and diplomatic deeds had come to be called, was well under way, and no longer was any effort being made to conceal the mutual animosity between Russia and the West.

CONSOLIDATION OF THE SOVIET BLOC.   The dropping of the pretense of unity was followed by the rapid consolidation of the Soviet bloc. The USSR began to draw her satellites closer by speeding up their transformation into people's democracies. (The term "people's democracy" was used by Moscow to classify a political and economic system in transition from a capitalistic to a soviet socialist state.) Albania and Yugoslavia had already become people's democracies in 1946; and between 1947 and 1949, Rumania, Bulgaria, Hungary, Czechoslovakia, and Poland, under pressure from the USSR, were converted into states of that classification. The process of change was often begun by the physical liquidation or imprisonment of those who stood in the way of Russian Communist control and was hastened by veiled or open threats of force against any further opposition.

The use of pressure by Russia resulted in one failure, brought about by the assertion of independence by Yugoslavia in 1948. Yugoslav Communists, having gained power with little aid from Russia, were inclined to think of themselves as masters in their own house. When Moscow attempted to bring them into line by accusing them of errors and heresies and demanding that they confess to their guilt, they proved stubbornly independent. In retribution, Moscow had the Yugoslav Communist Party expelled from the Cominform and its headquarters moved to Bucharest in June, 1948. Thereafter the USSR and the satellites waged a cold war against the defecting country.

Progress in Korea, Germany, and China helped to compensate for that one setback. Following the breakdown of American-Soviet negotiations in Korea, the Korean Communists, under Soviet protection, established the

Korean People's Democratic Republic[1] in September, 1948. Although the presence of American troops south of the 38th parallel limited the jurisdiction of the new republic to the area north of that parallel, it claimed to speak for the entire Korean people. However, under the safeguard of American troops, South Korea established a separate government, that of the Republic of Korea, claiming the same jurisdiction as that of the other government— all of Korea.

In Germany the process was repeated with variations. On May 8, 1949, representatives of the German population in the American, French and British zones of occupation adopted a constitution which was soon placed in operation as the fundamental law of the three zones, under the name of the Federal Republic of Germany. That was followed, on May 30, by the convening of an assembly of German delegates in the Soviet zone and its adoption of a constitution establishing the German Democratic Republic in that zone. The latter constitution, which followed the pattern of the constitutions of other people's democracies, came into force on October 7, 1949. The Federal Republic of Germany, the territory of which was still occupied by the troops of Western powers, was drawn into the Western bloc of nations; and the German Democratic Republic, the territory of which was still occupied by Soviet troops, was drawn into the Soviet bloc.

Meanwhile, the civil war in China was going in favor of the Communists. Early in 1949, the Communist armies succeeded in crushing the power of the Chinese Nationalist government on the mainland of China and forcing it to withdraw, with its remaining troops, to the island of Formosa. By September, the Chinese Communists had set up a new government on the mainland, the People's Republic of China, adding some 500 million people to the Soviet bloc.

As Communist political power was being extended, the USSR was tightening military and economic ties with the satellite countries. Czechoslovakia had signed a treaty of mutual assistance with the USSR in 1943, and Poland, in 1945. In 1948 similar treaties were concluded with Rumania, Hungary, Bulgaria and Finland. The provisions of those treaties followed a common pattern: the signatories promised military assistance to each other in the event of attack by Germany "or any state allied to the latter." Literally, they were not directed against the Western powers, but the clause "or any state allied to the latter" could be construed as indicating them. In Asia, the USSR already had a treaty of mutual assistance with the Mon-

---

[1] Countries that were classified as people's democracies might adopt one of three designations: "people's republic," "democratic republic," or "people's democratic republic."

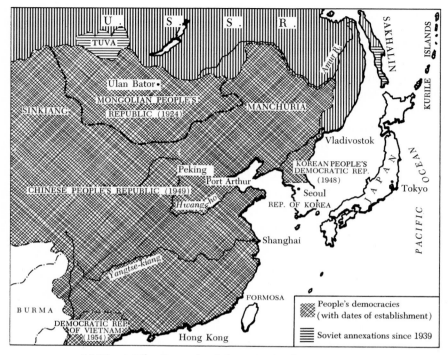

MAP 16. The Growth of Communist Power in Asia

golian People's Republic; and on February 14, 1950, she signed a treaty with the Chinese People's Republic, providing for mutual assistance in the event of an attack on either party by Japan "or states allied to it." In all cases, the treaties were followed by close military co-operation. The satellites adopted Soviet models for the manufacture of arms, copied Soviet forms of military training, and accepted, in many instances, Soviet officers as military advisers.

Likewise the economic life of the satellite countries had become more and more bound up with that of Russia. The connection was strengthened in Europe by the formation on January 25, 1949, of the Council for Economic Mutual Assistance (COMECON), consisting of representatives of the USSR, Czechoslovakia, Bulgaria, Hungary, Poland, and Rumania. In the Far East, the Chinese People's Republic agreed in March, 1950, to the formation of several Chinese-Soviet companies.

CONSOLIDATION OF THE WESTERN BLOC.   Meanwhile the Western powers moved on from economic to military collaboration, the high point in which was the signing of the North Atlantic Pact on April 4, 1949, by the United States, Canada, Great Britain, France, Belgium, The Netherlands, Luxemburg, Norway, Denmark, Iceland, Italy, and Portugal. The pact provided for (1) a military alliance guaranteeing the signatories aid if attacked in Europe or North America and (2) a permanent organization, the North Atlantic Treaty Organization (NATO), to maintain a military defense force composed of contingents supplied by the member nations.

Although the North Atlantic Pact did not so state, it was clearly a defensive alliance against Russia. Evidence of that was shown by efforts, begun in 1951, to bring the Federal Republic of Germany into the NATO. If war should come from the East, Germany would be one of the most important battlefields, and the West Germans might be a liability unless they could be won over to the support of the NATO.

While the Federal Republic of Germany was being brought into the camp of the Western powers a parallel undertaking was in process on the other side of the world, with Japan. In 1950 the United States and Great Britain undertook to break the long deadlock over peace terms for Japan by taking independent action to override the Soviet delaying tactics. They prepared drafts of a peace treaty and, after consultation with the interested countries, edited a final draft for submission to an international conference to be held in San Francisco in September, 1951. The highlights of the draft were (1) that Japan would renounce claim to southern Sakhalin and the Kurile Islands, leaving the way open for later formal cession of those areas to the USSR; (2) that Japanese sovereignty, including the right to rearm and to be free from foreign occupation, would be acknowledged; and (3) that foreign powers, by agreement with Japan, would have the right to station troops on Japanese territory (a provision understood to be particularly favorable to the United States).

When the conference convened, the Soviet representative, Andrei Gromyko, denounced the proposed treaty as "not a peace treaty but a treaty for the preparation of a new war in the Far East," and proposed radical changes in it. His proposals were rejected by the conference; and a peace treaty based on the Anglo-American proposals was signed by forty-eight nations on September 8, while the Soviet Union demonstratively refused assent to it.

THREATS TO PEACE.   The tension that accompanied the widening of the breach between the two antipathetic camps was increased by the urgency of acute, unresolved problems such as those resulting from the divisions in Germany, Austria, and Korea and from the ambiguous position of Trieste.

Negotiations on those problems had failed; yet open war was apparently considered neither feasible nor desirable by Russia.

In June, 1948, the Russians, in an effort to force agreement to Soviet demands in Germany, began to bar land and water shipments from Western Germany to the American, British, and French sectors of Berlin. Thereupon the other powers started sending in supplies by planes, which could not be stopped without the open use of force. Russia was then faced by the choice of reopening the transportation channels or making the first belligerent move. She made her choice in May, 1949, when, for the first time since December, 1947, the Council of Foreign Ministers met; she agreed then to abandon obstructionist tactics and to permit the resumption of routine deliveries to all sectors.

A year later the center of conflict between the Soviet bloc and the Western powers was shifted to Korea as a result of the invasion of the territory of the Republic of Korea by the army of the Korean People's Democratic Republic on June 25, 1950. The situation was taken under consideration by the Security Council of the United Nations, but the Soviet delegate to the Council, Jacob Malik, failed to attend the first meetings devoted to it. And when other members called upon the North Koreans to suspend hostilities and withdraw their troops and recommended that, if such steps were not taken, the members of the United Nations give military support to the Republic of Korea, Moscow denounced the action as illegal. The Western powers, however, followed the recommendations of the Security Council and began sending troops to Korea. The United States, whose troops were the first United Nations forces to become engaged, assumed the greatest responsibility in supplying leadership and men.

Even after the situation had become internationally prominent, the significance of the hostilities was not entirely clear. It was clear enough that the North Korean invasion was an act of aggression. And it was evident that the North Koreans were receiving the approval and support of Russia and of those countries oriented toward her: while proclaiming her neutrality, Russia offered logistical and political support; and Communist China sent a "volunteer" army to bolster the North Korean forces. However, neither the degree of Russia's responsibility for the initiation of the fighting nor the nature of her intentions with respect to the Korean venture could be satisfactorily gauged. Had Moscow endorsed the invasion? If so, had the Soviet leaders assumed that the United Nations would permit the destruction of the Republic of Korea? Or had they knowingly accepted the risk of a general war?

When Malik, in June, 1951, suggested that the hostilities could be ended by direct negotiations between the combatant forces, his words were taken by the West to mean that Russia did not want a general conflict. Negotiations were begun but soon bogged down over the question of the forcible repatriation of all prisoners in the hands of the United Nations forces. In October, 1952, no mutually satisfactory resolution of the issue having been reached, the talks were suspended while fighting continued as before, with no clear-cut military advantage for either side.

The domestic scene

RECONSTRUCTION. The immediate domestic task at the end of the war was reconstruction, a staggering task that many experts expected to require at least a decade, perhaps two. One of the many major problems was that of returning some 20 million persons to their homes and absorbing them into the economy. The number included more than 8 million demobilized soldiers, about 4.5 million persons who had been in the German labor force, army, or prison camps, and some 8 million who had been evacuated to Asiatic Russia. The conditions under which this movement of peoples took place were often primitive, and the circumstances to which they returned were harsh; but work was plentiful, and most of the returnees were soon involved in the great effort of reconstruction.

A major problem of a different order was that of the inflationary pressures caused by the wartime drop in the production of civilian goods and the inverse increase in civilian savings. The government dealt draconically with this problem by issuing new currency in December, 1947, exchanging the new for the old at a ratio of one new ruble for ten old ones, and by reducing the value of bank deposits and bonds by smaller ratios. At the same time, to offset in part the hardships brought about by the currency reform, rationing was ended, and the prices of many foods and goods were reduced.

A third major problem—a basic one—was the restoration of industry and agriculture to their prewar capacity. The Fourth Five-Year Plan (for 1946-50) included the ambitious objective of simultaneously completing reconstruction and exceeding prewar levels of production. By the end of 1950, prewar industrial levels were regained, indicating a remarkably rapid recovery in that area of the economy; housing, however, was still below prewar levels, and agricultural production was still unsatisfactory.

RETURN TO PEACETIME PROCEDURES. Most wartime practices were

transformed with as little delay as possible in order to facilitate the return to prewar routine. The State Committee of Defense was dissolved on September 4, 1945, and its functions were returned to the ordinary organs of party and state. Soon thereafter martial law was ended in all parts of the country except in those regions added to the USSR after 1939.

No elections had been held during the war, and the deputies elected to the Supreme Soviet in 1937 retained their seats until after the first postwar election, on February 10, 1946. As in former years the election results showed a high degree of unanimity, produced by lack of choice rather than by agreement: 99 per cent of the voters put checks on ballots that bore the name of only one candidate. When the newly elected Supreme Soviet met in March, it went through the formality of electing as the chief executive and legislative officials those persons selected in advance by the Politburo. The roster of elected officials indicated a fairly stable leadership: Stalin was reaffirmed as Premier, and Molotov remained in charge of foreign affairs. By and large, few changes were made in personnel. One of them resulted from the resignation of the popular Chairman of the Presidium of the Supreme Soviet, the aged and ailing Kalinin, who was replaced as titular head of the state by Nicholas Shvernik.

In some respects the return to peace did not bring the re-establishment of prewar routine. Although the party charter required that a congress, legally the source of authority, be convened every three years, there had been none since 1939, and there was no evidence that the calling of one was even considered at the end of the war. To be sure, party congresses had become empty formalities under Stalin, but it is noteworthy that even the formality was now apparently ignored.

A similar situation had developed with respect to the Central Committee. That body, which was required by party rules to meet at least once every four months, now rarely met. However, the fiction was maintained that major party decrees emanated from the committee when in fact they were decided by the Politburo or by Stalin. One decision, said to have been made by the Central Committee at a meeting in March, 1946, was particularly important as an indication of the political future of the country. It was the decision to raise Beria and Malenkov to full membership in the Politburo and to add as candidates Nicholas Bulganin, a former textile worker who had risen rapidly in political position during the war, and Alexis Kosygin, former Premier of the R.S.F.S.R. After those changes, the members of the Politburo were Stalin, Molotov, Voroshilov, Kaganovich, Mikoyan, Andreyev, Khrushchev, Zhdanov, Kalinin, Malenkov, and Beria; and the candidates were Voznesensky, Shvernik, Bulganin, and Kosygin. The inner core of the Soviet leadership had changed little since the late 1930's, and the few younger men who had been added could be depended upon to continue the policies established by the older ones.

READJUSTMENT OF POLITICAL CONTROLS. In directing the return to peacetime conditions, the Soviet leaders gave high priority to the strengthening, where necessary, of political controls that had been weakened or permitted to weaken, during the war. In the course of the war, for morale purposes, much of the ideological pressure that had been so characteristic of Soviet life had been relaxed. Marxism-Leninism had been deemphasized, old-fashioned nationalism encouraged, and religion treated with some consideration. It had seemed advisable, also, especially at the beginning of the war, to moderate the ideological attack on the capitalist powers: Stalin had gone so far as to say, in 1941, that ". . . England and the United States possess elementary democratic liberties." Moreover, during the war the people had picked up two disturbing notions: that the people of Western Europe and the United States were materially better off than those of the USSR (an observation made both by Red soldiers and by captured Soviet civilians) and that the war hardships of Soviet citizens should be rewarded by the provision of more material benefits and some relaxation of the drive under which they had been working. Now it was thought necessary to turn the minds of the people back to the proper appreciation of the Soviet system, to overcome their approval of Western ways, and to justify further deprivations.

Consequently, even before the final guns were fired, the Communist Party began a new ideological drive. The tenets of Marxism-Leninism were reaffirmed and restated, and the differences between Soviet Russia and the capitalist world rather than the likenesses were now underlined. On February 9, 1946, Stalin pointed out that World War II was the "inevitable result" of "modern monopoly capitalism," which could be expected to produce other wars—a point that had not been made since June, 1941. His pronouncement was the prelude to a campaign among writers, musicians, dramatists, scholars, and scientists against "subservience to bourgeois culture," "cosmopolitanism," and indifference to the political requirements of the party. Novels, symphonies, plays, and scholarly monographs were carefully examined, and any slip was immediately publicized and its perpetrator severely reprimanded. Prominent among those affected by official disapproval were the composers Shostakovich, Prokofiev, Khatchaturian, and Myaskovsky; the poetess Anna Akhmatova; the satirist Zoshchenko; and the dramatist Tikhonov. "The central task of Soviet literature and art," stated the party, "is the propagandizing of Soviet ideology, of the idea of the Bolshevik Party, of the political position of the party and the Soviet state. . . ." Since the party was supreme, its statement became the basis of accepted expression in all fields.

THE UNWILLING AND THE UNWANTED.   Although the great majority of those who left Russia during hostilities, either of their own will or against it, returned to their homes, about 500,000 (exact figures are not available) Russians, Ukrainians, Lithuanians, Latvians, and Estonians refused to go back. Some resisted the efforts of the Repatriation Missions because of fear of punishment for collaboration, some because of hatred for the Soviet regime. The non-returners formed a second generation of Soviet émigrés, often joining hands with the survivors of the first in organizations directed toward the overthrow of the Soviet system. Many, making homes in various parts of the world, foreswore politics in favor of assimilation by their new homelands.

For others no choice was possible. In the wake of the victorious Red Army, from 1943 on, there followed officials whose task was to conduct political mopping-up operations. The records of those who had lived under Axis occupation authority were examined for evidence of collaboration with the enemy; and the ones found guilty were treated with severity— sent to the gallows, deported, or assigned to labor camps. National groups in which the incidence of collaboration was exceptionally high were collectively punished without regard to individual guilt or innocence. Among them were Crimean Tatars, Kalmyks, Chechen, and Karachai, about 600,000 of whom were summarily deported from their homes to distant parts of Asiatic Russia.[1]

The areas annexed to the USSR since 1939 presented special problems. In some—Latvia, for example—Sovietization had barely begun when it was interrupted by the war; in others, such as Carpatho-Ukraine, it had now to be initiated. The government's current policy was to assimilate new territories into the Soviet system at a fast pace, accomplishing forthwith, in these areas, what had taken a generation elsewhere. The results, while quickly evident, were achieved only through the ruthlessness of wholesale arrests and deportation of those who resisted.

COMPROMISE AND CHANGE.   The trend toward stabilization and nationalism that had begun in the mid 1930's continued into the postwar

---

[1] In 1957 the Kalmyks, Chechen, and Karachai were permitted to return to their homes.

period, reinforced by certain lessons of the war. That fact indicated that those in power were prepared to set aside temporarily or even to jettison many of the changes brought about by the November Revolution if, while so doing, they could strengthen loyalties or assure themselves of stable social institutions and yet not sacrifice the goals that they considered indispensable.

One indication of their attitude was the dropping of appellations most closely associated with the early days of Communism. In 1946 the Supreme Soviet approved the substitution of the title "minister" for "people's commissar," thus bringing Soviet nomenclature into conformity with that in common use in Europe. In the same year, the names of the Red Army and the Red Navy were changed to the Soviet Army and the Soviet Navy.

When, at a reception for Soviet higher officers in May, 1945, Stalin proposed a toast to "the Russian people because it is the outstanding of all nations that constitute the Soviet Union," he broke with Communist tradition by singling out one nationality for preference. That sentiment, which once would have been condemned as the heresy of "Great Russian chauvinism," was probably prompted by the fact that the Great Russians had been the most loyal of the several nationalities during the war. In theory all Soviet nationalities still remained equal, but thereafter in Soviet usage the Great Russians were accepted as the "oldest brother in the family of Soviet peoples."

Seeking to retain the support of the religious-minded as well as to make use of the Church abroad, the Soviet Government continued its wartime concessions to religion: religious bodies were permitted to maintain their ecclesiastical organizations, train clerics, publish religious literature, and re-open many churches. Fanatic anti-religious activities became taboo. The basic attitude of the Soviet Government and the party, however, remained unchanged. Religion was still considered a remnant of superstition that would disappear in time. Complete separation of Church and state continued, and all the cultural resources of the state were employed toward rearing a nonreligious generation.

The attention that had been given to the strengthening of the family in the prewar period had not been lessened during the war years; in fact, the population losses during those years had increased the need for continuing the emphasis on large and stable families. Accordingly, on July 8, 1944, a law was enacted to encourage large families by means of special honors and grants. Increasing families were given progressively increasing money grants, and special services were provided to assist parents in the

An example of Stalinolatry: the "Victory Memorial," unveiled in 1950 (lower structure 110 feet high, statue 53 feet high), on a hill dominating Erevan, capital of the Armenian S.S.R.

care of large families. The same law imposed discriminatory taxes on bachelors, spinsters, and couples with fewer than three children. It also made marriage regulations more stringent by providing that common law marriages be no longer recognized and that divorces be granted thereafter only by court action.

Most important of all was the increasing trend toward social differentiation. By Soviet definition there could be no classes in the USSR; but social differentiation, as understood by Western social scientists, was growing sharper nonetheless and actually receiving encouragement from the government. It was produced in part by inequality in material rewards, which made for great disparities in the standards of living among the various wage groups. Income differentiation encouraged social differentiation; the factory director with his large apartment, automobile, and summer home, lived in a social world quite distinct from that of the unskilled laborer with his one-room apartment. Income differences were reinforced by overt status distinctions; for example, during the war and after, the practice of wearing uniforms indicating the position of the wearer was introduced among many of the personnel in the Ministry of Foreign Affairs, the procurators' offices, the coal and iron ore industries, and the railroad and river transport systems. Finally, it was becoming easier for those with high income and status to give their children a favored start in life. It is true that numerous scholarships made it possible for promising children of the poor to receive the education necessary for vocational advancement; but the system of tuition fees for secondary and higher education, introduced in 1940 as an allegedly emergency measure, was continued, and that fee might be an insuperable hurdle for the average poor child while no deterrent to the well-to-do. Social differentiation made for loyalty among the favored groups and added to social stability in general. Apparently that was what the Soviet leaders wanted, despite the probability of future difficulty in controlling the pressure that the socially favored would be likely to exert in order to gain more favors.

THE LAST YEARS OF STALIN. On December 21, 1949, millions of people in the USSR and elsewhere in the Communist world celebrated Stalin's seventieth birthday in extravagant style. Thousands of gifts and congratulatory messages poured into Moscow from every direction. A huge picture of the leader was suspended over the city from balloons. And Soviet and satellite dignitaries were more fulsome than ever in their public references to him, declaring that the day marked "the apotheosis of his [Stalin's] political success, power, and glory," extolling him as "a wholly unique strategist," "the organizer of the greatest, unprecedented victories in the history of world politics," and "the beloved leader and teacher of progressive humanity."

Stalin, at that time and in the remaining years of his life, held power that was practically unassailable. Many were opposed to the regime itself, and many objected to certain of its policies; but the country's political institutions effectively prevented the organization of opposition. So strong was the grip of the regime that the only way in which its policies could be changed was by the will of the leadership, and the leadership appeared to be unanimously committed to keeping them intact.

However, it later became evident that, as Russia entered the 1950's, some leaders privately interpreted many of the policies being followed as either self-defeating or inefficient. They were aware that the apparatus directing the economy was cumbersome and over-centralized. They were conscious of the heavy cost incurred by the Soviet insistence that the satellite states slavishly follow the Soviet model. They admitted to themselves the inadequacy of the current dogma according to which the experience of World War II, in which Stalin had proved himself to be "the greatest military genius of modern times," was the only useful guide to strategic preparation for future wars. They could not but observe that the Soviet arts had become sterile as a result of the mechanical application of the formula of "socialist realism." They had doubts about the wisdom of some of the country's policies in its relations with the Western bloc. And they were quite conscious of the fact that the younger generation, reared completely under the Soviet system, was in many respects a disappointment—apparently loyal but, to a marked degree, politically indifferent.

For the most part, the evident shortcomings had resulted from the rigid application of policies to which Stalin was committed, but not even his colleagues in the Politburo dared to take issue with him. For a period after the Great Purge, Stalin, without relaxing his firm mastery of the Politburo, had apparently used some circumspection in the application of his power. Later, however, he had become increasingly suspicious of the motives of those who failed to manifest sufficient support for his ideas and he was increasingly inclined to equate dissent with treason. This change had appeared evident in his dealings with Voznesensky, one of the younger leaders generally considered to be destined for a brilliant future. After Voznesensky had in some way aroused the suspicion of Stalin, he had been removed from his party and governmental posts in March, 1949, and then placed under arrest, subsequently (in September, 1950) to be shot—all this in strict secrecy from the public. If there had been any doubt among members of the Politburo about the means to which Stalin would resort in maintaining his unquestioned authority, the fate of Voznesensky removed it.

Not only did Stalin display increasing suspicion of his colleagues; he also encroached steadily on their share in the making of policy. He called meetings of the Politburo at irregular intervals and often met with only part of that body. He was clearly making considerable headway on a course he had begun during the Great Purge, concentrating effective control over both the party and the political police in his own hands. The ineffectiveness of the Politburo in this situation was compounded by the tendency of several members to play on Stalin's suspicions and to court his favor, thus advancing their own positions at the expense of the others.

Under the circumstances, the pattern of future development seemed inalterably fixed. When the Fifth Five-Year Plan was inaugurated, in 1951 (with fulfillment date set as 1955), few doubted that there would be a sixth five-year plan in 1956, a seventh in 1961, and so on into the indefinite future. In 1952, however, there were signs that Stalin himself was planning some changes. Portents were evident in the conduct and decisions of the long-overdue Nineteenth Congress of the All-Union Communist Party (Bolsheviks), which was held in October, 1952.

At this congress, Stalin sidestepped tradition by not delivering the chief report, a duty customarily performed by the acknowledged head of the party, but having George Malenkov present it. This act was interpreted as an indication that he thought of the younger man as his successor. Further deviation from tradition was signified when the congress adopted a new set of party rules, including three notable provisions: (1) the general strengthening of the higher party bodies in their control over the lower, (2) the changing of the formal name of the party to the Communist Party of the Soviet Union, dropping the designation "Bolsheviks," and (3) the changing of the name of the Politburo to "Presidium of the Central Committee." At the close of the congress, the newly elected Central Committee chose for the Presidium twenty-five members and eleven candidates, thus increasing the personnel of the party's policy-making body from twelve members and candidates. In addition, a small inner Buro was formed—although the new party rules had made no provision for it—to direct the work of the Presidium.

The enlargement of the policy-making body (the Presidium of the Central Committee was now three times the size of the old Politburo) was apparently part of a scheme whereby Stalin hoped to effect another major purge in the party and the government. The number of new members was

sufficient to form a large majority, which could overrule any efforts of resistance to Stalin that the other members, veterans of the Politburo, might
offer. Of the latter, there were only nine besides Stalin: Beria, Bulganin,
Kaganovich, Khrushchev, Malenkov, Mikoyan, Molotov, Shvernik, and
Voroshilov.[1] And only one of the candidates, Kosygin, was of the older
ranks. It was clear that the veteran party men could now offer little effective opposition if Stalin should choose—as it was believed that he would—
to remove some of his old comrades from office.

During the remaining months of 1952 there were many rumors of executions that had taken place or were to take place. Later many of the rumors
were substantiated. It was learned that during the summer a group of
prominent Jewish Communists, secretly imprisoned since 1948—among
them Solomon A. Lozovsky, a party leader of long standing; David Bergel-
son, probably the ablest of Soviet Jewish novelists; and a number of
others—had been condemned on spurious charges and executed. Their deaths
had followed four years of harassment of organized Jewish life in the USSR,
allegedly motivated by the conviction that Soviet Jews were guilty of
dividing their loyalty between the USSR and the newly formed state of
Israel. Following the Nineteenth Congress many persons, including a great
number of Jews, were secretly arrested on charges of espionage, wrecking,
or embezzlement. Of particular prominence were nine eminent doctors, who
were falsely accused of various kinds of misconduct: having ties with international Jewish organizations, with American intelligence, or with
British intelligence, and hastening the deaths of several high military and
naval officers. Under torture during the investigation, they confessed
to guilt for acts they had neither committed nor planned; and on January
13, 1953, the report of their arrest and confession was made public. Everything was being put in order for a public trial—possibly as a prelude to
many others. Soviet newspapers began to editorialize in the tone, and
often with the same words, used during the Great Purge, pointing out that
"predatory imperialists," in their attempt to "develop subversive activity,"
were making use of various "unreliable" elements in the Soviet population.
Such charges were accompanied by reminders of Stalin's well-known contention that, as long as the USSR continued to be encircled by the capitalist
world, it would be exposed to subversion by foreign agents.

---

[1] It will be noted that four men who had been on the roster of the Politburo in 1946
were not among those newly named to the Presidium. Kalinin and Zhdanov had died
of natural causes, and Voznesensky had been executed. Andreyev, apparently under criticism for errors of judgment, was not chosen for the Presidium but was elected, by the
congress, to the Central Committee.

SOVFOTO

Funeral of Joseph Stalin, March 1953
Pallbearers (left to right): Shvernik, Kaganovich, Bulganin, Molotov, Vasily
Stalin (son of Joseph Stalin), Malenkov, and Beria

While this promotion of sentiment for the public trial was still in process,
the country was shaken by an incident for which there had been no official
preparation. On March 5, 1953, Joseph Stalin died, of a brain hemorrhage.

The spontaneous response of the public to Stalin's death was that of
a people stricken by sincere grief at the loss of one whom they had been
taught to consider a great leader and benefactor. Among those who had
been officially associated with him, there were ostensibly similar sentiments;
many of these expressed sentiments, however, were to be revealed by later

developments as less than sincere. To almost all, it was evident that Russia's future would be different from her immediate past. Stalin, with his driving energy and implacable will, had indeed put his personal stamp on the Soviet system. Yet he had by no means enlisted as disciples all of the men of strength in the party and government, nor had he been able to rid officialdom of all potent enemies. Whoever might take up the duties of leadership and whatever might be the attitudes and ambitions of those to whom power was to come, the USSR was unavoidably headed for change. It was not to be expected that there would be a second Stalin.

THIRTY-ONE / THE USSR AFTER STALIN

S talin's sudden death imposed critical strains on the Soviet system for a
time. Of initial concern was the matter of succession: although Stalin
had given some indications that he favored Malenkov as his successor,
he had not made his intentions explicit, nor had he provided any means for
the transfer of his extensive personal power to the man or men who should
follow him. In addition, there was the pressing necessity of maintaining
governmental control; even a temporary weakening might be sufficient to
encourage open dissidence in the country, for there was an obvious prev-
alence of ill will toward the regime. To meet the exigencies of the situation
required both political skill and personal shrewdness, qualities that some
of the remaining leaders ably demonstrated. As a result, the regime was
proved resilient enough not only to meet the strains imposed by the sudden
change but also to increase in strength.

Transition

SUCCESSION.   The first acts of the post-Stalin period were directed by
eight members of the Presidium of the Central Committee, each of them
an experienced veteran of the Politburo: Beria, Bulganin, Kaganovich,
Khrushchev, Malenkov, Mikoyan, Molotov, and Voroshilov. Apparently,
during the last hours of Stalin's life, these men had privately planned to
assume the leadership, relegating to secondary roles their current associates
and former Politburo colleagues Kosygin and Shvernik. Their subsequent
actions indicated that, from the beginning, the policies by which they intended to administer the party and government were based on certain con-

stant considerations: (1) the wisdom of following quasi-legal procedure while keeping effective control in their own hands, (2) the necessity of preventing any one of their number from overpowering the others, (3) the need to correct certain of Stalin's policies, and (4) the urgency of presenting a united front to the country and the world. They lost no time on preliminary deliberations, but took up at once the task that they had commissioned themselves to perform.

The formalities of clothing the decisions of the new leaders with legal authority were the first to be carried out. On March 7, the day after the news of Stalin's death was made public, it was announced that a joint meeting of the Central Committee, the Council of Ministers, and the Presidium of the Supreme Soviet had made sweeping changes in official personnel and organization. They included, according to the official statement, the reduction of the number of members in the Presidium of the Central Committee from twenty-five to ten, the eight mentioned above and two others, Maxim Saburov and Michael Pervukhin; and of the number of candidates, from eleven to four: Shvernik (demoted from membership), Panteleimon Ponomarenko, Leonid Melnikov, and Mir Bagirov. The statement disclosed also this assignment of important posts: Malenkov was to serve as Premier; Bulganin, as Minister of Defense, with authority over army and navy; Beria, as Minister of Internal Affairs, with authority over both regular and political police;[1] Mikoyan, as Minister of Domestic and Foreign Trade; Voroshilov, as Chairman of the Presidium of the Supreme Soviet; Kaganovich, Beria, Molotov, and Bulganin, as First Deputy Chairmen of the Council of Ministers; and Khrushchev, as an official devoting himself exclusively to party administration. All changes were declared subject to final confirmation by the Supreme Soviet, a meeting of which was set for March 14.

The Supreme Soviet did not meet until the 15th, delayed probably by the behind-the-scenes struggle growing out of Malenkov's effort to realize

---

[1] The political police organization had undergone a series of changes in the twelve years preceding its coming under the authority of Beria. In February, 1941, the Chief Administration of State Security (political police) was separated from the NKVD and transformed into the People's Commissariat of State Security, but the coming of the war made it expedient to reunite the two bodies. In 1943 they were once more separated. Later, after the substitution of the term "ministry" for "people's commissariat," in 1946, they were given new names: Ministry of Internal Affairs (MVD, for *Ministerstvo Vnutrennikh Del*), handling the administration of labor camps and that of regular police; and the Ministry of State Security (MGB, for *Ministerstvo Gosudarstvennoi Bezopastnosti*), dealing with political police functions. Then, immediately after Stalin's death, the MGB was stripped of its separate identity and absorbed into the MVD. In 1962, the MVD was renamed the Ministry for Safeguarding Public Order (MOOP, for *Ministerstvo Okhrany Obshchestvennogo Poryadka*).

his hope of becoming Stalin's successor. His position at first appeared far from weak: as Premier, he was head of the government and, as the senior member of the Secretariat of the Central Committee, he had considerable power over the party apparatus. But his colleagues, by a concerted fight, succeeded in limiting his authority. On March 14, the Central Committee granted his "request" that he be relieved of membership in the Secretariat, and followed that action by approving a revised list of the remaining members. In the new list, Khrushchev, although nominally only one of five secretaries, was given first place, out of alphabetical order—a step preliminary to his being given, six months later, the designation of "first secretary," which would subsequently be capitalized as a title.[1] When the Supreme Soviet met, on the following day, it approved, with its customary unanimity, all changes in personnel and organization submitted to it. The first phase of the succession was now completed. Principal power was distributed among eight men, no one of whom was then in a position to dominate the others. Three of them, however, were in favored positions: Malenkov, as head of the government; Beria, as head of the police; and Khrushchev, as the chief figure in the party apparatus.

It was soon demonstrated that even this distribution of power was not to be an altogether stable one. Beria was the second to threaten the security of the other leaders, presumably trying to use the police as an instrument for attaining personal power. To meet the threat, his colleagues, backed by the leading army marshals, secretly arrested him and several of his police associates and charged them with acts of treason and espionage. Though the charges were probably false, they provided the accusers with quasi-legal grounds for removing Beria from his official positions. And, in December, 1953, after closed trials, he and six of his associates were shot.

Little more than a year later, Malenkov renewed his attempt to enhance his authority; and again he failed. In February, 1955, he was forced to resign his post as Premier in favor of Bulganin. The rebuff, in this case, was administered with much greater leniency than that accorded Beria: Malenkov was permitted to remain in the party Presidium.

For two and a half years after the Malenkov episode, power seemed to be agreeably distributed among the seven leaders and, on the surface at

---

[1] There is some question as to whether or not the title of "General Secretary" was in use at the time of Stalin's death. In any event, it was not used after his death. For a discussion of the matter, see Myron Rush, *The Rise of Khrushchev* (Washington: Public Affairs Press, 1958) 11-14.

least, relations among them were harmonious. Behind this appearance of stability, however, was concealed one disquieting development: Khrushchev's unobstrusive, but effective, accretion of power in the party through the placing of his supporters in key positions. Being seasoned party politicians, his colleagues were aware of what the First Secretary could do with his authority; yet they failed to appreciate the speed and efficiency with which he was gaining control of the party apparatus until it was too late. When the Twentieth Party Congress met, in February, 1956, Khrushchev could count on the support of a majority of the delegates, and, as might have been expected, they elected a Central Committee that would be subject to his influence. Still he either could not or would not use his influence to make an open attack on the position of his fellow leaders; and they were again elected, along with him, to the Presidium.

As the potential threat of Khrushchev's influence became more fully recognized, serious opposition developed and efforts were made to counter his growing strength. In June, 1957, at a meeting of the party Presidium, an anti-Khrushchev faction, led by Molotov, Malenkov, and Kaganovich, fought what proved to be the last battle to prevent his complete triumph. With a majority of the Presidium behind them, they sought to unseat him; and their efforts barely missed being successful. Khrushchev, however, managed to outmaneuver them. He insisted on, and won, consent for a meeting of the Central Committee, where he knew he could control a majority and use it to his own advantage. The results were as he had planned: the three leaders of the opposition were removed from both the Presidium and the Central Committee and replaced by men of Khrushchev's choice. Soon thereafter Molotov, Malenkov, and Kaganovich were consigned to minor governmental posts.

The First Secretary was now in fact—if not in name—the man in control, and he rapidly consolidated his power. He supplanted Bulganin as Premier, in March, 1958; and, with that act, he may be said to have achieved the union of the chief party and governmental posts in his own person—all within five years after Stalin's death. Soon Bulganin was dropped from the highest party organs and given an obscure post. Then, in May, 1960, Voroshilov was replaced as Chairman of the Supreme Soviet by Leonid Brezhnev, one of Khrushchev's protégés; and two months later Voroshilov was removed from the party Presidium. By the summer of 1960, only two of the eight men who had shared power after Stalin's death remained in prominent positions—Khrushchev and Mikoyan, the latter having somehow managed to protect himself from attack. Soviet leadership had reached another point of change.

SOVFOTO

Leading party officials at the Plenum of the Central Committee of the Communist Party of the Soviet Union, held in November 1962: (left to right, front) Kosygin, Brezhnev, Khrushchev, Kozlov, and Suslov

DE-STALINIZATION.   Although there were frequent shifts in leadership in the first five years after Stalin's death, there was a remarkable consistency, both during that period and thereafter, in implementing the original decision to correct those of Stalin's policies that the leaders considered harmful. The various actions they took toward that end are commonly grouped under the somewhat loose, but useful, term "de-Stalinization."

Until early in 1956, de-Stalinization was carried out quietly, without explicit admission that Stalin had erred or that his policies were being corrected. Though deliberately and assiduously abolishing many practices representative of the man who had dominated the party for a generation, the new leaders were careful not to dispel the public's belief in the dogma of party infallibility.

Particular attention was given to correcting abuses of "socialist legality"—abuses such as the employment of irresponsible power by the political police, and the unjust imprisonment or execution of persons in ill favor with the regime. Many of these practices were quickly ended, and the consequences of others were adjusted or undone. An amnesty (the first of three) for several categories of prisoners was issued without delay. Official exoneration was granted to the doctors whose arrest had been announced at the beginning of the year, and the new government declared that their confessions had been obtained by illegal means. With that act, the threat of a purge was ended, and public tension relaxed somewhat. Then in March, 1954, the administration of the political police was removed from the control of the MVD and placed under the newly created Committee of State Security (KBG, for *Komitet Gosudarstvennoi Bezopasnosti*), thus being made more strictly subordinate to party and governmental control than it had been in Stalin's last years.

Another phase of de-Stalinization that the new leaders recognized as important was one that required the utmost finesse: the depreciation of Stalin's prestige as accepted by the public and the termination of many of the practices by which he had been exalted. However, since it was politic for them to maintain the fiction that the government had passed into the hands of Stalin's official heirs, abrupt reversals that would arouse suspicion were to be avoided and, for a time, proper gestures of respect for the former leader were to be made. Shortly after his death, Stalin's body was placed beside that of Lenin in the mausoleum in Red Square, which had come to be the official Communist shrine, and he was extolled as "Lenin's comrade and the inspired continuer of his will." Very gradually thereafter was begun the careful process of changing the public conception of him as a figure to be hallowed. The first official efforts were made by omitting or toning down acts of homage to his memory and teachings; a typical instance was the failure of *Pravda* to mention his birthday on December 21, 1953. Another quietly executed measure was the leaders' alteration of their mode of living. In Stalin's lifetime, they had emulated his ways and maintained residence in the Kremlin, which had been closed to the public; in the year after his death, they gave up their residence within the walls, and before another year had passed, the historic Kremlin had opened its gates to the public.

A corollary to the reduction in Stalin's status was the formal return to "collective leadership"—that is, leadership by legally constituted bodies such as the Central Committee, rather than by individuals (Khrushchev's predominant influence was not interpreted as inconsistent with this policy).

After the new leadership assumed control, the Central Committee began to meet regularly—as it had not done for over fifteen years—and to take up major questions of policy. Other executive bodies followed suit.

Further acts of de-Stalinization involved the suspension of many taboos against intellectual inquiry, artistic expression, and certain contacts with the non-Communist world. The novelist Ilya Ehrenburg, whose works had often proclaimed changes in party policy, heralded this one with *The Thaw* (1954), a novel in which the theme suggested release from a harsh winter (to be interpreted as Stalinist restrictions) and the beginning of spring. The effects of the "thaw" in official policy were indeed evident in many places. In the armed forces, the high command undertook a critical review of Stalinist military thought. Writers were permitted to publish works criticizing certain phases of Soviet life; scholars, to establish some relations with their foreign counterparts; athletic teams, to participate again in international competitions; and Soviet entertainers and artists, to arrange exchange programs with those outside the Communist countries.

Beyond the Soviet borders, evidence of change was to be seen in the relaxation of Moscow's control over the satellites and in the urging of satellite leaders to promote de-Stalinization among their people. An important byproduct of this phase of the new policy was the resumption of friendly relations with Yugoslavia. Khrushchev himself went to Belgrade in May, 1955, and demonstratively formalized the change, at the same time apologizing for Stalin's "errors."

The effects of the changed course were felt even farther afield as the leaders began efforts to reduce tensions in the relations between the USSR and the non-Communist world. The first step was to end the fighting in Korea; this was accomplished by the signing of an armistice on July 27, 1953. Then, in August, Moscow announced that Germany would not be required to pay any more reparations after January 1, 1954; and in January, 1955, it declared the state of war with Germany at an end. In September, 1954, tension in the Far East was reduced by a Soviet agreement to turn over all rights in Manchuria to the Chinese People's Republic. In the following spring, the USSR offered to renew negotiations for an Austrian treaty, this time with serious intent; and on May 15, 1955, ten years after the end of hostilities, Austria was enabled to sign a treaty of peace with the USSR, the United States, Great Britain, and France, bringing to an end the four-power occupation. Four months later the Soviet Government announced the return of leased Porkkala to Finland—more than forty years before the expiration of the lease. And a month thereafter, a Soviet-Japanese pact was signed, ending the state of war that had been in effect between the two countries since 1945.

From almost any point of view, these positive actions by the USSR were impressive. Also impressive was the change in the general tone of Soviet diplomacy from the unyielding and often offensive attitude displayed by Soviet diplomats in Stalin's last years, to one that came to be known as "smiling diplomacy." Khrushchev emphasized the new tone with his frequent trips abroad and the conviviality and good fellowship he expressed.

It is evident that the Soviet leaders had certain aims in mind in this handling of foreign affairs: (1) to mitigate international hostility toward the USSR, (2) to disrupt the Western bloc—in particular, to end NATO, and (3) to win the friendship of those countries, such as India, that were in neither the Soviet nor the Western bloc. To achieve these ends they were ready to make concessions on issues considered to be of secondary importance, but not on those of primary importance—such as the future of Germany.

Because of this reservation, the Soviet Government was only partially successful in its efforts. Although it alleviated international hostility in some quarters and won the friendship of some neutral nations, it could not split the Western bloc while it refused to yield on major issues. In Southeast Asia, for instance, the ties of the Western bloc actually became firmer when the Southeast Asia Treaty Organization (SEATO), a counterpart of Europe's NATO, was formed as a result of Soviet efforts. Again, when the USSR proposed the dissolution of NATO and its replacement by an all-European organization (thereby eliminating American influence in Europe and tipping the balance toward the Soviet bloc), there was little support from NATO members. After that failure, the USSR formalized, by the Warsaw Pact, what was already a fact: the existence of a military organization in the Soviet bloc, which served as a counterbalance to NATO. This pact, a treaty of military alliance providing for a joint military command to be located in Moscow, was signed in Warsaw on May 14, 1955, by Albania, Bulgaria, Czechoslovakia, Hungary, the German Democratic Republic, Poland, Rumania, and the USSR.

THE CRITICAL YEAR, 1956. In some respects, this initial period of change following Stalin's death was like those that had followed the death of Nicholas I and of Plehve. In this instance, as in the former ones, the sequel to the death of the man who had symbolized authoritarian government was a series of governmental concessions that ultimately had the untoward effect of releasing forces of discontent. The Soviet Government's rapid succession of changes after March, 1953, though on the whole gratefully received by those concerned, led even loyal party members to question the infallibility of the party; and among those who had been critical and disaffected during the Stalin regime, they inspired hopes for further change. By 1956, troublesome problems were beginning to grow out of the situation. As it faced the problems it had created, the new government, to be sure, was not in the position of the tsarist government of 1855 and 1904. Now, there was no organized opposition, nor was there any practical or legitimate means by which dissent might be expressed; rather there was a single party with effective means for creating the appearance of unanimous public support for the regime, regardless of opposition. Nevertheless, the party and the government were to find it impossible, without reverting to Stalin's practices, to dissipate all the pressures they released by the program of de-Stalinization.

The party itself was responsible for forcing the pace of change and thus precipitating some of the difficulties produced by it. By 1956 there were appeals from within the organization to make explicit the criticism of Stalin that was being implied, and they finally brought results. At the Twentieth Party Congress, Khrushchev, who twenty years earlier had spoken of Stalin as "the hope, aspiration, and beacon of all advanced and progressive humanity," delivered a lengthy secret speech in which he charged the same man with having created a "cult of the individual," thereby making himself appear "a superman possessing supernatural characteristics"; with having so changed in his later years that he "absolutely did not tolerate collegiality in leadership and work;" and with giving vent to brutal and violent reactions "not only toward everything which opposed him, but also toward that which seemed to his capricious and despotic character, contrary to his concepts." The implication of these charges, that for nearly a generation the country had been under the leadership of a fanatic tyrant whom it had been forced to revere as well as to endure, was considered by the Soviet leaders to be too staggering for public consideration; and the text of the speech was therefore not released for publication.[1]

Although Khrushchev's speech was not made public, other anti-Stalin statements made at the congress were released; and, with their publication,

---

[1] Western sources were able to procure and publish an incomplete version of the speech.

the leaders dropped all pretense of upholding the former leader's policies, acknowledged the policy of de-Stalinization for what it was, and proceeded more openly and boldly in their new course, to which they now gave an aura of legitimacy by calling it a "return to Leninist principles." In the months immediately following the congress, there was a steady succession of breaks with the Stalinist past. The removal of the ubiquitous photographs, paintings, and statues of Stalin was begun,[1] thousands of party members who had been condemned and executed during the Great Purge were posthumously exonerated; many previously banned publications were reissued; the labor laws of 1940 (see p. 662) were repealed; tuition fees for secondary and higher education were dropped; for the first time since the 1930's, foreigners were freely admitted to the country; writers became more daring than before; the closing of the infamous labor camps was announced, and the return of political prisoners was speeded up.[2]

While carrying out these dramatic changes, the government was able, in most instances, to anticipate reaction and avoid any unplanned steps; but there were a few exceptions. One of the notable complications with which it had to deal arose in Georgia, Stalin's birthplace. Official attacks on the memory of the cherished native son provoked open hostility there, and force was required to suppress it.

Other unfavorable responses—and far more serious ones—were touched off in Poland and Hungary, where Communist control was so insecure, and the people so anxious for relief from it, that the sudden changes produced by de-Stalinization inspired mass outbursts. In July 1956, rioting broke out in Poland, and popular demonstrations began in Hungary. Attempts were made to pacify the rebellious by replacing some of the Communist officials who were recognized as being subservient to Moscow, by Communists who were known to be "Titoists"—that is, independent party members. In Hungary, the choice for leadership of the government was Imre Nagy, just released from imprisonment for "Titoism"; and in Poland, it was Wladyslaw Gomulka, also just out of prison. The results were not all that had been expected. The shift of leadership in Hungary failed to quell the revolt in that country: by the end of October it had taken on a character that was clearly pro-Western; and in deference to mass senti-

---

[1] Five years later, two special measures were taken to discourage the people's remembrance of Stalin: the removal of his body from the mausoleum it had shared with the body of Lenin, and the changing of the name of the city Stalingrad to Volgograd.

[2] Lacking an official statement of the number of prisoners in these labor camps, foreign experts have variously estimated the number, some setting it as high as 15 million, others as low as 3 million. The lower figure can be the more reliably supported.

ment, Nagy began to promise policies that would remove Hungary from the Soviet to the Western orbit. The Soviet answer to such developments, military force, produced much bloodshed and intensified ill will; but the Soviet army succeeded in subduing the rebels within a few weeks. Nagy himself was taken prisoner, by trickery, and shot. Following that, properly obedient Hungarian Communists were re-installed to rule the country, backed by the presence of Soviet troops. Meanwhile, in Poland events were following a different course. By the end of October, Gomulka and other nationalistic Communists were firmly in control of the government, and the government was in control of the country. The leaders were apparently willing to keep Poland in the Soviet bloc but not to permit Moscow to supervise Polish affairs in the future as it had in the past. Moreover, they were willing to fight for their terms; and Moscow, although it had the army with which to impose its will, decided to accept the terms. The outcome was that Poland regained some of her internal freedom but remained a people's democracy and a part of the Soviet orbit.

The revolts in Poland and Hungary threw some light on the limits to which de-Stalinization would be permitted to go. With respect to satellite countries, it was clear that though Moscow would countenance, even encourage, some deviations from the "one road to socialism," it would not permit withdrawal from the Soviet orbit, nor would it hesitate to use force, if expedient, to prevent withdrawal. Another limit revealed at the time of the revolts concerned the Soviet citizens themselves. Even before that time, a growing restiveness among students, writers, and artists had begun to make itself felt, as many of them sought to regain a measure of the freedom lost in the preceding years; and the revolts served to bring their discontent to the surface. Although the Hungarian revolt was officially described as the work of "counter-revolutionaries," some refused to credit official interpretations and demanded the facts. Since this questioning of authority coincided with the open antagonism of several writers towards the party's efforts to control their creative work, the leaders saw cause for concern. And, in the late summer, they began a campaign to bring the dissidents to heel. Khrushchev warned students against "unhealthy phenomena," and reminded writers that their first obligation was not to express themselves, but to help mold good Soviet citizens. Strictures and warnings of this nature, however, proved generally ineffective. Such novelists as Ilya Ehrenburg and Vera Panova, both of whom had written as if compliant to orders in Stalin's time, now demanded independence; such poets as Boris Pasternak, who had been silent during Stalin's ascendancy rather than write under command, began to express themselves more freely; younger writers —among them, Vladimir Dudintsev and Margaret Aliger—spoke up even more vigorously than their elders. And, although the party had crushed artistic defiance before and could still do so, it now took a singularly lenient attitude toward these continued evidences of daring. Apparently anxious to have the co-operation of the intellectual and artistic elite, Khrushchev and his colleagues held back from coercive measures and sanctioned a certain degree of nonconformity among them. Thus another limit of de-Staliniza-tion was tested and determined.

THE NEW COURSE DEFINED.   By the end of 1956, the features of the post-Stalinist regime had become reasonably clear. Although the leaders might speak of these features as marking "a return to Leninist principles," they were in fact Stalinist features, stripped of some of the more oppressive, irrational, and inefficient characteristics of the earlier regime. The structure of the Soviet system had not changed in its essentials, but the winds of change were blowing more freely than they had been for nearly a generation.

A decade of adjustment: 1956-1966

THE NEW LEADER.   Foremost in the new dispensation was Nikita Khrushchev. He was a shrewd man, a miner's son of modest education, un-sophisticated in both speech and manner. Although he had risen to promi-nence as one of Stalin's lieutenants, he dissociated himself completely from the ways of his former superior and worked energetically to implement the program begun after the change in leadership. He traveled extensively and, within a short time, became widely known as the personal representative of the "new" features of the Soviet regime.

THE ECONOMY.   Khrushchev's leadership did not change the economic goal of the USSR: to overtake and surpass the advanced capitalist countries. The Sixth Five-Year Plan (1956-60)[1] and the Seven-Year Plan (1958-65) were patterned after earlier plans. However, even though the Soviet leaders did not change their economic goal, they changed the methods used in reaching it. In 1957, they began to attack the country's most important problem, the inefficiency resulting from excessive centralization

---

[1] Because several of the targets of this plan could not be reached, it was terminated at the end of 1958 and replaced by a new plan, scheduled to begin in 1959 and to cover a period of seven years.

of economic authority. In May, they boldly undertook to decentralize management by abolishing twenty-five industrial ministries and dividing the country into 105 economic regions, each to be administered by a local Economic Council, or *Sovnarkhoz* (from *Soviet Narodnogo Khozyaistva*), with powers hitherto reserved to the central government.

While seeking to improve efficiency by decentralization, they sought also to improve productivity by raising morale. Among the more important steps taken in this direction were the re-establishment, in 1957, of the seven-hour workday (the eight-hour day had been in force since the beginning of the war); and, in March, 1958, the act granting collective farms the right to purchase agricultural machinery from the machine-tractor stations.

The results of these drastic and far-reaching economic changes were mixed. The responses to the adjustment of the length of the workday and to the granting of the right of machine purchase were favorably received. The new economic councils, however, did not satisfy expectations, and a swing back to centralization followed, the number of those bodies being reduced to forty-seven by the spring of 1963. And, at that time, a central economic agency, the USSR Supreme Council of the National Economy, defined as "the supreme state agency for guiding industry and construction," was established.

Despite these irregularities in its administration, the economy as a whole managed to show many striking gains. Agriculture, though it still lagged behind industry in progress, expanded more encouragingly than in the past, growing by some 60 per cent in the decade after Stalin's death. Industry grew even more rapidly in that period—so rapidly, in fact, that the USSR was enabled to "overtake and surpass" the leading capitalist countries in the production of coal and iron ore and in the manufacture of electric and diesel locomotives.

All in all, the gross national product doubled in the first ten years of the post-Stalin era. As in the past, the major part of the growth was in heavy industry, but the consumers were beginning to realize more benefit from the increase in national wealth, to enjoy some definite and substantial improvement in the standard of living.

As the economic trend improved, public attention was drawn more often to the development toward communism. In 1961, at its Twenty-second Congress, the party adopted a new program declaring, among other things:

The building of a communist society has become an immediate practical task for the Soviet people. . . .

Under communism all people will have equal status in society, will stand in the same relations to the means of production, will enjoy equal conditions of work and distribution, and will actively participate in the management of public affairs.

In addition to these qualitative goals, the program stated also quantitative ones for the coming twenty years, which, if achieved, would provide the material basis for communism. Industrial output was to increase by 500 per cent; agricultural output, by 250 per cent; real income, by 250 per cent—all this to be accomplished while the workday was being substantially decreased.

POLYCENTRISM.   Unquestionably, de-Stalinization had brought about a definite change in the relationship between the USSR and the satellite states. Relaxation of Soviet control, which was quite evident (even in Hungary, once the aftereffects of 1956 were erased), permitted the satellites to make domestic adjustments that in the long run gave their regimes greater internal strength than was possible in the days of Stalin. But there was no substantive change in the domestic institutions of these countries, nor was there any in their foreign policies.

The Soviet leaders spoke with increasing enthusiasm of the progress toward the realization of a "world socialist system" consisting, as the 1961 party program put it, of "free sovereign peoples pursuing the socialist and communist path, united by an identity of interests and goals and the close bonds of international socialist solidarity." Although the realities of the socialist system were as different from the pictured ideal as were the realities of "socialism" in Russia, the growing economic interdependence and co-operation between the USSR and the European satellite states could be considered one important step toward the ideal. The Council for Economic Mutual Assistance, which, under Stalin, had been used almost exclusively to exploit satellite economies, had now become a fairly effective instrument for the integration and co-ordination of the several economies.

On the other hand, while economic co-operation was proving advantageous as a centripetal force, other forces at work in the Soviet bloc were becoming all too clearly centrifugal in nature. There was evidence that Moscow's reiteration of the "identity of interests and goals" between the people's democracies and the USSR was no guarantee of such identity in all cases. Developments in the Chinese People's Republic were certainly a refutation. Shortly after Stalin's death, conflicts of views began to appear

between the governments in Moscow and in Peking; and the latter, unlike the European satellite governments, had sufficient military and political independence to support its position. Yet for about three years Peking,
though critical of the course followed by Stalin's successors, exercised
restraint in expressing its views. After the Soviet Government's open attack
on Stalin in 1956, however, it became more openly critical. The resulting
friction between the two supposedly friendly countries was, for several
years, concealed from the world while attempts were made to restore harmony. In 1957 and 1960, international meetings of Communist leaders
were held in Moscow for the purpose of finding some means of allaying the
internal discord, but they succeeded only in producing lengthy documents
proclaiming, but not producing evidence of, solidarity.

After the 1960 meeting, Peking increasingly followed policies independent of, and sometimes opposed to, those of Moscow. Peking also
courted the support of other members of the Soviet bloc and succeeded in
winning support from the neighboring governments of North Korea and
North Vietnam,[1] and from the government of Albania, quite safely out
of reach of Soviet reprisals. By the spring of 1963 the existence of two
large antipathetic groupings of Communists could no longer be concealed:
the principals were openly airing their quarrels, Peking accusing Moscow
of heresy in giving too much attention to peaceful co-existence between the
Communist and capitalist areas and not enough to the world revolutionary
struggle, and Moscow accusing Peking of irresponsibly flirting with the
danger of "world thermonuclear war." This exchange of accusations was
followed by a consideration of the issues at a meeting of Chinese and Soviet party leaders in Moscow, in July; still they were not resolved.

The Communist split now seemed almost irreparable. The close union of
the countries committed to the international Communist movement, as it had
existed under the leadership of Lenin and Stalin, had been replaced by two
powerful factions. Moreover, there was a possibility that these might, in
turn, subdivide, thus contributing to a condition, identified by political scientists as "polycentrism," that would further weaken Moscow's hope for a
socialist commonwealth.

ANNIHILATION OR ACCOMMODATION? Khrushchev's rise to power
did not produce any significant change in Soviet relations with the Western

---

[1] In 1954, after a protracted civil war between Communist and anti-Communist forces
in Vietnam, a *de facto* split was made in that country: the northern part, under a
Communist regime, calling itself the Democratic Republic of Vietnam; and the southern
part, under an anti-Communist regime, calling itself the Republic of Vietnam.

bloc. As before, the Soviet Government sought to extend its power without the risk of war and, at the same time, to expand its nuclear capabilities, which had been somewhat neglected during Stalin's last years. By 1957, it could point to encouraging results. In August, Moscow announced the completion of successful tests of an intercontinental ballistic missile capable of reaching targets in the United States. Two months later, the USSR successfully launched the world's first space satellite, *Sputnik*. Still another first was registered in April, 1961, when the first manned space satellite, with Yuri Gagarin at the controls, was put into orbit. With such advances in nuclear and space capacity, the USSR was approaching a position of parity with the Western powers in new methods of warfare.

While these achievements in military preparedness strengthened the country's position in international relations, they also increased the risks of a general nuclear war. The task of pursuing policies that extended Soviet power without, at the same time, inviting resistance from the powers in the Western bloc and precipitating a major conflict, grew seriously complex. Yet the USSR continued to court uncommitted nations in Africa, Asia, and Latin America; and to compete, in these areas, with the Western powers —particularly the United States—in offering technical and other types of assistance, effecting cultural exchanges, and disseminating political propaganda. This wooing and pursuing brought varied results. Egypt's response was typical of one extreme: she accepted Soviet economic aid but banned native Communists. Cuba's was typical of another: under the leadership of Fidel Castro, she accepted Communist ideology as well as Soviet military and economic aid. In fact, under the new regime, Cuba began to take on the characteristics of a people's democracy in both domestic and foreign affairs, and to become an integral part of the Soviet bloc. This fact was dramatically illustrated in the summer of 1962, when Soviet civilian and military experts secretly constructed nuclear missile sites on Cuban shores less than 100 miles from the United States mainland—a bold and dangerous move. In October of that year, the United States Government demanded that the sites be dismantled, and Moscow acquiesced rather than accept a challenge that might end in war.

Demonstrative as was the extension of Soviet influence to Cuba, it was intrinsically of far less importance than the continuing, unresolved competition for influence in Europe. In that area, the balance of power remained a precarious one, neither bloc being able to change it except by war or negotiation: the former, not acceptable; the latter, already shown to be without profit. Nonetheless, the Western bloc continued to make sporadic and fruitless attempts to negotiate major Soviet-Western differences. Moscow, for its part, concentrated on breaking the deadlock in Germany, making proposals that were, with one exception, doomed to failure, having been previously offered and rejected. The exception, a proposal made in 1957, called for the neutralization of Central and Eastern Europe—that is, the elimination of nuclear weapons from that area and the maintenance there of only a minimum stock of conventional arms. But this proposal was no more successful than the others. The only practical means by which Moscow, short of war, could hope to effect any change was by hammering away at the precarious Western position in Berlin, forcing the Western powers—and with them, the Federal Republic of Germany—out of the city. The benefit from such an eventuality would be the bolstering of the German Democratic Republic, which was being weakened by the continuing flight of East Germans to West Germany by way of Berlin.

Hoping to gain at least that benefit, Moscow repeated, in 1958 and 1961, what had been tried in 1948—the use of restrictive measures to force the Western powers out of Berlin. The result, in each instance, was another demonstration of Western determination not to budge. A stalemate having been thus once more established, Soviet troops helped the German Democratic Republic to build a menacing and avowedly impregnable wall between the Eastern and Western sectors of Berlin—a grim symbol of some sixteen years of failure to unify Germany and establish a stable peace in Europe.

In spite of the fact that, by the end of 1961, the impasse between the Soviet and Western blocs seemed as unbreakable as ever, both sides continued to seek a mutually agreeable way out of it. Since negotiations of major issues had yielded only negative results, certain leaders on both sides began to consider minor issues on which agreement might be expected, in the hope that instances of minor accord might make possible major agreements at some later date. The chance of success through such limited attempts was enhanced by the post-Stalin diplomacy that had led to certain noteworthy, though not extensive, mutual arrangements: among them, the Soviet-American cultural exchange arranged in 1958, which had led to a mood favoring expanded and improved diplomatic relations.

In 1963, the USSR, while remaining as stubborn as ever on major issues, manifested a readiness to compromise on little ones; likewise the United States and Great Britain were more anxious than ever to reach some accord, however modest. As a result, the three powers negotiated, in August, 1963, a treaty (open to other states as well) to ban the above-ground testing of nuclear weapons. Coming seventeen years after the establishment by the United Nations of the international Atomic Energy Commission, the purpose of which had been to ban the use of nuclear weapons altogether, this treaty could be interpreted only as a minor achievement. But, minor as it was, it inspired some hope for further positive achievements in international relations.

CHANGE IN SUCCESSION. Khrushchev's ascendancy came to a sudden end in October, 1964, when, during one of his absences from Moscow, a number of his colleagues, dissatisfied with some of his policies and disturbed by his excessive power, united to oust him.

In his place as First Secretary, they installed Brezhnev; in his place as Chairman of the Council of Ministers, Kosygin. And, for his personal future, they provided a status that he himself had, in the past, conferred on eclipsed political figures—comfortable obscurity. A year after these steps, Mikoyan, the only remaining one of the eight who had helped to launch the post-Stalin era, was relieved of the post to which he had moved, the chairmanship of the Presidium of the Supreme Soviet, and Nicholas Podgorny succeeded him. Then, at the Twenty-third Party Congress in 1966, Brezhnev's title was changed to General Secretary; and the Presidium of the Central Committee was renamed the Politburo.

Although these two latter changes were officially approved as a return to "Leninist" practices, some observers perceived in them the hint of a possible return to "Stalinist" practices. However, Brezhnev showed no subsequent signs of aspiring to Stalin's power, but shared the leadership with Kosygin; and both appeared to shun the limelight, refraining from actions suggestive of the "cult of personality."

Fifty years in review

THE SOVIET EVALUATION. Throughout 1967, the fiftieth anniversary of the revolution that established the Soviet regime was widely celebrated in the USSR. Of the many commemorative gatherings, none was more notable than the ceremonial session attended by members of the party's Central Committee and of the Supreme Soviets of the USSR and the RSFSR. Held early in November, it featured an address by General Secretary Brezhnev, who undertook to evaluate the country's accomplishments and indicate its expectations.[1]

[1] Cf. *The Current Digest of the Soviet Press*, November 22, 1967, pp. 3-20, for an English translation.

Under the leadership of the party, Brezhnev declared, Russia had been transformed from a backward nation into a "totally new world, a world of new, socialist relations, a world of the new, Soviet man"; from a "prison" of national minorities into a "voluntary association of peoples welded together in a common struggle for shared goals." The Soviet society, as he viewed it, had become one in which there no longer existed any exploitation, any privileged classes, or any estates.

Furthermore, he claimed, the USSR, "the birthplace of socialism," was building toward "the birthplace of communism," and steps were being taken to insure the requisite conditions: the elimination of distinctions between members of the working class, the peasantry on collective farms, and the intelligentsia; acceleration in the removal of differences between urban and rural standards of living and culture; and wider practical participation of workers in the administration of political, economic, and public affairs of the country.

In regard to the world revolutionary movement, he said that the road which "led Russia to socialism is the high road of world history, of the whole of human civilization." He went on to describe the preceding half century as a period during which a "revolutionary torrent" had transformed a third of the world into "a great commonwealth of socialist states." He designated as the "socialist states": Albania, Bulgaria, China, Cuba, Czechoslovakia, the German Democratic Republic, Hungary, the Korean People's Democratic Republic, Mongolia, Poland, Rumania, the USSR, the Democratic Republic of Vietnam, and Yugoslavia. Then, while admitting strains within this "commonwealth," he expressed confidence that they would pass and that, eventually, the "commonwealth" would encompass the whole world. As illustrations of the trend toward that eventuality, he noted that many of the newly independent states of Asia and Africa were "bypassing capitalism" in favor of a socialist orientation and that the "general crisis" of the shrinking capitalist world was becoming more serious. He qualified his optimism on this subject, however, by foreseeing "hard battles and persistent labor ahead on the path to the triumph of socialism and progress throughout the world" and by emphasizing that the USSR's most pressing task was "to prevent a new world war," because peace was a necessary condition "for accomplishing the tasks of the construction of socialism and communism and the development of the entire world revolutionary process."

The validity of much that Brezhnev affirmed as fact in this review of Soviet achievement was seriously questioned in many quarters beyond the borders of Russia.

RUSSIA, BIRTHPLACE OF SOCIALISM AND COMMUNISM? When the Bolsheviks gained power, they expected to create, within a generation, a democratic, socialist society based on true equality and capable of functioning without the services of a professional bureaucracy. But the USSR was, in fact, no nearer to the achievement of that expectation in 1967 than it had been in 1937, when Molotov announced that socialism had been achieved (see page 626). Political power still rested in the hands of a comparatively small group of men who continued the practice of using the election of officials—for positions in government, party, trade unions, and collective farms —as a means by which to tabulate ostensible support rather than as a means by which to determine the will of the voters. Although the size of the group that wielded power had grown between 1937 and 1967, the state of socialism, as defined in 1917, had by no means been achieved thereby.

If socialism had not been achieved by 1967, there could be no justification for the claim that the USSR was then on the road to communism, for the former was understood to be preliminary to the latter. There was evidence to support only the claim that the regime was taking some steps that could be characterized as communistic in nature.

At that time, the Soviet leaders, judged by their actions rather than their words, were steering a cautious domestic course, committed to the policies of de-Stalinization yet unwilling to permit broad play to the liberalizing forces that de-Stalinization had produced. Those forces were clearly represented by industrial managers pressing for greater authority in the making of economic decisions and by writers, artists, and scholars (energetically supported by some of the students in the universities) seeking greater freedom of expression. Other forces also were becoming identifiable. Among them, the youth of the country was considered sufficiently noteworthy to merit a place in Brezhnev's speech at the Twenty-third Party Congress: "Certain young people want to stand aloof from seething life, are parasitically minded, demand a great deal from the state but forget their duties to society and the people." The masses also, though with little opportunity to make themselves heard on major issues, were showing evidence of impatience for a faster rise in their standard of living. Still another significant, though subtle and less tangible, force was the heritage from Russia's past; it had not been expunged by years of repression and, at any relaxation of pressure, it stirred again—in religion, the family, the arts, the very rhythm of life.

The direction to be taken by the USSR, it appeared, would depend not only on the will of the leaders but also on the interaction of the various forces that were becoming recognizable as the regime moved on into the second half of its first century.

A GREAT COMMONWEALTH OF SOCIALIST STATES? In 1967, it was not to be denied that, in one-third of the world, there were regimes dominated by Communists, adhering to a common ideology and bound by many ties; or that, in Eastern Europe, the Warsaw Pact and the Council for Economic Mutual Assistance constituted strong and consequential ties. However, as has been seen, the "commonwealth" was seriously rent by continuing discord between Moscow and Peking and by developments that were leading countries like Rumania to demonstrate a growing independence of Moscow. There was, indeed, no assurance that efforts to prevent the growth of polycentrism would succeed.

TOWARD WORLD COMMUNISM? In 1967, it was not to be denied that the fifty-year accretion of Communist strength in the world had been considerable. But the admission of that fact could not be taken as support for the contention that the road which "led Russia to socialism is the high road of world history." The accretions had not proceeded in accordance with the Marxist-Leninist scheme of revolutionary development.

In no country except Russia (even with respect to Russia, there was room for debate), had the Communists achieved power as a result of a proletarian revolution. The industrial proletariat throughout the world had, in fact, shown little evidence of developing the revolutionary mentality that Marxism-Leninism had predicted. Furthermore, the "general crisis" in the capitalist world had not developed according to Marxist-Leninist predictions. Nor would the record sustain Brezhnev's contention that the fifty-year period had witnessed a "revolutionary torrent"; what it had witnessed was the growth of world communism in intermittent spurts. In brief, the successes achieved by communism had not confirmed the theories upon which predictions of ultimate victory had been based.

No amount of extravagant rhetoric in 1967 regarding the extent of Soviet concern with the "world revolutionary process" could obscure the fact that the USSR thus far during the post-Stalin period, just as during the earlier period, had placed more emphasis on the pursuit of Soviet national interest than on the promotion of international communism. It had sought to promote the latter only when the risks were low, and it had consistently shown itself ready to sacrifice Communist gains abroad when prudence indicated the need. In Soviet Russia's international policy, utopianism was still tempered by a strong infusion of political realism.

BIBLIOGRAPHY

General

REFERENCE WORKS

Florinsky, M. T., ed. *McGraw-Hill Encyclopedia of Russia and the Soviet Union*. New York: McGraw-Hill Book Co., 1961.

Utechin, S. V. *Everyman's Concise Encyclopedia of Russia*. New York: Dent, 1961.

BIBLIOGRAPHIES

American Bibliography of Slavic and East European Studies, 1957——.

Carew Hunt, R. N. *Books on Communism: a Bibliography*. London: Ampersand Ltd., 1959.

Grierson, P. *Books on Soviet Russia, 1917-1942*. London: Methuen & Co., Ltd., 1943.

Hammond, T. T. *Soviet Foreign Relations and World Communism*. Princeton: Princeton University Press, 1965.

Kerner, R. J. *Slavonic Europe*. Cambridge: Harvard University Press, 1918.

Morley, C. *Guide to Research in Russian History*. Syracuse: Syracuse University Press, 1951.

Shapiro, D. *A Select Bibliography of Works in English on Russian History, 1801-1917*. Oxford: Basil Blackwell, 1962.

GEOGRAPHY

Chew, A. F. *An Atlas of Russian History*. New Haven: Yale University Press, 1967.

Mirov, N. T. *Geography of Russia*. New York: John Wiley & Sons, Inc., 1951.

Shabad, T. *Geography of the USSR: a Regional Survey*. New York: Columbia University Press, 1951.

READINGS

Edie, J. M. et al., eds. *Russian Philosophy* (3 vols.). Chicago: Quadrangle Books, 1964. An anthology of intellectual history.

Harcave, S., ed. *Readings in Russian History* (2 vols.). New York: Thomas Y. Crowell Co., 1962.

Wiener, L. *Anthology of Russian Literature* (2 vols.) New York: G. P. Putnam's Sons, 1902-1903.

GENERAL HISTORIES

Charques, R. D. *A Short History of Russia*. New York: E. P. Dutton & Co., 1956.

Florinsky, M. T. *Russia: A History and an Interpretation* (2 vols.). New York: The Macmillan Co., 1953. An authoritative work covering developments up to 1917.

Klyuchevsky, V. O. *A History of Russia* (5 vols.). New York: Russell and Russell, 1960. A classic work, by one of Russia's greatest historians.

Pankratova, A. M., ed. *A History of the U.S.S.R.* (3 vols.). Moscow: Foreign Languages Publishing House, 1947-1948. Soviet secondary school textbook.

Pares, B. *A History of Russia*. New York: Alfred A. Knopf, 1953.

Platonov, S. F. *A History of Russia*. New York: The Macmillan Co., 1925.

Pokrovsky, M. N. *History of Russia from the Earliest Times to the Rise of Commercial Capitalism*. New York: International Publishers, 1931. A Marxist interpretation.

Rambaud, A. N. *A History of Russia from the Earliest Times to 1877* (2 vols.). New York: J. B. Alden, 1886. Authoritative work by an eminent French historian. Useful though somewhat out of date.

Sumner, B. H. *A Short History of Russia* (Rev. Ed.). New York: Harcourt, Brace & Co., 1949. Able work of synthesis, organized topically.

Vernadsky, G. and Karpovich, M. *A History of Russia*. New Haven: Yale University Press, 1943—. A major work, planned to be in 10 volumes, still in progress.

Weidlé, W. *Russia: Absent and Present*. London: Hollis and Carter, 1952. A brief interpretation.

HISTORIES OF SPECIAL TOPICS AND REGIONS

Allen, W. E. D. *The Ukraine: A History*. New York: The Macmillan Co., 1941. Objective study of a subject that usually receives partisan treatment.

Blum, J. *Lord and Peasant in Russia: from the Ninth to the Nineteenth Century*. Princeton: Princeton University Press, 1961. A history of agrarian relationships.

Cross, S. H. *Slavic Civilization through the Ages.* Cambridge: Harvard University Press, 1948. Essays on various related topics.

Dubnow, S. M. *History of the Jews in Russia and Poland from the Earliest Times until the Present Day* (3 vols.). Philadelphia: Jewish Publication Society of America, 1916-1920.

Dvornik, F. *The Slavs in European History and Civilization.* New Brunswick: Rutgers University Press, 1962.

Hrushevsky, M. *A History of Ukraine.* New Haven: Yale University Press, 1941. Translation of a work of a leading Ukrainian historian and nationalist.

Kovalevsky, M. M. *Modern Customs and Ancient Laws of Russia.* London: D. Nutt, 1891.

———. *Russian Political Institutions.* Chicago: University of Chicago Press, 1902. Survey of constitutional developments.

Lossky, N. O. *History of Russian Philosophy.* New York: International Universities Press, 1951. By a Russian theologian. Gives main attention to period since 1700.

Masaryk, T. G. *The Spirit of Russia* (2 vols.). New York: The Macmillan Co., 1955. Brilliant interpretation of Russian intellectual history, with chief emphasis on nineteenth century.

Mazour, A. G. *Modern Russian Historiography.* Princeton: D. Van Nostrand Co., 1958.

Skrine, F. H. B. and Ross, E. D. *Heart of Asia: a History of Russian Turkestan and the Central Asian Khanates from the Earliest Times.* London: Methuen & Co., 1899.

Spekke, A. *History of Latvia.* Stockholm: M. Goppers, 1957.

Uustalu, E. *The History of the Estonian People.* London: Boreas Publishing Co., 1953.

Vakar, N. P. *Belorussia.* Cambridge: Harvard University Press, 1956. A history of the White Russians, with emphasis on the last century.

Zenkovsky, V. V. *History of Russian Philosophy* (2 vols.). New York: Columbia University Press, 1953.

Social and Economic History

Eckhardt, H. von. *Russia.* New York: Alfred A. Knopf, 1932. Stimulating but not wholly reliable interpretation of social and economic history by a German political scientist.

Lyashchenko, P. I. *History of the National Economy of Russia to the 1917 Revolution.* New York: The Macmillan Co., 1949. Written by a Soviet historian as a text for Soviet higher schools. Most complete work on the subject in English, but somewhat marred by its conformity to official Soviet interpretation.

Mavor, J. *An Economic History of Russia* (2nd Ed., 2 vols.). Toronto: E. P. Dutton, 1925. Valuable as a supplement to Lyashchenko.

Mirsky, D. S. *Russia: A Social History*. London: Cresset Press, 1942. Analysis by a literary historian, giving special attention to non-Russian nationalities. Marxist in tone.

Religious History

Adeney, W. F. *The Greek and Eastern Churches*. New York: Charles Scribner's Sons, 1908. Historical survey, with some material on Russia.

Conybeare, F. C. *Russian Dissenters*. Cambridge: Harvard University Press, 1921. Survey of religious sects since the seventeenth century.

Fortescue, A. *Orthodox Eastern Church*. London: Catholic Truth Society, 1916. Good exposition of practices of the Orthodox Church.

French, R. M. *The Eastern Orthodox Church*. London: Hutchinson's University Library, 1951. A useful introduction.

Milyukov, P. *Outlines of Russian Culture*. (See entry under *Cultural History*.)

Cultural History

Alpatov, M. *Russian Impact on Art*. New York: Philosophical Library, 1950.

Leonard, R. A. *A History of Russian Music*. London: Jarrolds, 1957.

Milyukov, P. *Outlines of Russian Culture* (3 parts). Philadelphia: University of Pennsylvania Press, 1942. Historical survey of religion, literature, architecture, painting, and music, by one of Russia's foremost historians. A translation of portions of the second volume of his *Studies in the History of Russian Culture*.

Mirsky, D. S. *A History of Russian Literature*. New York: Alfred A. Knopf, 1949. Best short treatment of the subject.

Rice, T. T. *Russian Art*. London: Penguin Books 1949. Sculpture, painting and architecture treated historically.

Sokolov, Y. M. *Russian Folklore*. New York: The Macmillan Co., 1950.

Varneke, B. V. *History of the Russian Theatre*. New York: The Macmillan Co., 1951.

Diplomatic History

Bailey, T. A. *America Faces Russia: Russian-American Relations from Early Times to Our Day*. Ithaca: Cornell University Press, 1950. Emphasis on American attitudes toward Russia.

Lederer, I. J., ed. *Russian Foreign Policy*. New Haven: Yale University Press, 1962. Essays on various aspects of Tsarist and Soviet foreign policy.

Lobanov-Rostovsky, A. *Russia and Asia.* Ann Arbor: George Wahr Publishing Co., 1951. Historical survey of Russian relations with the Far East.

Marriott, J. A. R. *Anglo-Russian Relations, 1689-1943.* London: Methuen & Co., 1944.

Periodicals

The periodicals listed below carry scholarly articles, reviews of new books, and occasional bibliographies.

Russian Review, 1941—

Slavic Review (formerly *American Slavic and East European Review*), 1941—

Slavonic and East European Review, 1922—

Soviet Studies, 1950—

Part I: Growth of people and polity

SOURCE BOOKS

Cross, S. H. and Sherbowitz-Wetzor, O. P., trs. and eds. *The Russian Primary Chronicle.* Cambridge: The Mediaeval Academy of America, 1953.

Fedotov, G. P. *A Treasury of Russian Spirituality.* New York: Sheed and Ward, 1948. Collection of source materials.

Fennell, J. L. I., tr. and ed. *The Correspondence between Prince A. M. Kurbsky and Tsar Ivan IV of Russia, 1564-1579.* New York: Cambridge University Press, 1955.

Michel, R., and Forbes, R., trs. and eds. *Chronicle of Novgorod, 1016-1471.* London: Camden Society, 1914. English translation of one of the more important early historical chronicles.

Vernadsky, G., tr. and ed. *Medieval Russian Laws.* New York: Columbia University Press, 1947.

Zenkovsky, S. A., tr. and ed., *Medieval Russia's Epics, Chronicles, and Tales.* New York: E. P. Dutton & Co., 1963.

HISTORIES OF SPECIAL TOPICS

Cherniavsky, M. *Tsar and People: a Historical Study of Russian National and Social Myths.* New Haven: Yale University Press, 1961.

Fisher, R. H. *The Russian Fur Trade, 1550-1700.* Berkeley: University of California Press, 1943.

Howorth, H. H. *History of the Mongols from the 9th to the 19th Century* (5 vols.). London: Longmans, Green & Co., 1876-1927. Standard work, useful for background on the Mongols.

Lantzeff, G. V. *Siberia in the Seventeenth Century: a Study of Colonial Administration.* Berkeley: University of California Press, 1943.

Mongait, A. L. *Archaeology in the USSR.* Baltimore: Penguin Books, 1961. Survey of archaeological findings in Russia, by a Soviet scholar.

CULTURAL HISTORIES

Grekov, B. D. *The Culture of Kiev Rus.* Moscow: Foreign Languages Publishing House, 1947. Short study by a Soviet historian. Tends to minimize the importance of foreign influence on Russia.

Gudzy, N. K. *History of Early Russian Literature.* New York: The Macmillan Co., 1949. The work of a Soviet literary historian. Treats developments up to the seventeenth century.

RELIGION

Fedotov, G. P. *The Russian Religious Mind* (2 vols.). Cambridge: Harvard University Press, 1946-1966. Able consideration of Russian religious consciousness.

BIOGRAPHIES

Fennell, J. L. I. *Ivan the Great of Moscow.* New York: St. Martin's Press, 1961.

Vernadsky, G. *Bohdan, Hetman of Ukraine.* New Haven: Yale University Press, 1940. The life of Bogdan Khmelnitsky.

Waliszewski, K. *Ivan the Terrible.* Philadelphia: J. B. Lippincott Co., 1904. Still the soundest treatment in the English language, although not a definitive study.

Wipper, R. *Ivan Grozny.* Moscow: Foreign Languages Publishing House, 1947. Typical of current Soviet stress on the positive rather than the negative features of Ivan IV's reign.

Part II: Consolidation and expansion

SOURCE BOOKS

Catherine II. *The Memoirs of Catherine the Great.* New York: The Macmillan Co., 1955.

Putnam, P., ed. *Seven Britons in Imperial Russia, 1698-1812.* Princeton: Princeton University Press, 1952. First-hand account by seven British visitors to Russia.

Radishchev, A. *A Journey from St. Petersburg to Moscow.* Cambridge: Harvard University Press, 1958.

Reddaway, W. F., ed. *The Documents of Catherine the Great.* New York: The Macmillan Co., 1931.

HISTORIES OF PERIODS

Bain, R. N. *Daughter of Peter the Great, a History of Russian Diplomacy and of the Russian Court under the Empress Elizabeth Petrovna, 1741-1762.* New York: E. P. Dutton & Co., 1900.

————. *Pupils of Peter the Great, a History of the Russian Court and Empire from 1697 to 1740.* London: A. Constable, 1897. The works of Bain are neither even in quality nor free from error, but they are the only ones in English for the periods they present.

O'Brien, C. B. *Russia under Two Tsars, 1682-1689: the Regency of Sophia Alekseevna.* Berkeley and Los Angeles: University of California Press, 1952.

Sumner, B. H. *Peter the Great and the Emergence of Russia.* New York: The Macmillan Co., 1951. Admirable short study.

Thomson, G. S. *Catherine the Great and the Expansion of Russia.* New York: The Macmillan Co., 1950.

CULTURAL HISTORIES

Rogger, H. *National Consciousness in Eighteenth-Century Russia.* Cambridge: Harvard University Press, 1960.

Simmons, E. J. *English Literature and Culture in Russia, 1553-1840.* Cambridge: Harvard University Press, 1935.

Tompkins, S. R. *The Russian Mind: From Peter the Great through the Enlightenment.* Norman: University of Oklahoma Press, 1953.

DIPLOMATIC AND MILITARY HISTORIES

Golder, F. A. *Russian Expansion on the Pacific, 1641-1850.* Cleveland: Arthur H. Clark Co., 1914. Account of exploration and annexation.

Kaplan, H. H. *The First Partition of Poland.* New York: Columbia University Press, 1962.

Lobanov-Rostovsky, A. A. *Russia and Europe, 1789-1825.* Durham: Duke University Press, 1947. Valuable work, covering both diplomatic and military history for the period.

Lord, R. H. *The Second Partition of Poland.* Cambridge: Harvard University Press, 1915. Standard work. Good introduction to the foreign policy of Catherine II.

Pavlovsky, M. N. *Chinese-Russian Relations.* New York: Philosophical Library, 1949. Essays dealing with various aspects of the subject. Concerned mainly with late seventeenth and the eighteenth centuries.

Sumner, B. H. *Peter the Great and the Ottoman Empire.* New York: William Salloch, 1950. Succinct and useful account.

Tarle, E. *Napoleon's Invasion of Russia, 1812.* New York: Oxford University Press, 1942. Work of a noted Soviet historian, who was reprimanded by the Party in 1951 for the point of view presented in this book.

BIOGRAPHIES

Grey, I. *Peter the Great*. Philadelphia: J. B. Lippincott Co., 1960.
——. *Catherine the Great*. Philadelphia: J. B. Lippincott Co., 1962. Both of Grey's biographies are careful studies, based on recent scholarship.
Soloveytchik, G. *Potemkin*. New York: W. W. Norton & Co., Inc., 1947. Gives good understanding of the man and his times.
Waliszewski, K. *The Romance of an Empress, Catherine II of Russia*. New York: D. Appleton & Co., 1894. Dated, but still useful.

Part III: Bureaucratic Russia

SOURCE BOOKS

Czartoryski, A. J. *Memoirs of Prince Adam Czartoryski and his Correspondence with Alexander I* (2nd ed.). London: Remington & Co., 1888.
Herzen, A. *My Past and Thoughts: Memoirs* (6 vols.). New York: Alfred A. Knopf, 1924-1928. Excellent introduction to the spirit of intellectual Russia in the age of Nicholas I.
Kohn, H., ed. *The Mind of Modern Russia*. New Brunswick: Rutgers University Press, 1955. Selections covering the period from 1825 to 1917.
Pipes, R. E. *Karamzin's Memoir on Ancient and Modern Russia: a Translation and Analysis*. Cambridge: Harvard University Press, 1959.

HISTORIES OF PERIODS

Karpovich, M. *Imperial Russia, 1801-1917*. New York: Henry Holt & Co., 1932. Short and exceptionally lucid overview.
Kornilov, A. *Modern Russian History*. New York: Alfred A. Knopf, 1943. Fullest treatment in English of the period 1796-1894.
Nechkina, M. V., ed. *Russia in the Nineteenth Century*, Ann Arbor: J. W. Edwards, 1953. Translation of part of a text used in Soviet higher schools. Covers period from 1801 to end of the 1860's.
Pushkarev, S. *The Emergence of Modern Russia, 1801-1917*. New York: Holt, Rinehart and Winston, 1963.

HISTORIES OF SPECIAL TOPICS

Hare, R. *Pioneers of Russian Social Thought*. New York: Oxford University Press, 1951. Study of non-Marxian social thought in the nineteenth century.
Hecker, J. F. *Russian Sociology*. New York: Columbia University Press, 1915. Rev. ed., New York: John Wiley & Sons, 1934. History of Russian social thought in the nineteenth century. The 1934 edition is a revision from a Marxist viewpoint.

Laserson, M. M. *The American Impact on Russia: Diplomatic and Ideological, 1784-1917.* New York: The Macmillan Co., 1950. Scope much greater than indicated by title. Contains good analysis of Russian constitutional development.

Malia, M. *Alexander Herzen and the Birth of Russian Socialism, 1812-1855.* Cambridge: Harvard University Press, 1961.

Mazour, A. G. *The First Russian Revolution, 1825.* Berkeley: University of California Press, 1937. Excellent study of the Decembrist Revolt.

Monas, S. *The Third Section: Police and Society in Russia under Nicholas I.* Cambridge: Harvard University Press, 1961.

Riasanovsky, N. V. *Russia and the West in the Teachings of the Slavophiles.* Cambridge: Harvard University Press, 1952.

————. *Nicholas I and Official Nationality in Russia, 1825-1855.* Berkeley: University of California Press, 1959.

DIPLOMATIC AND MILITARY HISTORIES

Allen, W. E. D. and Muratoff, P. *Caucasian Battlefields: A History of the Wars on the Turco-Caucasian Border, 1828-1921.* Cambridge: Cambridge University Press, 1953.

Baddeley, J. F. *The Russian Conquest of the Caucasus.* New York: Longmans, Green & Co., 1908.

Gleason, J. H. *The Genesis of Russophobia in Great Britain.* Cambridge: Harvard University Press, 1950. Anglo-Russian relations from 1815 to 1841, with emphasis on the development of British public opinion of Russia.

Jelavich, B. *A Century of Russian Foreign Policy, 1814-1914.* Philadelphia: J. B. Lippincott Co., 1964.

Lobanov-Rostovsky, A. *Russia and Europe, 1825-1878.* Ann Arbor: George Wahr Publishing Co., 1954. Sequel to his *Russia and Europe, 1789-1825.*

Mosely, P. E. *Russian Diplomacy and the Opening of the Eastern Question in 1838 and 1839.* Cambridge: Harvard University Press, 1934.

Puryear, V. *England, Russia, and the Straits Question, 1844-1856.* Berkeley: University of California Press, 1931.

Skrine, F. H. *The Expansion of Russia* (3rd ed.). Cambridge: Cambridge University Press, 1915. General history of Russia in the nineteenth century with major emphasis on foreign policy.

Thomas, B. P. *Russo-American Relations, 1815-1867.* Baltimore: Johns Hopkins Press, 1930.

BIOGRAPHIES

Grunwald, Constantin de. *Tsar Nicholas I.* New York: The Macmillan Co., 1955.

Paléologue, G. M. *The Enigmatic Czar: the Life of Alexander I of Russia.* London: Hamish-Hamilton, 1938. Popular biography.

Raeff, M. *Michael Speransky.* The Hague: Martinus Nijhoff, 1957.

Strakhovsky, L. I. *Alexander I of Russia.* New York: W. W. Norton & Co., 1947. Supports thesis that Alexander did not die in 1825.

Waliszewski, K. *Paul the First of Russia.* Philadelphia: J. B. Lippincott Co., 1913.

Part IV: Russia in transition

SOURCE BOOKS

Browder, P. B. and Kerensky, A. F., eds. *The Russian Provisional Government, 1917: Documents* (3 vols.). Stanford: Stanford University Press, 1961.

Gankin, O. H., and Fisher, H. H., eds. *The Bolsheviks and the World War: the Origins of the Third International.* Stanford: Stanford University Press, 1940. Well-organized collection of documents.

Golder, F. A., ed. *Documents of Russian History, 1914-1917.* New York: Century Co., 1927.

Gurko, V. I. *Features and Figures of the Past: Government and Opinion in the Reign of Nicholas II.* Stanford: Stanford University Press, 1939. Memoirs of a tsarist official. Valuable.

Kokovtsov, V. N. *Out of My Past.* Stanford: Stanford University Press, 1935. Author was Chairman of the Council of Ministers.

Pobedonostsev, C. *Reflections of a Russian Statesman.* London: Grant Richards, 1898. Insight into the philosophy of reaction.

Witte, S. *The Memoirs of Count Witte.* Garden City: Doubleday & Co., 1921. Very valuable source.

HISTORIES OF PERIODS

Black, C. E., ed. *The Transformation of Russian Society: Aspects of Social Change since 1861.* Cambridge: Harvard University Press, 1960.

Charques, R. *The Twilight of Imperial Russia.* London: Phoenix House, 1958. A history of Russia during the reign of Nicholas II.

Florinsky, M. T. *The End of the Russian Empire.* New Haven: Yale University Press, 1931. Domestic history of Russia during World War I. Concluding volume of the "Russian Series" in the *Economic and Social History of the World War.* This is the only one of the series cited in this bibliography, but the entire series is recommended.

Harcave, S. *First Blood: The Russian Revolution of 1905.* New York: The Macmillan Co., 1964.

Pares, B. *The Fall of the Russian Monarchy*. New York: Alfred A. Knopf, 1939. Study of the deterioration of the monarchy during World War I.

Seton-Watson, H. *The Decline of Imperial Russia, 1855-1914*. New York: Frederick A. Praeger, 1952.

GOVERNMENT AND POLITICS

Curtiss, J. S. *Church and State in Russia: the Last Years of the Empire, 1900-1917*. New York: Columbia University Press, 1940.

Kennan, G. *Siberia and the Exile System* (2 vols.). New York: Century Co., 1891.

Kohn, H. *Pan-Slavism: Its History and Ideology*. Notre Dame: University of Notre Dame Press, 1953.

Kucherov, S. *Courts, Lawyers and Trials under the Last Three Tsars*. New York: Frederick A. Praeger, 1953.

Levin, A. *The Second Duma*. New Haven: Yale University Press, 1940.

Petrovich, M. B. *The Emergence of Russian Panslavism, 1856-1870*. New York: Columbia University Press, 1957.

Vasiliev, A. T. *The Ochrana*. Philadelphia: J. B. Lippincott Co., 1930. Popular description of the tsarist political police by one of its directors.

Vinogradoff, P. *Self-government in Russia*. London: Constable, 1915. Local organs of self-government in period after reforms.

THE LIBERAL AND REVOLUTIONARY MOVEMENTS

Anderson, T., ed. *Masters of Russian Marxism*. New York: Appleton-Century-Crofts, 1963. Selections from the writings of Plekhanov, Martov, Lenin, and others.

Baron, S. H. *Plekhanov: the Father of Russian Marxism*. Stanford: Stanford University Press, 1963.

Berdyaev, N. *The Origin of Russian Communism*. New York: Charles Scribner's Sons, 1937. Illuminating interpretation by a Russian religious philosopher.

Carr, E. H. *Michael Bakunin*. London: The Macmillan Co., 1937.

Fischer, G. *Russian Liberalism*. Cambridge: Harvard University Press, 1958.

Keep, J. L. H. *The Rise of Social Democracy in Russia*. Leiden: E. J. Brill, 1963.

Milyukov, P. *Russia and Its Crisis*. Chicago: University of Chicago Press, 1905. Valuable analysis of the state of Russia on the eve of the Revolution of 1905.

Popov, N. *Outline History of the Communist Party of the Soviet Union* (2 vols.). New York: International Publishers, 1934. The first volume of this prejudiced but useful work deals with the period up to 1917.

Tompkins, S. R. *The Russian Intelligentsia: Makers of the Revolutionary State*. Norman: University of Oklahoma Press, 1957.

Treadgold, D. W. *Lenin and His Rivals: the Struggle for Russia's Future, 1898-1906.* New York: Frederick A. Praeger, 1955.

Venturi, F. *Roots of Revolution: A History of the Populist and Socialist Movements in Nineteenth Century Russia.* New York: Alfred A. Knopf, 1961.

Von Laue, T. H. *Why Lenin? Why Stalin? A Reappraisal of the Russian Revolution, 1900-1930.* Philadelphia: J. B. Lippincott Co., 1964.

Wolfe, B. D. *Three Who Made a Revolution.* New York: Dial Press, 1948. Study of the political development of Lenin, Trotsky, and Stalin up to 1914.

Yarmolinsky, A. *Road to Revolution.* New York: The Macmillan Co., 1959. History of the revolutionary movement, to 1881.

SOCIAL AND ECONOMIC HISTORIES

Bruford, W. H. *Chekhov and His Russia: a Sociological Study.* New York: Oxford University Press, 1948. Author's purpose: "to see Russia through Chekhov's eyes and to see Chekhov as the product of a particular age and country."

Gordon, M. *Workers before and after Lenin.* New York: E. P. Dutton & Co., 1941. Survey of labor conditions and organizations.

Johnson, W. H. E. *Russia's Educational Heritage.* Pittsburgh: Carnegie Press, 1950.

Kaidanova-Berry, O. *Public Education in Russia since 1850.* Ann Arbor: Edwards, 1952.

Maynard, J. *Russia in Flux: Before October.* London: Victor Gollancz, Ltd., 1941. Penetrating essays on the intelligentsia and the peasantry. Portions of this book are reprinted in his *Russia in Flux.* New York: The Macmillan Co., 1948.

Miller, M. S. *The Economic Development of Russia, 1905-1914.* London: P. S. King & Son, Ltd., 1926.

Pavlovsky, G. *Agricultural Russia on the Eve of the Revolution.* London: George Routledge, 1930. Systematic treatment of the organization of agricultural life in period from 1900 to 1917.

Robinson, G. T. *Rural Russia under the Old Regime.* New York: Longmans, Green & Co., 1932. Excellent history of rural Russia from the Emancipation to World War I. Especially valuable for analyses of agrarian reforms.

Von Laue, T. H. *Sergei Witte and the Industrialization of Russia.* New York: Columbia University Press, 1963.

Walkin, J. *The Rise of Democracy in Pre-Revolutionary Russia: Political and Social Institutions under the Last Three Czars.* New York: Frederick A. Praeger, 1962.

MILITARY AND DIPLOMATIC HISTORIES

Buchanan, G. *My Mission to Russia and Other Diplomatic Memories* (2 vols.). Boston: Little, Brown & Co., 1923. Valuable recollections of the British Ambassador to Russia during World War I.

Churchill, R. P. *The Anglo-Russian Convention of 1907.* Cedar Rapids, Ia.: Torch Press, 1939.

Churchill, W. S. *The Unknown War: the Eastern Front.* New York: Charles Scribner's Sons, 1931. Best history in English of the fighting on the Eastern Front in World War I.

Kuropatkin, A. N. *The Russian Army and the Japanese War* (2 vols.). London: John Murray, 1909. Tendentious but useful work by one of the commanders in the war.

Langer, W. L. *The Franco-Russian Alliance, 1890-1894.* Cambridge: Harvard University Press, 1929.

Malozemoff, A. *Russian Far Eastern Policy, 1881-1904.* Berkeley: University of California Press. 1958.

Paléologue, G. M. *An Ambassador's Memoirs* (3 vols.). London: Hutchinson & Co., 1923-1925. Diary of the French Ambassador to Russia for the years 1914 to 1917.

Romanov, B. A. *Russia in Manchuria (1892-1906).* Ann Arbor: J. W. Edwards, 1952.

Smith, C. J. *The Russian Struggle for Power, 1914-1917: A Study of Russian Foreign Policy during the First World War.* New York: The Philosophical Library, 1957.

Sumner, B. H. *Russia and the Balkans.* New York: Oxford University Press, 1937.

Zabriskie, E. H. *American-Russian Rivalry in the Far East: a Study in Diplomacy and Power Politics, 1895-1914.* Philadelphia: University of Pennsylvania Press, 1946.

TRAVEL AND DESCRIPTION

Leroy-Beaulieu, A. *The Empire of the Tsars and the Russians* (3 vols.). New York: G. P. Putnam's Sons, 1893-1896. Valuable analysis of Russian institutions in the second half of the nineteenth century, based on travel and study.

Troyat, H. *Daily Life in Russia under the Last Tsar.* New York: The Macmillan Co., 1962.

Wallace, D. M. *Russia* (Rev. Ed.). New York: Henry Holt & Co., 1912. Deservedly famous description of Russian life by a discerning and experienced traveler. Especially good for picture of Russian life at end of nineteenth century.

Williams, R. H. *Russia of the Russians*. New York: Charles Scribner's Sons, 1915. Excellent description of Russia in period between 1905 and 1914.

BIOGRAPHIES

Graham, S. *Tsar of Freedom*. New Haven: Yale University Press, 1935. Popular biography of Alexander II.
Lowe, C. *Alexander III of Russia*. London: W. Heinemann, 1895.
Mosse, W. E. *Alexander II and the Modernization of Russia*. New York: The Macmillan Co., 1958.

Part V: Communist Russia

REFERENCE WORKS

Biographic Directory of the U.S.S.R. New York: Scarecrow Press, 1958.
Fitzsimmons, T. et al. *USSR: its People, its Society, its Culture*. New Haven: HRAF Press, 1960.
Hulicka, K. and I. *Soviet Institutions, the Individual, and Society*. Boston: The Christopher Publishing House, 1967.

Kulski, W. W. *The Soviet Regime*. Syracuse: Syracuse University Press, 1954. A valuable handbook on many aspects of the Communist system.
Malevsky-Malevich, P., ed. *Russia-USSR*. New York: W. P. Payson, 1933. Handbook prepared by émigré specialists. Useful for earlier portions of Soviet period.
Maxwell, R., ed. *Information U.S.S.R.* New York: The Macmillan Co., 1962. A translation of Volume 50 of *The Great Soviet Encyclopedia*.
Whiting, K. R. *The Soviet Union Today: a Concise Handbook*. New York: Frederick A. Praeger, 1962.
Who's Who in the USSR, 1961/62——. New York: Scarecrow Press, 1962——.

SOURCE MATERIALS

Bunyan, J. and Fisher, H. H., eds. *The Bolshevik Revolution, 1917-1918: Documents and Materials*. Stanford: Stanford University Press, 1934.
Bunyan, J., ed. *Intervention, Civil War, and Communism in Russia, April-December, 1918*. Baltimore: Johns Hopkins Press, 1936.
Current Digest of the Soviet Press, 1949——. Translations of articles in Soviet periodicals.
Daniels, R. V., ed. *A Documentary History of Communism*. New York: Random House, 1960.
Degras, J., ed. *Soviet Documents on Foreign Policy*. New York: Oxford University Press, 1951——.
——. *The Communist International, 1919-1943: Documents* (3 vols.). New York: Oxford University Press, 1957-1965.

Eudin, X. J. and Fisher, H. H., eds. *Soviet Russia and the West, 1920-1927: A Documentary Survey.* Stanford: Stanford University Press, 1957.

Eudin, X. J. and North, R. C., eds. *Soviet Russia and the East, 1920-1927: A Documentary Survey.* Stanford: Stanford University Press, 1957.

Gruliow, L., ed. *Current Soviet Policies.* New York: Frederick A. Praeger, 1953——. Translations of the stenographic reports of party congresses (beginning with the 19th), and of related materials.

Gsovski, V. *Soviet Civil Law* (2 vols.). Ann Arbor: University of Michigan Press, 1948-1949. Translation of and commentary on several of the Soviet civil codes.

Meisel, J. H. and Kozera, E. S., eds. *Materials for the Study of the Soviet System: State and Party Constitutions, Laws, Decrees, Decisions and Official Statements of the Leaders in Translation.* Ann Arbor: George Wahr Publishing Co., 1950.

Shapiro, L., ed. *Soviet Treaty Series.* Washington: Georgetown University Press, 1950——.

Sontag, R. J. and Beddie, J. S., eds. *Nazi-Soviet Relations, 1939-1941: Documents from the Archives of the German Foreign Office.* Washington, D.C.: Department of State, 1948.

Stalin's Correspondence with Churchill, Attlee, Roosevelt, and Truman, 1941-1945 (2 vols.). New York: E. P. Dutton & Co., 1958.

U.S. Department of State. *Foreign Relations of the U.S.: The Soviet Union, 1933-1939.* Washington: Government Printing Office, 1952.

GENERAL HISTORIES

Carr, E. H. *A History of Soviet Russia.* New York: The Macmillan Co., 1950——. A large-scale work of which only the first volumes have appeared.

Rauch, G. von. *A History of Soviet Russia.* New York: Frederick A. Praeger, 1957.

Schuman, F. L. *Russia since 1917.* New York: Alfred A. Knopf, 1957.

Treadgold, D. W. *Twentieth Century Russia.* Chicago: Rand McNally & Co., 1959.

REVOLUTION, CIVIL WAR, AND INTERVENTION, 1917-1921

Chamberlin, W. H. *The Russian Revolution, 1917-1921* (2 vols.). New York: The Macmillan Co., 1935. Most complete work on the subject.

Footman, D. *Civil War in Russia.* London: Faber and Faber, 1961.

Kennan, G. F. *Soviet-American Relations, 1917-1920.* Princeton: Princeton University Press, 1956——.

Kerensky, A. *The Catastrophe.* New York: Appleton, 1927.

Pipes, R. *The Formation of the Soviet Union: Communism and Nationalism, 1917-1923.* Cambridge: Harvard University Press, 1954.

Radkey, O. H. *The Agrarian Foes of Bolshevism: Promise and Default of the Socialist Revolutionaries, February to October 1917.* New York: Columbia University Press, 1958.

————. *The Sickle under the Hammer: the Russian Socialist Revolutionaries in the Early Months of Soviet Rule.* New York: Columbia University Press, 1963.

Reed, J. *Ten Days That Shook the World.* New York: Boni & Liveright, 1919. Near-classic description of the November Revolution by an admirer of the Bolsheviks who took part in the events.

Reshetar, J. *The Ukrainian Revolution (1917-1920).* Princeton: Princeton University Press, 1952.

Schapiro, L. *The Origin of the Communist Autocracy; Political Opposition in the Soviet State; First Phase, 1917-1922.* Cambridge: Harvard University Press, 1955.

Sukhanov, N. N. *The Russian Revolution 1917: a Personal Record.* New York: Oxford University Press, 1955. Probably the most valuable of all eye-witness accounts of the revolution.

Trotsky, L. *History of the Russian Revolution* (3 vols.). New York: Simon & Schuster, 1936. Very valuable but highly tendentious work.

Warth, R. D. *The Allies and the Russian Revolution.* Durham: Duke University Press, 1954.

White, J. A. *The Siberian Intervention.* Princeton: Princeton University Press, 1950.

WORLD WAR II, 1939-1945

Dallin, A. *German Rule in Russia, 1941-1945: a Study of Occupation Policies.* New York: St. Martin's Press, 1957.

Deane, J. R. *The Strange Alliance.* New York: Viking Press, 1947.

Feis, H. *Churchill, Roosevelt, Stalin: the War They Waged and the Peace They Sought.* Princeton: Princeton University Press, 1957.

Fischer, G. *Soviet Opposition to Stalin.* Cambridge: Harvard University Press, 1952.

Gallagher, M. P. *The Soviet History of World War II.* New York: Frederick A. Praeger, 1963.

Goure, L. *The Siege of Leningrad.* Stanford: Stanford University Press, 1962.

Guillame, A. *Soviet Arms and Soviet Power.* Washington, D. C.: Infantry Journal Press, 1949. Concerns the Red Army in World War II.

U. S. Department of the Army. *The German Campaign in Russia—Planning and Operations (1940-1942).* Washington: Department of the Army, 1955.

Werth, A. *The Year of Stalingrad.* London: Hamilton, 1946.

THE ECONOMY

Baykov, A. *The Development of the Soviet Economic System.* New York: The Macmillan Co., 1946. Fullest history of the subject.

Granick, D. *The Red Executive: a Study of the Organization Man in Russian Industry.* Garden City: Doubleday & Co., 1960.

Jasny, N. *The Socialized Agriculture of the U.S.S.R.* Stanford: Stanford University Press, 1949.

Nove, A. *The Soviet Economy: an Introduction.* New York: Frederick A. Praeger, 1961.

Schwartz, H. *The Soviet Economy Since Stalin.* Philadelphia: J. B. Lippincott Co., 1965.

Schwarz, S. M. *Labor in the Soviet Union.* New York: Frederick A. Praeger, 1951.

Wiles, P. J. *The Political Economy of Communism.* Cambridge: Harvard University Press, 1963.

RELIGION

Anderson, P. S. *People, Church, and State in Modern Russia.* New York: The Macmillan Co., 1944.

Curtiss, J. S. *The Russian Church and the Soviet State, 1917-1950.* Boston: Little, Brown and Co., 1953.

Hecker, J. F. *Religion and Communism.* London: Chapman & Hall, 1933.

Timasheff, N. S. *Religion in Soviet Russia, 1917-1942.* New York: Sheed & Ward, 1942.

THE ARTS

Borland, H. *Soviet Literary Theory and Practice during the First Five-Year Plan, 1928-1932.* New York: King's Crown Press, 1950. Good introduction to "planning" in literature.

Freeman, J., Kunitz, J., and Lozowick, L. *Voices of October: Art and Literature in Soviet Russia.* New York: Vanguard Press, 1928. Articles on the development of the arts in the 1920's.

London, K. *The Seven Soviet Arts.* New Haven: Yale University Press, 1938. Survey of the arts in the mid-1930's.

McLean, H. and Vickery, W. N., eds. and trs. *The Year of Protest, 1956: an Anthology of Soviet Literary Materials.* New York: Random House, 1961.

Macleod, J. *The New Soviet Theatre.* London: Allen & Unwin, 1943.

Reavey, G. *Soviet Literature Today.* New Haven: Yale University Press, 1947. Careful study of trends during and since World War II.

Struve, G. *Soviet Russian Literature, 1917-1950.* Norman: University of Oklahoma Press, 1951. Most complete historical survey.

GOVERNMENT AND PARTY

Armstrong, J. A. *The Politics of Totalitarianism: the Communist Party of the Soviet Union from 1934 to the Present*. New York: Random House, 1961.

Barghoorn, F. C. *Politics in the USSR*. Boston: Little, Brown and Co., 1966.

Batsell, W. R. *Soviet Rule in Russia*. New York: The Macmillan Co., 1929. Best study of government and party in 1920's.

Berman, H. J. *Justice in Russia* (Rev. Ed.). Cambridge: Harvard University Press, 1963.

Daniels, R. V. *The Conscience of the Revolution: Communist Opposition in Soviet Russia*. Cambridge: Harvard University Press, 1960.

Fainsod, M. *How Russia is Ruled* (Rev. Ed.). Cambridge: Harvard University Press, 1963. A basic work.

————. *Smolensk under Soviet Rule*. Cambridge: Harvard University Press, 1958. An important study of the local operations of the party and government.

Hazard, J. N. *Settling Disputes in Soviet Society*. New York: Columbia University Press, 1960. Development of legal institutions in the first decade of Soviet rule.

Meissner, B. *The Communist Party of the Soviet Union: Party Leadership, Organization, and Ideology*. New York: Frederick A. Praeger, 1956.

Schapiro, L. *The Communist Party of the Soviet Union*. New York: Random House, 1960. Historical treatment, the best work on the subject.

Scott, D. J. R. *Russian Political Institutions*. New York: Frederick A. Praeger, 1961. A useful introduction.

Towster, J. *Political Power in the U.S.S.R., 1917-1947*. New York: Oxford University Press, 1948. Fullest consideration of the development of government and party.

Vyshinsky, A. N. *The Law of the Soviet State*. New York: The Macmillan Co., 1949. Translation of a textbook on Soviet government used in the higher schools of the USSR.

Wolin, S. and Slusser, R. M., eds. *The Soviet Secret Police*. New York: Frederick A. Praeger, 1957.

IDEOLOGY

Barghoorn, F. C. *Soviet Russian Nationalism*. New York: Oxford University Press, 1956.

Bauer, R. A. *The New Man in Soviet Psychology*. Cambridge: Harvard University Press, 1952.

Black, C. E., ed. *Rewriting Russian History: Soviet Interpretations of Russia's Past*. New York: Frederick A. Praeger, 1955.

Bukharin, N. and Preobrazhensky, E. *The ABC of Communism*. London: Communist Party of Great Britain, 1922. In its time, the official interpretation of Communism.

Counts, G. S. and Lodge, N. *The Country of the Blind: the Soviet System of Mind Control*. Boston: Houghton Mifflin, 1949.

Gurian, W., ed. *The Soviet Union: Background, Ideology, Reality*. Notre Dame: University of Notre Dame Press, 1951. Articles by various experts.

Harper, S. N. *Civic Training in Soviet Russia*. Chicago: University of Chicago Press, 1929. Basic study of the process of creating the new Soviet citizen.

Inkeles, A. *Public Opinion in Soviet Russia*. Cambridge: Harvard University Press, 1950. Analysis of methods used in mobilizing public opinion.

Leites, N. *A Study of Bolshevism*. Glencoe: Free Press, 1953. Analysis of the Communist ideology.

Lenin, V. I. *Selected Works* (2 vols.). Moscow: Foreign Languages Publishing House, 1947. Selected basic writings.

Meyer, A. G. *Marxism: The Unity of Theory and Practice*. Cambridge: Harvard University Press, 1954.

――――. *Leninism*. Cambridge: Harvard University Press, 1957.

Moore, B., Jr. *Soviet Politics—the Dilemma of Power*. Cambridge: Harvard University Press, 1950. Study of change in ideology and practice.

Le Rossignol, J. E. *From Marx to Stalin*. New York: Thomas Y. Crowell Co., 1940. Development of Communist thought.

Monnerot, J. *Sociology and Psychology of Communism*. Boston: Beacon Press, 1953.

Stalin, J. *Leninism* (2 vols.). London: Allen & Unwin, Ltd., 1940. Collection of the most significant statements of the Soviet leader.

Timasheff, N. S. *The Great Retreat: the Growth and Decline of Communism in Russia*. New York: E. P. Dutton & Co., 1946. Study of the growing divergence between Soviet practice and professed ideology.

Trotsky, L. *The Revolution Betrayed*. Garden City: Doubleday, Doran & Co., 1937. Most comprehensive of his many attacks on Stalin.

Ulam, A. B. *The Unfinished Revolution: an Essay on the Sources of Influence of Marxism and Communism*. New York: Random House, 1960.

Webb, S., and Webb, B. *Soviet Communism: a New Civilization?* (2 vols.) New York: Charles Scribner's Sons, 1936. Voluminous description of Soviet institutions. Suffers from uncritical acceptance of official statements.

Wetter, G. A. *Dialectical Materialism: a Historical and Systematic Survey of Philosophy in the Soviet Union*. New York: Frederick A. Praeger, 1958.

EDUCATION

Counts, G. S. *The Challenge of Soviet Education*. New York: McGraw-Hill Book Co., 1957.

Kline, G. L., ed. *Soviet Education*. New York: Columbia University Press, 1957.

Pinkevich, A. *The New Education in the Soviet Republic*. London: Williams & Norgate, 1930.

Shore, M. J. *Soviet Education*. New York: Philosophical Library, 1947.

U. S. Department of Health, Education, and Welfare. *Education in the USSR*. Washington: U. S. Government Printing Office, 1957.

THE SOVIET ARMY

Dinerstein, H. S. *War and the Soviet Union: Nuclear Weapons and the Revolution in Soviet Military and Political Thinking*. New York: Frederick A. Praeger, 1959.

Ely, L. B. *The Red Army Today*. Harrisburg: The Military Service Publishing Company, 1949. Valuable work, based in large part on information supplied by former Soviet officers.

Erickson, J. *The Soviet High Command: a Military-Political History, 1918-1941*. New York: St. Martin's Press, 1962.

Garthoff, R. L. *Soviet Strategy in the Nuclear Age* (Rev. Ed.). New York: Frederick A. Praeger, 1962.

Liddell Hart, B. H., ed. *The Red Army*. New York: Harcourt, Brace, 1957. A collection of articles by various experts.

Wollenberg, E. *The Red Army*. New York: Transatlantic Arts, 1941. A history.

WORLD COMMUNISM

Borkenau, F. *World Communism*. New York: W. W. Norton & Co., 1939. History of the Comintern by a former German Communist.

Brzezinski, Z. K. *The Soviet Bloc* (3rd Ed.). Cambridge: Harvard University Press, 1967.

Fischer, R. *Stalin and German Communism*. Cambridge: Harvard University Press, 1948.

James, C. L. R. *World Revolution, 1917-1936: the Rise and Fall of the Communist International*. London: Secker and Warburg, 1937.

North, R. C. *Moscow and the Chinese Communists*. Stanford: Stanford University Press, 1953. •

Salvadori, M. *The Rise of Modern Communism*. New York: Holt, Rinehart, & Winston, 1952. A brief introduction.

Seton-Watson, H. *From Lenin to Khrushchev: the History of World Communism*. New York: Frederick A. Praeger, 1960.

————. *The Eastern European Revolution.* New York: Frederick A. Praeger, 1951.

Ulam, A. B. *Titoism and the Cominform.* Cambridge: Harvard University Press, 1952.

U. S. Eighty-fourth Congress, Second Session. *The Strategy and Tactics of World Communism.* Washington: U. S. Government Printing office, 1956.

DIPLOMATIC HISTORIES

Adams, A. E., ed. *Readings in Soviet Foreign Policy: Theory and Practice.* Boston: D. C. Heath & Co., 1961.

Beloff, M. *The Foreign Policy of Soviet Russia* (2 vols.). New York: Oxford University Press, 1947-1949. Covers the years from 1929 to 1941.

Browder, R. P. *The Origins of Soviet-American Diplomacy.* Princeton: Princeton University Press, 1953. Covers the period 1917-1935.

Dallin, D. J. *Soviet Foreign Policy after Stalin.* Philadelphia: J. B. Lippincott Co., 1961.

Dennis, A. L. P. *The Foreign Policies of Soviet Russia.* New York: E. P. Dutton & Co., 1924. Covers the years from 1917 to 1923.

Fischer, L. *The Soviets in World Affairs* (2 vols.). Princeton: Princeton University Press, 1951. Covers the years from 1917 to 1929.

Fleming, D. F. *The Cold War and its Origins* (2 vols.). New York: Doubleday & Co., 1961.

Mackintosh, J. M. *Strategy and Tactics of Soviet Foreign Policy.* New York: Oxford University Press, 1962.

Mosely, P. E. *The Kremlin and World Politics: Studies in Soviet Policy and Action.* New York: Vintage Books, 1960.

Taracouzio, T. A. *War and Peace in Soviet Diplomacy.* New York: The Macmillan Co., 1940. Study of the guiding principles of Soviet diplomacy.

Tompkins, P. *American-Russian Relations in the Far East.* New York: The Macmillan Co., 1949. Covers the years from 1914 to 1948.

Whiting, A. S. *Soviet Policies in China, 1917-1924.* New York: Columbia University Press, 1954.

NATIONAL MINORITIES

Armstrong, J. A. *Ukrainian Nationalism, 1939-1945.* New York: Columbia University Press, 1955.

Kohn, H. *Nationalism in the Soviet Union.* London: Routledge & Sons, 1933.

Kolarz, W. *Russia and Her Colonies.* New York: Frederick A. Praeger, 1952. A study of Soviet treatment of national minorities.

Schlesinger, R., ed. *The Nationalities Problem and Soviet Administration: Selected Readings on the Development of Soviet Nationalities Policies.* New York: Humanities Press, 1955.

Schwarz, S. M. *The Jews in the Soviet Union.* Syracuse: Syracuse University Press, 1951.

Smal-Stocki, R. *The Nationality Problem of the Soviet Union and Russian Communist Imperialism.* Milwaukee: Bruce Publishing Co., 1952.

Stalin, J. *Marxism and the National and Colonial Question.* New York: International Publishers, 1942.

MISCELLANEOUS

Bauer, R. A., Inkeles, A., and Kluckhohn, C. *How the Soviet System Works.* Cambridge: Harvard University Press, 1956.

Beck, F. and Godin, W. *Russian Purge and the Extraction of Confessions.* New York: The Viking Press, 1951. Aims and methods of political police practices.

Chamberlin, W. H. *Russia's Iron Age.* Boston: Little, Brown & Co., 1934. Russia during period of First Five-Year Plan.

———. *Soviet Russia.* Boston: Little, Brown & Co., 1930. Russia during the 1920's.

Dallin, D. J. *The Changing World of Soviet Russia.* New Haven: Yale University Press, 1956.

Dallin, D. and Nicolaevsky, B. *Forced Labor in Soviet Russia.* New Haven: Yale University Press, 1947.

Hendel, S. and Braham, R. L., eds. *The U.S.S.R. after 50 Years.* New York: Alfred A. Knopf, 1967.

Leonhard, W. *The Kremlin since Stalin.* New York: Frederick A. Praeger, 1962. A useful summary.

Maynard, J. *The Russian Peasant and Other Studies.* London: Victor Gollancz, 1942. Collection of thought-provoking essays on Soviet political development and on the agrarian problem. Parts are included in the author's *Russia in Flux.* New York: The Macmillan Co., 1948.

Mehnert, K. *Soviet Man and his World.* New York: Frederick A. Praeger, 1962.

Miller, W. R. *Russians as People.* New York: E. P. Dutton & Co., 1961.

Mosely, P. E., ed. *The Soviet Union, 1922-1962.* New York: Frederick A. Praeger, 1963. A collection of articles that originally appeared in the journal *Foreign Affairs.*

Reshetar, J. S. *Problems of Analyzing and Predicting Soviet Behavior.* Garden City: Doubleday & Co., 1955.

Simmons, E. J., ed. *Continuity and Change in Russian and Soviet Thought.* Cambridge: Harvard University Press, 1955.

Simon, E. D. et al. *Moscow in the Making.* New York: Longmans, Green & Co., 1937. Study of administration and municipal construction by a group of British experts.

PERSONAL ACCOUNTS

Alliluyeva, S. *Twenty Letters to a Friend.* New York: Harper & Row, 1967. Recollections of Stalin's daughter.

Barmine, A. *One Who Survived.* New York: G. P. Putnam's Sons, 1945. Recollections of a former Soviet diplomat.

Ehrenburg, I. *Memoirs: 1921-1941.* Cleveland: World Publishing Co., 1964. Recollections of a Soviet novelist.

Fischer, L., ed. *Thirteen Who Fled.* New York: Harper & Bros., 1949. Personal accounts of thirteen Soviet citizens who refused to return to Russia after World War II.

Gorbatov, A. V. *Years Off My Life.* New York: W. W. Norton and Co., 1965. Memoirs of a Soviet general.

Maisky, I. *Journey into the Past.* London: Hutchinson, 1962. Memoirs of a Soviet diplomat.

Trotsky, L. *My Life.* New York: Charles Scribner's Sons, 1930.

Weissberg, A. *The Accused.* New York: Simon and Schuster, 1951. Experiences of a former Austrian Communist in the USSR.

Yevtushenko, Y. *A Precocious Autobiography.* New York: E. P. Dutton & Co., 1963. By a young Soviet poet.

BIOGRAPHY

Deutscher, I. *The Prophet Armed: Trotsky, 1879-1921.* New York: Oxford University Press, 1954.

———. *The Prophet Unarmed: Trotsky, 1921-1929.* New York: Oxford University Press, 1959.

———. *The Prophet Outcast: Trotsky, 1929-1940.* New York: Oxford University Press, 1963.

———. *Stalin.* New York: Oxford University Press, 1949.

Fischer, L. *The Life of Lenin.* New York: Harper & Row, 1964.

Shub, D. *Lenin.* New York: Doubleday & Co., 1948.

Souvarine, B. *Stalin.* New York: Longmans, Green & Co., 1939.